IBM SPSS Statistics 18

Made Simple

Paul R. Kinnear & Colin D. Gray

School of Psychology

University of Aberdeen

Psychology Press
Taylor & Francis Group

HOVE AND NEW YORK

First published 2010 by Psychology Press
27 Church Road, Hove, East Sussex BN3 2FA

Simultaneously published in the USA and Canada
by Psychology Press
270 Madison Avenue, New York NY 10016

Psychology Press is an imprint of the Taylor & Francis Group, an informa business

Printed and bound in Great Britain by
TJ International Ltd, Padstow, Cornwall, from files supplied by the authors.
Cover design by Hybert Design.

This publication has been produced with paper manufactured to strict
environmental standards and with pulp derived from sustainable forests.

British Library Cataloguing in Publication Data
A catalogue record for this book is available from the British Library.

Library of Congress Cataloging in Publication Data
Kinnear, Paul R.
  IBM SPSS statistics 18 made simple / Paul R. Kinnear & Colin D. Gray.
    p. cm.
  ISBN 978-1-84872-047-3 (pb)
  SPSS (Computer file) 2. Social sciences--Statistical methods--Computer
  programs. I. Gray, Colin D. II. Title.
   HA32.K554 2010
   005.5'5--dc22
                                                          2010021481

ISBN: 978-1-84872-047-3 (pbk only)

Contents

CHAPTER 4 Describing and exploring your data 85

CHAPTER 5 Graphs and charts 132

CHAPTER 6   Comparing averages: Two-sample and one-sample tests *173*

CHAPTER 9   Within subjects experiments *312*

CHAPTER 10   Mixed factorial experiments *349*

CHAPTER 11   Measuring statistical association *395*

CHAPTER 14   Discriminant analysis and logistic regression *540*

CHAPTER 15   The search for latent variables: factor
analysis *580*

Preface

This book, *IBM SPSS Statistics 18 Made Simple*, is the latest in our *SPSS Made Simple* series. (In 2009, SPSS temporarily re-branded its software packages as *PASW* - Predictive Analytics SoftWare - but has reverted to *SPSS* once again.)

This edition retains the essentially practical and informal character of our previous books. No previous knowledge of SPSS is assumed. Throughout the book, we have made extensive use of annotated screen snapshots of the dialog boxes and the output in order to clarify the text. As in our two most recently published books *SPSS 16 Made Simple* and *PASW Statistics 17 Made Simple*, we have used numbered call-outs in the screen shots, which not only improves the clarity of the demonstrations, but also helps to communicate the correct sequencing of the procedure to the reader. The gratifyingly positive response to our previous book from our readers and students confirms that we have been successful in providing clear and useful advice, both for those who wish to get started with statistical computing and for the more experienced researcher. In the present edition, as always, the coverage of SPSS has been updated to reflect the improvements embodied in the most up-to-date version of this powerful software.

Although this is not a statistics textbook, the reader will find advice on the selection of appropriate statistical tests. *IBM SPSS 18 Statistics Made Simple* is not a cookbook: in addition to instructions on the implementation of each technique, the reader will find a clear, informal explanation of its rationale. The assumptions of the underlying statistical model are described and, where necessary, there is advice on how to proceed should the data fail to meet the model's requirements. There are also suggestions for further reading.

As well as showing the reader how to use SPSS to run statistical analyses, we have also provided guidance, in line with American Psychological Association (APA) recommendations (American Psychological Association, 2001) on how the results of each test should be presented in scientific papers and practical reports.

Over the years, we have expanded our coverage of statistical techniques in response to requests from our readers and reviewers, as well as student feedback. In recent editions, for example, we have placed greater emphasis upon the use of SPSS Syntax, a control language, not only to save time in repeated analyses, but also for running techniques, such as tests for simple effects, that are unavailable in the Windows dialogs. In this edition, we describe the use of AMOS, a structural equation modelling package available with the SPSS statistical software, to run path analysis and confirmatory factor analysis. Confirmatory factor analysis complements the exploratory factor analysis available on SPSS very nicely.

We have always provided many practice examples, both for the benefit of the reader studying the subject on an individual basis and for use by the instructor. The examples are of two kinds. Some are designed to consolidate the material of a specific chapter and are clearly labelled as such. Others, however, require the reader to analyse a data set without the cueing that a chapter context would provide and are intended to help promote a sense of strategy in data analysis. We had always wanted to provide more supplementary material of this kind, but for many years were prevented from doing so by considerations of space. In recent editions, therefore, we have transferred the examples to our website at www.psypress.com/spss-made-simple. There, the reader will find not only examples of the two types we have just described,

xvi   Preface

but also multiple-choice questions, PowerPoint presentations on various topics and some notes on some statistical terms in the SPSS output which tend to be perennial stumbling blocks.

Throughout the preparation of this book, as with previous editions, we have been most fortunate in having the advice, encouragement and computing expertise of John Lemon, Senior Computing Adviser at Aberdeen University's Directorate of Information Technology. We are also very grateful to Caroline Green, who has recently retired from her post of Senior Teaching Fellow, for her helpful observations on the Exercises and her reports of students' progress with them in the practical classes. We very much appreciate the unfailing support that Jim Urquhart and our Chief Technician, Peter Bates, have always given us and the encouragement we have received from Professor Peter McGeorge, Head of the School of Psychology in the College of Life Sciences and Medicine at the University of Aberdeen. Finally, we would like to express our gratitude to all those who, though too numerous to mention individually, have helped us in some way to produce this book.

Colin Gray and Paul Kinnear

June, 2010

CHAPTER 1

Introduction

1.1   MEASUREMENTS AND DATA

Since this book is about the analysis of data, we shall begin with a survey of the kinds of data that result from research and introduce some key terms.

1.1.1   Variables: quantitative and qualitative

A **variable** is a characteristic or property of a person, an object or a situation, comprising a set of different values or categories. Height is a variable, as are weight, blood type and gender. **Quantitative variables**, such as height, weight or age, are possessed in *degree* and so can sometimes be measured in units on an independent scale. In contrast, **qualitative** variables, such as sex, blood group or nationality, are possessed only in *kind*: they cannot be expressed in units on a scale. With qualitative variables, we can only make counts of the cases falling into the various categories, as when we might record that a theatre audience comprises 100 men and 300 women.

1.1.2   Levels of measurement: scale, ordinal and nominal data

A **data set** is a collection of numerical observations of variables. In this book, we shall use the term **measurement** to refer to the making of numerical records of any characteristic, whether quantitative or qualitative. The numbers in a data set can carry varying amounts of information about what is being recorded. Often, as as with heights or weights, they are measurements on an independent scale with units; but sometimes, as records of category membership, they serve merely as labels. It is useful to identify three **levels of measurement**:

1. At the highest level, **scale** or **continuous** data are measurements on an independent scale with units. Heights and weights are obvious examples. So also are performance scores, such as the number of times a participant hits a target, as well as IQs, responses to questionnaires and other psychometric data. In such a data set, each individual score (or **datum**) not only expresses the degree to which a property or characteristic is possessed, but also carries information independently of the other scores.

2. At the next level, come data in the form of ranks. Such **ordinal** data are also records of quantitative characteristics. For example, if two judges rank 10 similar objects according to their perceived weight, assigning the rank 1 to the heaviest and 10 to the lightest, the data set will consist of 10 pairs of ranks, one pair for each object. Ranks are not measures on an independent scale with units. Unlike a measurement such as a height or a weight, a rank has meaning only in relation to the other data in the set.

3. At the lowest level, **nominal** data relate to qualitative variables or attributes, such as gender or blood group, and are merely records of category membership, rather than true measurements. Nominal data, that is, are merely **labels**. They are numbers, but they do not express the degree to which any characteristic is possessed: they are arbitrary code numbers representing, say, different blood groups, genders or nationalities. Any other numbers (as long as they vary between categories) would have served the purpose just as well.

1.1.3   A grey area: ratings

Psychologists, market researchers and political pollsters frequently ask respondents to **rate** objects or people by assigning each to one of a set of ordered categories. There has been much debate about whether, from a statistical point of view, sets of ratings can be treated as scale data. Some argue that, unlike a rank, an individual rating carries information independently of the rest of the data. They do so on the grounds that raters are given reference or **anchor points** at the ends of the scale and are asked to express their judgements in relation to these. Others, however, would say that if 100 participants in a research project are asked to rate, say, 30 objects by placing each object in one of seven ordered categories, where 1 is very good and 7 is very bad, the operation will result in 100 sets of **ranks with ties**: that is, ratings are merely ordinal data and should be treated as such in the statistical analysis. In our view, the decision about which statistics to use depends upon several considerations, including the distribution of the data and the number of points on the rating scale.

Sometimes the term **categorical data** is used to include both purely nominal assignments and assignments to ordered categories. This term straddles the foregoing distinction between nominal and ordinal data and tends to blur the distinction between ranks and ratings.

1.1.4   Univariate, bivariate and multivariate data sets

It is useful to distinguish among data sets in terms of the number of measured variables they contain. In a **univariate** data set, all the data refer to just one variable. In a **bivariate** data set, there are measurements on two variables. In a **multivariate** data set, there are measurements on three or more variables.

This distinction among data sets is important, because it has implications for the researcher's choice of statistics. The three most important properties of a univariate data set (say, a set of heights, weights or scores on an attitude scale) are:

1. The **average** (as measured by the mean, the median, the mode or some other measure of **central tendency**).
2. The **spread** or **dispersion** of the scores about the average, as measured by the standard deviation, the variance or a range measure.
3. The shape of the **distribution** (symmetric, normal, skewed and so on).

With bivariate or multivariate data sets, interest shifts to the possibility of a statistical association, or **correlation**, between the variables that have been measured. Do people with higher incomes tend to score higher on psychometric tests? Is number of years of formal education an important factor in a person's income at the peak of his or her earning power? Is the amount of screen violence to which a child is exposed related to the child's own tendencies to actual violence?

With multivariate data sets, interest often centres on the extent to which certain variables can be accounted for or explained in terms of others in the data set. How well can we predict a person's final income from number of years of formal education, psychometric intelligence and parents' income? These are problems in **regression**.

1.2   EXPERIMENTAL VERSUS CORRELATIONAL RESEARCH

In this section, we shall consider a distinction which has important implications for the sorts of statistics the researcher will choose to describe and summarise a data set and to confirm the findings with statistical inference.

1.2.1   A simple experiment

Forty volunteers take part in an investigation designed to investigate the effects of caffeine upon skilled performance. Each volunteer is assigned, at random, to one of two groups. Twenty of the volunteers shoot at a target after ingesting a dose of caffeine. The remaining 20 volunteers also shoot at the target; but while the first group were receiving their caffeine, the second group were given a neutral saline solution as a **placebo**. Each volunteer receives a single accuracy score. Table 1 summarises the results of the experiment.

Table 1. Number of hits achieved by participants under caffeine and placebo conditions		
	Placebo	Caffeine
Mean number of hits	9.25	11.90
Standard deviation	3.16	3.28
Number of cases	20	20

The caffeine study has all the characteristics of a true **experiment**. An **experiment** is the collection of comparative data under controlled conditions. One variable, known as the **independent variable (IV)** is manipulated by the investigator in order to demonstrate that it has a causal effect upon another variable, which is known as the **dependent variable (DV)**. Here the dependent variable is performance and the independent variable is the group to which the participant was assigned. The Placebo condition serves as a comparison or **control** with reference to which the performance of the actively treated group can be compared.

The IV is controlled by the investigator, and its values are determined before the experiment is carried out. This is achieved either by **random assignment** of the participants to the pre-set conditions or by testing each participant under all conditions, if that is feasible. The DV, on the other hand, is measured during the course of the investigation.

In the planning of an experiment, the researcher applies the **rule of one variable**: that is, the conditions under which participants in the different groups are tested must differ only with respect to the independent variable. In a poorly designed experiment, variables other than the independent variable may have a causal effect upon the dependent variable. In a well designed experiment, such **extraneous variables** are neutralised, or under experimental **control**. The rule of one variable is one of the most important principles in experimental design. Random assignment to conditions is intended to ensure that any individual differences in ability between the experimental and control groups tend to cancel out, so that the two groups are comparable in aggregate.

There are other methods of controlling extraneous variables, such as testing the same participants under all conditions, so that each participant serves as his or her own control. In fact, good experiments can be run with only a single participant. The strategy the researcher should adopt depends on many factors, including the nature of the research question, the local situation and the resources available.

1.2.2 A more complex experiment

Table 2. Mean levels of performance on a skilled task by five groups of participants under five different conditions						
	Placebo	Drug A	Drug B	Drug C	Drug D	
Mean	8.00	7.90	12.00	14.40	13.00	GM* 11.06
SD	1.83	2.13	2.49	4.50	3.74	
						* Grand Mean

Suppose that in an investigation of the effects of four supposedly performance-enhancing drugs upon skilled performance, five groups of participants are tested:

- A control group, who have received a Placebo.
- A group who have received Drug A.
- A group who have received Drug B.

- A group who have received Drug C.
- A group who have received Drug D.

The results of the experiment are summarised in Table 2.

1.2.2.1 Factors, levels and measures

In experimental design, a **factor** is a set of related conditions or categories. The conditions or categories making up a factor are known as the **levels** of the factor, even though, as in the qualitative factors of gender or blood group, there is no sense in which one category can be said to be 'higher' or 'lower' than another. In the current drug experiment, there is one factor, Drug Condition, comprising five different conditions or levels: Placebo, Drug A, Drug B, Drug C and Drug D. In experimental design, the term **factor** has a meaning similar to the term **independent variable**, in the sense that the nature of the treatment is supposed to have a causal influence upon another variable, the **dependent variable (DV)**. In some experimental designs, however, (those having within subjects factors – see below), the dependent variable is known as a **measure**. In our current example, the dependent variable is the score that the participant achieved on the skilled task.

1.2.2.2 Between subjects and within subjects experiments

The 50 participants in the drug experiment were randomly assigned to the five conditions making up the treatment factor Drug Condition and each participant was tested only once. Such an experiment is said to be of **between subjects** design, in contrast to **within subjects** experiments, in which each participant is tested under all conditions.

1.2.3 Correlational research

In an experiment, the IV, unlike gender, blood group, or nationality, is not an intrinsic property of the participants: the participants are assigned at random to the experimental and control groups. Such random assignment to different conditions confers upon the experiment a great advantage: should a difference be found between the groups in their performance, the researcher may draw the inference that the active experimental treatment has had a causal effect upon the dependent variable.

1.2.3.1 A correlational study

Suppose that a researcher believes that exposure to screen violence promotes actual violence in children. Ethical and practical considerations rule out an experiment in which the independent variable of amount of exposure to screen violence is manipulated to determine its effects upon the incidence of violent behaviour. The investigator, therefore, decides upon a correlational strategy. Twenty-seven children are measured on two variables:
1. Their exposure to screen violence (Exposure).
2. Their actual violence (Actual).

The researcher measures these variables in the expectation that they will show a positive association: there should be a tendency for those with high Exposure also to score highly on Actual violence; those low on Exposure should also be low on Actual violence; and those with average Exposure should fall within the normal range on Actual violence. This strategy will not yield the strong evidence for causation that a true experiment would yield; however, an association would at least be consistent with the researcher's view that exposure to screen violence encourages actual violence in children.

1.2.3.2   A scatterplot

Correlational research like this results in a **bivariate** data set, which can be depicted in a **scatterplot**. The scatterplot of the children's actual violence against their exposure to screen violence is shown in Figure 1. In the scatterplot, each person is represented as a point, the coordinates of which are the person's scores on the Exposure and Actual scales, which are marked out on the horizontal and vertical axes, respectively.

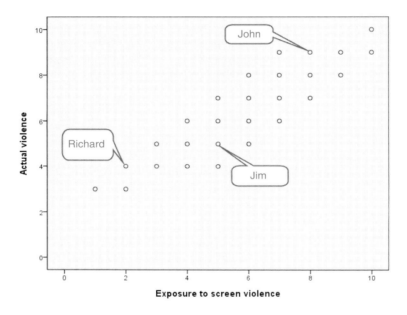

Figure 1. Scatterplot of Actual violence against Exposure to screen violence

In this second research scenario, as in the first, the research was motivated by the hypothesis that one variable has a causal effect upon another: in the drug example, the ingestion of Drug X improves memory; in the second, exposure to screen violence promotes actual violence. There is an important difference between the two situations, however: in the second scenario, neither variable was manipulated by the experimenter: both Exposure and Actual violence are measured as they occur in the participants.

From inspection of Figure 1, it is quite clear that there is a marked tendency for those (e.g. John) who score highly on Exposure also to score highly on Actual violence. Those who score low on Exposure (e.g. Richard) tend to have low scores on Actual. And those in the middle of the Exposure range (e.g. Jim) tend to have intermediate scores on Actual. Our scatterplot, that is, gives strong evidence of an association, or **correlation**, between the two variables.

1.2.4   The Pearson correlation coefficient

When a scatterplot is elliptical, there is, to at least some degree, a linear relationship between the two variables. The narrower the ellipse, the stronger is the relationship. If the relationship is perfect, the points all lie along a line. A circular cloud of points indicates dissociation between the variables.

The **Pearson correlation (r)** is a statistic designed to measure the strength of a supposed linear association between two variables measured at the scale or continuous level. The Pearson correlation is so defined that it can have values only within the range from −1 to +1, inclusive. A value of zero indicates dissociation between the variables.

The sign of a correlation reflects the orientation of the elliptical cloud of points in the scatterplot: if the principal axis of the ellipse has a positive slope, the correlation has a positive sign; if the axis has a negative slope, the correlation is negative. The sign of a correlation does not reflect the strength of the association between the two variables: the values −.6 and +.6 indicate the same level of association; but in the former case, one variable varies inversely with the other, whereas in the latter the relationship is positive.

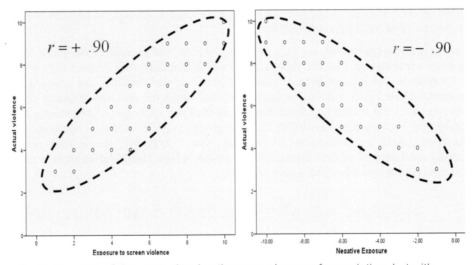

Figure 2. Scatterplots of data sets showing the same degree of association, but with correlations of opposite sign

Figure 2 shows two scatterplots: the first is the scatterplot of Actual violence upon Exposure to violence; the second is a scatterplot with the direction of the Exposure scale reversed (by multiplying the original Exposure scores by −1). In either case, the absolute value of the Pearson correlation is .90. A negative correlation of −.90 represents the same (strong) degree of linear association as a positive correlation of +.90.

A perfect linear association, with all the points in the scatterplot lying along the same straight line, would be reflected either in a correlation of +1 or a correlation of −1: either value would represent a perfect linear relationship.

1.2.5   Correlation and causation

When interpreting the results of correlational research, we should bear in mind the dictum that *correlation does not imply causation*. The researcher may believe that Actual violence is, to at least some extent, causally determined by Exposure to violence. That, however, is only one of several possible interpretations of the correlation. Other variables may be involved. Do children with high levels of Exposure tend to live in violent households or, at any rate, in households where parents, if not actually violent, watch and obviously enjoy a rich diet of screen violence? In correlation research, the direction of causality itself may itself be in doubt: violent people may watch violent television and films; but has viewing screen violence over the years made the viewers violent or are such programmes merely the preferred entertainment of those with a violent disposition?

1.2.6   Quasi-experiments

Does smoking shorten one's life? Researchers have conducted many studies comparing the longevity of smokers and non-smokers. In such research, those in the smoking and non-smoking groups are matched with respect to as many possible confounding variables as possible, such as socio-economic status, education, lifestyle and so on. In this way, it is hoped to achieve a comparison between two groups of people who differ only in their smoking category. A difference in longevity between smokers and non-smokers is taken as evidence for the hypothesis that smoking shortens life.

In such a **quasi-experiment**, as in a true experiment, the researcher attempts to control extraneous variables, so that the groups compared differ only with respect to the supposed causal variable. As in correlational research, however, the variables are properties of the participants: there is no random assignment to the smoking and non-smoking conditions. However careful the researchers have been to control the influence of extraneous variables, therefore, there remains the possibility that the groups may yet differ on some other crucial characteristic, such as personality or physical type. Arguably, the quasi-experiment is essentially a refinement of the correlational approach, where **statistical control** is used as an imperfect substitute for true experimental control.

1.3   CHOOSING A STATISTICAL TEST: SOME GUIDELINES

It is common for authors of statistical texts to offer advice on choosing statistical tests in the form of a flow chart, decision tree or similar diagram. The numerous schemes that have been proposed vary considerably, and sometimes seem to contradict one another. Almost any system of classification tends to break down when the user encounters cases that straddle category boundaries. In this area, moreover, the correct choice of statistical technique for certain types of data has been hotly disputed.

On one matter at least, there is general agreement: there is no such thing as a decision tree that will automatically lead the investigator to the correct choice of a statistical test in all circumstances. Some of the later chapters contain illustrations of the penalties that an automated, scheme-reliant approach can incur. At best, a decision tree can serve only as a rough guideline. Ultimately, a safe decision requires careful reflection upon one's own research aims and a thorough preliminary exploration of the data. *Get to know your data before you proceed to make any formal statistical tests.*

1.3.1   Considerations in choosing a statistical test

The choice of a statistical test depends upon several considerations, including:
1.   Your research question.
2.   The plan, or **design**, of your research.
3.   The nature of the data that you wish to analyse.

This list is by no means comprehensive; nor do we intend to imply that any fixed ordering of these three considerations is appropriate in all situations or that they are independent issues.

In general, an important consideration in deciding upon a statistical analysis is whether the research is experimental or correlational. The experimenter is usually interested in making comparisons between the average performance level of participants tested under different conditions. Statistical methods such as *t* tests and analysis of variance (ANOVA) were designed for the purpose of making comparisons. The correlational researcher typically seeks statistical **associations** among the variables in the study, with a view to imputing causality to theoretically important variables. Correlation and regression are suitable techniques for that purpose.

1.3.2   Five common research situations

We shall identify five basic research situations in which formal statistical tests can be applied (Figure 3). In this book, the techniques appropriate for these situations will be discussed more fully in the sections indicated in the figure.

The questions are as follows:
1.   Is a difference (between averages) significant? For example, is resting heart rate the same before and after a fitness course? (Section 1.4).
2.   How strongly are variables associated? For example, do tall parents tend to have tall children? (Section 1.5).
3.   Can scores on a target variable (or category membership, if the variable is qualitative) be predicted from data on other variables? For example, can university performance be predicted by scores on aptitude tests? (Section 1.6).
4.   From a single sample of data, what can be said about the population? For example, a child, asked to select the correct object from a choice of two over a series of fifty trials, does so on 35 occasions. Is this performance level better than chance? (Section 1.7).
5.   The user has a multivariate data set, perhaps people's scores on a battery of ability tests. Can these scores be accounted for (or classified) in terms of a smaller number of hypothetical latent variables or **factors**? For example, can performance in a variety of intellectual pursuits be accounted for in terms of general intelligence? (Section 1.8).

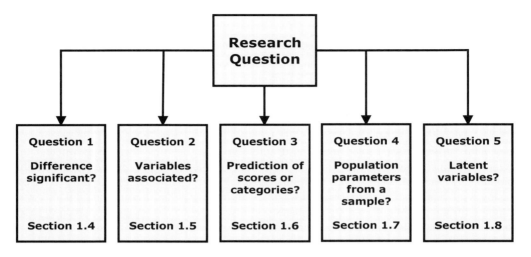

Figure 3. Five types of research situation

1.4   IS A DIFFERENCE SIGNIFICANT?

The question of whether two or more means are significantly different is one that arises naturally in the context of experimental or quasi-experimental research, where the performance of the participants under different conditions is being compared.

Suppose that in a drug experiment, performance under two different conditions (experimental and control) has been measured and that the means have somewhat different values. This may seem to support the experimenter's hypothesis; but would a similar difference be found if the experiment were to be repeated? Could the obtained difference merely be the result of sampling variability? Here the researcher wishes to test the statistical **significance** of the difference, that is, to establish that the difference is too large to have been merely a chance occurrence.

1.4.1   The design of the experiment: independent versus related samples

Of crucial importance in the choice of an appropriate statistical test for comparing levels of performance is the question of whether the experiment would have resulted in **independent** or **related samples** of scores.

1.4.1.1   Independent samples

Suppose we select, say, 100 participants for an experiment and randomly assign half of them to an experimental condition and the rest to a control condition. With this procedure, the assignment of one person to a particular group has no effect upon the group to which another is assigned. The two **independent samples** of participants thus selected will produce two independent samples of scores, each consisting of 50 values. A useful criterion for deciding whether you have independent samples of data is that there must be no basis for **pairing** the scores in one sample with those in the other. An experiment in which independent samples of participants are tested under different conditions is known as a **between subjects** experiment.

1.4.1.2   Related samples

Suppose that each of fifty participants shoots ten times at a triangular target and ten times at a square target of the same area. For each target, each participant will have a score ranging from 0 (ten misses) to 10 (ten hits). As in the previous example, there will be two samples of 50 scores. This time, however, each score in either sample can be paired with the same participant's score with the other target. We have here two **related** or **paired** samples of scores. The scores in two related samples are likely to be substantially correlated, because participants who are better shots will tend to have higher scores with either target than those who are poorer shots. An experiment like this, in which each participant is tested under both (or all) conditions, is known as a **within subjects** experiment. Within subjects experiments are also said to have **repeated measures** on the treatment factor (the shape of the target).

There are other ways of obtaining paired data. Suppose that in the current example, the participants were pairs of identical or fraternal twins: each participant shoots at only one target and the twin shoots at the other. This experiment will also result in two related samples of scores, because, as in the repeated measures experiment, there is a basis for pairing the data. Different statistical tests are appropriate for use with independent and related samples of data.

1.4.2   Flow chart for selecting a suitable test for differences between means

Figure 4 outlines *some* of the considerations leading to a choice of a statistical test of the significance of differences between means (or frequencies, if one has nominal data). If there are more than two conditions or groups, an analysis of variance (ANOVA) may be applicable. In this section, we shall consider only the comparison between two groups or conditions, such as male versus female, or experimental group versus control group.

To use the chart, begin at the START box and consider how many conditions there are in the experiment. If there are two conditions, proceed down the chart to the next stage. The next questions are whether the samples are independent or related and whether the data are **scale** or **nominal** data (see Section 1.1.2). The appropriate test is shown in the bottom box.

See Chap. 6

The tests for comparing scores under two conditions (*t* tests and their nonparametric equivalents) will be described in Section 1.9 of this chapter and in Chapter 6.

The tests for making comparisons among scores obtained under three or more conditions will be discussed in Chapters 7-10, which are concerned with analysis of variance (ANOVA).

See Chaps 7-10

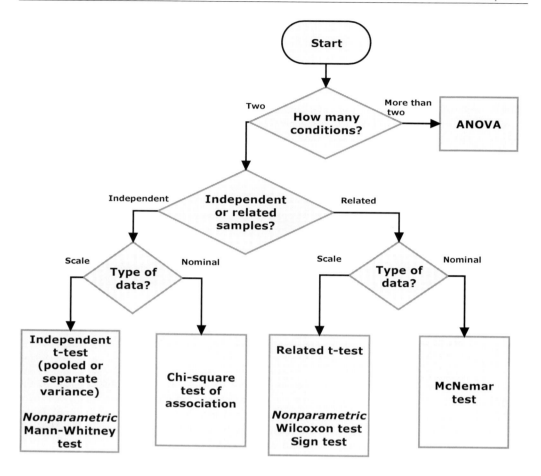

Figure 4. Flow chart showing the selection of a suitable test for differences between means or relative frequencies

In some schemes of this kind, there is a separate path for 'ordinal' data, along which the user is conducted to a choice of a nonparametric test, rather than a *t* test or analysis of variance. Ordinal data, however, are rare in experimental research, unless the researcher is working with ratings. Nonparametric tests can certainly be applied to scale data, but when this is done, the first step is the conversion of the original (scale) data to ranks, a process one might term 'ordinalization' of the data. For this reason, in the scheme of Figure 4, the nonparametric tests appear at the end of the path for scale data.

There are certainly those (including some journal editors) who insist that when the data are in the form of ratings, they must be regarded as ordinal rather than continuous, that is, as ranks with ties, and that a nonparametric test (such as the Mann-Whitney U test or the Wilcoxon matched-pairs test) should therefore be used, rather than a *t* test. Those who wish to have their papers published in such journals should bear this in mind.

1.5   ARE TWO VARIABLES ASSOCIATED?

Are those exposed to the most screen violence also the most violent in their actual behaviour? Do tall fathers tend to have tall sons, short fathers to have short sons and fathers of medium height to have sons of medium height?   These questions concern a possible statistical **association** between the two variables Father's Height and Son's Height.   To answer the question, you would need a data set comprising the heights of a substantial sample of fathers and those of their (first) sons.   For continuous or scale data such as these, the **Pearson correlation** measures the strength of association between the variables, provided the association is linear.

1.5.1   Flow chart for selecting a suitable test for association

Figure 5 outlines the questions one needs to answer in order to make a decision about an appropriate measure of association.

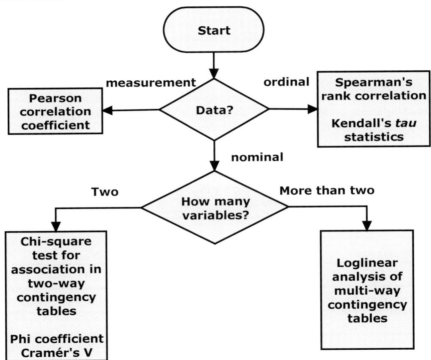

Figure 5. Flow chart showing measures of association

Begin at the START box and consider whether the data are scalar or ordinal. If the two variables are in the form of measurements, a Pearson correlation should be considered. However, as we shall see in Chapter 11, there are circumstances in which the Pearson correlation can be highly misleading. It is essential to examine the data first before proceeding to obtain the Pearson correlation coefficient.

See Chap. 11

1.5.2   Measuring association in ordinal data

The collection of truly ordinal data is more likely to occur in the context of correlational, as opposed to experimental, research. Suppose we ask two judges to rank twenty paintings in order of preference. We shall have a data set consisting of twenty pairs of ranks. Do the judges agree?

See Chap. 11

Again, our question is one of a statistical association. However, since the data in their original form are ordinal, a **rank correlation** is an appropriate statistic to use. The two most common kinds of rank correlation are:
  1.   **Spearman's rank correlation**;
  2.   **Kendall tau** statistics.
Both are considered more fully in Chapter 11.

1.5.3   Measuring association in nominal data: Contingency tables

A medical researcher suspects that the incidence of an antibody may be higher in patients of tissue type X, compared with its incidence in patients of tissue types, A, B and C. Seventy-nine patients are tissue-typed and tested for the presence of the antibody. Such an exercise will result in a set of nominal data on two qualitative variables or attributes, Tissue Type (A, B, C, X) and Presence (Yes, No). Here the scientific hypothesis is that there is an association between the two variables. Table 3 is a **contingency table**, which shows the joint classification on the two variables of the seventy-nine patients in the study. (SPSS uses the term **crosstabulation** to denote a table of this type.) The expected association is indeed evident in the table: there is a much higher incidence of the antibody in patients of tissue type X.

Table 3. A contingency table showing the incidence of an antibody in patients with four different types of tissue

Tissue type	Presence	
	No	Yes
A	14	8
B	11	7
C	5	7
X	6	21

The presence of an association can be confirmed by using a **chi-square** test (see Chapter 11). Since the value of the chi-square statistic depends partly upon the sample size, however, it is unsuitable as a measure of the *strength* of the association between two qualitative variables. Figure 5 identifies two statistics that measure strength of association between qualitative variables: **Cramér's V** and the **phi coefficient**. Both measures are discussed in Chapter 11.

See Chap. 11

1.5.4   Multi-way contingency tables

In recent years, there have been dramatic developments in the analysis of nominal data in the form of multi-way contingency tables. Previously, tables with three or more attributes were often 'collapsed' to produce two-way tables. The usual chi-square test could then be applied. Such 'collapsing', however, is fraught with risk, and the tests may give highly misleading results. The advent of modern **loglinear analysis** has made it possible to tease out the relationships among the attributes in a way that was not possible before (see Chapter 13).

> See
> Chap.
> 13

1.6   CAN WE PREDICT A SCORE FROM SCORES ON OTHER VARIABLES?

If there is an association between variables, it is natural to ask whether this can be exploited to predict scores on one variable from knowledge of those on another. For example, in some American universities, students take aptitude tests at matriculation and received an academic grade point average (GPA) at the end of their first year of study. Can students' GPAs be predicted from their earlier scores on the aptitude tests? Such prediction is indeed possible, and the methods by which this is achieved, which are known as **regression**, will be briefly reviewed in this section.

There are also circumstances in which one would wish to predict not scores on a target or criterion variable, but membership of a category of a qualitative variable. For example, it is of medical and actuarial interest to be able to assign individuals to an 'at risk' category on the basis of their smoking and drinking habits. Statistical techniques have been specially devised for this purpose also.

The purpose of the methods reviewed here is to predict a target, or **criterion** variable (the term **dependent variable** is also used in this context) from scores on other variables, known variously (depending on the context) as **regressors**, **predictors**, **independent variables**, or **covariates**. The predictors need not always be quantitative variables: qualitative variables, such as gender and blood group, are often included among the predictor variables in research of this kind.

1.6.1   Flow chart for predicting a score or category membership

To use the flow chart (Figure 6) for selecting the appropriate prediction procedure, begin at the START box and consider whether the target variable is qualitative (e.g. a set of categories such as Pass and Fail) or quantitative (e.g. examination scores, which are scale data).

Begin at the START box and consider the purpose of the test. If it is to test for goodness-of-fit, move down the left-hand side of the chart. If it is to estimate the population mean or its probable range, move down the right-hand side. The next consideration is the nature of the data: different types of data require different tests. If the target variable is quantitative, a **regression** method should be considered. In **simple regression**, there is one predictor; in **multiple regression**, there are two or more (Chapter 12). If the criterion variable is qualitative, the techniques of **discriminant analysis** and **logistic regression** must be considered (Chapter 14).

> See Chaps.
> 12 & 14

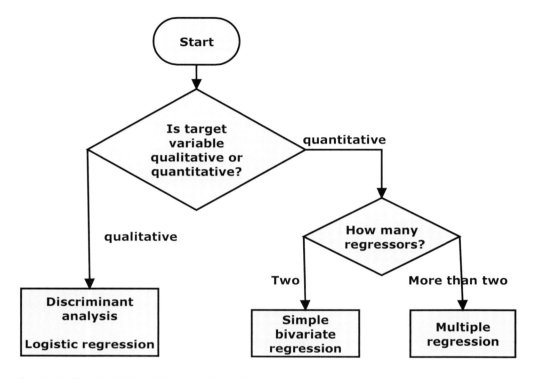

Figure 6. Flow chart showing procedures for prediction

1.6.2   Simple regression

In **simple regression**, a target or criterion variable is predicted from **one** predictor or regressor.

Suppose that, given a student's verbal aptitude score at matriculation, we want to predict the same student's grade point average a year later from the verbal aptitude score alone. Returning to our earlier example, can we predict a child's actual violence from the level of his exposure to screen violence? These are problems in simple regression, and the method is described in Chapter 12.

See Chap. 12

1.6.3   Multiple regression

A student's grade point average may be associated not only with verbal aptitude, but also with numerical ability. Can grade point average be predicted even more accurately when both verbal ability and numerical ability are taken into account? This is a problem in **multiple regression**. If grade point average is correlated with both verbal and numerical aptitude, multiple regression will produce (provided certain conditions are met) a more accurate prediction of a student's grade point average than will a simple regression upon either of the two regressors considered separately.

See Chap. 12

1.6.4   Predicting category membership: Discriminant analysis and logistic regression

Two statistical techniques designed to help the user make predictions of category membership are **discriminant analysis** and **logistic regression** (both of which are discussed in Chapter 14). In recent years, logistic regression, being a somewhat more robust technique than discriminant analysis, has become the preferred method.

See Chap. 14

1.7   FROM SAMPLE TO POPULATION

Much psychological research involves the collection of two or more samples of data. This is by no means always true, however: sometimes the researcher draws a **single** sample of observations in order to study just **one** population.

The situations in which one might use a one-sample test are of two main kinds:
1.   One may wish to compare a sample distribution with a hypothetical distribution, such as the normal. This is a question of **goodness-of-fit**.
2.   One may wish to make inferences about the **parameters** of a single population from the statistics of a sample.

1.7.1   Flow chart for selecting the appropriate one-sample test

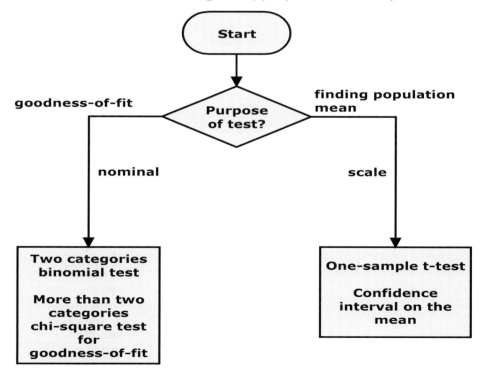

Figure 7. Flow chart of one-sample tests

Figure 7 summarises the circumstances in which a researcher might make various kinds of one-sample tests. The tests reviewed in this section are more fully considered in Chapters 6 and 11.

1.7.2 Goodness-of-fit: nominal data

Suppose a researcher wants to know whether 5-year-old children of a certain age show a preference for one of two types of toy (A or B). The choices of one hundred 5-year-olds are noted. Here the population comprises the choices (A or B) of 5-year-olds in general. Of the hundred children in the study, 60 choose toy A and 40 choose toy B. The null hypothesis states that the probability of choosing A (or B) is .5. More formally, as we shall see in Chapter 6, the null hypothesis states that we have sampled 100 times from a Bernoulli distribution with $p = .5$. Does this theoretical distribution fit our data? Figure 7 indicates that a **binomial test** can be used to test this hypothesis.

See Chap. 6

If, in the foregoing situation, there were three or more types of toys to choose from, the **chi-square** test of **goodness-of-fit** can be used to test the null hypothesis that the children have no preference for any particular toy.

1.7.3 Inferences about the mean of a single population

Suppose that a lecturer wishes to ascertain the typical reaction speed of first-year university students within a certain age group, say the 17 to 18 year-olds. The lecturer may have data on, say, two hundred first-year students; but the research question, being about the reaction speeds of first-year students in general, concerns the population of reaction times.

Figure 7 shows that a **one-sample *t* test** can be used to test the null hypothesis that a sample has been drawn from a population with a mean of a specified value. Often, however, as when the researcher is working with a non-standardised test, it may not be possible to specify any null hypothesis. The sample mean is a **point estimate** of the unknown population mean. The *t* distribution can also be used to build a **confidence interval** on the sample mean, so that the researcher has a range of values within which the true population mean can, with a specified degree of 'confidence', be assumed to lie.

See Chap. 6

The one-sample *t* test can also be used to test the difference between the means of two related samples of scores. If the difference between scores under the two conditions is found for each participant, we shall have a single sample of differences. If the null hypothesis is correct, the mean difference in the population is zero, which is equivalent to stating that, in the population, the mean scores under the two conditions have equal values. The related-samples *t* test and the one-sample *t* test, in fact, are exact equivalents and will produce exactly the same result.

1.8   THE SEARCH FOR LATENT VARIABLES

Suppose that 500 people are measured on twenty tests of ability and that the correlations between each test and every other test are arrayed in a square array known as a **correlation matrix (R-matrix)**. It is likely that, since those who are good at one thing tend also to be good at others, there will be substantial positive correlations among the tests in the battery.

Factor analysis (see Chapter 15) is a set of techniques which, on the basis of the correlations in an R-matrix, classify all the tests in a battery in terms of relatively few underlying (or **latent**) dimensions or **factors**. (The term factor has more than one meaning in statistics. In analysis of variance [ANOVA], a factor is an independent variable, that is, a set of related treatments or categories.) In **exploratory factor analysis**, the object is to find the minimum number of **factors** necessary to account for the correlations among the psychological tests. In **confirmatory factor analysis**, specified models are compared to see which of them gives the best account of the data.

See Chap. 15

While factors are hypothetical underlying dimensions, they are estimated, essentially, by sums of participants' scores on all the tests in the battery. Thus, in addition to scores on the tests, each person also receives one or more **factor scores**, each of which represents that person's endowment with the latent variable in question.

1.9   MULTIVARIATE STATISTICS

Factor analysis and canonical correlation belong to a set of techniques collectively known as **multivariate statistics**. While these methods arise naturally in the context of correlational research, however, they are also applicable to certain kinds of experimental data.

In Section 1.2, in which we considered experimental research, we spoke of the dependent variable (DV), which was measured during the course of the experiment and the independent variable (IV), which was manipulated by the experimenter with a view to showing that it had the power to affect the DV.

The DV in an experiment is often, in a sense, a representative or proxy variable. In a test of maze-learning proficiency, for instance, we may use the speed at which participants draw lines through the maze. Arguably, however, another aspect of performance, number of errors, also reflects maze-learning skill; indeed, in some situations there may be several reasonable potential dependent variables, any one of which could be taken as representative of proficiency.

Statistical methods designed for the analysis of data from experiments with a single DV are called **univariate statistics**. **Multivariate statistics** are methods designed for the analysis of data sets in which there are two or more DVs. In this context, however, the terms independent and dependent variable tend to be applied more generally to any research, whether experimental or correlational, in which some variables (the IVs) are thought to have a causal influence upon others (the DVs).

In experimental and quasi-experimental research, the *t* tests and ANOVA are generalised to **the multivariate analysis of variance** (**MANOVA**). In correlational research, factor analysis explains associations among the observed variables (the DVs) in terms of latent 'causal' variables known as **factors** which are, essentially, sums of the observed variables, but are taken to represent underlying psychological or health dimensions.

1.10   A FINAL WORD

In this chapter, we have offered some advice about using formal statistical tests to support the researcher's claim that what is true of a particular data set is likely to be true in the population.

At this point, however, a word of warning is appropriate. The making of a formal statistical test of significance always presupposes the applicability of a statistical **model**, that is, an interpretation (usually in the form of an equation) of the data set as having been generated in a specified manner. The model underlying the one-sample t test, for example, assumes that the data are from a normal population. To some extent, statistical tests have been shown to be robust to moderate violations of the assumptions of the models upon which they are based, that is, the actual error rates do not rise above acceptable levels. But there are limits to this robustness, and there are circumstances in which a result, declared by an incautious user to be significant beyond, say, the .05 level, may actually have been considerably more probable than that. There is no way of avoiding this pitfall other than by getting to know your data first (see Chapters 4 and 5) to ascertain their suitability for specified formal tests.

See
Chaps
4 & 5

Recommended reading

Terms and ideas in research design

There are available many excellent textbooks on research methodology. We have considered only those terms and principles that we consider to be essential for the purposes of data analysis with SPSS. (SPSS uses many of the terms we have introduced in this chapter.)

Field, A., & Hole, G. (2003). *How to design and report experiments*. London: Sage.

Chapter 1 discusses many of the methodological terms and issues touched upon in this chapter in greater depth and considers some more general issues in methodology.

Readable statistics texts

The reader with a limited mathematical background who is looking for a text on basic statistics is faced with a bewildering array of choices. We suggest the following book:

Sani, F., & Todman, J. (2006). *Experimental design and statistics for psychology: A first course*. Oxford: Blackwell.

For the reader who is more comfortable with algebraic notation, we suggest

Howell, D. C. (2007). *Statistical methods for psychology (6th ed.)*. Belmont, CA: Thomson/Wadsworth.

A useful dictionary of statistical terms

The following is a very useful reference book, with clear definitions.

Nelson, D. (2004). *The Penguin dictionary of statistics*. London: Penguin Books.

Some statistical terms and concepts

For the reader who, though familiar with such statistical terms as p-value, Type I and Type II errors, power and so on, is a little rusty on their meaning, we have provided some revision notes on our website at www.psypress.com/spss-made-simple.

CHAPTER 2

Getting started with IBM SPSS Statistics 18

2.1   OUTLINE OF AN SPSS SESSION

There are three stages in the use of SPSS :
1. The data are entered into the **SPSS Statistics Data Editor**.
2. Descriptive and statistical procedures are selected from the **drop-down menus**.
3. The output is examined and edited in the **SPSS Statistics Viewer**.

2.1.1   Entering the data

There are several ways of placing data in the **Data Editor**. They can be typed in directly or read in from SPSS data files that have already been created. SPSS can also read data from files produced by other applications, such as EXCEL, R and STATISTICA, as well as text files.

Once the data are in the **Data Editor**, the user has available a wide variety of editorial functions. Not only can the data be amended in various ways, but also selections from the original set can be targeted for subsequent analysis.

In this chapter, we shall give considerable attention to the **Data Editor**, because it enables the user to control important features of the output (such as the labelling of variables) which can make the results of a statistical analysis easier to interpret.

The user can also access important editing functions from an array of **drop-down menus** at the top of the screen.

2.1.2   Selecting the exploratory and statistical procedures

It is also from the drop-down menus that the user selects statistical procedures. The user is advised to explore the data thoroughly before making any formal statistical tests. SPSS offers many graphical methods for displaying a data set, some of which are described in Chapters 4 and 5. Graphs are of great assistance when you are getting to know your data.

2.1.3   Examining the output

The results of the analysis appear in the **SPSS Statistics Viewer**. The Viewer offers powerful editing facilities, which can be used to improve the appearance of the output and highlight the most important results.

From the SPSS Statistics Viewer, material can readily be transferred to files produced by other applications, such as Word, or printed out in hard copy.

2.1.4   A simple experiment

In this chapter, we shall illustrate the stages in a typical SPSS session by entering the results of a fictional experiment into the **Data Editor**, describing the data by choosing some statistics from the menu and examining the output. At this stage, we shall concentrate on the general procedure, leaving the details for later consideration.

Table 1 shows the results of an experiment designed to show the effects of a drug upon skilled performance.

Table 1. Results of an experiment designed to show whether a drug improves skilled performance							
Group							
Placebo				Drug			
Case	Score	Case	Score	Case	Score	Case	Score
1	6	6	3	11	8	16	8
2	5	7	2	12	6	17	6
3	5	8	4	13	6	18	7
4	1	9	5	14	7	19	5
5	2	10	1	15	6	20	10

The experiment, in which twenty participants attempted a test of skill, was of simple, two-group, between subjects design. Ten participants (cases) were assigned at random to one of two conditions:
1. A Placebo condition, in which the participant ingested a harmless saline solution;
2. A Drug condition, in which the participant ingested a small dose of a drug.

The dependent variable was the participant's score on the skilled task. The independent variable was the condition to which the participant was assigned: Drug or Placebo. The experimental hypothesis was that the group that had been assigned to the Drug condition would outperform the group assigned to the Placebo condition.

We shall shortly show how these data can be placed in the **SPSS Statistics Data Editor** and the results summarised with a few statistics.

2.1.5   Preparing data for SPSS

The data shown in Table 1 are not in a form that the SPSS Statistics Data Editor will accept. In a SPSS data set, each row must contain data on just one **case**, **subject** or **participant**. The data in Table 1 do not conform to this requirement: the first row of entries contains data from four different participants.

To make them suitable for analysis with SPSS, the data in Table 1 must be rearranged in a new format. In Table 2, the data in Table 1 have been re-tabulated, so that each row now contains data on only one participant.

Table 2. The data set of Table 1, recast in a form suitable for entry into SPSS

Participant	Condition	Participant's Score
1	1	6
2	1	5
3	1	5
4	1	1
5	1	2
6	1	3
7	1	2
8	1	4
9	1	5
10	1	1
11	2	8
12	2	6
13	2	6
14	2	7
15	2	6
16	2	8
17	2	6
18	2	7
19	2	5
20	2	10

In Table 2, the Condition variable identifies the group to which each participant belongs by means of an arbitrary code number, in this case 1 (for the Placebo condition) or 2 (for the Drug condition). Unlike the numbers in the Score column, which express level of performance, the code numbers in the Condition column serve merely as category labels: the Condition variable is a special kind of **categorical** variable (see Chapter 1) known as a **grouping variable**.

2.2   OPENING SPSS

There are several ways of beginning a session with SPSS, depending upon whether you intend to build a new file or access an old one. When SPSS is opened for the first time by clicking the SPSS icon, an introductory dialog box will appear with the title PASW Statistics 18 (the previous software Release was called PASW Statistics 17: the latest Release IBM SPSS Statistics 18 has not yet changed the titles of the dialog boxes).

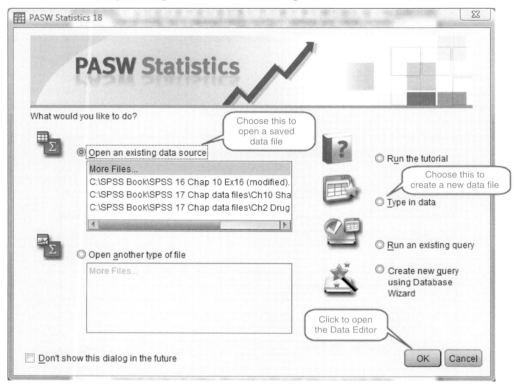

Figure 1. The **SPSS Statistics 18** opening dialog box

Underneath the title is the question: What would you like to do? Make your choice by clicking one of the six small radio buttons and then **OK** (Figure 1). Here we shall assume that you wish to enter data for the first time, in which case click the button labelled **Type in data**. When you click **OK**, the **Data Editor** will appear on the screen.

At a later stage, you may wish to omit the introductory dialog box, in which case click the square labelled **Don't show this dialog in the future** in the bottom left corner of the dialog box.

2.3   THE SPSS STATISTICS DATA EDITOR

The **Data Editor** provides two alternative spreadsheet-like arrays:

1. **Data View**, into which the user can enter new data or (if an old file has been accessed) view whatever data the file contains.
2. **Variable View**, which contains the names and details of the variables in the data set.

When you are creating a file for the first time, it is advisable to lay the foundations in **Variable View** first, so that when you come to enter data in **Data View**, the columns in the spreadsheet will already have been labelled, reducing the risk of transcription errors.

In this book, we shall use *italics* to indicate SPSS variable names and value labels that are to be typed into the **Data Editor**. We shall use a **bold** typeface for the names of menus, the names of dialog boxes and the captions therein.

2.3.1   Working in Variable View

When the **Data Editor** appears, you may find that you are in **Data View**. If so, click the tab labelled **Variable View** at the bottom left-hand side of the window and you will access **Variable View** (Figures 2a and 2b).

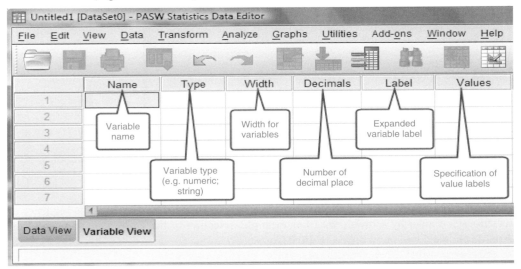

Figure 2a. Part of **Variable View** (For this figure, some of the columns have been narrowed.)

When the **Data Editor** first appears, the caption in the title bar reads, '**Untitled1 [DataSet0]** – **SPSS Statistics Data Editor**'. Any additional data sets (SPSS Statistics 18 allows more than one data set to be open during a SPSS session) would be numbered DataSet1, DataSet 2 and so on. When you finish entering your data (or preferably during data entry as a protection against losing data should the system crash), you can supply a name for the file by selecting the **Save As...** item from the **File** drop-down menu and entering a suitable name in the **File Name** box. After you have done this, the title bar will display your new name for the file.

Recent releases allow more than one data file to be available on the screen; though only one of them can be active at any one time. A file is activated by clicking anywhere within its window. The active file is marked with a green cross superimposed on the icon of a grid at the left-hand end of the title bar:

The word **Untitled** in the title bar is a warning to the user that the file has not yet been given a name and saved.

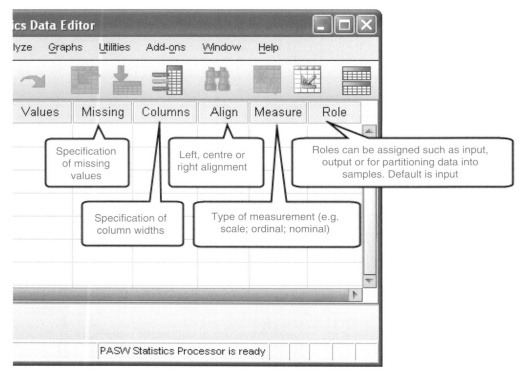

Figure 2b. Part of **Variable View** (For this figure, some of the columns have been narrowed.)

2.3.1.1   Notation for selecting from a menu

We shall adopt a notation for selecting items from a drop-down menu in which the sequence of selections is shown by arrows (➜). For example, selection of the **Copy** item from the **Edit** drop-down menu will be written as **Edit➜Copy**.

2.3.1.2   The Name and Labels columns

Some of the column headings in **Variable View** (such as number of places of decimals) are self-explanatory. The **Name** and **Labels** columns, however, require some explanation. A **variable name** is a string of characters (normally letters and spaces but it can include digits) which will appear at the head of a column in **Data View**, but not in the output. In other words, a variable name is a convenient shortened name for use only within **Data View** or when selecting items for analysis. In contradistinction, a **variable label** is a full, meaningful caption of the type you would wish to see in a book or a journal article.

There is a set of rules for naming variables, which can readily be accessed by entering SPSS's **Help** menu and choosing **Help➜Topics➜Index➜Variable names**. The main thing to remember is that a variable name must be a **continuous** sequence (no spaces) of up to 64 characters, *the first of which must be a letter*. Long variable names are not recommended. There can be any mixture of upper and lower case characters, and case is preserved for display purposes (e.g. TimeofDay). Phrasing can also be preserved in variable names by the use of an underline thus: Time_of_Day. (To obtain an underline, press and hold down the shift key, press the hyphen key.)   Although certain punctuation marks are permitted, it is simpler merely to remember to use letters and digits only.

2.3.1.3   Making entries in Variable View

- To name the variables Case, Group and Score, first check that there is a thickened border around the top leftmost cell (see Figure 2a). If it is not there, move the cursor there and click with the mouse.
- Type *Case* and press the ↓ cursor key to highlight the cell below to complete the entry of *Case* in the cell above. (Entry of information into a cell is only complete when the cursor is moved away to highlight another cell.)
- Type *Group* into the second cell with a thickened border and press the ↓ cursor key to highlight the cell below, completing the entry of *Group* in the cell above.
- Use the same procedure to enter the variable name *Score*.

SPSS will accept eight different **types** of variable, two of the most important being **numeric** (numerals with a decimal point) and **string** (e.g. names of participants, cities or other non-numerical material).   Initially, some of the format specifications of a variable are set by default, and the pre-set values will be seen as soon as the variable name has been typed and control transferred from the **Name** cell. Unless you specify otherwise, it will be assumed that the variable is of the numeric type.

The number of places of decimals that will be displayed in **Data View** is pre-set at 2. Since the scores in Table 2 are all integers, it would be tedious to read entries such as 46.00, 34.00 and 54.00, as opposed to 46, 34 and 54. It is better to suppress the display of decimals in **Data View** by clicking on the **Decimals** column to obtain the following display

By clicking twice on the downward-pointing arrow, you can replace the number 2 already in the cell with zero (see Figure 3). Note that this countermanding of the default specification will apply **only to the variable concerned**. Rather than over-riding the default specifications piecemeal in this way, you can reset the decimal display to zero for every numeric variable in the data set by choosing **Edit➔Options...➔Data** and resetting the number of decimal places to zero. See Chapter 3 for details.

See Chap. 3

Variable labels are assigned by using the **Label** column. In order to make the output as clear as possible, it is important to devise *meaningful* labels for all the variables in the data set. The labels shown in Figure 3, Case Number and Experimental Condition, are more informative than the corresponding variable names Case and Group, respectively, which are adequate for use within the **Data Editor**.

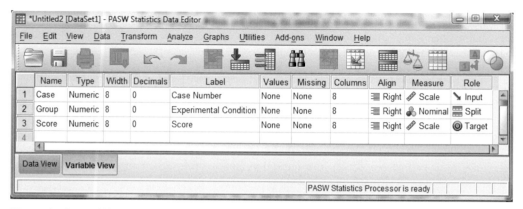

Figure 3. Part of **Variable View**, with entries specifying the names and details of the three variables

The **Values** column is for use with **grouping variables**. By clicking on **Values**, the user can supply a key to the meanings of the code numbers. In this case, the grouping variable is Experimental Condition and we can arbitrarily decide that 1 = Placebo and 2 = Drug. Click the first cell of the Values column to obtain the following display:

Note the grey area on the right with the three dots (…). Clicking this grey area will produce the **Values** dialog box (see Figures 4a and 4b).

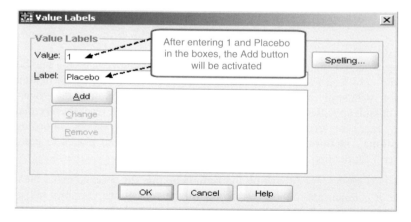

Figure 4a. How to enter value labels which, in the output, will replace the code numbers making up a grouping variable. The procedure is repeated for each value label e.g. 2 = "Drug"

Figures 4a and 4b show how to fill in the **Values** dialog box so that, in the output, the code number 1 will be replaced by the more informative value label Placebo. The same procedure is used to add Drug for value 2. In addition, when you switch to **Data View** and start entering data, the value labels will appear, provided either **Value Labels** within the **View** drop-down menu is ticked or you have clicked the value labels icon in the toolbar.

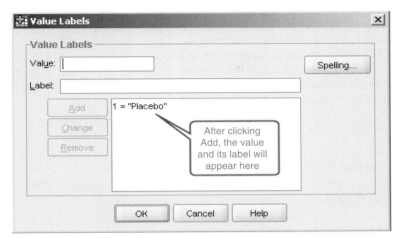

Figure 4b. The outcome after doing the steps outlined in Figure 4a

2.3.1.4   The Width column

With string variables, the **Width** column controls the maximum length (in number of characters) of the string you will be allowed to enter when you are working in **Data View**. (The setting in Width has no effect upon the number of characters you can type in when working with a numeric variable, just upon the number you can see.)

The default setting for Width is 8, but this can be changed by choosing **Edit➔Options➔Data** and changing the **Width** setting there. For more details, see Chapter 3. If a string is too long for the set width, you will find that you will not see the extra letters when you go into **Data View**.

See Chap. 3

Note that when you are working in either Variable View or Data View, you can easily widen the columns at any time by clicking and dragging on their boundary lines.

2.3.1.5   The Columns column

The cells of this column display the actual widths, for all the variables in the data set, of the columns that will appear in **Data View**. Initially, the cells in **Columns** will show the same setting as the **Width** column: 8. Were you to create a new numeric variable with a name whose length exceeded the preset width, only part of the name would be displayed in the **Name** column of **Variable View**. Moreover, in **Data View**, only part of the variable name would be visible at the head of the column for that variable.

To specify wider columns for a variable in **Data View** while working in **Variable View**, click the appropriate cell in **Columns** and adjust the setting there.

2.3.1.6   The Align column

This determines whether the data are **Left**, **Right** or **Centre** aligned. The default setting is **Right**.

2.3.1.7 The Measure column

This enables the user to declare whether the data are **Scale** (i.e. measurements), **Ordinal** or **Nominal** (see Section 1.1.2 Levels of measurement: scale, ordinal and nominal data). The default measure is **Scale**. It is important to declare categorical variables such as sex or blood group as **Nominal** and categorical variables such as rating scales as **Ordinal**, especially if a graphic (e.g. an item from **Chart Builder** or the **Tables** procedure) is going to be used. For our example, Case and Score would be entered in the Measure column as **Scale** and Group would be entered as **Nominal**.

See
Section
1.1.2

2.3.1.8 The Role column

Variables can be assigned roles such as input or output, or for partitioning data into samples. These roles will then assist in the selection of variables in certain dialog boxes. By default, all variables are assigned the **Input** role. Further details are available in SPSS's **Help** menu (**Help➜Topics➜roles**).

2.3.1.9 Copying settings

Values in the cells of **Variable View** can be copied and pasted to other cells using the standard Windows methods (see Section 2.3.3). For example, having adjusted the **Columns** setting to, say, 15 characters for one variable of the data set, the new setting can be applied to other variables by copying and pasting the contents of the cell with the entry 15 into the cells for the other variables.

Modified settings can also be copied to **Columns** from the **Width** Column. Having adjusted an entry in the **Width** column to, say, 16, the new setting can be copied and pasted into **Columns** in the usual way. The effect will be to widen the columns in **Data View** for the variables to which the new **Columns** setting has been copied.

2.3.2 Working in Data View

Once the appropriate specifications have been entered in **Variable View**, click the **Data View** tab at the bottom of the **Variable View** window to enter **Data View** (Figure 5). At this stage it is a good precaution to save the data file (see Section 2.3.3.8). When **Data View** is accessed, the variable names Case, Group and Score will be seen at the heads of the first three columns as specified in **Variable View**. The default name *var*, which appears in the third, fourth and fifth columns, indicates that those columns have yet to be assigned to specified variables.

Running along the bottom of the **Data View** window is a horizontal band, in which various messages appear from time to time. When SPSS is accessed, the message reads: **SPSS Processor is ready**. The horizontal band is known as the **Status Bar**, because it reports not only whether SPSS is ready to begin, but also on the stage that a procedure has reached. If, for example, a large data set is being read from a file, progress is continually monitored, in blocks of cases, in the status bar.

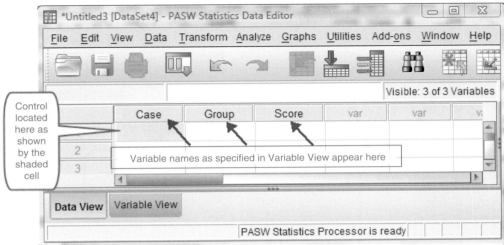

Figure 5. Part of **Data View**, showing the variable names and active cell

2.3.3   Entering the data

Figure 6 shows a section of **Data View**, in which the data in Table 1 have been entered. The first variable, Case, represents the case number of the participants. Enter the number of each participant from 1 to 20. The second variable Group, identifies the condition under which each participant performed the task: 1 = Placebo; 2 = Drug. Enter ten 1's into the first ten rows of the Group variable, followed by ten 2's. Do this in the manner described in Section 2.3.3.1.

In the first ten cells of the Score column, enter the scores of the ten participants who performed the task under the Placebo condition, followed by those of the ten participants who performed under the Drug condition.

Notice that in Figure 6, location of control is indicated by the shaded cell in the 12th row of the second column. The value in this cell is 6. The contents of this cell are also displayed in a white area known as the **cell editor** just above the column headings. The value in the **cell editor** (and the cell itself) can be changed by clicking in the **cell editor**, selecting the present value, typing a new one and pressing ⏎. The new value will appear in the grid.

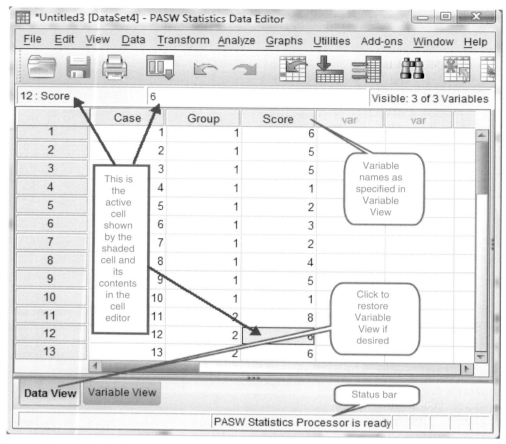

Figure 6. Part of **Data View** after the results in Table 1 have been entered

2.3.3.1 Blocking, copying and pasting

Initially, only one cell in **Data View** is highlighted. However, as we have seen, it is possible to highlight a whole block of cells, or even an entire row or column. This **blocking** operation (when all the cells appear in **inverse video**, with the characters printed in white against a black background) is achieved either by clicking and dragging with the mouse or proceeding as follows:

- To highlight a *whole row or column*, click the grey box containing the row number or the column heading.
- To highlight a *block of cells* within a row or column, click on the first cell and (keeping the left button of the mouse pressed down) drag the pointer to the cell at the end of the block. The same result can be obtained by clicking the first cell in the block, pressing the **Shift** key and keeping it held down while using the appropriate cursor key ($\uparrow$ or $\downarrow$) to move the highlighting along the entire block.

The blocking operation can be used to copy the values in one column into another or to place them elsewhere in the same column.

- Highlight a column of values that you wish to copy and then choose **Edit➔Copy**.
- Next, highlight the cells of the target column and choose **Edit➔Paste**.

The values in the source column will now appear in the target column. (Make sure that the number of highlighted target cells is equal to the number of cells copied.) For example, the successions of 1's and 2's identifying the Placebo and Drug conditions could have been entered as follows.

- Place the value 1 in the topmost cell of the Group column. Move the black rectangle away from the cell to complete the entry of the value and return the highlight to the cell, which will now contain the value 1.
- Choose **Edit➔Copy** to store the value 1 in the clipboard.
- Highlight cells 2 to 10 and choose **Edit➔Paste** to place the value 1 in all the highlighted cells.

2.3.3.2 Using key combinations to copy and paste

Copying and pasting can also be carried out by using the key combinations **Ctrl + C** (hold the **Ctrl** key down, then press C) and **Ctrl + V**, respectively.

2.3.3.3 Deletion of values

Whether you are working in **Variable View** or in **Data View**, entries can be removed by selecting the target items in the manner described above and pressing the **Delete** key. Note that a period (.) indicates a missing value.

2.3.3.4 Switching between Data View and Variable View

You can switch from one **Data Editor** display to the other at any point. While in **Data View**, for instance, you might want to return to **Variable View** to name further variables or add further details about existing ones. Just click the **Variable View** tab. When you have finished the new work in **Variable View**, click **Data View** to continue entering your data.

2.3.3.5 Creating more space for entries in Data View

While the widths of the columns in **Data View** can be controlled from **Variable View** in the manner described above, you can also control column width while working in **Data View**. To widen a column, click on the grey cell containing the variable name at the top of the column and click and drag the right-hand border to the right.

2.3.3.6 Displaying value labels in Data View

The values assigned to the numerical values of a grouping variable can be displayed in **Data View** by clicking the icon in the toolbar or by choosing **View➔Value Labels**.

Should the Group column in **Data View** not be sufficiently wide to show the value labels completely, create more space by placing the cursor in the grey cell at the head of the column containing the label Group and click and drag the right-hand border of the cell to the right.

2.3.3.7 Using the display of values in the Data Editor as a guide when entering data

Having specified the variable type as numeric when in **Variable View**, you will find that **Data View** will accept, in the first instance, only numerical entries. After you have typed in the value 1, however, you can display its value label as described in Section 2.3.3.6 . You will now see the label Placebo in the cell. You can now copy and paste this label to the other nine cases in the Placebo group in the usual way. When you come to the Drug group, however, you will need to type in 2 which, when you click another cell, will then appear as the value Drug. Data View will not accept the word *Drug* typed in directly. You can then copy and paste the second numerical label to the remaining cases in the Drug group. This procedure can be useful if, momentarily, as when your SPSS session has been interrupted, you have forgotten the number-label pairings you assigned in **Variable View**. It also helps you to avoid transcription errors when transferring your data from response sheets.

2.3.3.8   Saving the data file

Save your work frequently. Even modern computers can freeze up and you can lose hours of work. While entering your data, save your work by choosing **Save As…** from the **File** drop-down menu, selecting an appropriate drive and/or folder and then entering a suitable name in the **File Name** box. After you have done this, the title bar of the Data Editor will display the name you assigned to the file. Note that if you do not do this before ending the session, you will be prompted to supply a name for the data file at that point. If you are working in the Data Editor and save your work to a named file, you can update the contents of the file easily by clicking the disk icon in the toolbar underneath the drop-down menus at the top of the window. In this way, you can continually update the file and so keep most of your work safe from mishaps.

2.3.3.9   SPSS tutorials

For an animated step-by-step tutorial on entering data into SPSS, readers can work through the tutorial provided by SPSS. Click the **Help** drop-down menu, select **Tutorial** and then **Using the Data Editor**. The arrow buttons in the right-hand bottom corner of each page of the tutorial enable the user to navigate forward and backward through the tutorial.

2.4   A STATISTICAL ANALYSIS

2.4.1   An example: Computing the group means

In this section, we shall use SPSS to summarise the results of the experiment by obtaining some descriptive statistics such as the mean and standard deviation of the scores for each treatment group (Placebo and Drug).

Several SPSS routines, including **Descriptives**, calculate means and standard deviations. In our case, however, the data contain a grouping variable and we want to compare the group means and other aspects of the group distributions. The **Means** procedure will do this for us; in fact, in order for the procedure to run, **Means** requires that the data set includes a grouping variable, which the user will be prompted to specify. **Descriptives** would be the wrong choice here, because it calculates the means of entire columns only.

- From the drop-down **Analyze** menu, choose **Compare Means➔Means …** as shown in Figure 7.
- Click **Means…** to access the **Means** dialog box (Figure 8).

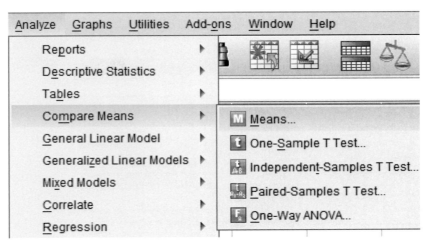

Figure 7. Finding the **Means** menu

Initially, in the left-hand panel the variable names are obscured; but you can view the entire label by touching it with the screen pointer.

- Click on Score to highlight it and then on the arrow pointing to the **Dependent List** box. The variable name and label will then be transferred to the Dependent List box. Alternatively, the variable names can be dragged and dropped into the appropriate panel.

- In a similar manner, transfer the variable Experimental Condition to the **Independent List** box (see Figure 9).

- Click **OK** to run the analysis. The results will appear in a new window called the **SPSS Statistics Viewer**, a section of which is shown in Output 1.

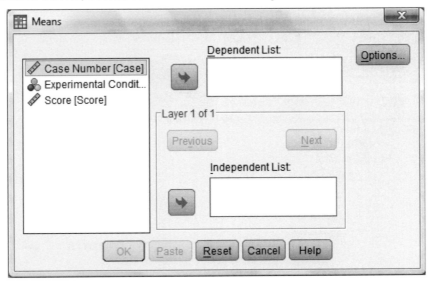

Figure 8. The **Means** dialog box showing the three variables in the data set

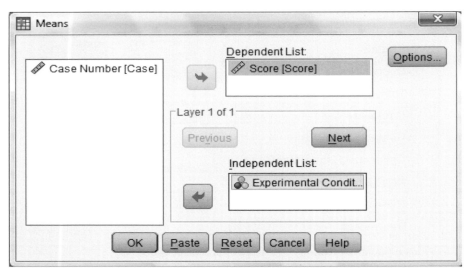

Figure 9. The completed **Means** dialog box for computing the mean scores for the two experimental conditions

The **SPSS Statistics Viewer** window is divided into two 'panes' by a vertical grey bar. The left pane shows the hierarchical organisation of the contents of the **Viewer**. The right pane contains the results of the statistical analysis and various other items. If some of the contents labels are not fully visible, the bar can be dragged to the right by moving the cursor on to it, pressing the left cursor button and dragging the bar as far as necessary. The contents of the **Viewer** on both sides of the bar can be edited.

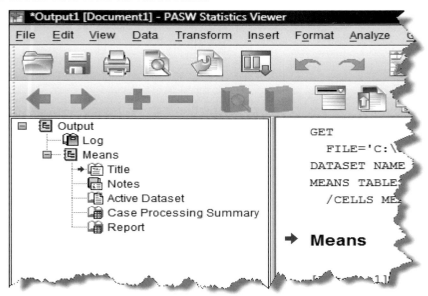

Output 1. Part of the **SPSS Statistics Viewer** window showing the list of output items in the left pane. The output tables appear in the right pane

For the moment, however, the main item of interest is the **Report** (Output 2), which appears in the right pane. From the **Report**, it can be seen that the mean performance of those tested under the Drug condition was over twice the level of those tested under the Placebo condition.

Report

Score

Experimental Condition	Mean	N	Std. Deviation
Placebo	3.40	10	1.838
Drug	6.90	10	1.449
Total	5.15	20	2.412

Output 2. The **Report** table showing the mean, number of scores and standard deviation in each of the two groups

It would seem, therefore, that the results of the experiment support the hypothesis. This, however, is insufficient: formal tests are necessary to confirm the appearance of the data. It should be noted, however, that before the researcher makes any formal statistical tests, the data should first be thoroughly explored. SPSS has an exploratory data analysis procedure, **Explore**, which offers a wide range of useful statistics. **Explore** can be run by choosing **Analyze➔Descriptive Statistics➔Explore…**.

We shall consider **Explore** more fully in Chapter 4.

See Chap. 4

2.4.1.1   Editing the output in SPSS Statistics Viewer

The **SPSS Statistics Viewer** offers powerful editing facilities, some of which can radically alter the appearance of a default table such as that shown in Output 3. Many of the tables in the output are **pivot tables**, that is, tables in which the columns and rows can be transposed and to which other radical alterations can be made.

Report

Variables Score ▼

Experimental Condition	Mean	N	Std. Deviation
Placebo	3.40	10	1.838
Drug	6.90	10	1.449
Total	5.15	20	2.412

Output 3. An item which has been prepared for editing. On double-clicking the item, a dotted border appears around it

Suppose, for example, that you would prefer the experimental conditions Placebo and Drug to be column headings and the group means, standard deviations and N's to be below them. If you double-click the **Report**, a dotted border will appear around the table (Output 3). You will notice that, along the drop-down menus at the top of the **Viewer** window, a new menu, **Pivot**, has appeared.

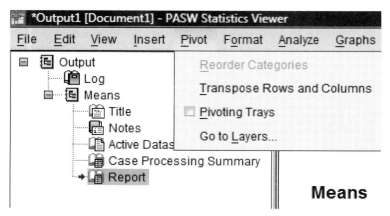

Figure 10. The **Pivot** drop-down menu with **Transpose Rows and Columns** selected

- Choose **Pivot➜Transpose Rows and Columns** (Figure 10).

The effect (see Output 4) is dramatic! The descriptive statistics now occupy the rows and the experimental conditions the columns.

The **Pivot** menu can be used to edit complex tables with three, four or more dimensions of classification. Such manipulation can be of great assistance in bringing out the most important features of your results.

Report

Score

	Experimental Condition		
	Placebo	Drug	Total
Mean	3.40	6.90	5.15
N	10	10	20
Std. Deviation	1.838	1.449	2.412

Output 4. The transposed **Report** table

2.4.2   Keeping more than one application open

One useful feature of Windows is that the user can keep several applications open simultaneously. It is therefore quite possible to be writing a document in **Word** while at the same time running **SPSS** and importing output such as the **Report** in the previous section. If more than one application is open, the user can move from one to another by clicking on the appropriate button on the **Taskbar** (usually located at the foot of the screen). Alternatively, you can hold down the **Alt** key and press the **Tab** key repeatedly to cycle control through whatever applications may be open.

2.5   CLOSING SPSS

SPSS is closed by choosing **Exit** from the **File** menu. If you have not yet saved the data or the output at any point, a default dialog box will appear with the question: **Save contents of data editor to untitled?** or **Save contents of output viewer to Output 1?** You must then click the **Yes**, **No** or **Cancel** button. If you choose **Yes**, you will be given a final opportunity to name the file you wish to save. Beware of saving unselected output files because they can occupy considerable storage space, especially if they contain graphics.

2.6   RESUMING WORK ON A SAVED DATA SET

There are several ways of resuming work on a saved data set. After opening SPSS and obtaining the introductory **SPSS Statistics 18** dialog box, you can click the radio button **Open an existing data source** (Figure 1). A list of saved files with the extension *.sav* will appear in the upper **More Files** window. Select the appropriate file and click **OK**. The data file will then appear in **Data View**. Other kinds of file, such as SPSS output files, can be retrieved from the lower **More Files** window by clicking on the radio button labelled **Open another kind of file**. While you are in the **Data Editor**, it is always possible to access files by choosing **Open** from the **File** menu. A quicker method of accessing a SPSS data file is to double-click its icon. The data will immediately appear in **Data View**.

Exercises

Exercise 1 *Some simple operations with SPSS Statistics 18* and Exercise 2 *Questionnaire data* are available in www.psypress.com/spss-made-simple and click on Exercises.

CHAPTER 3

Editing data sets

3.1   MORE ABOUT THE SPSS STATISTICS DATA EDITOR

3.1.1   Working in Variable View

In Section 2.2, we introduced the **Data Editor**, which has two alternative displays, **Variable View** and **Data View**. Here we describe some additional features of **Variable View** (see Section 2.3.1).

> See Section 2.3.1

3.1.1.1   Inserting new variables

An additional variable can be inserted in **Variable View** by highlighting any row (click the grey cell on the left), and choosing **Data➔Insert Variable**.

The new variable, with a default name such as VAR00004 (i.e. the next free name), will appear **above** the row that has been highlighted.

In **Data View,** the new variable will appear in a new column **to the left** of the variable that was highlighted in **Variable View**.

3.1.1.2   Rearranging the order of variables in Variable View

In Figure 1, is a section from **Variable View**, in which the top-to-bottom ordering of the variables determines their left-to-right order of appearance in **Data View**, which is Case, Group, then Score.

	Name	Type	Width	Decimals
1	Case	Numeric	8	0
2	Group	Numeric	8	0
3	Score	Numeric	8	0

Figure 1. The arrangement of the variables in **Variable View** determines their order of appearance in **Data View**

Suppose that you want to change the sequence of the variables in **Data View**: you want Score to appear to the left of Group. In **Variable View**, click the grey box to the left of the Score variable to highlight the whole row. Holding the left mouse button down, drag the screen pointer upwards. A red line will appear above the Group row. On releasing the mouse button, the variable Score will appear immediately under Case (Figure 2). In **Data View**, the variable Score will now appear to the left of the variable Group.

	Name	Type	Width	Decimals
1	Case	Numeric	8	0
2	Score	Numeric	8	0
3	Group	Numeric	8	0

Figure 2. The arrangement of variables after moving Score above Group

3.1.1.3   Large data sets: inserting case numbers

In the small data set we considered in Chapter 2, each row had a number and could be taken as representing one particular case or person. Suppose, however, that we had a much larger data set, containing thousands of cases. Suppose also that, from time to time, cases were to be removed from the data set or that the data were to be sorted and re-sorted on different criteria. As a result, any particular row in the data set, say the 99th row, may not always contain data on the same person throughout the exercise.

With a large data set like this, especially one that is continually changing, it is good practice to create, as the first variable, one with a name such as Case, which records each participant's original case number: 1, 2, ..., and so on. The advantage of doing this is that, even though a given person's data may occupy different rows at different points in the data-gathering exercise, the researcher always knows which data came from which person.

Should the accuracy of the transcription of a participant's data into SPSS later be called into question, that person's data can always be identified and checked throughout the entire process of data entry.

Suppose you wish to add case numbers to a data set. This is easily done, however large the data set may be, by using the **Compute Variable** procedure as follows:

- Create a new variable named Case to the left of the first variable in Data View.
- Choose **Transform➔Compute Variable...** to open the **Compute Variable** dialog box.

- Place the cursor in the **Target Variable** slot and enter the variable name *Case*.

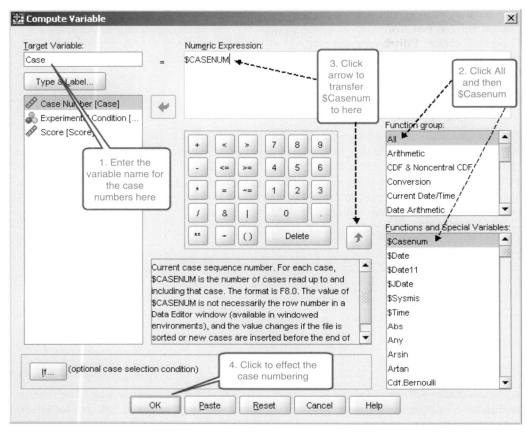

Figure 3. Part of the **Compute Variable** dialog box for generating case numbers

- Follow the instructions shown in Figure 3 and click **OK**.
- Click the **Data View** tab to confirm that, on the extreme left, a new variable named Case has appeared, containing the counting numbers 1, 2, … .

Note that this procedure cannot be used for creating case numbers in an empty data file. If you want to create case numbers before entering data, then you can proceed as follows.

- Create a new variable named Case.
- Enter an arbitrary first value, such as 1.
- Copy the contents of the first cell to the buffer with **Edit➔Copy**.
- Select as many cells as you need to make up the total number of cases.
- Paste the value into the selected cells by choosing **Edit➔Paste**.
- Choose **Transform➔Compute Variabe** and $CASENUM as before to insert the case numbers, which will replace the repeated value in the Case variable.

The default settings for variable width and the number of places of decimals are 8 and 2, respectively. If you wish to enter several new variables and display them all as whole numbers (integers), choose **Edit➜Options➜Data** and change the pre-set values. Figure 4 shows the top of the **Options** dialog box.

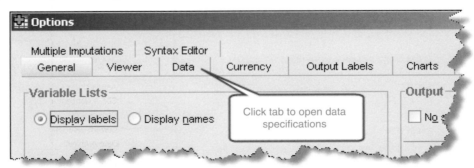

Figure 4. The top of the **Options** dialog box

- Click the tab labelled **Data**. In the new dialog box is an area headed **Display Format for New Numeric Variables** (Figure 5), in which both the width and number of decimal places can be amended.
- In the box containing the number of **Decimal Places**, click the downward arrow on the right until 0 appears. Click **OK** and the **Options** dialog box will close. The changes you have specified will apply only to any **new** numeric variables that you may create. You will find that, even after amending the default settings in **Options**, the appearance of numerical data already in **Data View** is unchanged.
- At the foot of the **Data** dialog box, is a button labelled **Apply**, which is activated when you change the settings. The purpose of the **Apply** button is to register the changes you have made **without closing the dialog box**. You can then click other tabs and make whatever changes you wish to make in those before leaving **Options** by clicking on **OK**.

If you are working on a networked computer where the software and settings are held on a central server, any changes you may make by changing the entries in **Options** may apply only for the duration of your own session: when you log off, the system will restore the original default values.

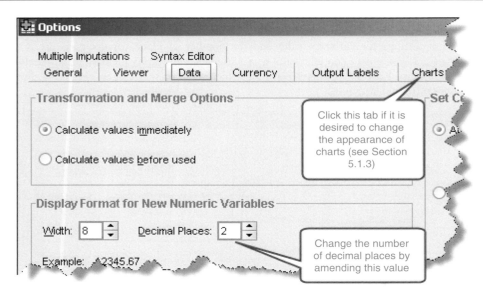

Figure 5. The **Options** dialog box showing the panel for adjusting the **Display Format for New Numeric Variables**

3.1.1.5   Changing the type of variable (the Type column)

In **Variable View**, there is a column headed **Type**. The **Type** column specifies the general form that an entry for a particular variable will take when it appears in the data set. By default, the variable type is assumed to be **numeric**, but seven other types can be specified in SPSS.

A **string** is a sequence of characters, such as a person's name, which is treated as a qualitative variable (not as a numeric variable) by the system. Had we entered, in the variable Name, the names of all the participants taking part in the drug experiment, Name would have been a **string variable**.

To create a string variable, proceed as follows:
- After typing in the name of the variable, highlight the cell in the **Type** column thus

- Click the grey area with the three dots to the right of **Numeric** to open the **Variable Type** dialog box (Figure 6).
- In the dialog box is a list of eight variable types, each with a radio button. Initially, the **Numeric** button will be marked.
- Descriptions of the different types of variable will be found by clicking the **Help** button in the dialog box.

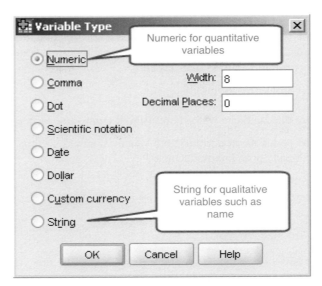

Figure 6. The **Variable Type** dialog box

- Click the **String** radio button at the foot of the list. The **Width** and **Decimal Places** boxes will immediately be replaced by a box labelled **Characters**.
- Change the default value 8 in the **Characters** box to some larger number such as 20 to accommodate the longest likely name. Do this by moving the cursor into the number box, selecting the 8 and typing in 20.
- Click **OK**. In **Variable View**, the variable type String will now appear in the **Type** column and the cell for the Name variable in the **Width** column will now show 20.
- Click the **Width** column and copy the specifications either by choosing **Copy** from the **Edit** menu or with the key combination **Ctrl + C**.
- Click on **Columns** and paste the new **Width** specification (20) there either by choosing **Paste** from the **Edit** menu or with the key combination **Ctrl + V**. The effect of this move will be to make sufficient space available in **Data View** to see the longest name in the data set. Alternatively, in **Data View**, the right-hand edge of the box containing the variable Name can be dragged to the right by holding down the left mouse button and dragging it as far as desired.

3.1.1.6 Missing values (the Missing column)

SPSS assumes that all data sets are complete (i.e. that the cells in every row and every column have something in them). The user, however, may not have entries for every case on every variable in the data set (e.g. a participant's age might not have been recorded). Such missing entries are marked by SPSS with what is known as a **system-missing** value, which is indicated in the **Data Editor** by a full stop. SPSS will exclude system-missing values from its calculations of means, standard deviations and other statistics.

It may be, however, that for some purposes the user wishes SPSS to treat certain responses actually present in the data set as missing data. For example, suppose that, in an examination, some candidates either walked out the moment they saw the paper or, having attempted at least some of the examination, earned only a nominal mark (say 20% or less) from the examiner. In either case, you might wish to treat the candidate's response as a missing value, but for some purposes you might want to retain information about the relative frequencies of the two responses in the output. In SPSS terminology, the user wants certain responses to be treated as **user-missing** values (as opposed to **system-missing** values).

Suppose you want SPSS to treat as missing:
1. Any marks between 0 and 20.
2. Cases where the candidate walked out without giving any written response at all.

A walk-out could be coded as an arbitrary, but salient, number, such as -9: the negative sign helps the number to stand out as impossible mark.

To define such user-missing values:
- In **Variable View**, move the cursor to the **Missing** column and click on the appropriate cell for the variable concerned.
- Click the grey area with the ellipsis █ to the right of **None** to open the **Missing Values** dialog box.
- Initially, the **No missing values** radio button is marked. The three text boxes underneath give the user the opportunity to specify up to three **Discrete Missing Values**, referred to in SPSS as 'missing (1)', 'missing (2)', and 'missing (3)'. These may either be numerical, as with a grouping variable, or short string variables (up to 8 characters in length), but they must be consistent with the original variable type. In the case of a string variable, the procedure is case sensitive. The other options in the dialog box are for scale (quantitative) variables: the user may define a missing value as one falling within a specified range, or one that falls either within a specified range or within a specified category.
- Click the **Range plus one discrete missing value** button. Enter the values 0 and 20 into the **Low** and **High** boxes, respectively, and –9 into the **Discrete value** box. The completed dialog box is shown in Figure 7.
- Click **OK** and the values will appear in the **Missing** column cell.

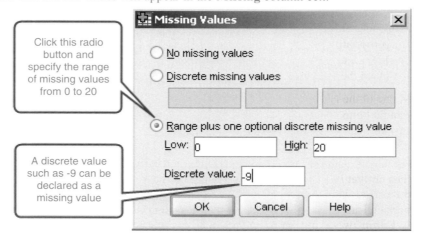

Figure 7. The completed **Missing Values** dialog box showing a range of missing values between 0 and 20 and a discrete value of -9

As with the attributes of number of decimals places and width, missing value specifications can be copied to other variables by pasting them into the appropriate cells.

3.1.1.7   Data alignment (the Align column)

In **Data View**, by default, numbers are right-aligned and strings are left-aligned.   These settings can be changed by clicking on the appropriate cell in the **Align** column and choosing **Left**, **Right** or **Center**.

3.1.1.8   Measurement level (the Measure column)

The default measurement level is **Scale** for numeric variables and **Nominal** for **String** variables.   Although a grouping variable refers to a set of qualitative categories, its representation in SPSS is still numeric, because it is a set of code numbers for the groups or conditions and should be specified as **Nominal** in the **Measure** column in **Variable View**.   In most chart-drawing and table-producing procedures, it is imperative that category variables are specified as **Nominal**.

3.1.1.9   The Role column

Variables can be assigned roles such as input or output, or for partitioning data into samples. These roles will then assist in the selection of variables in certain dialog boxes. By default, all variables are assigned the **Input** role. Further details are available in SPSS's **Help** menu (**Help➔Topics➔roles**).

3.1.2   Working in Data View

In Sections 2.3.2 and 2.3.3, the entry of data in **Data View** was briefly considered. Here we shall describe some additional features of **Data View**.

> See
> Sections
> 2.3.2 &
> 2.3.3

3.1.2.1   Reading in SPSS files

- When the opening SPSS window appears, select **Open an existing data source**.
- Select the appropriate file. (If you are working on a networked computer, you may have to click **More files …** and locate the file or folder containing the file.)
- Click **OK** to load the data file into **Data View**.

Alternatively, one of the following methods can be used:

- Click the radio button of the opening SPSS window labelled **Type in data** and then **OK** to bring **Data View** to the screen.
- Select **File➔Open➔Data** to show the **Open File** dialog box. The target file can then be specified.
- If SPSS has not yet been opened, you can use the Windows **Find** menu or **My Computer** to locate the file, which should open SPSS with the data loaded in **Data View** (or the variables loaded in **Variable View**) when the file name is double-clicked. Sometimes, especially with networked computers, it may be necessary to open SPSS first. While data are being read into **Data View** from a file, the hour-glass will appear and messages will appear in the **Status Bar** at various stages in the operation. The message **SPSS Processor is ready** signals the end of the reading process.

3.1.2.2   Entering data into Data View before specifying variables in Variable View

Although we strongly recommend that you lay the foundations in **Variable View** before actually entering the data in **Data View**, it is possible to begin immediately to enter data into **Data View**. It is also possible to copy blocks of data directly into **Data View**, which can be useful when you are importing data from another application which does not have one of the many data formats recognised by SPSS. The details of the variables can be added in **Variable View** later.

- Choose **File➜New** to create an empty SPSS data file.
- Enter **Data View** and type the value 23 into the cell in the second row of the fourth column. **Data View** will now appear as in Figure 8.

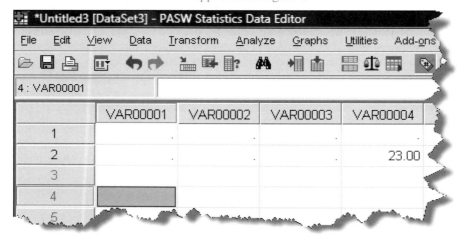

Figure 8. The appearance of **Data View** after entering a datum without previously naming variables in **Variable View**

The fourth variable has now been given the default name *VAR00004*. Notice that SPSS has assumed that we have a 2×4 matrix of data and filled in the blank cells with the system-missing symbol. Should you type values into cells to the right of the fourth column, more default variable names will appear as SPSS expands the supposed data matrix to include the new column and row. If you click on a cell underneath the lowest row of dots, more rows of dots will appear, the lowest of which contains the cell you have just clicked.

To assign meaningful names and labels to the default variables visible in **Data View**, switch to **Variable View** and assign the specifications there. You can either enter **Variable View** in the usual way by clicking the **Variable View** tab at the bottom of **Data View** or double-click the default heading of the variable you wish to name. Either way, when you enter **Variable View**, you will see that the default variable names have been entered there. In other words, the two display modes of the **Data Editor** are interchangeable in the order in which they are completed.

To add a new variable **to the right of those already in Data View**, you have only to type a value into a cell to the right of the present matrix of data. To add a new column **between two of those within the present data set**,

- Highlight the variable **to the right of** the intended position of the new variable.
- Choose **Edit➜Insert Variable** to create a new, empty, variable to the left of the variable you have highlighted.

Suppose that in **Data View**, the order of the variables is Case, Group and Score, and you want to change the order to Case, Score and Group. We recommend that you do this in **Variable View** (see Section 3.1.1), but the following procedure works in **Data View**.

- Create a new, empty variable to the left of Group in the manner described above.
- Click on the grey cell at the head of the Score column to highlight the whole column.
- Choose **Edit➜Cut** to remove the Score variable and place it in the clipboard.
- Click the grey cell at the head of the new, empty variable to highlight the whole column.
- Use **Edit** and **Paste** to move the Score variable including its data and definitions into its new position to the left of Group.

Columns can be lengthened by choosing **Edit➜Insert cases** which will have the effect of adding new empty rows underneath the existing columns. If you need to insert a substantial number of new cases, proceed as in Section 3.1.1.3.

There are occasions, however, when you may want to place rows for additional cases in the middle of the data set. Suppose that, in the drug experiment described in Chapter 2, you want to add data on an additional participant who has been tested under the Placebo condition. So you want to insert a new row of data at the foot of the scores of the participants in the Placebo group just above the scores of the Drug group. Proceed as follows.

- Click the grey cell on the left of the row of data **above** which you want to insert the new case. (This will be the row of data for the first participant who performed under the Drug condition.) The row will now be highlighted.
- Choose **Edit➜Insert Cases** to create a new empty row above the one you highlighted.

You can now type in the data from the additional placebo participant. Actually, new cases can be added anywhere in the data set and re-ordered later by using **Data➜Sort Cases** (see Section 3.3.3).

When entering data into a data file, especially a large file, it is only too easy to mistype a value (e.g. 100 instead of 10) or, when adding more data, to duplicate a case number. In this subsection, we shall look at a way of checking for aberrant data and in the next subsection a way of detecting duplicate values.

SPSS provides a means of checking the validity of data within the **Validation** item in the **Data** menu where various rules can be specified, either for individual variables or across all variables. The procedure is in two parts: the first part consists of defining as many rules as desired, the second part applies these rules to specified variables. For example, suppose we wish to check that no case number greater than 50 and no score greater than 20 has been entered into our data set.

- From the drop-down **Data** menu, choose **Validation➔Define Rules...** (Figure 9) to access the **Define Validation Rules** dialog box (Figure 10).
- Within the **Rule Definition** window, type *Range of Case Numbers* to replace the **Name** SingleVarRule1, and enter the values 1 and 50 into the **Minimum** and **Maximum** boxes respectively.
- Click **New** and then repeat the procedure but this time replacing SingleVarRule1 with *Range of Scores* and enter the values 1 and 20 into the **Minimum** and **Maximum** boxes respectively. The names of the rules are arbitrary. Additional rules can be added as desired.
- Finally click **OK**.

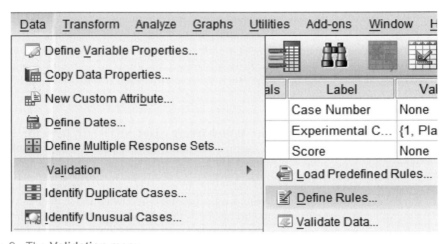

Figure 9. The **Validation** menu

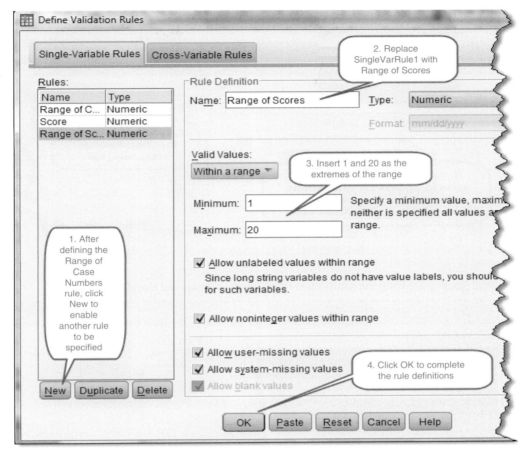

Figure 10. The **Define Validation Rules** dialog box with two rules defined

Having defined the rules, the next step is to validate the target variables in the data set by applying the appropriate rules. For illustration, imagine that three more cases had been entered in the data file: one with a case number of 21 and a score of 15; another with a case number of 22 and a score of 30 (this is outside the range of scores); and third with a case number of 200 (this is outside the range of case numbers) and a score of 8.

Proceed as follows:

- From the drop-down **Data** menu (Figure 9), choose **Validation→Validate Data...** to access the **Validate Data** dialog box.
- Select the variable Case Number in the **Variables** box and click the arrow to transfer it to the **Analysis Variables** box. Do likewise with Score (Figure 11) and then click the **Single-Variable Rules** tab to open the **Single-Variables Rules** dialog box (Figure 12).
- Click the variable names and the check boxes as shown in Figure 12 and then **OK**.

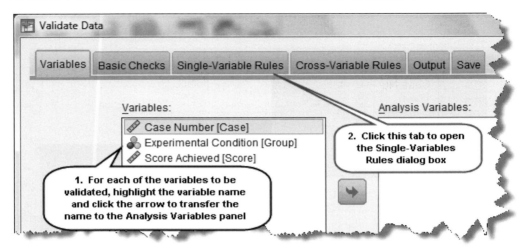

Figure 11. Part of the **Validate Data** dialog box showing the transfer of variable names of variables to be validated

The final stage is applying the appropriate rule(s) to the appropriate variables.

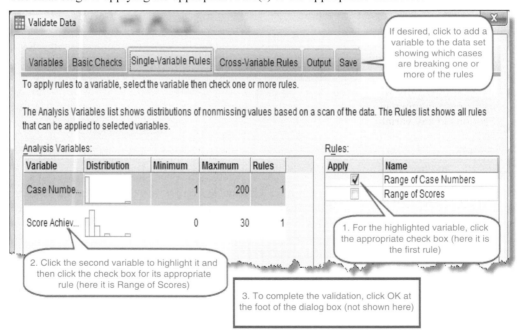

Figure 12. The **Validate Data** dialog box for associating variables and rules

The output (Output 1) of the validation begins with warnings and variable checks, and a table of **Rule Descriptions** (not reproduced here). These are followed by two tables listing the number of violations and their row numbers in the data set (SPSS refers to these as Case) for each variable analysed (Output 1). One invalid Case Number and one invalid Score have been detected.

Variable Summary

	Rule	Number of Violations
Case Number	Range of Case Numbers	1
	Total	1
Score	Range of Scores	1
	Total	1

Case Report

	Validation Rule Violations
Case	Single-Variable[a]
22	Range of Scores (1)
23	Range of Case Numbers (1)

a. The number of variables that violated the rule follows each rule.

Output 1. Two of the tables in the output showing that one Case Number and one Score were invalid. The Case Report identifies the row number (Case) with the invalid Score and the row number with the invalid Case Number

3.1.2.7   Identifying duplicate cases

Sometimes, especially when incrementing a data set with fresh cases, it is useful to ensure that the same case number is not duplicated. SPSS provides a routine for checking for possible duplications in any variable.

- From the drop-down **Data** menu, choose **Identify Duplicate Cases …** (Figure 9) to access the **Identify Duplicate Cases** dialog box (Figure 13). Click the variable name Case Number and transfer it to the **Define matching cases by** window.
- Assuming that later cases with the same case numbers have been incorrectly numbered, click the radio button **First case in each group is primary** to replace the default option that the **Last case in each group is primary**.
- Click **OK**.

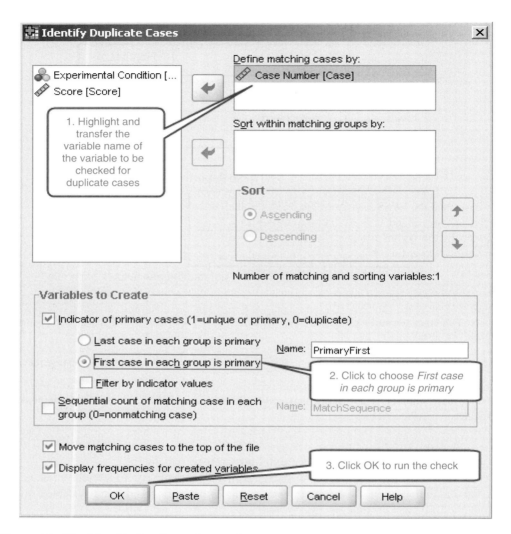

Figure 13. The **Identify Duplicate Cases** dialog box with the variable Case Number and the **First Case in each group is primary** option selected

For illustration, assume that another case had been added to the file with a case number of 20. After clicking **OK** in the **Identify Duplicate Cases** dialog box, the data file would appear with the duplicated cases at the top (Figure 14). The case in row 1 is the original case, the most recently added case in row 2 is the one with the duplicate case number. The **SPSS Statistics Viewer** also contains tables (not reproduced) showing how many duplicated cases there are.

	Case	Group	Score	PrimaryFirst
1	20	Drug	10	Primary Case
2	20	Placebo	8	Duplicate Case
3	1	Placebo	6	Primary Case
4	2	Placebo	5	Primary Case

Figure 14. The first few cases of the data set showing the original and the duplicated cases

3.2   MORE ON THE SPSS STATISTICS VIEWER

We described the **SPSS Statistics Viewer** in part of Section 2.4.1 and how the output can be edited. The **Viewer** consists of two panes (see Output 1 in Chapter 2), the widths of which can be adjusted by clicking and dragging the vertical bar separating them. The left pane lists the items of output in order of their appearance in the right pane, each item having an icon and a title.

> See
> Section
> 2.4.1

The icon shows whether the item is visible in the right pane (open-book icon) or invisible (closed-book icon). By double-clicking the icon, the item can be made visible or invisible in the right pane, where all actual output is presented. The output can also be rearranged by moving the appropriate icons around in the left pane by clicking and dragging them. A single click on an item in the left pane will bring the item into view in the right pane. Unwanted items in the output can be deleted by highlighting them in the left pane and pressing the **Delete** key. In this book, only selections from the right pane will normally be reproduced.

Report

Score

Experimental Condition	Mean	N	Std. Deviation	Median
Placebo	3.40	10	1.838	3.50
Drug	6.90	10	1.449	6.50
Total	5.15	20	2.412	5.50

Output 2. Output from **Compare Means** procedure, with means, sample sizes, standard deviations and medians

In Section 2.4.1 we tabulated the results of the Drug experiment using the **Compare Means** procedure. Here (see Output 2) we have added a column of medians by clicking **Options...** in the **Means** dialog box and transferring Median from the **Statistics** panel to the **Cell Statistics** panel. (It is often a good idea, when exploring data, to compare means with medians: if they have similar values, symmetrical distributions are suggested. Here, however, the medians have been included merely to demonstrate some editing in the **Viewer**.)

3.2.1   Editing the output

In Section 2.4.1, we demonstrated that the output in the **SPSS Statistics Viewer** could be edited by showing the effect of a pivoting procedure. Here we consider some more ways of improving the appearance of the output.

To edit an item, say a table, in the **Viewer**, double-click it. The table will now be surrounded by a dotted box indicating that you are now in the **Viewer**'s editor. Once a selected item has been surrounded by a dotted box, the following changes can be made:

* To **widen or narrow columns**, move the cursor on to a vertical line in the table and click and drag the line to the left or the right.
* **Items** can be **deleted** by highlighting them and pressing the **Delete** key.
* **Whole columns or rows** can be **deleted** by highlighting them and pressing the **Delete** key (see below for details).
* **Text** can sometimes be altered by double-clicking an item and deleting letters or typing in new ones.
* If values are listed, it is possible to re-specify the number of decimal places shown by highlighting the numbers concerned in a block, pressing the **right-hand** mouse button, selecting **Cell Properties...** and changing the specification in the **Cell Properties** dialog box.

For example, suppose that, in the **Report** table (Output 2), we want to dispense with the third row (Total) containing the statistics of all twenty scores in the data set considered as a single group and also the column of Medians.

* Click the first value (5.15) in the bottom row so that it is highlighted.
* Press the **Ctrl** button and, keeping it pressed, click the other value cells in the Total row so that they are all highlighted (Output 3).
* Press the **Delete** key. If this key does not work, an alternative way of deleting the material is to click the right-hand mouse button and select **Clear** from the drop-down menu. Note that titles of columns and rows disappear if their values are deleted.
* Delete the values in the Median column in a similar manner.
* Click outside the shaded border to leave the **Editor**. The **Report** table will now appear as in Output 4.

Report

Variables Score ▼

Experimental Condition	Mean	N	Std. Deviation	Median
Placebo	3.40	10	1.838	3.50
Drug	6.90	10	1.449	6.50
Total	5.15	20	2.412	5.50

Output 3. Highlighting material to be deleted

Score

Experimental Condition	Mean	N	Std. Deviation
Placebo	3.40	10	1.838
Drug	6.90	10	1.449

Output 4. The edited **Report** table after removing the Total row and Median column

3.2.2   More advanced editing

The **Data Editor** offers even more powerful editing facilities than those we have considered so far, some of which can radically alter the appearance of a default table such as the **Report** table we have been editing. Many of the tables in the output are **pivot tables**, that is, tables in which the columns and rows can be transposed and to which other radical alterations can be made.

In Chapter 2, we showed how, by choosing **Pivot➜Transpose Rows and Columns** we could change the rows of the default **Report** table into columns and vice versa (see Section 2.4.1). Here we illustrate the manipulation of a three-way table of means.

See
Section
2.4.1

3.2.2.1   A three-way table of means

It is well known that females are generally better at recalling verbal material and males are better at recalling graphic material. An experiment was carried out recalling verbal or graphic items after either a short, medium or long period of inspection of the items. Male and female participants were each divided into six subgroups looking at verbal or graphic items for the three inspection times.

Coding variables for Sex, Task, and Inspection Time were named in **Variable View** along with Score for the number of items recalled. Corresponding **Labels** were specified as Sex, Type of Task, Inspection Time and Number of Items Recalled. The **Means…** procedure with Number of Items Recalled entered in the **Dependent List** and each of Sex, Type of Task and Inspection Time entered as layers in the **Independent List** generated Output 5 when only Mean was selected for the **Cell Statistics** box within **Options**.   The rows for Total have been edited out of Output 5 for simplicity.

Report

Mean

Sex	Type of Task	Inspection Time	Number of Items Recalled
Male	Verbal	Short	4.00
		Medium	5.00
		Long	5.00
	Graphic	Short	2.67
		Medium	3.67
		Long	4.00
Female	Verbal	Short	5.33
		Medium	5.67
		Long	6.33
	Graphic	Short	1.67
		Medium	2.33
		Long	3.33

Output 5. The output from the **Mean** procedure

It is possible to effect a simple transposition of all the rows in Output 5 into columns and vice versa by choosing **Transposing rows and Columns** from the **Pivot** menu. There is little to be gained from this, however, because of the complexity of the table. To improve the clarity of the table, we want to select individual variables for transposition. This finer control is achieved by using the **Pivoting Trays** procedure.

- After highlighting the **Report** table (Output 5) by double-clicking anywhere within it, choose **Pivot→Pivoting Trays** to obtain the **Pivoting Trays** display shown in Figure 15.

The icons and titles show their locations in the **Report** table. The icons can be dragged to other locations and their order can be changed within the same location. The best way to see how the pivoting trays work is to click and drag the icons to other grey borders in the display and observe the resulting changes in the **Report** table of means.

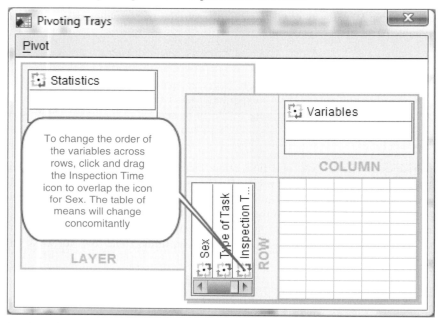

Figure 15. The **Pivoting Trays** dialog box showing what is/are located in layers, rows and columns. The sequence of variables and their locations can be changed by dragging the icons appropriately

From left to right, the three icons in the ROW list represent the variables Sex, Type of Task and Inspection Time respectively, which is the order in which these three dimensions appear in the table. This order can be changed by clicking and dragging an icon to a different position. For example, if we click and drag the present rightmost icon (Inspection Time) to the left of the other two icons (Figure 15), that dimension will now appear in the leftmost position in the **Report** table (Output 6).

Report

Mean

Inspection Time	Sex	Type of Task	Number of Items Recalled
Short	Male	Verbal	4.00
		Graphic	2.67
	Female	Verbal	5.33
		Graphic	1.67
Medium	Male	Verbal	5.00
		Graphic	3.67
	Female	Verbal	5.67
		Graphic	2.33
Long	Male	Verbal	5.00
		Graphic	4.00
	Female	Verbal	6.33
		Graphic	3.33

Output 6. The appearance of the table after the order of the icons in the **ROW** list has been changed (compare with Output 5)

In Outputs 5 and 6, the labels of the three factors in the experiment are all in rows. Should we wish to retain the levels of Sex and Type of Task in rows, but move those of Inspection Time into columns, we need only click and drag the icon for Inspection Time from the **ROW** list to the **COLUMN** list (Figure 16).

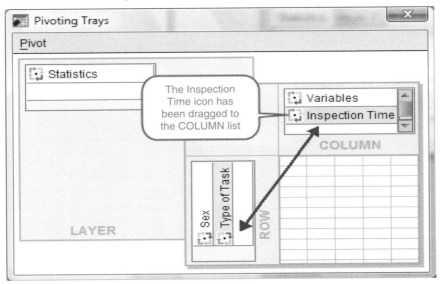

Figure 16. The Inspection Time icon has been dragged to the **COLUMN** list

The effect of this manipulation is that, whereas the two types of Sex and Type of Task will appear in rows as before, the three levels of Inspection Time now appear at the heads of three columns (Output 7).

Report

Mean

		Number of Items Recalled		
		Inspection Time		
Sex	Type of Task	Short	Medium	Long
Male	Verbal	4.00	5.00	5.00
	Graphic	2.67	3.67	4.00
Female	Verbal	5.33	5.67	6.33
	Graphic	1.67	2.33	3.33

Output 7. Edited table in which Inspection Time has been transposed to columns

The leftmost part of Figure 16 contains the **LAYER** list. A **layer** is a tabulation at one particular level of another factor. In the tables we have looked at so far, all the dimensions have been shown. Suppose, however, that we want to view the two-way table of means for Type of Task and Inspection Time for each level of Sex. Simply click and drag the Sex icon from the **ROW** list to the **LAYER** list (Figure 17). The table will now appear as in Output 8.

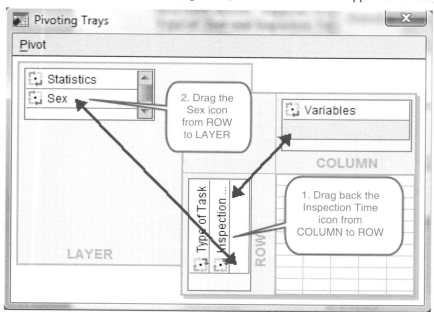

Figure 17. The Sex icon has been dragged from ROW to LAYER and Inspection Time icon restored from COLUMN to ROW

We can see the means for Type of Task and Inspection Time only for the Male level of Sex. To see the means for Female, simply click on the arrow to the right of Male and select Female.

Report

Statistics	Mean ▼	
Sex	Male ▼	

Type of Task	Inspection Time	Number of Items Recalled
Verbal	Short	4.00
	Medium	5.00
	Long	5.00
Graphic	Short	2.67
	Medium	3.67
	Long	4.00

Output 8. A layered table, in which the means for Type of Task and Inspection Time are displayed at only one level of Sex. The means for Female can be seen by clicking the arrow to the right of Male and selecting Female

3.2.3   Tutorials in SPSS

The SPSS package now includes some excellent tutorials on various aspects of the system, including the use of the **Viewer** and the manipulation of pivot tables.

To access a tutorial choose **Help➜Tutorial** and double-click to open the tutorial menu. The buttons in the right-hand bottom corner of each page of the tutorial enable the user to see the list of items (magnifier) and to navigate forward and backward through the tutorial (right and left arrows).

3.3   SELECTING CASES, REARRANGING DATA AND COMBINING FILES

So far, the emphasis has been upon the construction of a complete data set, the saving of that set to a file on disk, and its retrieval from storage. There are occasions, however, on which the user will want to operate selectively on the data. It may be, for instance, that only some of the cases in a data set are of interest (those contributed by the participants in one category alone, perhaps); or the user may wish to exclude participants with outlying values on specified variables. In this section, some of these more specialised manoeuvres will be described.

Transformation and recoding of data will be discussed in Chapter 4.

3.3.1   Selecting cases

Let us assume that, in **Data View**, we have the results of the Drug experiment. In the original data set, there were two variables: Experimental Condition and Score. Suppose, however, that a Gender variable has been added, where 1 = Male and 2 = Female, and that we want to examine the data from the female participants only.

- Choose **Data➜Select Cases…** to obtain the **Select Cases** dialog box (see Figure 18).
- Initially, the **All cases** radio button is marked. Click the **Select Cases: If** button and complete the **Select Cases: If** dialog box as shown in Figure 19. Click **Continue** to return to the **Select Cases** dialog box.
- Click **OK** to select only the female participants for analysis.

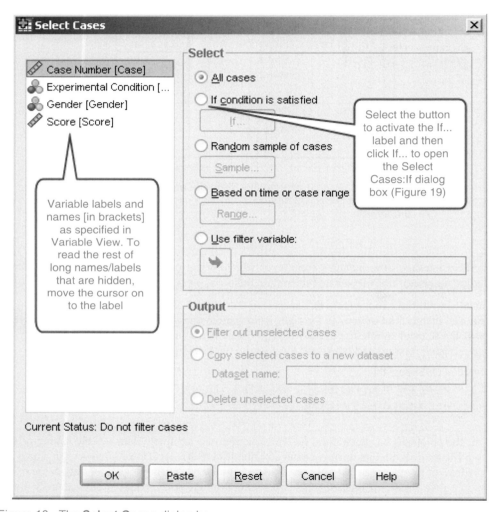

Figure 18. The **Select Cases** dialog box

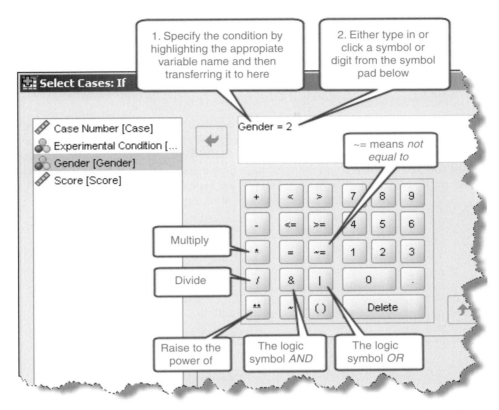

Figure 19. Part of the **Select Cases: If** dialog box with the expression for selecting only Gender 2 (the female participants)

A section of **Data View** is shown in Figure 20. Another column, headed filter_$, has now appeared, containing the entries Not Selected and Selected. Note that, although the name filter_$ will appear in subsequent dialog boxes, it should not be selected as a variable for analysis because it will only report the number of selected cases.

	Case	Group	Gender	Score	filter_$
1	1	Placebo	Male	6	Not Selected
2	2	Placebo	Female	5	Selected
3	3	Placebo	Male	5	Not Selected
4	4	Placebo	Female	1	Selected
5	5	Placebo	Male	2	Not Selected
6	6	Placebo	Female	3	Selected
7	7	Placebo	Male	2	Not Selected

Figure 20. **Data View**, showing that only the scores of the female participants will be included in the analysis. The oblique bars are deselected cases

The row numbers of the unselected cases (the males) have been marked with an oblique bar. This is a useful indicator of **case selection status.** The status bar (if enabled at the foot of **Data View**) will carry the message **Filter On**. Any further analyses of the data set will exclude cases where Gender = 1.

Case selection can be **cancelled** as follows:
- From the **Data menu**, choose **Select Cases** and (in the **Select Cases** dialog box) click **All cases**.
- Click **OK**.

3.3.2   Aggregating data

In a School of Business Studies, students take a selection of five courses each. (There is a degree of choice, so that different students may take somewhat different selections of courses.) On the basis of their performance, the students are marked on a percentage scale. We shall be concerned with the marks of ten of the students, whose marks on the five courses they took are contained in the SPSS data file *Students marks* and reproduced in www.psypress.com/spss-made-simple. Figure 21 is a section of **Data View**, showing some of their marks.

	Student	Course	Mark
1	Anne	Accountancy	80
2	Rebecca	Accountancy	78
3	Susan	Accountancy	87
4	Anne	Computing	49
5	Fred	Computing	55
6	Rebecca	Computing	65
7	Susan	Computing	56
8	Anne	German	40
9	Fred	German	72
10	Jim	German	73

Figure 21.   Part of the file Students marks in **Data View**

3.3.2.1   Finding course averages: The Aggregate procedure

Suppose we want to find the mean mark for each of the courses that were taken. SPSS's **Aggregate** procedure groups cases according to the nominal variable specified (e.g. Course) and then aggregates the values of the quantitative variable specified (e.g. Mark). Various options are available for how the aggregation is done (e.g. mean, median, percentage above a specified value). We shall use the **Aggregate** procedure to group the marks according to course and calculate the mean mark for each course.
- Choose **Data➔Aggregate…** to obtain the **Aggregate Data** dialog box.
- In the **Aggregate Data** dialog box, the **Break Variable** is the variable on the basis of which the marks are to be grouped (i.e. Course).
- The **Aggregated Variable** is the mark that a student received (i.e. Mark).

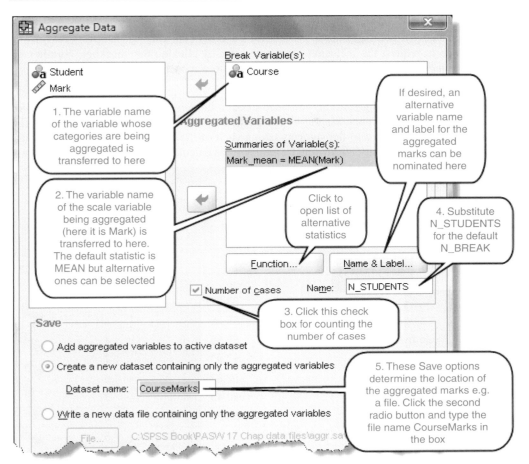

Figure 22. The completed **Aggregate Data** dialog box. The results of the aggregated marks for courses will be saved in the variable Mark_Mean within the dataset CourseMarks along with the count of cases in the variable N_STUDENTS

- Since in this exercise, we are interested in courses rather than individuals, we shall save the course means in a separate file. Note, however, that if the upper radio button in the Aggregate Data dialog is activated, the mean course marks will appear in the file of students' individual marks. A new dataset is created by clicking the radio button **Create a new dataset containing only the aggregated variables** in the **Save** panel of the dialog box. Type in a name for the dataset such as *CourseMarks* – see Figure 22 for the completed dialog box.

Notice that in the **Aggregated Variable(s)** panel is the expression Mark_mean = MEAN(Mark). Unless otherwise instructed, SPSS will calculate the mean mark for each course. You can choose another statistic (such as the Median) by clicking on the **Function…** button and changing the specification. You can also change the variable name and specify a variable label by clicking **Name & Label…** and completing the dialog box.

Since the students had a degree of choice and some courses were more popular than others, the means calculated by the **Aggregate** procedure are based on varying sample sizes. It is therefore wise to request the inclusion of sample sizes by clicking the checkbox **Number of cases** and changing the variable name from N_Break to a more meaningful one by typing in N_Students. Finally click **OK**.

To see the results of the aggregation, you need to open the new dataset *CourseMarks* (Figure 23) by clicking Untitled[CourseMarks] along the foot of the screen. The dataset shows the mean mark (Mean) awarded to the students taking each of the courses that were selected and the size of the sample of marks from which the mean was calculated in the column N_Students.

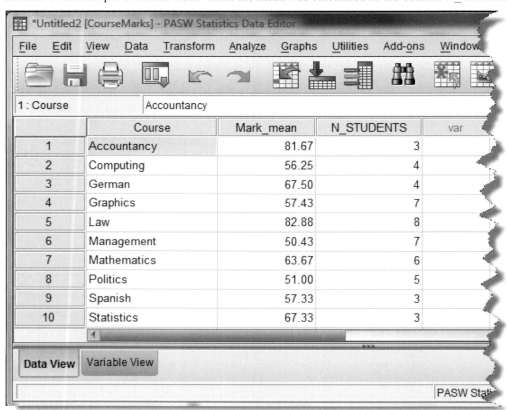

Figure 23. Mean mark on each of the courses together with the number of students who took each course in the new dataset CourseMarks

Note that if the **Add aggregated variables to active dataset** button in Figure 22 had been selected instead of the **Create a new dataset**... button, the mean marks would have appeared in the *Students marks* file in a column alongside the students' individual marks, thus allowing comparisons with the mean marks of all those who took the same courses.

3.3.3   Sorting data

Suppose that, in order to appraise the courses, you want to list them in order of the mean marks the students achieved.

- With the data file *CourseMarks* in the **Data Editor**, choose **Data→Sort Cases...** to obtain the **Sort Cases** dialog box. Figure 24 shows the completed dialog box.

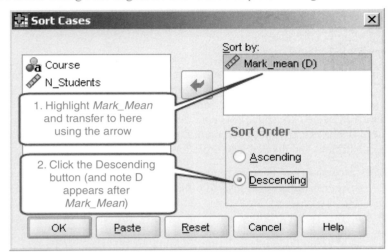

Figure 24. The completed **Sort Cases** dialog box

- Since you will probably want the marks to be arranged with the highest at the top and the lowest at the bottom, we have marked the **Descending** button in **Sort Order**. (Note, however, that in **file merging** – see below – the sort order must be the same as the file to be merged.)
- Click **OK** to see the mean marks listed in descending order of magnitude (Figure 25).

	Course	Mean	N_Students
1	Law	82.88	8
2	Accountancy	81.67	3
3	German	67.50	4
4	Statistics	67.33	3
5	Mathematics	63.67	6
6	Graphics	57.43	7
7	Spanish	57.33	3
8	Computing	56.25	4
9	Politics	51.00	5
10	Management	50.43	7

Figure 25. Results of the sorting procedure. The courses are now listed in descending order of their mean marks

3.3.4   Merging files

SPSS offers a powerful procedure known as **file merging**, which enables the user to import data into a file known as the **working file** from an **external** file. The **File Merge** procedure has two principal uses:

1. You can use it to import extra data (i.e., more cases) on *the same set of variables*.
2. You can use it to import data on *extra variables* that are not already in the working file.

3.3.4.1   Using Merge Files to import more cases of the same variables from an external file

In Chapter 2, an experiment was described in which the skilled performance of ten people who had ingested a small quantity of a supposedly performance-enhancing drug was compared with the performance of a placebo group of the same size. The scores of the twenty participants were stored in a file named *Drug Experiment*. Suppose, however, twenty more participants were to be tested under exactly the same conditions (ten under the Placebo condition and ten under the Drug condition) and the new data stored in a file named *Drug more data*.

The **Merge Files** procedure can be used to import the new data from the file *Drug more data* into the file *Drug Experiment*, so that, instead of having ten scores for each condition we shall have twenty. The success of this type of file-merging operation requires that **the specifications for the two variables must be exactly the same in both files**. Before attempting the following exercise, check both files in **Variable View** to make sure that the specifications (name, width, type, values) of the variables Case, Group and Score are identical.

Ensure that the file containing the original data *Drug Experiment* is in the **Data Editor**. Then
- Choose **Data➔Merge Files➔Add Cases ...** to obtain the **Add Cases to [dataset name]** dialog box (Figure 26).

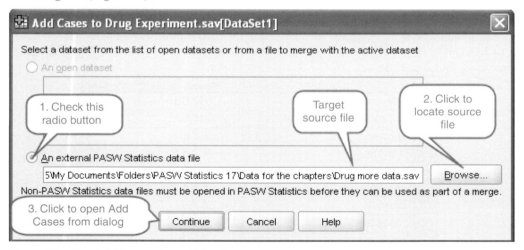

Figure 26. The **Add Cases to...** dialog box

- Use **Browse...** to select the file *Drug more data* from wherever it is stored and click **Continue** to obtain the **Add Cases from [dataset name]** dialog box (Figure 27).
- Since both data files contain only the variables Case, Group and Score, the right-hand panel headed **Variables in New Active Dataset** contains Case, Group and Score and no variable names appear in the left-hand panel headed **Unpaired Variables**. Had the external file contained an extra variable (or variables), or a variable specification did not

match between the two files, its unmatched name (or names) would have appeared in the left-hand panel.

- Click **OK** to obtain the merged file, a section of which is shown in Figure 28.
- If desired, the cases can be sorted to list all the Drug scores and then all the Placebo scores using **Sort Cases...** in the **Data** menu.

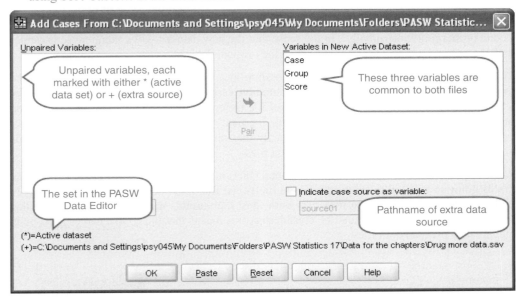

Figure 27. The **Add Cases from** ... dialog box listing the variables existing in both files

Figure 28 shows a section of Data View after the extra data have been imported. There are now 20 scores in the Drug group and 20 in the Placebo group.

	Case	Group	Score
18	18	Drug	7
19	19	Drug	5
20	20	Drug	10
21	1	Placebo	5
22	2	Placebo	3
23	3	Placebo	6

Figure 28. A section of the merged file showing the first three cases from the file Drug more data added on beneath the last three cases from the file Drug Experiment

3.3.4.2   Using Merge Files to add extra variables

We have just described the use of the **Merge Files** procedure to add further cases to a data set from a file containing more data on exactly the same variables. We can think of this operation as one of merging 'vertically', in the sense that the columns in the original data set become longer, but the number of columns (variables) in the data set remains the same.

Returning now to our hypothetical business school, however, suppose that, at the end of the year, the students had been asked to rate their courses on quality of teaching on a scale from 1 to 10. Our administrator used SPSS's Aggregate procedure to obtain the mean ratings for each course and saved the mean ratings to a file called *Course mean ratings*. How can these mean ratings be imported into the *Students marks* file, so that, in addition to the students' names, courses taken and marks achieved, there is also, opposite the name of each student, the mean of the ratings given by the students who took the course? We can think of this operation as one of merging 'horizontally', in the sense that the new data set will contain more variables than the original and will thus be wider than the original data set.

To make the addition of extra variables possible in a 'horizontal' merge, the two files (the original and the target) must contain one common variable. This common variable is to be used as a 'key' to 'look up' data in the target file (referred to by SPSS as the **keyed file**) and import them into the original file. As with 'vertical' merging (i.e., the addition of further cases), the common variable must have exactly the same specifications (Name, Width, Type and – where applicable – Values) in both data files.

Another point to bear in mind with 'horizontal' merging, is that the key variable, ie., the one that is going to be used to 'look up' data in the keyed file, must be sorted in the same way in both the active and the source files. In both files, the variable must be sorted in 'ascending order'. In the examples we shall be considering, this means that the course names must be in alphabetical order in both files.

- Open the file *Students marks*.
- Choose **Data➔Merge Files➔Add Variables ....** This will access the **Add Variables to** dialog box (Figure 29).

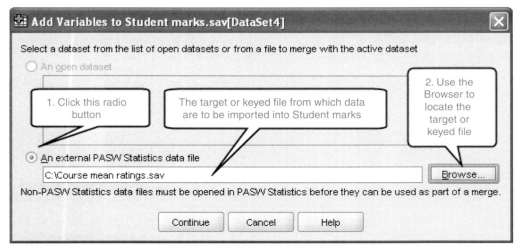

Figure 29. The **Add Variables to** dialog box

- Follow the instructions in Figure 29. On clicking the Continue button, the **Add Variables from** dialog box will appear (Figure 30). Note that the **Key Variable** Course has been transferred from its initial position in **Excluded variables**. (It also appeared in **New Active Dataset**.)

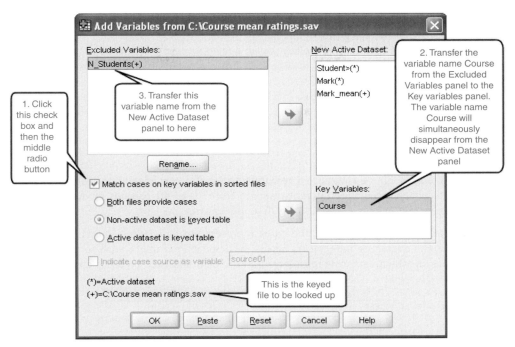

Figure 30. The **Add Variables** from dialog box

- Click **OK**. The *Students marks* file will now appear as in Figure 31.

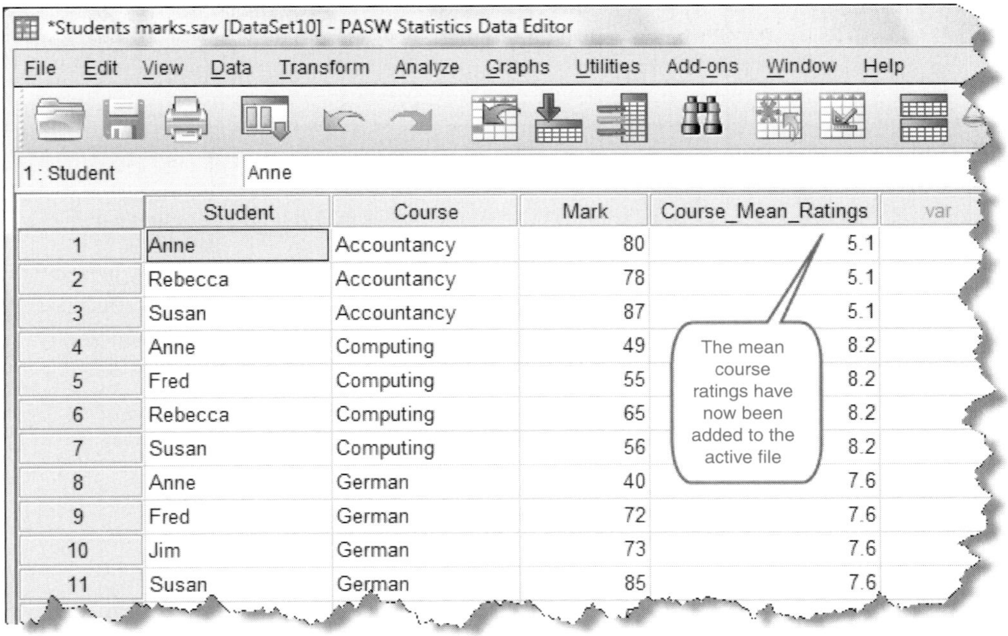

Figure 31. The Student marks file to which have been added, by a file-merging operation, the course mean ratings

The success of this second, 'horizontal' kind of file-merging operation has two essential prerequisites:

    1.   The specifications of the key variable must be exactly the same in both files.

    2.   The cases in both files must be sorted in ascending order of the key variable.

In the present example, both the active *Students marks* and the passive *Course mean ratings* files must previously have been sorted by Course, since that is the key variable that is to be used to look up the mean ratings in the keyed file *Course mean ratings*.

3.3.5   Transposing the rows and columns of a data set

In an experiment on time estimation, a researcher asks nine participants to make five verbal estimates of each of seven time intervals ranging from 10 to 40 seconds in duration. Each participant, therefore, makes a total of thirty-five judgements.

In the data set shown in Figure 32, the cases represent particular time intervals. For some purposes, such as averaging judgements across participants, we might wish to transform this data set to one in which each row represents a participant and each column represents a time interval.

	Interval	Amy	Fred	Joe	Stephen
1	10	8	120	7	8
2	10	6	10	9	7
3	10	5	20	6	10
4	10	7	5	8	9
5	10	5	10	6	11
6	15	15	25	10	13
7	15	6	8	9	12
8	15	14	12	10	12
9	15	7	8	12	12
10	15	14	10	12	15
11	20	20	60	15	18
12	20	10	18	14	15

Figure 32. A section of **Data View**, showing verbal estimates of the time intervals specified by the first variable Interval

- Choose **Data➔Transpose…** to view the **Transpose** dialog box (Figure 33).

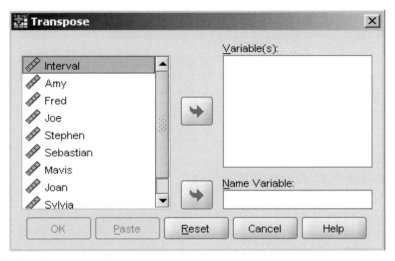

Figure 33. The **Transpose** dialog box

- Select all the variables and transfer them to the **Variable(s)** box on the right by clicking the central black arrow.
- Click **OK** to view the transposed matrix (Figure 34).

It can be seen from Figure 34 that SPSS has created a new variable CASE_LBL containing not only the names of the participants but also the Interval variable.   The row containing the Interval variable should now be deleted and the default names var001, var002, ...   replaced (in **Variable View**) by typing in names such as *Ten1*, *Ten2*, ..., *Fifteen1*, *Fifteen2*, ... remembering that SPSS will not allow duplication of variable names.   In addition, the first variable CASE_ LBL should be renamed *Name*.   Part of the final transformed data set is shown in Figure 35.

1 : CASE_LBL		Interval			
	CASE_LBL	var001	var002	var003	var004
1	Interval	10	10	10	10
2	Amy	8	6	5	7
3	Fred	120	10	20	5
4	Joe	7	9	6	8
5	Stephen	8	7	10	9
6	Sebastian	6	5	7	6

Figure 34. The transposed data set, in which the data from the participants are now contained in rows

	Name	Ten1	Ten2	Ten3	Ten4	Ten5	Fifteen1	Fifteen2
1	Amy	8	6	5	7	5	15	6
2	Fred	120	10	20	5	10	25	8
3	Joe	7	9	6	8	6	10	9
4	Stephen	8	7	10	9	11	13	12
5	Sebastian	6	5	7	6	5	9	9
6	Mavis	10	8	10	8	10	15	10

Figure 35. Part of the transformed data set in which the columns and rows of the original data set have been transposed

3.4   IMPORTING AND EXPORTING DATA

It is possible to import data into SPSS from other applications or platforms such as Microsoft EXCEL. SPSS can also read ASCII tab-delimited or comma-delimited files, with values separated by tabulation symbols or fixed format files with variables recorded in the same column locations for each case. It is also possible to export SPSS data and output into other applications such as word processors and spreadsheets.

3.4.1   Importing data from other applications

3.4.1.1   Importing EXCEL files

When importing files from EXCEL, the following points should be observed:
1.   If the first row of the EXCEL file does not contain variable/column names or data, then the material may not be read into SPSS properly. Either delete blank rows or amend the **Range** in SPSS's **Opening Excel Data Source** dialog box after selecting the EXCEL file to be read.
2.   Dates must be formatted as *DD-MMM-YYYY in EXCEL.
3.   It may be necessary to make several attempts to ensure a satisfactory import. For example, some file types may need changing   (e.g. from **String** to **Numeric**) within **Variable View**.

To import the EXCEL file named *test1.xls*, which is stored in the authors' folder *SPSS STATISTICS 18 Chap data files*:
*   Choose **File➔Open➔ Data…** to obtain the **Open File** dialog box (Figure 36).
*   Click the directory of file types in the **Files of type:** box and highlight Excel (*.xls).
*   Select the appropriate **Look in** folder.
*   A list of Excel files will then appear in the white panel above. Click the appropriate file and its name will appear in the **File name:** box.

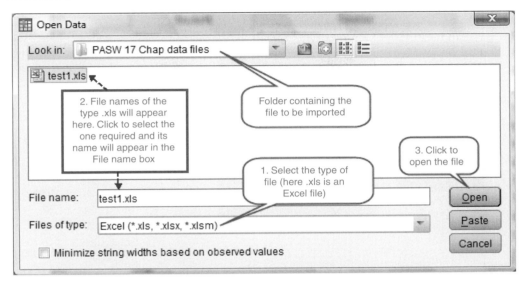

Figure 36. The **Open File** dialog box with Excel [*.xls] selected as the type of file and the file test1 selected from the folder SPSS 18 Chap data files

- Click **Open** to open the **Opening File Options** dialog box (Figure 37). Activate the **Read variable names** check box to transfer the EXCEL variable names into the SPSS **Data Editor**.

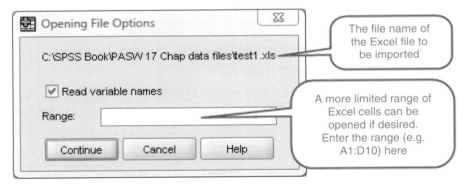

Figure 37. The **Opening File Options** dialog box with **Read variable names** selected

- If the EXCEL file has more than one worksheet, the **Opening File Options** dialog box will contain an extra panel labelled **Worksheet**

  Worksheet: Sheet1 [A1:N7893]   ∨ . Different worksheets can then be selected by clicking the directory arrow.
- If an error message appears stating that SPSS cannot load an EXCEL worksheet, it may be necessary to return to EXCEL and re-save the file in the format of a different version of EXCEL, to copy and paste columns of data directly into SPSS **Data View**, or to re-format the cells.

- Click **OK** to transfer the file into SPSS. **Variable View** will list the variable names and their types, and **Data View** will show the transferred data and variable names (Figure 38). It may be necessary to change variable types in **Variable View**. The **SPSS Statistics Viewer** will list the names, types and formats of the variables. Note that SPSS Statistics Viewer may initially obscure the data file beneath.
- The file can then be saved as an SPSS data file.

	A	B	C	D
1	**Name**	**Sex**	**Age**	**Score**
2	Brown, G	m	25	87
3	Green, F	m	18	78
4	Mason, P	f	23	100
5	Sampson, G	m	24	67
6	Winston, P	f	20	50

	Name	Sex	Age	Score
1	Brown, G	m	25	87
2	Green, F	m	18	78
3	Mason, P	f	23	100
4	Sampson, G	m	24	67
5	Winston, P	f	20	50

Figure 38. Transfer of an EXCEL file (left) to SPSS (right)

It is also possible to copy columns of data from an EXCEL file by highlighting the data (but not the column headings), selecting **Copy** from EXCEL's **Edit** menu and then within SPSS, selecting **Paste** from SPSS's **Edit** menu and pasting the data into **Data View**. (Again, do not include the cell at the head of the SPSS column in the selection.) The variables can then be named in the usual manner within **Variable View**. Should the EXCEL columns contain strings (e.g. names), make sure that, in **Variable View**, you change the **Type** of variable to **String** before pasting. Other types of file can be transferred in a similar manner.

3.4.1.2 Exporting data from SPSS to EXCEL

The **Save As** procedure allows you to save an SPSS file (or a selection of data) as an EXCEL file. The procedure is entirely straightforward.

SPSS data can also be prepared for export to another application or platform by saving it to a wide range of formats, including **SPSS portable (*.por)**. Full details of importing and exporting files are available in SPSS's **Help** facility.

3.4.2 Copying output

SPSS Statistics 18 offers a facility for exporting output. To copy output, proceed as follows:

- Ensure that the item of output in **SPSS Statistics Viewer** has a box around it by clicking the cursor anywhere within the table or graphic. If you wish to copy more than one table, then ensure that all the desired tables are boxed by holding down the **Ctrl** key whilst clicking on each table in turn.
- Choose **File➜Export…** (Figure 39) to obtain the **Export Output** dialog box (Figure 40).

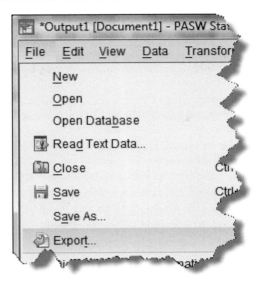

Figure 39. The location of the **Export...** item

- Complete the **Export Output** dialog box (Figure 40) by naming the file to where the output is going and its format (e.g. *.doc for a Word file; *.xls for an Excel file; *.ppt for a Powerpoint file; *.htm for a HTML file). Either type in the file name or use the **Browse...** to locate the appropriate folder (a **Save As** dialog box will appear from which the folder can be selected: insert a file name in the **File Name** panel and click **Save** to return to the **Export Output** dialog box).

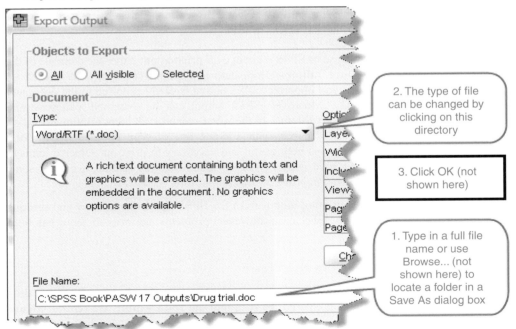

Figure 40. The **Export Output** dialog box for naming the output file and selecting its format

Alternatively, to **copy a table**, proceed as follows:

- Ensure that the table of output in SPSS Statistics Viewer has a box around it by clicking the cursor anywhere within the table or graphic. If you wish to copy more than one table, then ensure that all the desired tables are boxed by holding down the **Ctrl** key whilst clicking on each table in turn.
- Click **Copy** in the **Edit** menu.
- Switch to the word processor and ensure that the cursor is located at the intended insertion point.
- Select **Paste Special...** in the word processor's **Edit** menu and then **Formatted Text (RTF)** if it is desired to edit or format the table within the word processor.
- Alternatively, select **Paste Special...** in the word processor's **Edit** menu and then **Picture.** The picture can be repositioned and resized within the word processor but it cannot be edited. However the quality of the image is higher than it is when **Paste** is used.

To **copy a graphic**, proceed as follows:

- Ensure that the graphic in the **SPSS Statistics Viewer** has a box around it by clicking the cursor anywhere within it. If you wish to copy more than one graphic, ensure that all the desired graphics are boxed by holding down the **Ctrl** key whilst clicking on each chart or graph in turn.
- Click **Copy** in the **Edit** menu.
- Switch to the word processor and ensure that the cursor is located at the insertion point.
- Click **Paste Special...** and select **Bitmap**. The item can then be centred, enlarged or reduced by clicking it so that it acquires a box around it with the usual Windows tabs. To centre the box, click and drag it to the desired position. To enlarge or reduce the size of the graphic, drag one of the tabs in the appropriate direction.

3.5   PRINTING FROM SPSS

It is possible to make extensive use of SPSS without ever printing out either the contents of the **Viewer** or the data in the **Data Editor**. Both data and output can easily be backed up electronically by saving to disk; and important SPSS output is easily exported to the document you actually want to print out. Moreover, SPSS output can be extremely extensive and indiscriminate printing can be very wasteful. In the worst scenario, an inept printing operation could result in dozens of sheets of paper, with a single line of print on each. There are, nevertheless, occasions on which it is both useful and necessary to print out selected items in the **Viewer** window or even a hard copy of the raw data. In this section, we offer some suggestions to help you control and improve printed output from SPSS.

There are differences between printing output from the **SPSS Statistics Viewer** and printing data from the **Data Editor**. In either case, however, problems can arise if there has been insufficient editorial control.

3.5.1   Printing output from the Viewer

We shall illustrate some aspects of printing from the **Viewer** with the data from the drug experiment. Suppose that, having entered the data into the **Data Editor**, we run the **Means** procedure, with requests for several optional extras such as medians, range statistics, measures of effect size and one-way ANOVAs to increase the extent of the output.

We strongly recommend that, before you print any output, you should make full use of the **Viewer**'s editing facilities to *remove all irrelevant material*. When using SPSS, one invariably requests output which, at the end of the day, proves to be superfluous. Moreover, as we have seen, radical changes in tables and other output can be made (and great economies in space) by using the **Viewer**'s powerful editing facilities. Since some of the output tables can be very wide, unnecessary columns can be removed. Some pivoting may help not only to make a table more readable but also more manageable for a printing operation.

For some kinds of material, it is better to use **landscape** orientation for the sheet, that is, have the shorter side vertical, rather than the more usual **portrait** orientation. It is easy to make such a specification while working in the **Viewer** before printing anything out. To clarify a batch of printed output, we also recommend that you add explanatory captions, such as *Output for the Drug Experiment*. Otherwise, it is only too easy to accumulate pages of SPSS output, the purpose of which becomes increasingly unclear as time passes. All these things can easily be done while you are working in the **Viewer**. Often, however, even after you have edited and severely pruned the **Viewer**'s contents, you will only be interested in printing out a **selection** of the items.

3.5.1.1   Using Print Preview

- To ascertain the content of each page of the output that will be printed before any selection of items has been made, choose **File➜Print Preview…** to view the content of the first page in the **Viewer (all visible output) box** (Figure 41).
- The contents of the other pages can be viewed by pressing the **PgDn** key as often as you need. Alternatively, you can click on the **Next Page** button in the row of buttons at the top of the dialog box. You will see that, when no item has been selected, the output extends to several pages.

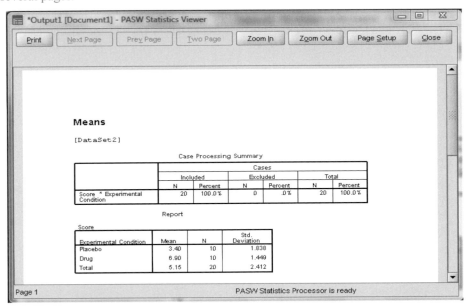

Figure 41. Part of the **Print Preview** dialog box (shrunk horizontally and vertically) for viewing the output before printing from the **SPSS Statistics Viewer**

3.5.1.2   Selecting items for printing

To select two or more items, click the first and, pressing the **Ctrl** key and keeping it held down, click the other items that you wish to select. (You will also need to hold down the **Ctrl** key if you are clicking icons in the left pane to achieve a multiple selection.) The items need not be adjacent. If you now choose **Print Preview**, you will see that it shows only the items you have selected, and it is only those items that will actually be printed. There are two ways of selecting items: you can click the item's icon in the left pane of the **Viewer**; or you can click the item itself in the right pane. Either way, a rectangle with a single continuous border will appear around the item or items concerned. It is, perhaps, easier to click on the items in the right pane directly to make it immediately clear what has been selected.

Try selecting any item in the **Viewer** and choose **Print Preview**, to see the **SPSS Statistics Viewer (selected output)** window, which will display only the item you have selected. If you return to the **Print** dialog box, you will see that the **Selection** radio button in the **Print range** panel has now been activated. Were you to click **OK** at this point, only the selected item would be printed.

3.5.1.3   Deleting items from the Viewer

Items are removed from the **Viewer** by selecting them and pressing the **Delete** key. After a multiple selection, pressing the **Delete** key will remove all the selected items.

3.5.1.4   Re-arranging the items in the Viewer

Items can be rearranged very simply by clicking and dragging them in the left-hand pane, a red arrow showing where the item will be relocated as you drag. Alternatively items in the right-hand pane can be cut and pasted in the usual manner by selecting the item, choosing **Cut** from the **Edit** menu, moving the cursor to the desired new position and choosing **Paste** from the **Edit** menu. Key combinations of **Ctrl + X** for cutting and **Ctrl + V** for pasting can also be used.

3.5.1.5   Inserting page breaks

You can also exert some control over the appearance of the output in the **Viewer** by creating a **page break** between items that clearly belong to different categories.
- Click the item above which you want to create a page break.
- Choose **Insert➜Page Break**.
- Return to the **Viewer** and click outside the selection rectangle to cancel the selection.

If you now return to **Print Preview**, you will see that a page break has been created and the item you selected is now at the top of a fresh page. Used in conjunction with re-ordering, page breaks can help you to sort the items in the **Viewer**. Bear in mind, however, that creating page breaks always increases the number of sheets of paper in the printed output.

3.5.1.6   Changing from portrait to landscape using Page Setup

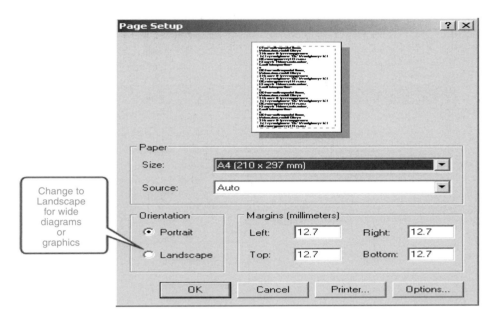

Change to
Landscape
for wide
diagrams
or
graphics

Figure 42. The Page Setup dialog box

- Click either the **Page Setup** button at the top of the **Print Preview** dialog box or **Page Setup** in the **File** menu to enter the **Page Setup** dialog box (Figure 42).
- In the **Orientation** panel, is the radio button for changing from **Portrait** to **Landscape** orientation. Sometimes, for printing purposes, the landscape orientation can accommodate particularly wide tables that will not fit in portrait orientation.
- Click **OK** to return to the **Viewer**.

3.5.1.7   The SPSS Statistics Viewer's Print dialog box

- Access the SPSS Statistics Viewer's **Print** dialog box (Figure 43) by choosing **File➔Print…**.

By default, the radio button labelled **All visible output** is active, which means that pressing **OK** will result in the *entire contents* of the **SPSS Statistics Viewer** being printed out indiscriminately. The default setting of copies is 1, but obviously an increase in that value to 2 will double the volume of the printed output.

This **Print** dialog box differs from the dialog you will receive when you print from the **Data Editor**, in which you would be offered the choice of printing either the entire output or the pages within a specified range. It is also possible to print out only the current page. However, no page range is offered in the dialog shown in Figure 43. When you are printing from the **SPSS Statistics Viewer**, the radio button marked **Selection** will only become active when a selection from the items in the **Viewer** has been made.

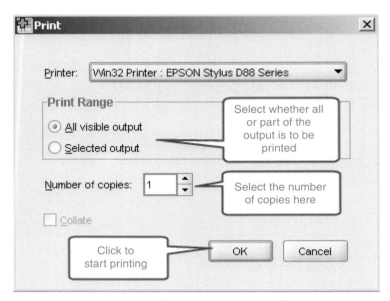

Figure 43. The **Print** dialog box for printing output from the **SPSS Statistics Viewer**

3.5.2   Printing from the Data Editor

It is possible to print out data from **Data View**. There are, however, several problems with this approach. Most notably, if there are too many variables to fit on to one page of printed output and hundreds of cases, it can be difficult to keep track of the output. It sometimes helps to add dummy columns, each cell of which contains a single numerical value, but this can be quite tedious.

To print only selected parts of the data set, use the click-and-drag method to define the target sections by highlighting them to display the material in reverse video. This requires a little practice; but it will be found that when the screen pointer touches the lower border of the window, the latter will scroll down to extend the blackened area to the desired extent. If the pointer touches the right border, the window will scroll to the right across the **Data Editor**. When the **Print** dialog box (Figure 43) appears, the marker will now be on **Selection** (the lowest radio button). Click **OK** to obtain a hard copy of the selected areas.

3.5.3   Transferring data to the Viewer for printing

An alternative way of obtaining a hard copy of the raw data is to print the data from the **Viewer**.

- Choose **Analyze➜Reports➜Case Summaries…** to obtain the **Summarize Cases** dialog box (Figure 44).

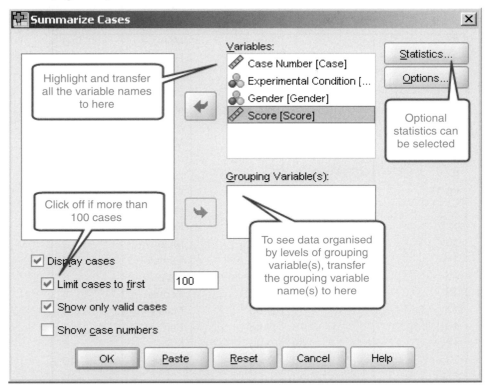

Figure 44. The **Summarize Cases** dialog box

- To see the data arranged as in **Data View**, transfer all the variable names into the **Variables** box. Alternatively, the data can be reorganised by levels of the grouping variables by transferring the grouping variable names to the **Grouping Variable(s)** box. To see all the data, click off the **Limit case to first** check box.
- The **Case Summary** table is shown in Output 9.

Case Summaries

		Experimental		
	Case Number	Condition	Gender	Score
1	1	Placebo	Male	6
2	2	Placebo	Female	5
3	3	Placebo	Male	5
4	4	Placebo	Female	1
5	5	Placebo	Male	2
6	6	Placebo	Female	3
7	7	Placebo	Male	2
8	8	Placebo	Female	4
9	9	Placebo	Male	5
10	10	Placebo	Female	1
11	11	Drug	Male	8
12	12	Drug	Female	6
13	13	Drug	Male	6
14	14	Drug	Female	7
15	15	Drug	Male	6
16	16	Drug	Female	8
17	17	Drug	Male	6
18	18	Drug	Female	7
19	19	Drug	Male	5
20	20	Drug	Female	10
Total N	20	20	20	20

Output 9. The **Case Summaries** of the data from the drug experiment

Exercises

Exercise 3 *Merging files – adding cases & variables* is available in www.psypress.com/spss-made-simple and click on Exercises.

CHAPTER 4

Describing and exploring your data

4.1   INTRODUCTION

Description and exploration of your data are essential preliminaries to the making of any formal statistical tests. This chapter tells you how to use SPSS to describe various kinds of data.

We saw in Chapter 1 that the kinds of statistics the researcher uses to capture the most important features of a data set will depend very much on the nature of the data. For scale or continuous data, interest centres on the distribution of the data. What is the average value? To what extent are scores spread out around the average? What is the shape of the distribution? With categorical data, on the other hand, the questions change. How many participants fell into the different categories? Did a greater proportion of cases fall into Category A compared with Category B?

Different statistics are appropriate for data of different types: there is little point in finding the mean of a set of ranks, for example, because the resulting average would depend solely upon the number of people (or objects) in the sample.

Before embarking even upon a descriptive analysis, it is vital to check the integrity of the data. There may have been transcription errors (e.g. 100 instead of 10). Failure to spot highly deviant scores can result in a set of statistics that misrepresent the data. There are circumstances in which the mean and standard deviation are poor measures of central tendency and dispersion. This can occur when the distribution is markedly skewed, or when extreme cases known as **outliers** exert undue **leverage** upon the values of these statistics.

In recent years, statisticians have devised a set of robust statistical methods specially designed for the purpose of examining small, unruly data sets. Together, they are known as **Exploratory Data Analysis (EDA)**. (For a readable account of EDA, see Howell, 2007, Chapter 2.) EDA statistics have now found their way into all good statistical computing packages, including SPSS. The EDA statistics are particularly good for capturing the most important characteristics of data sets with skewed distributions and highly deviant scores. As well as robust statistics, EDA includes a set of table-graph hybrids which EDA authors refer to as **displays**. We shall consider some EDA techniques and displays in this chapter.

A powerful and versatile system such as SPSS can usually offer several approaches to the solution of a problem in data analysis. Graphs, for instance, can be produced by procedures in either the **Analyze** or the **Graphs** menus. Over the years, many new procedures have been added to the menus, the output of which overlaps with that of older routines. Some of the latter, however, continue to be useful. Once in the **Analyze** menu, for example, the user wishing to draw a graph can choose between the **Legacy dialogs** and the newer **Chart Builder**. The Chart Builder offers many additional facilities; but the Legacy dialogs offer quick and easy access. Descriptive statistics are available on several different procedures. The old **Crosstabs** procedure is still very useful for producing contingency tables; but the newer **Table** command gives the user rather more control over the output.

Table 1. The Blood Group, Sex, Height and Weight data in Data View

Height	Weight	Sex	Blood_group	var
181.16	34.95	1	1	
184.27	39.08	1	1	
173.05	40.64	2	2	
172.16	40.85	2	2	
171.45	42.01	2	2	
186.92	49.58	1	1	
192.91	56.90	1	2	
169.14	41.99	2	2	
180.70	48.27	2	2	
172.16	43.85	2	1	
167.47	41.42	2	3	
169.32	42.51	2	2	
172.00	44.46	2	1	

In this chapter, we shall not attempt a comprehensive coverage of all that SPSS has to offer in the way of descriptive statistics, displays and graphs. Instead, we shall offer the reader some general guidelines for the selection of appropriate routines.

To illustrate how SPSS can be used to describe and explore data, we shall first make use of a large data set comprising two continuous variables, Weight and Height, and two categorical variables, Gender and Blood Group. (Later, we shall turn out attention to a small data set.) Table 1 shows the first few lines of the large data set, which contains 2000 cases. To save space, we have omitted the variable Case from the screen shot. (The entire data set is available at www.psypress.com/spss-made-simple.) Note that some graphical procedures require that the level of measurement (scale, ordinal or nominal) must first be specified in **Variable View**. It is best, therefore, to specify the level of measurement as a matter of routine. In the **Measure** column of Variable View, the variables of Gender and Blood group must be set at the **Nominal** level. There is no need to make an entry for Weight or Height, because by default, all numerical variables are set at the **Scale** level of measurement.

4.2 DESCRIBING NOMINAL DATA

Two of the variables in the data set, Gender and Blood Group, are categorical. In this section, we shall show how SPSS can be used to describe records of categorical variables, that is, **nominal** data.

Questions about nominal data are questions about frequencies: How many cases were there in each blood group? How many males and females were there in the two samples? Was the ratio of the number of males to the number of females the same in the different blood groups?

To answer the first two questions, we shall require tables showing the frequencies of observations in each category. Graphical displays, however, will also be helpful. A **bar chart**, for example, can be used to display the profile of frequencies of observations across groups. (A bar chart is a versatile type of graph, which can also be used to compare summaries of the distribution – means, medians – of a continuous or scale variable across categories. When used with nominal data, however, the bar chart becomes effectively a **bar graph**, which depicts a discrete frequency distribution.)

The third question is one of the possible **association** between two categorical variables or attributes, namely, Sex and Blood Group. To answer the question, we shall need a **contingency table** or **cross-tabulation** (Chapter 1), depicting the bivariate frequency distribution of the two attributes.

4.2.1 Describing nominal data relating to one attribute

Our first question about a data set containing a variable such as Gender or Blood group is: How many cases were there in each category? We can use the **Frequencies** procedure to answer this one. The Frequencies procedure can provide not only tables of frequencies, but also bar charts, which can bring out the frequency distribution more clearly. Proceed as follows.

- Choose **Analyze→Descriptive Statistics→Frequencies...** to open the **Frequencies** dialog box.
- Follow the steps shown in Figure 1.

- Click **Charts** to obtain the **Frequencies: Charts** dialog box (Figure 2) and select the **Bar Chart(s)** radio button. There is also the choice of frequencies or percentages for the *y*-axis in the **Chart Values** box. Take the frequencies option.
- Click **Continue** to return to **Frequencies** and then **OK** to run the procedure.

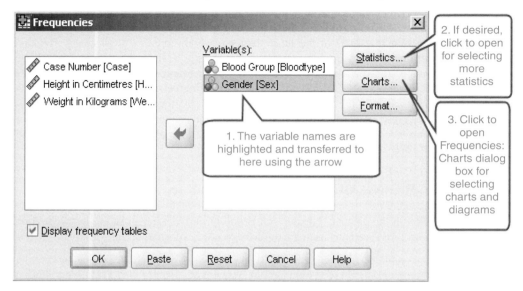

Figure 1. The **Frequencies** dialog box for Gender and Blood Group

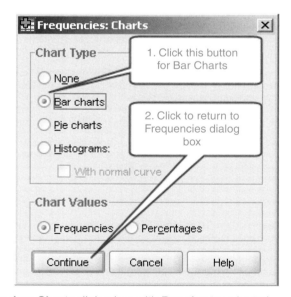

Figure 2. The **Frequencies: Charts** dialog box with **Bar charts** selected

The output consists of two tables (Output 1). The bar chart for Blood group is shown in Output 2. (The chart for Gender is not shown here.) A bar chart can also be requested directly with the **Bar** procedure in the **Graphs** menu. It is possible to edit a bar chart in order to centre or change the axis labels, the title, the shading of the boxes and other aspects of the graph. More details about the editing of graphs will be given in the next chapter.

Blood_group

		Frequency	Percent	Valid Percent	Cumulative Percent
Valid	Group O	880	44.0	44.0	44.0
	Group A	840	42.0	42.0	86.0
	Group B	200	10.0	10.0	96.0
	Group AB	80	4.0	4.0	100.0
	Total	2000	100.0	100.0	

Gender

		Frequency	Percent	Valid Percent	Cumulative Percent
Valid	Male	1000	50.0	50.0	50.0
	Female	1000	50.0	50.0	100.0
	Total	2000	100.0	100.0	

Output 1. Frequency listings for Blood Group and Gender

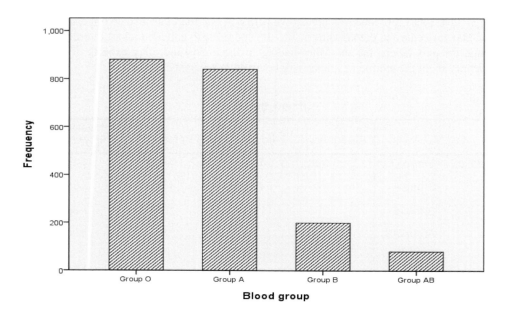

Output 2. Bar Chart for Blood Group

Note that the graph shown in Output 2 is usually known a **bar graph**, that is, a depiction of a discrete frequency distribution. A clear distinction must be made between a bar graph and a **histogram**, which is used to depict a *continuous* distribution. With continuous data, bar charts do not depict distributions: instead, they compare a statistical summary of the distribution of the same continuous variable across the categories of qualitative (or categorical) variables.

4.2.2   Obtaining contingency tables

In this subsection, we shall describe the use of two procedures to obtain contingency tables: (1) **Crosstabs**; (2) **Custom Tables**. **Crosstabs** is in the **Descriptive Statistics** menu and **Custom Tables** is in the **Tables** menu. We shall begin by using the **Crosstabs** procedure to obtain a contingency table for Blood Group and Gender.

4.2.2.1   Contingency tables with Crosstabs

- Choose **Analyze➜Descriptive Statistics➜Crosstabs...**   to open the **Crosstabs** dialog box.
- Transfer the variable names as shown in Figure 3 and click **OK**. If one of the variables has more than about four categories, it is better to use it for **Rows** rather than **Columns**, otherwise the output will be too wide for printing on a single page. In this example, a narrower table is produced if Blood Group is nominated for **Rows**.
- The contingency table is shown in Output 3.

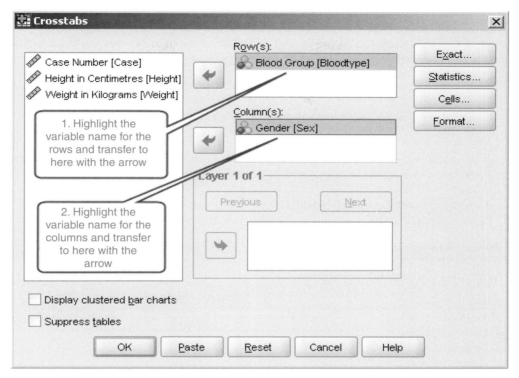

Figure 3. The completed **Crosstabs** dialog box

Gender * Blood_group Crosstabulation

Count

		Blood_group				Total
		Group O	Group A	Group B	Group AB	
Gender	Male	448	413	101	38	1000
	Female	432	427	99	42	1000
Total		880	840	200	80	2000

Output 3. Contingency table from **Crosstabs** for Gender and Blood Group

The table shown in Output 3 is the simplest possible contingency table. When completing the dialog in Figure 3, you can click the **Cells...** button to access the **Cell Display** dialog box and request several additional tabulations, such as row and column frequencies. The simple table in Output 3, however, shows very clearly that, although there is considerable variation in the numbers of cases in the different Blood Group categories, there are similar numbers of males and females in each group. There would appear to be no association between Blood Group and Gender.

An excellent feature of the **Custom Tables** procedure is that the user gets a preview of the format of the table requested, in the form of an outline of the titles of rows and columns and representations of the positions of the counts or percentages that have been requested.

To obtain a table of frequencies with percentages, proceed as follows:

- Choose **Analyze➔Tables➔Custom Tables...** to open the **Custom Tables** dialog box (Figure 4). If the warning box about labels appears, click **OK**. (You will, of course, have made sure that the level of measurement of all variables has already been specified in Variable View.)
- Highlight and drag the variable name as shown in Figure 5. The cursor with the variable name needs to be made to hover over the Columns or Rows box until the border changes colour.
- To obtain percentages as well as counts, follow the steps described in Figures 6 and 7.
- Finally click **OK**. The contingency table is shown in Output 4.

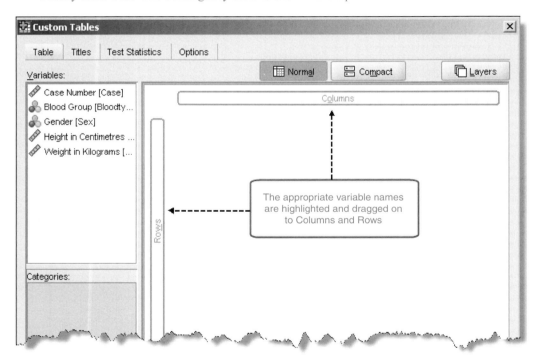

Figure 4. The upper part of the **Custom Tables** dialog box

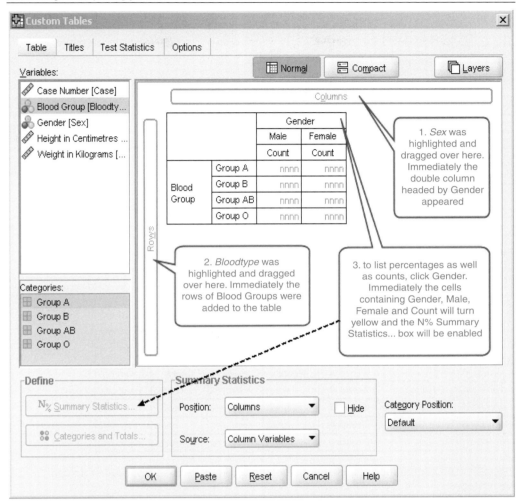

Figure 5. The **Custom Tables** dialog box partially completed by dragging Gender and Blood Group to **Columns** and **Rows** respectively

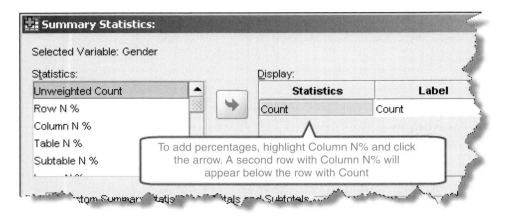

Figure 6 After clicking the **N% Summary Statistics…** button in Figure 5, the **Summary Statistics** dialog box opens (the top half is shown here). Add column percentages as described and then click the **Apply to Selection** button at the foot of the dialog box (not shown) to return to the **Custom Tables** dialog box

		Gender			
		Male		Female	
		Count	Column ...	Count	Column ...
	Group A	nnnn	nnnn.n%	nnnn	nnnn.n%
Blood Group	Group B	nnnn	nnnn.n%	nnnn	nnnn.n%
	Group AB	nnnn	nnnn.n%	nnnn	nnnn.n%
	Group O	nnnn	nnnn.n%	nnnn	nnnn.n%

Figure 7. The appearance of the inner part of the **Custom Tables** preview after adding percentages

		Gender			
		Male		Female	
		Count	Column N %	Count	Column N %
Blood_group	Group O	448	44.8%	432	43.2%
	Group A	413	41.3%	427	42.7%
	Group B	101	10.1%	99	9.9%
	Group AB	38	3.8%	42	4.2%

Output 4. Frequencies and percentages of Blood Group for each Gender

Tables such as that shown in Output 4 quickly show whether the data have been entered correctly, since the blood group counts in the tables can be compared with those in the original data set. Checks should also be made on the other variables in the data set: e.g. check the minimum and maximum heights by using the **Descriptives** procedure for Height as shown in Section 4.3. A height of over 200 cm or under 100 cm prompts a scrutiny of the data in **Data View** for a possible transcription error.

4.3   DESCRIBING CONTINUOUS OR SCALE DATA

There are many procedures for describing and exploring data in the form of measurements on an independent scale with units. With such continuous or scale data, as with nominal data, we shall want to supplement the statistics with graphical displays. The histograms of the heights and weights of the males and the females can be expected to show approximate normality of distribution of either variable. Bar charts can be used to compare summaries of the height and weight distributions of males and females.

Since long bones tend to weigh more than short ones, we can expect the variables of Height and Weight to be correlated. As a preliminary to the investigation of the association between the two variables, we shall need the scatterplots of the bivariate distributions for the Males and Females separately.

The present data contains records of the heights of 1000 men and 1000 women. While it would, of course, be possible to ignore the Gender variable and simply describe the data on all 2000 cases using either the **Descriptives** or the **Frequencies** procedures, the statistics of combined samples from different populations are rather uninformative. We shall therefore describe the characteristics of the male and female distributions separately.

4.3.1   Histograms of the distributions of height and weight for the males and females

We shall describe a variety of the most recent SPSS graphics routines in the next chapter. Here, we shall make use of some older procedures that can produce useful graphs very quickly. (In Chapter 5, however, we shall meet other graphs, such as **back-to-back histograms**, which can be very useful for depicting data of the kind that we are describing in this section.)

The basis of a histogram is a table called a **frequency distribution**, which divides the total range of values into arbitrary **class intervals** and gives the frequency of measurements that fall within each interval, that is, have values between the upper and lower **bounds** of the interval concerned. With data on height recorded in centimetres, for example, the total range would be divided into a sequence of class intervals such as 140–149, 150–159, 160–169, …, and so on, and the frequency distribution would give the frequencies of heights within each of these ranges.

In a bar graph (such as Output 2), the bars are separated to clarify the fact that the horizontal axis contains no scale of measurement; in fact, the order of the bars in Output 3 is arbitrary, since the Group AB bar could as well have followed the Group A bar, rather than vice versa, as in the figure. A histogram on the other hand, is appropriate for continuous or scale data. The class intervals are stepped out along the horizontal axis and above each interval a bar is drawn whose height represents the number of people whose measurements fell within that interval. In a histogram, as compared with a bar graph, the bars touch one another, reflecting the continuity of the scale of measurement.

To obtain histograms of the distributions of Height in the Males and the Females, proceed as follows:

- Choose **Data➔Select Cases** to select the data for the Males only. In the **Select Cases** dialog box, set Sex = 1, which is the code number for the Males in the data set.
- Choose **Legacy dialogs➔Histogram** and, in the Histogram dialog box, transfer the variable Height to the Variable slot at the top of the dialog. Check the box labelled **Display Normal Curve**. Click **OK** to produce the histogram, an edited version of which is shown in Output 5.
- To obtain the histogram of the distribution of the heights of the females (not shown), proceed in a similar way, setting Sex = 2 in the **Select Cases** dialog,.

Histograms are offered by several other SPSS procedures, including **Frequencies**, **Explore** and the **Chart Builder**, which we shall discuss in detail in Chapter 5.

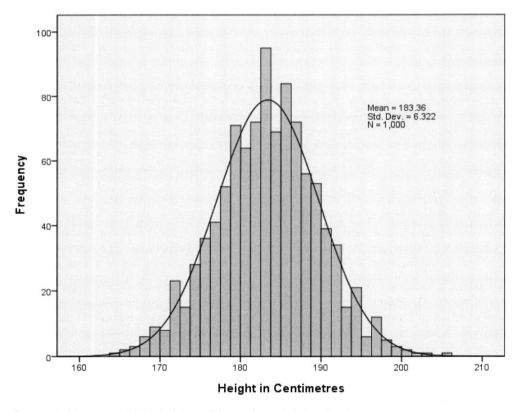

Output 5. Histogram of the heights of the males (slightly edited)

The histogram of the distribution of Height in the Males shows an approximately bell-shaped, normal distribution. The same is true of the histogram of Height in the Females. It will also be found that the distributions of Weight in the Males and Females are similarly bell-shaped.

4.3.2   Obtaining scatterplots of weight against height

To obtain the scatterplots of weight against height for the males and females separately, proceed as follows.

- Select the data for the females only by setting Gender = 2 in the **Select Cases** dialog.
- Choose **Legacy dialogs➜Scatter/Dot➜Simple Scatter** and, in the **Scatterplot** dialog box, place Weight in the Y-axis box and Height in the X-axis box (since we have speculated that Weight is partly determined by height). Click **OK** to run the Scatterplot routine.
- Select the data for the males only and proceed as above to obtain the scatterplot of Weight against Height for the Males. (Only the scatterplot for the females is shown.)

The scatterplot is shown in Output 6.

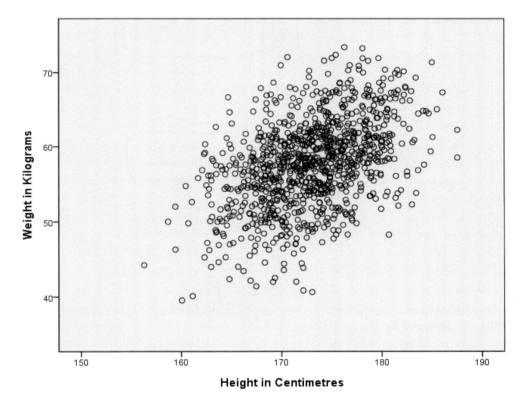

Output 6. Scatterplot of Weight against Height for the females

From Output 6, we can tell from inspection alone that there is a substantial correlation between the variables of Weight and Height in the region of .4 to .6   The topic of correlation, including the interpretation of a scatterplot, is discussed further in Chapter 11. An elliptical plot like that in Output 6 indicates that the Pearson correlation is a suitable statistic for use with this data set.

- Choose **Analyze➜Correlate➜Bivariate** to open the **Bivariate Correlations** dialog box.

- Complete the dialog as shown in Figure 8 and click **OK** to run the procedure.

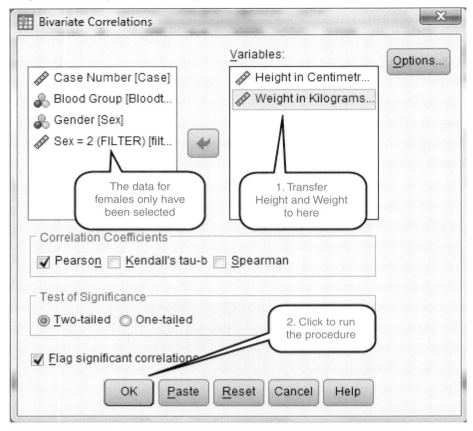

Figure 8. The completed **Bivariate Correlations** dialog

The correlation turns out to be .456, as can be seen in Output 7. (We report: $r(1000) = .456$; $p < .01$. See Chapter 11.)

Correlations

		Height in Centimetres	Weight in Kilograms
Height in Centimetres	Pearson Correlation	1	.456**
	Sig. (2-tailed)		.000
	N	1000	1000
Weight in Kilograms	Pearson Correlation	.456**	1
	Sig. (2-tailed)	.000	
	N	1000	1000

**. Correlation is significant at the 0.01 level (2-tailed).

Output 7. The Pearson correlation between Height and Weight in a thousand women

4.3.3   Obtaining the statistics of the height distributions of males and females

This is a large data set, which the preliminary graphs have shown to be free of any obvious problems such as skewed distributions or many extreme scores. A good procedure here for exploring the data further is **Frequencies**, which offers a selection of useful statistics, such as the mean, the median, quartiles and user-specified percentiles. The **Frequencies** procedure gives a much better selection of statistics than does **Descriptives**.

Proceed as follows:
- Select the data on the males by choosing   **Data➔Select Cases** and, in the **Select Cases** dialog box, set Gender = 1, which will select the data on the Males only.
- Choose **Analyze➔Descriptive Statistics➔Frequencies** to open the **Frequencies** dialog box.
- In the **Frequencies** dialog, uncheck the **Display frequency tables** box (Figure 9). If you omit to do this, the output will include a long list of scores.
- Click the Statistics button to access the **Frequencies: Statistics** dialog box and complete that dialog as shown in Figure 10.
- Click **OK** to run the procedure.

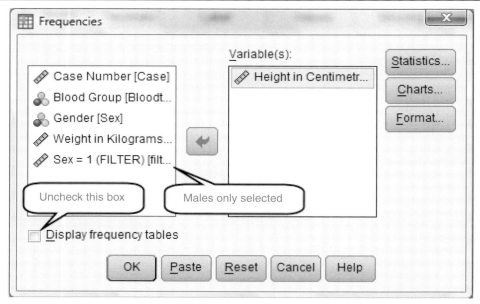

Figure 9. The **Frequencies** dialog box with the **Display frequency tables** box unchecked

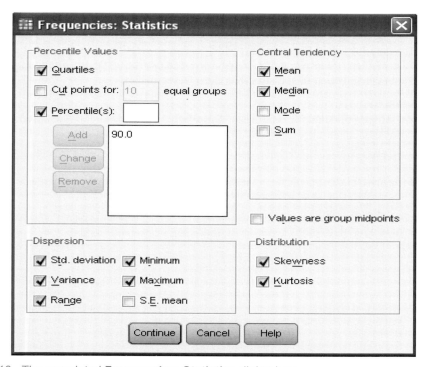

Figure 10. The completed **Frequencies: Statistics** dialog box

The requested statistics are shown in Output 8. Note that the mean and median have similar values, indicating that the distribution is symmetrical. The median is about half way between the upper and lower quartiles, which is another indication of symmetry.

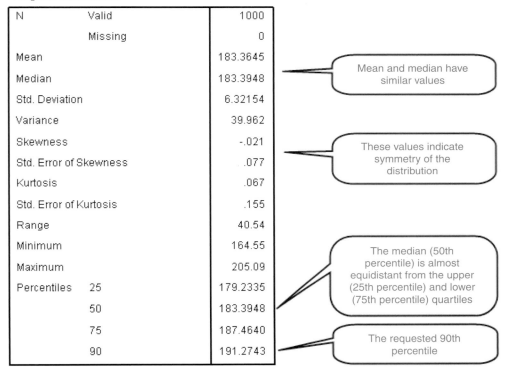

Statistics

Height in Centimetres

N	Valid	1000
	Missing	0
Mean		183.3645
Median		183.3948
Std. Deviation		6.32154
Variance		39.962
Skewness		-.021
Std. Error of Skewness		.077
Kurtosis		.067
Std. Error of Kurtosis		.155
Range		40.54
Minimum		164.55
Maximum		205.09
Percentiles	25	179.2335
	50	183.3948
	75	187.4640
	90	191.2743

Mean and median have similar values

These values indicate symmetry of the distribution

The median (50th percentile) is almost equidistant from the upper (25th percentile) and lower (75th percentile) quartiles

The requested 90th percentile

Output 8. The statistics from the **Frequencies** procedure

4.4   DESCRIBING SMALL DATA SETS

In the previous subsections, we explored a large data set using the **Frequencies** procedure, which is very useful for that purpose. Often, however, our data are much less plentiful than we would wish and, should scarcity of data be combined with such features as skewness of distribution and the presence of markedly atypical scores in the samples, statistics such as the mean and standard deviation can present a misleading picture of the data. For small and unruly data sets, a set of special statistics has been devised, which are referred to collectively as **Exploratory Data Analysis (EDA)**. These special EDA statistics are much more resistant to the leverage exerted by outliers and asymmetry of distribution than are the traditional statistics.

Another feature of EDA is a set of diagrams or **displays**, which might best be described as hybrids of tables and graphs. The EDA counterpart of the histogram, devised for use with small data sets, is the **stem-and-leaf display**. The counterpart of the bar chart is the **boxplot**, which summarises distributions of the same continuous variable such as height or weight in the different categories of a qualitative attribute such as gender or blood group.

The **Explore** procedure (in the **Descriptive Statistics** menu) can be regarded as a general exploratory data analysis procedure and can be used with any size of data set. **Explore** offers many of the facilities already illustrated with other procedures; moreover, like **Means** and **Compare Means**, it allows quantitative variables to be subdivided by the categories of a qualitative variable such as gender. If, for example, a data set contains the heights of 50 men and 50 women collected into a column headed Height and (in another column) code numbers making up the grouping variable Sex, **Explore** will produce statistical summaries of the distributions of Height in the Males and Females considered separately. As well as traditional statistics and graphs, **Explore** also offers some EDA statistics and displays, which can be used to explore small data sets.

4.4.1   Stem-and-leaf displays

Output 9 (annotated) shows a **stem-and-leaf display** of a small data set of the weights of females using the **Explore** procedure (see Section 4.4.3).

```
          Weight in Kilograms Stem-and-Leaf Plot


          Frequency     Stem &  Leaf

              2.00 Extremes     (=<42)          57 Kg      59 Kg
              7.00         4 .  6678999
              9.00         5 .  011124444
             24.00         5 .  5555666677777778888899999
             14.00         6 .  00012222222334
             11.00         6 .  55666677777
              2.00         7 .  03
                                                    Class interval
          Stem width:     10.00
          Each leaf:       1 case(s)
```

14 females had weights between 60 Kg and 64 Kg inclusive

Output 9. A stem-and-leaf display

In the **stem-and-leaf display**, the central column of numbers (4, 5, 5, 6, 6, 7) is the **stem**, on which the class intervals are stepped out across the entire range. The numbers on the stem are often leading digits only: in this example, each number represents so-many tens: 4 represents 40 Kg, 6 represents 60 Kg. Each number on the stem denotes the lower bound of a class interval: for example, the first number, 4, represents the lower bound of the class interval from 46 – 49 Kg, the second number is the lower bound of the interval from 50 – 54 Kg, the third is the lower bound of the interval from 55 – 59 kg, and so on. The numbers in the column headed **Leaf** are the final digits of the women's weights, to the nearest Kg. The column headed **Frequency** lists the number of cases falling within each class interval. The row at the stem value 6, for example, signifies that 14 women had weights in the range from 60 – 64 Kg, inclusive. There were two 'extreme' cases, with weights less than or equal to 42 Kg. The stem-and-leaf display is very useful for displaying information about small data sets, but is ponderous with larger data sets, for which the histogram is the more suitable diagram.

4.4.2   Boxplots

The structure of a typical boxplot is shown in Table 2. The box itself represents that portion of the distribution falling between the 25th and 75th percentiles, i.e. the **lower** and **upper** **quartiles** (in EDA terminology these are known as **hinges**). (The xth percentile is the value below which x% of the distribution lies, so 50% of the heights lie between the 25th and 75th percentiles.) The thick horizontal line across the interior of the box represents the median. The vertical lines outside the box, which are known as **whiskers**, connect the largest and smallest values that are not outliers or extreme cases.

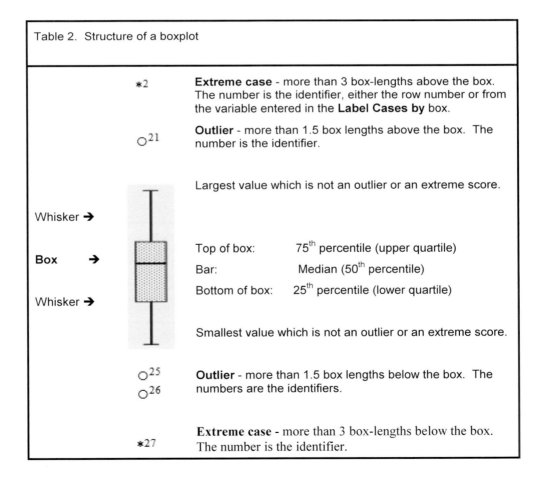

Table 2. Structure of a boxplot

*2   **Extreme case** - more than 3 box-lengths above the box. The number is the identifier, either the row number or from the variable entered in the **Label Cases by** box.

○21   **Outlier** - more than 1.5 box lengths above the box. The number is the identifier.

Largest value which is not an outlier or an extreme score.

Whisker →

Box   →   Top of box: 75th percentile (upper quartile)
Bar: Median (50th percentile)
Bottom of box: 25th percentile (lower quartile)

Whisker →

Smallest value which is not an outlier or an extreme score.

○25   **Outlier** - more than 1.5 box lengths below the box. The
○26   numbers are the identifiers.

*27   **Extreme case** - more than 3 box-lengths below the box. The number is the identifier.

The boxplot in Table 2 shows three **outliers** and two **extreme cases**. An **outlier** (marked as an o) is defined as a value more than 1.5 box-lengths away from the box; whereas an **extreme case** (*) is more than 3 box-lengths away from the box. The number(s) alongside o and * are the case numbers of the deviant observations concerned. The case numbers are either (by default) the row numbers in **Data View** or the identifiers from the variable entered in the **Label Cases by** box.

Skewness is indicated by an eccentric location of the horizontal median bar in the box. The distribution depicted in Table 2 is positively skewed: the median bar is considerably nearer to the upper hinge than to the lower hinge. Boxplots are particularly useful for identifying outliers and extreme cases in data sets, and can be requested directly by choosing **Graphs➔Chart Builder** and selecting **Box** from the gallery, as described in more detail in Section 5.4 of the next chapter.

4.4.3   Exploring a small data set

In this section, we shall use the **Explore** procedure to investigate a small data set consisting of data on 32 people (16 men and 16 women). As before, the variables are Height, Weight and Blood Group. With small samples, it can be difficult to tell from a histogram whether a variable is normally distributed or not. The stem-and-leaf display, however, often presents a clearer picture. Similarly, a boxplot offers a much more informative comparative summary of the distribution of a variable across different categories than can a bar chart showing only the means or medians of the distributions.

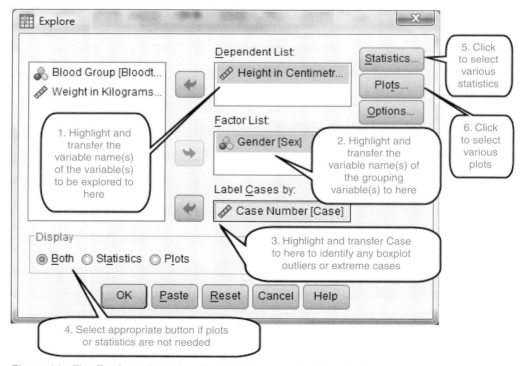

Figure 11. The **Explore** dialog box for Height categorised by Gender

To run the **Explore** routine, proceed as follows:

- Choose **Analyze→Descriptive Statistics→Explore…** to open the **Explore** dialog box.
- Follow the steps shown in Figure 11.
- If there is a variable identifying the cases (e.g. Case), then click Case and transfer it with the arrow to the **Label Cases by** box. Outliers or extreme cases are identified in boxplots by their row numbers by default or by the identifier in the variable entered in the **Label Cases by** box.
- Click **Plots** to open the **Explore: Plots** dialog box (Figure 12). The default setting for the **Boxplots** is a side-by-side (**Factor levels together**) plot for each level of the factor (i.e. Female and Male) and **Stem-and-leaf** table.
- Click **Continue** and then **OK**.

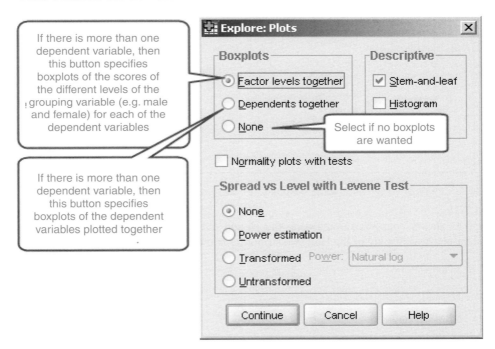

Figure 12. The **Explore: Plots** dialog box

Should you wish to have boxplots of two dependent variables side-by-side (e.g. Height and Weight) at each level of a classificatory variable (e.g. Gender or Blood Group), both dependent variables must be entered into the **Dependent List** box, and (in the **Boxplots** dialog box) the **Dependents together** radio button must be selected. In the present example, of course, it would have made no sense to plot boxplots of Height and Weight side-by-side at each level of Gender, since height and weight measurements have quite different scales.

4.4.4   Some of the statistical output from Explore

The table of statistics for the Males only is shown in Output 10. Its contents overlap considerably with those of a similar table in the output from the **Frequencies** routine. The **5%**

Trimmed Mean (an EDA statistic) is the mean of the scores from which the extreme values at either end of the distribution have been removed. (A tenet of the philosophy of EDA is that it is better to describe 95% of the data well than 100% of them badly.) The trimmed mean, the traditional mean and the median all have similar values, suggesting that the distribution is reasonably symmetrical.

Descriptives

Gender				Statistic	Std. Error
Height in Centimetres	Male	Mean		176.63	3.12
		95% Confidence Interval for Mean	Lower Bound	169.98	
			Upper Bound	183.27	
		5% Trimmed Mean		177.31	
		Median		179.00	
		Variance		155.32	
		Std. Deviation		12.46	
		Minimum		145.00	
		Maximum		196.00	
		Range		51.00	
		Interquartile Range		14.50	
		Skewness		-.95	.56
		Kurtosis		1.64	1.09

Output 10. Some of the statistical output from **Explore**: summary of the statistics for the Males only

Output 11 shows boxplots summarising the Height distributions in the Males and Females. The stem-and-leaf display of the Height distribution in the males is shown on the right.

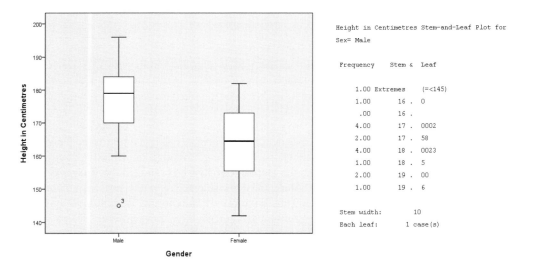

Output 11. Boxplots of the Height distributions for the Males and Females. (A stem-and-leaf display of the Height distribution of the Males is shown on the right.)

The Female distribution appears symmetrical, with the median bar equidistant from the upper and lower hinges. The Male distribution, however, shows a hint of negative skewness: the median bar is definitely nearer to the upper hinge. There is also an outlier at the lower end of the distribution contributed by participant number 3. The impression of negative skewness is reinforced by the appearance of the stem-and-leaf display of the male data; and the same outlier is picked up by that display also.

4.5 DESCRIBING DATA FROM MULTIPLE RESPONSE QUESTIONNAIRES

Some questionnaires contain items in the form of checklists from which the respondent can choose two or more items. For example, when asked which means of transport you use to get to work, you may be allowed to tick up to seven items from the following list: walking, cycling, taking the bus, driving a car on your own, using a motorbike, sharing a car and taking the train. On each working day, some commuters may use all seven methods to get to their work; whereas others may use just one. Most, however, will fall between these limits: Respondent A might drive his car to a station and then take a train; Respondent B might walk to a bus stop, take the bus to the railway station, take the train to a railway station near work and finally take another bus to complete her journey; and so on.

When a questionnaire includes questions in the form of a checklist allowing the respondent to tick one or more items, one cannot transcribe the responses to such a questionnaire into one variable of an SPSS data set, since we are allowed to enter only one value for each variable. Instead, we must create several elementary or **component** variables (e.g. Do you walk? Do you cycle?), one for each form of transport. There are two methods of coding responses. In the **multiple-dichotomy** method, which we shall follow in this section, the same code value (usually 1) is used for the positive response to every component question: e.g., if, for the question: 'Do you cycle?', the code value 1 indicates Yes, the same will be true for the question: 'Do you take the train?'. To capture a respondent's response to the checklist, we shall need as many variables as there are items in the list. The researcher can then enter a value of 1 for each of the items in the checklist that the respondent ticked.

The process of creating sets of component variables to capture a respondent's choices from a list is, of course, very laborious – particularly if there are several checklists in a questionnaire. Fortunately, special software is available for making the process less burdensome. In the example we shall use as an illustration in this section, we shall start with a data set containing a set of component variables for a single checklist that has been created by using the SNAP package of proprietary software.

We could, of course, proceed to analyse responses to the component variables separately by using SPSS procedures such as **Frequencies** and **Crosstabs**. Since the frequencies of positive responses to the items in the checklist are free to vary independently, there would certainly be something be gained from doing that. On the other hand, taken together, the questions form a meaningful set and there is even greater merit in treating them, to some extent, as a coherent composite variable in the analysis. When comparing men and women in their use of various modes of transport, for example, there is interest not only in whether men use, say, cars more than women or vice versa, but also whether there is a difference in their selections of other modes of transport for parts of their journey to work.

The SPSS **Multiple Response** command integrates the component variables that carry responses to a checklist into a variable-like group known as a **multiple response set**. Up to 20 such sets can be defined. Were a questionnaire to present the respondent with 20 checklists, it would be reasonable to define 20 multiple response sets, each capturing the respondent's choices from one of the checklists. Should the researcher have a question about a subset of the listed items, however, a smaller multiple response set can easily be defined. For example, one might define a set containing only non-mechanised modes of transport (walk; cycle; run) and another containing mechanised modes of transport (bus; car; train). Like an ordinary variable, a multiple response set can be processed by some SPSS routines to display frequencies and optional percentages for its component items in univariate tables and multivariate crosstabulations. Defined multiple response sets can be crosstabulated either with elementary variables or with other defined multiple response sets. The **Multiple Responses Crosstabs** procedure can produce cell, row, column and total counts and the corresponding percentages. The cell percentages can be based upon cases or upon responses. Such information can provide additional insights over and above any analysis with any single variable alone.

It should be noted that, although a multiple response set behaves like a categorical variable, it is supported by two SPSS routines only, namely, **Custom Tables** and the **Chart Builder**. A multiple response set is a special construct within a data file, which cannot be read by other SPSS routines such as **Crosstabs** and **Frequencies**. Multiple response sets can be saved in data files, but they cannot be sent to or imported from other file formats.

4.5.1   Data for the Multiple Response procedure

We shall illustrate the **Multiple Response** procedure with a data set (in a file named *Multiple Responses*) consisting of records of age, age group, sex and how the respondents travel to work. Our analysis begins at the stage where the details of how the respondents get to work have already been coded (by the software SNAP) into seven binary variables: Travel_walk, Travel_cycle, …, Travel_train (Figure 13).

Travel_walk	Numeric	8	0	Do you walk?	{1, Yes}...
Travel_cycle	Numeric	8	0	Do you cycle?	{1, Yes}...
Travel_bus	Numeric	8	0	Do you take the bus?	{1, Yes}...
Travel_drivecar	Numeric	8	0	Do you drive a car?	{1, Yes}...
Travel_motorbike	Numeric	8	0	Do you drive a motorbike?	{1, Yes}...
Travel_sharecar	Numeric	8	0	Do you come by car with others	{1, Yes}...
Travel_train	Numeric	8	0	Do you come by train?	{1, Yes}...

Figure 13. Part of **Variable View** showing the variables specifying seven modes of travel

Were you to click on the **Values** cell of any of the seven Travel variables listed in Figure 13, you would see the value 1 only: there is no zero (Figure 14). This is a peculiarity of the SNAP software, which has consequences for the appearance of **Data View**.

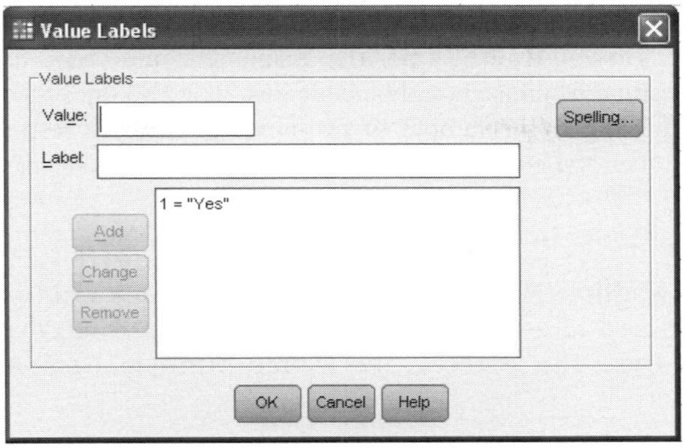

Figure 14. The **Value Labels** window for one of the component variables

Inspection of Data View, a section of which is shown in Figure 15 will show, in addition to case numbers and the grouping variables, seven columns, each headed with one of the variable names shown in Figure 12. In each column, a value of 1 signifies whether a respondent uses the mode of transport specified by the column heading. Where a respondent does not use this mode of transport, however, a missing value will be recorded, rather than a zero. Had the researcher created the component variables without using the SNAP software, zeros for negative responses would have been entered in Data View, and the value label No would have been assigned to the code value 0 in the Values column of Variable View.

Travel_walk	Travel_cycle	Travel_bus	Travel_drivecar	Travel_motorbike	Travel_sharecar	Travel_train
.	1	.	.	.	.	.
1	1	.	.	.	.	.
.	.	1	.	.	.	.
.	.	1	.	.	.	.
.	.	1	.	.	.	.
1	.	1	.	.	.	.

Figure 15. A section of Data View in a file created by the SNAP software

The **Multiple Response** procedure has no problem at all with missing values in Data View. We should note, however, that some standard SPSS procedures such as **Compute Variable** cannot cope with missing values. Should we wish to run **Compute Variable**, we should have to replace the system-missing values in Data View with zeros. (This, as we shall see, can easily be done by using the **Recode** procedure.) The use of **Compute Variable** is necessary if the researcher has questions about the frequencies of specific combinations of different modes of travel. The **Multiple Response** procedure cannot answer questions of this type and we must use other methods to answer them.

Before we proceed to define a multiple response set, we should note that the **multiple-dichotomy** method of coding that we have chosen is the method of choice for recording responses to checklists, as in our current example. To understand the **Multiple Response Sets** dialog, however, we need to be aware that there is another method of coding, called **multiple-category** coding, by which you create a set of component variables, one for each mode of transport, but have a different value for the positive response for each component variable: thus, to the question, 'Do you walk?', a positive response could coded as 1; to the question, 'Do you cycle?', a positive response could be coded as 2; and so on. Such **multiple category sets** are used when the maximum number of responses given by a respondent to a survey is significantly less than the total number of possible responses.

4.5.2   Creating a multiple response set

The first step in the **Multiple Response** procedure is to create a **Multiple Response Set** for the type of transport used to get to work. To do this, select **Analyze➜Tables➜Multiple Response Sets...** (Figure 16) to access the **Define Multiple Response Sets** dialog box (Figure 17).

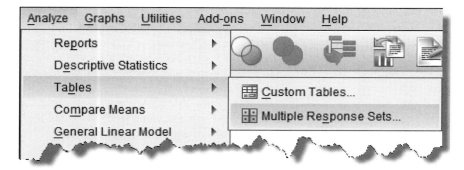

Figure 16. The **Multiple Response Sets** item in the **Analyze** menu

Complete the dialog box as shown in Figure 17 (assuming multiple dichotomy formatting, in which the value 1 always means Yes), remembering to enter the value 1 in the Counted Value slot. Click **OK** to run the procedure. Confirmation of the creation of a new Response Set named Travel_Mode with a label Travel to Work will appear in **SPSS Statistics Viewer** (Output 12).

(Had the variables been in multiple categories format [1 = Walk for the first variable, 2 = Cycle for the second variable, and so on], the radio button marked **Labels of counted value** in the left-hand **Category Labels Source** panel would have been clicked instead of the default **Variable labels** - see Figure 17.)

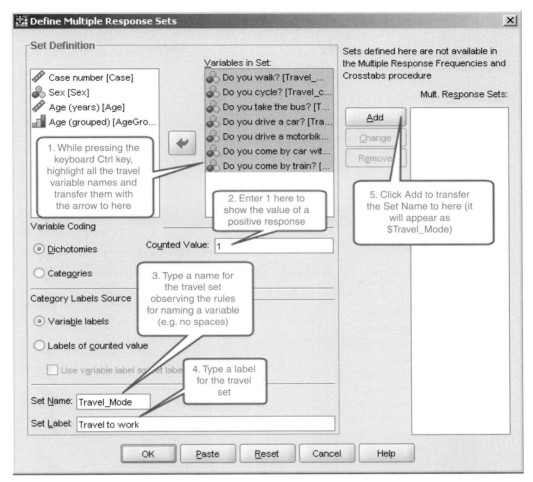

Figure 17. The **Define Multiple Response Sets** dialog box. Clicking **Add** will complete the dialog by transferring the Set Name to the right-hand panel

Multiple Response Sets

Name	Label	Coded As	Counted Value	Data Type	Elementary Variables
$Travel_Mode	Travel to Work	Dichotomies	1	Numeric	Do you walk? Do you cycle? Do you take the bus? Do you drive a car? Do you drive a motorbike? Do you come by car with others? Do you come by train?

Output 12. Confirmation that a multiple response set named Travel_Mode with a label Travel to Work has been created

Note that, despite the confirmation in the Output Viewer that a multiple response set has been created, this new variable does not appear in the Data Editor. A multiple response set is a special construct that the **Multiple Response Sets** procedure builds and stores within the data file. It is supported by the **Custom Tables** and **Chart Builder** procedures only and cannot be used by other SPSS procedures.

4.5.3   Obtaining the crosstabulations

Now that a Multiple Response Set has been created, the researcher can make a crosstabulation of the Response Set Travel to Work with the ordinary grouping variables Sex and AgeGroup. The **Custom Tables** routine will do this for us.

- Select **Analyze→Tables→Custom Tables…** to open the **Custom Tables** dialog box (Figure 18).

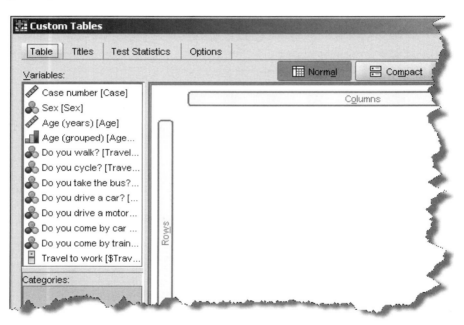

Figure 18. Part of the **Custom Tables** dialog box

- Complete the dialog box as shown in Figure 19 and click **OK**. Figure 20 offers further guidance. As each variable name is dragged into either the **Columns** or the **Rows** panels, the display changes to show the constituent levels of the variables (Figure 20).

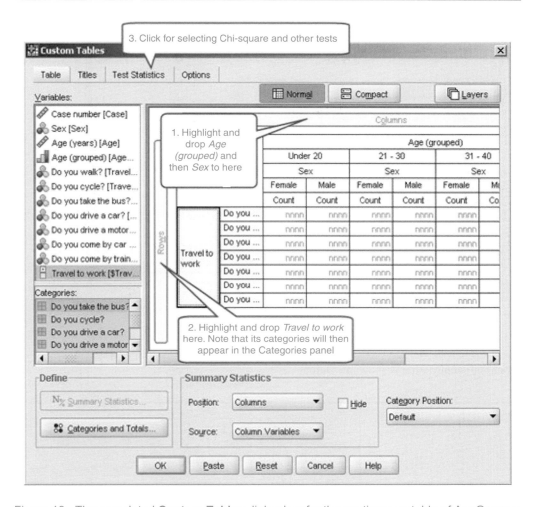

Figure 19. The completed **Custom Tables** dialog box for the contingency table of AgeGroup × Sex ×Travel to work

Age (grouped)			
Under 20	21 - 30	31 - 40	41 - 50
Count	Count	Count	Count
nnnn	nnnn	nnnn	nnnn

Age (grouped)			
Under 20	21 - 30	31 - 40	41 - 50
~~Count~~	~~Count~~	~~Count~~	~~Count~~
nnnn	nnnn Sex [Sex]	nnnn	nnnn

Figure 20. Hover Age(grouped) over the Columns box (left). Then hover Sex until horizontal coloured lines appear (right). Release the mouse button.

Various statistical tests can also be selected, as shown in Figure 21.

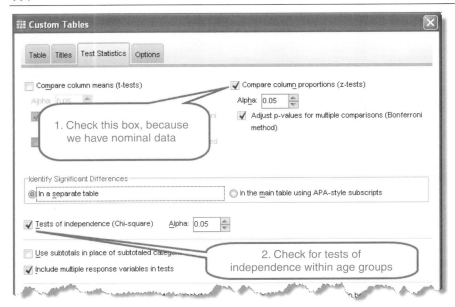

Figure 21. Click the check boxes for the appropriate test statistics, then click **OK** at the foot of the dialog box

The contingency table is shown in Output 13.

		Age (grouped)							
		Under 20		21 - 30		31 - 40		41 - 50	
		Sex		Sex		Sex		Sex	
		Female	Male	Female	Male	Female	Male	Female	Male
		Count	Count	Count	Count	Count	Count	Count	Count
How to get to work	Do you walk?	153	76	207	167	26	17	10	7
	Do you cycle?	5	13	22	33	7	8	5	5
	Do you take the bus?	69	39	72	41	14	6	8	2
	Do you drive a car?	46	28	67	57	44	34	41	16
	Do you drive a motorbike?	0	0	3	2	0	0	1	0
	Do you come by car with others?	8	5	8	4	2	1	3	1
	Do you come by train?	0	4	1	7	1	2	2	1

Output 13. The contingency table of the various ways of getting to work categorised by Sex and AgeGroup

The chi-square test of independence (Output 14) shows that there are significant differences among the responses for How to get to work between the sexes in the two younger age groups but not in the two older ones. These differences are further teased out (Output 15) showing that cycling and taking the train are the critical responses for some of the age groups as shown by the letter A.

Pearson Chi-Square Tests

		Age (grouped)			
		Under 20	21 - 30	31 - 40	41 - 50
		Sex	Sex	Sex	Sex
Travel to work	Chi-square	21.258	17.581	3.675	5.456
	df	6	7	6	7
	Sig.	.002' a	.014' a	.720a	.605a.b

Results are based on nonempty rows and columns in each innermost subtable.

*. The Chi-square statistic is significant at the 0.05 level.

a. More than 20% of cells in this subtable have expected cell counts less than 5. Chi-square results may be invalid.

b. The minimum expected cell count in this subtable is less than one. Chi-square results may be invalid.

Output 14. The chi-square tests showing sex differences for Travel to work for the Under 20 and 21-30 Age Groups only

Comparisons of Column Proportions[b]

		Age (grouped)							
		Under 20		21 - 30		31 - 40		41 - 50	
		Sex		Sex		Sex		Sex	
		Female	Male	Female	Male	Female	Male	Female	Male
		(A)	(B)	(A)	(B)	(A)	(B)	(A)	(B)
How to get to work	Do you walk?								
	Do you cycle?		A		A				
	Do you take the bus?								
	Do you drive a car?								
	Do you drive a motorbike?	a	a			a	a		a
	Do you come by car with others?								
	Do you come by train?	a			A				

Results are based on two-sided tests with significance level 0.05. For each significant pair, the key of the category with the smaller column proportion appears under the category with the larger column proportion.

a. This category is not used in comparisons because its column proportion is equal to zero or one.

b. Tests are adjusted for all pairwise comparisons within a row of each innermost subtable using the Bonferroni correction.

Output 15. The column proportions tests. The letter A shows which proportions are significantly different

Other statistics such as percentages can be selected by highlighting sections of the table (e.g. Sex) in the dialog box (Figure 19), clicking **N% Summary Statistics** in the **Define** panel to open the **Summary Statistics** dialog box (see Figure 6 in Section 4.2), selecting one (or more) of the options within the **Statistics** panel (e.g. **Row Valid N %**), clicking the arrow to transfer the chosen statistic to the next available row (or rows) in the **Display** panel, and clicking the **Apply to Selection** button. You will then be returned to the **Custom Tables** dialog box, where newly selected statistics are shown in the display. Finally click **OK** to obtain the contingency table. Care needs to be taken in selecting percentages: there are many options and the resulting table can easily become cluttered and difficult to read.

The Response Set can also be used as one of the variables in a graph such as a clustered bar chart. This is illustrated in Output 16, which shows the Response Set plotted with Sex and AgeGroup.

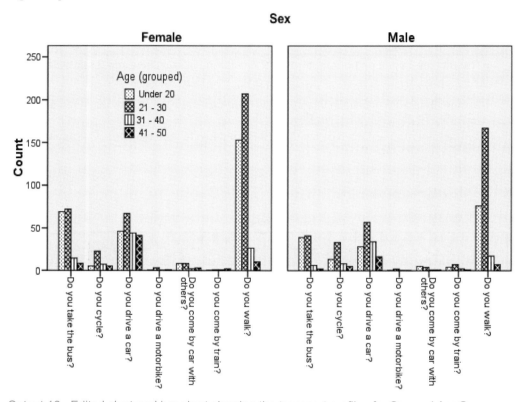

Output 16. Edited clustered bar chart showing the transport profiles for Sex and AgeGroup

4.5.4   Finding the frequencies of specific transport profiles

(Before reading the following subsection, we suggest the reader might first read Section 4.6, which describes the **Recode** and **Compute Variable** procedures.)

A respondent is quite likely to use more than one mode of transport to get to work. We might want to analyse the frequencies with which different *combinations* of modes of transport are used and compare these frequency profiles across groups: how many people cycle and take the bus? How many walk, cycle and drive? To determine the frequencies of the various combinations of modes of travel, we shall have to define a new composite variable with a name such as 'Combination', consisting of a set of new values, each value labelling one particular combination of modes of travel. After making a preliminary adjustment to the data set, we shall use the **Compute Variable** procedure to construct a new variable, Combination, which will code the various combinations of modes of travel.

The first step is to use the **Recode** procedure to convert the system-missing values in Data View into zeros. This is necessary because the **Compute Variable** procedure cannot run with system-missing values (represented as dots) in Data View. Proceed as follows.

- Choose **Transform➜Recode into the same variables** to open the **Recode into Same Variables** box.
- Transfer the names of the seven modes of transport variables into the **Numeric Variables** panel on the right.
- Click the **Old and New Values** button underneath the Numeric Variables panel to open the **Recode into Same Variables: Old and New Values** dialog box (Figure 22).
- Check the **System-missing** radio button on the left. In the **New Value** slot enter the value zero. Click the **Add** button to add SYSMIS $\rightarrow$ 0 to the **Old to New** panel on the right.
- Click **Continue** to return to the **Recode into Same Variables** box and click **OK** to effect the recoding.

You will see that, in **Data View**, the periods indicate that missing values have been replaced with zeros.

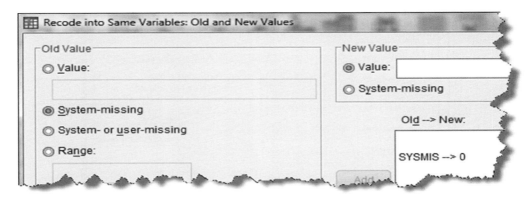

Figure 22. The completed Recode into Same Variable: Old and New Values dialog box

4.5.4.1   Constructing the new Combination variable

We want to identify each combination of possible modes of transport with a distinct code number. We can achieve this by creating a new variable named Combination, which is defined as a linear function of the seven modes of transport variables, in which each coefficient is a power of ten thus:

$$Combination = 10^0 Travel\_walk + 10^1 Travel\_cycle + 10^2 Travel\_bus + ...$$
$$... + 10^3 Travel\_drivecar + 10^4 Travel\_motorbike + ...$$
$$... + 10^5 Travel\_sharecar + 10^6 Travel\_train$$

For a commuter who used all seven modes of transport, the value for the Combination variable would be:

$$Combination = 1 + 10 + 100 + ...$$
$$... + 1000 + 10,000 + ...$$
$$... + 100,000 + 1,000,000$$
$$= 1111111$$

The reason for the increasing powers of ten in the formula for the Combination variable is this: we do not want two respondents, both of whom chose, say, three modes of travel but selected different methods, to receive the same value for the Combination variable. Weighting the modes of travel with ascending powers of ten ensures that the sum will be different in the two cases.

We can now proceed with the **Compute Variable** procedure as shown in Figure 23. Simply build the formula for Combination into the Numeric Expression window, selecting the variable names on the left and clicking the arrow on the central pillar to transfer them to the appropriate places in the formula.

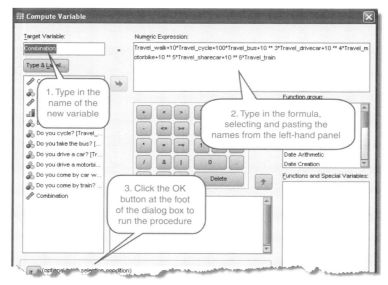

Figure 23. Using **Compute Variable** to calculate values of the new variable Combination

The number of combinations is large, but with perseverance it is possible to enter a value label in **Variable View** for every possible combination of modes of travel: for example, the combination of walking and taking the bus is 1 + 100 = 101. A fragment of the **Values** window in Variable View is shown in Figure 24.

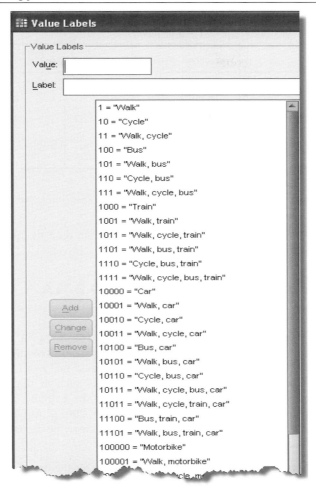

Figure 24. A fragment of the Value Labels window showing combinations with their value labels

The structure of the new variable named Combination enables the researcher to answer questions that cannot be answered by the **Multiple Response Sets** procedure. Suppose we want to compare the three age groups with respect to the number of respondents who travel to work by walking only. This question is different from any we have considered so far, because it is a question about a combination of responses. It is quite distinct from the question of how many respondents from each age group walked to get to work, because that might have been just one of several means of transport that they used. Proceed as follows:

- Choose **Data** ➔**Select Cases** and, in the **Select Cases: If** window, set Combination = 1. (This is the code for walking only.)
- Choose **Analyze**➔**Descriptive Statistics**➔**Frequencies** and, to the **Variables** panel on the right-hand side of the dialog box, transfer the variables AgeGroup and Combination = 1. (This choice, rather than Combination, ensures that only those who said they made their entire journey to work by foot will be selected.) Click **OK** to run the procedure. The frequency distribution is shown in Output 17.

Age (grouped)

		Frequency	Percent	Valid Percent	Cumulative Percent
Valid	Under 20	126	32.6	32.6	32.6
	21 - 30	232	60.1	60.1	92.7
	31 - 40	24	6.2	6.2	99.0
	41 - 50	4	1.0	1.0	100.0
	Total	386	100.0	100.0	

Output 17. The numbers of respondents in the different age groups for whom walking was their only means of transport

It would appear from Output 17 that most of those for whom the sole method of transport to work was walking were in their twenties.

4.6   SELECTING AND TRANSFORMING DATA

4.6.1   Reducing and transforming data

After a data set has been entered into SPSS, it may be necessary to modify it in certain ways. For example, an exploratory data analysis may have revealed that one or two extreme cases have exerted undue leverage upon the values of statistics such as the mean and standard deviation. One approach to this problem is to de-select the extreme cases and repeat the analysis with the remaining scores (cf. Tabachnick & Fidell, 2007). Any exclusions, however, should be mentioned in the experimental report. Cases can easily be dropped from the analysis by using the **Select Cases** command (Section 3.3.1).

Sometimes, in order to satisfy the distribution requirements for the use of a particular statistic, it may be necessary to **transform** the values of a variable. For example, a distribution of response latencies is often **positively skewed,** i.e., it has a long tail to the right; whereas the distribution of the logarithms of the raw scores is more symmetrical. Transformations are easily implemented with the **Compute** procedure (Section 4.6.2).

Finally, it is sometimes convenient to combine or alter the categories making up a variable measured at the nominal or ordinal level. This is achieved with the **Recode** procedure, which can construct a new variable with the new category assignments (Section 4.6.3).

4.6.2   The COMPUTE VARIABLE procedure

4.6.2.1   Transforming the data

Many statistical tests are predicated upon assumptions about the data, one of which is normality of distribution. In some areas of research, the distribution of the measure or DV is typically skewed and it is common practice to work, not with the raw data, but with transformations that have a more symmetric distribution. While it has been shown that non-normality itself has rather little effect upon Type I or Type II error rates, a transformation that symmetrises the distribution sometimes stabilises the within groups variances, which is highly desirable, since marked heterogeneity of variance (particularly in combination with unequal sample sizes) can affect the error rates.

Tukey (1977) showed that even data with a markedly skewed distribution can be symmetrised by applying one of the transformations in a scheme called the **ladder of transformations** (see Figure 25). In the centre is x, the original variable. On the right of x, are transformations that correct for negative skewness, that is, a long tail to the left. The further away a transformation is from x on the 'ladder', the more marked its effect upon the distribution. Thus if a distribution is only slightly skewed in the positive direction (tail to the right), the mild square root transformation may be sufficient to symmetrise it. In such cases, a stronger transformation might overcorrect the skewness, producing a distribution with a tail to the left. The stronger transformations are only appropriate when the distribution is very asymmetrical, with a long tail in either direction; otherwise, they will overcorrect.

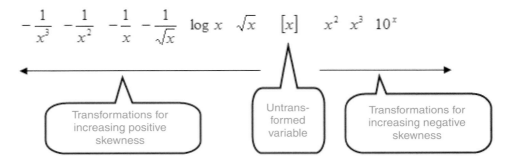

Figure 25. Tukey's ladder of transformations. The nearer the transformation of the original variable x to the head of either arrow, the stronger the effect upon the shape of the distribution

Notice the minus signs in front of the reciprocal transformations. This is because a reciprocal transformation reverses the order of magnitude of the values: the bigger the denominator, the smaller the value of the reciprocal. The negative sign is necessary to restore the original order.

The **Compute Variable** procedure was used in Chapter 3 to number the cases in a data set. The same procedure can also be used to effect many different kinds of transformations of the original data set. New variables of transformed data can be created, or the values of existing variables can be replaced by the transformed values. We do not recommend the second approach, because the original values for the variable cannot then be recovered. The **Compute Variable** procedure also allows transformation of subsets of the original data set that have been specified by logical conditions.

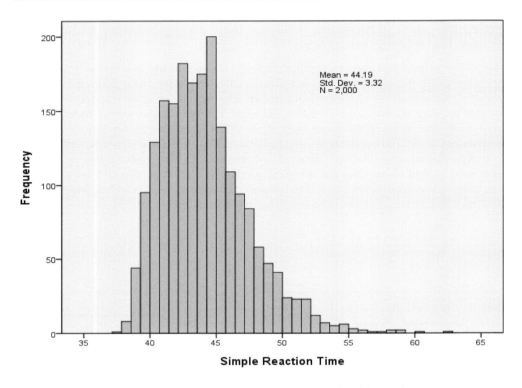

Mean = 44.19
Std. Dev. = 3.32
N = 2,000

Simple Reaction Time

Output 18. Histogram (edited) of the simple reaction times of 2000 people

Output 18 shows a histogram of the simple reaction times of 2000 people. Typically, such data show a positively skewed distribution, with a tail to the right. For the purposes of statistical testing, the investigator might want to transform the original data to make the distribution more symmetrical. Such normalisation can often be achieved by taking the logarithms, square roots, reciprocals and other functions of the original scores. These transformations, however, have different effects upon distribution shape, as the following exercise will demonstrate. We shall begin by using the **Compute Variable** procedure to calculate the natural logarithms of the raw data.

Assuming the data set is present in the **Data Editor**,
• Choose **Transform➜Compute Variable...** to open the **Compute Variable** dialog box (the completed version is shown in Figure 26).
• Follow the steps described in Figure 26.
• Click **OK**.

A new column LogLatency, containing the natural logs of the values of Latencies, will appear in **Data View**. You may wish to add a label (e.g. Log of Latency) for this new variable and to change the number of decimal places – see Section 2.3.1. A setting of two decimal places works well in this example; but with a reciprocal transformation (see below), four places of decimals would be required. Output 19 shows the histogram of the logs of the latencies. The transformation has clearly reduced the skewness of the distribution; although it has not removed it altogether.

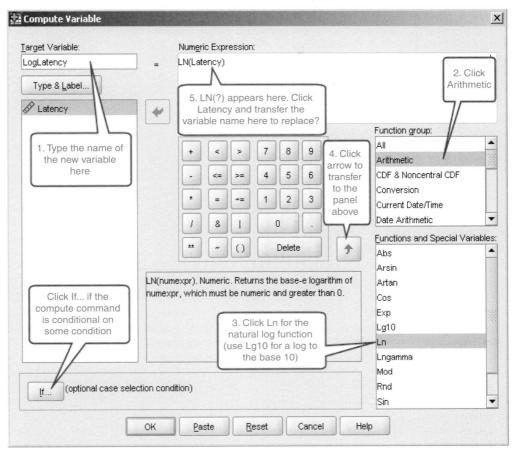

Figure 26. The completed **Compute Variable** dialog box for computing the natural logarithm of Latency

We can move further to the left along Tukey's ladder, trying the repicrocal transformations: $-1/x^4$ and $-1/x^8$. The effects of these are shown in Output 20. The first transformation (on the left) achieves a fairly symmetrical distribution; but the second (on the right) overcorrects the original positive skew by producing a distribution with negative skew.

We should also note that a transformation must involve a legitimate and meaningful algebraic operation. For example, if the data set contains zero values, a log transformation cannot be implemented, since log 0 is $-\infty$; and since one is not allowed to divide by zero, none of the reciprocal transformations is defined for zero entries. The log of a negative value is not defined and a negative number has no square root, with obvious implications for those transformations. The problem of zero values can be overcome by adding a small positive constant (say, +.5) to every score in the data set before trying any transformations. Negative values can arise when the data are in the form of difference scores. The problem of negative values can be solved by adding a constant k to all values, where k is sufficiently large to ensure that all values in the data set are positive.

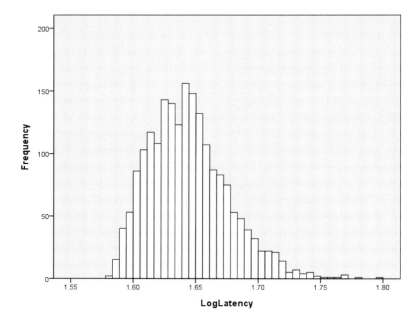

Output 19. Histogram showing the distribution of the natural logs of the response latencies. The distribution is more symmetrical than that of the untransformed values of Latency

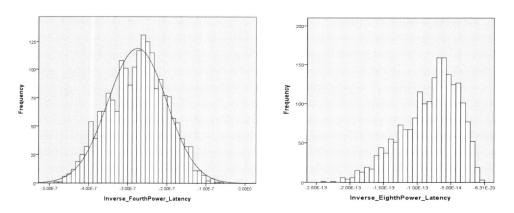

Output 20. Two reciprocal transformations of the simple reaction time data.

4.6.2.2   Using Compute Variable to obtain functions of several variables

Compute Variable can also be used to combine values of variables. Suppose you have a data set comprising the marks of schoolchildren in their French, German and Spanish examinations. You might be interested in averaging each child's score over the three examinations.

One way of doing this is to write your own numerical expression in the **Numerical Expression** box of the **Compute Variable** dialog box (e.g. name the new variable MeanMark and enter the expression (French + German + Spanish)/3.   Should any child not have taken all three examinations, however, the mean would not be calculated and a system-missing mark would appear in **Data View** instead of a value for the mean.

Another way of obtaining the mean is to paste the **MEAN** function from the **Functions and Special Variables** list (Figure 26) into the **Numerical Expression** box and transfer the variable names French, German and Spanish into the pasted function taking care to have a comma between each name and to ensure that ? is no longer present [e.g. **MEAN**(French, German, Spanish)]. Should a child's mark be missing, the mean of the other two marks will be calculated. The function MEAN, therefore, calculates the mean from whatever valid values may be present. Only if a child has sat none of the three examinations, will a system-missing value for the mean be recorded.

Figure 27 is a section of **Data View** comparing the results of using the two methods of finding the mean. The variable MeanbyDiv contains the values of the mean from the first method and the variable MEAN contains the values of the mean from the second method.

ChildsN	French	German	Spanish	MeanbyDiv	MEAN
Fred	67	78	23	56.00	56.00
Mary	50	50	.	.	50.00
John	.	.	.	.	.
Peter	0	50	50	33.33	33.33
Amy	0	.	.	.	.00
Jack	23	.	.	.	23.00

Figure 27. Two ways of computing the means of three variables

It can be seen from Figure 27 that the add-then-divide way only works when there are marks on all three examinations. It fails with Mary, John, Amy and Jack. The MEAN way fails to produce a result only with John, who did not sit any of the examinations. The MEAN function also makes a clear distinction between zeros and missing values: Mary correctly receives the mean of 50 and 50 (50); whereas Peter correctly receives the mean of 0, 50 and 50 (33.33). Jack correctly receives a mean of 23, even though he sat only one examination.

4.6.2.3   Conditional computations

A medical researcher has gathered some data on the drinking and substance intake of patients. Figure 28 shows a section from **Data View**. (The code values corresponding to the value labels displayed are: 0 = No Abuse and 1 = Abuse.)

	Patient	Alcohol	Substances
1	Sarah	No Abuse	No Abuse
2	Alan	Abuse	No Abuse
3	Jim	No Abuse	Abuse
4	Joe	Abuse	Abuse

Figure 28. A section of the data set for substance abuse in patients

The researcher wants to create a third variable, Addict, with values as follows:

> 0 for patients with No Abuse on both variables
> 1 for patients with Abuse on Alcohol but No Abuse on Substances
> 2 for patients with No Abuse on Alcohol but Abuse on Substances
> 3 for patients with Abuse on both variables.

The problem can be solved in several ways. We could begin by letting Addict = Alcohol + Substances + 1. We could then instruct the **Compute Variable** routine to proceed as follows. If either (Alcohol = Substances = 0) or (Alcohol = 1 and Substances = 0), subtract 1 from Addict. This will solve the problem, because the remaining combinations would fail to meet either condition and no subtraction would take place.

- Choose **Transform➜Compute Variable** to access the **Compute Variable** dialog box.
- Type *Addict* into the **Target Variable** box.
- Transfer the variable names Alcohol and Substances to the **Numeric Expression** box and create the expression Alcohol + Substances + 1 (see Figure 29).
- Click **OK**.

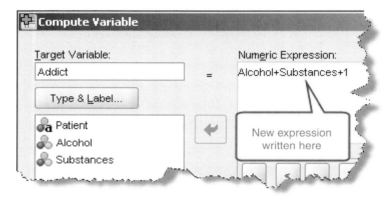

Figure 29. Part of the **Compute Variable** dialog box for computing values for the new variable Addict

The values of Addict will then appear in **Data View** as shown in Figure 30.

	Patient	Alcohol	Substances	Addict
1	Sarah	No Abuse	No Abuse	1
2	Alan	Abuse	No Abuse	2
3	Jim	No Abuse	Abuse	2
4	Joe	Abuse	Abuse	3

Figure 30. **Data View** showing the newly computed variable Addict

These values for Addict are correct except for Sarah and Alan who should have a value of 0 and 1 respectively. We therefore have to modify the computation of these values of Addict by subtracting 1 from the total when both variables have 0, or if Alcohol = 1 and Substances = 0. This is done by constructing a conditional expression in the **Compute Variable: If Cases** dialog box.

- Return to the **Compute Variable** dialog box and change the Numeric Expression entry to Addict – 1.
- Click the **If...** button to open the **Compute Variable: If Cases** dialog box.
- Click the radio button labelled **Include if Case satisfies condition:**
- In the box on the right enter the expression:
        (Alcohol = 0 & Substance = 0) | (Alcohol = 1 & Substances = 0).
  In this logical expression, the ampersand symbol **&** denotes **AND** and the symbol |
  denotes **OR**. Care must be taken when inserting brackets in the conditional expression to
  ensure that the logical operators **AND** and **OR** operate appropriately.
- The top part of the completed dialog box will appear as in Figure 31.
- Click **Continue** to return to the **Compute Variable** dialog box.
- Click **OK** to compute the altered values of Addict.

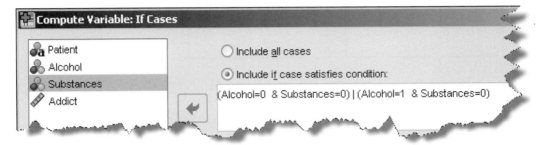

Figure 31. Top part of the **Compute Variables: If Cases** dialog box with the specially written
conditional expression

The entries in **Data View** will now appear as shown in Figure 32.

	Patient	Alcohol	Substances	Addict
1	Sarah	No Abuse	No Abuse	0
2	Alan	Abuse	No Abuse	1
3	Jim	No Abuse	Abuse	2
4	Joe	Abuse	Abuse	3

Figure 32. The desired values for Addict after using a conditional expression in the **Compute
Variable** dialog box

An alternative method would be to compute Addict = Alcohol*10 + Substances and then use
the **Recode** procedure (next Section) to recode the resulting set of values.

4.6.3   The RECODE procedure

We have seen that the **Compute Variable** procedure operates upon one or more of the
variables in the data set, so that there will be as many values in the transformed variable as
there were in the original variable. Sometimes, however, rather than wanting a transformation
that will systematically change all the values of a variable, the user may want to assign
relatively few code numbers to values that fall within specified ranges of the variable.

For example, suppose we have a set of 18 children's examination marks on a scale from 0 to
100 (Table 3). We shall recode these into three **bins** or intervals: 0-49 are Fails; 50-74 are

Passes; 75-100 are Good. This can easily be done by using the **Recode** procedure on the **Transform** menu.

Table 3. Children's examination marks					
Child	Mark	Child	Mark	Child	Mark
1	62	7	70	13	50
2	51	8	40	14	50
3	40	9	63	15	42
4	68	10	81	16	65
5	38	11	62	17	30
6	40	12	78	18	71

4.6.3.1   Using the Recode procedure

Enter the data into **Data View** in variables named Case and Marks and then:

- Choose **Transform➜Recode into Different Variables...** to open the **Recode into Different Variables** dialog box (Figure 33). Just as in the case of the **Compute Variable** procedure, it is possible to change the values in the same variable to the recoded values but we recommend placing the recoded values in a new variable, named Grade.
- Click Marks and the arrow to transfer the name into the **Numeric Variable➜Output Variable** box.
- Type the name of the output variable Grade into the **Name** box and click **Change** to insert the name into the **Numeric Variable➜Output Variable** box (Figure 33).
- Click the **Old and New Values** box to open the **Recode into Different Variables: Old and New Values** dialog box (Figure 34).
- Follow the steps in Figure 35 for defining the old and new values. These will categorise all exam marks less than 50 as Fail, 50-74 as Pass and 75 and over as Good. The defined criteria are shown in Figure 36.
- Click **Continue** and **OK**.

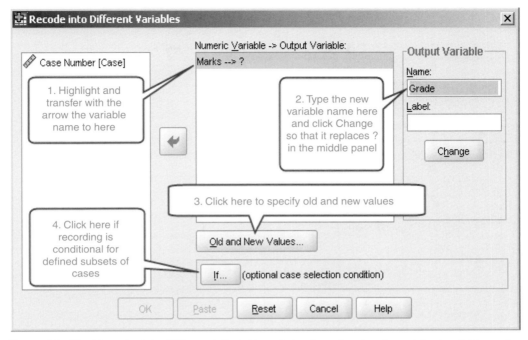

Figure 33. The **Recode into Different Variables** dialog box showing the original variable and the one to which the recoded values will be placed

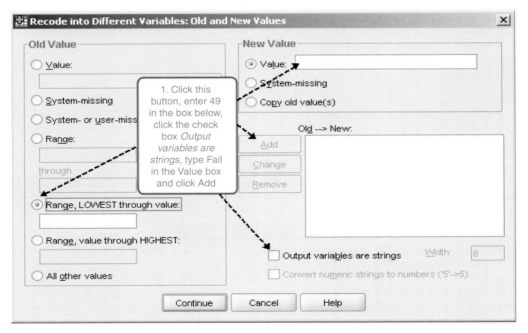

Figure 34. The **Old and New Values** dialog box with the first stage in defining ranges for Pass, Fail and Good

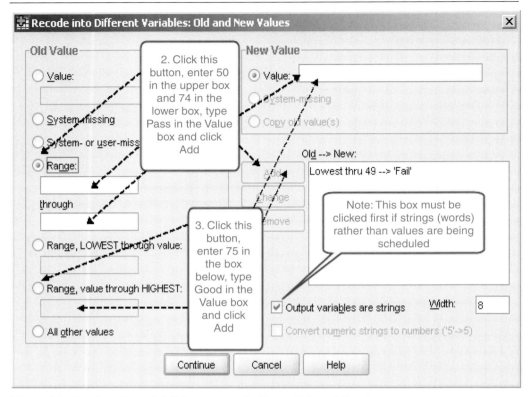

Figure 35. Continuation of defining ranges for Pass, Fail and Good

Figure 36. The appearance of the **Old -> New** panel after entering all the criteria

A new string variable Grade containing the recoded labels Pass, Fail and Good will appear in **Data View** (Figure 37).

	Case	Marks	Grade
8	8	40	Fail
9	9	63	Pass
10	10	81	Good
11	11	62	Pass
12	12	78	Good

Figure 37. Part of **Data View** showing the new string variable Grade with the labels Pass, Fail and Good

4.7   A FINAL WORD

In this chapter, we have described the use of SPSS Statistics 18 to describe various kinds of data in large and small data sets. Different statistics are appropriate for the description of data at the continuous (scale) and nominal levels of measurement.

Graphs and other displays can often reveal aspects of a distribution that a numerical statistical summary misses. For large sets of scale or continuous data, the histogram is a very useful graph for depicting the distribution of scale data; for small data sets, on the other hand, EDA displays such as the stem-and-leaf and the boxplot often present a truer picture of the distribution. The **Explore** procedure offers several EDA statistics and displays.

Association between categorical variables involves the construction of a contingency table. Contingency tables are readily available in the **Legacy dialogs**, the **Table** procedure and in the **Chart Builder**, which we shall concentrate upon in the next chapter.

SPSS can be used to discern patterns of multiple responses (**multiple response sets**) among variables, especially by comparing the patterns of responses across the levels of one or more of the other variables (e.g. across gender; across age groups).

The **Compute Variable** procedure in the **Transform** menu is very useful for transforming single variables in the original data set and for creating new variables by combining those in the original data set in specified ways. The **Recode** procedure can map the values of a categorical variable into a new set of categories.

Exercises

Exercise 4 *Correcting and preparing your data* and Exercise 5 *Preparing your data (continued)* are available in www.psypress.com/spss-made-simple and click on Exercises.

CHAPTER 5

Graphs and charts

5.1   INTRODUCTION

SPSS offers a wide range of graphs and charts, some of which we made use of in Chapter 4 when describing and exploring data. In this chapter, we shall build on those foundations and consider some general points about graph-drawing in SPSS using some of the most recent procedures. It is worth noting that the fanciest graphs do not necessarily provide the clearest picture of the results of an investigation. Three-dimensional effects, for example, though they may be aesthetically attractive, require careful handling; otherwise, they may actually obscure your presentation.

5.1.1   Graphs and charts on SPSS

There are several different ways of producing graphics with SPSS. There is a selection of procedures on the **Graphs** menu (Figure 1); but graphs also appear as options within analytical procedures. For instance, there is a **Charts** option in the **Frequencies** procedure and a **Profile Plot** option in the ANOVA procedures. The standard graphs that these routines produce can be edited to a considerable extent.

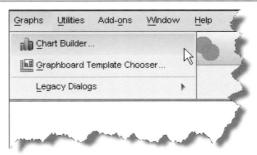

Figure 1. The **Graphs** menu

Even greater control of graphical output is afforded by the **Chart Builder** and the **Graphboard Template Chooser**. In this chapter, we shall concentrate on the use of **Chart Builder**. A gallery of charts and graphs is obtained by clicking on the **Chart Builder** item in the **Graphs** menu (Figure 2). If the gallery does not appear immediately, click the **Gallery** tab at the left of the **Chart Builder** dialog box.

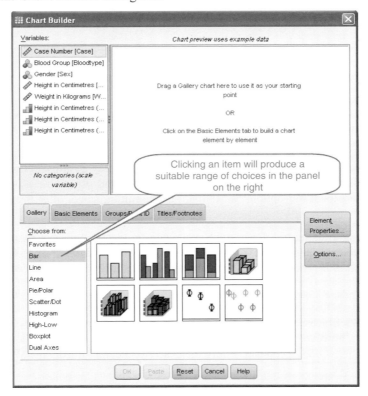

Figure 2. Options available in the **Chart Builder** dialog box

Readers who have used the graphic procedures in earlier releases of this software may be comforted to see that they are still available in the **Legacy Dialogs** submenu (Figure 3). We saw in Chapter 4 that the Legacy dialogs continue to offer quick and easy access to useful graphs such as the histogram and the scatterplot.

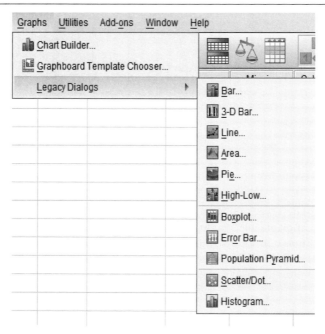

Figure 3. The list of graphical procedures in the **Legacy Dialogs** submenu

Before any graphics procedures are run, the data set should first be carefully prepared in the Data Editor. It is easier to change variable names and labels in **Variable View** than it is later, when you are editing a chart.

If there are missing data, specify beforehand whether they should be included in the chart. They can be excluded from graphs by turning off the **Display groups defined by missing values** box in the **Options** dialog box. Once you are in a chart procedure, it is often easier to add a title within the **Title** option, rather than at the editing stage, after the chart has been produced.

When completing a dialog box for a graph, you can often leave some boxes unchecked. The acid test of whether enough information has been specified in a dialog box is whether the **OK** button is enabled: if it is not, more information is needed before the chart procedure will run.

5.1.2   Viewing a chart

A chart in **SPSS Statistics Viewer** may occasionally disappear from the screen. You can easily retrieve it, however, by clicking its icon in the left-hand pane of the Viewer. If you are working in another window, you can restore the chart by selecting it from the **Window** menu at the top of the screen.

You can make a chart narrower by clicking it and dragging the right-hand handle of the surrounding frame leftwards. (This move, however, can adversely affect the appearance of labels and captions.) If you wish to change the aspect ratio of **all** charts to make them narrower, select **Edit➔Options➔Charts** and amend the value in the **Chart Aspect Ratio** box. The default value is 1.25, but if you change that to, say, 1, graphs and charts will appear narrower.

Images use up memory. Bear in mind that images can always be recreated from saved data files. Save only those that you are likely to need later.

Once a dialog box for a chart has been completed, the **command syntax** (see Chapter 8) can be saved to a syntax file by clicking **Paste**. The (unedited) graph can be produced at any time by running the syntax. Edited graphs can be stored as **chart templates** for future use. Chart templates are very useful for generating whole sets of similar graphs for analogous tables of data, such as those at different layers of a multi-way table.

5.1.3 Editing charts and saving templates

SPSS provides a special **Chart Editor** for graphical output which allows a wide range of changes to be made to a graph or chart; though proficiency requires some practice. Enter the **Chart Editor** by double-clicking anywhere in the image. A single click will draw a single frame around the image. After double-clicking, the original image is shaded and a copy of it is shown in the **Chart Editor**.

The **Chart Editor** allows the user to change text, colours, style of line, type of marker, title, axis ticks and labels, and other features. Many of these changes are made by double-clicking the item in the chart and completing dialogs.

For black-and-white printing, it is usually best to use the **Chart Editor** to remove the colours and replace them with patterns. Alternatively, the default setting for charts can be changed from cycling through colours to cycling through patterns. To do this
- Choose **Edit→Options...** and select the **Charts** tab in the **Options** dialog box.
- Within the **Style Cycle Preference** selection panel, select **Cycle through patterns only**.
- Click **Fills...** . Select whichever pattern you want for **Simple Charts** and delete the empty pattern box in **Grouped Charts** by clicking the radio button for **Grouped Charts**, selecting the empty box pattern and clicking **Remove**. Click **Continue**.
- Click **Apply**, then **OK**.

Should your computer be part of a networked system, this change will apply to the current session only.

If it is likely that the same chart will be required on subsequent occasions for the presentation of fresh data, you may wish to save the edited version as a **Chart Template**, which can be applied to the later charts. Instructions about how to save and use a template will be given in Section 5.2.6.

5.2 BAR CHARTS

This section describes the production of simple bar charts, clustered bar charts, panelled bar charts and 3-D charts.

5.2.1 Simple bar charts

A bar chart for comparing the means scores of groups of participants such as those in the drug experiment (Table 1 in Section 2.1.4) can be obtained as follows:
- Choose **Graphs→Chart Builder...**.

- A warning box (Figure 4) will appear asking the user to ensure that each variable has been defined in the **Measure** column of **Variable View** as **Scale**, **Ordinal** or **Nominal**, and that values of categorical variables have been labelled. By default, **Variable View** assumes variables are at **Scale** level, so it may be necessary to set categorical variables to **Nominal** either in **Variable View** or by clicking on **Define Variable Properties...** in the Chart Builder's warning box. Click **OK** to continue.

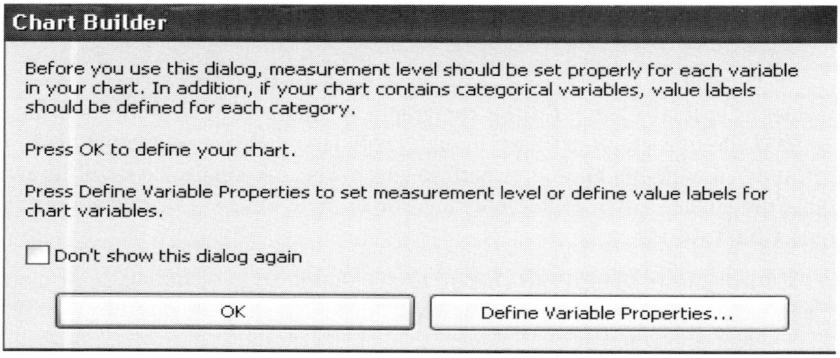

Chart Builder

Before you use this dialog, measurement level should be set properly for each variable in your chart. In addition, if your chart contains categorical variables, value labels should be defined for each category.

Press OK to define your chart.

Press Define Variable Properties to set measurement level or define value labels for chart variables.

☐ Don't show this dialog again

| OK | Define Variable Properties... |

Figure 4. The warning box when **Chart Builder** is opened

- Ensure that the illustrations correspond to **Bar** by checking that **Bar** is highlighted in the **Choose from** panel (Figure 5). Click the first (top left) picture of simple bars to highlight it and then drag it to the **Chart preview** in the panel above. In addition, an **Element Properties** dialog box will also appear (Figure 6).
- Click the variable name Score to highlight it and then drag it to the **Y-Axis** box. Similarly, move Experimental Condition to the **X-Axis** box.
- To include the 95% Confidence Intervals on the means, click the **Display error bars** box in the **Element Properties** dialog box (Figure 6) and select the first radio button.
- To add a title, click **Titles/Footnotes** (middle of **Chart Builder** dialog box) and then click **Title 1** in the list of check-boxes that will appear in place of the gallery of graphics choices. A panel will appear in the **Element Properties** dialog box, where a title such as *Means and 95% Confidence Intervals* can be typed in. Click **Apply**, followed by **Close**. Notice that **T1** will appear at the top of the preview (Figure 5) if a title has been requested.
- Finally click **OK** in the **Chart Builder** dialog box to create the chart (Output 1).

If the chart is to be printed in black and white, it is best to use the **Chart Editor** to change the colours of the graph to shades of grey. In fact, we have found it most effective to change the fill colour to white and mark the bars with distinguishing fill patterns. Alternatively, changing the default **Chart** options to **Cycle through patterns only** as described in Section 5.1.3 renders such editing unnecessary.

A simple bar chart summaries the distributions of a scale variable at different levels of one categorical variable only, in this case the Experimental Condition under which the participants in the study performed. Additional category variables can be included by using the options in **Groups/Point ID** in Figure 5: select **Rows** panel variable or **Columns** panel variable and then transfer the appropriate variable name into the box that will appear on the right of the bar chart in the **Chart** preview. Alternatively, opt for **Clustered bar charts** as described in the next subsection by clicking on the second figure in the **Chart Builder** dialog box (Figure 5).

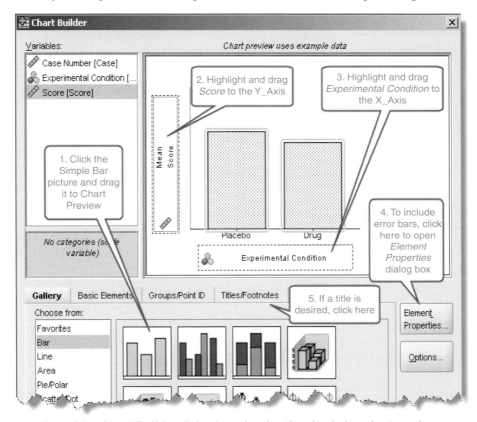

Figure 5. Part of the **Chart Builder** dialog box showing the simple bar chart preview

If there is a second categorical variable such as sex, the **Rows panel variable** option enables the user to plot bar charts one-above-the-other (Rows); the **Columns panel variable** option results in a side-by-side (Columns) arrangement.

When **Clustered** is used, the bars are clustered in a single graphic whereas the **panel** facility displays the levels of the second category variable in separate graphics. An example of panelled bar charts is shown in the **Panelled bar chart** subsection after the **Clustered bar charts** subsection.

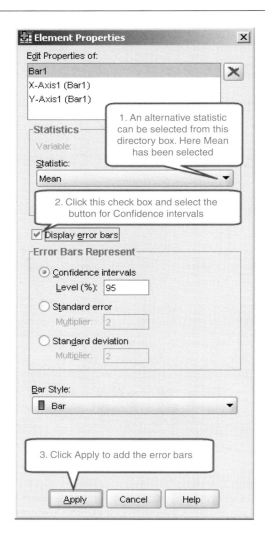

Figure 6. The **Element Properties** dialog box for changing the statistic to be used for the bars and selecting error bars

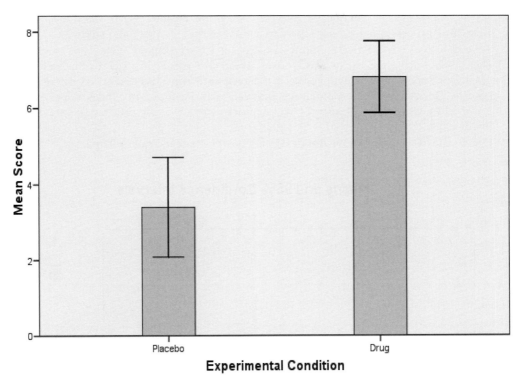

Means and 95% Confidence Intervals

Output 1. A simple bar chart with error bars representing optional 95% confidence intervals. Experimental Condition is the category variable

5.2.2   Clustered bar charts

A **clustered bar chart** shows two category variables in the same chart, as explained in the previous subsection. Suppose that, in addition to the Experimental Condition variable, we also knew the Gender of the participants. A clustered bar chart could then be plotted with Experimental Condition as the first category variable subdivided (or **clustered**) according to the second category variable Gender. Output 2 shows a clustered bar chart summarising the results of the drug experiment. On the horizontal axis, as before, is the independent variable Experimental Condition. In addition, the variable Gender has been used to cluster the data under the separate Placebo and Drug conditions.

To obtain such a clustered bar chart, open **Chart Builder** (see Section 5.2.1) and then:

- Ensure that the illustrations correspond to **Bar** by checking that **Bar** is highlighted in the **Choose from** panel. Click the second picture of Clustered Bar to highlight it and then drag it to the **Chart preview** in the panel above. In addition, an **Element Properties** dialog box will also appear.

- Click the variable name Score to highlight it and then drag it to the **Y-Axis** box. Do likewise with Experimental Condition to the **X-Axis** box and with Gender to the **Cluster: set pattern** box.
- To include the 95% Confidence Intervals, click the **Display error bars** box in the **Element Properties** dialog box (Figure 6) and then select the first radio button.
- To add a title, click **Titles/Footnotes** (middle of **Chart Builder** dialog box) and then click **Title 1** from the list of check-boxes which will appear in place of the gallery of graphics choices. A panel will appear in the **Element Properties** dialog box where a title such as 'Means and 95% Confidence Intervals' can be typed in. Then click **Apply**, followed by **Close**. Notice that **T1** will appear at the top of the preview (Figure 5) if a title is requested.
- Finally click **OK** in the **Chart Builder** dialog box to create the chart (Output 2).

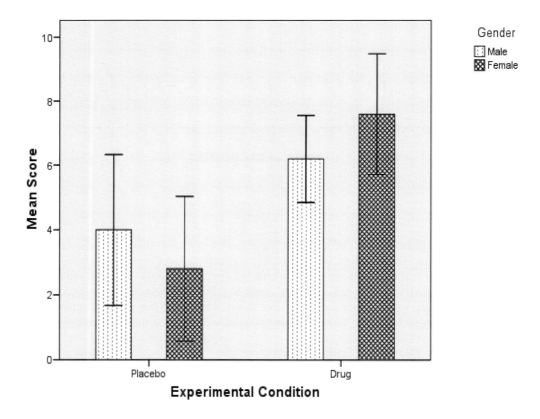

Output 2. A clustered bar chart and optional error bars representing 95% confidence intervals with Experimental Condition as the category variable and Gender as the cluster variable

5.2.3   Panelled bar charts

Yet another way of including a second or third independent variable in bar charts is to **panel** them either by rows or by columns. For example, the data used in Chapter 8 investigating the effects upon simulated driving performance of two new anti-hay fever drugs when male and female drivers are either alert or tired could be graphed as shown in Output 3. To obtain a panelled bar chart, open **Chart Builder** (see Section 5.2.1) and proceed as follows:

- Ensure that the illustrations correspond to **Bar** by checking that **Bar** is highlighted in the **Choose from** panel. Click the second picture of Clustered Bar to highlight it, then drag it to the **Chart preview** in the panel above. At that point, an **Element Properties** dialog box will also appear.

- Click the variable name Driving Performance to highlight it, then drag it to the **Y-Axis** box. Similarly drag Alertness to the **X-Axis** box and and Sex to the **Cluster: set pattern** box.

- Click **Groups/Point ID** in the middle of the **Chart Builder** dialog box, then click the **Columns panel variable** box. This will result in another box labelled **Panel** appearing in the **Chart preview** panel. Click Drug to highlight it, then drag it to the **Panel** box.

- To include the 95% Confidence Intervals, click **Element Properties** and in the dialog box (Figure 6) check **Display error bars** and click the first radio button.

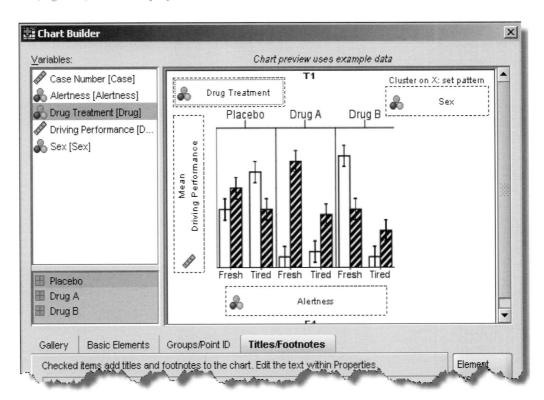

Figure 7. The **Chart preview** panel for the panelled clustered bar chart shown in Output 3 with the variable names transferred to the appropriate panels

- To add a title, click **Titles/Footnotes** (middle of **Chart Builder** dialog box) and then click **Title 1**. A panel will appear in the **Element Properties** dialog box, where a title such as *Means and 95% Confidence Intervals* can be typed in. Click **Apply**, followed by **Close**. Notice that **T1** appears at the top of the preview (Figure 7).
- Finally, click **OK** in the **Chart Builder** dialog box to create the chart (Output 3).

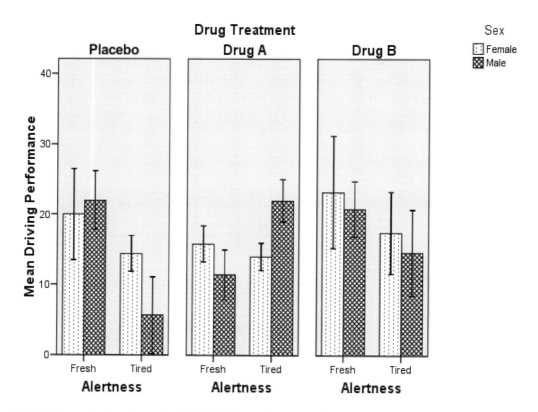

Output 3. A clustered bar chart divided into column panels

Note that simple bar charts can also be panelled so that this option could be used instead of a clustered bar chart. For example, we could have presented the data in Output 2 as simple bar charts for the Experimental Condition with Males in one row and Females in another row.

5.2.4   3-D charts

The **Chart Builder** can also be used to draw more exotic figures such as three-dimensional bar charts. As an example, a 3-D chart of Height against Blood Group and Gender can be drawn by selecting the image of a Simple 3-D Bar (first in second row) and filling in the variable names as shown in Figure 8. The output is shown in Output 4.

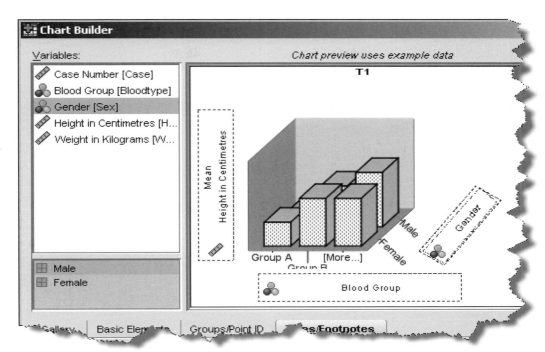

Figure 8. The upper part of the **Chart Builder** dialog box showing the selection of variables for a 3-D bar chart

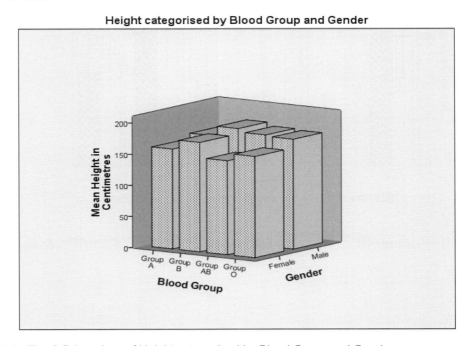

Output 4. The 3-D bar chart of Height categorised by Blood Group and Gender

5.2.5   Editing a bar chart

- Double-click the chart (or right-click and select **SPSS Chart Object→Open**) to open the **Chart Editor** (Figure 9).
- To change, say, the bars representing Males, click within the Sex key the identification for Male. All the bars representing males will then appear with a purple frame.

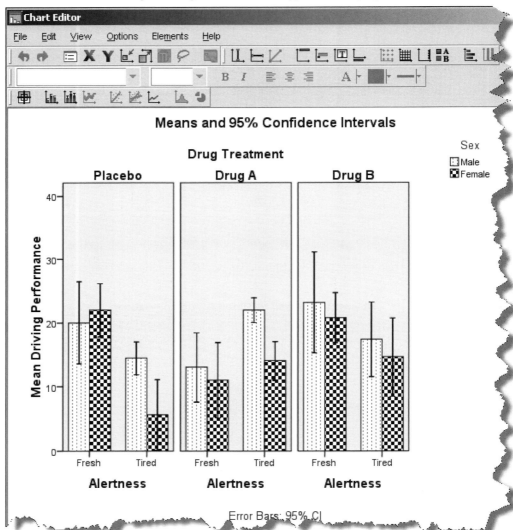

Figure 9. The **Chart Editor** window

- Double-click any of the bars or right-click to open the **Properties** dialog box (Figure 10). Note that within the **Bar Options**, it is possible to change the width of the bars and the size of the gaps between clusters by moving the sliders or changing the numbers in the **%** boxes.

- To change the colour and fill of the bars, click the **Fill & Border** tab to open a dialog box for selecting fill colours, border colours and fill patterns.
- To change the fill colour, click the **Fill** box and then select a colour from the right-hand palette of colours, white and black.
- To change the fill pattern, click the **Pattern** box and select a fill.
- Click **Apply** to make these changes in the chart without leaving the editor.
- The variable bars can be rearranged by clicking the **Variables** tab, selecting the variable to be moved, pressing the right-hand mouse button, and then selecting the move to be made. For example, you can see what the chart would look like if the clustering was done by Experimental Condition rather than by Sex.
- Other changes can also be made, such as alterations to the axis labels and the bar identification key.

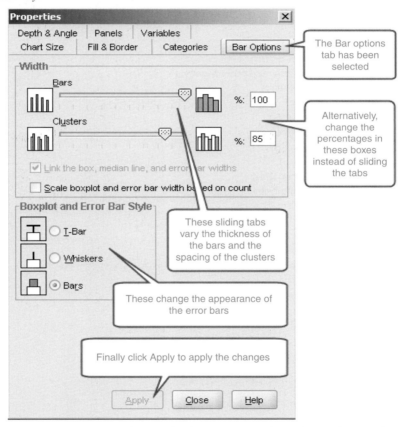

Figure 10. The **Properties** dialog box for **Bar Options** showing the various editing options for features of a graphic

5.2.6   Chart templates

Should you wish to save time by applying these editing changes to future bar chart requests, save the final format as a **Chart Template** and invoke the template each time a similar bar chart is requested.

- While still in **Chart Editor**, select **File➜Save Chart Template...** to open the **Save Chart Template** dialog box (Figure 11).
- Click the **All settings** check box and type a description of the template in the panel at the foot of the dialog box e.g. *Panelled clustered bar chart with error bars*. Click **Continue**.
- The **Save Template** dialog box will appear. Choose suitable folder and file names (e.g. Panelled clustered bar chart) for the template and click **Save**. The user of a networked computer will have to store the file in portable memory (e.g. a memory stick) in order to have it available on a later occasion.
- Close the **Chart Editor** to return the chart to **Output1 – SPSS Statistics Viewer**.

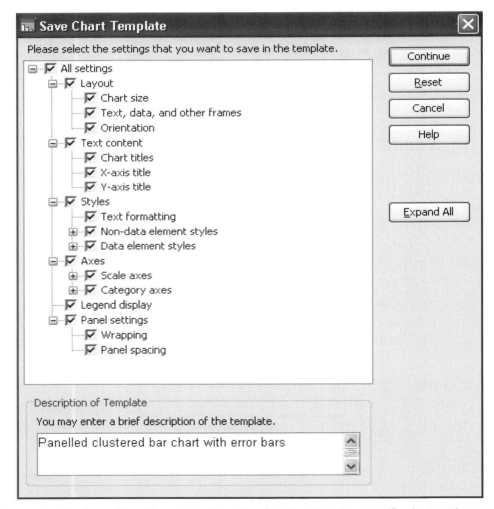

Figure 11. The **Save Chart Template** dialog box for selecting all or specific chart settings

5.2.6.1   Invoking a chart template

There are three ways of invoking a previously saved chart template. It can be installed as the default template in the **Charts** section of the **Options** dialog box (**Options** is the last item in the **Edit** drop-down menu). It can be specified in the **Chart Builder** dialog box. It can be ordered in the **Chart Editor** window.

To apply our saved chart template for another panelled clustered bar chart (e.g. for a new data set), we shall illustrate the use of the **Chart Builder** dialog box. To obtain a panelled bar chart, open **Chart Builder** (see Section 5.2.1) and then:

- Click the **Options** box on the right-hand side of the **Chart Builder** dialog box to open the **Options** dialog box.
- Click the box labelled **Add...** to open the **Find Template Files** option box.
- Locate the appropriate file and click **Open** to return to the **Options** dialog box. The file name of the template file will now appear in the panel (Figure 12).
- Click **OK** to draw the panelled clustered bar chart.

The new chart will appear with the changes made to the original chart incorporated in it.

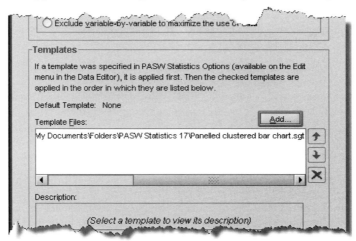

Figure 12. The **Template** section of the **Clustered Bar Chart: Options** dialog box showing the template name

5.2.6.2   Chart prototypes (SPSS calls them 'Favorites')

SPSS also has a facility for saving chart prototypes in the **Chart Builder** portfolio of images. For example, if the user wants to create a number of graphics in the same style from different data sets, then the original graphic acts as a prototype (a 'favorite'), which can then be invoked from the **Favorites** panel in the **Chart Builder** dialog box.

To save a prototype, proceed as follows:

- While still in the **Chart Builder** dialog box after completing all the details (such as including 95% confidence intervals and specifying a title), move the cursor to anywhere in the Chart preview panel and right-click to open a small choice panel (Figure 13).
- Select **Add to Favorites...** , then enter a file name for the template (SPSS refers to it as **prototype**) such as 'Clustered panelled bar chart' and click **OK**. The template will then appear in a panel in the **Chart Builder** dialog box with **Favorites** highlighted in the **Choose from** directory.

Figure 13. The choice panel for saving a chart template to **Add to Favorites...**

To apply our saved panelled clustered bar chart template to another data set, we shall illustrate the use of our newly created **Favorite** in the **Chart Builder** dialog box. To do so, open **Chart Builder** (see Section 5.2.1) and then:

- Ensure that the illustrations correspond to **Favorites** by checking that **Favorites** is highlighted in the **Choose from** panel. Click the picture of the panelled clustered bar graphic and drag it to the **Chart preview** in the panel above. In addition, an **Element Properties** dialog box will also appear.

- The various variable names must then be transferred, but it is not necessary to specify either the title or the 95% confidence intervals.

- Click **OK** to draw the panelled clustered bar chart using the new data set.

The new chart will appear with the changes made to the original chart incorporated.

SPSS offers helpful tutorials on editing charts. You can access these by clicking **Help→Tutorial** and then double-clicking each of **Tutorials→Creating and Editing Charts**.

The usual buttons in the right-hand bottom corner of each page of the tutorial enable the user to see the index (the magnifying glass), the table of contents (the house icon) and to navigate forward and backward through the tutorial (the right and left arrows).

5.3   ERROR BAR CHARTS

An alternative to a bar graph is an **Error Bar chart**, in which the mean of the scores in a particular category is represented by a single point and the spread (the user can choose the confidence interval on the mean, multiples of the standard deviation or multiples of the standard error of the mean) is represented by a vertical line (T-bar or whiskers) passing through the point. Output 5 is a clustered error bar chart summarising the results of the drug experiment.

To obtain an error bar chart, open **Chart Builder** (see Section 5.2.1) and then:

- Ensure that the illustrations correspond to **Bar** by checking that **Bar** is highlighted in the **Choose from** panel. Click the fourth picture of the second row (clustered error bars shown in green and blue – see Figure 2) to highlight it and then drag it to the **Chart preview** in the panel above. An **Element Properties** dialog box will now appear.

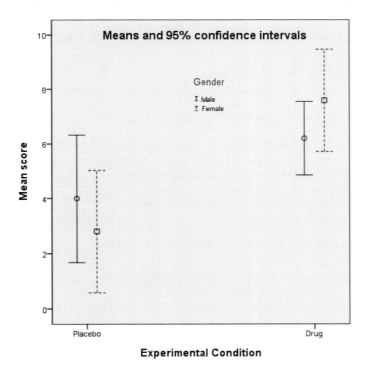

Output 5. A clustered error bar chart with Experimental Condition as the category variable and Gender as the cluster variable

- Click the variable name Score to highlight it and then drag it to the **Y-Axis** box. Do likewise with Experimental Condition to the **X-Axis** box and with Gender to the **Cluster: Set symbol** box.
- **95% Confidence Intervals** is the default setting appearing in the **Element Properties** dialog box. The percentage can be changed or the user can select Standard error or

Standard deviation (together with the desired multiplier). If a change from the default is selected, it will be necessary to click **Apply**.

- To add a title, click **Titles/Footnotes** (middle of **Chart Builder** dialog box) and then click **Title 1**. A panel will appear in the **Element Properties** dialog box where a title such as Means and 95% Confidence Intervals can be typed in. Then click **Apply** followed by **Close**. Notice that **T1** would appear at the top of the preview if a title is requested.
- Finally click **OK** in the **Chart Builder** dialog box to create the chart (Output 5).

The symbols used for the means and the form of the lines used for the error bars can be changed by double-clicking anywhere within the graphic to open the **Chart Editor**. Double-clicking on the appropriate symbol or line in the Gender key will open the corresponding **Properties** dialog box where changes can be made.

You will notice that in Output 5, there are no lines linking the error bars. This is entirely appropriate, since the bars represent qualitatively distinct categories. In other circumstances, however, as when the categories are ordered, it may be desirable to join up the points (when there are more than two) with interpolation lines. This is easily achieved in the **Chart Editor** by clicking the means to highlight them, selecting the **Elements** drop-down menu and clicking **Interpolation line** (or alternatively clicking the ⤳ icon).

5.4   BOXPLOTS

Three types of boxplots are available in **Chart Builder**, a single boxplot (called **1-D Boxplot** in the gallery), **simple boxplot** for plotting the boxplots across categories of a grouping variable and **clustered boxplot** for plotting boxplots across categories of two grouping variables. Here we shall illustrate the procedure by plotting a boxplot of Height in Centimetres categorised by Gender. The structure of a boxplot is shown in Table 2 in Chapter 4.

See Table 2 in Chapter 4

To obtain a clustered boxplot, open **Chart Builder** (see Section 5.2.1) and then:

- Follow the steps in Figure 14.
- To add a title, click **Titles/Footnotes** (middle of **Chart Builder** dialog box) and then click **Title 1**. A panel will appear in the **Element Properties** dialog box where a title such as 'Boxplots of Height categorised by Sex' can be typed in. Click **Apply**, followed by **Close**. Notice that **T1** appears at the top of the preview (Figure 14).
- Finally click **OK** in the **Chart Builder** dialog box to create the boxplot (Output 6).

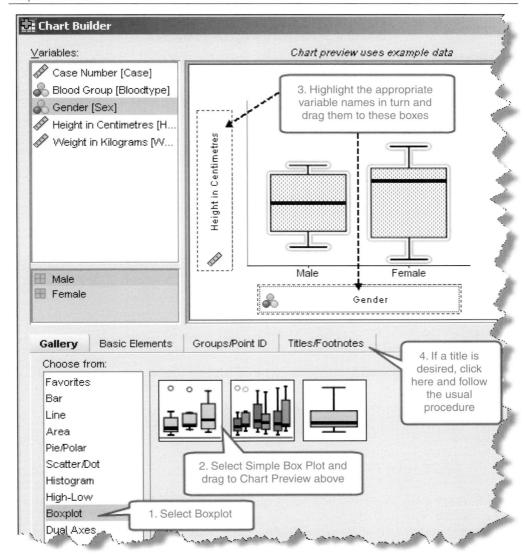

Figure 14. The completed **Chart Builder** dialog box for plotting a boxplot of Height for each Sex

Notice in the output that there is one case identified as an outlier with 'o'. Any extreme case would have been identified with an asterisk (*).

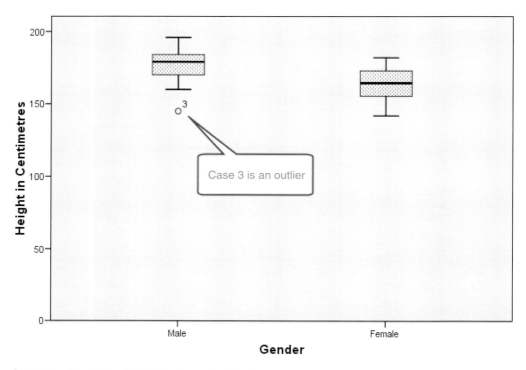

Output 6. Boxplots of Height categorised by Sex

5.5   PIE CHARTS

The **pie chart** is an alternative to a bar graph that provides a picturesque display of the frequency distribution of a qualitative variable.   It is a particularly valuable kind of graph for displaying the relative frequencies of observations in the same set of categories over time or for bringing out the varying compositions of two things, such as conservative versus risky investment portfolios. Pie charts can be panelled in a similar way to bar charts as previously described in Section 5.2.

See Section 5.2

To illustrate the production of a pie chart, we shall use the data set of blood group, gender, height and weight.

To draw a pie chart of the categories within Blood Group, open the **Chart Builder** (see Section 5.2.1) and proceed as follows:

• Ensure that the illustration corresponds to **Pie/Polar** by checking that **Pie/Polar** is highlighted in the **Choose from** panel. Click the picture and drag it to the Chart preview in the panel above. In addition, an **Element Properties** dialog box will also appear.

- Click the variable name Blood Group to highlight it and drag it to the **Slice by?** box. The **Angle Variable?** box will then change to **Count**.

- To change **Count** to **Percentages**, click the arrow to the right of Count in the **Statistic** panel within **Element Properties**, select **Percentage (?)** and then click **Apply**.

- To add a title, click **Titles/Footnotes** (middle of **Chart Builder** dialog box) and then click **Title 1**. A panel will appear in the **Element Properties** dialog box where a title such as Blood Group Percentages can be typed in. Then click **Apply** followed by **Close**. Notice that **T1** would appear at the top of the preview if a title is requested.

- Finally click **OK** in the **Chart Builder** dialog box to create the chart (Output 7).

Blood Group Percentages

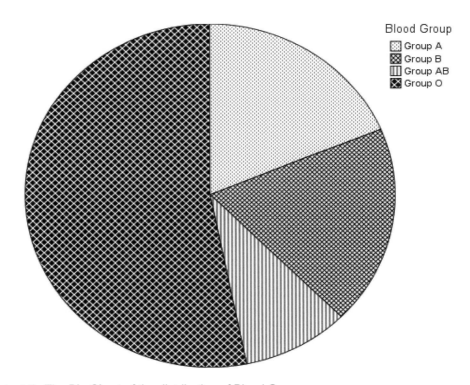

Output 7. The **Pie Chart** of the distribution of Blood Group

The pie chart in Output 7 can be edited (see Section 5.1.3) to change the fill patterns, to rotate the slices if it is desired to bring a particular slice to the top, to insert labels and to 'explode' a slice as shown in Output 8. If desired, the changes can be stored as a **Chart Template**, which can be invoked for future pie chart drawings of fresh data on the same categories.

See Section 5.1.3

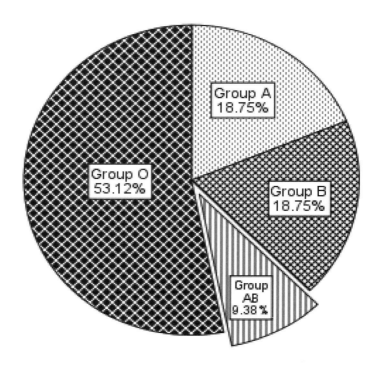

Output 8. The edited **Pie Chart** with slice labels, percentages and one slice (for Group AB) exploded

5.6   LINE GRAPHS

Like a scatterplot, a **line graph** depicts the relationship between two continuous or scale variables, such as weight and height. In a **line graph**, as in a histogram, the entire range of a one variable (say height) is stepped out in equal intervals along the horizontal axis. Above of the midpoint of each interval, in the body of the graph, a point is placed with height on the y-axis proportional to the average weight of all cases with heights falling within the interval. Finally, the points above adjacent intervals are joined by straight lines.

Line graphs can be drawn with just one line or more than one line in the graph; and like bar charts and pie charts, they can also be panelled.

In this section, we shall use the Chart Builder to draw line graphs depicting the relationship between weight and height in the men and women in one of the data sets we explored in Chapter 4. To do this, we must first divide the total range of height into equal intervals, a task for which a special procedure is available.

5.6.1   The Visual Binning procedure

In order to draw the line graphs, we must first divide the entire range of the variable that is going to be on the horizontal axis of the graph (height) into equal intervals and specify a representative value for each interval. This is done automatically by SPSS's **Histogram** procedure. In the histogram, the intervals are known as **class intervals**. Elsewhere, however, class intervals are known as **bins** and we shall need to use a special procedure known as **binning** to divide the total range of height into bins, with fixed **bin width**.

We shall use SPSS's **Visual Binning** procedure to divide the total range of the men's heights into intervals or bins, the largest and smallest of which are open-ended, so that all scores are included. Proceed as follows.

Choose **Transform➜Visual Binning** to open the initial **Visual Binning** dialog box and transfer the variable Height to the **Variables to bin** box on the right. (See Figure 15.)

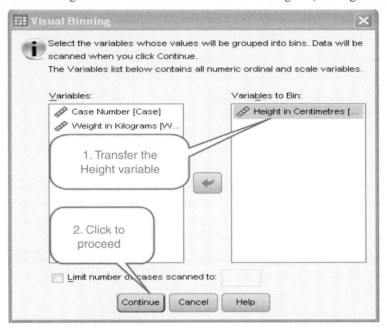

Figure 15. The initial **Visual Binning** dialog box

Click the **Continue** button to enter the main **Visual Binning** dialog box, which shows a histogram of the distribution of Height, tells us that 32 cases have been scanned and gives the minimum and maximum values of Height in our data set as 142cm and 196cm, respectively (See Figure 16).

The appearance of the histogram in the main Visual Binning dialog box tells us that we need to specify rather few bins and a wide bin width to avoid zero means for some bins, which would spoil the plot. (This is because the data set is small. With a sizeable data set, we should want many more bins, which would produce a better line graph. We would normally want about 12 bins.) The cutpoints will appear in the histogram as the bins are specified. We are going to enter, as Values in the Value column, the upper limits of the intervals. If we want five bins, we shall need to specify only four cutpoints.

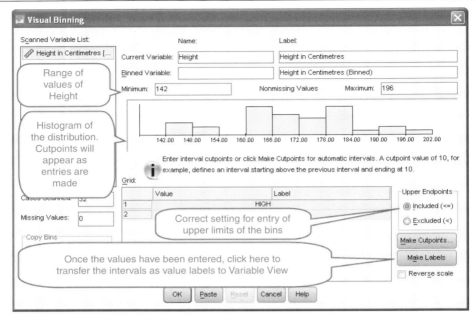

Figure 16. The main **Visual Binning** dialog box, with uncompleted dialog

The completed main Visual Binning dialog box is shown in Figure 17. Note that a single value (155, 165, …) is entered in each row. The **Make Labels** button enters the full value labels into the table, on the right of the single numerical values. As each value is entered, the row with the entry HIGH is displaced downwards in the table.

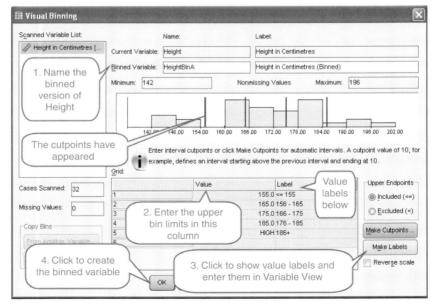

Figure 17. The completed main **Visual Binning** dialog

By choosing **View➜Value labels**, you can see, in Data View, the bin intervals shown in the Label column of the Visual Binning dialog. (These intervals also appear in the Values column of Variable View for the variable HeightBin.) With Value labels inactive, you would see only the ordinal numbers of the intervals. If, while in Variable View, you look in the Measure column, you will see that the binned version of Height has been automatically entered as an ordinal variable.

We have illustrated the binning procedure with an admittedly rather mechanical approach, which requires the user to enter a value for each interval. You will find that if you click the **Make Cutpoints** button, enter 155 as your initial value, specify the number of cutpoints as 4 and specify a bin width of 10, you will obtain exactly the same result as with the procedure above, but much more quickly.

5.6.2   Plotting line graphs

We have used the Visual Binning procedure to divide the total range of heights of the participants into five bins: ≤ 155, 156-165, 166-175, 176-185, ≥ 186. This binned version of the Height variable has been stored as the ordinal variable HeightBin. (HeightBin is fine for a variable name, provided the technical term **bin** does not appear in the variable label. You may need to edit the variable label in Variable View: a label such as 'Height in Centimeters (binned)' should be avoided.)   Since the heights of men and women tend to fall within slightly different ranges, a panelled Simple Line graph is preferable to a multiple line graph.

To plot a line graph of mean weight against height bins, open the **Chart Builder** (see Section 5.2.1) and proceed as follows:

- Ensure that the illustrations correspond to **Line** by checking that **Line** is highlighted in the **Choose from** panel (Figure 2). Click the first picture (Simple Line) and drag it to the **Chart preview** in the panel above. An **Element Properties** dialog box will now appear.
- Click the variable name Weight in kilograms to highlight it and then drag it to the **Y-Axis** box. Move Height in centimetres (binned) to the **X-Axis** box. (See Figure 18.)
- Click the tab labelled **Groups/Point ID** and check the **Rows panel variable** box. In the Chart preview panel, a box will appear labelled 'Panel?'. Click and drag Sex into this panel box.
- To add a title, click the **Titles/Footnotes** tab (in the middle of **Chart Builder** dialog box) and then click **Title 1**. A panel will appear in the **Element Properties** dialog box where a title such as Line Graphs of Weight against Height for Males and Females can be typed in. Click **Apply** followed by **Close**. Notice that **T1** now appears at the top of the preview (Figure 18).
- Finally click **OK** in the **Chart Builder** dialog box to create the chart (Output 9).

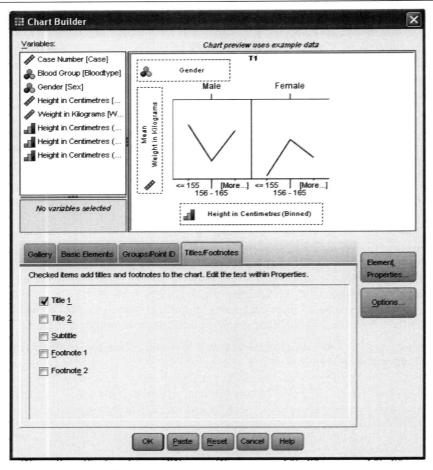

Figure 18. The completed **Chart Builder** dialog for panelled line graphs.

The edited line graph is shown in Output 9. The editing operations included the following:

1. Re-setting the y-scale with a minimum of 0. This is achieved by double-clicking the graph to open the **Chart Editor**, double-clicking on the y-scale values, clicking the **Scale** tab within the **Properties** dialog box, clicking off the **Minimum** auto box, entering 0 in the **Custom** box alongside, and finally clicking **Apply**.

2. Inserting circles for the means by clicking on the **Show Line Markers** icon ![icon]. Initially unfilled circles will appear; but these could easily have been made solid by clicking on them and changing **Fill** to black in the **Properties** box.

All such changes can be saved as a **Chart Template** – see Section 5.2.6.

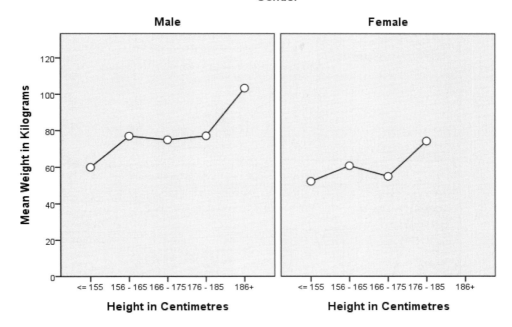

Output 9. Panelled line graphs (edited) of Weight against Height for Males and Females

5.7   SCATTERPLOTS AND DOT PLOTS

5.7.1   Scatterplots

Another diagram for displaying the relationship between two variables is the **scatterplot,** in which the scales of values of the two variables (such as height and weight) are set out on the horizontal and vertical axis and each person is represented as a point whose co-ordinates are his or her particular height and weight. As with the other charts, scatterplots can also be panelled. A scatterplot should always be plotted and examined before a correlation coefficient is calculated (Chapter 11) or a regression analysis is carried out (Chapter 12).

See Chaps. 11 & 12

To plot a simple scatterplot, open **Chart Builder** (see Section 5.2.1) and then:

- Ensure that the illustrations correspond to **Scatter/Dot** by checking that **Scatter/Dot** is highlighted in the **Choose from** panel (Figure 2). Click the first picture of a Simple Scatter to highlight it and then drag it to the **Chart preview** in the panel above (Figure 19). In addition, an **Element Properties** dialog box will also appear.
- Click the variable name Height in Centimetres to highlight it and then drag it to the **Y-Axis** box. Do likewise with Weight in Kilograms to the **X-Axis** box.

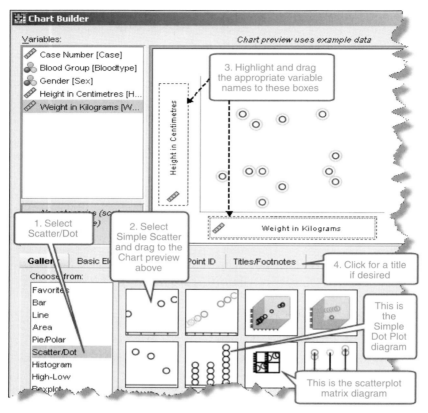

Figure 19. The **Chart Builder** dialog box with **Scatterplot/Dot** highlighted to show the various scatterplots options and with a simple scatterplot of Height against Weight prepared in the preview panel

- To add a title, click **Titles/Footnotes** (middle of **Chart Builder** dialog box) and then click **Title 1**. A panel will appear in the **Element Properties** dialog box where a title such as *Scatterplot of Height against Weight* can be typed in. Click **Apply**, followed by **Close**. Notice that **T1** would appear at the top of the preview if a title has been requested.
- Finally click **OK** in the **Chart Builder** dialog box to create the chart (Output 10).

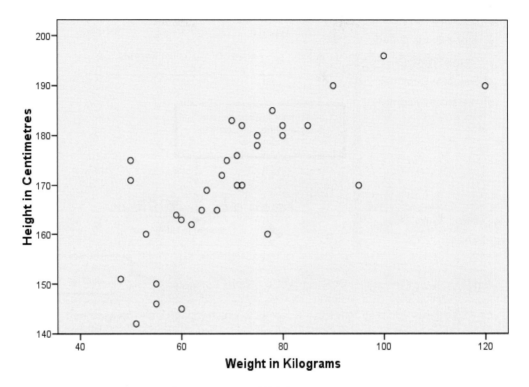

Output 10. The Scatterplot of Height against Weight

Inspection of the scatterplot shows that the line graph in Output 9, although bringing out a clear positive relationship between height and weight when average weights are considered, masks considerable individual variability. The heights of people of around 50 kg in weight range from just over 140 cm to 175 cm in height.

5.7.2   Dot plots

A **dot plot** plots one variable on a scale axis. The cases are represented by points that are stacked at the variable values. Thus weights for each sex could be plotted in charts side-by-side by choosing **Chart Builder** (see Section 5.2.1) and then:

- Ensure that the illustrations correspond to **Scatter/Dot** by checking that **Scatter/Dot** is highlighted in the **Choose from** panel. Click the second picture in the second row of a Simple Dot Plot to highlight it and then drag it to the **Chart preview** in the panel above (Figure 20). In addition, an **Element Properties** dialog box will also appear.

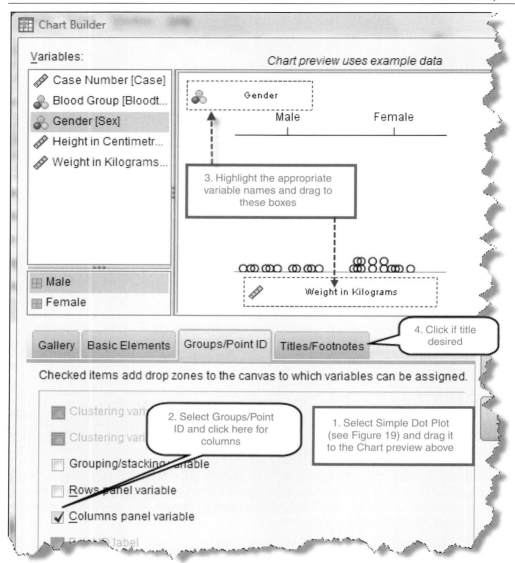

Figure 20. The upper part of the **Chart Builder** dialog box with **Groups/Point ID** highlighted to show the panel options for a simple dot plot of Weight for each sex prepared in the preview panel

- Follow the steps in Figure 20.
- To add a title, click **Titles/Footnotes** (middle of **Chart Builder** dialog box) and then click **Title 1**. A panel will appear in the **Element Properties** dialog box where a title such as Dot plot of Weight for each Sex can be typed in. Then click **Apply** followed by **Close**.
- Finally click **OK** in the **Chart Builder** dialog box to create the chart (Output 11).

Dot plot of Weight for each Sex

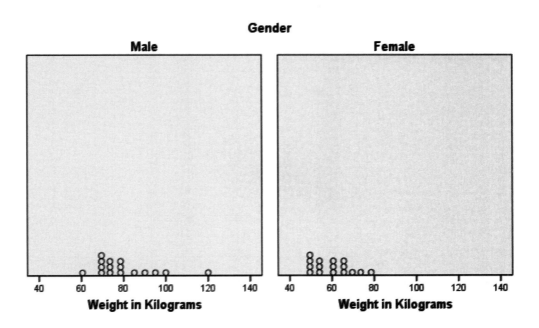

Output 11. A panelled dot plot showing the weights of males and females

5.8   DUAL Y-AXIS GRAPHS

SPSS Statistics 18 has a facility for plotting dual y-axis charts. For example, we could plot weight and height for each sex. Here we shall illustrate the procedure using the data set from Chapter 15 to see whether competence in Latin is associated with competence in modern foreign languages such as French and German.

To plot a dual y-axis graph, open **Chart Builder** (see Section 5.2.1) and then:

- Ensure that the illustrations correspond to **Line** by checking that **Line** is highlighted in the **Choose from** panel. Click the first picture (Simple Line) to highlight it and then drag it to the **Chart preview** in the panel above. In addition, an **Element Properties** dialog box will also appear.
- Click **Basic Elements** in the middle of **Chart Builder** and then click the dual y-axis picture (the one with Y1 and Y2) to highlight it. Drag it to the **Chart preview** above (Figure 21).

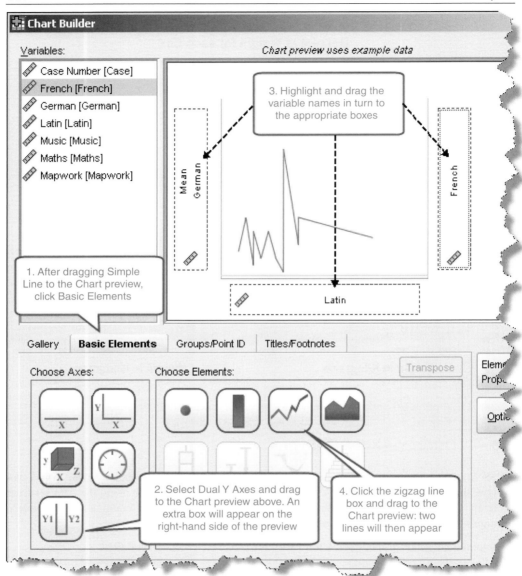

Figure 21. The **Chart Builder** dialog box for plotting two y-axis variables

- Follow the steps in Figure 21.
- To add a title, click **Titles/Footnotes** (middle of **Chart Builder** dialog box) and then click **Title 1**. A panel will appear in the **Element Properties** dialog box where a title such as French and German against Latin can be typed in. Then click **Apply** followed by **Close**. Notice that **T1** would appear at the top of the preview if a title is requested.

- Click **OK** to plot the graph (Output 12). The line for German has been edited to differentiate it from the line for French because the colour coding is lost in a grey-scale reproduction. Annotations have also been added.

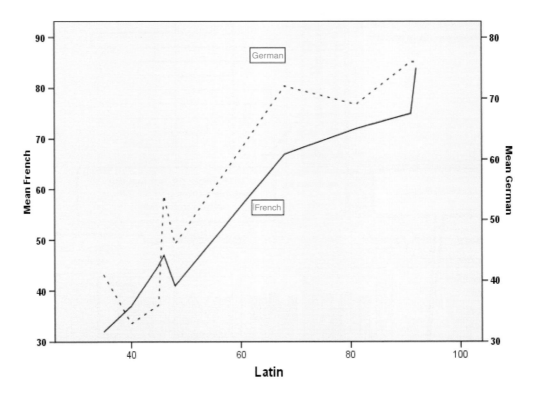

Output 12. The edited dual Y-Axis plot of French and German against Latin

5.9   HISTOGRAMS

Various types of histogram are easily plotted in **Chart Builder**. For example, we could plot the heights of males and females back-to-back. To plot a **Population Pyramid** (i.e., back-to-back histograms), open **Chart Builder** (see Section 5.2.1) and then:

- Follow the steps in Figure 22.
- To add a title, click **Titles/Footnotes** (middle of **Chart Builder** dialog box) and then click **Title 1**. A panel will appear in the **Element Properties** dialog box where a title such as Histograms of height for each sex can be typed in. Then click **Apply** followed by **Close**.
- Click **OK** to plot the histograms (Output13).

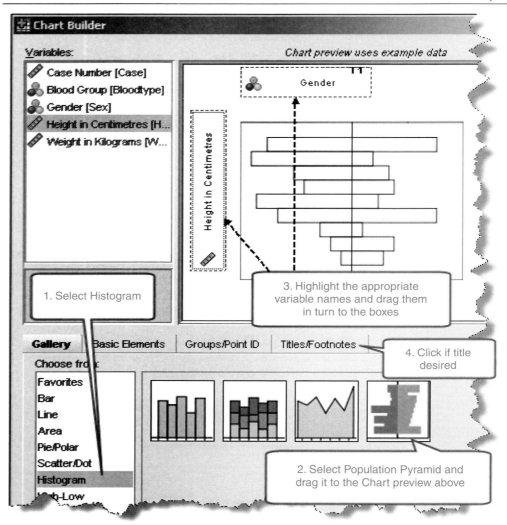

Figure 22. The upper part of the **Chart Builder** dialog box for drawing a population pyramid (back-to-back histograms) of height for men and women

The great advantage of the population pyramid over, for example, side-by-side panelled **histograms, is that** the histograms are drawn to the same scale, which makes it easier to **compare the distributions.**

Histograms of Height for each Sex

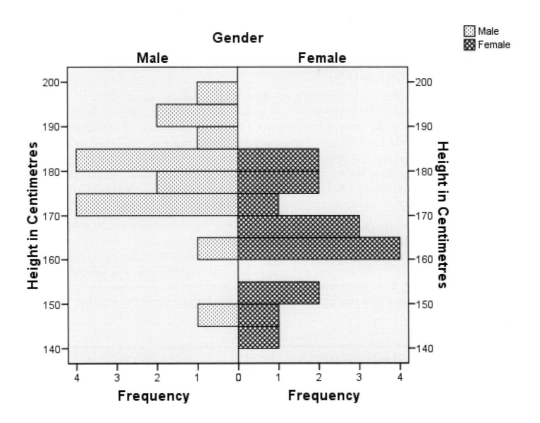

Output 13. The population pyramid of height for each sex

5.10   Receiver-Operating-Characteristic (ROC) Curve

The **ROC curve** arises in **signal detection theory**, which was originally developed during the Second World War to understand and improve the detection, by the **operator** of a radar system, of the presence of enemy vessels. What factors determine the correct detection of **signals** against a background level of disturbance, or **noise**? Signal detection theory has been used in psychophysics for studying the detection of weak signals, in memory research for measuring recognition of previously presented material and, in medical research, for validating diagnostic tests and investigating the efficacy of drugs.

A major problem with the traditional, one-value sensory threshold is that its value is affected by many factors, including response bias. Some people, for example, will only report that they have perceived a signal when they are absolutely certain that one was present; whereas others, in contrast, will respond positively to the smallest spot on a radar screen. How can one determine an operator's sensitivity independently of response bias? The solution is to use an experimental paradigm in which signals are presented on some of the trials only, so that the **hit rate** (saying 'yes' when a signal is present) and the **false alarm rate** (saying 'yes' when a signal is absent) can be determined. We can expect that if a signal is strong, the hit rate should increase. In a sensitive operator, the hit rate should increase faster than the false alarm rate as signal strength increases, so the the graph of Hits against False Alarms, that is, the operator's **ROC** curve, should rise steeply, before eventually levelling off. In an insensitive operator, an increase in the hit rate will be accompanied by an equally rapid increase in the false alarm rate, so that the ROC curve is a straight line, rather than a curve.

In signal detection theory, it is assumed that the probability distributions of level of disturbance with noise alone and with signal plus noise overlap. The less the overlap, the stronger the signal and the greater the operator's ability to detect it. The separation of the peaks of the two distributions is termed d' (**d-prime**), the formula of which will be given later. It is quite possible to map the range of d-prime on to specific shapes of the ROC curve. In summary, signal detection theory replaces the traditional point value of the threshold in classical psychophysics with an ROC curve, from which a measure of sensitivity (d-prime) can be calculated, which is relatively independent of response bias.

We shall look at the hypothetical development of a test for detecting pathology of the retina (retinopathy). Ideally the test should identify those with retinopathy 100% of the time and those without retinopathy 100% of the time but in the real world there are likely to be patients with retinopathy who pass the test and persons without retinopathy who will fail the test. Thus the aim is to establish a cut-off point on the test scale such that the clinician can be about 80% certain that the person tested has the condition (an 80% hit rate) thus keeping the false alarm rate at 20% or below.

Table 1. The contingency table for the type of observer and passing or failing the test			
Test Result	**Type of Observer**		
	Retinopathy	No Retinopathy	Total
Fail	A ('Hit')	B ('False Alarm')	A+B
Pass	C ('Miss')	D (Correct: no signal)	C+D
Total	A+C	B+D	A+B+C+D

We define sensitivity as the probability of a failed test among patients with retinopathy and specificity as the probability of a passed test among those without retinopathy. If we collate frequencies in a 2 × 2 table (Table 1), then *sensitivity* = probability of a hit for retinopathy i.e. A/(A+C) and *specificity* = probability of a true passed test for persons with no retinopathy i.e. D/(B+D). Ideally we want high *sensitivity* and high *specificity* i.e. a low value of (1 − *specificity*), the false alarm rate.

5.10.1   The SPSS ROC curve

The SPSS ROC curve is a plot of *sensitivity* (hit rate) against *1 − specificity* (false alarm rate). High discrimination is represented by a curved line almost reaching into the top left-hand corner of the ROC graph space and zero discrimination by a diagonal line at 45° to the horizontal. As an example, suppose a new computer-based test of defective colour vision has been devised and is given to twenty patients with retinopathy and twenty persons without retinopathy. The aim is to find out whether the test can be used to discriminate these two categories of observers and if so, what cut-off point of errors should be adopted. The data are given in Table 2.

Table 2. Colour vision error scores for persons with and without retinopathy							
Retinopathy				No Retinopathy			
40	43	36	45	34	35	31	25
35	35	33	39	36	30	36	19
34	37	45	35	32	31	29	23
34	20	50	37	28	23	29	32
25	40	30	35	24	24	32	29

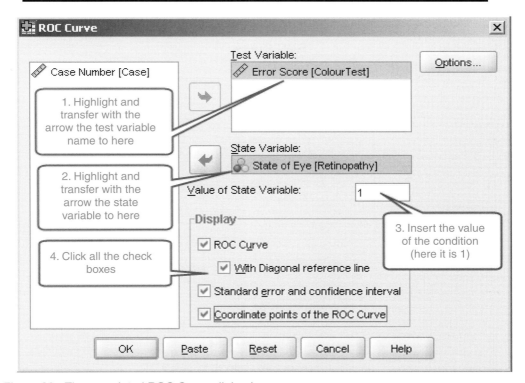

Figure 23. The completed **ROC Curve** dialog box

Three variables are created in the **Data Editor**: 1. a scale variable Case; 2. a grouping variable named Retinopathy (variable label State of Eye), with value labels: 1 = Retinopathy; 2 = No Retinopathy; 3. a scale variable named ColourTest with variable label Error Score.

To plot the ROC Curve

- Choose **Analyze→ROC Curve…** to open the **ROC Curve** dialog box.
- Complete the dialog box as shown in Figure 23.

The first table in the output (Output 14) shows the **Case Processing Summary** – here we have 20 cases with retinopathy and 20 cases without retinopathy.

Case Processing Summary

State of Eye	Valid N (listwise)
Positive[a]	20
Negative	20

Larger values of the test result variable(s) indicate stronger evidence for a positive actual state.

a. The positive actual state is Retinopathy.

Output 14. The Case Processing Summary table

The next output item is the **ROC Curve** (Output 15).

ROC Curve

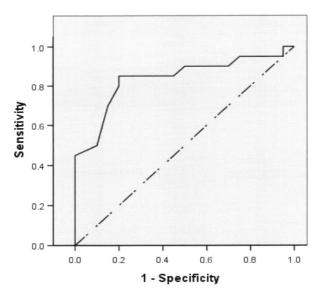

Diagonal segments are produced by ties.

Output 15. The **ROC Curve**

Output 16 is a table listing statistics relating to the area under the ROC Curve. **Area** is the probability that a randomly chosen retinopathy patient exceeds a randomly chosen person without retinopathy (here it is .838 i.e. 83.8%) and **Asymptotic Sig.** is the probability that the test is better than guessing is less than .0005, i.e. is highly significant.

Area Under the Curve

Test Result Variable(s): Error Score

Area	Std. Error[a]	Asymptotic Sig.[b]	Asymptotic 95% Confidence Interval	
			Lower Bound	Upper Bound
.838	.067	.000	.707	.968

The test result variable(s): Error Score has at least one tie between the positive actual state group and the negative actual state group. Statistics may be biased.

a. Under the nonparametric assumption

b. Null hypothesis: true area = 0.5

Output 16. Statistics relating to the area under the **ROC Curve**

Finally there is a table of co-ordinates of the curve (Output 17 on next page). Notice that a cut-off value of 33.5 in the table of co-ordinates represents a sensitivity of .800 (80%) and a false alarm rate (1 – Specificity) of .200 (20%). If it was desired to restrict the false alarm rate to 10%, it would be necessary to increase the error score to 35.5 but then the sensitivity for detecting retinopathy would be reduced to 50%.

5.10.2   The d' statistic

The statistic d' (d-prime) is often calculated in such applications. It is given by the formula

$$d' = \frac{|\mu_2 - \mu_1|}{\sqrt{(\sigma_1^2 + \sigma_2^2)/2}}$$

and is easily computed in SPSS by entering the means and standard deviations into a new data file and then using **Compute** to calculate d' (Figure 24). For this example, $d' = 1.24$.

RetMean	RetSD	NormMean	NormSD	dPrime
36.400	6.809	29.100	4.778	1.241

Figure 24. The calculation of d'

The highest possible d' (greatest sensitivity) is nearly 7 but typical values are usually no higher than 2.0: thus our value of 1.24 is typical.

Coordinates of the Curve

Test Result Variable(s): Error Score

Positive if Greater Than or Equal To[a]	Sensitivity	1 - Specificity
18.00	1.000	1.000
19.50	1.000	.950
21.50	.950	.950
23.50	.950	.850
24.50	.950	.750
26.50	.900	.700
28.50	.900	.650
29.50	.900	.500
30.50	.850	.450
31.50	.850	.350
32.50	.850	.200
33.50	.800	.200
34.50	.700	.150
35.50	.500	.100
36.50	.450	.000
38.00	.350	.000
39.50	.300	.000
41.50	.200	.000
44.00	.150	.000
47.50	.050	.000
51.00	.000	.000

The test result variable(s): Error Score has at least one tie between the positive actual state group and the negative actual state group.

a. The smallest cutoff value is the minimum observed test value minus 1, and the largest cutoff value is the maximum observed test value plus 1. All the other cutoff values are the averages of two consecutive ordered observed test values.

Output 17. The table of co-ordinates of the ROC Curve

Exercises

Exercise 6 *Charts and graphs,* and Exercise 7 *Recoding data; selecting cases; line graph* are available in www.psypress.com/spss-made-simple and click on Exercises.

CHAPTER 6

Comparing averages: Two-sample and one-sample tests

6.1   OVERVIEW

In Chapter 1, five research scenarios were described (Section 1.3.2, Figure 3). In the first, the researcher has **two or more samples** of scores and wants to know whether the means are significantly different. As a guide to choosing an appropriate test in this kind of situation, we offered a flow chart (Section 1.4.2, Figure 4). (When using such a chart, however, it is important to bear in mind that the making of any statistical test assumes that a statistical model is applicable to your particular data set. A preliminary analysis may be necessary to establish this.) The first question in the flow chart concerned the number of groups or conditions. The main purpose of this chapter is to show you how to implement the tests recommended by the chart when there are two samples of scores.

See Section 1.4.2

In the fourth scenario in Section 1.3.2, the researcher has only a single sample of scores, on the basis of which he or she wishes either to make an inference about the mean of the population or to decide whether the distribution of the sample is sufficiently well fitted by a theoretical distribution. One-sample tests, however, can sometimes be relevant to situations where there are two samples of scores. Where there are two related samples of scores in the form of continuous or scale data, for instance, the appropriate *t* test for comparing the two means can be viewed as a one-sample test.

Table 1 identifies the appropriate SPSS menu items for the various two-sample tests. The left half of the table lists **parametric tests**, which make assumptions about population distributions and parameters. The right half of the table lists **non-parametric tests**, which make fewer assumptions. Each half of the table is subdivided according to whether the samples are independent or related. (Incidentally, in the context of the *t* test, SPSS uses the term **paired samples** rather than **related samples**; elsewhere, as in the menu for nonparametric tests, we find the term **related samples**.)

Table 1. Comparing the averages of two samples: The SPSS menus			
Assumptions			
Populations assumed to have normal distributions and equal variances		No specific assumptions about the population distributions	
Independent samples	Paired samples	Independent samples	Related samples
SPSS submenus and procedures			
Compare Means		Nonparametric Tests	
Independent Samples T Test...	Paired-Samples T Test...	2 Independent Samples...	2 Related Samples...

6.2   COMPARING MEANS: THE INDEPENDENT SAMPLES T TEST WITH SPSS

To illustrate the running of a *t* test on SPSS, we shall use the data that were the basis of the table summarising the results of the caffeine experiment described in Chapter 1 (Table 1, Section 1.2.1).

We shall need to have two variables in **Data View**:
  (1)   a variable containing the scores that the participants achieved (the dependent variable);
  (2)   a grouping variable, consisting of code numbers indicating the conditions under which each score was achieved.

6.2.1   Preparing the data file

The complete data set is shown in Table 2.

Prepare the data file from this data set in Table 2 as follows:
* In **Variable View**, enter the variable names as *Case* for the case number, *Group* for the grouping (independent) variable, and *Hits* for the dependent variable.

See
Section
2.3

- In the **Label** column, enter the variable labels *Case Number*, *Treatment Group* and *Number of Hits*.
- In the **Values** column, define the values and their labels for the variable Group as follows: 1 = Placebo, 2 = Caffeine.
- In the **Measure** column, change the setting for Group from **Scale** to **Nominal**.
- Open **Data View** and, for each participant, type in the case number, the value for Group and number of hits.

Table 2.	Number of hits for the Placebo and Caffeine groups						
Case	Placebo	Case	Placebo	Case	Caffeine	Case	Caffeine
1	5	11	9	21	2	31	13
2	6	12	9	22	8	32	13
3	6	13	10	23	9	33	13
4	7	14	10	24	9	34	13
5	7	15	10	25	10	35	14
6	8	16	11	26	11	36	14
7	8	17	11	27	11	37	15
8	8	18	11	28	12	38	15
9	8	19	12	29	12	39	15
10	9	20	20	30	12	40	17

6.2.2   Exploring the data

Before running the *t* test, it is important to check the data for anomalies such as extreme values or skewed distributions. Such considerations are particularly important with small data sets such as this one. Since this data set contains a grouping variable, the **Explore** procedure (Chapter 4, Section 4.4.3) is appropriate. (Unlike **Descriptives**, **Explore** requires a grouping variable.)

See
Section
4.4.3

- Choose **Analyze→Descriptive Statistics→Explore…** to open the **Explore** dialog box (see Chapter 4, Figure 11).
- Transfer the dependent variable Number of Hits in the left-hand box to the **Dependent List:** box. Transfer the grouping variable Treatment Group to the **Factor List:** box.
- Click **Plots…** to open the **Explore: Plots** dialog box, deselect the **Stem-and-leaf** check box and select the **Histogram** check box. Click **Continue** to return to the **Explore** dialog box.
- Click **OK** to run the **Explore** procedure.

Output 1 and Output 2 show some interesting results.

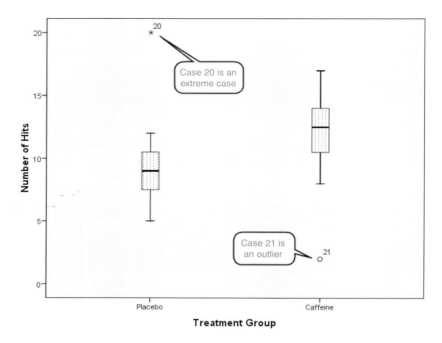

Output 1. The boxplots from the **Explore** procedure

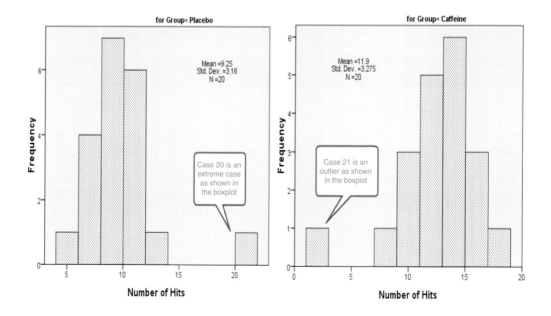

Output 2. The histograms from the **Explore** procedure

In Output 1, the Placebo boxplot shows an extreme value for case 20 ($*^{20}$ means, 'Case 20 is an extreme value').

In Output 2, which shows histograms of the same distributions, the same extreme value appears as the isolated right-hand box in the Placebo histogram. Another score, for Case 21, appears as an outlier (o^{21} means, 'Case 21 is an outlier') in the Caffeine boxplot and is shown as the isolated left-hand vertical rectangle in the Caffeine histogram.

See Table 2, Chap. 4

With such a small sample, the presence of the markedly atypical scores of Cases 20 and 21 is likely to exert undue leverage on the values of the statistics summarising the data set. We shall therefore de-select Cases 20 and 21 before running the *t* test. This is easily done using the **Select Cases** procedure described in Chapter 3, Section 3.3.1.

See Section 3.3.1

- Choose **Data➔Select Cases…** to open the **Select Cases** dialog box (see Chapter 3, Figure 18).
- Click the **If condition is satisfied** radio button and then **If…** to open the **Select Cases: If** dialog box.
- Transfer Case to the conditional statement box. Type in the expression *Case ~= 20 & Case ~= 21* to select all cases except 20 and 21. Click **Continue** to return to the **Select Cases** dialog box.
- Click **OK**.

Inspection of the data in **Data View** will show that cases 20 and 21 have been de-selected, as indicated by diagonal lines through those case numbers and values of zero in those rows of the new column headed filter_$. (The value 1 in the other rows indicates selection.) Now we can continue with the *t* test.

6.2.3   Running the *t* test

- Choose **Analyze➔Compare Means➔Independent-Samples T Test …** (Figure 1) to open the **Independent-Samples T Test** dialog box (Figure 2).

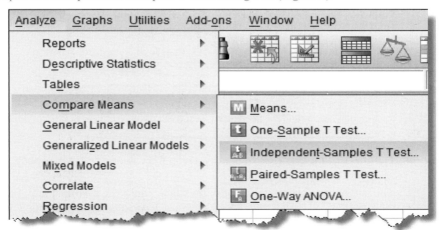

Figure 1. The **Compare Means** menu

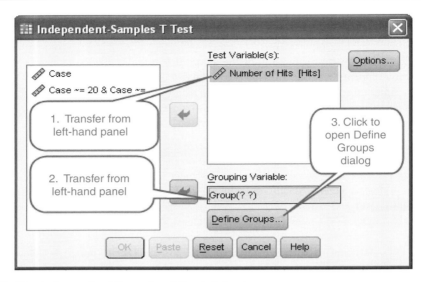

Figure 2. The **Independent-Samples T Test** dialog box

- Follow the steps in Figure 2.
- Define the values of the groups by clicking **Define Groups** to obtain the **Define Groups dialog box** (Figure 3).

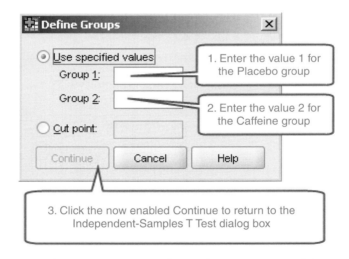

Figure 3. The **Define Groups** dialog box before defining the values of the two groups

- Type the value 1 into the **Group 1** box and the value 2 into the **Group 2** box, and click **Continue**. The values 1, 2 will then appear in brackets after Group in the **Grouping Variable** box:

  Grouping Variable:
  Group(1 2)

- Click **OK** to run the *t* test.

6.2.4 Interpreting the output

Early in the output, a table of **Group Statistics** (Output 3) will appear, listing some statistics of the two samples, including the means (8.68 and 12.42). (Notice that the values of all four statistics are different from those in Table 1 Chapter 1. The present values describe the **reduced** data set, that is, the original data, minus the outliers.)

Group Statistics

	Treatment Group	N	Mean	Std. Deviation	Std. Error Mean
Number of Hits	Placebo	19	8.68	1.945	.446
	Caffeine	19	12.42	2.364	.542

Output 3. Summary table of group statistics

The two means are certainly different but are they significantly different? Output 4 summarises the results of the *t* tests. The first thing to notice is that there are two rows of results which, in this particular example, give values of *t* (– 5.32) which agree to two places of decimals. The upper row, labelled **Equal variances assumed**, gives the results of the traditional *t* test, with the pooled variance estimate; the lower row, labelled **Equal variances not assumed**, gives the results of the test with the **Behrens-Fisher statistic** *T*, in which the variance estimates are not pooled. Notice too that, although the values of *t* agree closely, the degrees of freedom of *T* are given as 34.71, because they have been adjusted downwards with the **Welch-Satterthwaite formula**.

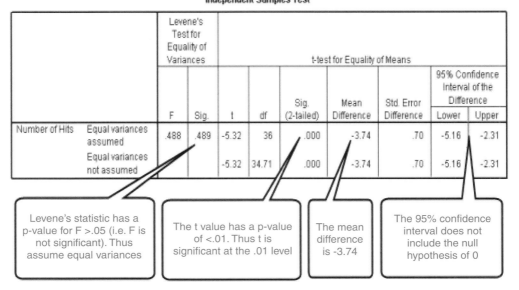

Output 4. T test output for **Independent Samples**

Notice that the first two columns of Output 4 refer to **Levene's test**. This is not the result of the *t* test proper: Levene's test is a test of the assumption of **homogeneity of variance** and its purpose is to help us decide whether to accept the result of the *t* test in the upper, **Equal variances assumed** row, or that given in the lower, **Equal variances not assumed** row. Notice too that, in Levene's test, the test statistic is *F*, not *t*. For the moment, we need only look at the *p*-value of *F*, which is .49. Since the *p*-value of *F* is greater than .05, the variances can be assumed to be homogeneous and the **Equal Variances** row of values for the *t* test can be used.

In summary:
- Since the Levene test gave $p > 0.05$, the homogeneity of variance assumption is tenable, and we can accept the report of the *t* test in the upper row of Ouput 4.
- Had *p* been less than .05, the homogeneity of variance assumption would have been untenable and we should have had to accept the report of the test in the lower row of Output 4.

The reader will have observed that in this example, both the p-values and *t*-values for **Equal variance assumed** and **Equal variance not assumed** are identical to several places of decimals. That would not have been the case had the variances been heterogeneous: the two *t* tests can lead to different decisions about the null hypothesis.

Turning now to the *t* test itself (upper row in Output 4), we see that *t* (*df* = 36) is – 5.321. The negative value arises because, when we were completing the dialog in Figure 3, we entered the code value 2 of the Caffeine group into the slot labelled **Group 2** and the code value 1 of the Placebo group into the slot labelled **Group 1**. That meant that, in the computation of *t*, the Caffeine mean would be subtracted from the Placebo mean. Had we entered the value 2 into the **Group 1** slot and the value 1 into the **Group 2** slot, the value of *t* in Output 4 would have been positive, because the Placebo mean would have been subtracted from the Caffeine mean.

6.2.5   Two-tailed and one-tailed *p*-values

In Output 4, the *p*-value is given under the column headed **Sig. (2-tailed)**. In a two-tailed test, the critical region for the test statistic is divided between the two tails of the distribution, so that the probability, under the null hypothesis, of a value in either tail is .025. In other words, we shall reject the null hypothesis if the value of *t* is either less than the 2.5[th] percentile or above the 97.5[th] percentile. This is entirely reasonable if the null hypothesis states that the two means are equal: a large difference in either direction casts doubt upon that hypothesis. That is why, although the value of *t* in Output 4 was negative, we were able to ignore the sign.

If we ignore the sign of *t*, its *p*-value will always lie in the **upper tail** of the distribution above our obtained value of *t*. This is a **one-tailed *p*-value**. But, since, under the null hypothesis, large negative values of *t* are just as likely as large positive values, an absolute value at least as great as the one we have obtained is actually twice as probable as the one-tailed *p*-value. SPSS calculates the **two-tailed *p*-value** by multiplying the one-tailed *p*-value by two.

Advocates of one-tailed tests will argue that, in general, the alternative hypothesis should coincide with the scientific hypothesis. That is not the case in our example: the researcher expects the Caffeine mean to be higher than, not simply different from, the Placebo mean. Arguably, therefore, the critical region should be placed entirely in the upper tail of the distribution: that is, the critical value of *t* should be the 95th (rather than the 97.5[th]) percentile.

The one-tail tester must subtract only in the direction dictated by the scientific hypothesis – the sign of t is now absolutely crucial. Note also that if the scientific or alternative hypothesis H_1 is that μ_2 (the Caffeine mean) is greater than μ_1 (the Placebo mean), the null hypothesis H_0, being the negation of H_1, is that μ_2 is not greater than μ_1, that is, H_0 must state that μ_2 is less than or equal to μ_1. We must write these directional hypotheses as follows:

$$H_1 : \mu_2 > \mu_1$$
$$H_0 : \mu_2 \leq \mu_1$$

When calculating the value of t, therefore, you must always subtract the Placebo mean from the Caffeine mean, even if the former has the greater value, with the result that t is negative. Moreover, however large the absolute value of t, the negative sign forces the researcher to accept the null hypothesis. This is the problem with one-tailed tests: they cannot confirm an unexpected result.

6.2.6   The effects of extreme scores and outliers in a small data set

The t test we have described was run on a data set with two outliers removed. You might wish to re-run the test on the complete data set (Table 2). You would find that the value of t is smaller: $t(38) = 2.60$; $p = .01$ (two-tailed), $p < .01$ (one-tailed).

The t value from the full data set is smaller than the value calculated from the reduced data set. The inclusion of the outlier and the extreme score has the effect of increasing the standard error of the difference (the denominator of t) from .70 to 1.02. The difference between the means also increases; but in small data sets such as this, the presence of outliers, even when they result in a greater difference between the means, typically increases the denominator of the t statistic more than the numerator and so may sometimes reduce the value of t to insignificance. (This did not happen with the full data set in the present example.) The relatively greater effect of outliers upon the denominator of the t statistic arises because variances are calculated from the *squares* of deviations from the mean, and large deviations continue to exert a disproportionate leverage, even after the square root operation has been carried out.

6.2.7   Measuring effect size

The mean performance level of the Caffeine group was 3.74 units higher than that of the Placebo mean. We have seen that this is a significant difference; but is it also a *substantial* difference? Is it worth reporting?

6.2.7.1   Cohen's *d* statistic

For the simple two-group between subjects experiment, Cohen (1988) suggested as a measure of effect size the statistic d, where

$$d = \frac{\mu_1 - \mu_2}{\sigma} \quad \text{- - - (1)   \textbf{Cohen's effect size index}}$$

Since Cohen's measure expresses the difference between the two population means in units of standard deviation, studies in which the same dependent variable has been measured in different units can be compared. Cohen's measure d is therefore much used in **meta-analysis**, the combination of statistics from several independent studies with a view to integrating all the evidence into a coherent body of knowledge. Cohen's index d is defined in terms of parameters, rather than statistics; but in practice, the parameters μ_1, μ_2 and σ are estimated from the means of the two samples and an estimate of the supposedly homogeneous population standard deviation.

As our estimate of σ, we can use the square root of the pooled variance estimate in the independent samples t test which, when the sample sizes are equal, is simply the mean of the two sample variances. Using the values given in Output 3, we have

$$s_{pooled} = \sqrt{\frac{s_1^2 + s_2^2}{2}} = \sqrt{\frac{1.945^2 + 2.364^2}{2}} = 2.16$$

Now, substituting the sample means in Output 3 and the pooled estimate of the standard deviation we have just calculated into formula (1), we have

$$d = \frac{M_1 - M_2}{s_{pooled}} = \frac{12.42 - 8.68}{2.16} = 1.73$$

We should note that if the sample sizes are unequal, the calculation of s_{pooled} is a little more complicated:

$$s_{pooled} = \sqrt{\frac{s_1^2(n_1 - 1) + s_2^2(n_2 - 1)}{n_1 + n_2 - 2}} \quad \text{- - - (2)}$$

**Making a pooled estimate of σ
when the sample sizes are unequal**

You can see from (2) that in our estimate, we are weighting the contribution of each sample variance with its relative contribution to the total degrees of freedom of the t statistic. If you substitute the values in Output 3 into formula (2), you will get exactly the same value for the estimated of the pooled standard deviation as we did by simply taking the square root of the mean of the two sample variances:

$$s_{pooled} = \sqrt{\frac{s_1^2(n_1 - 1) + s_2^2(n_2 - 1)}{n_1 + n_2 - 2}} = \sqrt{\frac{1.945^2(18) + 2.364^2(18)}{36}} = 2.16 \text{, as before.}$$

6.2.7.2   Interpreting values of d

On the basis of a study of a considerable body of published literature, Cohen (1962, 1988) has suggested a categorisation of effect size as shown in Table 3:

Table 3. Cohen's categories of effect size		
Effect size (d)	**Size of Effect**	**In words, ...**
$.2 \leq d < .5$	Small	Less than .2 is Trivial
$.5 \leq d < .8$	Medium	.2 to .5 is Small
$d \geq .8$	Large	.5 to .8 is Medium
		.8 or more is Large

Our value of d for the caffeine experiment is 1.73. Our experiment, therefore, has found caffeine to have a 'Large' effect upon performance.

6.2.8   Reporting the results of a statistical test

Your research report may be read by someone who may not agree with your statistical analysis of the results. The general principle to follow is to try to provide the reader with sufficient information to understand exactly what you have done, so that they will be free to make up their own minds about the implications of the results of your study.

You may, for instance, have decided to make a one-tailed test. If so, your report must make it clear that your reported p-value is the one-tailed p-value, so that your reader, who may not accept your justification for a one-tailed test, is free to multiply the given value by two and evaluate your results accordingly.

6.2.8.1   Provide the descriptives

The reader should never be confronted with a bald statement of the results of a statistical test (or, worse, a list of test results) without also being given access, on the same page, to the corresponding descriptive statistics. Where possible, the descriptives should be given in the same paragraph as the test results; but failing that, they should appear in a table nearby, so that the reader can fully understand the meaning of the test result.

6.2.8.2   Provide a full report

It is insufficient merely to report that a t test has found a difference to be significant. Your report must include, not only the value of t, but also the p-value, the degrees of freedom and a statement of whether the result is significant and beyond which level. There should also be some measure of effect size. When reporting the results of a t test, for example, include the value of Cohen's d or an equivalent index. This will allow the reader to appraise your results in relation to those reported by other researchers and evaluate them accordingly.

The p-value should be reported to two or three places of decimals, even for non-significant results. (The examples given in the APA Handbook imply that values should be given to two decimal places; but this is not explicitly stated and some would certainly feel that three places of decimals is more appropriate.) A reported p-value of .95, for example, conveys the important information that the result of the test came nowhere near significance; whereas a value of .06, although statistically insignificant, casts some doubt upon the null hypothesis – especially if a scarcity of data indicates that the test was of low power.

Very small *p*-values should be reported as inequalities (<) thus: $p < .01$; or, if the writer is reporting *p*-values to three places of decimals, $p < .001$.

6.2.8.3   A sample report

The *t* test that we have just carried out on the results of the caffeine experiment might be reported as follows:

> The mean score of the Caffeine group (M = 12.42; SD = 2.364) was significantly higher than that of the Placebo group (M = 8.68; SD = 1.945): $t(36) = 5.32$; $p <$ .01 (two-tailed). Cohen's $d = 1.73$, a 'large' effect. Two cases were excluded from the analysis: one was an extreme score; the other was an outlier. This result confirms the hypothesis that shooting accuracy is improved by the ingestion of caffeine.

When an analysis is reported to be based upon a reduced data set, some reviewers like to see a report of an analysis with the full data set as well. In our current example, both analyses lead to the same conclusions about the results, namely, that the ingestion of caffeine improves shooting accuracy. Be ready to provide the results of both analyses, should that be requested.

Some reviewers and journal editors like reports to contain confidence intervals as well. Confidence intervals are included in the SPSS output. A confidence interval is equivalent to a test of significance, in the sense that if a difference is significant beyond, say, the .05 level, but not beyond the .01 level, the 95% confidence interval will not include zero, but the 99% interval will. A confidence interval, however, provides a whole range of possible values for the true population difference, any of which is compatible with the results of a particular study. Clearly, therefore, a confidence interval can be a useful addition to the report.

6.3   THE RELATED-SAMPLES (OR PAIRED-SAMPLES) T TEST WITH SPSS

In an experiment on lateralisation of cortical functioning, a participant looks at a central spot on a computer screen and is told to press a key on recognition of a word that may appear on either side of the spot.

The experimental hypothesis is that words presented in the right visual field will be more quickly recognised than those in the left visual field, because the former are processed by the left cerebral hemisphere, which is thought to be better adapted to the processing of verbal information. For each participant, the median response time to forty words in both the right and the left visual fields is recorded, as indicated in Table 4.

Also shown in Table 4 are the differences resulting from subtracting the right field scores from the left field scores. As the researcher had hoped, there is indeed a clear tendency for the differences to be positive, that is, the right field times tend to be shorter.

Here, since each participant was tested with words in both visual hemifields, we have two related samples of scores. A **related-samples *t* test** is therefore appropriate. (SPSS calls this test the **paired-samples t test**.)

Table 4. Median reaction times for words presented in the left and right visual fields

Case	Left Field	Right Field	Difference (d)
1	323	304	19
2	512	493	19
3	502	491	11
4	385	365	20
5	453	426	27
6	343	320	23
7	543	523	20
8	440	442	− 2
9	682	580	102
10	590	564	26

6.3.1   Preparing the data file

Proceed as follows:

- Using the techniques described in Chapter 2 (Section 2.3), open **Variable View** and enter the variable names *Case*, *LeftField* and *RightField*. To improve the output, add fuller variable labels, such as *Case Number, Left Visual Field* and *Right Visual Field*.

See Section 2.3

- Now switch to **Data View** (which will now show the variable names) and enter the data.

Notice that, since in this example the same participants perform under both the Left Visual Field and the Right Visual Field conditions, there is no grouping variable. Notice too that there has been (and will be) no opportunity either to name or to label the dependent variable, Median Reaction Time.

6.3.2   Exploring the data

Since each participant has performed under both conditions, we can expect some consistency in level of performance across conditions: those who are quickest to recognise words in the Left Visual Field should also be among the quickest to recognise words in the Right Visual Field; those who are slowest in Left Visual Field recognition should also be among the slowest in Right Visual Field recognition. We can therefore expect a **positive correlation** (see Section 1.2.3) between reaction times under Left Visual Field and Right Visual Field conditions.

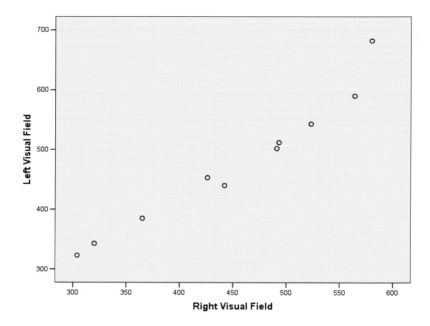

Output 5. The scatterplot of Left Visual Field against Right Visual Field

This positive correlation should be reflected in the appearance of the scatterplot (Output 5), in which (for large samples) the cloud of points should take the shape of an ellipse with the principal axis sloping up from left to right.

To check for anomalies in the data before running the *t* test, use the Chart Builder or the Legacy dialogs to obtain a scatterplot as described in Section 5.7. The pattern is indicative of a strong linear relationship between scores for the left and right visual fields, which is what we should expect, since each pair of scores comes from the same participant.

See Section 5.7

6.3.3   Running the *t* test

Proceed as follows:
- Choose **Analyze➔Compare Means➔Paired-Samples T Test ...** (see Figure 1) to open the **Paired-Samples T Test** dialog box (the completed version is shown in Figure 4).
- Transfer the variable labels to the **Paired Variables** box on the right of the dialog as described in Figure 4. (They can be selected in pairs by using the Control button and transferred together to the **Paired Variables** panel.)
- Click **OK**.

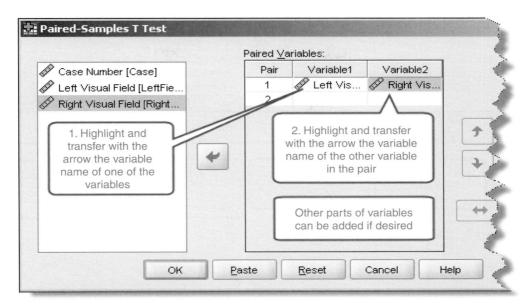

Figure 4. The **Paired-Samples T Test** dialog box for pairing Left Visual Field and Right Visual Field

6.3.4   Interpreting the output

Since it is possible to run *t* tests on several pairs of variables at the same time, the output specifies the pair under consideration in each sub-table. In this example, there is only one pair. The upper part of Output 6, **Paired Samples Statistics**, tabulates the statistics for each variable. The second output table (lower part of Output 6), **Paired Samples Correlations,** gives the value of the correlation coefficient, which is 0.97.

Paired Samples Statistics

		Mean	N	Std. Deviation	Std. Error Mean
Pair 1	Left Visual Field	477.30	10	112.09	35.45
	Right Visual Field	450.80	10	97.09	30.70

Paired Samples Correlations

		N	Correlation	Sig.
Pair 1	Left Visual Field & Right Visual Field	10	.97	.00

Output 6. Paired samples statistics and correlations

The final table (Output 7), **Paired Samples Test,** shows various statistics and their *p*-values.

Paired Samples Test

			Paired Differences						
						95% Confidence Interval of the Difference				
		Mean	Std. Devia- tion	Std. Error Mean	Lower	Upper	t	df	Sig. (2-tailed)
Pair 1	Left Visual Field - Right Visual Field	26.50	27.81	8.80	6.60	46.40	3.01	9	.015

The mean difference between pairs of values

The SD of the differences between pairs of values

The 95% confidence interval does not contain the null hypothesis of 0.

The p-value for t is 0.015. Thus the result is significant at the .05 level

Output 7. T test output for paired samples

6.3.5   Measuring effect size

As with the independent samples t test, effect size is measured with the statistic d, where d is estimated with

$$d = \frac{M_1 - M_2}{s_{pooled}}$$

From the upper table in Output 6, we have

$$s_{pooled} = \sqrt{\frac{s_1^2 + s_2^2}{2}} = \sqrt{\frac{112.09^2 + 97.09^2}{2}} = 104.86$$

Substituting the values in Output 6 and our estimate of the population standard deviation into formula (1), we have

$$d = \frac{M_1 - M_2}{s_{pooled}} = \frac{477.30 - 450.80}{104.86} = .25$$

From Table 3, we see that this is a 'small' effect – only a quarter of a standard deviation.

6.3.6   Reporting the results of the test

We can report the results of the test as follows.

> The mean response latency for the Left Visual Field (M = 477.30, SD = 112.09) was greater than the mean for the Right Visual Field (M = 450.80, SD = 97.09). A related-samples t test showed significance beyond the .05 level: t(9) = 3.01; p = .02 (two-tailed). The 95% confidence interval on the difference was [6.60, 46.40], which does not include the value of zero specified by the null hypothesis. Cohen's d = .25, which is a small effect.

6.3.7   A one-sample test

The related-samples t test is actually a one-sample test. The null hypothesis of equality of the two treatment means is restated as the proposition that we have a single sample from a population of differences d with a mean of zero. All the statements in Output 7, therefore, refer to the set of differences d, rather than the raw scores X.

Notice the entry called the 'Std. Error Mean'. Its value, 8.80, was obtained as follows:

$$s_{M_d} = \frac{s_d}{\sqrt{n}} = \frac{27.81}{\sqrt{10}} = 8.80$$

We see that the value of t (on 9 degrees of freedom) is 3.01, and that the p-value, 'Sig. (2-tailed)', is 0.015. The result of the t test is significant beyond the .05 level.

6.4   THE MANN-WHITNEY U TEST

The t test is an example of a **parametric test**: that is, it is assumed that the data are samples from two normally distributed populations with the same variance. Other tests, known as **nonparametric tests**, are predicated upon models that do not make so many assumptions about population distributions. (Nonparametric counterparts of parametric tests, however, do make some assumptions about the distributions.)   A nonparametric alternative to the independent-samples t test is the **Mann-Whitney U test**. (An equivalent test is the **Wilcoxon Rank Sum Test**.)   Two nonparametric alternatives to the related-samples t test are the **Wilcoxon Signed-Ranks test** and the **Sign test**.

Planned experiments usually produce scale or continuous data. Occasionally, however, one might have a situation in which each participant attempts a task and either a pass or a fail is recorded. If so, a two-group experiment will yield two independent samples of **nominal data**. Here the research question is still one of the significance of differences, albeit differences between relative frequencies, rather than differences between means.   With independent samples, a **chi-square test for association** will answer the question of whether the success rates in the two groups are significantly different (see Chapter 11).

See Chap. 11

6.4.1   Nonparametric tests in SPSS

SPSS offers a wide selection of nonparametric tests in the **Nonparametric Tests** submenu of **Analyze**.   A new feature in SPSS 18 is a simplification which automatically chooses the appropriate test after the user has specified the experimental design as **One Sample**, **Independent Samples** or **Related Samples** (see Figure 5) and has then transferred the appropriate variable names into the **Test Fields** panel.   The default output does not list the value of the test statistic; but should that be required (and many journals expect the values of test statistics to be given), double-click the output to open the **Model Viewer** (Output 9), which also includes a bar chart for each of the levels of the grouping variable.   Users accustomed to previous versions of SPSS can still find the various nonparametric options in **Legacy Dialogs**.   You can also select a particular test by clicking on the **Settings** tab in Figure 6.

6.4.1.1   The Mann-Whitney, Sign and Wilcoxon tests

The **Mann-Whitney** test is an alternative to the independent samples *t* test; the **Sign** and **Wilcoxon** tests are nonparametric counterparts of the paired-samples *t* test.   Most nonparametric methods are more resistant than their parametric counterparts to the influence of outliers and skewness.   The down side is a loss in the power of the test to reject the null hypothesis should that be false.   This is likely to be a real issue with the sorts of small, badly behaved data sets upon which the researcher would be most likely to consider running nonparametric tests rather than the *t* tests.

6.4.1.2   'Asymptotic' p-values

With large samples, several of the most common nonparametric test statistics have sampling distributions approximating to known continuous distributions and the approximation is close enough to provide serviceable estimates of *p*-values. (The term **asymptotic** means that the approximation to the theoretical distribution becomes ever closer as the sample size grows larger.) With small samples, however, the approximation can be very poor and the incautious user runs a heightened risk of make a false inference.

Fortunately, with the usual reports of the approximate, **asymptotic** *p*-values, SPSS can also provide **exact** *p*-values.   We recommend that, when the data are scarce, you should choose exact tests and report the exact *p*-values for nonparametric tests, rather than the asymptotic *p*-values.

6.4.2   Independent samples: the Mann-Whitney U test

Here we will use the original data set shown in Table 2, rather than the 'cleaned-up' set (minus the two outliers) that we used for the *t* test.

With the data in **Data View**,

- Choose **Analyze→Nonparametric Tests→Independent Samples...** (Figure 5) to open the **Nonparametric Tests: Two or More Independent Samples** dialog box (Figure 6).

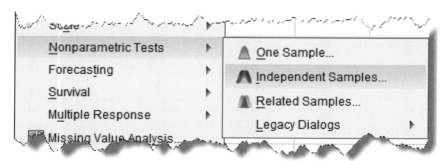

Figure 5. The **Nonparametric Tests** menu in the **Analyze** menu

- Click the **Fields** tab to open the next dialog box (Figure 7).
- Complete the dialog box as shown in Figure 7.

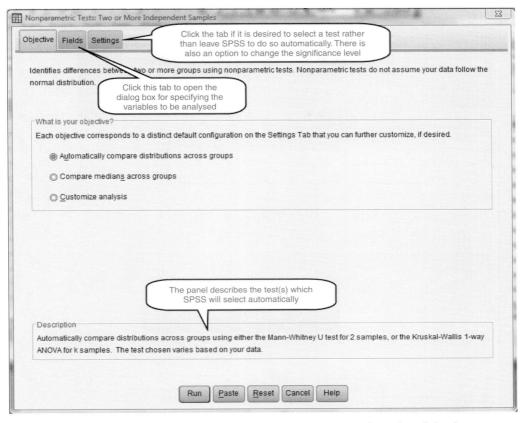

Figure 6. The **Nonparametric Tests: Two or More Independent Samples** dialog box

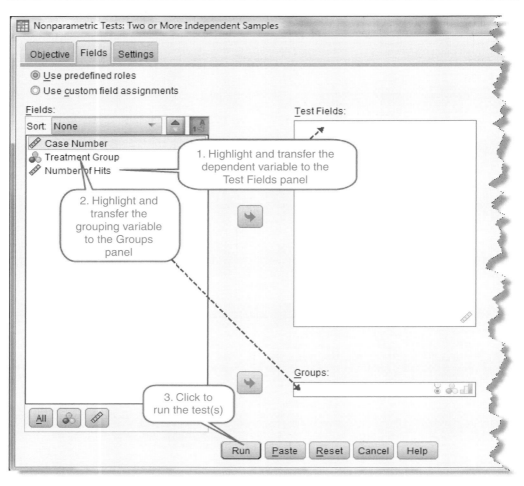

Figure 7. Specifying the **Test Fields** and **Groups** variables

6.4.3   Output for the Mann-Whitney U test

The initial output is shown in Output 8. If more details are required, double-click the output to open the **Model Viewer** output (Output 9). This includes back-to-back histograms and a table of values, including the value of the Mann-Whitney U statistic and the asymptotic *p*-value.

Hypothesis Test Summary

	Null Hypothesis	Test	Sig.	Decision
1	The distribution of Number of Hits is the same across categories of Treatment Group.	Independent-Samples Mann-Whitney U Test	.001	Reject the null hypothesis.

Asymptotic significances are displayed. The significance level is .05.

Output 8. The output for the automatic version of the **Two Independent Samples** test

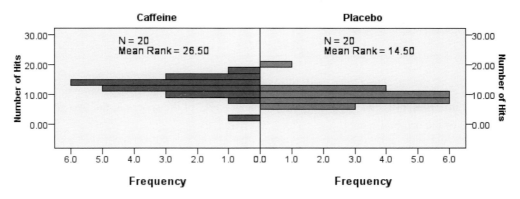

Total N	40
Mann-Whitney U	320.000
Wilcoxon W	530.000
Test Statistic	320.000
Standard Error	36.800
Standardized Test Statistic	3.261
Asymptotic Sig. (2-sided test)	.001

Output 9. The **Model Viewer** output after double-clicking on the output shown in Output 8

In the process of determining the value of the test statistic U, all the scores in the data set are first ranked in order of magnitude, after which the means of the ranks of the scores in each of the two groups are calculated.   The mean rank of the scores obtained under the Placebo condition is very considerably less than that of the scores obtained under the Caffeine condition, as shown beside each of the histograms in Output 9. We see from the asymptotic p-value that the **Mann-Whitney** tests shows significance.

6.4.4   Effect size

Several indices of effect size for use with the Mann-Whitney U test have been proposed. Let M_1 and M_2 be the mean ranks for Group 1 and Group 2, respectively. As a measure of effect size, King and Minium (2003) advocate the Glass rank biserial correlation coefficient r_g, where

$$r_g = \frac{2(M_1 - M_2)}{n_1 + n_2} \quad \text{--- (3)}$$

The Glass rank biserial correlation coefficient

Note that in formula (3), M_1 and M_2 are the mean *ranks* of the scores in the two groups, not the means of the original scores.

In our current example,

$$r_g = \frac{2(M_1 - M_2)}{n_1 + n_2} = \frac{2(26.5 - 14.5)}{40} = +.6$$

Cohen (1988) offers guidelines for interpreting the value of a correlation. In Chapter 11, it is explained that, although the value of a correlation is in itself a perfectly good measure of effect strength, the square of the correlation, which is termed the **coefficient of determination** is also useful, because it expresses the proportion of the total variance of either variable that is shared between the two variables. (In Chapter 12, it is observed that the coefficient of determination is also the proportion of the variance of one variable that is accounted for or explained by **regression** upon another variable.)

Table 5 below is an interpretation of Cohen's guidelines for interpreting a correlation.

Table 5. Guidelines (from Cohen, 1988) for classifying association strength, as measured by a correlation coefficient		
Absolute value of r	r squared	Size of effect
$.1 \leq |r| < .30$	$.01 \leq r^2 < .09$	Small
$.30 \leq |r| < .50$	$.09 \leq r^2 < .25$	Medium
$|r| \geq .50$	$r^2 \geq .25$	Large

In words ...

A correlation less than .1 is trivial.

If a correlation is between .1 and .3 (ignoring the sign), the association is SMALL. Between 1% and 8% of the variance is shared.

If a correlation is between .3 and .5, the association is MEDIUM. Between 9% and 25% of the variance is shared.

If a correlation is .5 or greater, the association is LARGE. At least 25% of the variance is shared.

It is clear from Table 5 that the obtained difference in mean ranks is a Large effect.

6.4.5   The report

The report of the result of the significance test should include not only the details of the test statistic and the *p*-value, but also the value of r_g (or an equivalent measure) and its classification in terms of effect size.

Your report of the results of the **Mann-Whitney U test** might read as follows:

> The mean number of hits for the Placebo group (M = 9.25, SD = 3.16) was less than the mean number of hits for the Caffeine group (M = 11.90, SD = 3.275). A Mann-Whitney U test showed this difference to be significant: U = 80.0; exact *p* < .01 (two-tailed).   The Glass rank biserial correlation = +.6, a 'large' effect in Cohen's (1988) classification.

6.5   THE WILCOXON MATCHED-PAIRS TEST

We turn now to the comparison of performance levels when the data are from an experiment of **within subjects** design, that is each participant is tested under both conditions. The **Wilcoxon Matched-Pairs Test** is applicable to data of this kind and carries fewer assumptions about the distribution of the data than does the related-samples (or paired samples) *t* test.

6.5.1   The Wilcoxon matched-pairs test in SPSS

With the data from Table 4 (the lateralisation data) in **Data View**,
- Choose **Analyze→Nonparametric Tests→Related Samples...** (Figure 5) to obtain the **Nonparametric Tests: Two or More Related Samples** dialog box (which is similar to the one shown in Figure 6).
- Click the **Fields** tab to open the next dialog box (Figure 8).

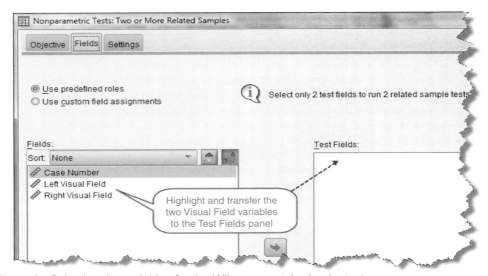

Figure 8. Selecting the variables for the Wilcoxon matched-pairs test

- Click **Run** to run the test.

6.5.2   The output

The initial output (Output 10) summarises the result of the test. Notice that the null hypothesis is about the medians (not the means) of the populations. On double-clicking on the initial output, you will access the **Model Viewer** and obtain the information shown in Output 11.

Hypothesis Test Summary

	Null Hypothesis	Test	Sig.	Decision
1	The median of differences between Left Visual Field and Right Visual Field equals 0.	Related-Samples Wilcoxon Signed Ranks Test	.007	Reject the null hypothesis.

Asymptotic significances are displayed. The significance level is .05.

Output 10. The initial output of the **Two Related Samples** test

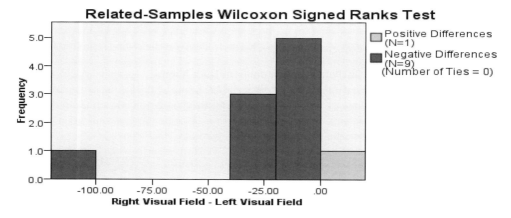

Total N	10
Test Statistic	1.000
Standard Error	9.798
Standardized Test Statistic	-2.705
Asymptotic Sig. (2-sided test)	.007

Output 11. The **Model Viewer** for the **Wilcoxon** test after double-clicking Output 10

In the **Wilcoxon test**, each participant's score under the Right Visual Field condition is paired with the same person's score under the Left Visual Field condition. A set of difference scores is obtained by consistently subtracting the Left Visual Field score in each pair from the Right Visual Field score. The middle histogram in Output 11 shows that in 9 out of 10 cases, the Left Visual Field score was greater than that for the Right Visual Field. The differences are then ranked in order of their absolute values: that is, they are ranked in order of magnitude, regardless of sign. The signs are then restored and the sums of the positive and negative ranks taken. The test statistic W is the smaller of the two sums of ranks of the same sign: in this case, $W = 1$.

The asymptotic p-value (**Asymptotic Sig.**) specifies the two-tailed p-value for the test statistic. Clearly the test has shown significance beyond the .01 level.

6.5.3 Effect size

As a measure of effect size following the Wilcoxon Matched-Pairs test, King and Minium (2003; p.457) prescribe the **matched-pairs rank biserial correlation**. If the sums of the positive and negative ranks are R_+ and R_-, respectively, T is the smaller of these two values, and N is the number of pairs of scores, the formula for the correlation r is:

$$r = \frac{4\left|T - \left(\frac{R_+ + R_-}{2}\right)\right|}{N(N+1)} \quad \text{- - - (4)}$$

The matched-pairs rank biserial correlation

In formula (4), the vertical lines denote the absolute value of the expression inside: that is, even if the difference is negative, the value is treated as if it were positive.

Substituting the values given in Output 11 into formula (4), we have

$$r = \frac{4\left|T - \left(\frac{R_+ + R_-}{2}\right)\right|}{N(N+1)} = \frac{4\left|1 - \left(\frac{1+54}{2}\right)\right|}{10(11)} = .96$$

Since this index of effect size is a correlation, we can interpret its size by using Table 5. In this case, however, we can see immediately that this is very strong effect indeed.

6.5.4 The report

In Output 11, the Standardized Test Statistic is the basis of the asymptotic p-value. Since we also have available the exact p-value, however, that is the value we shall report. Your report of the results of this test might read as follows:

A Wilcoxon matched-pairs, signed ranks test showed that the difference between the median response time for words presented in the left visual field (Md = 477.50 ms, Range = 359ms, Min, max = 323, 682) and the right visual field (Md = 466.50 ms; Range = 276 ms, Min, max = 304, 580) was significant beyond the .01 level: exact $p < .01$ (two-tailed). The sums of ranks were 54 and 1 for the negative and positive ranks, respectively, therefore $W = 1$. The matched-pairs rank biserial correlation is .96, which is a 'large' effect.

6.6   THE SIGN AND BINOMIAL TESTS

While the Wilcoxon matched pairs test assumes neither normality of distribution nor homogeneity of variance, it does assume that, in the population, the positive and negative differences have identical distributions. Like the Mann-Whitney test, the Wilcoxon test is vulnerable to the influence of extreme scores or outliers. In this subsection, we shall describe a test which carries no assumptions about the original distributions.

In this section, we shall describe a nonparametric test in which even more information is shed from the original data set. The **sign test** is yet another alternative to the related- or paired-samples *t* test, and is applicable to a data set such as the hemifield data in Table 4. (This test is actually an application of the **binomial test**, which we shall describe later in this section.)

Recall that in the related-samples *t* test, the basis of the analysis is a column of difference scores, obtained by consistently subtracting Left Visual Field scores from the Right Visual Field scores (or vice-versa). In the Wilcoxon Matched-Pairs Test, those differences were transformed to ranks and the test statistic was the smaller of the sums of the negative and positive ranks. In the sign test, the only information used is the signs of the ranks, so that the starting point for the test is a string of pluses and minuses (Table 6).

Table 6. Table of differences	
Difference (d)	Sign
−19	−
−19	−
−11	−
−20	−
−27	−
−23	−
−20	−
+ 2	+
−102	−
−26	−

If the null hypothesis is true and the populations of response times for the right and left visual fields are identical, there should, in the long run, be as many positive signs as there are negative signs: that is, the proportion of either sign in the population of signs should be ½ . Even in this small data set, that null hypothesis seems false, but a formal test is necessary to confirm the pattern of predominance of positive signs.

6.6.1   The sign test in SPSS

With the data in **Data View**,

- Choose **Analyze→Nonparametric Tests→Related Samples...** to obtain the **Nonparametric Tests: Two or More Related Samples** dialog box, which is similar to Figure 6.
- Click the **Fields** tab and transfer the variables as shown in Figure 8.
- Click the **Settings** tab to open the dialog box for selecting a test and follow the steps shown there (Figure 9). Click **Run** to run the Sign test.

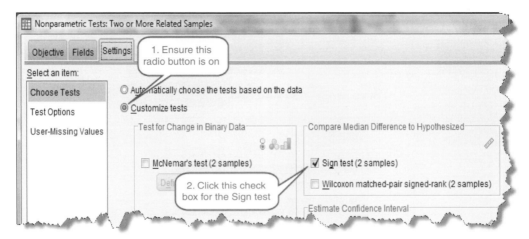

Figure 9. Selecting **Sign test** in the **Nonparametric Tests: Two or More related Samples Settings** dialog box

6.6.1.1   The output

The result of the sign test is shown in Outputs 12 and 13. The exact *p*-value is .021, so there is evidence against the null hypothesis; the asymptotic *p*-value (.027) also shows significance well beyond the .05 level.

Hypothesis Test Summary

	Null Hypothesis	Test	Sig.	Decision
1	The median of differences between Right Visual Field and Left Visual Field equals 0.	Related-Samples Sign Test	.021[1]	Reject the null hypothesis.

Asymptotic significances are displayed. The significance level is .05.

[1] Exact significance is displayed for this test.

Output 12. The output for the automatic version of the **Sign test**

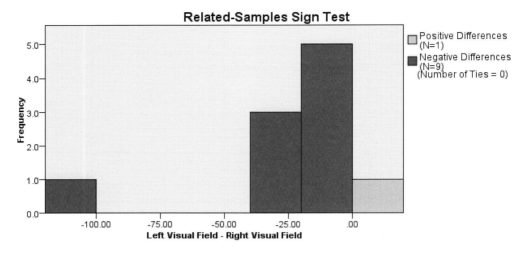

Total N	10
Test Statistic	1.000
Standard Error	1.581
Standardized Test Statistic	-2.214
Asymptotic Sig. (2-sided test)	.027
Exact Sig. (2-sided test)	.021

1. The exact p-value is computed based on the binomial distribution because there are 25 or fewer cases.

Output 13. The Model Viewer for the **Sign test**

6.6.1.2   Effect size

An index of effect size following the binomial and sign tests, Cohen (1988; pp.147–151) suggests the statistic g, which is the difference between P, the proportion of outcomes in the target category and p, the probability of the outcome under the null hypothesis:

$$g = |P - p| \quad \text{- - -} \ (5)$$

Cohen's Effect size index (two-sided) for binomial test

To evaluate a value of g, Cohen suggests that we can regard the values .05, .15 and .25 as Small, Medium and Large effects, respectively. This advice can be interpreted as shown in Table 7.

Table 7. Guidelines (from Cohen, 1988) for interpreting the effect size index g	
Value of g	Size of effect
$.05 \leq g < .15$	Small
$.15 \leq g < .25$	Medium
$g \geq .25$	Large
In words ... A value less than .05 is trivial. A value between .05 and .15 is a Small effect. A value between .15 and .25 is a Medium effect. A value of at least .25 is a Large effect.	

Output 13 shows that 90% of participants showed negative difference scores; whereas the proportion under the null hypothesis is .5. Substituting in formula (5), we have

$$g = |P - p| = .9 - .5 = .4$$

which, according to Table 7 is a Large effect.

6.6.1.3 The report

Our report of the results of the sign test might read as follows:

The Median response time was higher for words presented in the left visual field (Md = 477.50 ms, Range = 359ms, Min, max = 323, 682) than it was for words in the right visual field (Md = 466.50 ms; Range = 276 ms, Min, max = 304, 580). When the response times for the left visual field were consistently subtracted from those for the right visual field, there were nine negative differences and one positive difference. A sign test showed an exact *p*-value of .02. Cohen's $g = .4$, a 'large' effect.

6.6.2 Bernoulli trials: the binomial test

If a coin is tossed, say, 20 times, and the outcome (H or T) noted each time, we may end up with a sequence such as H, H, T, T, T, T, H, T, T, T, H, H, T, H, H, T, T, T, H, H.

This set of trials has the following properties:
1. There is a fixed number of identical experiments or trials.
2. The outcomes of every trial can be divided into the same two dichotomous categories, one of which can be regarded as a 'success', the other as a 'failure'. ('Heads you win, tails you lose.')

3. The outcomes of the trials are independent.
4. The probability of a 'success' is the same on all trials. If the coin is fair, that fixed probability is ½ .

Such a series is known as a set of **Bernoulli trials**. Note that property (2) does not imply that there are only two possible outcomes, only that we can divide the outcomes into two categories. Suppose that a candidate sitting a 50-question multiple-choice examination with six alternatives per question were (having no knowledge of the topic) to choose the answer by rolling a die each time. In that case, although there are six outcomes per question, they can be classified dichotomously into Pass (with a probability of 1/6) and Fail (with a probability of 5/6). Here too, we have a set of Bernoulli trials.

The **binomial probability model** enables us to assign probabilities to specified numbers of heads or tails over *n* Bernoulli trials. Is a coin biased? Suppose we were to obtain 16 heads in 20 tosses. The binomial model can give us the probability, given that p = ½ , of obtaining more than 15 heads or fewer than five heads in 20 tosses. If that probability is less than .05, we have evidence against the claim that the coin is fair.

Returning to the hemifield example and supposing that the null hypothesis is true, we can think of the random selection of ten participants for the experiment as ten Bernoulli trials, because on each trial we can classify the outcome in the same way as + or − . If there is indeed no tendency in the population for response times to be different for the right and left visual fields, the probability of a + (or a –) on each trial is ½ . In our experiment, we obtained nine − signs and one + sign. The binomial model shows that the two-tailed probability of such a bias under the null hypothesis is less than .05. (The 'two-tailed *p*-value' is obtained by multiplying the probability of at least nine minus signs by two. We shall want to report a marked difference between the hemifield scores, regardless of direction.)

As a second example, suppose that a researcher wants to know whether 5-year-old children of a certain age show a preference for one of two toys (A or B). The choices of one hundred 5-year-olds are noted, of whom 60 choose toy A and 40 toy B. Can we confirm the apparent preference for toy A by means of a formal statistical test?

If the null hypothesis is true so that, in the population, there is no tendency for children to prefer toy A, we can regard the selection of the children and the noting of the preference (A or B) of each child as a set of 100 Bernoulli trials. Under the null hypothesis, the probability of any child preferring toy A is ½ . The binomial probability model can give us the probability that at least 60 children (or less than 40 children) would say they preferred toy A.

We should note that, in the sign test, the application of the binomial probability model tests only the null hypothesis that $p = ½$. In the **binomial test** procedure, which we shall now describe, the value of p can be set to any value between 0 and 1.

6.6.2.1   The binomial test in SPSS

To illustrate the binomial test, we shall use our first example of the children's choices between two toys. Of the 100 five-year-olds studied, 60 chose toy A and 40 chose toy B. Proceed as follows:

*   Assign code numbers to the two choices, say 1 to toy A and 2 to toy B.
*   In **Variable View**, name a variable *Toy*, give the values 1 to Toy A and 2 to Toy B and assign variable labels to the values. Change **Scale** to **Nominal** in the **Measure** column.

- Name a second variable *Frequency* for the number of choices.
- Enter the data in **Data View**.
- In order to ensure that, in the statistical analysis, the two choices will be weighted by their frequencies of occurrence, select **Weight Cases...** in the **Data** menu to obtain the **Weight Cases** dialog box, select the **Weight Cases by** radio button, transfer Frequency to the **Frequency Variable** box, and click **OK**. Note that if each child's choice were to be entered individually into the data set (a more realistic scenario), there would be no need to use the **Weight Cases** procedure.

With the data in **Data View**,

- Choose **Analyze→Nonparametric Tests→One Sample...** (Figure 5) to obtain the **One-Sample Nonparametric Tests** dialog box (Figure 10).
- Click the **Fields** tab to open the variable selection dialog box and transfer the variable name Toy to the **Test Fields** panel. (See Figure 10.)

Click the **Settings** tab to open the dialog box for selecting a test (Figure 11). Click the radio button marked **Customize tests** and check the box describing the binomial test.

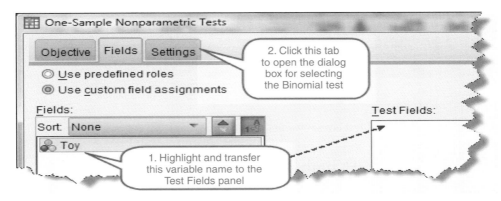

Figure 10. The **One-Sample Nonparametric Tests** dialog box for selecting the variable name

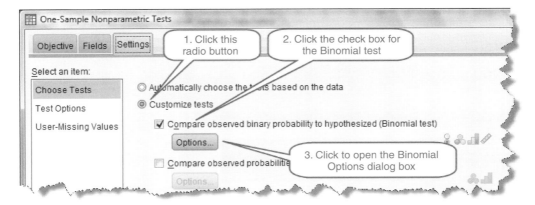

Figure 11. The **One-Sample Nonparametric Tests** dialog box for selecting the Binomial test

After clicking the **Options** box, the **Binomial Options** dialog box will appear (Figure 12). With a null hypothesis of two equally likely options, the default probability level of 0.5 applies. This is appropriate for the present test, because if the experiment was conducted properly and the children had no preference, the probability of each choice is .5. In other situations, however, that would not be the case, as when a candidate is guessing the correct answers to the questions in a multiple-choice examination, in which case, if there were four choices, the **Test Proportion** would be .25.

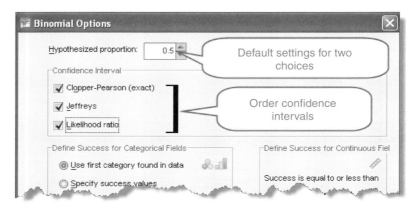

Figure 12. The **Binomial Options** dialog box

6.6.2.2   The output

The results of the binomial test are shown in Outputs 14, 15 and 16.

Hypothesis Test Summary

	Null Hypothesis	Test	Sig.	Decision
1	The categories defined by Toy = Toy A and Toy B occur with probabilities 0.5 and 0.5.	One-Sample Binomial Test	.057	Retain the null hypothesis.

Asymptotic significances are displayed. The significance level is .05.

Output 14. The initial output for the Binomial test

One-Sample Binomial Test

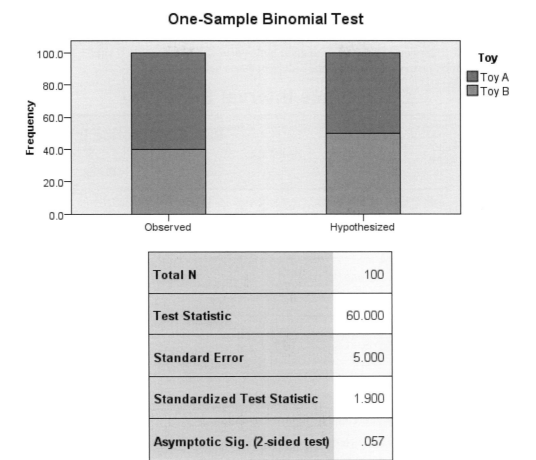

Output 15. The **Model Viewer** for the **Binomial Test**

Notice that the symptotic p-value is given in Output 14. With large samples, as in our example with $n = 100$, the exact and asymptotic p-values agree to many places of decimals; with a small sample, however, the two p-values can be far from identical and could lead to different conclusions about the null hypothesis. In such a case, both p-values would be included in the output. In our example, since the p-value is approximately .057, the null hypothesis cannot be rejected.

On double-clicking the initial output, the **Model Viewer** will appear giving further statistics and a stacked bar chart showing the observed frequencies of choices of Toy A and Toy B with the expected frequencies under the null hypothesis for comparison.

From the left-hand bar in the bar chart in Output 15, we see that the value of Cohen's statistic g is $.6 - .4 = .2$. This is an effect of medium size.

At the base of the left-hand pane of the Model Viewer is a drop-down menu initially set at **Hypothesis Summary View**. Reset this to **Confidence Interval Summary View** to see the requested confidence intervals on the proportion of 'successes' in the sample. The three requested confidence intervals are shown in Output 16. It can be seen that all three intervals agree that the 95% confidence interval is [.5 to .7], inclusive. In other words, a range of values up to .7 are compatible with the data; but so also is the *ex hypothesi* value .5. We have not got compelling evidence against the null hypothesis here.

Confidence Interval Summary

Confidence Interval Type	Parameter	Estimate	95% Confidence Interval	
			Lower	Upper
One-Sample Binomial Success Rate (Clopper-Pearson)	Probability (Toy=Toy A).	.600	.497	.697
One-Sample Binomial Success Rate (Jeffreys)	Probability (Toy=Toy A).	.600	.502	.692
One-Sample Binomial Success Rate (Likelihood)	Probability (Toy=Toy A).	.600	.502	.693

Output 16. The confidence intervals

The result of the binomial test could be reported as follows:

> Although more children (60%) chose toy A than toy B (40%), a binomial test failed to reject the hypothesis that there is no preference: Exact p = .06 (two-tailed). Cohen's g = .2, an effect of Medium size.

6.7   EFFECT SIZE, POWER AND THE NUMBER OF PARTICIPANTS

The power P of a statistical test is the probability that the null hypothesis will be rejected if it is false. When planning an experiment, the researcher must decide upon the numbers of participants necessary to ensure that statistical tests have sufficient power. There is a fair consensus that tests should have a power level of at least .75.

Since the power of a test depends upon the difference, in the population, between the means under the null and alternative hypotheses, the researcher must decide upon the smallest difference that is worth confirming by tests and reporting as a contribution to knowledge.

6.7.1   How many participants shall I need in my experiment?

Suppose that you plan to carry out an experiment comparing the performance of a group of participants who have taken a supposedly performance-enhancing drug with that of a placebo group. You wish to make a *t* test that will reveal an effect of medium size (i.e. Cohen's d is at least .5) and achieve a power of .75. How many participants will you need? It is quite possible to answer questions like this by using the cumulative distribution functions in the SPSS Compute menu, but one needs a clear grasp of the underlying statistical theory and the conventions for specifying these functions. An easier approach is to use a dedicated software package such as **G*Power 3**, which is freely available on the Internet and can be downloaded on to your computer (Erdfelder *et al.*, 1996; Faul *et al.*, 2007).

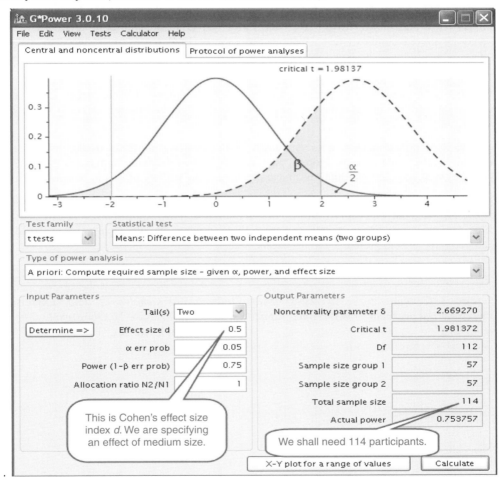

Figure 13. The **G*Power** window

G*Power asks the user to enter values for several of the effect size indices suggested by Cohen (1988). To obtain the answer to the present question, we must type the value .5 in the *d* slot. The output is shown in the lower right part of Figure 13.

6.8   A FINAL WORD

In this chapter we have described tests for comparing the performance levels of participants in experiments with two groups or treatment conditions. We first considered the **parametric *t* tests**. A difference between the means in a between subjects experiment can be tested with an **independent-samples *t* test**. A difference between the means in a within subjects experiment can be tested with a **related- or paired-samples *t* test**.

The parametric *t* tests carry several assumptions (such as homogeneity of variance and normality of distribution), which are often not true of data sets. For this reason, there are those who advocate nonparametric alternatives to the *t* tests, which carry fewer assumptions about the data.   The **Mann-Whitney U test** is a nonparametric alternative to the independent-samples *t* test and the **Wilcoxon Matched-Pairs test** is a nonparametric alternative to the related- or paired-samples *t* test.   In both tests, the original scores are reduced to ranks, a process which reduces the power of a nonparametric test to reject the null hypothesis if that is false.

The **Sign test** is another alternative to the related-samples *t* test in which even more information from the original data is shed, only the signs of the differences being retained in the analysis.

Advocates of nonparametric tests emphasise their greater robustness to the influence of skewness, outliers and extreme scores. They are not, however, totally immune to the leverage exerted by outliers; moreover their use incurs an immediate penalty of loss in power.

There has been much controversy about the use of nonparametric tests instead of *t* tests with some kinds of data, especially ratings. Many journal editors would insist that ratings, with which the values of group means constrain the variances, should always be analysed by nonparametric tests in preference to the *t* tests.

Exercises

Exercise 8 *Comparing the averages of two independent samples of data,* Exercise 9 *Comparing the averages of two related samples of data* and Exercise 10 *One-sample tests* are available in www.psypress.com/spss-made-simple and click on Exercises.

CHAPTER 7

The one-way ANOVA

7.1   INTRODUCTION

In Chapter 6, we discussed the use of the *t* test and other techniques for comparing mean performance levels under two different conditions.   In this chapter, we shall also be describing techniques for comparing means, but in the context of more complex experiments with three or more conditions or groups.

7.1.1   A more complex drug experiment

Like the *t* tests, the analysis of variance (ANOVA for short) is a technique (actually a set of techniques) for comparing means.   The ANOVA, however, was designed for the analysis of data from more complex experiments, with three or more groups or conditions.

In Chapter 1 (Section 1.2.2), we described an experiment in which each of five groups of participants performed under a different drug-related condition: a comparison, placebo condition and four different drug conditions: A, B, C and D. In Table 1 here, the raw data are also given, as well as the group means and standard deviations.   Does any of the four drugs affect level of performance? Our scientific hypothesis is that at least one of them does.   The null hypothesis, however, (and the one directly tested in ANOVA) is the negation of this assertion. H_0 holds that none of the drugs affects performance: in the population (if not in the sample), the mean performance score is the same under all five conditions.   By analogy with the two-group experiment, we write:

$$H_0: \mu_1 = \mu_2 = \mu_3 = \mu_4 = \mu_5 \ \text{- - -} \ (1)$$

Null hypothesis for a five-group experiment

The **ANOVA** provides a direct test of this null hypothesis.

Table 1. The results of a one-factor, between subjects experiment

	Placebo	Drug A	Drug B	Drug C	Drug D	
	10	8	12	13	11	
	9	10	14	12	20	
	7	7	9	17	15	
	9	7	7	12	6	
	11	7	15	10	11	
	5	12	12	24	12	
	7	7	14	13	15	
	6	4	14	11	16	
	8	9	11	20	12	
	8	8	12	12	12	
Mean	8.00	7.90	12.00	14.40	13.00	GM* 11.06
SD	1.83	2.13	2.49	4.50	3.74	

*Grand Mean

7.1.2   ANOVA models

The meaning of **factor, level, between subjects factors, within subjects factors** and other terms in experimental design was explained in Chapter 1, Section 1.2.2. Our current drug experiment is of **one-factor, between subjects** or **completely randomised** design and will produce five independent samples of scores.

Every statistical test is predicated upon an interpretation, or **model**, of the data.   If the data do not meet the assumptions of the model, there is a heightened risk of drawing a false inference from the results of the test.   Different models are applicable to data sets from experiments of different experimental design.

In the next section, we shall discuss the model underlying the **one-way** or **completely randomised ANOVA**.

7.1.3   The one-way ANOVA

In this subsection, we introduce some key terms in the analysis of variance.

7.1.3.1   Between groups and within groups variance

In Table 1, the treatment means show considerable variability, or variance. This variance among the treatment means is termed **between groups variance**. Within any of the five treatment groups, however, there is also dispersion of the scores about their group mean. This **within groups variance** reflects, among other things, individual differences. When several people attempt exactly the same task under exactly the same conditions, their performance is likely to vary considerably, provided the task is at the right level of difficulty and there is no floor or ceiling effect. There is also random **experimental error**, that is, random variation arising from such things as sudden background noises, changes in the tone or clarity of the experimenter's tone of voice and so on. Together, individual differences and random experimental error contribute to **error variance**, that is, variability among the scores that is not attributable to variation among the experimental conditions. Error variance is sometimes referred to as **data noise**.

In the one-way ANOVA, it is assumed that the within groups or error variance σ_e^2 is homogeneous across treatment groups. This is the same assumption of **homogeneity of variance** that underlies the pooling of the two variance estimates in the independent-samples t test. Since sampling entails sampling variability or sampling error, the five group sample variances in the current example can be expected to vary. If, however, they are all estimates of the supposedly constant variance σ_e^2, they can be pooled (as in the t test) to give a combined estimate of within groups variance. Note that, since the variance estimates are each based on the deviations of the individual scores within a group about their group mean, the pooled variance estimate is unaffected by any differences between the values of the group means. A treatment mean, however, is calculated from raw scores. The values of the group means and the between groups variance, therefore, also reflect, in part, within groups or error variance.

A second determinant of the between groups variance is the magnitude of any real differences there may be among the population means for the five treatment groups. If a sample of ten scores is taken from each of two populations centred on different mean values, we can expect the sample means to have different values; and the greater the difference between the population means, the greater the difference between the sample means is likely to be. Real differences between population means inflate differences between sample means beyond what would be expected from sampling error alone.

The one-way ANOVA works by comparing the between groups variance with the within groups variance. In the ANOVA, a variance estimate is known as a **mean square (MS)**. The numerator of the mean square is known as a **sum of squares (SS)**, and the denominator as the *degrees of freedom (df)*, so that

$$MS = \frac{SS}{df} \ \text{---} \ (2)$$

ANOVA notation for a variance estimate

In the one-way ANOVA, two variance estimates are calculated:

- The **between groups mean square** $MS_{between}$, which is calculated from the values of the group means only;

- The **within groups mean square** MS_{within}, which ignores the values of the treatment means and is calculated exclusively from the spreads of the individuals' scores around their group means.

The larger the value of $MS_{between}$ compared with that of MS_{within}, the stronger the evidence against the null hypothesis.

7.1.3.2   The *F* ratio

ANOVA compares these two variance estimates by means of a statistic known as an ***F* ratio**, where

$$F = \frac{MS_{between}}{MS_{within}} \quad - - - (3) \textbf{ An } \textbf{\textit{F} ratio}$$

The denominator of the F statistic is known as the **error term**. If the null hypothesis is true, both mean squares reflect merely within groups or error variance and the value of F should be around (though not exactly) 1. If the null hypothesis is false, the numerator of F will be inflated by real differences among the population means and F may be very large. If so, there is evidence against the null hypothesis (Figure 1).

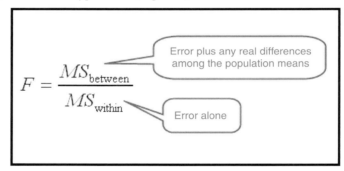

Figure 1. What *F* is measuring

It is clear from Figure 1 that if there are real differences among the population means, the numerator of F will be inflated in relation to the denominator and the value of F will therefore be greater (perhaps much greater) than 1. If, on the other hand, the null hypothesis is true, both mean squares will reflect only random error and the value of F will usually be close to unity.

7.1.3.3   The partition of the total sum of squares

The rationale of the one-way ANOVA becomes clearer on consideration of the sums of squares, that is, the numerators of the variance estimates which, since they are all calculated from the same data can themselves be regarded, in relation to one another, as measures of variability. In particular, there is an important relationship between the ANOVA sums of squares which affords insight not only into the workings of the one-way ANOVA, but also some of the statistics used in various follow-up analyses.

The total sum of squares SS_{total} is the sum of the squares of the deviations of all the scores in the data set from the grand mean:

$$SS_{total} = \sum_{\text{all scores}} (X - M)^2 \quad \text{- - - (4)} \quad \textbf{Total sum of squares}$$

We can think of SS_{total} as measuring the total variability of the scores in the entire data set of 50 scores.

The building block of the total sum of squares is the **total deviation** $X - M$. Each of these 50 total deviations can be broken down (or partitioned) into two components:

(1) a **between groups deviation**, that is, the deviation of the mean for group j from the grand mean $(M_j - M)$;

(2) a **within groups deviation**, that is, the deviation of the individual score from the group mean $(X - M_j)$.

The total deviation of each score in the data set can be written thus:

$$X - M = (M_j - M) + (X - M_j) \quad \text{- - - (5)}$$

$$\begin{bmatrix} \text{total} \\ \text{deviation} \end{bmatrix} \quad \begin{bmatrix} \text{between} \\ \text{groups} \\ \text{deviation} \end{bmatrix} \quad \begin{bmatrix} \text{within} \\ \text{groups} \\ \text{deviation} \end{bmatrix}$$

Breakdown of the total deviation

The breakdown in formula (5) applies to each of the 50 scores in the data set – though bear in mind that, because there are only five treatment means, there are only five values for the between groups deviation and that every member of each group will have the same value for the between groups deviation.

If we take the sum of the squares of all fifty total deviations in the data set, we have a measure of the total spread or dispersion of the scores. It can be shown that this total sum of squares is the sum of the between and within sums of squares, a relationship known as the **partition of the total sum of squares**:

$$SS_{total} = SS_{between} + SS_{within} \quad \text{- - - (6)}$$

$$\begin{bmatrix} \text{total} \\ \text{variability} \end{bmatrix} \quad \begin{bmatrix} \text{between groups} \\ \text{variability} \end{bmatrix} \quad \begin{bmatrix} \text{within groups} \\ \text{variability} \end{bmatrix}$$

Partition of the total sum of squares

The partition of the total sum of squares divides the total variability among the scores into between groups and within groups components.

The following are the values of the total, between and within sums of squares in the current data set:

$$SS_{total} = \sum (X - M)^2$$
$$= (10 - 11.06)^2 + (9 - 11.06)^2 + \ldots + (12 - 11.06)^2$$
$$= 786.820$$

$$SS_{between} = \sum (M_j - M)^2$$
$$= 10^* (8.00 - 11.06)^2 + 10(7.90 - 11.06)^2 + \ldots + 10(13.00 - 11.06)^2$$
$$= 351.520$$

$$SS_{within} = \sum (X - M_j)^2$$
$$= (10 - 8.00)^2 + \ldots + (12 - 13.00)^2$$
$$= 435.30$$

* The multiplier 10 in the second calculation is the number of participants in each group: each individual's score is contributed to by the deviation of their group mean from the grand mean, and that deviation is the same for every member of that particular group.

The one-way ANOVA can be represented schematically as shown in Figure 2. (In other kinds of ANOVA, the total sum of squares is partitioned differently, sometimes in quite complex ways.)

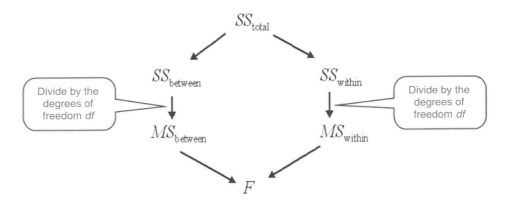

Figure 2. Schematic picture of the one-way ANOVA

7.1.3.4   Degrees of freedom of the total, between and within sums of squares

Since there are 50 scores, the degrees of freedom of the total sum of squares is 49 (i.e. 50 – 1) because, of the 50 deviations from the grand mean, only 49 are free to vary independently. Although there are also fifty terms in the between groups sum of squares, there are only five *different* treatment means and the values of four of their deviations from the grand mean fully determine the value of the remaining deviation. The degrees of freedom of the between groups sum of squares is therefore $5 - 1 = 4$. Turning now to the within group sum of squares, there are 10 scores in each group, but only 9 of their deviations about their group mean are free to vary independently. Over the entire data set, therefore, deviations about the group means have $5 \times 9 = 45$ degrees of freedom.

It is worth noting that the total degrees of freedom can also be partitioned in the manner of the total sum of squares:

$$df_{total} = df_{between} + df_{within} \quad \text{- - - (7)}$$

Partition of the total degrees of freedom

In ANOVA, much of what is true of the sums of squares is true also of the degrees of freedom. A knowledge of the degrees of freedom of the various sources of variance, therefore, is of great assistance when one is interpreting the SPSS output for more complex ANOVA designs.

7.1.3.5   The Mean Squares and the F statistic

The between and within groups mean squares are obtained from their respective sums of squares by dividing them by their respective degrees of freedom. The F statistic is the between groups mean square divided by the within groups mean square:

$$MS_{between} = \frac{SS_{between}}{df_{between}} = \frac{351.520}{4} = 87.880$$

$$MS_{within} = \frac{SS_{within}}{df_{within}} = \frac{435.30}{45} = 9.673$$

$$F = \frac{MS_{between}}{MS_{within}} = \frac{87.880}{9.673} = 9.09$$

7.1.3.6   Testing F for significance

The value of F that we have calculated from the data (9.09) is nine times the expected value of F under the null hypothesis, which is about 1. But is this value of F large enough for us to be able to reject H_0?

Suppose that the null hypothesis is true and that our drug experiment were to be repeated many times. Through sampling error, we can expect very large values of F (much greater than 9.09) to occur occasionally. The distribution of F is known as its **sampling distribution**. To make a test of significance, we must locate our obtained value within the sampling distribution of F so that we can determine its **p-value**, that is, the probability, under the null hypothesis, of obtaining a value at least as extreme as the one we obtained.

7.1.3.7   Parameters of the F distribution

To specify a particular F distribution, we must assign values to its **parameters**.

The F distribution has *two* parameters:

1.   The degrees of freedom of the between groups mean square $df_{between}$;
2.   The degrees of freedom of the within groups mean square df_{within} .

An F distribution is positively skewed, with a long tail to the right (Figure 3). In our own example, in order to make a test of the null hypothesis that, in the population, all five means have the same value, we must refer specifically to the F distribution with 4 and 45 degrees of freedom, which we shall denote with the expression: $F(4, 45)$.

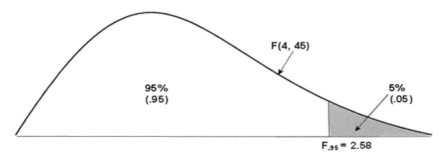

95th percentile of F distribution

Figure 3. Distribution of F with 4 and 45 degrees of freedom. The critical value of F (2.58) is the 95th percentile of this distribution

7.1.3.8   The critical region and the critical value of F

Since a variance, which is the sum of squared deviations, cannot have a negative value, the value of F cannot be less than zero. On the other hand, F has no upper limit. Since only large values of F cast doubt upon the null hypothesis, we shall be looking only at the *upper* tail of the distribution of F.

It can be seen from Figure 3 that, under the null hypothesis, only 5% of values in the distribution of $F(4, 45)$ have values as great as 2.58. Our obtained value of F, 9.09, greatly exceeds this critical value; in fact, fewer than 1% of values of F are as large as this.

The *p*-value of 9.09 (made available by editing the SPSS output) is 0.000018, which is very small indeed. The null hypothesis of equality of the treatment means is therefore rejected.

7.1.3.9   The ANOVA summary table

It is useful for the researcher to have what is known as a **summary table**, which includes, not only the value of F, but also the between groups and within groups sums of squares and mean squares, with their respective degrees of freedom. The ANOVA summary table is not usually included in the body of a research paper; nevertheless, the full summary table, which is included in the SPSS output, is a valuable source of information about the results of the analysis.

Table 2 shows the ANOVA summary table for our present example.

Table 2. The ANOVA Summary Table					
	Sum of squares	df	Mean square	F	p-value*
Between groups	351.520	4	87.880	9.085	< 0.01
Within groups	435.30	45	9.673		
Total	786.820	49			
*SPSS calls the *p*-value 'Sig.'					

7.2   THE ONE-WAY ANOVA (COMPARE MEANS MENU)

There are several ways of running a one-way ANOVA on SPSS. The easiest method is to select an option in the **Compare Means** menu (Figure 4).

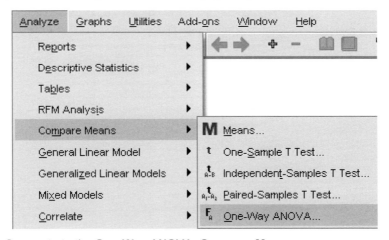

Figure 4. One route to the **One-Way ANOVA: Compare Means** menu

7.2.1   Entering the data

In **Variable View**, as with the independent samples *t* test, you will need to define two variables:

1. A variable with a name such as Score, which contains all the scores in the data set. This is the dependent variable. It can be given a more informative variable label, such as Performance Score.
2. A grouping variable with a simple variable name such as Group or Drug, which identifies the condition under which a score was achieved. (The grouping variable should also be given a more meaningful variable label such as Drug Condition, which will appear in the output.)

The grouping variable will consist of five values (one for the placebo condition and one for each of the four drugs). We shall arbitrarily assign value labels thus: 1 = Placebo; 2 = Drug A; 3 = Drug B; 4 = Drug C; 5 = Drug D. The captions attached to the numerical values are known as **value labels** and are assigned by making entries in the **Values** column in Variable View.

Proceed as follows:

- Open **Variable View** first and amend the settings so that when you enter **Data View**, your variables will already have been labelled and the scores will appear without unnecessary decimals. When you are working in **Data View**, you will have the option of displaying the value labels of your grouping variable, either by checking **Value Labels** in the **View** menu or by clicking on the easily-identifiable **label icon** (it looks like a suitcase label) at the top of the window.

- In the **Values** column, assign clear value labels to the code numbers you have chosen for grouping variables (Figure 5). When you are typing data into **Data View**, having the value labels available can help you to avoid transcription errors.

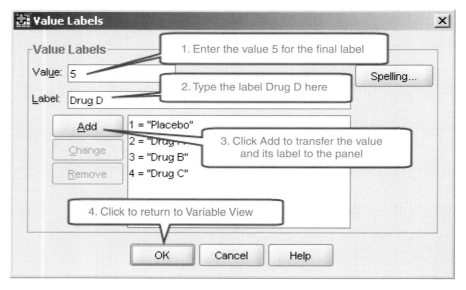

Figure 5. Assigning value labels to the code numbers making up the grouping variable. The figure shows the last label being assigned to the value 5

- Set **Decimals** to zero for both variables: we want to see integers only in Data View.

- In the **Measure** column of **Variable View**, specify the level of measurement of your grouping variable, which is at the nominal level of measurement (Figure 6). (The values that we have assigned are quite arbitrary and serve merely as numerical labels for the five different treatment conditions.)

	Name	Type	Width	Decimals	Label	Values	Missing	Columns	Align	Measure
1	Group	Numeric	8	0	Drug Condition	{1, Placebo}...	None	8	Right	Nominal
2	Score	Numeric	8	0		None	None	8	Right	Scale

Figure 6. The completed **Variable View** window, specifying the nominal level of measurement for the grouping variable Drug Condition

Notice that in Figure 6, the variable label for the dependent variable has been omitted. This means that in the SPSS output, the variable name Score will appear; whereas the grouping variable will appear under its full variable label Drug Condition.

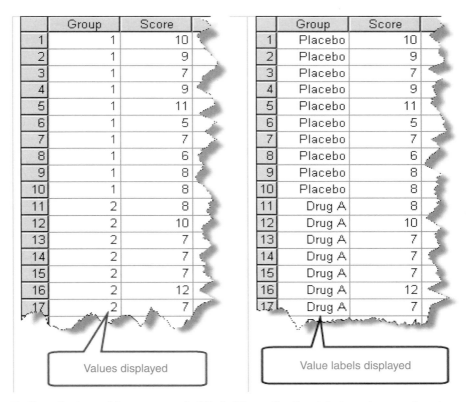

Figure 7. Two displays of the same part of **Data View** after the data have been entered: on the left, in the Group column, the values are shown; on the right, in the same column, the value labels are shown

Having prepared the ground in this way while in **Variable View**, you will find that when you enter **Data View**, the names of the variables appear at the heads of the first two columns. When you type in the values of the grouping variable, you can view their labels by checking the **Value Labels** option in the **View** menu or by clicking the ![icon] icon. Figure 7 shows the same part of **Data View** after the data have been entered, with and without value labels.

7.2.2   Running the one-way ANOVA

Click **Compare Means** to open the **One-Way ANOVA** dialog box (Figure 8). The basic ANOVA can be requested very easily as shown. Click **OK** to run the ANOVA.

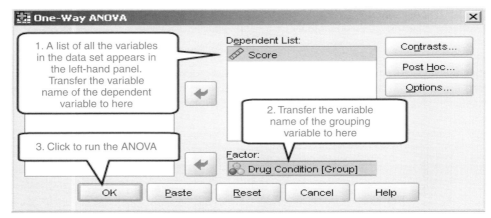

Figure 8. Completing the **One-Way ANOVA** dialog box

7.2.3   The output

In the **ANOVA summary table** (Output 1), the values of F, the SS, the MS and df are the same as those we calculated earlier. Confirm also that the values in the **Mean Square** column are the **Between Groups** and **Within Groups** sums of squares divided by their respective degrees of freedom. The value of F has been obtained by dividing the **Between Groups** mean square by the **Within Groups** mean square.

In the df column, confirm that, as we showed earlier, the between groups sum of squares has 4 degrees of freedom and the within groups sum of squares has 45 degrees of freedom.

Notice that in Output 1, the p-value is given as .000. The exact p-value can be obtained by double-clicking on the ANOVA table in the output, choosing **Cell Properties** and resetting the number of decimal places to a higher value. We stress that a p-value should never be reported as it appears in Output 1: write, '$p < 0.01$' or (in this case) '$p < .001$' .

ANOVA

Score

	Sum of Squares	df	Mean Square	F	Sig.
Between Groups	351.52	4	87.88	9.08	.000
Within Groups	435.30	45	9.67		
Total	786.82	49			

Notice that the Total Sum of Squares is the sum of the Between Groups and Within Groups values

The associated p-value for F is <.01 (i.e. significant at the .01 level). Write it as 'p<.01'

Output 1. The **One-way ANOVA** summary table

7.2.4   Effect size

Several measures of effect size for use with the ANOVA have been proposed, the earliest of which was a statistic known as **eta squared** (η^2), where eta is known as the **correlation ratio**.

7.2.4.1   Eta and eta squared

The eta squared statistic is the between groups sum of squares divided by the total sum of squares:

$$\eta^2 = \frac{SS_{between}}{SS_{total}} = \frac{SS_{between}}{SS_{between} + SS_{within}} \quad \text{- - - (8)}$$

Eta squared

It can readily be seen from the partition of the total sum of squares that eta squared is the proportion of the total variability (as measured by the total sum of squares) that is accounted for by differences among the sample means.

Using the values in the ANOVA summary table (Output 1), we have

$$\eta^2 = \frac{351.520}{786.820} = .447$$

the square root of which (the value of the correlation ratio itself) is:

$$\eta = \sqrt{\frac{SS_{between}}{SS_{between} + SS_{within}}} = \sqrt{.447} = .67$$

The term **correlation ratio** is not particularly transparent. Eta, however, is indeed, as we have just seen, a ratio. Moreoever, the statistic is also a correlation. If each of the fifty scores in our data set is paired with its group mean, the correlation between the scores and the group means has the value of eta. You can confirm this very easily and quickly by using the **Aggregate** command in the **Data** menu to place, opposite each score in Data View, its group mean. (Use the grouping variable as the **break variable**.) You will find that the **Pearson correlation** between the column of scores and the column of means is .66840, the square of which is .447, the value of eta squared, as calculated above.

The Pearson correlation (Chapter 11) was designed as a measure of a supposed linear relationship between two scale or continuous variables. In this special situation, however, you will notice that the value of the correlation is unaffected by the ordering of the groups, which are identified by arbitrary code numbers. Eta can be regarded as a **function-free correlation** expressing the total regression (linear and curvilinear) of the scores upon the treatments, which are represented as arbitrary code numbers. For reasons that will be fully explained in Chapter 12, eta squared can also be symbolised as R^2 and is referred to as such in the SPSS output. This is because eta is, in fact, a **multiple correlation coefficient**. A multiple correlation is the Pearson correlation between predictions from regression and the target variable. In this case, the target variable is the set of raw scores. The predictors are grouping variables carrying information about group membership. Multiple regression of the scores upon the grouping variables will predict, as the estimate of each score, its group mean.

Thus the multiple correlation coefficient (eta) is the correlation between the scores and their group means, which explains why eta cannot have a negative value.

7.2.4.2   Bias in eta squared

As measures of effect size, the statistics eta and eta squared are purely descriptive of the data set in hand. As estimates of effect size in the population, however, they are positively biased. We shall see when we investigate the use of the **General Linear Model (GLM)** procedure to run the one-way ANOVA, that in the output a statistic called **adjusted R^2** appears. This is a better estimate of effect size than the unadjusted values of eta and eta squared, because it incorporates an adjustment for the positive bias in eta squared. Adjusted R^2, however, is relevant only to the one-way ANOVA. For some ANOVA designs with more than one treatment factor, the statistic known as **omega squared** $\hat{\omega}^2$ (see Section 7.2.4.5) can be calculated. While omega squared also incorporates a correction for positive bias, however, there are ANOVA designs for which the calculation of that statistic is difficult or impossible. The omega squared statistic is not an option in SPSS.

In the following section, where the term eta squared appears, we shall be referring to effect size *in the population*, rather than the positively biased estimate calculated from the statistics of any particular data set.

7.2.4.3   Cohen's f statistic

Cohen (1988) suggested another measure of effect size which he called f. While eta squared estimates the variance of the population treatment means as a proportion of the total variance, that is, the variance of the population means plus error, Cohen's f estimates the ratio of the standard deviation of the population treatment means to the error standard deviation. Since both statistics are defined in terms of exactly the same parameters, one can readily be transformed to the other and vice versa:

$$\eta^2 = \frac{f^2}{1 + f^2}$$

$$\eta = \sqrt{\frac{f^2}{1 + f^2}} \qquad \text{- - - (9)}$$

$$f = \sqrt{\frac{\eta^2}{1 - \eta^2}}$$

Relation between Cohen's f, eta and eta squared

We have found that for the results of the drug experiment, the value of eta squared is .447. Assuming that this is the best estimate of effect size available, we substitute this value into formula (9) to obtain

$$f = \sqrt{\frac{.447}{1 - .447}} = .90$$

Cohen (1988) has offered guidelines for the interpretation of values of his own statistic *f* and equivalent values of eta squared (both defined in terms of population parameters). His guidelines are interpreted in Table 3 below.

Table 3.   Guidelines for assessing values of eta squared (or bias-corrected measures such as omega squared) and the equivalent values of Cohen's *f*.

Size of Effect	Eta squared	Cohen's *f*
Small	$0.01 \leq \eta^2 < 0.06$	$0.10 \leq f < 0.25$
Medium	$0.06 \leq \eta^2 < 0.14$	$0.25 \leq f < 0.40$
Large	$\eta^2 \geq 0.14$	$f \geq 0.40$

Since our obtained value for eta squared is .45, the treatment factor of Drug Condition can be said to have had a 'large' effect. Since several treatments were involved, however, this fact conveys a limited amount of information.   Did all four drugs have an effect or just some of them? How large were the effects of the different drugs considered individually? We shall return to the question of effect size when we consider the making of comparisons among the individual treatment means.

The value of omega squared can be calculated directly from the value of F by means of the following formula:

$$\hat{\omega}^2 = \frac{(k-1)(F-1)}{(k-1)(F-1)+kn} \quad \text{--- (10) \textbf{Omega squared}}$$

where *k* is the number of treatment groups, and *n* is the number of participants in each group. Substituting the values given in Output 1 into formula (10), we have

$$\hat{\omega}^2 = \frac{(5-1)(9.085-1)}{(5-1)(9.085-1)+50} = .39$$

Notice that the value of omega squared is less than that of eta squared, because it corrects for positive bias.

The square root of the omega squared statistic can be viewed as an estimate of the correlation ratio in the population and, as such, is an improvement upon the sample value of eta.   The value of omega squared can be interpreted by using the ranges of values for eta squared given in Table 3.

In Chapter 6, the reader was advised never to present the results of a statistical test without also giving the descriptives, either in the same paragraph or in a nearby table on the same page. We would urge that this rule should be followed a fortiori with reports of the results of ANOVA, where the absence of the descriptives makes a bald statement of the test results even more opaque. The fact that F is significant gives no indication of where the difference or differences among an array of means might lie.

Even if F is significant and it seems clear from the descriptives that only a few of the differences are large enough to account for the significant value of F, further follow-up tests are necessary to confirm these impressions. We shall discuss such tests later in the chapter. For now, we suggest that a report of the results of the one-way ANOVA might begin as follows:

> The mean performance level for the placebo was M = 8.00 (SD = 1.83) and for the four drug conditions A, B, C and D, the means were M = 7.90 (SD = 2.13); M = 12.00 (SD = 2.49); M = 14.40 (SD = 4.50); M = 13.00 (SD = 3.74), respectively. The one-way ANOVA showed F to be significant beyond the .01 level: $F(4, 45) = 9.08$; p <.01. Eta is .67 which, according to Cohen's (1988) classification, is a 'large' effect.

7.2.6   The two-group case: equivalence of F and t

Since the one-way ANOVA is a technique which enables us to test the null hypothesis of equality of treatment means, it is natural to consider its application to data from an experiment with only two groups, as when we are comparing the performance of a group performing under an active or experimental condition with that of a comparison or control group. In Chapter 6, we saw that the null hypothesis of equality in the population of the two group means could be tested by using an independent-samples t test. Would the one-way ANOVA lead to the same decision about the null hypothesis as the independent-samples t test? In fact, it would.

In Chapter 6, we compared the mean level of performance of a group of 20 participants who had ingested a dose of caffeine (the Caffeine group) with that of another group of 20 participants who had ingested a neutral saline solution (the Placebo group). An analysis of the complete data set (including the two outliers), shows that the Caffeine group (Mean 11.90, SD 3.28) outperformed the Placebo group (Mean 9.25, SD 3.16). The independent-samples t test confirms that there is a significant difference between the mean levels of performance for the Drug and Placebo groups: $t(38) = 2.604$; $p = 0.013$. (Here we have given the p-value to three places of decimals for the purposes of comparison later.)

If a one-way ANOVA is run on the same data set, the summary table appears as in Table 4.

Table 4. Summary table of the ANOVA of the data from the two-group Caffeine experiment					
	Sum of squares	df	Mean square	F	p-value
Between groups	70.225	1	70.225	6.781	0.013
Within groups	393.550	38	10.357		
Total	463.775	39			

The p-value from the ANOVA is exactly the same as the p-value from the t test: the two tests lead to exactly the same decision about the null hypothesis. Notice also that $F = 6.781$. This value is the square of the value of t: thus $2.6042^2 = 6.781$. The t distribution has a mean of zero and an infinite range of values in the positive and negative directions. The distribution of t^2, however, has a minimum value of zero and an infinite range of values in the positive direction only. It can be shown the square of the distribution of t on 38 degrees of freedom is distributed as $F(1, 38)$. In general,

$$t^2\left(df\right) = F\left(1, \ df\right) \ \text{- - - (11)}$$

Relation between t and F
in the special case of two groups

Note also that the p-value of F is equal to the *two-tailed* p-value of t: thus, although the critical region of F lies in the upper tail of the distribution only, a sufficiently large difference between the means in *either* direction will result in a large positive value of F.

7.3   THE ONE-WAY ANOVA (GLM MENU)

The **General Linear Model** (GLM) menu offers, in addition to the basic one-way ANOVA, many more statistics, including measures of effect size (eta squared and partial eta squared), as well as other important techniques, such as **Analysis of covariance (ANCOVA)**. In this subsection, we shall describe how to run the one-way ANOVA in GLM. The GLM dialog assumes that the user is familiar with some technical terms that do not appear in the One-Way ANOVA dialog.

The preparation of the data in the **Data Editor** for **GLM**, we should note, is exactly as it was for the ANOVA in **Compare Means**.

7.3.1   Factors with fixed and random effects

The selection of experimental conditions for an experiment is usually driven either by theory or by the need to resolve some practical issue. A factor consisting of a set of theoretically-determined conditions is said to have **fixed effects**. Most factors in experimental research are fixed effects factors.

There are occasions, however, on which the conditions making up a factor can be viewed as a random sample from a large (perhaps infinitely large) pool of possible conditions. In research on reading skills, for example, an investigator studying the effects of sentence length upon passage readability may select or prepare some passages which vary systematically in sentence length. With such a procedure, however, reading performance may reflect passage properties other than sentence length; moreover, these additional properties cannot be expected to remain the same from passage to passage. The effects of using different passages should, arguably, be included as a factor in the analysis, even though the experimenter is not primarily interested in this nuisance variable. Since passage characteristics other than average sentence length can be viewed as a random sample from a pool of possible conditions, the passage factor is said to have **random effects**. Factors with random effects arise more commonly in applied, correlational research and their presence has important implications for the analysis.

7.3.2   The analysis of covariance (ANCOVA)

A **covariate** is a variable which, because it can be expected to correlate (i.e. 'co-vary') with the DV, is likely to add to the variability (or 'noisiness') of the data and inflate the error term, resulting in a reduction of the power of the statistical test to reject the null hypothesis. An obvious example of a covariate is IQ, which can be expected to correlate substantially with almost any measure of cognitive or skilled performance and add considerably to the 'noisiness' of the data.

The **analysis of covariance** (**ANCOVA**) is a technique whereby the effects of a covariate upon the DV are removed from the data, thus reducing error and increasing the power of the *F* test. The manner in which this is achieved is described in statistical texts such as Winer, Brown & Michels (1991) and Keppel & Wickens (2004).

7.3.3   Univariate versus multivariate statistical tests

In all the experiments we have considered so far, there has been a single DV. In the current example, the DV is the score a participant achieves on a task. The one-way ANOVA and the *t test* are **univariate tests**, because they were designed for the analysis of data from experiments with a single DV. If, however, we had also recorded the time the participant took to complete the task, there would have been two DVs. **Multivariate tests** are techniques designed for the analysis of data from experiments with two or more DVs. An example of a multivariate technique is **Multivariate Analysis of Variance (MANOVA)**, which is a generalisation of the univariate ANOVA to the analysis of data from experiments with several DVs. This technique is described and illustrated in Chapter 10 (Section 10.4).

7.3.4   The one-way ANOVA with GLM

The **General Linear Model** (GLM) menu is shown in Figure 9. The **Univariate** option is clearly appropriate for our example, since there is only one dependent variable.

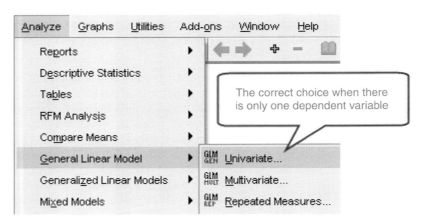

Figure 9. The **General Linear Model** menu

In this section, we shall use **GLM** to run the basic one-way ANOVA only, so that we can compare the output with the **Compare Means** One-Way ANOVA summary table. Proceed as follows:

- Choose **Analyze➔General Linear Model➔Univariate...** to open the **Univariate** dialog box (the completed box is shown in Figure 10).
- As before, the left panel of the dialog box will contain a list of all the variables in the data set. Transfer the variable labels as shown in Figure 10. In our example, the Drug Condition factor has fixed effects, since its levels were selected systematically.
- Click **OK** to run the basic one-way ANOVA.

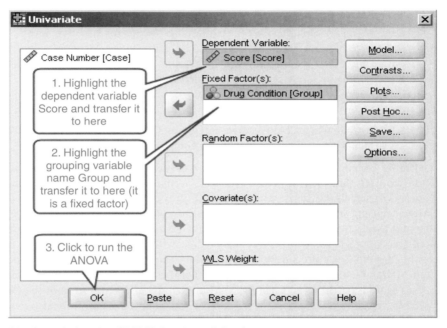

Figure 10. Completing the **GLM Univariate** dialog box

7.3.5   The GLM output

7.3.5.1   Design specifications

The GLM output includes a table of design specifications. These should be checked to make sure that you have communicated the experimental design correctly to SPSS. Output 2 shows the specifications of the independent variable, the Drug Condition factor.

Between-Subjects Factors

		Value Label	N
Drug Condition	1	Placebo	10
	2	Drug A	10
	3	Drug B	10
	4	Drug C	10
	5	Drug D	10

Output 2. Design specifications: the values and value labels of the grouping variable Drug Condition

Check this table to make sure that SPSS agrees that the factor has five levels, that 10 participants were tested at each level and that the code numbers are correctly paired with the five conditions. Incorrect specifications in **Variable View** can emerge at this point. Transcription errors in **Data View** could result in incorrect entries in the N column.

7.3.5.2   The ANOVA summary table

The **GLM ANOVA** summary table is shown in Output 3, with the table from the **Compare Means One-Way ANOVA** procedure below it for comparison.

The GLM table contains some additional terms: **Corrected Model, Intercept, Corrected Total** and **Type III Sum of Squares**. These are terms from another statistical technique called **regression**, which is discussed in Chapter 12. It is quite possible to recast the one-way ANOVA (or, indeed, *any* ANOVA) as a problem in regression and make exactly the same test of the null hypothesis. If that is done (as in the GLM procedure), the mean squares, their degrees of freedom, the value of *F* and the *p*-value will all be exactly the same as those produced by the ANOVA procedure. In the GLM summary table, the rows labelled as **Corrected Model, Group, Error** and **Corrected Total** contain exactly the same information that we shall find in the **Between Groups, Within Groups** and **Total** rows of the One-Way ANOVA table reproduced underneath it for comparison. The values of *F* are also exactly the same in both tables.

Output 3 contains yet another item that is missing from the table we obtained from the **One-Way** procedure in **Compare Means** (Output 1). Underneath the table is the information that **R Squared** (that is, η^2) = .447 and **Adjusted R Squared** = .398. As a measure of effect size in the report, adjusted R squared is the better statistic to report, because it incorporates a correction for bias.

Univariate Analysis of Variance

Tests of Between-Subjects Effects

Dependent Variable: Score

Source	Type III Sum of Squares	df	Mean Square	F	Sig.
Corrected Model	351.52[a]	4	87.88	9.08	.000
Intercept	6116.18	1	6116.18	632.27	.000
Group	351.52	4	87.88	9.08	.000
Error	435.30	45	9.67		
Total	6903.00	50			
Corrected Total	786.82	49			

a. R Squared = .447 (Adjusted R Squared = .398)

Oneway

The sums of squares in the grey area have the same values in both tables. The corrected total sum of squares in the GLM table is the same as the total in the ANOVA table.

The values of *F* are the same

ANOVA

Score

	Sum of Squares	df	Mean Square	F	Sig.
Between Groups	351.52	4	87.88	9.08	.000
Within Groups	435.30	45	9.67		
Total	786.82	49			

Output 3. Comparison of the **Univariate ANOVA** summary table from the **GLM** menu (upper panel) with the **One-Way ANOVA** summary table from the **Compare Means** menu (lower panel).

7.3.6   Requesting additional items

The basic ANOVA output includes little other than the ANOVA summary table. We shall require several other statistics, which can be selected from the GLM **Univariate** dialog box (Figure 10). For clarity, we shall consider these measures separately here; but they would normally be requested along with the basic ANOVA. Among the items we shall select are the **descriptive statistics** (including the means and standard deviations for the five conditions in the experiment), **homogeneity tests** (testing the assumption of homogeneity of variance among the levels of the DV), **estimates of effect size** and a **profile plot** (a line graph of the treatment means). These are obtained by making the appropriate responses in the **Univariate** dialog box.

The first three recommended options are obtained by clicking **Options…** in the **Univariate** dialog box (Figure 10) to open the **Options** dialog box (Figure 11).

When the box labelled **Estimates of effect size** is checked in **Options**, the ANOVA summary table will include **partial eta squared (η_p^2)** which, in the context of the one-way ANOVA, is identical with eta squared (R^2 in Output 3). You may wish to confirm that when the **Estimates of effect size** box is checked, the output will give the value of partial eta squared as .447.

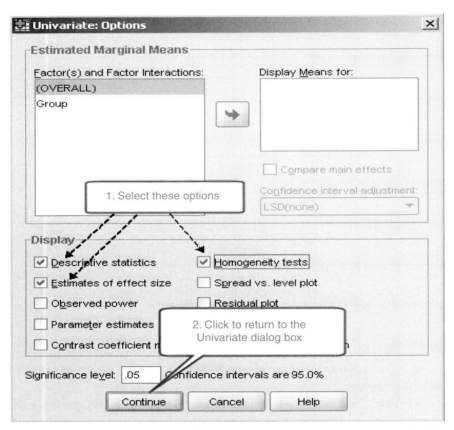

Figure 11.   The **Options** dialog box with **Descriptive statistics**, **Estimates of effect size** and **Homogeneity tests** selected

Click **Plots…** (Figure 10) to open the **Profile Plots** dialog box (Figure 12) and follow the procedure shown in Figure 12.

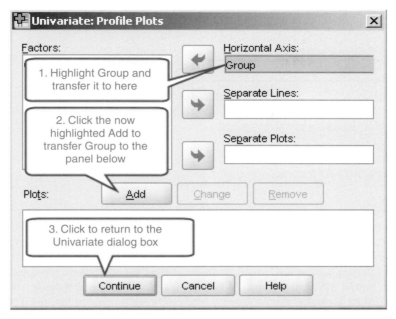

Figure 12. Requesting a **Profile Plot** of the means

7.3.7   Additional output from GLM

7.3.7.1   Descriptive statistics

Output 4 tabulates the requested **Descriptive statistics**.

Descriptive Statistics

Dependent Variable:Score

Drug ...	Mean	Std. Deviation	N
Placebo	8.00	1.826	10
Drug A	7.90	2.132	10
Drug B	12.00	2.494	10
Drug C	14.40	4.502	10
Drug D	13.00	3.742	10
Total	11.06	4.007	50

Output 4. The **Descriptive Statistics** output: means and standard deviations for the five groups

7.3.7.2   The Levene test

Output 5 shows the result of Levene's test for homogeneity of variance.

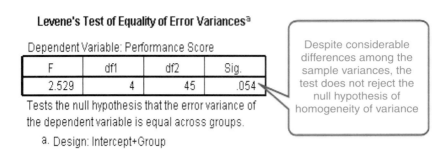

Levene's Test of Equality of Error Variances[a]

Dependent Variable: Performance Score

F	df1	df2	Sig.
2.529	4	45	.054

Tests the null hypothesis that the error variance of the dependent variable is equal across groups.

a. Design: Intercept+Group

Despite considerable differences among the sample variances, the test does not reject the null hypothesis of homogeneity of variance

Output 5. **Levene's Test** for homogeneity of variance

The non-significance of the **Levene F Statistic** for the test of equality of error variances (homogeneity of variances) indicates that the assumption of homogeneity of variance is tenable; however, considerable differences among the variances are apparent from inspection. The one-way ANOVA is to some extent robust to violations of the assumption of homogeneity of variance, especially when, as in the present example, there are equal numbers of observations in the different groups. When there are marked differences in sample size from group to group, however, this robustness tends to break down and the true Type I error rate may increase to an unacceptable level. We shall return to this matter later, in Section 7.4.1.1.

7.3.7.3   The profile plot of the means

The requested profile plot of the means is shown in Output 6. Observe that the zero point of the vertical scale does not appear on the axis. This is something that still happens in default profile plots on SPSS. Always be suspicious of such a graph, because it can give the appearance of a strong effect when actually there is very little happening. The difficulty can easily be remedied by double-clicking on the graph to bring it into the **Chart Editor**, double-clicking on the vertical axis and specifying zero as the minimum point on the vertical scale (Output 7).

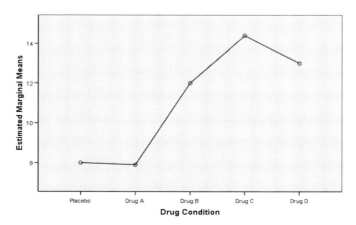

Output 6. The plot of the means as originally shown in SPSS output

In this case, although the profile plot has flattened somewhat, unequal levels of performance among the groups are still evident. The effect of including the zero point on the vertical scale, however, can sometimes be quite dramatic: with some data sets, an exciting-looking range of peaks suddenly becomes a featureless plain. In this case, however, it is clear that even when the zero point is shown on the vertical axis, something is really happening in this data set.

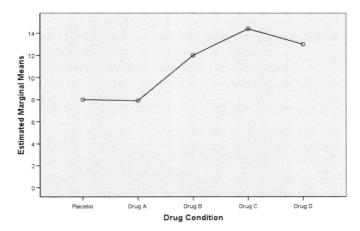

Output 7. The plot of the means with the ordinate scale now including zero

It is important to be clear that the profile plot in Output 7 is not to be seen as depicting a functional relationship between the five conditions in the experiment and the mean scores: the five conditions making up the single factor in the experimental design are *qualitative* categories, which have no intrinsic order. The results of the ANOVA would be exactly the same were we to rearrange the data so that, in the Score column in Data View, the scores obtained under Drug C followed those for the Placebo condition; in fact, *any* ordering of the data from the five conditions in the **Data Editor** would produce exactly the same result from the ANOVA. What we learn from the profile plot in Output 7 is that there are marked differences among the five group means and we can expect this to be reflected in the value of *F*. The more mountainous the profile of means, the more reason we have to doubt the null hypothesis of equality.

7.3.7.4   Report of the primary analysis

The report of the primary analysis (enhanced by the addition of measures of effect size) might read as follows:

> The mean performance level for the placebo was M = 8.00 (SD = 1.83) and for the four drug conditions A, B, C and D, the means were M = 7.90 (SD = 2.13); M = 12.00 (SD = 2.49); M = 14.40 (SD = 4.50); M = 13.00 (SD = 3.742), respectively. The one-way ANOVA showed *F* to be significant beyond the .01 level: $F(4, 45) = 9.08$; $p < .01$. Estimated omega squared = .39. Adjusted eta squared = .40 . These values are Large effects in Cohen's system.

Notice that the omega squared and adjusted eta squared statistics have very similar values.

7.4   MAKING COMPARISONS AMONG THE TREATMENT MEANS

We have found evidence against the null hypothesis (H_0: All five means in the population have the same value) but what can we conclude from this? If H_0 states that all the means are equal, the alternative hypothesis is simply that they are not all equal. The falsity of H_0, however, does not imply that the difference between any and every pair of group means is significant. If the ANOVA F test is significant, there should be at least one difference *somewhere* among the means; but we cannot claim that the mean for any particular group is significantly different from the mean of any other group. Further analysis is necessary to confirm whatever differences there may appear to be among the individual treatment means. In this section, we shall describe some methods for testing comparisons among the group means.

7.4.1   Planned and unplanned comparisons

Before running an experiment such as the one in our current example, the experimenter may have some very specific questions in mind. It might be expected, for example (perhaps on theoretical grounds), that the mean score of every group who have ingested one of the drugs will be greater than the mean score of the Placebo group. This expectation would be tested by comparing each drug group with the Placebo group. Perhaps, on the other hand, the experimenter has theoretical reasons to suspect that Drugs A and B should enhance performance, but Drugs C and D should not. That hypothesis could be tested by comparing the Placebo mean with the average score for groups A and B combined and with the average score for groups B and C combined. These are examples of **planned comparisons**.

Often, however, the experimenter, perhaps because the field has been little explored, has only a sketchy idea of how the results will turn out. There may be good reason to expect that *some* of the drugs will enhance performance; but it may not be possible, a priori, to be more specific. Unplanned, or **post hoc**, comparisons are part of the 'data-snooping' that inevitably follows the initial analysis of variance.

7.4.1.1   The per comparison and familywise Type I error rates

When we use the t test to compare two means, the significance level α is the probability of a Type I error, that is, the rejection of the null hypothesis when it is actually true. When, however, we intend to make several comparisons among a group of means, we must distinguish between the individual comparison and the whole set, or **family**, of comparisons that we intend to make. It can be shown that if we make a set of comparisons, the probability, under the null hypothesis, of *at least one* of them being significant may be considerably greater than α. We must, therefore, distinguish between the Type I error rate **per comparison** (α) and the **familywise** Type I error rate (α_{family}). If we intend to make c comparisons, the **familywise** Type I error rate can be shown to be approximately $c\alpha$

$$\alpha_{family} \approx c\alpha \quad - - - (12)$$

The familywise Type I error rate

It is clear from equation (12) that, when the researcher is making many comparisons among the treatment means of data from complex experiments, the probability of at least one test showing significance can be very high: with a large array of treatment means, the probability of obtaining at least one significant difference might be .8, .9 or greater, even when there are no differences in the population at all! It is therefore essential to control the familywise Type I error rate by making data-snooping tests more conservative. Several procedures for doing this have been proposed.

7.4.1.2   The Bonferroni correction

Equation (12) is the basis of the **Bonferroni method** of controlling the familywise Type I error rate. If c is the number of comparisons in the family, the p-value for each test is multiplied by c. Alternatively, we can fix the alpha-rate per comparison at α/c. This procedure obviously makes the test of a comparison more conservative. For example, suppose that, having decided to make 4 comparisons, we were to make an ordinary t test of one comparison and find that the p-value is .04. In the Bonferroni procedure, we must now multiply this p-value by 4, obtaining .16, a value well above the desired familywise error rate of .05. We must, therefore, accept the null hypothesis (or, at any rate, not conclude that we have evidence to reject it). Alternatively, rather than set the per comparison significance level at .05, we could set it at .05/4 = .01, approximately. Our p-value of .04 is not small enough to justify rejection of the null hypothesis on this conservative test, because we must multiply it by four to maintain the per family Type I error rate at .05 .

It is common practice, following the running of an experiment with several different conditions, to make unplanned or **post hoc** multiple pairwise comparisons among the treatment means: that is, the difference between every possible pair of means is tested for significance. Here, the Bonferroni method can result in extremely conservative tests, because in this situation c (the size of the comparison family) is arguably the number of different pairs that can be drawn from the array of k treatment means; otherwise we risk capitalising upon chance and making false claims of differences among the population means.

The great problem with the Bonferroni correction is that when the array of means is large, the criterion for significance becomes so exacting that the method finds too few significant differences. In other words, the Bonferroni tests are conservative to the point that they may have very little power to reject the null hypothesis. The **Tukey** tests and the **Newman-Keuls** test are less conservative, the Tukey test itself (or a variant known as Tukey-b) being generally preferred for post hoc tests of pairwise differences following the one-way ANOVA. For more complex comparisons, such as the comparison of one mean with the mean of several others, the **Scheffé test** is highly regarded; but it is thought to be over-conservative when used for pairwise comparisons.

The situation may arise in which the researcher wishes to compare performance under each of several active conditions with that of a baseline control group. The **Dunnett test**, described in Howell (2007; p.374), is regarded as the most powerful test available for this purpose.

These tests (and many others) are available in SPSS. While several of them are also available in the One-Way procedure, we shall confine ourselves to GLM, which offers a better selection of options.

7.4.1.3   Unplanned or post hoc multiple comparisons with SPSS

Click **Post Hoc…** (Figure 10) to open the **Post Hoc** dialog box (Figure 13). Follow the directions in Figure 13 in order to run the **Bonferroni**, **Tukey** and **Dunnett** tests.

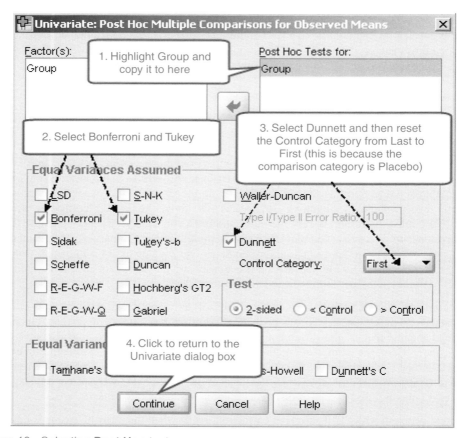

Figure 13. Selecting **Post Hoc** tests

Output 8 is only part of an extensive table of the results of multiple pairwise comparisons with the **Tukey**, **Bonferroni** and **Dunnett** tests. The most conservative test of the three, the Bonferroni, has the widest confidence intervals and the largest p-values; the least conservative test, the Dunnett test, which is the most powerful test, has the narrowest confidence intervals and the smallest p-values.

Output 9 shows a second part of the output for the **Tukey** test. The output shows that there are two subgroups of tests. Within each subgroup there are no significant pairwise differences; on the other hand, any member of either subgroup is significantly different from any member of the other subgroup. For example, there are no differences among Drugs B, C and D; but each of those is significantly different from both the Placebo and Drug A. In fact, of the four drugs tested, the only one not to produce an improvement over the Placebo was Drug A.

Multiple Comparisons

Dependent Variable: Score

	(I) Drug Condition	(J) Drug Condition	Mean Difference (I-J)	Std. Error	Sig.	95% Confidence Interval Lower Bound	95% Confidence Interval Upper Bound
Tukey HSD	Placebo	Drug A	.10	1.391	1.000	-3.85	4.05
		Drug B	-4.00*	1.391	.046	-7.95	-.05
		Drug C	-6.40*	1.391	.000	-10.35	-2.45
		Drug D	-5.00*	1.391	.007	-8.95	-1.05
Bonferroni	Placebo	Drug A	.10	1.391	1.000	-4.01	4.21
		Drug B	-4.00	1.391	.061	-8.11	.11
		Drug C	-6.40*	1.391	.000	-10.51	-2.29
		Drug D	-5.00*	1.391	.008	-9.11	-.89
	Drug A	Placebo	-.10	1.391	1.000	-4.21	4.01
		Drug C	-1.40	1.391	1.000	-5.51	2.71
Dunnett t (2-sided)a	Drug A	Placebo	-.10	1.391	1.000	-3.62	3.42
	Drug B	Placebo	4.00*	1.391	.021	.48	7.52
	Drug C	Placebo	6.40*	1.391	.000	2.88	9.92
	Drug D	Placebo	5.00*	1.391	.003	1.48	8.52

Based on observed means.

*. The mean difference is significant at the .05 level.

a. Dunnett t-tests treat one group as a control, and compare all other groups against it.

Output 8. Comparison of the outputs for the **Tukey**, **Bonferroni** and **Dunnett** tests

Homogeneous Subsets

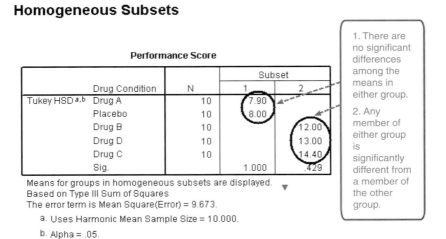

Performance Score

	Drug Condition	N	Subset 1	Subset 2
Tukey HSD a,b	Drug A	10	7.90	
	Placebo	10	8.00	
	Drug B	10		12.00
	Drug D	10		13.00
	Drug C	10		14.40
	Sig.		1.000	.429

Means for groups in homogeneous subsets are displayed.
Based on Type III Sum of Squares
The error term is Mean Square(Error) = 9.673.

a. Uses Harmonic Mean Sample Size = 10.000.

b. Alpha = .05.

1. There are no significant differences among the means in either group.

2. Any member of either group is significantly different from a member of the other group.

Output 9. The two subgroups of treatment means identified by the **Tukey** multiple comparisons test

We suggest your report of the results of the Tukey test might read as follows:

The Tukey HSD test was used to make pairwise comparisons among the individual treatment means, with the familywise significance level set at .05. The test confirmed the differences between the Placebo mean and those for Drugs B, C and D; but the difference between the Placebo and Drug A means is insignificant. The conservative p-values for the differences between the Plabeco mean and those for Drugs A, B, C and D are, respectively, 1.00, .046, < .001 and .007. The differences between the Placebo mean and those for Drugs B, C and D are 4.0, 6.4 and 5.0, respectively. If the population standard deviation is estimated as the square root of the within groups mean square (3.11), the values of Cohen's d statistic for the three differences are 1.29, 2.06 and 1.61, respectively. All these differences are 'large' in Cohen's classification.

To remind the reader of Cohen's guidelines for d, we reproduce Table 3 from Chapter 6 in Table 5 below.

Table 5. Cohen's categories of effect size		
Effect size (d)	**Size of Effect**	**In words, …**
$.2 \leq d < .5$	Small	Less than .2 is Trivial .2 to .5 is Small
$.5 \leq d < .8$	Medium	.5 to .8 is Medium
$d \geq .8$	Large	.8 or more is Large

7.4.2   Linear contrasts

We have data from a one-factor between subject experiment with five treatment groups. Let M_1, M_2, M_3, M_4 and M_5 be the mean performance levels for the Placebo, Drug A, Drug B, Drug C and Drug D conditions, respectively.

A comparison between two of an array of k treatment means (or combinations of the means) can be expressed as a **linear contrast**, that is, a linear sum of the five treatment means, with the constraint that the coefficients (weights) add up to zero. Suppose we want to compare M_1 with M_2. The difference $M_1 - M_2$ can be expressed as the linear contrast ψ_1, where

$$\psi_1 = (1)M_1 + (-1)M_2 + (0)M_3 + (0)M_4 + (0)M_5 \quad \text{- - - (13)}$$

A linear contrast

Since we are interested in comparing only two of the five means, the inclusion of all five means in equation (13) may seem highly artificial; but we need to develop a notation for a whole *set* of contrasts that might be made among a given set of treatment means. We must have the same number of terms in all contrasts, even if we have to have coefficients of zero for the irrelevant terms. In a situation such as our current example, in which there are five treatment means, one of which is a control or comparison, the researcher may wish to compare the control mean with each of the others. Such pairwise contrasts are known as **simple contrasts**. As in equation (13), the formulation of each of a set of simple contrasts must include all the treatments means, the irrelevant means having coefficients of zero:

$$M_2 - M_1 = (-1)M_1 + (+1)M_2 + (0)M_3 + (0)M_4 + (0)M_5$$
$$M_3 - M_1 = (-1)M_1 + (0)M_2 + (+1)M_3 + (0)M_4 + (0)M_5$$
$$M_4 - M_1 = (-1)M_1 + (0)M_2 + (0)M_3 + (+1)M_4 + (0)M_5$$
$$M_5 - M_1 = (-1)M_1 + (0)M_2 + (0)M_3 + (0)M_4 + (+1)M_5$$

This set of four simple contrasts can be represented more compactly by the four rows of coefficients alone:

$$\begin{pmatrix} -1 & +1 & 0 & 0 & 0 \\ -1 & 0 & +1 & 0 & 0 \\ -1 & 0 & 0 & +1 & 0 \\ -1 & 0 & 0 & 0 & +1 \end{pmatrix}$$

The same notation extends easily to more **complex contrasts**, that is, contrasts involving three or more treatment means. If we wish to compare M_3 with the mean of M_1 and M_2, the difference $M_3 - \dfrac{(M_1 + M_2)}{2}$ can be expressed as the complex linear contrast ψ_2, where

$$\psi_2 = (-0.5)M_1 + (-0.5)M_2 + (1)M_3 + (0)M_4 + (0)M_5 \quad \text{- - - (14)}$$

A complex linear contrast

It is worth bearing in mind that although in (14) three of the five treament means have non-zero coefficients, the contrast is between only *two* means: (1) M_3 and (2) a composite mean derived from M_1 and M_2. This has the important implication that a contrast sum of squares must always have one degree of freedom, however complex the contrast and however many means may be involved. We shall return to this point when we discuss the testing of contrasts for significance.

In general, for a set of k treatment means M_j, any contrast ψ can be represented as

$$\psi = \sum_j^k c_j M_j = c_1 M_1 + c_2 M_2 + \ldots + c_k M_k \quad \text{- - - (15)}$$

General equation for a linear contrast

where c_j is the coefficient of the treatment mean M_j and $\Sigma c_j = 0$. If there are k treatment means, there are k terms in the summation.

7.4.2.1   Sums of squares for contrasts

Associated with a particular contrast ψ is a sum of squares SS_ψ, the formula for which is

$$SS_\psi = \frac{n\psi^2}{\sum c_j^2} = \frac{n\left[\sum_j c_j M_j\right]^2}{\sum c_j^2} \quad \text{- - - (16)}$$

A contrast sum of squares

This sum of squares can be thought of as the variability of the scores that can be attributed to the difference between the two means (or composite means) that are being compared. The term $\sum_j c_j^2$ in the denominator acts as a scaling factor, ensuring that the sum of squares attributable to a particular contrast can be compared in magnitude with the ANOVA between groups mean square $SS_{between}$.

Table 6 shows the application of formula (16) to the first contrast that we considered (formula 13).

Table 6. Steps in calculating a contrast sum of squares					
	Placebo	**Drug A**	**Drug B**	**Drug C**	**Drug D**	
Mean	8.00	7.90	12.00	14.40	13.00	
c_j	1	−1	0	0	0	$\sum_j c_j^2 = 2$
$c_j M_j$	8.00	-7.90	0	0	0	$\sum_j c_j M_j = 0.10$

Substituting the values from Table 6 into formula 16, we have

$$\psi_1 = (1)M_1 + (-1)M_2 + (0)M_3 + (0)M_4 + (0)M_5 = 8.00 - 7.90 = 0.10$$

$$SS_1 = \frac{n\psi_1^2}{\sum c_j^2} = \frac{10(0.10^2)}{2} = .5$$

7.4.2.2   Testing a contrast for significance

A contrast is a comparison between two means. In this special two-group case, therefore, we can either make an independent samples t test to test the difference for significance or we can run a one-way ANOVA – the two procedures will produce the same decision about the null hypothesis. The value of F will be the square of the value of t; but the p-value will be the same for both statistics.

Since any contrast is a comparison between two means, a contrast sum of squares always has one degree of freedom. This means that, in this special case, the mean square has the same value as the sum of squares, so that

$$F_{contrast} = \frac{MS_{contrast}}{MS_{within}} = \frac{SS_{contrast}}{MS_{within}} \quad \text{- - - (17)}$$

_F_ ratio for a contrast

where the degrees of freedom of $F_{contrast}$ are 1 and df_{within}.

We can therefore make the test of the contrast in Table 6 with the statistic $F(1,45)$, where

$$F(1,45) = \frac{MS_1}{MS_{within}} = \frac{SS_1}{SS_{within}} = \frac{0.05}{9.673} = .005$$

Alternatively, we can make the test with $t(45)$, where t is the square root of F:

$$t(45) = \sqrt{F(1,45)} = \sqrt{0.005} = 0.07$$

The _p_-value of either statistic is 0.943.

Since SPSS gives the result of the t test rather than the F test, we should perhaps look a little more closely at the t test. In the equal-n case, the usual formula for the independent-samples t statistic is:

$$t = \frac{M_1 - M_2}{\sqrt{MS_{within}\left(\frac{1}{n} + \frac{1}{n}\right)}} = \frac{M_1 - M_2}{\sqrt{2MS_{within}/n}} \quad \text{- - - (18)}$$

Independent-samples _t_ statistic (equal n case)

When we are making a test of a contrast, the numerator of (18) is replaced by the value of the contrast, i.e., $\sum_j c_j M_j$. The denominator changes too, the constant 2 being replaced with $\sum_j c_j^2$. The t statistic for testing the contrast is therefore

$$t = \frac{\sum_j c_j M_j}{\sqrt{\sum_j c_j^2 MS_{within}/n}} \quad \text{- - - (19)}$$

The _t_ statistic for a contrast

Substituting the values we calculated in Table 6 into (19) and putting $MS_{within} = 9.673$, we have

$$t = \frac{0.10}{\sqrt{2 \times 9.673/10}} = 0.07$$

which is the value we obtained above simply by taking the square root of F.

We have seen that, when the F test from the one-way ANOVA has shown significance, we can obtain some idea of overall effect size by calculating a measure such as Cohen's f, eta squared or an equivalent statistic such as adjusted R^2 or estimated omega squared. Such overall measures, however, are of limited value. They may confirm that something substantial is going on, but they do not tell us exactly *what* is going on.

Planned contrasts confirm that, in our drug experiment, some drugs resulted in a very substantial improvement in performance, whereas others did not. The addition of a measure of effect size to a significant contrast arguably makes a greater contribution to knowledge than any overall measure of effect size.

Since any contrast, however complex, is basically a comparison between two means, Cohen's d statistic affords a useful measure of effect size here also. In Chapter 6, we saw that Cohen's d statistic was defined as the difference between the two means divided by the supposedly constant population standard deviation. The formula for d is reproduced below.

$$d = \frac{\mu_1 - \mu_2}{\sigma} \quad - - - (20)$$

Cohen's effect size index

In practice, we would estimate the within groups standard deviation with the square root of the average of the sample variances, incorporating, where necessary, a weighting for sample size. The pooled variance estimate s^2_{pooled} in the usual t test formula can be replaced by the ANOVA within groups mean square MS_{within}. If n is the size of each sample, the formulae for Cohen's d and the t statistic can be rewritten as follows:

$$d = \frac{M_1 - M_2}{\sqrt{MS_{within}}}; \qquad t = \frac{M_1 - M_2}{\sqrt{2MS_{within} / n}} \quad - - - (21)$$

**Cohen's d statistic and the
independent samples t statistic**

It follows from formula (21) that, if we already have the value of t, we can obtain that of Cohen's d very quickly from the following formula, in which n is the size of each sample:

$$d = t\sqrt{2 / n} \quad - - - (22)$$

Obtaining the value of d from that of t

In Chapter 6, we found that, when two scores had been removed from the Caffeine data set, t = 5.32 and d = 1.73. Applying formula (22) to this value of t, we have

$$d = t\sqrt{2 / n} = 5.32\sqrt{2/19} = 1.73$$

as before.

In the unequal-n case, the multiplier $\sqrt{2 / n}$ must be replaced with $\sqrt{\left(\dfrac{1}{n_1} + \dfrac{1}{n_2}\right)}$.

Turning now to contrasts, in the equal-n case, we must replace the factor $\sqrt{2/n}$ with

$$\sqrt{\sum_{j}^{k} c_j^2 / n} \,, \quad \text{where } c_j \text{ is the contrast coefficient for group } j \text{ and } k \text{ is the number of groups.}$$

The formula for obtaining the value of d from that of t now becomes:

$$d = t\sqrt{\sum_{j}^{k} c_j^2 / n} \quad \text{- - - (23)}$$

Cohen's d for a contrast

Returning to the simple contrast tested in Section 7.4.2.2, we saw in Table 6 that $t = .07$, $n = 10$ and

$$\sum_{j} c_j^2 = 2. \quad \text{Substituting in formula (23), we have}$$

$$d = t\sqrt{\sum_{j}^{k} c_j^2 / n} = .07\sqrt{2/10} = .03$$

In Cohen's classification, the value .03 is trivially small. (See Table 5.)

7.4.2.4   Helmert contrasts

Suppose, as in our present example, we have an array of five treatment means. We construct a set of **Helmert contrasts** as follows:
1. We compare the first mean with the average of the other four means.
2. We drop the first mean and compare the second mean with the average of means three, four and five.
3. We drop the second mean and compare the third with the average of means four and five.
4. Finally, we compare the fourth mean with the fifth.

This set of contrasts can be represented by four rows of coefficients as follows:

$$\begin{pmatrix} +1 & -1/4 & -1/4 & -1/4 & -1/4 \\ 0 & +1 & -1/3 & -1/3 & -1/3 \\ 0 & 0 & +1 & -1/2 & -1/2 \\ 0 & 0 & 0 & +1 & -1 \end{pmatrix}$$

We can remove the fractions by multiplying each of the coefficients in the first row by 4, those of the second by 3, and those of the third by two thus:

$$\begin{pmatrix} +4 & -1 & -1 & -1 & -1 \\ 0 & +3 & -1 & -1 & -1 \\ 0 & 0 & +2 & -1 & -1 \\ 0 & 0 & 0 & +1 & -1 \end{pmatrix}$$

While multiplying the coefficients by four multiplies the value of the contrast by the same factor, the value of $\sum c^2$ in the denominator of formula (16) also increases, so that the value of the contrast sum of squares is unaltered.

Helmert contrasts have, as we shall see, a very important property.

7.4.2.5   Orthogonal contrast sets

In a set of Helmert contrasts, each contrast is independent of the others: that is, its value is neither constrained by, nor does it constrain, those of any of the other contrasts in the set. The first contrast does not affect the value of the second, because the first mean is not involved in the second contrast. Similarly, the values of neither of the first two contrasts affect the value of the third, because the latter involves neither of the first two means. Finally, the fourth contrast is independent of the first three because the first three means have now been dropped.   Taken together, these Helmert contrasts are said to make up a set of **orthogonal contrasts**.

In either version of the set of Helmert contrasts (the matrix containing the fractions or the matrix with the whole numbers), the sum of the products of the corresponding coefficients in any two rows is zero. For contrasts 1 and 2, for instance, if we let c_1 and c_2 be the coefficients in row 1 and row 2, respectively, $\sum c_1 c_2 = 0$. This is the criterion for the orthogonality (independence) of a set of contrasts. You might wish to confirm, for example, that the sum of products of the corresponding coefficients in the first two rows of either matrix is zero; moreover, you can easily check that the sum of products is zero for *any* two rows.

In our current example, with five treatment means, we were able to construct a set of four orthogonal contrasts. In general, with k treatment means, sets of only $(k - 1)$ orthogonal contrasts are possible; though it may be possible to construct more than one orthogonal set. The limit to the size of any one set of orthogonal contrasts is, of course, the degrees of freedom of the between groups sum of squares.

7.4.2.6   Attributing variability to the contrasts in an orthogonal set

An advantage of orthogonal contrasts is that it is possible to assign to each contrast a sum of squares that is attributable to that contrast alone and to none of the others in the set. Moreover, when the sums of squares of the $(k - 1)$ orthogonal contrasts are added together, we shall obtain the between groups treatment sum of squares. With a set of orthogonal contrasts, therefore, we can partition the between groups sum of squares into several components, each representing the contribution of one particular contrast. The details of how this is done are given in Appendix 7.4.2.6 at the end of this chapter.

7.4.2.7   Testing contrasts in the One-Way ANOVA procedure

To make a test of a few specified contrasts, however, we shall first turn to the **One-Way ANOVA** procedure in the **Compare Means** menu. In the **One-Way ANOVA** dialog box (Figure 8), click on the **Contrasts ...** button at the top right of the dialog box and proceed as shown in Figure 14.

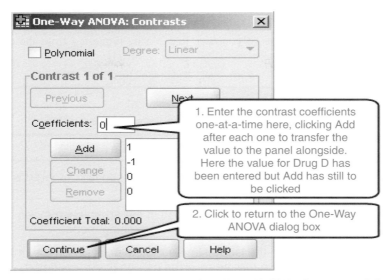

Figure 14. Specifying a simple contrast in the **One-Way ANOVA: Contrasts** dialog box

Output 10 shows the result of the t test of the contrast ψ_1. In the upper panel, the coefficients of the contrast ψ_1 are listed. The t-value (.07) agrees with the result of our previous calculation.

Contrast Coefficients

Contrast	Drug Condition				
	Placebo	Drug A	Drug B	Drug C	Drug D
1	1	-1	0	0	0

Contrast Tests

		Contrast	Value of Contrast	Std. Error	t	df	Sig. (2-tailed)
Score	Assume equal variances	1	.10	1.391	.072	45	.943
	Does not assume equal	1	.10	.888	.113	17.584	.912

Output 10. Result of the test of the contrast ψ_1

You will notice that on the second row of the table in Output 10, another t test is reported. Here the **Behrens-Fisher statistic T** has been used to test the null hypothesis of no difference, with the degrees of freedom adjusted downwards from 45 to 17.584 by the **Welch-Satterthwaite formula**, as described in Chapter 6.

Table 7 shows the different types of contrasts that can be requested from the GLM dialog box.

Table 7. The types of contrast sets available on GLM	
Type	**Description**
Simple	A pre-specified reference or control mean is compared with each of the other means.
Helmert	Starting from the leftmost mean in the array, each mean is compared with the mean of the remaining means.
Difference (Reverse Helmert)	Starting from the leftmost mean in the array, each mean is compared with the mean of the means that preceded it.
Repeated	First with second, second with third, third with fourth, ...
Deviation	Each mean is compared with the grand mean.

We shall illustrate the procedure by requesting a set of simple contrasts. Click **Contrasts...** (Figure 10) to open the **Contrasts** dialog box (Figure 15) and follow the directions in Figure 15.

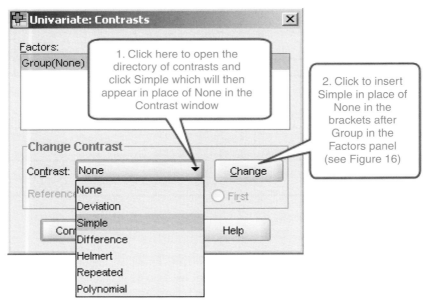

Figure 15. Requesting simple contrasts

The **Contrasts** dialog box will now appear as in Figure 16. To specify the Placebo category as the **Reference Category**, you will need to click the appropriate radio button at the foot of the dialog box and click **Change** to complete the specification (Figure 16, lower slot).

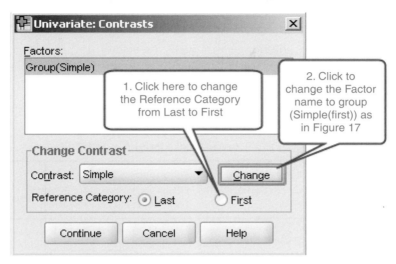

Figure 16. Completing the specifications of simple contrasts with Placebo as the reference category

In Figure 17, it is clear from the entry in the upper panel not only that **Simple** contrasts have been specified, but also that the reference category is now the Placebo group, with which all the other means (that is the means of the four drug conditions) will each be compared.

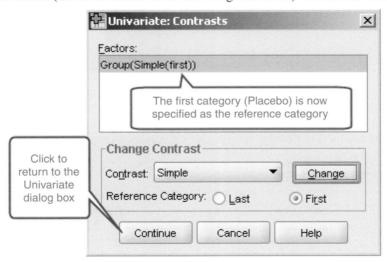

Figure 17. The **Univariate: Contrasts** dialog has now been completed, with the first (Placebo) condition as the reference category

Output 11 shows part of the table of results of the set of simple contrasts. No *t*-values are given; but if the 95% confidence interval fails to include zero, the contrast is significant. The first test reported in Output 11 is the one we made by specifying the same contrast in the **One-Way ANOVA** procedure. To obtain the value of *t*, we need only divide the 'Contrast Estimate' by the 'Std. Error':

$$t(35) = \frac{-0.10}{1.391} = -0.07 \quad \text{(as before)}$$

Custom Hypothesis Tests

Contrast Results (K Matrix)

			Dependent Variable
Drug Condition Simple Contrast[a]			Performance Score
Level 2 vs. Level 1	Contrast Estimate		-.100
	Hypothesized Value		0
	Difference (Estimate - Hypothesized)		-.100
	Std. Error	Not significant since p-value >.05	1.391
	Sig.		.943
	95% Confidence Interval for Difference	Lower Bound	-2.901
		Upper Bound	2.701
Level 3 vs. Level 1	Contrast Estimate		4.000
	Hypothesized Value		0
	Difference (Estimate - Hypothesized)		4.000
	Std. Error	Significant since p-value <.05	1.391
	Sig.		.006
	95% Confidence Interval for Difference	Lower Bound	1.199
		Upper Bound	6.801
Level 4 vs. Level 1	Contrast Estimate		6.400

Output 11. Part of the **Simple Contrasts** output with *Placebo* as the reference category

7.5   TREND ANALYSIS

In the data sets that we have been considering so far, the sets of categories or conditions making up the treatment factor differ qualitatively, so that, as far as the results of the analysis are concerned, the order in which the levels of the factor are defined in the **Labels** column in **Variable View** and the consequent order of entry of the data into the Score column in **Data View** are entirely arbitrary. In our example, suppose that the levels of the Drug factor had been defined in the order: Drug C, Placebo, Drug D, Drug B, Drug A. The outcome of the one-way ANOVA would have been exactly the same as it was before.

Now suppose that the levels making up a treatment factor are equally-spaced points on a single *quantitative* dimension, so that the treatment factor is a continuous independent variable, rather than merely a set of unordered categories. Suppose, for example, that in our drug experiment, the factor or independent variable had consisted not of a set of active conditions with different drugs, but of different dosages of the same drug. Our five treatment conditions now make a set of **ordered categories** equally spaced at different points on the same quantitative dimension. The purpose of such an investigation is no longer simply to establish whether differences exist among the group treatment means, but to investigate the precise nature of the functional relationship between the factor (independent variable) and the measure (dependent variable). We now have a continuous independent variable, Drug Dosage, as well as the original continuous dependent variable, Score.

At this point, it may be appropriate to review the possible types of functional relationships that might obtain between the independent variable (the Drug dosage factor) and Score (the measure or dependent variable). (The reader who is familiar with the term **polynomial** may wish to skip the next section.)

7.5.1   Polynomials

A **polynomial** is a sum of terms, each of which is a product of a constant and a power of the same variable: e.g. $y = 6 + 2x$, $y = 2 + x + 3x^2$, $y = -4 + 3x^2 - 4x^3$ and $y = 3 - x - x^2 - 2x^3 - x^4$ are all polynomials. The general definition of a polynomial is as follows:

$$y = a_0 + a_1 x + a_2 x^2 + \ldots + a_n x^n \quad \text{- - - (24)}$$

General equation of a polynomial

where a_0 is a constant, and $a_1, a_2, \ldots, a_n$ are the **coefficients** of the single variable x, which is raised to increasing powers, up to a maximum of n.

The highest power n of x is known as the **order** or **degree** of the polynomial. The graph of the equation of a polynomial of the first degree, such as $y = x - 3x$, is a straight line (Figure 18, leftmost panel): a first order polynomial is thus a **linear function**.

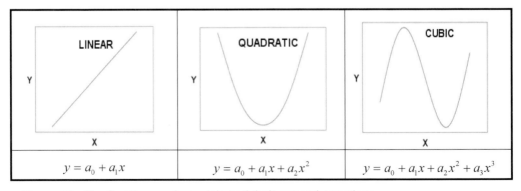

Figure 18. The first three polynomials and their general equations

A straight line obviously does not change direction at all. By choosing the right values for the constants a_0 and a_1, however, a straight line can be made to fit any *two* points in the plane of the graph that are separated along the x-axis.

A polynomial of the second degree, such as $y = 7 + x - 6x^2$ (Figure 18, middle panel), is known as a **quadratic function**. The graph of a quadratic function is a curve which changes direction only once. Although a quadratic curve changes direction only once, values for the three constants can always be found so that the curve will fit any three points that are separated along the x-axis. The graph of a polynomial of the **third degree**, such as $y = -14 + x - 8x^2 + 20x^3$ (Figure 18, rightmost panel), is termed a **cubic function**. The graph of a cubic function changes direction *twice*. Although the graph of a cubic function changes direction only twice, values of the four constants can always be found so that the curve fits any four points separated along the x-axis. In general, a polynomial of degree n changes direction $(n - 1)$ times and can be made to fit any $(n + 1)$ points separated along the x-axis.

The graphs in Figure 18 depict polynomial relationships in their pure forms. In a real data set, however, more than one kind of relationship, or **trend** may be evident: for example, the graph of a data set may be of linear shape in the middle of the range of values, but have a curve at one end, suggesting the presence of both linear and quadratic trends. In **trend analysis**, it is possible to attribute portions of the total variability of the scores to specific polynomial relationships in the data and to test these components of trend for significance.

In a trend analysis, a special set of orthogonal contrasts, known as **orthogonal polynomial coefficients** is constructed. In any row, the coefficients are values of a polynomial of one particular order: the first row is a first order (linear) polynomial; the second row is a second order (quadratic) polynomial and so on. Since each row of coefficients is a contrast, the coefficients sum to zero; moroever, as with all orthogonal sets, the products of the corresponding coefficients in any two rows also sum to zero. The sum of squares associated with each contrast (row) captures one particular type of functional trend in the data; moreover, because we have an orthogonal set, each contrast sum of squares measures that kind of trend and no other. The sum of squares for the first row captures the linear component of trend, the SS for the second row the quadratic component, that for the third row the cubic and so on. As in the ANOVA of data from an experiment with a qualitative treatment factor, it is possible to partition the between groups sum of squares into the sums of squares associated with the different contrasts and test each contrast for significance; in trend analysis, however, each test confirms the presence of a specific polynomial relationship in the data.

In Appendix 7.5.1 at the end of this chapter, there is an illustrative example of a trend analysis.

7.6   POWER AND EFFECT SIZE IN THE ONE-WAY ANOVA

When planning research, it is now standard practice to calculate the numbers of observations that will enable tests of sufficient power to be made. (The power of a statistical test is the probability that the test will show significance if the null hypothesis is false.) One determinant of the power of a test is the size of the effect that is being studied: a given test has greater power to obtain significance when there is a large effect than when there is a small one. In order to plan a test with a specified power, a decision must be made about the minimum size that effects must reach before they are sufficiently substantial to be worth reporting.

There are several other determinants of the power of a statistical test. The factor most under the control of the researcher, however, is usually the size of the sample: the more data you have, the greater the power of your statistical tests.

Statistical textbooks show that the sample sizes necessary to achieve an acceptable level of power (at least 0.75) for small, medium and large effects vary considerably: to be sufficiently powerful to reject the null hypothesis when there is a small effect, a sample must be several times as large as one necessary to reject the null hypothesis when there is a large effect. The higher the level of power you require, the greater the differential in sample sizes needed for the three different minimum effect sizes (Keppel & Wickens, 2004; p.169, Figure 8.1).

7.6.1 How many participants shall I need? Using G*Power 3

The easiest way to answer questions about power and sample size is to use a dedicated statistical package such as **G*Power 3** (Erdfelder, Faul & Buchner, 1996; Faul, Erdfelder, Lang & Buchner, 2007). The answers G*Power gives to questions about power and sample size agree with those that you would obtain if you were to consult standard tables or use a statistical computing package such as SPSS .

Questions about power and sample size cannot be answered without specifying the minimum effect size for which a test at a specified level of power is to be made. As a measure of minimum effect size, G*Power requires the user to specify a value of Cohen's f statistic.

G*Power also requires the user to input a value for the **noncentrality parameter**, which we shall now consider.

7.6.1.1 The central F distribution

When the null hypothesis is true, the expected value of F is *about* 1. (More precisely, the expected value of F is $df_{error}/(df_{error} - 2)$, which approaches unity as the error degrees of freedom become large.) The expected value of F under the null hypothesis is the mean of the **central F distribution**, that is, the sampling distribution of F that is 'centred' around the expected value under the null hypothesis.

7.6.1.2 The noncentral F distribution

If the null hypothesis is false, the distribution of F is centred on a value greater than $df_{error}/(df_{error} - 2)$ and is said to be distributed as **noncentral F**. The noncentral F distribution has three parameters: $df_{between}$, df_{within}, and the **noncentrality parameter (lambda λ)**, which is related to Cohen's f according to:

$$\lambda = f^2 \times N \quad ---(25)$$

The noncentrality parameter

In formula (25), N is the *total* sample size.

The noncentrality parameter, as it were, locates the centre of the noncentral F distribution on the real number line somewhere to the right of that of the central F distribution. The larger the value of f, the less overlap there will be between the two distributions, the lower will be the Type II error rate and the greater will be the power of the F test to reject the null hypothesis if that is false.

Open G*Power 3, and select **Tests➜Means➜Many groups: ANOVA: One-way (one independent variable)** to open the dialog box (Figure 19). Then follow the steps shown in Figure 19. Figure 19 shows the output from G*Power 3, with the central and noncentral F distributions at the top and, in the right-hand lower panel, the total sample size necessary to achieve a power level of .75 to detect an effect of 'medium' size, that is a Cohen's f of at least .25. (These specifications are entered in the appropriate slots of the left-hand lower panel labelled **Input Parameters**.) In the **Output Parameters** panel at bottom right, we see that 180 participants will be required, that is, 36 participants in each of the five groups.

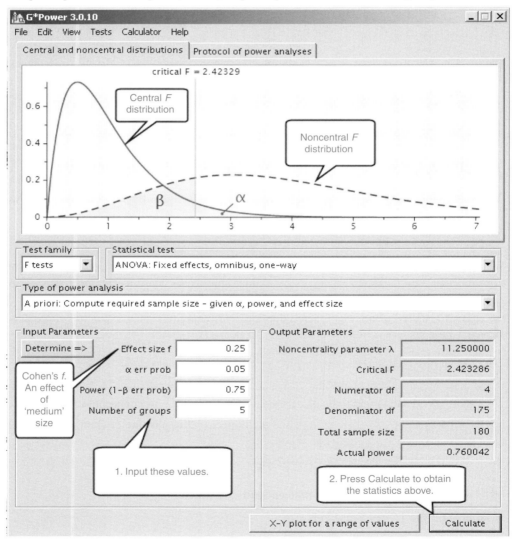

Figure19. The **G*Power** window for the ANOVA F test

7.7   ALTERNATIVES TO THE ONE-WAY ANOVA

Monte Carlo studies have shown that the one-way ANOVA is, to some extent, robust to small to moderate violations of the assumptions of the model and will tolerate some heterogeneity of variance and skewness of distribution. The general import of these studies is that, if the sample sizes are similar in the various groups, and the distributions of the populations are, if not normal, at least similar from group to group, variances can differ by a factor of four without the Type I or Type II error rates rising unacceptably (see Howell, 2007; p.316).

The risk of error, however, increases considerably in data sets with unequal sample sizes in the groups. Occasionally, a data set, even when 'cleaned up' to the greatest possible extent by the removal of obviously aberrant extreme scores, may still show contraindications against the use of the usual one-way ANOVA.

The techniques described by Welch (1951) and Brown & Forsythe (1974) were specially designed for use with data sets showing marked heterogeneity of variance. They are thought to keep the error rates within acceptable limits in most circumstances. Both are available within SPSS and we feel that these (rather than nonparametric tests) should generally be one's first port of call when there are strong contraindications against the usual ANOVA procedure.

When the data are in the form of ratings, however, some journal editors and reviewers would object to the use of any kind of parametric method (even a robust test, such as those of Welch or Brown and Forsythe).

The **Kruskal-Wallis** test is a nonparametric alternative to the one-way ANOVA. It assumes neither normality of distribution nor homogeneity of variance. It should be noted, however, that although the Kruskal-Wallis test is less vulnerable to the presence of extreme scores and outliers than is the one-way ANOVA, it is by no means immune to their influence.

The Kruskal-Wallis method does not test the null hypothesis of equality, in the population, of the treatment means: the hypothesis actually tested is that all samples have been drawn from the same population. Although the test is tolerant of skewness, the distributions of scores in the various groups must have the same shape.

It is also worth remembering that the first step in the running of a test such as the Kruskal-Wallis is the conversion of the original scale data to ranks, a process which might be termed 'ordinalisation'. Such ordinalisation incurs the immediate penalty of a loss in power, which is a consideration when the data are scarcer than the researcher would have liked.

7.7.1   The Kruskal-Wallis k-sample test

Proceed as follows:
- Choose **Analyze➜Nonparametric Tests➜K Independent Samples…** (Figure 20) to open the **Tests for Several Independent Samples** dialog box (the completed version is shown in Figure 21).

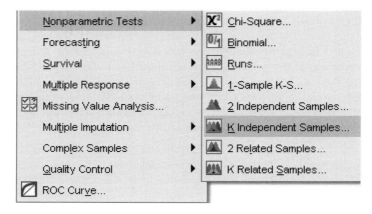

Figure 20. Part of the **Analyze** menu showing **Nonparametric Tests** and its submenu with **K Independent Samples** selected

- Transfer the variable labels and define the range of the grouping variable as shown in Figure 21.

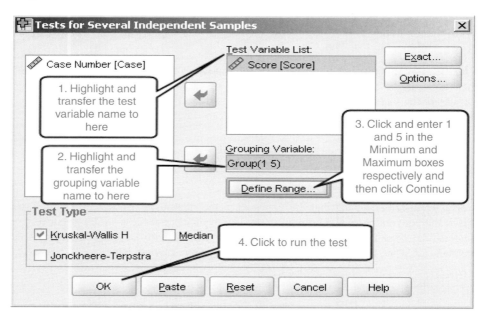

Figure 21. The **Tests for Several Independent Samples** dialog box

- An **Exact** test can be ordered by clicking the **Exact** button and choosing the **Exact** option in the **Exact Tests** dialog. Exact tests, however, can run very slowly and are very demanding of computer memory; moreover, after waiting for some time, you may receive the message that memory was insufficient for the exact test! Here we shall content ourselves with the default asymptotic test.
- Click **OK**.

The test results are shown in Output 12.

Kruskal-Wallis Test

Ranks

	Drug Condition	N	Mean Rank
Score	Placebo	10	12.95
	Drug A	10	13.10
	Drug B	10	31.50
	Drug C	10	36.60
	Drug D	10	33.35
	Total	50	

Test Statistics[a,b]

	Performance Score
Chi-Square	25.376
df	4
Asymp. Sig.	.000

With a p-value <.01, the result is significant at the .01 level

a. Kruskal Wallis Test

b. Grouping Variable: Drug Condition

Output 12. The **Kruskal-Wallis One-Way ANOVA** output

The first subtable, **Ranks**, tabulates the mean rank for each group. The second subtable, **Test Statistics**, lists the value of Chi-Square, its *df* and its *p*-value (**Asymp. Sig.**). Since the *p*-value is much smaller than .01, the Kruskal-Wallis test agrees with the parametric test in confirming that the five groups do not perform equally well.

The test statistic for the Kruskal-Wallis test is *H*, which is calculated from the sums of the ranks in the different groups and *N*, the total number of participants, as follows:

$$H = -3(N+1) + \frac{12}{N(N+1)} \sum_{i=1}^{k} \frac{R_i^2}{n_i} \quad \text{--- (26)}$$

Test statistic for the Kruskal-Wallis test

In formula (26), R_i is the sum of the ranks in group *i*, and *N* is the total number of participants. The values given in Output 12 are the means of the ranks of the scores in the five treatment groups. We can obtain the five values of R_i from Output 12 by muliplying each of the rank means by ten. Substituting in formula (26), we obtain

$$H = -3(51) + \frac{12}{50(51)} \left(\frac{129.5^2 + 131^2 + \ldots + 333.5^2}{10} \right)$$

$$= 25.04$$

The statistic H is distributed approximately as chi-square on $k - 1$ degrees of freedom, where k is the number of groups. You will notice, however, that the value of H we have just calculated does not quite match that given for chi-square in the output (25.376). We can easily see, by choosing **Analyze→Descriptives→Frequencies**, that our current data set contains several tied observations: for example the value 12 occurs 10 times. When there are tied observations, a modification H* of the test statistic is used, which incorporates a correction for the number of ties (Neave & Worthington, 1988: p.249). The value of H* is given by $H^* = H/C$, where

$$C = 1 - \frac{\sum t^3 - \sum t}{N(N^2 - 1)} \quad --- (27)$$

Correction factor for H with tied observations

In formula (27), t is the number of times a value occurs in a tie so that, for example, for the value 12, t = 10, because ten of the scores in the data set had that value. In our current example, we find that $\Sigma t = 45$ and $\Sigma t^3 = 1701$, so that

$$C = 1 - \frac{1701 - 45}{50(2499)} = .9867, \text{ and } H^* = \frac{25.04}{.9867} = 25.38$$

which is the value of chi square given in the output.

7.7.1.2   Effect size

As an overall measure of effect size following a significant Kruskal-Wallis test result, King and Minium (2003, p. 459) offer a statistic known as epsilon-squared (E^2) as an appropriate measure. Its formula is

$$E^2 = \frac{H(N+1)}{(N^2 - 1)} \quad --- (28)$$

**The epsilon-squared measure of effect size
for the Kruskal-Wallis test**

In formula (28), H is the test statistic for the Kruskal-Wallis test and N is the total number of participants.

Substituting our calculated value of H into formula (28), we have

$$E^2 = \frac{H(N+1)}{(N^2 - 1)} = \frac{25.04(51)}{2499} = .51$$

Unfortunately, the calculation of epsilon squared requires the value of H, rather than H^*, the value for chi-square that is given in the SPSS output. There is, however, a way of obtaining the value of epsilon without having to calculate the value of H first. Epsilon is the exact analogue, for ranks, of eta squared, where eta is the correlation ratio. If all the raw scores are ranked, irrespective of their groups, and each score's overall rank is paired with the mean of the ranks in its group, the correlation between the overall ranks and the group mean ranks is the square root of epsilon.

Proceed as follows.

- Choose **Transform→Rank Cases** and transfer the variable label Score to the upper right-hand panel of the **Rank Cases** dialog box, leaving the lower panel empty (Figure 22). This will produce a column containing the rank of every score in the data set, irrespective of which group it came from.

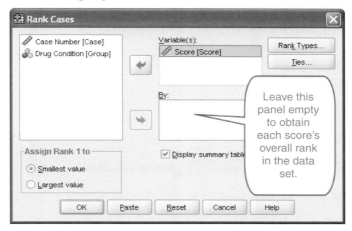

Figure 22. The **Rank Cases** dialog box

SPSS will automatically create a new variable, with variable name RScore and variable label Rank of Score (Figure 23).

	Name	Type	Width	Decimals	Label
1	Case	Numeric	8	0	Case Number
2	Group	Numeric	8	0	Drug Condition
3	Score	Numeric	8	0	Score
4	RScore	Numeric	9	3	Rank of Score

Figure 23. **Variable View**, showing that a new variable has been named and labelled

- Select **Data→Aggregate** to enter the **Aggregate Data** dialog box (Figure 24). Move the variable label Rank of Score to the Summaries of Variable(s) panel on the right and Drug Condition to the Break Variable(s) panel. Click the OK button. This will have the effect of creating another new variable, named RScore_mean (Figure 25).

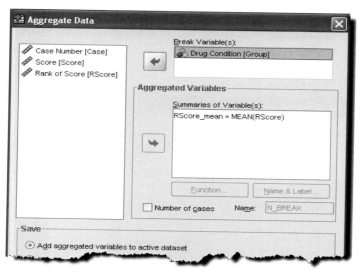

Figure 24. **Aggregate Data** dialog box

	Name	Type	Width	Decimals	Label
1	Case	Numeric	8	0	Case Number
2	Group	Numeric	8	0	Drug Condition
3	Score	Numeric	8	0	Score
4	RScore	Numeric	9	3	Rank of Score
5	RScore_mean	Numeric	8	2	

Figure 25. **Variable View**, showing that a second new variable has been named and labelled

Check in Data View to see that the two new variables have been added to the original data set (Figure 26).

	Case	Group	Score	RScore	RScore_mean	var
1	1	Placebo	10	21.000	12.95	
2	2	Placebo	9	17.500	12.95	
3	3	Placebo	7	8.000	12.95	
4	4	Placebo	9	17.500	12.95	
5	5	Placebo	11	25.000	12.95	
6	6	Placebo	5	2.000	12.95	
7	7	Placebo	7	8.000	12.95	
8	8	Placebo	6	3.500	12.95	
9	9	Placebo	8	13.500	12.95	

Figure 26. **Data View** showing that two new columns of values have been added

- Select **Analyze➔Correlate➔Bivariate** to access the **Bivariate Correlations** dialog box (Figure 27). Transfer the two new variables, RScore and RScore_mean, to the **Variables** panel on the right of the dialog.

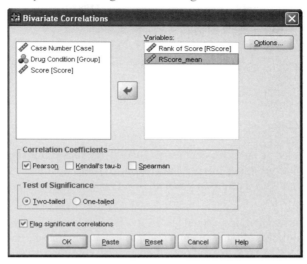

Figure 27. The **Bivariate Correlation** dialog box, with two rank variables in the right-hand panel

The output will show that the correlation between the overall ranks of the scores and their group mean ranks is .72, the square of which is .52 which, within rounding error, is the value of epsilon squared.

A significant result for the Kruskal-Wallis test can be followed up with multiple pairwise comparisons using the **Mann-Whitney** test, between, say, the Placebo group and the each of the four active drug conditions. The Bonferroni correction can be used to control the familywise Type I error rate. Were every possible pairwise comparison to be made, however, the Bonferroni test would be very conservative. A more feasible approach would be to plan, in advance, to compare the Control group with each of the four drug groups, in which case the *p*-value for each test would only have to be multiplied by four. Otherwise, since there are 10 possible pairings from five treatment groups, we should have to multiply the *p*-value by 10 to make every possible comparison!

The procedure for making a Mann-Whitney U test has already been described in Chapter 6, Section 6.4.3. When a test of a pairwise comparison with the Mann-Whitney U test has shown significance, a Glass rank correlation can be calculated as an index of effect size and interpreted with references to Cohen's table in the usual way.

7.7.1.3   Report of the result of a Kruskal-Wallis test

One potential problem with some of the statistics in the output for a nonparametric test is that neither ranks nor mean ranks have any meaning beyond the data from which they have been calculated. From Output 12, we see that the mean ranks for the Placebo and Drug C groups were 12.95 and 36.6, respectively. While it is quite clear that performance under the Drug C condition was markedly superior to that of the Placebo group, it would be difficult to compare the difference with one reported in another study with the same conditions, but different numbers of participants. It is therefore best, in the tables and graphs in the body of the paper, to report the usual statistics such as the means and standard deviations of the original scores, rather than the rank statistics. The report of the test itself, however, might include the rank statistics thus:

> The mean rank under the Placebo condition is 12.95 and for Drugs A to D the mean ranks are respectively 13.10, 31.50, 36.60 and 33.35. The Kruskal-Wallis chi-square test is significant beyond the .01 level: χ^2 (4) = 25.38; $p < .01$. Epsilon squared is .52 which, in Cohen's classification, is a 'large' effect.

7.7.2   Dichotomous nominal data: the chi-square test

Suppose that participants in an experiment are divided randomly into three equally-sized groups: two experimental groups (Group A and Group B) and a Control group (Group C). Each participant is tested with a criterion problem, a 1 being recorded if they pass, and a 0 if they fail.

This experiment would result in a nominal data set. With such data, a **chi-square test** for association can be used to test the null hypothesis that, in the population, there is no tendency for the criterion problem to be solved more often in one condition than in the other (see Chapter 11).

7.8   A FINAL WORD

The one-way ANOVA provides a direct test of the null hypothesis that, in the population, all treatment or group means have the same value. When the value of F is sufficiently large to cast doubt upon the null hypothesis, further questions arise, the answers to which require further testing. The ANOVA itself is therefore merely the first step in the process of statistical analysis.

A significant value of F, while implying that, in the population, there is a difference *somewhere* among the treatment means, does not locate the difference for us, and it would be illegitimate to infer, on the basis of a significant F, that any two means (or combinations of means) are significantly different. On the other hand, the process of data-snooping, that is, the making of follow-up statistical tests, runs a heightened risk of a **Type I error**. A key notion here is the *familywise* Type I error rate. This is the probability, under the null hypothesis, of obtaining *at least one* significant result when several tests are made subsequently. The familywise Type I error rate may be very much higher than the *per comparison* Type I error rate, which is usually set at 0.05. It is essential to distinguish the Type I error rate per comparison with the Type I error rate familywise. Several ways of achieving control over the familywise Type I error rate were discussed.

Since statistical significance and a small p-value do not necessarily mean that a substantial effect has been found, the report of the results of a statistical test is now expected to include a measure of effect size, such as eta squared or (if possible) omega squared. The researcher should also ensure that sufficient numbers of participants are tested to allow statistical tests of adequate power to be made.

When there are strong contraindications against the use of the normal one-way ANOVA, as when the sample variances and sizes vary markedly, the researcher must consider more robust methods, some of which are available as alternatives to the ANOVA in the same SPSS program. These robust variants of ANOVA should be the first alternatives to be considered. There are also available nonparametric counterparts of the one-way ANOVA which, since they involve an initial process of converting scores on the original scale to ranks, incur an automatic loss in power. The case for their use, arguably, is strongest for data in the form of ratings.

When the conditions making up the treatment factor vary along a continuous dimension, as when different groups of participants perform a skilled tasks after ingestion of varying doses of the same drug, the technique of trend analysis can be used to investigate the polynomial components of the functional relationship between the independent and dependent variables. In trend analysis, the components of trend are captured in contrasts whose coefficients are values of polynomials of specified order. These contrasts (and the trends they capture) can be tested for significance in the usual way.

Recommended reading

There are available many textbooks on analysis of variance. Two excellent examples are:

Howell, D. C. (2007). *Statistical methods for psychology (6th ed.)*. Belmont, CA: Thomson/Wadsworth.

Keppel, G., & Wickens, T. D. (2004). *Design and Analysis: A researcher's handbook (4th ed.)*. Upper Saddle River, New Jersey: Pearson/Prentice Hall.

Both books also present ANOVA in the context of the **general linear model** (GLM).

Exercise

Exercise 11 *One-factor between subjects ANOVA* is available in www.psypress.com/spss-made-simple and click on Exercises.

Appendix 7.4.2.6

Partition of the between groups sum of squares into the sums of squares of the contrasts in an orthogonal set

If we apply formula (11) to the set of four Helmert contrasts and calculate the sum of squares for each contrast, you may wish to confirm that four contrast sums of squares add up to 351.52, the between groups sum of squares given in the ANOVA summary table.

$$
\begin{pmatrix}
 & M_1 & M_2 & M_3 & M_4 & M_5 & \sum c_j^{\,2} & \sum c_j M_j & SS_{contrast} \\
Contrast & 8.00 & 7.90 & 12.00 & 14.40 & 13.00 & & & \\
1 & +4 & -1 & -1 & -1 & -1 & 20 & -15.3 & 117.04 \\
2 & 0 & +3 & -1 & -1 & -1 & 12 & -15.7 & 205.41 \\
3 & 0 & 0 & +2 & -1 & -1 & 6 & -3.4 & 19.27 \\
4 & 0 & 0 & 0 & +1 & -1 & 2 & 1.40 & 9.80 \\
 & & & & & & & & 351.52
\end{pmatrix}
$$

> The sum of the contrast sums of squares is equal to $SS_{between}$ in the ANOVA summary table

What we have shown is that the partition of the total ANOVA sum of squares can be extended in the following way:

$$SS_{between} = SS_1 + SS_2 + SS_3 + SS_4$$

Partition of the between groups SS into
component contrast sums of squares

where the sums of squares on the right-hand side of the equation are those associated with each of the four contrasts in the orthogonal set.

Appendix 7.5.1

An illustration of trend analysis

The purpose of the drug experiment was essentially to compare the performance of participants who had ingested different drugs with a comparison, Placebo group. For our second example, the purpose of the investigation changes. This time, the investigator wishes to determine the effects upon performance of varying the dosage of a single drug – possibly the one that seemed to have the strongest effect in the first experiment. Suppose that, in a drug experiment of similar design to our running example, the groups vary, in equal steps of 2 units, in the size of the dosage of a single drug that they have ingested: zero (the Placebo), 2mg, 4mg, 6mg and 8mg. The profile plot appears as in Output 13. It is important to be clear about the differences between this second experiment and the previous one. In the first experiment, the Drug Condition factor was a set of qualitative (and therefore unordered) categories, so that the order in which the 'levels' were defined in the (value) Labels column and the consequent ordering of the groups of scores in the Score column in Data View were entirely arbitrary. The results of the analysis would be the same regardless of the order. In this new experiment, the five conditions are equally spaced points on a quantitative dimension: Drug Dosage. Here, the ordering of the data is crucial, because the purpose of the exercise is to investigate (and confirm) any possible functional relationships between the scores and the dosage level that might emerge. Does performance increase continuously as the dosage increases? Or does it increase at first, but fall off with higher dosages?

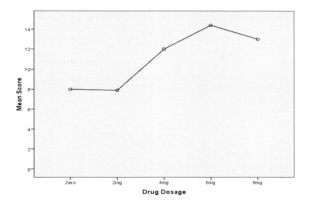

Inspection of the profile plot suggests that the means show a basically linear trend in the middle of the range; the changes in direction at the extremes of the Drug Dosage scale, however, may indicate the presence of an additional (perhaps cubic) component.

Almost any standard statistics textbook will contain a table of sets of orthogonal polynomial coefficients for a wide range of values of k, where k is the number of levels in the quantitative treatment factor. (We should note that the use of such tables assumes that the levels of the factor are equally spaced on the scale of the continuous independent variable.) When, as in the present example, there are five conditions, the set of orthogonal polynomial coefficients contains only four rows because, as we have seen, a polynomial of the 4th order will fit any five points:

$$\begin{pmatrix} -2 & -1 & 0 & 1 & 2 \\ 2 & -1 & -2 & -1 & 2 \\ -1 & 2 & 0 & -2 & 1 \\ 1 & -4 & 6 & -4 & 1 \end{pmatrix}$$

The top row of coefficients captures the linear trend, the second row captures the quadratic trend and so on. Each contrast is tested in the manner described in Section 7.4.

Trend analysis with SPSS

SPSS offers powerful facilities for the running of trend analyses. It is, of course, possible to run a trend analysis with GLM. As with the basic one-way ANOVA, however, it may, in the first instance, be more illuminating to run a trend analysis on the **One-Way ANOVA** procedure in the **Compare Means** menu.

In the **One-Way ANOVA** dialog box, trend analysis is accessed by clicking the **Contrasts** button (Figure 28). When requesting a trend analysis in the **One-Way ANOVA: Contrasts dialog box** (Figure 29), check the **Polynomial** box and (after the first row of coefficients has been entered) adjust the **Degree** setting to the polynomial of the next order of magnitude. So start with the Linear coefficients and continue with the Quadratic, Cubic and finally the fourth order coefficients. When all four sets of coefficients have been entered, click **Continue** to return to the **One-Way ANOVA** dialog

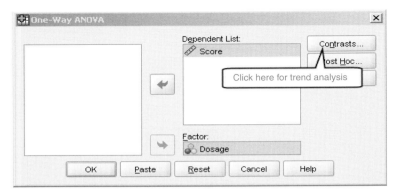

Figure 28. Ordering a trend analysis

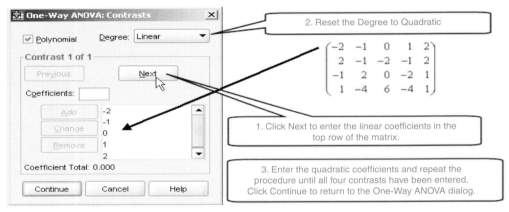

Figure 29. Specifying the components of trend in the **One-Way ANOVA: Contrasts** dialog box

Output of a trend analysis

The first item in the output (not shown) is the full ANOVA summary table. Since this data set is exactly the same as the one we used for the basic one-way ANOVA, the table is identical with Output 1. We shall need to recall, however, that the between groups sum of squares is 351.520. The output also contains a table of **Contrast Coefficients** (not shown). Check the entries in the table to make sure that you specified the contrasts correctly. The results of the trend analysis itself are contained in two tables, the first of which is the full ANOVA table, in which the between groups sum of squares (with value 351.520 as above) is broken down into the sums of squares accounted for by each of the four orthogonal polynomial contrasts (Output 14). It is clear from the table that the statistical tests have confirmed the linear and cubic components of trend in the data.

ANOVA

Performance

			Sum of Squares	df	Mean Square	F	Sig.
Between Groups	(Combined)		351.520	4	87.880	9.085	.000
	Linear Term	Contrast	272.250	1	272.250	28.144	.000
		Deviation	79.270	3	26.423	2.732	.055
	Quadratic Term	Contrast	13.207	1	13.207	1.365	.249
		Deviation	66.063	2	33.031	3.415	.042
	Cubic Term	Contrast	64.000	1	64.000	6.616	.013
		Deviation	2.063	1	2.063	.213	.646
	4th-order Term	Contrast	2.063	1	2.063	.213	.646
	Within Groups		435.300	45	9.673		
	Total		786.820	49			

The between groups sum of squares is the sum of the four contrast sums of squares

The linear and cubic components of trend have been confirmed by the statistical tests.

Output 14. The full ANOVA table, showing that statistical tests have confirmed the presence of linear and cubic trends

There is also a **Contrast Tests** table, which reports t tests of the same four contrasts (Output 15). The values of t in the upper part of this table are the square roots of the corresponding values of F reported in the full ANOVA table. The values of t in the lower part of the table, however, were calculated differently, because heterogeneity of variance had indicated that the assumption of homogeneity of variance was untenable and a pooled variance estimate was not used to estimate the standard error of the difference. Consequently, the usual relationship between t squared and F no longer holds. The degrees of freedom have been adjusted downwards by application of the Satterthwaite formula. Even on these more conservative tests, however, the linear and cubic trend components are still confirmed.

Contrast Tests

		Contrast	Value of Contrast	Std. Error	t	df	Sig. (2-tailed)
Performance	Assume equal variances	1	16.50	3.110	5.305	45	.000
		2	-4.30	3.680	-1.168	45	.249
		3	-8.00	3.110	-2.572	45	.013
		4	3.80	8.229	.462	45	.646
	Does not assume equal variances	1	16.50	3.068	5.378	21.299	.000
		2	-4.30	3.450	-1.246	29.217	.223
		3	-8.00	3.414	-2.343	17.205	.031
		4	3.80	7.989	.476	22.802	.639

The degrees of freedom have been reduced because of heterogeneity of variance

The linear and cubic components are confirmed even by conservative tests

Output 15. Results of t tests of the four components of trend

The results of this trend analysis might be reported as follows.

"A trend analysis confirmed the linear appearance of the profile plot: for the linear component, $t(21.30) = 5.38$; $p < .01$;   for the cubic component, $t(17.21) = 3.34$; $p = .03$".

Note, once again, the manner in which small p-values are reported: avoid expressions such as '.000' and give the probability to two places of decimals, using the inequality sign $<$ for probabilities that are less than .01.

Trend analysis with GLM

We have recommended that you make your first acquaintance with trend analysis through the **One-way ANOVA** procedure in the **Compare Means** menu. We did so because the exercise should help to clarify the link between contrasts and trend analysis. On the other hand, this approach requires the user to look up tables to produce a set of orthogonal polynomial coefficients. On GLM, the whole process is automatised, so that the user is not required to enter the coefficients as required in the **One-Way ANOVA** approach. We think, however, that working through the procedures we have described will make the output of trend analysis with GLM easier to understand.

CHAPTER 8

Between subjects factorial experiments

8.1   INTRODUCTION

Experiments with two or more factors are known as **factorial** experiments. In the simplest case, there is a different sample of participants for each possible combination of conditions. This arrangement is known as a **between subjects** (or **completely randomised**) **factorial** experiment. In this chapter, we shall discuss between subjects factorial experiments with two and three factors. For the analysis of data from such experiments, the **two-way** and the **three-way ANOVA** are appropriate techniques.

8.1.1   An experiment with two treatment factors

Suppose that a researcher has been commissioned to investigate the effects upon simulated driving performance of two new anti-hay fever drugs, A and B. It is suspected that at least one of the drugs may have different effects upon fresh and tired drivers, and the firm developing the drugs needs to ensure that neither drug has an adverse effect upon driving performance.

The researcher decides to carry out a two-factor factorial experiment, in which the factors are:
1.   Drug Treatment, with levels Placebo, Drug A and Drug B;
2.   Alertness, with levels Fresh and Tired.

All participants are asked to take a flavoured drink containing either (in the Drug A and Drug B conditions) a small quantity of the drug or (in the control or Placebo condition) no drug. Half the participants are tested immediately on rising; the others are tested after doing without sleep for twenty-four hours. A different sample of ten participants is tested under each of the six treatment combinations: (Fresh, Placebo); (Fresh, Drug A); (Fresh, Drug B); (Tired, Placebo); (Tired, Drug A); (Tired, Drug B).

In this experiment, each level of either factor is to be found in combination with every level of the other; the two factors, that is, are said to **cross**. There are experimental designs in which the factors do not cross (not all combinations of conditions or groups are present), but such designs will not be considered in this book. The two-factor between subjects factorial experiment can be represented as a table in which each row or column represents a particular level of one of the treatment factors, and a **cell** of the table (i.e. a single rectangle in the grid) represents one particular treatment combination (Table 1). In Table 1, the cell on the bottom right represents the combination (Tired, Drug B). The ten participants in Group 6 were tested under that particular treatment combination.

Table 1. A completely randomised, two-factor factorial experiment on the effects of two factors upon simulated driving performance			
	Levels of the **Drug Treatment** factor		
Levels of the **Alertness** factor	Placebo	Drug A	Drug B
Fresh	Group 1	Group 2	Group 3
Tired	Group 4	Group 5	Group 6

The mean scores of the participants are shown in Table 2. The row and column means are known as **marginal means**. They are the means of all the scores at each level of either factor, ignoring the other factor in the classification. Inspection of the column means shows that the mean score of all those who ingested Drug B, irrespective of whether they were fresh or tired, is 19.0, a higher level of performance than that of the Placebo or Drug A groups. Inspection of the row means shows that the mean score of the Fresh participants, ignoring the drug group to which they had been assigned, is greater than that of the Tired participants.

Table 2. Mean scores achieved by the participants in the drugs experiment				
	Placebo	Drug A	Drug B	Mean
Fresh	21.0	12.0	22.0	18.3
Tired	10.0	18.0	16.0	14.7
Mean	15.5	15.0	19.0	16.5

To say that the mean for the fresh participants is greater than that for the tired participants does not, of course, imply that this superiority is necessarily true of the scores at any particular level of the Drug Treatment factor. In fact, when we move from consideration of the marginal means to the cell means in the body of the table, we see that with the scores achieved under the Drug A condition, the opposite is the case: the Tired participants outperformed the Fresh participants!

The most interesting features of the data from factorial experiments often emerge from consideration of the cell means in the body of the table, rather than the marginal means. This is because the cell means show how the factors in a factorial experiment interplay or **interact**, often in complex ways. The interaction of the factors is a source of variance over and above any main effect and the possibility of such an interaction is often the principal motivation for a factorial experiment.

8.1.2 Main effects and interactions

The introduction of a second factor into the experimental design extends the range of questions that can be investigated. In this two-way factorial experiment, there are two kinds of effects, both of which can be tested with an appropriate F statistic:

1. **main effects**;
2. the **interaction**.

Main effects may be evident from inspection of the marginal means. Should at least one of the differences among the column means for the three levels of the Drug factor be sufficiently great as to indicate a difference in the population and should this pattern be confirmed by statistical testing, the Drug Treatment factor is said to have a **main effect**. Similarly, a large difference between the two row means would indicate that the Alertness factor also has a main effect. Since Table 2 shows that there are indeed marked differences among both row and column marginal means, it looks as if both factors have main effects. Not surprisingly the fresh participants, on average, outperformed the tired participants. In the participants as a whole, Drug A did not produce a higher overall level of performance in comparison with the mean score of those participants who received a placebo. Drug B, on the other hand, did produce a higher overall level of performance.

8.1.2.1 Simple main effects

The effect of one treatment factor (such as Alertness) at one particular level of another factor (e.g. on the Drug A participants only) is known as a **simple main effect**. From inspection of Table 2, it would appear that the Alertness factor has different simple main effects at different levels of the Drug factor: its effect is diminished with Drug B and actually reversed with Drug A: the ingestion of the drug actually *impairs* performance compared with the Placebo group.

8.1.2.2 Interactions

When the simple main effects of one treatment factor are not homogeneous at all levels of another, the two factors are said to **interact**. An interaction between two factors, such as Drug Treatment and Alertness, is indicated by a multiplication sign thus: Drug Treatment × Alertness. (In computer output, multiplication is indicated by an asterisk: Drug Treatment*Alertness.) The results of the drug experiment, therefore, suggest the presence of a Drug Treatment × Alertness interaction.

8.1.3 Profile plots

The interaction pattern that we have just described can be depicted graphically, as plots of the cell means for the Fresh and the Tired participants against Drug Treatment (see Figure 1). Such graphs are called **profile plots**. In the present example, the Fresh participants' performance profile is V-shaped, plunging under the Drug A condition. The Tired participants' profile, on the other hand, rises to higher levels under both the Drug A and Drug B conditions. The presence of an interaction is indicated by **profile heterogeneity** from level to level of one of the factors, that is, by *non-parallel* profiles. This is certainly the case with the profiles of the Fresh and Tired participants in the present example across the three Drug Treatment conditions.

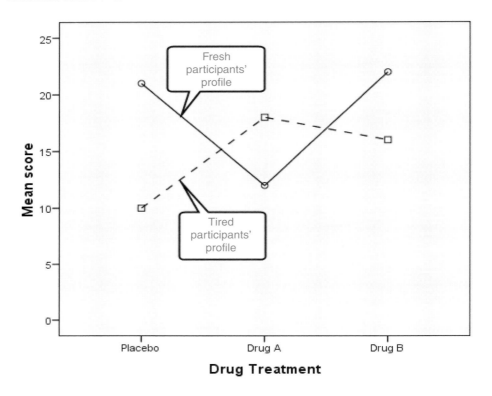

Figure 1. A pattern of cell means suggestive of an interaction

It is important to be clear that an interaction effect is a source of variance over and above the effect of either factor considered alone or, indeed, the main effects of both factors combined. Main effects and interactions are independent: it is quite possible to obtain significant main effects without any significant interaction between the factors; it is also possible to have significant interactions without any significant main effects. As well as showing an interaction pattern, however, the appearance of the profiles in Figure 1 is affected partly by the presence of main effects. Had there been an even greater difference in overall performance level between the Fresh and Tired participants, for example, the Fresh and Tired profiles might have become completely separated at all three levels of the Drug Treatment factor. It is the *convergence* or *divergence* of the profiles, rather than their separation or slope, that indicates the presence of an interaction: there is no need for the profiles to cross one another. When the profiles are parallel, there is no interaction – even if they both slope sharply upwards or downwards or are widely separated on the vertical axis of the graph. Either of those tendencies indicates a main effect, not an interaction.

8.2 HOW THE TWO-WAY ANOVA WORKS

In Figure 2, we reproduce Figure 2 from Chapter 7, Section 7.1.3.3, which is a graphical summary of the one-way ANOVA.

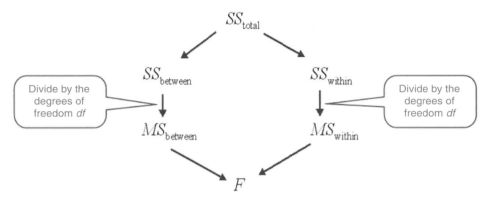

Figure 2. Schematic picture of the one-way ANOVA

In the one-way ANOVA, the total sum of squares, that is, the sum of the squares of the deviations of the scores from the grand mean, is divided into two components: the **between groups** sum of squares, which is calculated from the deviations of the treatment means from the grand mean; and the **within groups** sum of squares, which is based upon the deviations of the individual scores from their group means.

8.2.1 The two-way ANOVA

As in the one-way ANOVA, a within subjects (error) sum of squares can be calculated by averaging the variances of the scores in the individual cells, i.e., their dispersion about their group means.

In the two-way ANOVA, the counterpart of the between groups sum of squares is the sum of squares of the deviations of the *cell means* from the grand mean. This between groups sum of squares, however, can itself be further divided into three components:
1. a **main effect** sum of squares for the Drug Treatment factor;
2. a **main effect** sum of squares for the Alertness factor;
3. an **interaction** sum of squares.

The two main effect sum of squares and the interaction sum of squares are now divided by their respective degrees of freedom to obtain mean squares, that is, variance estimates for the main effects and the interaction. As in the one-way ANOVA, the within groups sum of squares can be divided by its degrees of freedom to obtain an estimate of the error (within cell) variance. Finally, the two main effects and the interaction are tested with three F statistics, each of which has the same within groups mean square as its error term or denominator:

$$F_{\text{Alertness}} = \frac{MS_{\text{Alertness}}}{MS_{\text{within}}}$$

$$F_{\text{Drug}} = \frac{MS_{\text{Drug}}}{MS_{\text{within}}} \qquad \text{- - - (1)}$$

$$F_{\text{Alertness} \times \text{Drug}} = \frac{MS_{\text{Alertness} \times \text{Drug}}}{MS_{\text{within}}}$$

The three F tests in the two-way ANOVA

Figure 3 summarises the two-way ANOVA. (In the Figure, the specific labels Drug, Alertness and Alertness × Drug have been replaced by the more compact symbols A, B and A × B.)

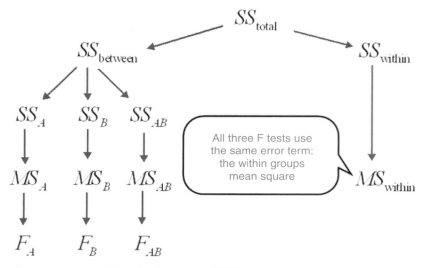

Figure 3. Diagram summarising the two-way ANOVA

8.2.2   Degrees of freedom

In more complex designs, it is particularly important to be clear about the degrees of freedom of the various sources; otherwise it can be difficult to follow the reports of tests in the output.

8.2.2.1   Degrees of freedom of the main effects

In the one-way ANOVA of data from an experiment with k treatment groups, the degrees of freedom df of the between groups mean square is the number of treatment groups minus one: $df = k - 1$. In a similar way, in a two-way ANOVA, the degrees of freedom of each of the source mean squares for main effects is the number of levels making up the source, minus one: thus for the Alertness factor (Fresh, Tired), $df = (2 - 1) = 1$; for the Drug Treatment factor (Placebo, Drug A, Drug B), $df = (3 - 1) = 2$.

Turning now to the degrees of freedom of the interaction, the rule is as follows: the degrees of freedom of an interaction mean square is the product of the degrees of freedom of the factors involved. Since $df_{\text{Alertness}} = 1$ and $df_{\text{Drug}} = 2$, $df_{\text{interaction}} = 1 \times 2 = 2$.

In general, if Factor A and Factor B have a and b levels, respectively, the degrees of freedom of their interaction are given by:

$$df_{\text{interaction}} = (a-1)(b-1) \quad \text{- - - (2)}$$

Formula for the degrees of freedom of the interaction

In words, we obtain the degrees of freedom of the interaction by multiplying the degrees of freedom of the factors involved in the interaction.

In the two-way ANOVA, the within groups mean square is the average of all the cell variances. In the present example, there are 6 cells, each cell representing a different combination of the factors of Alertness and Drug Treatment. Each of the six cells yields a variance estimate which, since it is based upon ten observations, has 9 degrees of freedom. The pooled within cells variance estimate, therefore, has $6 \times 9 = 54$ degrees of freedom.

In general, suppose we have a factorial A $\times$ B design, in which factors A and B have a and b levels, respectively. There are n participants in each group, that is, each combination of treatments or cell of the design. There are ab groups, for each of which there is a variance estimate from (n – 1) scores. The within subjects mean square is the average of all the variance estimates and its degrees of freedom are therefore given by:

$$df_{\text{within}} = ab(n-1) \quad \text{- - - (3)}$$

Formula for the degrees of freedom
of the within groups mean square

In the two-way ANOVA, the within cell pooled variance estimate MS_{within} is the error term in all three F tests.

Table 3 shows the ANOVA summary table for the data summarised in Table 2. Notice that there are three F statistics: one for each of the two factors considered separately; the third for the interaction. Consistent with our inspection of Table 2, the two-way ANOVA has shown that all three tests show significance beyond the .05 level; and the Alertness factor and the interaction are significant beyond the .01 level.

The precise manner in which the quantities in Table 3 are calculated is lucidly described in many excellent textbooks, such as Howell (2007) and Keppel & Wickens (2004).

Table 3. The two-way ANOVA summary table						
Source	df	SS	MS	F	p	Partial eta squared
Main effects						
Alertness (A)	1	201.67	201.67	8.71	<.01	.14
Drug (D)	2	190.00	95.00	4.10	.02	.13
Interaction						
Interaction (A × D)	2	763.33	381.67	16.49	<.01	.38
Error						
Within groups (Error)	54	1250.00	23.15			
Total	59	2405.0				

The two-way ANOVA has confirmed the most interesting feature of the data, namely, the presence of an interaction between the Drug Treatment and Alertness factors: while the drug improved the performance of the tired participants, it impeded the performance of the fresh participants. It is this ability to confirm the existence of an interaction that accounts for the fact that the factorial ANOVA is one of the most widely used statistical techniques in some fields of research, such as experimental psychology; indeed, the main effects of factors considered separately are often of little interest in themselves. It is not surprising, for example, to learn that fresh participants outperform tired participants; but it is of considerable interest to learn that while a drug improves the performance of tired participants, this effect is reversed with fresh participants.

The entries under the heading **Partial eta squared** (an option in SPSS) are included in Table 3 at this point for the sake of completeness. Partial eta squared is a measure of effect size. We shall return to the measurement of effect size in a later section.

8.3   THE TWO-WAY ANOVA WITH SPSS

Table 4 shows the raw data from the two-factor factorial Drug × Alertness experiment.

Table 4. Results of the Drug Treatment × Alertness factorial experiment			
Levels of the **Alertness** factor:	Levels of the **Drug Treatment** factor:		
	Placebo	A	B
Fresh	24 25 13 22 16	18 8 9 14 16	27 14 19 29 27
	23 18 19 24 26	15 6 9 8 17	23 19 17 20 25
Tired	13 12 14 16 17	21 24 22 23 20	21 11 14 22 19
	13 4 3 2 6	13 11 17 13 16	9 14 11 21 18

8.3.1 Entering the data into the Data Editor

Since there are two factors, two **grouping variables**, Alertness and Drug Treatment, will be required to specify the treatment combination under which each score was achieved. The dependent variable or measure is Driving Performance. In the **SPSS Statistics Data Editor**, we shall need a column for case numbers, two for the grouping variables, and a fourth column for Driving Performance.

Proceed as follows:

- In **Variable View**, use the **Name** column to assign names to the variables, as described in Chapter 2, Section 2.3. Here, the variables Case Number, Drug Treatment and Driving Performance must be given more compact variable names such as Participant, Drug and DrivingPerf, respectively, comforming to the requirement that a variable name must be a single string with no spaces. (The shift and hyphen keys, however, can be used to achieve partial separation among the characters, as in Driving_Perf.)

> See Section 2.3

- The full variable label, however, not the variable name, will appear in the output, so the variable name can be quite cryptic, so long as the variable label is explicit.
- In the **Decimals** column, change the values to 0 to display whole numbers.
- In the **Label** column, enter the full variable labels: *Participant Number, Alertness, Drug Treatment,* and *Driving Performance.* This is essential for the quality of the output.
- In the **Values** column, enter the values and labels for the grouping variables, such as 1 and 2 (with labels Fresh and Tired, respectively) for the Alertness factor and 1, 2, and 3 (with labels Placebo, Drug A, and Drug B, respectively) for Drug Treatment.
- In the **Measure** column, specify that Participant and DrivingPerf are Scale variables, and that Drug and Alertness are Nominal variables.
- Enter **Data View**. To display the labels for the values entered for the grouping variables, check the View menu to make sure that **Value Labels** is ticked.

Some of the data in **Data View** are shown in Figure 4. Note that the values for the grouping variables Alertness and Drug have been replaced by their corresponding labels. For example, in case 28, the value 1 has been replaced by Fresh and 2 has been replaced by Drug B. Likewise, in case 31, the value 2 has been replaced by Tired and 1 by Placebo.

	Participant	Alertness	Drug	DrivingPerf	
27	27	Fresh	Drug B	19	
28	28	Fresh	Drug B	17	
29	29	Fresh	Drug B	20	
30	30	Fresh	Drug B	25	
31	31	Tired	Placebo	13	
32	32	Tired	Placebo	12	
33	33	Tired	Placebo	14	
34	34	Tired	Placebo	16	
35	35	Tired	Placebo	17	

Figure 4. Part of **Data View** showing some of the data from Table 4

8.3.2   Exploring the data: boxplots

Before running the ANOVA, it is important to explore the data to check for any problems with the distributions.   To obtain the boxplots under each of the six treatment combinations, proceed as follows:

- Choose **Graphs➔Chart Builder...** and select **Boxplot** from the gallery.
- Drag the **Clustered Boxplot** image to the **Chart preview** and from the left panel, drag the variable label Driving Performance to the **Y-Axis** box, the label Drug Treatment to the **X-Axis** box and the variable label Alertness to the **Cluster: set pattern** box.
- Complete the details as in Section 5.4 to obtain the boxplot (Output 1).

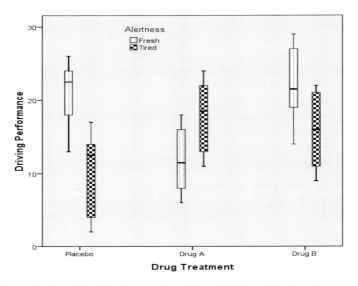

Output 1. Boxplots clustered for Alertness at each level of Drug Treatment

These boxplots show no extreme cases, each of which would have been flagged with an asterisk. (See Chapter 4, Table 2, for details of the structure of a boxplot.) None of the distributions is markedly skewed. There is therefore no need to remove any cases or apply a transformation to make the distribution more symmetrical. We can safely proceed with the ANOVA.

See
Table 2
in
Chap. 4

8.3.3 Choosing a factorial ANOVA

In SPSS, a factorial ANOVA is run by choosing from the **General Linear Model (GLM)** menu (see Figure 9 in Chapter 7).

For a between subjects factorial ANOVA, we must choose the **Univariate** option, bearing in mind that, although there are two independent variables (factors), namely, Drug Treatment and Alertness, this is still essentially a **univariate data** set, because there is only one dependent variable, Driving Performance. See Figure 10 in Chapter 7 for details.

8.3.3.1 Completing the Univariate dialog box

The **Univariate** dialog box has already been discussed in Chapter 7, and the meanings of terms such as **fixed factor** and **covariate** were explained in Section 7.3. For the two-way ANOVA, the names of both factors, Alertness and Drug Treatment, are transferred to the **Fixed Factor(s)** panel on the right of the dialog. The procedure and completed dialog are shown in Figure 5.

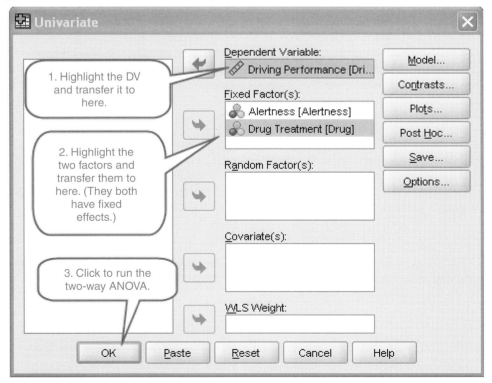

Figure 5. The completed **Univariate** dialog

To obtain a profile plot of the means, click **Plots…** in the **Univariate** dialog box (Chapter 7, Figure 10) to open the **Univariate: Profile Plots** dialog box and follow the steps in Figure 6.

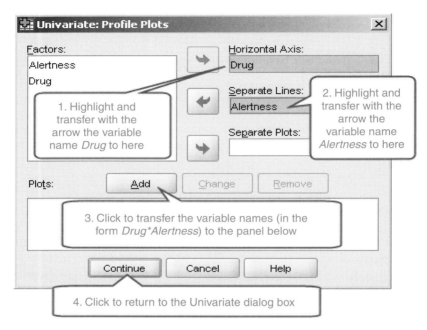

Figure 6. The **Profile Plots** dialog box for plotting the two Alertness profiles against Drug Treatment, the three levels of which will appear on the horizontal axis

Note that by completing the dialog as we have in Figure 6, we have requested the profile plot shown in Figure 1, with the three drug conditions on the horizontal axis and the profiles of the fresh and tired participants across the three conditions. For some purposes, however, we might want to profile the three drug conditions over the two states of alertness, in which case we should have transferred Alertness to the slot labelled **Horizontal Axis** and Drug Treatment to the **Separate Lines** slot. We shall do that later in the chapter.

The results are shown in Output Listings 2-5. The earliest items require close attention, because they show whether the nature of the experimental design and the variables in the data set have been clearly communicated to SPSS.

The table in Output 2, **Between-Subjects Factors**, lists the factor names and their value labels, together with the number of cases in each cell of the design.

Between-Subjects Factors

		Value Label	N
Alertness	1	Fresh	30
	2	Tired	30
Drug Treatment	1	Placebo	20
	2	Drug A	20
	3	Drug B	20

Output 2. The table of **Between-Subjects Factors**

8.3.4.2 Descriptive statistics

Output 3 is the table of descriptive statistics requested from **Options…** .

Descriptive Statistics

Dependent Variable: Driving Performance

Alertness	Drug Treatment	Mean	Std. Deviation	N
Fresh	Placebo	21.00	4.29	10
	Drug A	12.00	4.42	10
	Drug B	22.00	4.94	10
	Total	18.33	6.35	30
Tired	Placebo	10.00	5.66	10
	Drug A	18.00	4.64	10
	Drug B	16.00	4.78	10
	Total	14.67	5.97	30
Total	Placebo	15.50	7.47	20
	Drug A	15.00	5.38	20
	Drug B	19.00	5.65	20
	Total	16.50	6.38	60

Output 3. The table of **Descriptive Statistics**

8.3.4.3 The ANOVA summary table

The table in Output 4, **Tests of Between-Subjects Effects**, is the ANOVA summary table, which tabulates the sources of variation, their **Sums of Squares**, degrees of freedom (*df*), mean squares, *F* ratios and *p*-values (**Sig.**). Note that, in the between subjects factorial ANOVA, each *F* ratio is the Mean Square for the source divided by the Error Mean Square (23.15). The final column **Partial Eta Squared** is the estimate of effect size (explained in Section 8.3.5).

The table in Output 4 was edited in **SPSS Viewer** to reduce the display of values from three decimal places to two decimal places. This was done by double-clicking the whole table so that it showed a hashed border, highlighting the five columns of numbers so that they appeared in inverse video, clicking the right-hand mouse button to show a menu, selecting the item **Cell Properties…**, selecting in the **Format** box the item **#.#**, changing the number of decimals shown in the **Decimals** box to 2, and finally clicking **OK**.

The terms **Corrected Model** and **Intercept** refer to the regression method used to carry out the ANOVA and can be ignored. The three rows **Alertness, Drug** and **Alertness*Drug** are of most interest, since these report tests for the two main effects and the interaction. Note the **Sig.** (i.e. p-value, or tail probability) for each F ratio. There are significant main effects for both the Alertness and Drug Treatment factors: the former is significant beyond the .01 level, the latter beyond the .05 level, but not beyond the .01 level. In addition to main effects of both treatment factors, there is a significant interaction. The p-value is given as .000, which means that it is less than 0.0005. Write '$p < .01$', not '$p = .000$'. Clearly, the Drug Treatment factor has different effects upon Fresh and Tired participants. To ascertain the nature of these effects, however, we shall need to examine the pattern of the treatment means more closely.

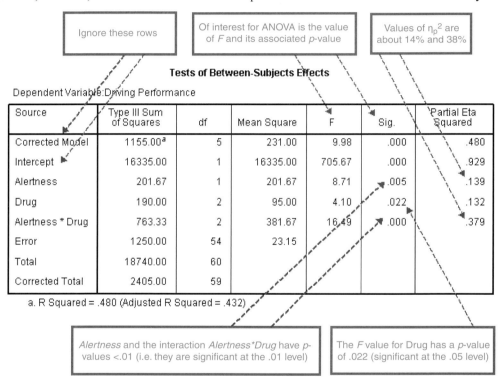

| Ignore these rows | Of interest for ANOVA is the value of F and its associated p-value | Values of η_p^2 are about 14% and 38% |

Tests of Between-Subjects Effects

Dependent Variable:Driving Performance

Source	Type III Sum of Squares	df	Mean Square	F	Sig.	Partial Eta Squared
Corrected Model	1155.00a	5	231.00	9.98	.000	.480
Intercept	16335.00	1	16335.00	705.67	.000	.929
Alertness	201.67	1	201.67	8.71	.005	.139
Drug	190.00	2	95.00	4.10	.022	.132
Alertness * Drug	763.33	2	381.67	16.49	.000	.379
Error	1250.00	54	23.15			
Total	18740.00	60				
Corrected Total	2405.00	59				

a. R Squared = .480 (Adjusted R Squared = .432)

| *Alertness* and the interaction *Alertness*Drug* have p-values <.01 (i.e. they are significant at the .01 level) | The F value for Drug has a p-value of .022 (significant at the .05 level) |

Output 4. The **ANOVA** summary table

8.3.5   Measuring effect size in the two-way ANOVA

In Chapter 7, we introduced the measure of effect size known as **eta-squared** (η^2), which is the proportion of variance in the dependent variable accounted for by differences in the levels of the independent variable. In the case of the one-way ANOVA, η^2 is defined as follows:

See Section 7.2

$$\eta^2 = \frac{SS_{\text{treatment}}}{SS_{\text{total}}} = \frac{SS_{\text{between}}}{SS_{\text{total}}} \quad \text{- - - (4)}$$

Eta squared in the one-way ANOVA

Let Factor A and Factor B be the factors in a two-way ANOVA. We have seen that in the two-way ANOVA, there are three between groups sources of variance: the two main effect sources and the interaction. For Factor A, the measure of effect size known as **complete eta squared** (η^2) is defined as follows:

$$\eta^2 = \frac{SS_A}{SS_{total}} = \frac{SS_A}{SS_A + SS_B + SS_{A \times B} + SS_{within}} \quad \text{- - - (5)}$$

Complete eta squared

Applying formula (5) to the information in Table 3, we find that, for the Alertness factor,

$$\eta^2 = \frac{SS_{Alertness}}{SS_{total}}$$

$$= \frac{SS_{Alertness}}{SS_{Alertness} + SS_{Drug} + SS_{Alertness \times Drug} + SS_{within}}$$

$$= \frac{201.67}{2405.00} = .08$$

There are two major problems with complete eta squared. One is that its value is affected by the variance arising from the presence of the other factors in the experiment, which would make it difficult to compare the effect size of the same factor in two experiments with different numbers of factors. Some authors therefore advocate an alternative form of η^2, called **partial** η^2 or η_p^2 in which the variance of the sums of squares for a particular effect is expressed as a proportion, not of the *total* sum of squares, but of the sum of squares of *that effect alone* plus the error sum of squares:

$$\eta_p^2 = \frac{SS_A}{SS_A + SS_{within}} \quad \text{- - - (6)   \textbf{Partial eta squared}}$$

Applying formula (6) to the information in Table 3, we find that, for the Alertness factor, the value of partial eta squared is

$$\eta_p^2 = \frac{201.667}{201.667 + 1250} = .139$$

which is the value given in Table 3. The value of partial eta squared is, of course, appreciably larger than that of complete eta squared for the same effect. SPSS includes partial eta squared as an option (**Estimates of effect size**) in the **Options...** dialog box. The choice between the **complete η^2** and **partial η^2** statistics depends upon the design of the experiment and purpose of the investigation (see Keppel & Wickens, 2004; p.235). As we shall see, however, better measures of effect size are available for some designs.

8.3.5.3   Estimated omega squared

The other major problem with eta squared (and this applies to both the complete and partial versions) is that it is a purely descriptive measure and overstates the strength of the effect in the population. The estimated omega squared statistics correct this positive bias and allow for shrinkage with re-sampling.

The estimated omega squared statistics corresponding to eta squared and partial eta squared are, respectively, **complete omega squared** $\left(\hat{\omega}^2\right)$ and **partial omega squared** $\left(\hat{\omega}_{p}^2\right)$ – see Keppel & Wickens, 2004; pp.232–233.

The formula for the estimate of complete omega squared is

$$\hat{\omega}_{source}^2 = \frac{df_{source}(F_{source}-1)}{\displaystyle\sum_{\substack{all\ treatment \\ sources}} df_{source}(F_{source}-1)+abn} \quad \text{- - - (7)}\ \textbf{Complete omega squared}$$

Applying Formula (8) to the information in Table 3, we see that, for the Alertness factor, the value of the estimate of complete omega squared is

$$\hat{\omega}_{Alertness}^2 = \frac{df_{Alertness}(F_{Alertness}-1)}{\displaystyle\sum_{\substack{all\ treatment \\ sources}} df_{source}-1)+abn}$$

$$= \frac{1(7.712)}{1(7.712)+2(3.10)+2(15.49)+60} = .07$$

The formula for partial omega squared is as follows:

$$\hat{\omega}_{source}^2 = \frac{df_{source}(F_{source}-1)}{df_{source}(F_{source}-1)+abn} \quad \text{- - - (8)}\ \textbf{Partial omega squared}$$

where a, b and n are the number of levels of Factor A, the number of levels of Factor B and the number of observations per cell, respectively.

Returning to Table 3, we see that, for the Alertness factor, partial eta squared is given as .14. Applying Formula (8), we find that the estimate of partial omega squared for the same source is

$$\hat{\omega}_p^2 = \frac{df_{Alertness}(F_{Alertness}-1)}{df_{Alertness}(F_{Alertness}-1)+(2\times3\times10)}$$

$$= \frac{1\times7.712}{1\times7.712+60} = .114$$

As we should expect, this value is somewhat less than the value of partial eta squared for the same source, because the estimate of omega squared incorporates a correction for positive bias.

Since the estimate of complete omega squared has the full denominator and incorporates the correction for bias, we can expect it to be the smallest of the four estimates that we have calculated.

8.3.5.4 Interpreting values of eta squared and omega squared: equivalent ranges of Cohen's f

In Chapter 7, in addition to eta squared and omega squared, we introduced a third measure of effect size, **Cohen's *f*.** We did so because values of *f* are required as input for **G*Power 3**, a package which computes the sample sizes necessary to achieve specified levels of power to reject the null hypothesis in the presence of effects of specified minimum size.

Here (Table 5) we reproduce the table from Chapter 7 comparing the size ranges for Cohen's measure of effect size *f* with those for eta squared and omega squared. In terms of population parameters, eta squared and omega squared are identical; the estimate of partial omega squared, however, corrects for the positive bias in partial eta squared.

Table 5. A scheme for assessing values of partial eta squared/omega squared and Cohen's *f*

Size of Effect	Partial eta squared (or partial omega squared)	Cohen's *f*
Small	$0.01 \leq \eta^2 < 0.06$	$0.10 \leq f < 0.25$
Medium	$0.06 \leq \eta^2 < 0.14$	$0.25 \leq f < 0.40$
Large	$\eta^2 \geq 0.14$	$f \geq 0.40$

8.3.6 Reporting the results of the two-way ANOVA

The results of the three F tests shown in Table 3 should be reported by specifying the name of the factor, followed by the value of the *F* ratio (with the *df* of the numerator and denominator separated by a comma in brackets), the *p*-value and a measure of effect size as follows:

For the Alertness factor:	$F(1, 54) = 8.71$; $p < .01$; partial eta squared = .14.
For the Drug factor:	$F(2, 54) = 4.10$; $p = .02$; partial eta squared = .13.
For the interaction:	$F(2, 54) = 16.49$; $p < .01$; partial eta squared = .38.

A reader, however, should never be confronted with the result of a statistical test (or, worse, a list of results like this) without also being given instant access to the descriptive statistics, either in the body of the text or in a table or figure nearby. A measure of effect size should also be included. The following report embodies these requirements; though a table would have made it less cluttered. The main thing is, the descriptives must be available as well as the test results. Note that *p*-values are given to two places of decimals only; with probabilities less than .01, the inequality sign < is used thus: $p < .01$. Probabilities *greater* than .05 should also be given (to two places of decimals). Insignificant results are also of interest. The report might read as follows:

The mean Driving Performance scores for the Fresh (M = 18.33, SD = 6.35) and Tired (M = 14.67, SD = 5.97) conditions of the Alertness factor differed significantly beyond the .01 level: $F(1, 54) = 8.71$; $p < .01$. Partial eta squared = .14, a 'large' effect. The means and standard deviations of the three conditions making up the Drug Treatment factor were: Placebo (M = 15.5, SD = 7.47); Drug A (M = 15.0, SD = 5.38); Drug B (M = 19.00, SD =

5.65). The Drug Treatment factor had a significant main effect: $F(2, 54) =$ 4.10; $p = .02$. Partial eta squared $= .13$, a 'large' effect. There was also a significant Alertness $\times$ Drug interaction: $F(2, 54) = 16.49$; $p < .01$. Partial eta squared $= .38$, a 'large' effect.

8.4   FURTHER ANALYSIS

In Chapter 7, we observed that the ANOVA itself is just the first stage in the analysis of a set of data from a complex experiment: inevitably, further analysis will be required to clarify the result of the initial ANOVA F test. This is true, *a fortiori*, of the factorial ANOVA. In the first place, the researcher will wish to establish (using measures such as those discussed above) the strengths of the effects that the experiment has demonstrated. It will also be necessary to pinpoint and confirm differences among the group means. Should a significant interaction be obtained, it may be necessary to 'unpack' it by making comparisons among the individual cell means.

8.4.1   The danger with multiple comparisons

A data set from a complex experiment with two or more treatment factors may well show some interesting patterns: the more complex the experiment, in fact, the more likely you are to find something interesting in the results. Unfortunately, this 'discovery' might be the result of sampling error! You will therefore want to follow up the original ANOVA with additional analysis and make several (perhaps many) additional tests of significance. The problem with that procedure, however, is that the more significance tests you make, the more significant results you will obtain – even if the null hypothesis is true!

By making many tests of significance without taking certain precautions, the researcher is 'capitalising upon chance'. In order to avoid that mistake, the researcher must make conservative tests in order to control the **per family** Type I error rate, that is, the probability, under the null hypothesis, that at least one test will show significance. There has been much dispute about which of several possible strategies one should follow and none has emerged as a clear winner. Here, we outline just one approach.

8.4.2   Unpacking significant main effects: post hoc tests

If the two-way ANOVA has shown a factor with three or more levels to have a significant main effect, the researcher may wish to make further comparisons among the individual marginal means. Unplanned or post hoc pairwise (or more complex) comparisons can be run by clicking the **Post Hoc** button in the **Univariate** dialog box.

The optional **Tukey** Post Hoc test results for the Drug Treatment factor are shown in Output 5. It can be seen that the means for Drug A and Drug B differ significantly from one another, but neither differs significantly from the Placebo mean.

Multiple Comparisons

Dependent Variable: Driving Performance

Tukey HSD

(I) Drug Treatment	(J) Drug Treatment	Mean Difference (I-J)	Std. Error	Sig.
Placebo	Drug A	.50	1.52	.942
	Drug B	-3.50	1.52	.064
Drug A	Placebo	-.50	1.52	.942
	Drug B	-4.00*	1.52	.029
Drug B	Placebo	3.50	1.52	.064
	Drug A	4.00*	1.52	.029

Based on observed means.

*. The mean difference is significant at the .05 level.

> The only difference with a p-value <.05 is *Drug A* and *Drug B*.
> Note these rows are highlighted with *

Output 5. Multiple Comparisons with the **Tukey Post Hoc** test for the Drug Treatment factor

8.4.3 The analysis of interactions

When the two-way ANOVA has confirmed a significant interaction between the two factors, it is often necessary to 'unpack' the interaction to determine which differences among the individual treatment or group means are significant.

8.4.3.1 An alternative profile plot

In Figure 7, we have re-plotted the means from the drug experiment, so that the profiles are now the three different Drug Treatment conditions and on the horizontal axis are the levels of the Alertness factor. Having the factor with the greater number of levels on the horizontal axis, as in Figure 1, is normally more aesthetically pleasing. We have re-plotted the means with the scales reversed, however, because ultimately we shall want to make comparisons among the means for the three drug conditions and the new arrangement helps to highlight the key comparisons.

From the graph it is clear that, in the Fresh participants, performance is considerably better under the Placebo and Drug B conditions than it was under Drug A; whereas in the Tired participants, performance with both drugs seems superior to performance under the Placebo condition. Are these differences significant: that is, would these patterns survive a replication of the experiment?

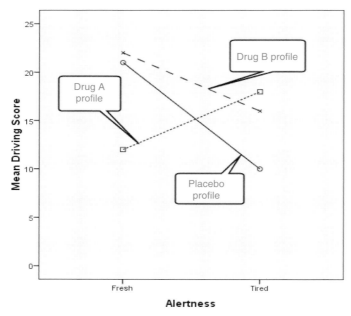

Figure 7. Profile plots of the three drug treatments against levels of Alertness

One approach to the problem of making conservative multiple comparisons among the individual means is to pretend that this is really a one-factor experiment with six groups and request a **Tukey** test. (That would entail adding a new grouping variable with six values to the data set.) The problem with that approach is that, even with an array of six means, the number of possible pairwise comparisons is quite large (15) and this is reflected in a large critical value for the **studentized range statistic (q)**. The **Bonferroni correction** imposes an even tougher criterion for significance. In the next subsection, we shall describe another strategy, which provides a justification for defining a smaller comparison 'family', thus enabling the user to make tests of greater power.

8.4.3.2   Testing for simple main effects

The ANOVA summary table has confirmed the interaction pattern that was strikingly evident in Figure 1 (and in Figure 7). Further analysis, however, is necessary in order to confirm the differences among the cell means. We have seen that in a factorial experiment, a **simple main effect** is the effect of a factor at one particular level of another. It would appear from Figure 7 that there is a simple main effect of the Drug Treatment factor at each of the two levels of the Alertness factor. If we could demonstrate that each of these effects is robust, we should have a justification for defining the comparison families on the basis of three means, rather than six, and so run more powerful **Tukey** (or perhaps **Bonferroni-corrected**) pairwise multiple comparisons tests.

Tests for simple main effects cannot be run simply by completing dialogs in the windowed ANOVA procedure. To test for a simple main effect of the Drug Treatment factor with the Fresh participants only, one could select the data for the fresh participants only and run a one-way ANOVA on those data alone. Subdividing the data in this way, however, entails a loss in power. The use of SPSS control language, or syntax, to test for the presence of simple main effects is the preferred approach.

8.5   TESTING FOR SIMPLE MAIN EFFECTS WITH SYNTAX

So far throughout this book, the statistics provided by SPSS have been accessed by opening windows and completing dialog boxes. Although this is the easy way to learn SPSS, there is another approach which, though it requires practice, has considerable advantages, both short-term and long-term.

It is possible to run SPSS procedures and analyses by writing instructions in a control language known as **SPSS syntax**. (In fact, until a few years ago, the only way of using any of the major statistical packages was by using control language.) It is still useful to learn how to use syntax, if only because some SPSS routines are available through syntax only. Moreover, the syntax for a particular analysis (even one set up initially from dialog boxes – see below) can be saved as a syntax file and re-used later, with enormous savings in time.

8.5.1   The Syntax Editor

The commands are written in a special window known as the Syntax Editor, either by typing them in from the keyboard or by pasting them in from syntax files. The SPSS Statistics Syntax Editor window can be opened by making a selection from the File drop-down menu as shown in Figure 8.

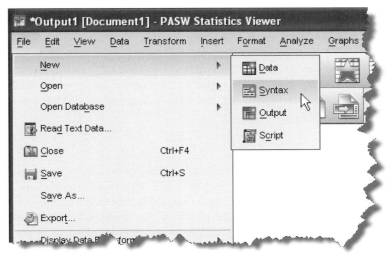

Figure 8. Accessing the syntax window

The window of the **SPSS Statistics Syntax Editor** is shown in Figure 9.

When a particular command in the window has been highlighted, it can be run by clicking the **Selection** icon ▶ . The **Run** drop-down menu gives finer control over the selection and running of multiple commands in the syntax window: e.g., the commands in the Editor can be run step by step, either from the beginning or from a specified current position.

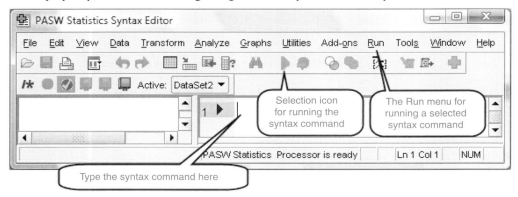

Figure 9. The **Syntax Editor**

8.5.2   Building syntax files automatically

You can make good use of syntax without actually writing any commands at all! If an analysis has been set up from dialog boxes, pressing **Paste** (instead of **OK**) in the main dialog box will paste the hitherto hidden syntax into the **syntax window** from which it can be saved to a file in the usual way. Once a SPSS data file is active, the syntax file can be opened and the procedure can be run immediately: there is no need to complete any dialog boxes. For a syntax file to run, the Data Editor must contain an active data set. This can be a data set that has already been saved to a file: there is a GET FILE command, which can activate a saved data set automatically. It is also possible to run syntax commands by entering a minute data set containing a single score into the syntax editor itself. In no time at all, you will become practised in the use of syntax and familiar with the general form of syntax commands. We believe that the easiest way to learn SPSS syntax is by working from the dialog boxes in this way, rather than ploughing through the available texts on the topic, which tend to be rather compendious and are better left until one has already acquired a working knowledge of the language.

8.5.3   Using the MANOVA command to run the univariate ANOVA

In the ANOVA, there is just one dependent variable or measure, no matter how many independent variables or factors there may be. The ANOVA, therefore, is a **univariate** statistical technique – even though there may be several factors in the design. In **multivariate statistics**, there are two or more dependent variables. The **multivariate analysis of variance (MANOVA)** is a generalisation of the ANOVA to data sets in which there are two or more dependent variables or measures.   We shall have more to say about MANOVA in later chapters. For present purposes, it is only necessary to bear in mind that, for some purposes, the ANOVA can be viewed as a special case of MANOVA and can be run with the MANOVA command. Simple effects analysis for the ANOVA, in fact, can only be accessed by taking the MANOVA route: tests for simple effects are not an option in the ANOVA command itself.

SPSS Statistics 18.0 has a new syntax editor. When the first letter of a command is typed, a directory of command names will appear and the user can select the one required by clicking on it. The command keyword (e.g. MANOVA) appears in red type and remains red until the command is syntactically complete and correct.

A command may be syntactically correct, yet still will not run. If, in the **Syntax Editor** window, a variable name does not correspond to the one in the data set, the command will not run and an error message will appear, both in a box at the foot of the Syntax Editor window and in the **Statistics Viewer** window. An SPSS command always begins with a **command keyword**, which SPSS must recognise for the procedure to run. Within each command, there are **subcommands**, each of which must be preceded by a forward 'slash' / sign. Note also that a subcommand will not run on its own: it must appear within a recognised command. Like a sentence in English, to be syntactically complete, every SPSS command must end in a full stop or period. The command keyword will remain in red until the full stop has been added. (Actually, should the user forget the full stop, SPSS will sometimes add one and the command may run anyway. Don't depend on it, though!)

Figure 10 shows a syntax command that will run a two-way ANOVA on the same drug and alertness data that we have already analysed, but under the aegis of the MANOVA command. Note the following points. The first word of the syntax must be the command keyword MANOVA and the command must end with a full stop or period. In the middle of the command is the keyword BY, on the left of which is the measure or dependent variable and on the right is the list of between subjects factors. The numbers in brackets after each factor name are the lowest and highest code numbers assigned to the groups or conditions.

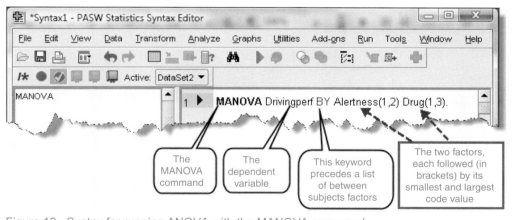

Figure 10. Syntax for running ANOVA with the MANOVA command

The ANOVA summary table is shown in Output 6. The values of the sums of squares, the mean squares, the degrees of freedom and F are exactly as they were in Output 4. The term UNIQUE indicates that the ANOVA has been run by using the MANOVA command. This is a special application of MANOVA: the MANOVA output normally looks different from this.

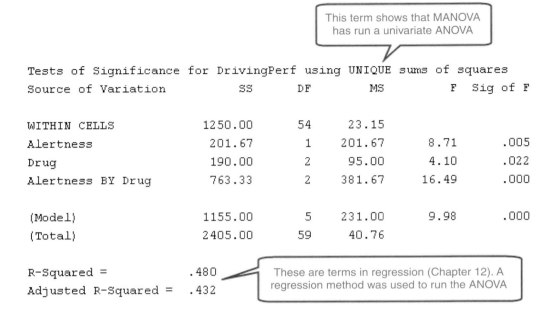

Output 6. The **ANOVA summary table** obtained from running the MANOVA command

8.5.3.3   Including simple effects in a MANOVA subcommand

There is more than one way of writing the syntax for simple main effects. The easiest way is shown in Figure 11.

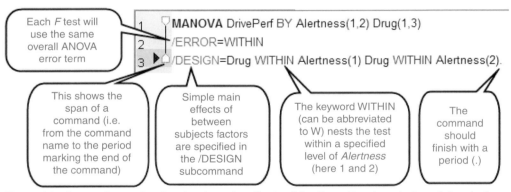

Figure 11. Syntax for testing for simple main effects of the Drug Treatment at each level of Alertness

The subcommand /DESIGN is used for tests of simple main effects. The commands for all the simple main effects of one factor at the different levels of another can be included within the same /DESIGN subcommand.

Note carefully the subcommand /ERROR. If this subcommand is not included, MANOVA will use a composite error term that includes an extra RESIDUAL component. The inclusion of the /ERROR subcommand is not the only way of avoiding this problem: as we shall see, it is possible to absorb the residual component of the error term into the effect sums of squares by amending the /DESIGN subcommand.

8.5.3.4 Output for the simple main effects analysis

Part of the output from the simple effects analysis is shown in Output 7.

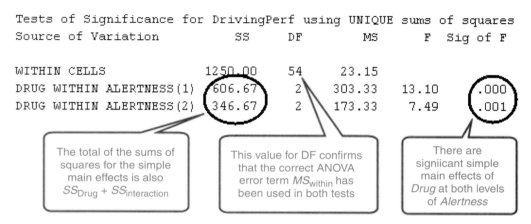

```
Tests of Significance for DrivingPerf using UNIQUE sums of squares
Source of Variation                 SS      DF       MS       F   Sig of F

WITHIN CELLS                     1250.00    54     23.15
DRUG WITHIN ALERTNESS(1)          606.67     2    303.33   13.10    .000
DRUG WITHIN ALERTNESS(2)          346.67     2    173.33    7.49    .001
```

The total of the sums of squares for the simple main effects is also $SS_{Drug} + SS_{interaction}$

This value for DF confirms that the correct ANOVA error term MS_{within} has been used in both tests

There are signiicant simple main effects of *Drug* at both levels of *Alertness*

Output 7. Results of tests for simple main effects of the Drug Treatment factor at each level of Alertness

The analysis has confirmed the presence of simple effects of the Drug Treatment factor at both levels of Alertness: both *p*-values are very small. The correct error term has been used, as requested in the /ERROR subcommand. (Compare with the values of SS and DF in the full two-way ANOVA summary table in Output 6.)

The comparison of the values in Output 7 with the ANOVA summary table in Output 6 also confirms another interesting identity. Earlier, we observed that the appearance of profile plots (such as those in Figure 1 p.270) reflects the presence of the main effect of the factor whose simple main effects we are testing, as well as the interaction. In Output 7, you can see that

$$SS_{Drug\ at\ Alertness(1)} + SS_{Drug\ at\ Alertness(2)} = 606.666 + 346.666$$
$$= 953.33$$

This is the total of the sums of squares for the Drug Treatment factor and the interaction in the ANOVA summary table (Output 6):

$$SS_{Drug} + SS_{Alertness \times Drug} = 190.00 + 763.33$$
$$= 953.33$$

The above comparison illustrates the general point that, in a factorial experiment of A × B design, the sums of squares of the simple main effects of A at B_1, A at B_2, ..., across all levels of B, add up to the sum of squares for the main effect of A plus the sum of squares for the interaction:

$$\sum_k SS_{A \text{ at } B_k} = SS_{A \text{ at } B_1} + SS_{A \text{ at } B_2} + ... + SS_{A \text{ at } B_k} \qquad \text{- - - (9)}$$

$$= SS_A + SS_{AB}$$

Simple main effects reflect main effect plus interaction

Effectively, the simple main effects terms in Output 7 have replaced the main effect and interaction terms in the full ANOVA shown in Output 6.

8.5.3.5   An alternative syntax for testing simple main effects

The manner in which the ANOVA run by the MANOVA procedure has re-divided (or, to use the technical term, **re-partitioned**) the sums of squares becomes explicit when another wording of the MANOVA syntax command is used to test for the same simple main effects.

We have seen that the full ANOVA can be run from the MANOVA command with a single line of syntax, namely,

MANOVA DrivingPerf BY Alertness(1,2) Drug(1,3).

The same result can also be achieved by adding a /DESIGN subcommand, as in Figure 12.

Figure 12. Ordering a full ANOVA by specifying the components in the DESIGN subcommand

The same simple effects analysis discussed above can also be implemented by rewriting the /DESIGN subcommand to re-partition the between groups sum of squares into a main effect of Alertness, plus simple effects of the Drug Treatment factor at each level of Alertness (see Figure 13). Notice that the explicit main effect of the drug factor and interaction term have disappeared: they have been replaced by the simple main effects.

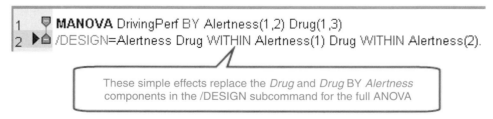

Figure 13. Specifying tests for simple main effects without also specifying the error term

Output 8 shows the result of the analysis. Several features of the output are worthy of note. The source labelled WITHIN + RESIDUAL is actually the WITHIN error term in the full ANOVA, as you can see from the degrees of freedom (54) and the agreement between the sum of squares value (1250) and that given as WITHIN CELLS in Output 7. The sums of squares for ALERTNESS and (Total) have exactly the same values as those given in the full ANOVA summary table (Output 6). Once again, the sums of squares for the simple effects of the Drug Treatment factor at the different levels of Alertness sum to the total of the Drug and Drug × Alertness sums of squares in the full ANOVA.

```
Tests of Significance for DrivingPerf using UNIQUE sums of squares
Source of Variation            SS      DF     MS        F   Sig of F

WITHIN+RESIDUAL              1250.00   54    23.15
ALERTNESS                    201.67    1    201.67     8.71   .005
DRUG WITHIN ALERTNESS(1)     606.67    2    303.33    13.10   .000
DRUG WITHIN ALERTNESS(2)     346.67    2    173.33     7.49   .001

(Model)                     1155.00    5    231.00     9.98   .000
(Total)                     2405.00   59    40.76

R-Squared =          .480
Adjusted R-Squared =  .432
```

These sources replace the main effect of Drug and the Drug*Alertness interaction in the full ANOVA summary table

Output 8. Tests for simple effects in a model re-dividing the sum of squares of the main effect of the Drug factor plus that of the Drug × Alertness interaction

8.5.3.6   Multiple comparisons following tests of simple main effects

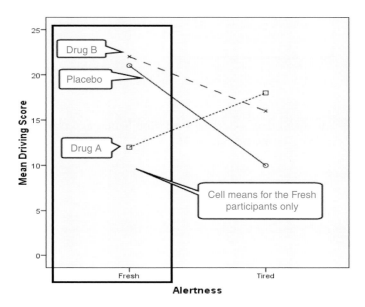

Figure 14. Profile plots showing the effect of the Drug Treatment factor upon the Fresh participants

Figure 14 is an alternative set of profile plots of the two-way table of means for the Drug and Alertness experiment, with the profiles for the three different drug conditions being plotted against the two levels of the Alertness factor on the horizontal axis. From the graph, it would appear that, with the Fresh participants, Drug A lowered the performance level in comparison with the Drug B and Placebo conditions, which produced similar levels of performance.

Now that we have established that there is a significant simple main effect of the Drug Treatment factor with the Fresh participants, we can proceed with post hoc pairwise comparisons on the basis that the comparison 'family' is the number of possible pairs in the three cell means for the Fresh participants. From Figure 14, we can expect that the mean for Drug A will turn out to be significantly less than the means for the Placebo and Drug B groups; whereas it seems likely that there is no significant difference between Drug B and the Placebo.

To select Fresh participants only, choose **Data→Select Cases…** and click the **If condition satisfied** radio button to open the **Select Cases: If** dialog box (Figure 15). Follow the instructions in Figure 15 and then click **OK** in the **Select Cases** dialog box.

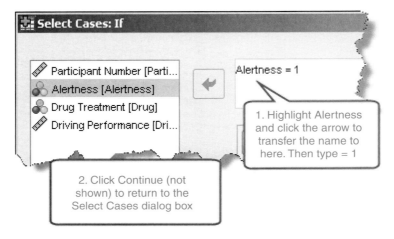

Figure 15. Selecting the data from the Fresh participants only

Back in the **Univariate** dialog box, click the **Post Hoc** button and choose the **Tukey** test, specifying the factor as Drug Treatment (Figure 16).

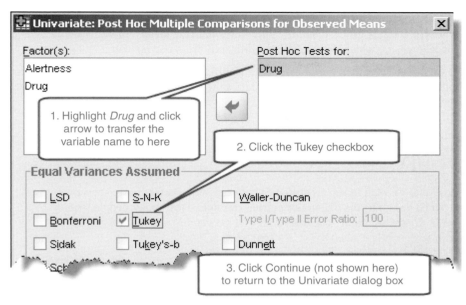

Figure 16. Choosing **Tukey** post hoc tests for the Drug Treatment factor

8.5.3.7   Output for the Tukey test

Output 9 shows that the **Tukey** test has identified two subgroups:

1.   The mean for Drug A;
2.   The means for the Placebo and Drug B groups.

Should you require further details for your report, the SPSS output includes another table showing the *p*-values and confidence intervals for these tests.

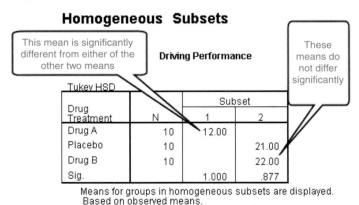

Output 9. Summary of the results of the **Tukey** test

The **Tukey** test has clearly confirmed that, in the data from the Fresh participants only, the mean for the Drug A group is significantly lower than the means for either the Drug B group or the Placebo group, which do not differ significantly from one another.

Since the Drug Treatment factor also has a significant main effect upon the Tired participants, a similar Tukey test can be run on those data as well to confirm the pattern of differences that appears in Figure 1.

8.6   HOW MANY PARTICIPANTS SHALL I NEED FOR MY TWO-FACTOR EXPERIMENT?

Suppose that we plan to run a two-factor between subjects factorial experiment of the same design as the one in our current example. How many people would we need to test in order to achieve, say, a power of .75 for an effect of medium size, that is, Cohen's $f = .25$ (see Section 7.6)?

See Section 7.6

When deciding upon the numbers of participants necessary to achieve a specified level of power for, say, an effect of 'medium' size ($f = .25$) the user should bear in mind that in factorial experiments, the tests of the various effects do not always have the same power to reject the null hypothesis: e.g. if both factors have three or more levels, the test for an interaction will have less power than a test for a main effect. You may have sufficient participants to achieve a power of at least .75 for your tests of main effects; but your test for an interaction may have lower power. Since the interaction is often the main focus in a factorial experiment, the researcher should give this effect source special attention.

As with the earlier versions, **G*Power 3** will answer questions about the power of an experimental design with specified numbers of participants and about the numbers of participants that will be needed to achieve tests at a minimum specified level of power. Open G*Power 3 and select **Tests→Means→Many groups: ANOVA: Main effects and interactions (two or more independent variables)**. Returning to our original question, we shall need to enter the following items: the effect size (.25); the alpha-level (.05); the desired power level (.75); the numerator degrees of freedom (in the present example, $df_{interaction} = 2$); the total number of groups (six). In the output, we shall learn that a total sample size of 141 will be required. In practical terms, this means we shall actually require 24 participants in each group, i.e. 144 participants in all.

8.7   MORE COMPLEX EXPERIMENTS

SPSS can readily be used to analyse data from more complex factorial experiments, with three or more treatment factors. In Section 8.2, we described the two-way ANOVA, which we illustrated with data from an imaginary investigation of the effects of two new anti-hay fever drugs, A and B, upon simulated driving performance. It was suspected that at least one of the drugs might have different effects upon fresh and tired drivers, and the firm developing the drugs needed to ensure that neither had an adverse effect upon driving performance. It was found that Drug A did indeed have different effects upon fresh and tired participants: it improved the performance of tired drivers; but it impaired the performance of fresh drivers. The two-factor drugs-and-driving experiment demonstrated the presence of an interaction between the two treatment factors of Alertness (Fresh, Tired) and Drug Treatment (Placebo, Drug A, Drug B).

Our hypothetical researcher was aware that much of the previous research on the hay fever drugs had used male participants. Recent pilot work, however, had suggested that the striking interaction between Alertness and Drug Treatment might not occur in female drivers. It was therefore decided to include females in a new investigation and run a **three-factor between subjects factorial experiment**, in which the factors were:
1. Drug Treatment, with levels Placebo, Drug A and Drug B.
2. Alertness, with levels Fresh and Tired.
3. Sex, with levels Female and Male.

An experiment with three factors allows the investigation of more complex hypotheses than does a two-factor experiment: in particular, the addition of the third factor brings the possibility of a complex interplay among all three factors known as a **three-way interaction**.

8.7.1   Three-way interactions

In a factorial experiment with three factors, the interaction between two factors at one particular level of the third factor is known as a **simple interaction**. For example, the interaction between the Drug Treatment and Alertness factors in the female participants only is a simple interaction, as is the interaction between the same two factors in the male participants.

8.7.1.1   Three-way interactions

A **three-way interaction** is said to occur when the simple interactions between two factors are not the same at all levels of a third factor. This is exactly what is implied by the investigator's hypothesis: we can expect a three-way interaction among the factors of Alertness, Drug Treatment and Sex because we have reason to suspect that the simple interaction between Drug Treatment and Alertness is not the same in the two sexes.

It is quite clear from the graphs (Figure 17) that the two-way interaction between the Alertness and Drug Treatment factors is different in the female and male participants: while the simple interaction is strikingly evident in the males, it is not apparent in the data from the females. Here we have what appears to be a three-way interaction among the factors Alertness, Drug Treatment and Sex. We can hope that the three-way ANOVA will confirm this complex interaction.

In the males, Drug A had a dampening effect on the performance of the fresh participants; whereas the same drug improved the performance of the tired participants. In the female participants, there is little sign of an interaction; though the Drug A profile is shallower than those of the Drug B or Placebo groups. There is here no evidence that either drug boosted the performance of tired female drivers.

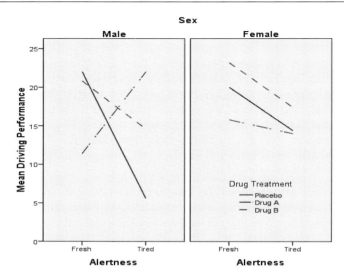

Figure 17. The two-way graphs for the female and male participants, illustrating a three-way interaction among the factors of Alertness, Drug Treatment and Sex

8.7.2   The three-way ANOVA

The results of the experiment are shown in Table 6.

Table 6. Results of a three-way factorial experiment				
Levels of the **Alertness** factor:	Levels of the **Sex** factor:	Levels of the **Drug Treatment** factor:		
		Placebo	A	B
Fresh	Male	23 18 19 24 26	11 16 11 8 11	23 19 17 20 25
	Female	24 25 13 22 16	14 18 15 18 14	27 14 19 29 27
Tired	Male	13 4 3 2 6	21 19 25 21 24	9 14 11 21 18
	Female	13 12 14 16 17	13 16 14 15 12	21 11 14 22 19

The three-way ANOVA summary table is shown in Table 7. It is worth examining Table 7 carefully and comparing it with the two-way table. There are now tests for three main effects: Drug Treatment, Alertness and Sex. There are also tests for each of the three possible two-way interactions: Alertness × Drug Treatment, Alertness × Sex and Drug Treatment × Sex. Finally, there is a test for a three-way interaction.

The most interesting result in Table 7 is the significance of the three-way interaction, which is consistent with the research hypothesis. The result of this F test would be reported in the manner described for the two-way ANOVA:

$$F(2, 48) = 11.15; p < .01$$

A measure of effect size (partial eta squared or partial omega squared) would also be included.

Source	df	SS	MS	F	p
Table 7. Three-way ANOVA table for the data in Table 6					
Main effects					
Alertness (A)	1	264.60	264.60	17.49	<.01
Drug (D)	2	150.53	75.27	4.97	.01
Sex (S)	1	29.40	29.40	1.94	.17
Two-way interactions					
A × D	2	617.20	308.60	20.39	<.01
A × S	1	.60	.60	.04	.84
D × S	2	78.40	39.20	2.59	.09
Three-way interaction					
A × D × S	2	337.60	168.80	11.15	<.01
Error term					
Within groups (Error)	48	726.40	15.13		
Total	59	2204.73			

In this context, it is worth observing that a list of ANOVA test results means very little without a clear demonstration of the patterns of differences responsible for each result. The mere fact that the three-way interaction is significant does not necessarily mean that the cell means show the patterns of those in Figure 17. Rather than presenting the reader of your report with a long list of results of the seven F tests, you should 'talk the reader through' the patterns of means in a graph such as Figure 17 or a table, explaining the relevant significant (and insignificant) results with reference to the descriptive statistics.

8.7.3   How the three-way ANOVA works

The rationale of the three-way ANOVA is a simple extension of that of the two-way ANOVA.

In the three-way ANOVA, the between groups sums of squares is partitioned into three main effects sums of squares, three two-way interaction sums of squares and the three-way interaction sum of squares. In our current example, the partition is:

$$SS_{between} = SS_{Alertness} + SS_{Drug} + SS_{Sex} + SS_{A \times D} + SS_{A \times S} + SS_{D \times S} + SS_{A \times D \times S} \quad \text{- - -} (10)$$

Partition of the total sum of squares in the three-way ANOVA

As with the one-way and two-way ANOVA, the mean squares are obtained by dividing the sums of squares by their degrees of freedom. The general form of the F statistic for any between subjects factorial design is as follows:

$$F\left(df_{source}, df_{within}\right) = \frac{MS_{source}}{MS_{within}} \quad \text{- - -} (11)$$

General form of the F statistic in the between subjects factorial ANOVA

It is important, with complex experimental designs especially, to be clear about the degrees of freedom of the various sources in the ANOVA. This knowledge is very helpful when you are interpreting the SPSS output, or when you want to use a package such as **G*Power 3** to determine the number of participants that will be needed in a study you plan to run.

The degrees of freedom are obtained in a manner analogous with the one-way and two-way ANOVA. For main effects, df is the number of conditions or groups minus 1.

$$df_A = (a-1); \quad df_B = (b-1); \quad df_C = (c-1) \quad \text{- - -} \quad (12)$$

Degrees of freedom of main effects

In our current example,

$$df_{\text{Drug}} = (3-1) = 2; \quad df_{\text{Alertness}} = (2-1) = 1; \quad df_{\text{Sex}} = (2-1) = 1$$

For two-way interactions, the df is the product of the degrees of freedom of the main effects of the sources involved in the interaction:

$$df_{A \times B} = (a-1)(b-1); \quad df_{A \times C} = (a-1)(c-1); \quad df_{B \times C} = (b-1)(c-1) \quad \text{- - -} \quad (13)$$

Degrees of freedom of two-way interactions

In our current example,

$$df_{\text{Alertness} \times \text{Drug}} = (2-1)(3-1) = 2;$$
$$df_{\text{Alertness} \times \text{Sex}} = (2-1)(2-1) = 1;$$
$$df_{\text{Drug} \times \text{Sex}} = (3-1)(2-1) = 2$$

The degrees of freedom of the three-way interaction is the product of the degrees of freedom of the three component sources.

$$df_{A \times B \times C} = (a-1)(b-1)(c-1) \quad \text{- - -} \quad (14)$$

Degrees of freedom of the three-way interaction

In our current example, if A, B and C are the Alertness, Drug Treatment and Sex factors, respectively, a = 2, b = 3, c = 2 and

$$df_{A \times B \times C} = (2-1)(3-1)(2-1) = 2$$

As in the two-way ANOVA, all the F tests in the three-way ANOVA have the same denominator, namely, MS_{within}. As in the one-way and two-way ANOVA, the within groups mean square is the average of the variance estimates calculated from each sample of participants.

In general, if the three factors A, B and C have a, b & c levels, respectively, n is the number of participants in each combination of conditions and N is the total number of observations, there will be $a \times b \times c = abc$ combinations of treatments, that is, cells in the design. In our example,

$abc = 2 \times 3 \times 2 = 12$. If n is the sample size (in our fictitious example, $n = 5$), the total number of observations is $N = abcn$. In our example, $N = 2 \times 3 \times 2 \times 5 = 60$.

As in the one-way and two-way ANOVAs, the error term in the three-way ANOVA is a pooled estimate of the supposedly uniform population variance σ_e^2. In general, since there are abc cells in the design, there will be abc variance estimates, each with $(n-1)$ degrees of freedom. The degrees of freedom of the within groups mean square MS_{within} is therefore given by

$$df_{within} = abc(n-1) = N - abc \quad \text{- - - (15)}$$

Degrees of freedom of the
within groups mean square

In our current example,

$$df_{within} = 60 - 12 = 48$$

which is the value given in Table 7.

8.7.4   Measures of effect size in the three-way ANOVA

Since the various measures of effect size are defined and calculated as simple generalisations from the two-way ANOVA, we shall only consider partial omega squared here.

$$\hat{\omega}_{source}^2 = \frac{df_{source}\left(F_{source}-1\right)}{df_{source}\left(F_{source}-1\right) + abcn} \quad \text{- - - (16)}$$

Partial omega squared for the three-way ANOVA

Note that, in the denominator of (16), we must introduce the multiplier c, the number of levels making up the third factor, into the rightmost term.

8.7.5   How many participants shall I need?

Proceed with **G*Power 3** in a manner similar to the two-factor ANOVA, supplying the degrees of freedom for the various sources and the error term as described in Section 8.6.

8.7.6   The three-way ANOVA with SPSS

8.7.6.1   Entering the data

For the three-way ANOVA, the data set in **Data View** will now include three grouping variables (Alertness, Sex, and Drug), as well as a column for the dependent variable DrivingPerf. (It is good practice also to include a column of case or participant numbers as well.) Figure 18 shows a section of **Data View**, showing the third grouping variable Sex, representing the third factor in the experimental design.

	Participant	Alertness	Drug	Sex	DrivingPerf	
1	1	Fresh	Placebo	Female	24	
2	2	Fresh	Placebo	Female	25	
3	3	Fresh	Placebo	Female	13	
4	4	Fresh	Placebo	Female	22	
5	5	Fresh	Placebo	Female	16	
6	6	Fresh	Placebo	Male	23	
7	7	Fresh	Placebo	Male	18	
8	8	Fresh	Placebo	Male	19	
9	9	Fresh	Placebo	Male	24	

Figure 18. Part of **Data View** showing some of the data in Table 6

To run the three-factor ANOVA, proceed as follows:

- Open the **General Linear Model - Univariate** dialog box and complete it as in Chapter 7, Figure 10, moving Driving Performance to the **Dependent Variable** box and the three grouping factors Alertness, Drug Treatment and Sex to the **Fixed Factors** box.
- Select the optional **Descriptive statistics** and **Estimates of effect size** check boxes from **Options…** and the **Tukey Post Hoc** test for Drug Treatment from **Post Hoc…**, clicking **Continue** each time to return to the **Univariate** dialog box.
- To obtain the profile plots of the means that we have shown in Figure 17, click **Plots…** to open the **Univariate: Profile Plots** dialog box. Select Alertness for the **Horizontal Axis** box, Drug Treatment for the **Separate Lines** box and Sex for the **Separate Plots** box. Click **Add** to add the plot to the **Plots** list and then **Continue** to return to the **Univariate** dialog box. (Note that, should you want to have the Drug Treatment factor on the horizontal axis of the graphs and show the profiles of the two Alertness conditions, you would transfer Drug Treatment to the Horizontal Axis box, Alertness to the **Separate Lines** box and Sex to the **Separate Plots** box as before.)
- Click **OK**.

8.7.6.2   Output for the three-way ANOVA

The first table in the output lists the factors in the experiment, their value labels and the number of cases in each cell (Output 10). Check this information carefully to ensure that there have been no transcription errors and that the design specifications have been correctly communicated to SPSS.

Between-Subjects Factors

		Value Label	N
Alertness	1	Fresh	30
	2	Tired	30
Drug Treatment	1	Placebo	20
	2	Drug A	20
	3	Drug B	20
Sex	1	Male	30
	2	Female	30

Output 10. The table of **Between-Subjects Factors**

The next table in the output (not reproduced here) shows the descriptive statistics you should always request in the **Options...** dialog box.

Ignore these rows

Of interest for ANOVA is the value of *F* and its associated p-value

The values of η_p^2 are all $\geq 10\%$ except for *Sex* and *Alertness*Sex*

Tests of Between-Subjects Effects

Dependent Variable: Driving Performance

Source	Type III Sum of Squares	df	Mean Square	F	Sig.	Partial Eta Squared
Corrected Model	1478.33ª	11	134.39	8.88	.000	.671
Intercept	16867.27	1	16867	1114.58	.000	.959
Alertness	264.60	1	264.60	17.48	.000	.267
Drug	150.53	2	75.27	4.97	.011	.172
Sex	29.40	1	29.40	1.94	.170	.039
Alertness * Drug	617.20	2	308.60	20.39	.000	.459
Alertness * Sex	.60	1	.60	.04	.843	.001
Drug * Sex	78.40	2	39.20	2.59	.085	.097
Alertness * Drug * Sex	337.60	2	168.80	11.15	.000	.317
Error	726.40	48	15.13			
Total	19073.00	60				
Corrected Total	2204.73	59				

a. R Squared = .671 (Adjusted R Squared = .595)

Alertness, the interaction *Alertness*Drug* and the triple interaction have p-values <.01 (i.e. significant at the .01 level)

Drug has a p-value between .05 and .01 (i.e. significant at the .05 level) but *Sex* and its interactions have p-values >.05 (i.e. not significant)

Output 11. The three-way factorial **ANOVA** summary table

The ANOVA summary table (Output 11) shows that of the three main effects, Alertness and Drug are significant but Sex is insignificant. Of the three two-way interactions, Alertness × Drug is significant, but neither Alertness × Sex nor Drug × Sex is significant. There is a significant three-way interaction, in line with the experimental hypothesis.

The full SPSS ANOVA summary table is a useful source of information for the researcher who is analysing data with a view to publishing a research paper. Such a table, on the other hand, would rarely appear in the body of the text of a paper; moreover, little would be achieved by including, in the body of the text, a comprehensive list of all the test results in the ANOVA summary table. Instead, the reader should be guided through only those results that are relevant to the principal research hypotheses, each result being explained with reference to the appropriate descriptive statistics.

Whether a table or a graph is the more suitable vehicle for the descriptive statistics is a matter of opinion and journal editors can differ on this issue. With a complex experiment such as the present one, we think it makes life easier for the reader to be referred to a graph such as Figure 17, rather than a complex table; but others would certainly disagree.

8.7.7   Follow-up analysis following a significant three-way interaction

Having obtained a three-way interaction, you will certainly want to follow this up with further analysis. In an experiment of this degree of complexity, however, the perils of data-snooping are even greater than they are in a two-factor experiment. As far as we can see from our study of the literature, there seems to be, in this situation, no generally acceptable way of avoiding inflation of the **Familywise Type I error** rate to at least some extent. The following suggestions, though defensible, would certainly not be accepted by everyone.

In general, we think that the risk of capitalising upon chance is reduced by following a multistage decision process, in which tests at any stage are only made if the previous stage has shown a significant result. For example, only if the three-way interaction has proved significant, would one proceed to test for simple interactions between Drug Treatment and Alertness at each level of Sex. Should you obtain a significant simple interaction only with the males, this would provide additional confirmation of the research hypothesis. As with testing for simple main effects in the two-factor experiment, the **Bonferroni correction** could be used to make a more conservative test for simple two-way interactions in the three-factor experiment. Since there are two possible simple interactions, one for the males, the other for the females, you would require that each test should show significance beyond the .025 level, rather than merely beyond the .05 level.

Should a simple interaction prove to be significant, you will naturally wish to make unplanned comparisons among the individual cell means. In the two-factor experiment, there was the difficulty that if one bases the size of the comparison family upon the set of means involved in the entire interaction, the criterion for significance is very stringent. Arguably, a significant test for a simple main effect might justify basing the size of the comparison family upon those means at one level only of the other factor. The same problem arises in the analysis following a significant three-way interaction. In order to justify limiting the size of the comparison 'family', you could proceed to test for a main effect of the Drug Treatment factor at specific combinations of the factors of Alertness and Sex. Should you find, for example, that there is a significant main effect of the Drug Treatment factor in those participants who were both Fresh and Male, you could then proceed to run a **Tukey** test on the three cell means involved, basing the size of the comparison family upon those means alone, rather than upon all those involved in the interaction. A test for a main effect of one factor at a specific combination of two other factors is known as a **simple, simple main effect**. A significant simple, simple main effect would arguably justify reducing the size of the comparison family when making unplanned multiple comparison among the cell means. Once again, the test for a significant simple, simple main effect should be protected by the **Bonferroni** procedure: in the present example, the test would have to show significance beyond the .025 level, rather than the .05 level.

In the next section, we shall describe the use of SPSS syntax to test for simple interactions and simple, simple main effects.

8.7.8   Using SPSS syntax to test for simple interactions and simple, simple main effects

Tests for simple effects of various kinds in completely randomised factorial experiments are accessed by the use of the DESIGN subcommand within the MANOVA command. Here we shall consider the syntax for simple interactions and simple, simple main effects separately. In practice, of course, both types of subcommand could be included in the same MANOVA command.

8.7.8.1   The full two-way ANOVA with syntax

The full ANOVA can be run with a one-line MANOVA command very similar to the one we used for the two-factor ANOVA (Figure 19):

Figure 19. The MANOVA command for the three-way ANOVA

The ANOVA summary table is shown in Output 12. The values given, of course, agree exactly with the corresponding values in the GLM output (Output 11).

```
Tests of Significance for DrivingPerf using UNIQUE sums of squares
Source of Variation              SS        DF       MS         F   Sig of F

WITHIN CELLS                  726.40       48      15.13
Alertness                     264.60        1     264.60     17.48     .000
Drug                          150.53        2      75.27      4.97     .011
Sex                            29.40        1      29.40      1.94     .170
Alertness BY Drug             617.20        2     308.60     20.39     .000
Alertness BY Sex                 .60        1        .60       .04     .843
Drug BY Sex                    78.40        2      39.20      2.59     .085
Alertness BY Drug BY          337.60        2     168.80     11.15     .000
  Sex

(Model)                      1478.33       11     134.39      8.88     .000
(Total)                      2204.73       59      37.37


R-Squared =            .671
Adjusted R-Squared =   .595
```

Output 12. Results of the three-way ANOVA from the MANOVA procedure

8.7.8.2   Testing for simple interactions

Figure 20 shows the syntax for tests of simple interactions at each level of the Sex factor. In the /DESIGN subcommand, the keyword BY is used to specify an interaction.

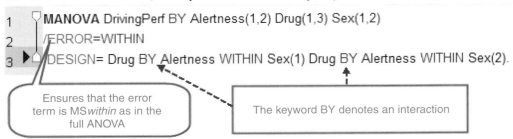

```
1    MANOVA DrivingPerf BY Alertness(1,2) Drug(1,3) Sex(1,2)
2    /ERROR=WITHIN
3    /DESIGN= Drug BY Alertness WITHIN Sex(1) Drug BY Alertness WITHIN Sex(2).
```

Ensures that the error term is MS*within* as in the full ANOVA

The keyword BY denotes an interaction

Figure 20. Tests for the simple Drug Treatment × Alertness interaction at each level of Sex

The results of the tests for simple interactions are shown in Output 13.

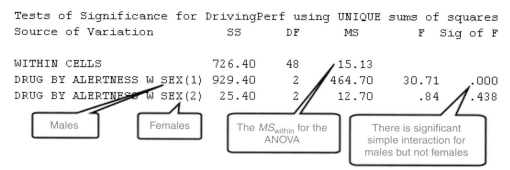

Output 13. Tests for a simple interaction between Drug Treatment and Alertness at each level of Sex

There is a significant simple Drug Treatment × Alertness interaction in the Males, but not in the Females. This result is consistent with the experimenter's hypothesis that the interaction may not occur in Female drivers.

Notice that if we add the sums of squares for the two simple interactions, we obtain the sum of the sums of squares for the Drug × Alertness interaction and the Drug × Alertness × Sex interaction from the full ANOVA summary table. Simple effects confound the target interaction with certain lower-order effects: simple main effects confound the two-way interaction with the main effect; simple interactions confound the three-way interaction with the two-way interaction. Simple effects, then, are a blend of effects at different levels, and it is for that reason that some are opposed to their use.

8.7.8.3 Testing for a simple, simple main effect of the Drug Treatment factor at each level of Sex

Figure 21 shows the syntax for testing for simple, simple main effects. A specific combination of Alertness and Sex is specified by a second use of the keyword WITHIN.

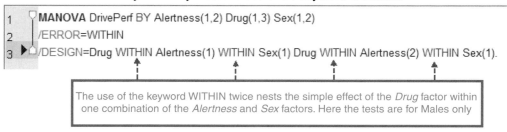

Figure 21. Testing for simple, simple main effects of the Drug Treatment factor at different combinations of Alertness and Sex

The results of the tests for simple, simple main effects are shown in Output 14.

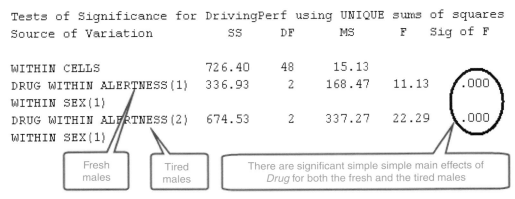

Tests of Significance for DrivingPerf using UNIQUE sums of squares
Source of Variation   SS   DF   MS   F   Sig of F

WITHIN CELLS   726.40   48   15.13
DRUG WITHIN ALERTNESS(1)   336.93   2   168.47   11.13   .000
WITHIN SEX(1)
DRUG WITHIN ALERTNESS(2)   674.53   2   337.27   22.29   .000
WITHIN SEX(1)

Fresh males | Tired males | There are significant simple simple main effects of *Drug* for both the fresh and the tired males

Output 14. Tests (edited) for simple, simple main effects of the Drug Treatment factor at each level of Alertness in the Male participants only

Since both tests show significance beyond the .01 level, there is, some would argue, justification for making unplanned multiple comparisons among the three cell means at either level of Alertness.

8.7.9   Unplanned multiple comparisons following a significant three-way interaction

We have seen that the appearance of the cell means in Figure 1 has been confirmed by the finding that there is a significant simple interaction between the factors of Drug Treatment and Alertness among the male participants. We have also found that there is a significant simple, simple main effect of the Drug Treatment factor in the data from the Fresh Males. We now want to unpack the interaction more completely by making unplanned multiple comparisons among the Placebo, Drug A and Drug B cell means from the data on the Fresh Males only. The first step is to filter out all the data except the scores obtained by the Fresh Male participants. Figure 22 shows the appropriate **Select Cases: If** command.

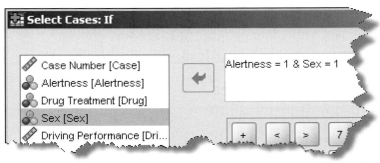

Figure 22. Selecting only those performance scores that were produced by the Fresh Males in the study

Figure 23 shows the appearance of part of **Data View** with the filter in operation. It will be seen that only the data from the Fresh Males have been selected for the **Tukey** analysis.

	Case	Alertness	Drug	Sex	DrivingPerf	filter_$
8	8	Fresh	Placebo	Male	19	Selected
9	9	Fresh	Placebo	Male	24	Selected
10	10	Fresh	Placebo	Male	26	Selected
11	11	Fresh	Drug A	Female	14	Not Selected
12	12	Fresh	Drug A	Female	18	Not Selected
13	13	Fresh	Drug A	Female	15	Not Selected
14	14	Fresh	Drug A	Female	18	Not Selected
15	15	Fresh	Drug A	Female	14	Not Selected
16	16	Fresh	Drug A	Male	11	Selected
17	17	Fresh	Drug A	Male	16	Selected

Figure 23. The appearance of **Data View** after the user has selected the data from the Fresh Males only

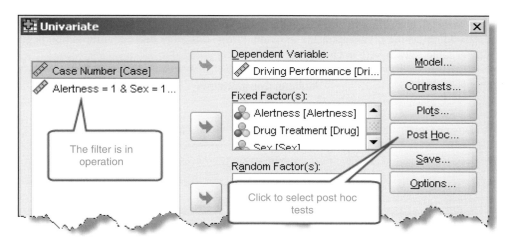

Figure 24. Accessing **Post Hoc** tests from the **Univariate** dialog box

The **Tukey** test can now be run from the by clicking **Post Hoc** to access a wide choice of **Post Hoc** tests (Figure 24).

In the **Univariate: Post Hoc Multiple Comparisons for Observed Means** dialog, move the variable label Drug Treatment to the right-hand panel and check the **Tukey** box (see Figure 16). The results of the Tukey test are shown in Output 15.

Homogeneous Subsets

Driving Performance

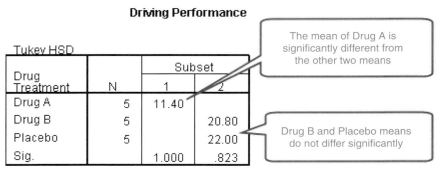

Tukey HSD

Drug Treatment	N	Subset 1	Subset 2
Drug A	5	11.40	
Drug B	5		20.80
Placebo	5		22.00
Sig.		1.000	.823

The mean of Drug A is significantly different from the other two means

Drug B and Placebo means do not differ significantly

Means for groups in homogeneous subsets are displayed.
Based on observed means.
The error term is Mean Square(Error) = 10.000.

Output 15. Results of **Tukey** post hoc tests following a significant simple, simple main effect of Drug Treatment in the Fresh Male participants

The **Tukey** tests have confirmed that the mean for Drug A is significantly less than the means for the Drug B and Placebo groups, which do not differ significantly. Should it be felt necessary to report the *p*-values for the individual tests, this more detailed information is given in another table, shown here in Output 16.

Multiple Comparisons

Driving Performance
Tukey HSD

(I) Drug Treatment	(J) Drug Treatment	Mean Difference (I-J)	Std. Error	Sig.	95% Confidence Interval Lower Bound	95% Confidence Interval Upper Bound
Placebo	Drug A	10.60*	2.000	.001	5.26	15.94
	Drug B	1.20	2.000	.823	-4.14	6.54
Drug A	Placebo	-10.60*	2.000	.001	-15.94	-5.26
	Drug B	-9.40*	2.000	.001	-14.74	-4.06
Drug B	Placebo	-1.20	2.000	.823	-6.54	4.14
	Drug A	9.40*	2.000	.001	4.06	14.74

Based on observed means.
The error term is Mean Square(Error) = 10.000.

*. The mean difference is significant at the 0.05 level.

Output 16. Details of the **Tukey** multiple comparison tests, including confidence intervals and *p*-values

8.8   A FINAL WORD

In this chapter, we have tried to convey something of the power of factorial experiments to answer complex scientific questions. The interpretation of the results of complex experiments, however, particularly unplanned tests made during the data-snooping phase following the ANOVA proper, is fraught with risk and there is a heightened risk of capitalising upon chance.

We strongly recommend that you should try to avoid factorial designs with more than three factors. While we agree that participants' scores are likely to depend on many variables, it is usually possible to arrange that theoretically unimportant potential sources of variance, such as positional and sequential contingencies, can be neutralised by careful experimental design and need not emerge explicitly as factors in the analysis.

There are several good reasons for avoiding complex factorial designs with four or more factors. Four-way interactions are exceedingly difficult to interpret. Moreover, although the follow-up methods we have described can, in principle, be extended to the analysis of more complex experiments, there remains the potential problem of over-analysis and hence capitalising upon chance. The more factors there are, the greater the risk that the analysis will turn up an unexpected and striking effect that would not be confirmed by a re-run of the experiment. If a comparison is of such vital theoretical importance, there is much to be said for designing a new, simpler experiment to confirm that it has nor arisen merely through sampling error.

Some would certainly disapprove of the use of simple effects analysis to reduce the size of the comparison 'family' when one is unpacking a significant interaction; and the testing of simple, simple main effects for the purpose of reducing the size of the comparison family when unpacking a significant three-way interaction is even more questionable. Others, however, would agree that if such analyses are untaken only after an interaction (or simple interaction) has proved to be significant, the risk of capitalising upon chance has at least been reduced. In our view, an experiment of complex factorial design is perhaps most appropriate when the hypotheses driving the research are still somewhat tentative. At a later stage, when the focal hypothesis has crystallised, the researcher should test it with an experiment of simpler design.

Recommended Reading

In this chapter, we could do no more than touch upon the analysis of data from complex factorial experiments. Howell (2007; Chapter 13) gives a lucid treatment of the analysis of interactions.

Howell, D. C. (2007). *Statistical methods for psychology (6th ed.)*.   Belmont, CA: Thomson/Wadsworth.

Exercise

Exercise 12 *Between subjects factorial ANOVA (two-way ANOVA)* is available in www.psypress.com/spss-made-simple Click on Exercises.

CHAPTER 9

Within subjects experiments

9.1   INTRODUCTION

In this chapter, we turn to experiments in which each participant (or subject) is tested under all the different conditions in the experimental design. Such repeated testing obviously makes fullest use of the participant's presence. As we shall see, however, the taking of **repeated measures** on the same participants also has disadvantages.

9.1.1   Rationale of a within subjects experiment

A potential problem with between subjects experiments (Chapters 7 & 8) is that if there are large individual differences in performance, searching for a meaningful pattern in the data can be like trying to listen to an old-fashioned radio against a loud background crackle of interference. For example, in a Drug experiment such as the one described in Chapter 7, some of the scores obtained by participants in the Placebo condition may well be higher than those of participants tested under any of the drug conditions. There are some people who can bring a natural dexterity and flair to almost any test of skill; in others, on the other hand, those qualities are consistently less evident. Since, in a between subjects experiment, a different sample of participants performs under each condition, variation in natural aptitude is likely to introduce considerable **noise** into the data and inflate the error terms of the F statistics.

Another drawback with the between subjects experiment is that it is wasteful of participants: if the experimental procedure is a short one, a participant may spend more time travelling to and from the place of testing than actually performing the experimental task. We shall now consider another experimental strategy which not only allows the researcher to make fuller use of the participant's time, but also results in more powerful statistical tests.

A researcher wishes to investigate the effects upon shooting accuracy of the shape of a target. Participants are asked to shoot twenty times at each of four differently-shaped targets. Since each participant is tested under all the conditions making up the factor of target shape, this experiment is said to be of **within subjects** design, or to have **repeated measures** on the factor of target shape. Table 1 compares the design of this one-factor, within subjects experiment with that of a one-factor between subjects experiment similar to the drug experiment in Chapter 7.

Table 1. Between subjects and within subjects experiments in which there is one treatment factor with four levels				
(a) A one-factor between subjects experiment				
	Levels of the Drug factor			
	Control	Drug A	Drug B	Drug C
Participants	Group 1	Group 2	Group 3	Group 4
(b) A one-factor within subjects experiment				
	Levels of the Shape factor			
	Circle	Square	Triangle	Diamond
Participants	The same participants perform with all four shapes. The order of presentation of the four conditions is varied, or **counterbalanced**, so that each condition occurs with equal frequency in each of the four ordinal positions across all the participants in the study.			

The variance in the scores from our experiment on target shape and shooting accuracy will certainly reflect individual differences every bit as marked as they are likely to be in the drug experiment. There is, however, an important difference between the two experiments. In being tested under every condition, each participant is effectively serving as his or her own control. That person's average performance over all conditions can serve as a baseline against which their performance under the different conditions can be evaluated.

While the within subjects experiment has obvious advantages over the between subjects experiment, it should also be said that this data-gathering strategy raises problems that are not encountered with the between subjects experiment. All these difficulties stem ultimately from the fact that within subjects experiments yield correlated data. The manner in which the data are correlated has important implications, both for the making of the statistical tests in the ANOVA itself and for such considerations as the measure of power and effect size.

9.1.2 How the within subjects ANOVA works

In Figure 1, we reproduce from Chapter 7 a diagram of the one-way between subjects ANOVA. In the one-way ANOVA, two estimates of variance are made: the between groups mean square ($MS_{between}$), which is calculated from the values of the group means only; and the within groups means square (MS_{within}) , which is the average of the variances of the individual scores within the groups. The null hypothesis of equality, in the population, of the treatment means was tested with the statistic F, where $F = MS_{between} / MS_{within}$.

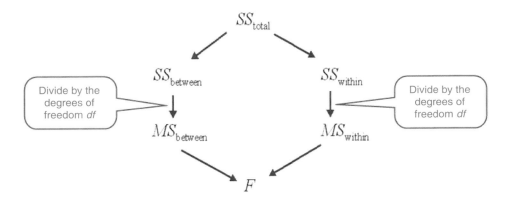

Figure 1. Summary of the one-way (between groups) ANOVA

Figure 1. Summary of the one-way (between groups) ANOVA

In the one-factor within subjects ANOVA, the participants are not grouped, so there is no between groups sum of squares. The participants are tested under all conditions, however, which makes it possible to calculate a mean score for each participant. Since each participant is tested at all levels of the treatment factor, we could regard Subjects as a second factor which **crosses** with Treatments, that is, every combination of Subjects and Treatments is present in the design of the experiment. In fact, we can think of the within subjects experiment as a two-factor experiment with one observation per cell, which is why some textbooks refer to this design as being of the 'Subjects × Treatments' type.

The Subjects × Treatments designation makes explicit the possibility of an interaction between the Subjects 'factor' and the true treatments factor. If there are n participants, the Subjects factor has n levels. If the treatment factor has k levels, the interaction between the Subjects and Treatments factors has $(n-1)(k-1)$ degrees of freedom.

It is this interaction between Subjects and Treatments that serves as the error term for the F test in the one-factor, within subjects ANOVA. The corresponding variance estimate is known as the **residual** mean square, because it represents what remains of the total variance when the contributions of the treatment factor and the Subjects factor have both been removed.

$$MS_{residual} = MS_{Subjects \times Treatments} = \frac{SS_{residual}}{df_{residual}} = \frac{SS_{residual}}{(n-1)(k-1)} \quad \text{- - - (1)}$$

The error term in the
one-factor within subjects experiment

Figure 2 summarises the one-factor within subjects ANOVA:

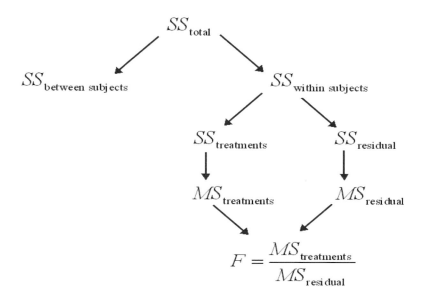

Figure 2. Summary of the one-factor within subjects ANOVA

It can be seen from Figure 2 that in the one-factor within subjects ANOVA, no estimate of the between subjects variance is actually made. However, the between subjects sum of squares is removed from the total sum of squares and the mean squares for the treatment factor and the error term are both calculated from the within subjects sum of squares.

If Subjects is a 'factor', it is one with **random effects**: that is, the participants in the experiment are assumed to be a random sample from a large pool of possible participants. This is why the residual (Subjects × Treatments) mean square is suitable as the error term for the F test. (Howell, 2007, gives a lucid discussion of the rationales of the F tests in the ANOVA, including the within subjects ANOVA.)

When we compare Figure 2 with Figure 1 (the diagram of the one-way ANOVA), it is clear that the within subjects design allows the extraction of a considerable amount of the variance from the data and results in an error term that does not reflect the main effect of the Subjects factor. (The residual error term, however, does reflect the interaction between Treatments and Subjects.)

In our within subject experiment, the treatment factor has four levels. If there are ten participants or subjects, the experiment will result in forty scores. The equivalent one-factor between subjects experiment would have forty participants, one group of ten for each of the four treatment conditions. In the within subjects ANOVA, the residual sum of squares has only $(10 - 1)(4 - 1) = 27$ degrees of freedom; whereas in the one-way (between subjects) ANOVA, the within groups mean square MS_{within} has $4(9) = 36$ degrees of freedom.

Since the degrees of freedom of the residual sum of squares are less than the df of MS_{within}, the critical value for F is larger. In practice, however, the partialling out of a major part of the variance arising from individual differences results in an increase in the power of the F test, so that the power efficiency (that is, power in relation to the number of participants) of the within subjects experiment is greater than that of the between subjects experiment.

In summary, therefore, the within subjects experiment has two advantages over the between subjects experiment:

1. It makes more efficient use of time and resources, requiring fewer participants and making more use of those participants.
2. It cuts down data noise, resulting in a test of greater power in relation to the number of participants in the experiment.

The within subjects experiment, however, also has disadvantages, which in some circumstances can outweigh considerations of convenience and the maximisation of the signal-to-noise ratio. One of these problems is discussed in Section 9.1.4.

See Section 9.1.4

9.1.3 A within subjects experiment on the effect of target shape on shooting accuracy

Table 2 shows the results of an experiment on the effects of target shape on shooting accuracy. (In this experiment, there were three target shapes only.) The order of presentation of the three targets was counterbalanced across participants in an attempt to neutralise any order effects.

Table 2. Results of a one-factor within subjects experiment			
Participant (Subject)		Target	
	Circle	Square	Triangle
1	10	12	14
2	18	10	16
3	20	15	16
4	12	10	12
5	19	20	21
6	25	22	20
7	18	16	17
8	22	18	18
9	17	14	12
10	23	20	18

The ANOVA summary table is shown in Table 3.

Table 3. The ANOVA summary table					
Source	df	SS	MS	F	p
Shape	2	39.267	19.633	4.86	.02
Subjects	9	370.170	40.608		
Residual (Shape × Subjects)	18	72.730	4.04		
Total	29	482.167			

We can report the result of the F test as follows:

The factor of Target Shape had a significant main effect: $F(2, 18) = 4.86$; $p = .02$.

In a scientific report, this result would be accompanied by the descriptive statistics (preferably in a table or graph) and some measure of effect size such as partial eta squared or partial omega squared.

9.1.4 Order effects: counterbalancing

A potential problem with repeated measures is that a participant's performance on one task may be affected by the experience of having performed another task, particularly when the two tasks are attempted in close succession. Such an effect upon performance is an example of a **carry-over** (or **order**) **effect**. Sometimes, of course, carry-over effects are of focal interest, as in memory research, where the researcher might wish to demonstrate the proactive interference of learning one list of words with the recall of the words in another list learned subsequently. Usually, however, carry-over effects in within subjects experiments are potential **confounds**, whose influence can be difficult to disentangle from that of the treatment factor itself.

If participants are tested on a succession of tasks, their performance on the later tasks may improve through a **practice effect**. Practice effects, however, are only one type of carry-over effect. Not all carry-over effects are positive: proactive and retroactive interference in memory are negative carry-over effects. In within subjects experiments, carry-over effects are potential **extraneous variables**, whose effects may be confounded with those of the treatment factor.

The possibility of carry-over effects confounding the effects of the treatment factor is reduced by the procedure known as **counterbalancing**, in which the order of the conditions making up a within subjects factor is varied from participant to participant, in the hope that carry-over effects will balance out across conditions. Counterbalancing is not always effective, however, because order effects can be very asymmetrical. There are also situations in which a within subjects strategy would be quite inappropriate: the drug experiment in Chapter 7 is a good example.

9.1.5 Assumptions underlying the within subjects ANOVA: homogeneity of covariance

We shall not describe the model underlying the within subjects ANOVA explicitly here. Recall, however, that in the model for the one-way ANOVA, certain assumptions are made about the random error component of each score, such as normality of distribution and homogeneity of variance.

Another important assumption in the one-way ANOVA is the independence of the error components of different scores. The within subjects ANOVA, however, is based upon a model of a situation in which the same participant is tested under all experimental conditions. Here, the assumption of independence of the error components is untenable. The within subjects model, while acknowledging that the data are correlated, makes an additional assumption about the scores, namely, that they have the property of **homogeneity of covariance**, or **sphericity**.

9.1.5.1   The covariance

Since the same participants shoot at all three targets, we can expect a positive correlation between the scores that the participants achieved under any two of the conditions: high scores with one target are likely to be paired with high scores on the other; and low scores on one target are likely to be accompanied by low scores on the other. The actual correlations among the scores for the three targets confirm this expectation: the correlation between the scores on the Circle and Square targets is .802; the correlation between Circle and Triangle is .729; and the correlation between Square and Triangle is .826.

The **covariance** is a measure of strength of association which, unlike the correlation coefficient (actually a special case of the covariance), has no upper or lower limits. For a bivariate data set comprising n (X, Y) pairs, the covariance between X and Y, $COV(X, Y)$ is given by

$$COV(X,Y) = \frac{\sum(X - M_X)(Y - M_Y)}{n-1} \quad \text{- - - (2)} \quad \textbf{The covariance}$$

Formula (2) resembles the formula for the sample variance, except that the sum of the squared deviations from the mean has been replaced by the sum of the products of the deviations of X and Y from their respective means. In fact, the variance is the covariance of a variable with itself!

9.1.5.2   The variance-covariance matrix

In Table 4, are shown the covariances of each of the three conditions in the experiment with the other two conditions.

Table 4. Variance-covariance matrix for the scores in Table 2			
	Circle	Square	Triangle
Circle	**21.60**	15.91	10.38
Square	15.91	**18.23**	10.80
Triangle	10.38	10.80	**9.38**

In the cells on the **principal diagonal** of this array or matrix, that is, the diagonal that runs from top left to bottom right, are the variances of the scores for each condition: each diagonal cell, that is, contains the covariance of the scores achieved under one particular condition with themselves. The off-diagonal elements contain the covariances between heterogeneous pairs of conditions. In summary, the values in bold along the diagonal (21.60; 18.23; 9.38) are the variances; the off-diagonal elements are the covariances.

Notice the symmetry of the variance-covariance matrix: the covariance of X with Y is identical with the covariance of Y with X, so the entries in the cells below the principal diagonal duplicate those in the cells above it.

The values in the variance-covariance matrix must show a uniformity or consistency known as **homogeneity of covariance** or **sphericity**: that is, there should be comparable levels of association among the scores at different levels of the treatments factor. If this assumption is violated, the **Type I error rate** (i.e. the probability of rejecting H_0 when it is true) may be inflated. Tests for homogeneity of covariance are made on the variance-covariance matrix. For this purpose, SPSS uses the **Mauchly Sphericity Test**. Should the data fail the sphericity test (i.e. p-value < 0.05), the ANOVA F test must be modified to make it more **conservative** (less likely to reject the null hypothesis). SPSS offers three such conservative tests, varying in their degree of conservativeness: the **Greenhouse-Geisser**, the **Huynh-Feldt**, and the **Lower-bound**. All three tests reduce the degrees of freedom of the numerator and the denominator of the F ratio (by multiplying them by a factor termed **epsilon**), thus increasing the value of F required for significance.

9.2   A ONE-FACTOR WITHIN SUBJECTS ANOVA WITH SPSS

The one-factor within subjects ANOVA is accessed through **Repeated Measures...** in the **General Linear Model** menu. As always, however, we strongly recommend that you begin your analysis by getting to know your data first, before embarking on any formal statistical tests.

9.2.1   Entering the data

Since the participants have not been divided into groups, no grouping variable is required for entry of these data into the **SPSS Statistics Data Editor**. In **Variable View**, using the procedures described in Section 2.3, enter the variables *Case* (or *Participant*), *Circle*, *Square* and *Triangle*. Using the **Label** column, expand the variable names to *Case Number*, *Circle Target*, *Square Target* and *Triangle Target*. Set the number of decimal places displayed to zero to avoid clutter in Data View. In **Data View**, enter the data from Table 3 into the first four (pre-labelled) columns.

See Section 2.3

9.2.2   Exploring the data: Boxplots for within subjects factors

- To draw boxplots of the data at the various levels of a within subjects factor, select **Analyze➔Descriptive Statistics➔Explore...** to open the **Explore** dialog box (Figure 3).
- Follow the steps shown in Figure 3.
- In the **Explore: Plots** dialog box (Figure 4), click on the **Dependents together** button and click off the **Stem-and-leaf** check box. Click **Continue** and then **OK**.

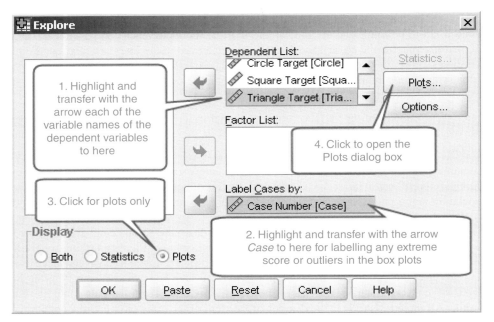

Figure 3. The **Explore** dialog box with the dependent variable names transferred to the **Dependent List** panel and the **Plots** button checked

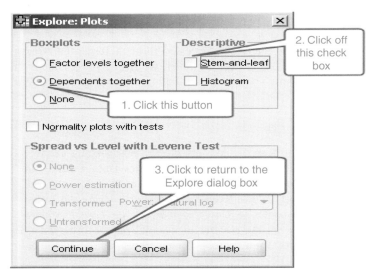

Figure 4. The **Explore: Plots** dialog box with **Dependents together** selected and **Stem-and-leaf** deselected

The boxplots (Output 1) reveal no extreme cases (which would have been flagged by * - see Table 2 in Section 4.4.2 for details of the structure of a boxplot). None of the distributions is markedly skewed. There is therefore no need to remove any cases or apply any transformation to symmetrise the distribution. We can carry on with the ANOVA.

See Table 2 in Section 4.4.2

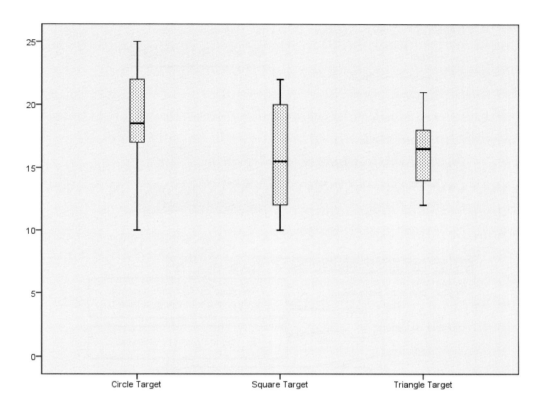

Output 1. Boxplots of the data for the three shapes

9.2.3   Running the within subjects ANOVA

So far, we have merely created a data set in Data View consisting of three variables: Circle, Square and Triangle. Hitherto, SPSS will have assumed that the values in the Circle, Square and Triangle variables are related to three quite different properties or characteristics. There is no mention of the treatment factor Shape anywhere in this data set, in contrast to the appearance of Data View before a one-way ANOVA, in which the treatment factor is one of the named variables. SPSS must now be informed that these data are all Accuracy scores and are the results of a within subjects experiment with one treatment factor (Shape) consisting of three levels. When we do this, SPSS will present a frame into which we can insert the names Circle, Square and Triangle as the names of the three levels of the treatment factor Shape.

The within subjects ANOVA is selected as follows:

- Select **Analyze➜General Linear Model➜Repeated Measures...** (Figure 5) to open the **Repeated Measures Define Factors** dialog box (Figure 6).
- Follow the steps described in Figure 6 to obtain the situation in Figure 7.
- Click **Define** to return to the **Repeated Measures ANOVA** dialog box (the upper half of which is shown in Figure 7).

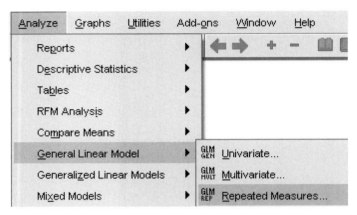

Figure 5. The **General Linear Model** menu

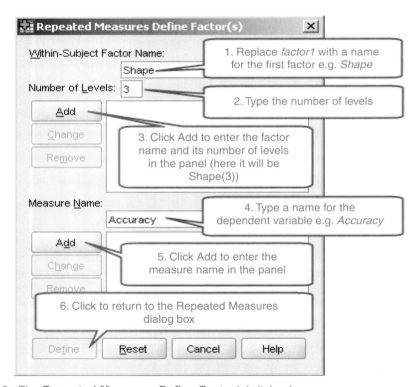

Figure 6. The **Repeated Measures Define Factor(s)** dialog box

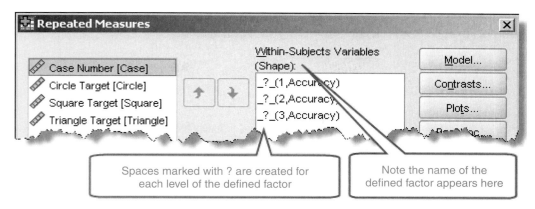

Figure 7. The upper half of the **Repeated Measures** dialog box after defining the **Within-Subjects Variables** factor as Shape with three levels and naming the measure as Accuracy

- Highlight the variables Circle, Square and Triangle (Figure 8) by clicking-and-dragging the cursor down over them and clicking the arrow to transfer all three into the **Within Subjects Variables [Shape]** box. The question marks will be replaced by the variable names as shown in Figure 8.

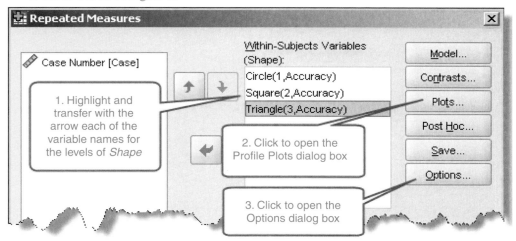

Figure 8. The completed **Repeated Measures** dialog box

- There are some useful options with a repeated measures ANOVA. For example, you can obtain a profile plot of the levels of the within subjects factor by clicking **Plots...** and following the steps shown in Figure 9. Click **Continue** to return to the original dialog box.

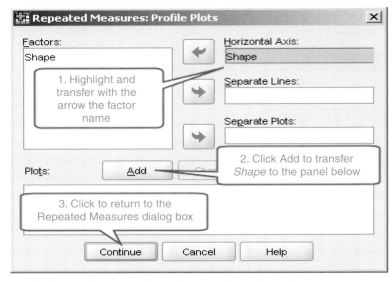

Figure 9. The **Profile Plots** dialog box for a plot at each level of a factor

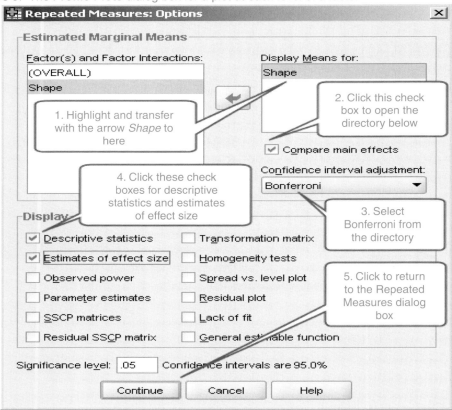

Figure 10. The completed **Options** dialog box requesting **Descriptive statistics**, **Estimates of effect size** and **Bonferroni** comparisons

- A table of **Descriptive statistics**, **Estimates of effect size** and a table of **Bonferroni adjusted pairwise comparisons** among the levels of the within subjects factor are requested by clicking **Options...** in the **Repeated Measures** dialog box and following the steps shown in Figure 10. See Section 9.2.4.5 regarding the choice of the Bonferroni test. Click **Continue** to return to the original dialog box.

See
Section
9.2.4.5

- Click **OK** to run the procedure.

9.2.4   Output for a one-factor within subjects ANOVA

The output is extensive, but not all of it is required for a within subjects ANOVA.

9.2.4.1   The SPSS Statistics Viewer

Output 2 shows the left-hand pane of the **SPSS Statistics Viewer**, in which are itemised the various subtables that appear in the right-hand pane. Three of the tables should be deleted immediately by highlighting each in turn and pressing the **Delete** key on the keyboard: **Multivariate Tests**; **Tests of Within-Subjects Contrasts**; **Tests of Between-Subjects Effects** (in this example, there are no between subjects factors). The **Multivariate Tests** in **Estimated Marginal Means** can also be deleted.

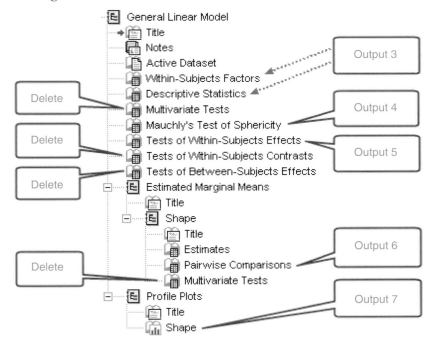

Output 2. The left-hand pane of the **SPSS Statistics Viewer** for the Repeated Measures (within subjects) analysis

Output 3 shows the **Title**, the **Within-Subjects Factors** list for the measure Accuracy and the specially requested **Descriptive Statistics** table.

Within-Subjects Factors

Measure: Accuracy

Shape	Dependent Variable
1	Circle
2	Square
3	Triangle

Descriptive Statistics

	Mean	Std. Deviation	N
Circle Target	18.40	4.648	10
Square Target	15.70	4.270	10
Triangle Target	16.40	3.062	10

Output 3. The **Within-Subjects Factors** list and **Descriptive Statistics** table

9.2.4.3   The Mauchly Test of Sphericity

Output 4 reports the result of the **Mauchly's Test of Sphericity**, a test for homogeneity of covariance (see Section 9.1.5). There are two possible results. If the p-value (**Sig.**) is greater than .05, the null hypothesis of homogeneity of covariance (sphericity) is accepted. If the p-value is less than .05, the null hypothesis of homogeneity of covariance is rejected. The result of Mauchly's Test indicates how we should read the final ANOVA summary table.

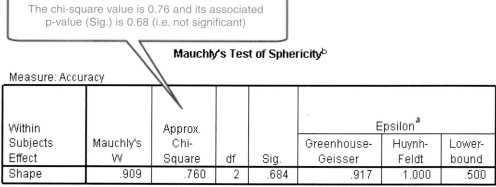

The chi-square value is 0.76 and its associated p-value (Sig.) is 0.68 (i.e. not significant)

Mauchly's Test of Sphericity[b]

Measure: Accuracy

Within Subjects Effect	Mauchly's W	Approx. Chi-Square	df	Sig.	Epsilon[a]		
					Greenhouse-Geisser	Huynh-Feldt	Lower-bound
Shape	.909	.760	2	.684	.917	1.000	.500

Tests the null hypothesis that the error covariance matrix of the orthonormalized transformed dependent variables is proportional to an identity matrix.

a. May be used to adjust the degrees of freedom for the averaged tests of significance. Corrected tests are displayed in the Tests of Within-Subjects Effects table.

b.
Design: Intercept
Within Subjects Design: Shape

Output 4. **Mauchly's Test of Sphericity** and values of epsilon for conservative **ANOVA** *F* tests

9.2.4.4   The ANOVA summary table

The ANOVA summary table (Output 5) shows the results of four F tests of the null hypothesis that, in the population, shooting accuracy for all three shapes is the same.

The results of the tests are given in separated rows, labelled **Sphericity Assumed**, **Greenhouse-Geisser**, **Huynh-Feldt** and **Lower-Bound**. In the lower part of the table, the same row labels are used for the error terms of the four F statistics reported in the top half of the table. Each F ratio was obtained by dividing the treatment mean square in its row by the error mean square in the row of the same name in the lower half of the table. If Mauchly's Test does not show significance, we need only read, in the ANOVA summary table, the rows labelled **Sphericity Assumed**. If Mauchly's Test does show significance, we suggest that, in the ANOVA summary table, you read only the rows labelled **Greenhouse-Geisser**.

The conservative test only makes a difference when:
1.   There is heterogeneity of covariance (i.e. Mauchly's Test is significant).
2.   The F with unadjusted degrees of freedom (i.e. the values shown in the **Sphericity Assumed** rows) is barely significant beyond the .05 level.

Should F have a low tail probability (say $p < 0.01$), the null hypothesis can be safely rejected without making a conservative test. In the present case, Mauchly's Test gives a p-value of .68, so there is no evidence of heterogeneity of covariance. The usual ANOVA F test can therefore be made.

Tests of Within-Subjects Effects

Measure:Accuracy

Source		Type III Sum of Squares	df	Mean Square	F	Sig.	Partial Eta Squared
Shape	Sphericity Assumed	39.27	2	19.63	4.86	.021	.351
	Greenhouse-Geisser	39.27	1.83	21.41	4.86	.024	.351
	Huynh-Feldt	39.27	2.00	19.63	4.86	.021	.351
	Lower-bound	39.27	1.00	39.27	4.86	.055	.351
Error(Shape)	Sphericity Assumed	72.73	18	4.041			
	Greenhouse-Geisser	72.73	16.50	4.41			
	Huynh-Feldt	72.73	18.00	4.04			
	Lower-bound	72.73	9.00	8.08			

Since the Mauchly result was not significant, the Sphericity Assumed rows apply. The other rows could be deleted

For F=4.86 with a p-value of 0.02, the factor *Shape* is significant

The value of partial eta squared is 35% (i.e. a large effect size)

Output 5. The **ANOVA** summary table for the **Within-Subjects Effects**

The main result in Output 5 is the value of **F** and its associated *p*-value (**Sig.**) for the within subjects factor Shape. This table has been edited to reduce the number of decimal places to two in some of the columns and to narrow some columns.

The value of 18 for the error *df* can be seen in the row labelled **Error (Shape) Sphericity Assumed**. In the present case, there was no need to make a conservative *F* test because Mauchly's Test was not significant. It is apparent from the **Sig.** column that *in this particular example* the conservative tests make no difference to the result of the ANOVA *F* test.

In the case of the factor Shape, note that the *p*-value for *F* in the **Sphericity Assumed** row is .021: that is, the obtained value of *F* is significant beyond the five per cent (.05) level, but not beyond the .01 level. We can therefore conclude that Shape does affect shooting accuracy. We can write this result as follows:

> The mean scores for the three shapes of target differed significantly at the 5% level: $F(2, 18) = 4.86$; $p = .02$ Partial eta squared = .35, which is a large effect.

9.2.4.5   Unplanned multiple comparisons

There is some doubt as to whether, following significant main effects of within subjects factors, the **Tukey test** affords sufficient protection against inflation of the per family type I error rate. Monte Carlo studies have indicated that the **Bonferroni** correction affords better protection. The next table (Output 6) shows the results of Bonferroni-corrected tests of pairwise comparisons.

Pairwise Comparisons

Measure: Accuracy

(I) Shape	(J) Shape	Mean Difference (I-J)	Std. Error	Sig.[a]	95% Confidence Interval for Difference[a] Lower Bound	Upper Bound
1	2	2.70*	.90	.044	.075	5.325
	3	2.00	1.01	.238	-.966	4.966
2	1	-2.70*	.90	.044	-5.325	-.075
	3	-.70	.78	1.000	-2.974	1.574
3	1	-2.00	1.01	.238	-4.966	.966
	2	.70	.78	1.000	-1.574	2.974

Based on estimated marginal means

*. The mean difference is significant at the .05 level.

a. Adjustment for multiple comparisons: Bonferroni.

Only one comparison has a p-value (Sig.) <.05

Output 6. The Bonferroni adjusted **Pairwise Comparisons** among the levels of the within subjects factor Shape for the measure Accuracy

It can be seen from Output 6 that of the three possible pairwise comparisons among the three treatment means, only the difference between the means for the Circle and Square conditions is significant. The other two comparisons fall well short of significance.

9.2.4.6   The profile plot

The requested profile plot is shown in Output 7, which is an edited version of the default plot, adjusted to include zero on the vertical scale. The default plot, with only a small section of the scale on the vertical axis, makes the differences among the means look enormous.

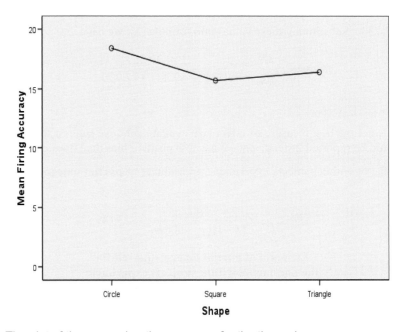

Output 7. The plot of the mean shooting accuracy for the three shapes

9.2.5   Effect size in the within subjects ANOVA

We have seen that the one-factor within subjects ANOVA can be viewed as a Subjects × Treatments factorial experiment with one observation per cell. We need to take that view in order to understand the measures of effect size that have been proposed. Even when there is only one treatment factor, the presence of the Subjects factor in the design means that the question of a partial (rather than a complete) measure of effect size arises. For the one-factor within subjects experiment, partial measures express the variance attributable to the treatment factor as a proportion, not of the total variance, but of the source variance plus the residual variance.

In some within subjects designs, the omega squared measure (which corrects for positive bias) is difficult or impossible to apply. In such situations, the partial eta squared measure (which is provided by SPSS) should be reported.

9.2.5.1 Partial eta sqared

As with the between subjects ANOVA, SPSS provides, as a measure of the size of the effect of a treatment source (a factor or an interaction), the statistic known as **partial eta squared** η_p^2, where

$$\eta_p^2 = \frac{SS_{treatment}}{SS_{treatment} + SS_{residual}} \quad \text{- - - (3) \textbf{ Partial eta squared}}$$

From Table 3 (the ANOVA summary table), we find that $SS_{Shape} = 39.267$ and $SS_{residual} = 72.730$. Substituting these values into formula (3), we have

$$\eta_p^2 = \frac{SS_{treatment}}{SS_{treatment} + SS_{residual}} = \frac{39.267}{39.267 + 72.730} = .35$$

9.2.5.2 Partial omega squared

Eta squared is not the best measure of effect size available and we suggest that **partial omega squared** should be reported instead, since it has less positive bias than does eta squared.

For the one-factor within subjects experiment, an estimate of **partial omega squared** is given by

$$\hat{\omega}^2_{treatments} = \frac{(k-1)(F-1)}{(k-1)(F-1) + kn} \quad \text{- - - (4)}$$

**Estimate of partial omega squared for
the one-factor within subjects experiment**

In the current example,

$$\hat{\omega}^2_{treatments} = \frac{(3-1)(4.86-1)}{(3-1)(4.86-1) + 3 \times 10} = 0.20$$

Note that, because the estimate of partial omega squared incorporates a correction for positive bias, its value is lower than that of partial eta squared.

Below, in Table 5, we reproduce Table 5 from Chapter 8, which gives guidelines for the interpretation of values of omega squared and Cohen's f.

Table 5. Guidelines for assessing values of eta squared (or bias-corrected measures such as omega squared) and the equivalent values of Cohen's f		
Size of Effect	Eta squared	Cohen's f
Small	$0.01 \leq \eta^2 < 0.06$	$0.10 \leq f < 0.25$
Medium	$0.06 \leq \eta^2 < 0.14$	$0.25 \leq f < 0.40$
Large	$\eta^2 \geq 0.14$	$f \geq 0.40$

We should note that, although the eta squared measures can readily be extended to within subjects designs with two or more factors, the estimation of omega squared is deeply problematic. (See, for example, Keppel & Wickens, 2004; p.427.) For a detailed discussion of these issues, see Dodd & Schultz (1973).

9.3 POWER AND EFFECT SIZE: HOW MANY PARTICIPANTS SHALL I NEED?

The correlated nature of the data from within subjects experiments has implications for the determination of power and effect size. To determine the power of the F test in a within subjects experiment, we also need to be able to locate the critical value for F in the noncentral F distribution, where its cumulative probability is beta, the Type II error rate, and (1 – beta) is the power of the test. In Chapter 7, we saw that for the kind to data to which the one-way ANOVA is applicable, the noncentrality parameter lambda is simply the square of Cohen's f statistic multiplied by N, the total sample size. In the one-factor within subjects experiment, which will yield correlated data, matters are by no means as simple. The noncentrality parameter is affected by several factors, including the average correlation among the scores at the different levels of the treatment factor. It is also affected by epsilon, the multiplier for the degrees of freedom that is obtained from the variance-covariance matrix. The import of all this is that, in order to determine, a priori, the power of a within subjects experiment that you are planning to run, you will require information that may not readily be available unless you have already run some pilot studies of the measures you intend to use in your experiment.

The **G*Power 3** package, which is available freely on the Internet (Erdfelder, Faul & Buchner, 1996; Faul, Erdfelder, Lang & Buchner, 2007), can also answer questions about power and effect size in within subjects experiments. Suppose that you are planning to run a within subjects experiment with three treatment conditions. You want to make a test with a power of at least .75 to reject the null hypothesis for an effect of 'medium' size (Cohen's f = .25). You have set the alpha-level at .05. How many participants will you need? In G*Power 3, select **Test→Means→Repeated measures: within factors, ANOVA approach** to get the dialog box with **ANOVA: repeated measures: within factors** in the Statistical test window and **A priori: Compute required sample size – given α, power and effect size** in the Type of power analysis window.

In the **Input Parameters** panel on the left, you will be asked to enter values for the Number of groups and the Repetitions. In this case, the number of groups is 1, because there is a single sample of participants. The number of repetitions is three, the number of levels in the within subjects treatment factor. There are no problems there; but in addition, you will be required to supply the average correlation among the three levels of the treatment factor and the value of epsilon. You might, of course, decide on some plausible level for the correlation, such as .6, and set epsilon at 1, which would be justified should the data from such an experiment be 'spherical', that is, have the property of homogeneity of covariance. Without additional information, however, you cannot know this; nor can one know how closely the scores in the three different conditions are correlated. The question of the degree of correlation, however, is important, because the higher the inter-correlation, the greater is the power of the test for a given number of participants. Some pilot work with the planned measures, of course, would enable the researcher to supply the necessary information.

After clicking the **Calculate** button, the **Output Parameters** panel will show 20 in the **Total sample size** window and .75 in the **Actual Power** window. This suggests that you would be advised to use at least 20 participants.

9.4   NONPARAMETRIC EQUIVALENTS OF THE WITHIN SUBJECTS ANOVA

As with the one-factor completely randomised experiment, nonparametric methods are available for the analysis of ordinal and nominal data. Once again, we suggest that if your measurements are on a continuous scale, the first possibility to consider is the running of the within subjects ANOVA on a cleaned-up data set, rather than 'ordinalising' the data by converting them to ranks, which is effectively what happens when one runs a nonparametric test. The decision to opt for a nonparametric test incurs the immediate penalty of a loss of power. In the next example, however, the raw data are ranks in the first place and the researcher has no option but to use a nonparametric test.

9.4.1   The Friedman test for ordinal data

Suppose that six people rank five objects in order of 'pleasingness'. Their decisions might appear as in Table 6.

Table 6. Six people's ranks of five objects in order of 'pleasingness'				
	Object 1	Object 2	Object 3	Object 4	Object 5
Person 1	2	1	5	4	3
Person 2	1	2	5	4	3
Person 3	1	3	4	2	5
Person 4	2	1	3	5	4
Person 5	2	1	5	4	3
Person 6	1	2	5	3	4

If we assume that the highest rank is given to the most pleasing object, it would appear, from inspection of Table 6, that Object 3 is more pleasing to most of the raters than is Object 1. Since, however, the numbers in Table 6 are not independent measurements but ranks, the one-factor within subjects ANOVA cannot be used here.

9.4.1.1   Running the Friedman test

The Friedman test is suitable for such ordinal data.

In **Variable View**, name the variables *Object1, Object2, ... Object5* (with no spaces before the digits). In **Data View**, enter the data in the usual way.

To run the Friedman test:

- Choose **Analyze→Nonparametric Tests→K Related Samples...** to obtain the **Tests for Several Related Samples** dialog box (Figure 11).

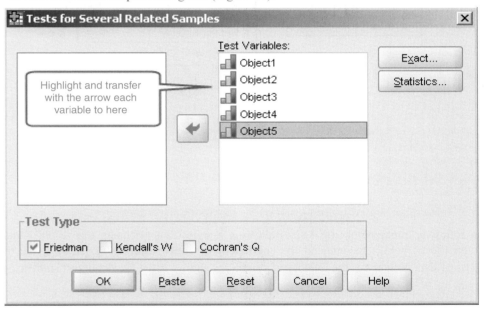

Figure 11. The **Tests for Several Related Samples** dialog box with the **Friedman** Test selected

- In the panel on the left, a list of the variables will appear. This list should include the items Object1, Object2, ..., Object5, which will contain the numbers shown in Table 6. Simply transfer these names to the **Test Variables:** box in the usual way. Make sure the **Friedman** check box has been ticked.
- Click the **Exact...** button to see the **Exact Tests** dialog box and activate the **Exact** radio button. Click **Continue** and then **OK**.

The **Friedman Test** results are shown in Output 8.

Clearly the rankings differ significantly across the objects since the *p*-value is less than .01. We can write this result as:

$$\chi^2 (4) = 17.2; p < .01.$$

Friedman Test

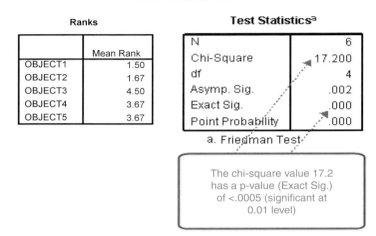

Output 8. **Friedman** test results

9.4.1.2   Measuring effect size with the coefficient of concordance

As a follow-up measure of effect size following a significant Friedman test result, King & Minium (2003; p.462) recommend the **coefficient of concordance (*W*)**. If *N* is the total number of data points, *k* is the number of conditions and χ^2 is the Friedman test statistic, the formula for *W* is

$$W = \frac{\chi^2}{N(k-1)} \; \text{---} \; (5)$$

The coefficient of concordance

Substituting the values in Output 8 for χ^2, *N* and *k* in formula (5), we have

$$W = \frac{\chi^2}{N(k-1)} = \frac{17.2}{6(4)} = .72$$

The coefficient of concordance can take values in the range from zero to 1, inclusive. To interpret a value of *W*, therefore, we can use the usual Cohen benchmarks (Chapter 6, Table 5) for classifying the size of a correlation and, since *W* is greater than .5, conclude that a value of .72 represents a 'large' effect.

Following a significant result of the Friedman test, pairwise multiple comparisons can be made among the different conditions by using the Wilcoxon signed–ranks test, applying the Bonferroni correction to protect against inflation of the familywise Type I error rate. For example, if Object 1 is regarded as a comparison object, we could compare the level of ranking for Object 1 with those for Objects 2, 3, 4 and 5, setting our per comparison Type 1 error rate at $.05/4 = .01$.

9.4.2   Cochran's Q test for nominal data

Suppose that six children were asked to imagine they were in five different situations and had to choose between Course of Action A (coded 0) and B (coded 1). The results might appear as in Table 7. From inspection of Table 7, it would seem that B (i.e. cells containing 1) is chosen more often in some scenarios than in others. A suitable confirmatory test is **Cochran's Q** test, which was designed for use with related samples of dichotomous nominal data.

Table 7. Courses of action chosen by six children in five scenarios					
	Scene 1	Scene 2	Scene 3	Scene 4	Scene 5
Child 1	0	0	1	1	1
Child 2	0	1	0	1	1
Child 3	1	1	1	1	1
Child 4	0	0	0	1	0
Child 5	0	0	0	0	0
Child 6	0	0	0	1	1

To run Cochran's Q test:

- Choose **Analyze➔Nonparametric Tests➔K Related Samples...** to bring the **Tests for Several Related Samples** dialog box to the screen (Figure 11), click off the **Friedman** check box and click the **Cochran** check box.
- Click the **Exact...** button to see the **Exact Tests** dialog box and activate the **Exact** radio button. Click **Continue** and then **OK**.

The results are shown in Output 9.

It is clear that the same course of action is not taken in all five scenarios:

$$\text{Cochran } Q = 9.82; \ df = 4; \ p = .04.$$

Cochran Test

Frequencies

	Value	
	0	1
SCENE1	5	1
SCENE2	4	2
SCENE3	4	2
SCENE4	1	5
SCENE5	2	4

Test Statistics

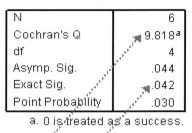

N	6
Cochran's Q	9.818[a]
df	4
Asymp. Sig.	.044
Exact Sig.	.042
Point Probability	.030

a. 0 is treated as a success.

The Q value 9.818 has a p-value (Exact Sig.) of 0.042 (significant at the 0.05 level)

Output 9. **Cochran Test** results

9.4.2.2   Further analysis following a significant value of Cochran's Q

Note that, as always, we must be cautious in our statement of the implications of statistical significance. We can reject the null hypothesis that there is, in the population, no difference among the five scenarios, confirming the variation among the scenarios apparent in Table 7. We cannot, however, conclude from this that the difference between any two particular scenarios is also significant. Further pairwise post hoc comparisons could be made by using the **Sign Test**, controlling the **Type I error rate** with the **Bonferroni** procedure previously described.

9.5   THE TWO-FACTOR WITHIN SUBJECTS ANOVA

An experiment was designed to investigate the effects of the shape and solidity of patterns shown on a screen upon the ease with which they are detected. The dependent variable (DV) was the Number of Errors made in responding to a pattern. There were two treatment factors: Shape (Circle, Square, or Triangle) and Solidity (Outline or Solid). Each participant was tested under all six combinations of the two treatment factors: that is, both factors were within subjects. The results are shown in Table 8.

Table 8. Results of a two-factor within subjects experiment

SHAPE:-	Circle		Square		Triangle	
SOLIDITY:-	Solid	Outline	Solid	Outline	Solid	Outline
Participant						
1	4	2	2	8	7	5
2	3	6	2	6	8	9
3	2	10	2	5	5	3
4	1	8	5	5	2	9
5	4	6	4	5	5	10
6	3	6	4	6	9	12
7	7	12	2	6	4	8
8	6	10	9	5	0	10
9	4	5	7	6	8	12
10	2	12	12	8	10	12

The ANOVA summary table for the data of Table 8 is shown in Table 9 below.

Table 9. Summary table for the ANOVA of the data in Table 8

Source	Degrees of freedom	Sum of squares	Mean square	F	p
Subjects	9				
Shape	2	46.03	23.02	2.98	.08
Error (Shape)	18	138.97	7.72		
Solidity	1	117.60	117.60	54.56	<.01
Error (Solidity)	9	19.40	2.16		
Shape × Solidity	2	23.70	11.85	1.41	.27
Error (Shape × Solidity)	18	151.30	8.41		

There are three treatment sources of variance in this ANOVA: the two main effect sources, Shape and Solidity; and the Shape × Solidity interaction. The F test for each of these sources has its own error term. The error term is always the interaction between the source (i.e. Shape, Solidity or Shape × Solidity) and Subjects. So the error term for Shape is the Shape × Subjects interaction, with $2 \times 9 = 18$ degrees of freedom; the error term for Solidity is the Solidity × Subjects interaction, with $1 \times 9 = 9$ degrees of freedom; the error term for Shape × Solidity is Shape × Solidity × Subjects, with $2 \times 1 \times 9 = 18$ degrees of freedom.

A full explanation of this rule for finding the correct error term lies beyond the scope of this book. Basically, the Subjects source can be regarded as a factor with random effects, so that the various combinations of Subjects and treatments do not cancel out across the experiment as a whole. The interaction, therefore, adds to the expected value of the treatments sum of squares. (For more on this, see a statistical textbook such as Howell, 2007 or Keppel & Wickens, 2004.)

9.5.1   Preparing the data set

The first four rows of data in **Data View** appear as in Figure 12.

Case	CircleSolid	CircleOutline	SquareSolid	SquareOutline	TriangleSolid	TriangleOutline
1	4	2	2	8	7	5
2	3	6	2	6	8	9
3	2	10	2	5	5	3
4	1	8	5	5	2	9

Figure 12. Part of **Data View** for the two-factor within subjects ANOVA

Extra care is needed when entering data from experiments with two or more within subjects factors. It is essential to ensure that SPSS understands which data were obtained under which combination of factors. In the present example, there are six scores for each participant, each score having being achieved under one combination of the two factors. We can name the data variables in the data set *CircleSolid*, *CircleOutline*, *SquareSolid*, *SquareOutline*, *TriangleSolid* and *TriangleOutline*, representing all possible combinations of the shape and solidity factors. Such systematic, left-to-right naming not only helps to avoid transcription errors at the data entry stage, but also prevents incorrect responses when you are in the **Repeated-Measures Define Variable(s)** dialog box and are naming the within subjects factors.

Note that the left-to-right ordering of the variable names is exactly the order in which they appeared in the original table of results (Table 8).

9.5.2   Running the two-factor within subjects ANOVA

- Select **Analyze➜General Linear Model➜Repeated Measures...** and complete the various dialog boxes by analogy with the one-factor example, defining a second within subjects (repeated measures) factor and naming the dependent measure as Errors.
- The completed **Repeated Measures Define Factor(s)** dialog box, with the two within subjects factor names Shape and Solidity, is shown in Figure 13, together with the measure name Errors.
- After **Define** has been clicked, the **Repeated Measures** dialog box appears with the six variables listed in alphabetical order on the left. (The top half is reproduced in Figure 14).

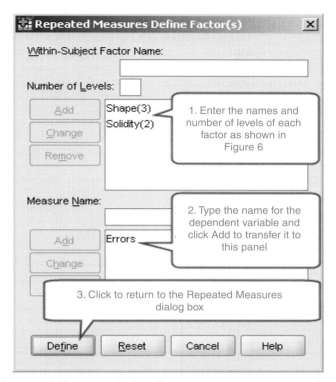

Figure 13. The **Repeated Measures Define Factor(s)** dialog box with two factors and their numbers of levels defined as well as a name for the dependent variable

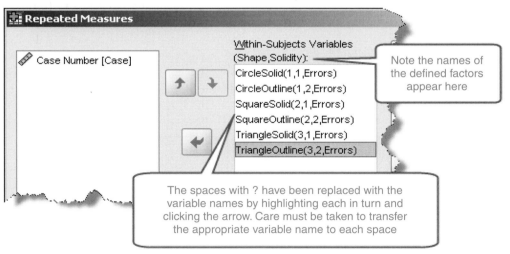

Figure 14. The top half of the **Repeated Measures** dialog box for two factors Shape and Solidity after transferring the variable names

On the right (Figure 14), in the box labelled **Within-Subjects Variables [Shape, Solidity]**, appears a list of the various combinations of the code numbers representing the levels of each of the two treatment factors. It will be noticed that, as one reads down the list, the first number in each pair changes more slowly than the second. When there is more than one within subjects factor, it is inadvisable immediately to transfer the variable names in a block from the left-hand box to the **Within-Subjects Variables** box by a click-and-drag operation, as in the one-factor situation. Check that the downward order of the variable names in the left-hand panel matches the order of the names in **Variable View** (or **Data View**).

Should your experiment be more complex, with more levels in the factors, it is safer to transfer the variables to the **Within-Subjects Variables** slots one at a time, noting the numbers in the square brackets and referring to the names of the newly defined within subjects factors (in this case Shape and Solidity) inside the square brackets in the caption above the **Within-Subjects Variables** box.

A table such as Table 10 clarifies the numbering of the levels of within subjects factors. Thus the variable CircleSolid is [Shape 1, Solidity 1] i.e. [1,1], CircleOutline is [1,2] and so on.

Table 10. Numbering of levels in within subjects variables						
Shape Factor	Shape 1 (Circle)		Shape 2 (Square)		Shape 3 (Triangle)	
Solidity Factor	Solidity 1 (Solid)	Solidity 2 (Outline)	Solidity 1 (Solid)	Solidity 2 (Outline)	Solidity 1 (Solid)	Solidity 2 (Outline)
Variable name	Circle Solid	Circle Outline	Square Solid	Square Outline	Triangle Solid	Triangle Outline

- There are some useful options associated with a repeated measures ANOVA. Request a profile plot of the levels of one of the factors across the levels of the other factor by clicking **Plots...** and following the steps shown in Figure 15. Click **Continue** to return to the original dialog box.
- A table of **descriptive statistics**, **estimates of effect sizes** and a table of post hoc **Bonferroni pairwise comparisons** among the levels of within subjects factors with more than two levels (here only Shape) are requested by clicking the **Options...** button in the **Repeated Measures** dialog box and following the steps shown earlier in Figure 10. Click **Continue** to return to the original dialog box and then **OK**.

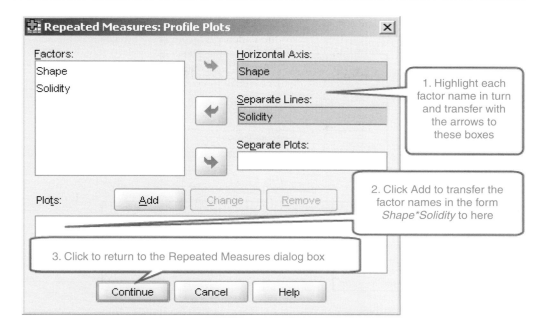

Figure 15. Part of the **Profile Plots** dialog box for requesting a profile plot Shape*Solidity

9.5.3 Output for a two-factor within subjects ANOVA

As in the case of the one-factor within subjects ANOVA, the output is extensive, and not all of it is required. You can make life easier by pruning some items and removing others altogether. Three of the subtables in the left-hand pane of the **SPSS Statistics Viewer** can be immediately deleted by highlighting each in turn and then pressing the **Delete** key on the keyboard: **Multivariate Tests**; **Tests of Within-Subjects Contrasts**; **Tests of Between-Subjects Effects** (in this example, there are no between subjects factors).

See
Output 2
in Section
9.2.4

9.5.3.1 Experimental design and descriptive statistics

Output 10 shows the **Title**, **Within-Subjects Factors** list and the specially requested **Descriptive Statistics** table.

Within-Subjects Factors

Measure: Errors

Shape	Solidity	Dependent Variable
1	1	CircleSolid
	2	CircleOutline
2	1	SquareSolid
	2	SquareOutline
3	1	TriangleSolid
	2	TriangleOutline

Descriptive Statistics

	Mean	Std. Deviation	N
Solid Circle	3.60	1.838	10
Outline Circle	7.70	3.268	10
Solid Square	4.90	3.446	10
Outline Square	6.00	1.155	10
Solid Triangle	5.80	3.190	10
Outline Triangle	9.00	3.018	10

Output 10. The **Within-Subjects Factors** list and **Descriptive Statistics** table

9.5.3.2 Results of the Mauchly test

The next table (Output 11) reports the result of the **Mauchly's Test of Sphericity** for homogeneity of covariance (see Section 9.2).

The table is more extensive than that in Output 5, because there are two factors. Notice that the test is not applied when a factor has only two levels (as in the case of Solidity) because, when there is only a single covariance, the question of homogeneity of covariance does not arise. The test does not show significance (i.e. there is no evidence of heterogeneity of covariance), either for Shape or for the interaction between Shape and Solidity, so the significance levels in the rows labelled **Sphericity Assumed** can be accepted. You should now remove from the ANOVA table the rows giving the results of the various conservative F tests.

9.5.3.3 The ANOVA summary table

The edited ANOVA summary table (minus the rows with the conservative tests and the words Sphericity Assumed) for the within subjects factors Shape and Solidity, and their interaction is shown in Output 12. Notice that, in contrast with a two-factor between subjects ANOVA, there are three error terms, one for each main effect and one for the interaction.

The chi-square values and their associated p-values (Sig.) show that none is significant. Note the test does not apply to factors with only two levels (e.g. *Solidity*)

Mauchly's Test of Sphericity[b]

Measure: Errors

Within Subjects Effect	Mauchly's W	Approx. Chi-Square	df	Sig.	Epsilon[a]		
					Greenhouse-Geisser	Huynh-Feldt	Lower-bound
Shape	.67	3.25	2	.197	.750	.866	.500
Solidity	1.00	.00	0	.	1.000	1.000	1.000
Shape * Solidity	.90	.82	2	.663	.911	1.000	.500

Tests the null hypothesis that the error covariance matrix of the orthonormalized transformed dependent variables is proportional to an identity matrix.

a. May be used to adjust the degrees of freedom for the averaged tests of significance. Corrected tests are displayed in the Tests of Within-Subjects Effects table.

b.
Design: Intercept
Within Subjects Design: Shape+Solidity+Shape*Solidity

Output 11. **Mauchly's Test of Sphericity** and more conservative statistics for Shape and for the interaction between Shape and Solidity

Tests of Within-Subjects Effects

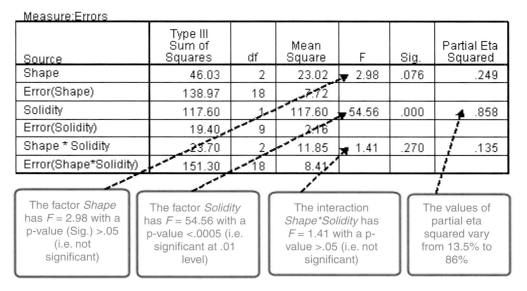

Measure:Errors

Source	Type III Sum of Squares	df	Mean Square	F	Sig.	Partial Eta Squared
Shape	46.03	2	23.02	2.98	.076	.249
Error(Shape)	138.97	18	7.72			
Solidity	117.60	1	117.60	54.56	.000	.858
Error(Solidity)	19.40	9	2.16			
Shape * Solidity	23.70	2	11.85	1.41	.270	.135
Error(Shape*Solidity)	151.30	18	8.41			

The factor *Shape* has $F = 2.98$ with a p-value (Sig.) >.05 (i.e. not significant)

The factor *Solidity* has $F = 54.56$ with a p-value <.0005 (i.e. significant at .01 level)

The interaction *Shape*Solidity* has $F = 1.41$ with a p-value >.05 (i.e. not significant)

The values of partial eta squared vary from 13.5% to 86%

Output 12. The edited **ANOVA** summary table for the **Within-Subjects Effects**

Output 12 shows that the factor Shape has no significant main effect, since the *p*-value for *F* in the column headed **Sig.** is greater than .05. We can write this result as follows:

There was no significant effect of the Shape factor: $F(2, 18) = 2.98$; $p = .082$.

The factor Solidity is significant, since its *p*-value is less than .01 (the output value 0.000 means that the *p*-value is less than .0005). We can write this result as:

The Solidity factor had a main effect that was significant beyond the 1% level: $F(1, 9) = 54.6$; $p < .01$. Partial eta squared = .86. This is a large effect.

As we said earlier, it would be desirable to be able to use the partial omega squared measure instead of eta squared; however, as Keppel & Wickens observe (2004; p427), we almost never have sufficient information about the sources of random error to be able to supply the necessary estimates for the equations. It is, therefore, better to report the values of partial eta squared (biased though they are) than no measures of effect size at all.

Finally, there was no significant Shape × Solidity interaction: $F(2, 18) = 1.41$; $p = .27$. Since the factor Shape is not significant, the **Bonferroni pairwise comparisons** table should be ignored.

9.5.3.4   Profile plots

The edited profile plot is shown in Output 13. An interaction is indicated when the profiles cross one another, diverge or converge. The slight convergence and divergence of the profiles here was apparently insufficient for a statistically significant interaction.

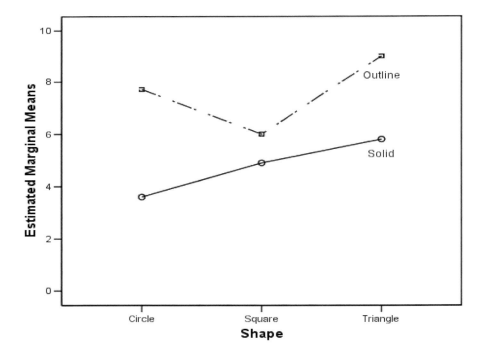

Output 13. The profile plots of the two levels of Solidity across the three shapes

In conclusion, Output 12 shows only the Solidity factor to have had a significant effect: neither the other factor, Shape nor its interaction with Solidity was significant.

9.5.4 Unpacking a significant interaction with multiple comparisons

In the example we have just considered, the question of unplanned multiple comparisons among the means for combinations of the two treatment factors did not arise, because the interaction was insignificant. In fact, since the only significant source of variance was Solidity, which had only two levels, no further analysis was necessary, since a significant main effect implies that the difference between the two means is significant.

Table 11 shows an alternative set of results from the Shape and Solidity experiment.

Table 11. An alternative set of results from the Shape and Solidity experiment						
SHAPE:-	Circle		Square		Triangle	
SOLIDITY:-	Solid	Outline	Solid	Outline	Solid	Outline
Participant						
1	8	2	3	8	5	7
2	7	6	3	6	6	11
3	6	10	3	5	3	5
4	5	8	6	5	2	11
5	8	6	5	5	3	12
6	7	6	5	6	7	14
7	11	12	3	6	2	10
8	10	10	10	5	0	12
9	8	5	8	6	6	14
10	6	12	13	8	8	14

The profile plots of the two different conditions of Solidity against the Shape factor are shown in Output 14. The ANOVA of this set of results (we shall not show the summary table here) confirms the presence of a marked interaction between the factors Solidity and Shape.

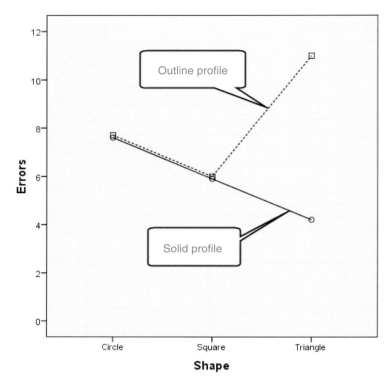

Output 14. Profile plots of the two Solidity conditions suggesting a striking simple main effect of Solidity when the target is a triangle

The appearance of the profiles in Output 14 suggest that if we test for simple main effects of Solidity at each of the three levels of the Shape factor, we can expect to confirm the existence of an effect with the triangle only. The SPSS syntax for testing for simple main effects of Solidity at the Circle, Triangle and Square levels of Shape is shown in Figure 16.

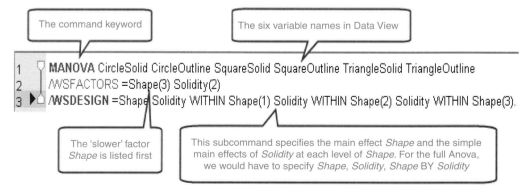

Figure 16. Syntax for testing simple main effects of Solidity at the Circle, Triangle and Square levels of Shape. Note that for within subjects factors, the subcommand /WSDESIGN replaces /DESIGN

The results of the tests for simple main effects are shown in Output 15. They are entirely consistent with the pattern that is so evident in the graph in Output 14: there is a significant simple main effect of Solidity at the Triangle level of Shape, but none at the Square or Circle levels.

```
Tests involving 'SOLIDITY W SHAPE(1)' Within-Subject Effect.

Tests of Significance for T4 using UNIQUE sums of squares
Source of Variation          SS         DF         MS          F    Sig of F

WITHIN+RESIDUAL            56.45         9         6.27
SOLIDITY W SHAPE(1)         .05         1          .05        .01       .931
```
No simple main effect of *Solidity* at Shape(1)

```
Tests involving 'SOLIDITY W SHAPE(2)' Within-Subject Effect.

Tests of Significance for T5 using UNIQUE sums of squares
Source of Variation          SS         DF         MS          F    Sig of F

WITHIN+RESIDUAL            51.45         9         5.72
SOLIDITY W SHAPE(2)         .05         1          .05        .01       .928
```
No simple main effect of *Solidity* at Shape(2)

```
Tests involving 'SOLIDITY W SHAPE(3)' Within-Subject Effect.

Tests of Significance for T6 using UNIQUE sums of squares
Source of Variation          SS         DF         MS          F    Sig of F

WITHIN+RESIDUAL            44.80         9         4.98
SOLIDITY W SHAPE(3)       231.20         1       231.20      46.45      .000
```
A significant simple main effect of *Solidity* at Shape(3)

Output 15. The results of tests (edited) for simple main effects of the Solidity factor at the three levels of Shape

The confirmation of a simple main effect of one factor at one particular level of another might be regarded as a justification for calculating the size of the comparison family from the cell means at that level only. The **Bonferroni** correction might be made on that basis.

9.6   A FINAL WORD

In this chapter, we have considered the analysis of variance of data from within subject experiments, in which the participant performs at all levels of the treatment factors. Despite the practical efficiency of this research strategy and the increase in power that results from using participants as their own controls, the within subjects ANOVA encounters problems that do not arise with between subjects experiments.

Within subjects experiments produce correlated data; and therein lies the heart of the difficulty. The within subjects ANOVA model carries the additional assumption of homogeneity of variance. Violation of this requirement can have serious consequences for the ANOVA, arising from the failure of the F statistics to have the distributions specified by the degrees of freedom, with consequent inflation of the error rates. There are available tests for homogeneity of covariance and adjustments that can be made to the F tests as a result of violation of this assumption. Heterogeneity of covariance, however, has ramifications that extend far beyond the ANOVA itself which, as we have pointed out, is usually merely the first stage in the analysis of a set of data. The measurement of effect size, power and the making of specific contrasts are all problematic; even if the data meet the requirement of sphericity, the researcher is pressed for information that may be difficult or impossible to obtain.

There is, however, another approach to the analysis of the data from within subjects experiments. Rather than viewing the participant's performance under the k different conditions making up a treatment factor as values of one dependent variable measured under different conditions, the same data could be viewed as measures on k different dependent variables. The **Multivariate Analysis of Variance** (or **MANOVA** for short) is a generalisation of ANOVA, which is applicable to correlated experimental data and yet does not require homogeneity of covariance. In the final section of the next chapter, we shall take a closer look at the MANOVA and its application to within subjects experiments.

Recommended reading

There are available several readable textbooks with clear yet comprehensive accounts of within subjects ANOVA. The treatments of ANOVA in the following books are particularly accessible.

Field, A. (2009). *Discovering statistics using SPSS (3rd ed.)*. London: Sage.

Howell, D. C. (2007). *Statistical methods for psychology (6th ed.)*. Belmont, CA: Thomson/Wadsworth.

Keppel, G., & Wickens, T. D. (2004). *Design and analysis: A researcher's handbook (4th ed.)*. Upper Saddle River, NJ: Pearson Prentice Hall.

Tabachnick, B.G., & Fidell, L.S. (2007). *Using multivariate Statistics (5th ed.)*. Boston: Allyn & Bacon (Pearson International Edition).

Two useful additional references

Dodd, D. H., & Schultz, R. F. (1973). Computational procedures for estimating magnitude of effect for some analysis of variance designs. *Psychological Bulletin, 79*, 391-395.

Faul, F., Erdfelder, E., Lang, A-G., and Buchner, A. (2007). G*Power 3: A flexible statistical power analysis program for the social, behavioral and biomedical sciences. *Behavior Research Methods, 39*, 175 – 191.

Exercises

Exercise 13 *One-factor within subjects (repeated measures) ANOVA* and Exercise 14 *Two-factor within subjects ANOVA* are available in www.psypress.com/spss-made-simple and click on Exercises.

CHAPTER 10

Mixed factorial experiments

10.1   INTRODUCTION

In the factorial designs we have considered so far, all the factors have been either between subjects or within subjects: in the **between subjects** factorial experiment, they are all between subjects; in the **within subjects** factorial experiment they are all within subjects.   In this chapter, we shall consider **mixed factorial** experiments, in which there are both between subjects and within subjects factors.

10.1.1   A mixed factorial experiment

A researcher designs an experiment to explore the hypothesis that engineering students, because of their training in two-dimensional representation of three-dimensional structures, have a more strongly developed sense of shape discrimination than do psychology students, whose training places a greater emphasis upon verbal and numerical skills. This, he reasons, should enable the engineers to make more accurate drawings of projections in the fronto-parallel plane of the gable-ends of buildings photographed from varying angles.   The investigator creates a set of solid building-like structures with triangular, square and rectangular 'gable-ends' and the participant is required to judge which of a set of comparison shapes presented on a screen is the correct projection, in the fronto-parallel plane, of the gable-end of the object. A scoring system is devised which assigns the highest marks for selections that are closest to the correct projection of the gable end of the real structure. The dependent variable (or measure) is the participant's score. The results of the experiment are shown in Table 1.

It can be seen from Table 1 that there were two factors in this experiment:

1. Student Category, with levels Psychology and Engineering.
2. Shape, with levels Triangle, Square and Rectangle.

Student Category is, of course, a between subjects factor; but since each participant was tested with all three shapes, Shape is a within subjects factor. It is very common for factorial designs to have within subjects (repeated measures) factors on *some* (but not *all*) of their treatment factors, in which case they are said to be of **mixed factorial** design. An older term for this kind of design is **split-plot**, a term which reflects the agronomic setting in which this type of experiment originated.

Group	Case	Triangle	Shape Square	Rectangle
Table 1. Results of a two-factor mixed factorial experiment with one within subjects factor and one between subjects factor				
Psychology	1	2	12	7
	2	8	10	9
	3	4	15	3
	4	6	9	7
	5	9	13	8
	6	7	14	8
Engineering	7	13	3	35
	8	21	4	30
	9	26	10	35
	10	22	8	30
	11	20	9	28
	12	19	8	27

10.1.2   Classifying mixed factorial designs

In this chapter, we shall follow a common convention for labelling different kinds of mixed factorial designs, in which the between subjects factors are represented by letters without brackets and the within subjects factors are bracketed. The present experiment, for example, is of design A × (B), where Factor A is Category of Student, Factor B is Shape and the brackets around B indicate that there are repeated measures on Shape. Later in the chapter, we shall consider more complex mixed factorial experiments with three factors:

1. Design A × (B × C), which has one between subjects factor and two within subjects factors;
2. Design A × B × (C), which has two between subjects factors and one within subjects factor.

In the same notation, the completely randomised one-factor experiment is of type A, the two-factor between subjects factorial experiment is of type A × B and the two-factor within subjects factorial experiment is S × A × B. (Subjects crosses with the treatment factors.)

In Table 2, are shown three experimental designs with two factors, A and B. The two-factor mixed factorial experiment of which our current experiment is an example, is depicted schematically in Table 2c. This design is clearly a hybrid of the completely randomised and within subjects designs. It is like a between subjects one-factor between subjects experiment, except that each participant, instead of being tested just once, undergoes a within subjects S × B (Subjects by Treatments) experiment and is tested three times, once at each level of factor B.

Table 2. Completely randomised, within subjects and mixed factorial experimental designs

(a) Completely randomised two-factor factorial experiment (design A × B)

Factor A	Factor B		
	B1	B2	B3
A1	Group 1	Group 2	Group 3
A2	Group 4	Group 5	Group 6

(b) Two-factor, within subjects factorial experiment (design S × A × B)

A1			A2		
B1	B2	B3	B1	B2	B3

Each participant is tested under all combinations of the two treatment factors. The ordering of the treatment combinations would be counterbalanced, so that, across all the participants, each combination occurs equally often in each serial position (1st, 2nd,..., 6th).

(c) Two-factor, mixed factorial experiment [design A × (B)]

Factor A (group)	Factor B		
	B1	B2	B3
A1	Each participant is tested at all three levels of factor B		
A2	Each participant is tested at all three levels of factor B		

10.1.3   Rationale of the mixed ANOVA

The ANOVA of the data in Table 1 is a hybrid of the ANOVA for the between subjects and within subjects experiments. If we were to ignore the Shape factor, calculate the mean performance of each participant across the three shapes and treat that mean as a single score, we should have data suitable for a one-way ANOVA, the results of which are shown in Output 1.

ANOVA

Mean

	Sum of Squares	df	Mean Square	F	Sig.
Between Groups	359.343	1	359.343	98.952	.000
Within Groups	36.315	10	3.631		
Total	395.657	11			

Output 1. The ANOVA summary table for the one-way ANOVA of the mean scores of participants in the two groups

In Chapter 9, we saw that in the two-factor within subjects S × A × B experiment, the Subjects 'factor' crosses with the two treatment factors, so that the correct error term for the F-test of the interaction A × B is the three way interaction A × B × S, remembering that the Subjects factor (S) has random effects. In the present case, however, it is clear that the Subjects 'factor' (S) does not cross with the Group factor, so that there can be no A × B × S interaction; there is, however, a B × S (i.e. Shape × Subjects) interaction nested within levels of the group factor A. These nested interactions are pooled to give the error term for the F tests for the within subjects sources. (It can be shown that, because the Subjects 'factor' has random effects, the expected value of this pooled error term includes not only an A × B component, but also a three-way A × B × S component. This pooled mean square is therefore also the appropriate error term for the test for the presence of a two-factor interaction. For a full explanation, see a statistics textbook such as Howell, 2007, or Keppel & Wickens, 2004.)

The ANOVA summary table is shown in Table 3. There are both between subjects and within subjects sources. We have already seen that the between groups sources are Group and the Within Groups error term. Within each professional group, are the results of a Subjects × Treatments (one-factor within subjects) experiment, with Shape as the single factor. In the experiment as a whole, however, the Group and Shape factor cross, so that we can include the Group × Shape interaction as another within subjects source of variance in the analysis of variance.

In this mixed two-factor ANOVA, there are three F tests:
1. A test for a main effect of the group factor, Category of Student;
2. a test for a main effect of the Shape factor;
3. a test for an interaction between Shape and Category of Student.

In the first test, the error term is the usual one-way ANOVA within groups mean square (Output 1). In the second and third tests, the error term is the pooled Shape by Subjects interaction, which is called Error (Shape) in the SPSS output.

Table 3. ANOVA summary table for the data in Table 1

Source	df	SS	MS	F	p
Between subjects					
Group	1	1078.03	1078.83	98.95	<.01
Error: Within Groups	10	108.94	10.89		
Within subjects					
Shape	2	533.56	266.78	32.62	<.01
Shape × Group	2	1308.22	654.11	79.99	<.01
Error (Shape): Pooled Shape × Subjects	20	163.56	8.18		

We said earlier that the term Error (Shape) is a pooled variance estimate constructed from the Shape × Subjects interactions in the two groups. You can see this from the degrees of freedom: since there are six participants (subjects) within each group, the degrees of freedom of the error term for either one-factor within subjects experiment is $(6 - 1)(3 - 1) = 10$. Pooling across both groups doubles this value, producing the tabled *df* value of 20 for the within subjects error term Error (Shape).

10.2 THE TWO-FACTOR MIXED FACTORIAL ANOVA WITH SPSS

In Chapter 9, we saw that the within subjects ANOVA is available in the **General Linear Model** menu, under **Repeated Measures**. The mixed ANOVA is also run with the **Repeated Measures** procedure.

See Chap. 9

10.2.1 Preparing the SPSS data set

In Table 1, we represented the experimental design with the levels of the within subjects factor arrayed horizontally (as column headings) and those of the between subjects factor stacked vertically (as row labels), with Engineering under Psychology. We did so because this arrangement corresponds to the way in which the results will be arranged in **Data View**.

As always, the first column of **Data View** will contain the case numbers. The second column will contain a single grouping variable Category representing the Psychologists (code value: 1) and the Engineers (code value: 2). The third, fourth and fifth columns will contain the results at the three levels of the Shape factor (Triangle, Square, and Rectangle).

Using the techniques described in Chapter 2, Section 2.3, enter **Variable View** and name five variables: *Case* (or *Participant*), *Category* (the grouping variable), *Triangle*, *Square*, and *Rectangle*. Use the **Label** column to assign more meaningful variable names (Case Number, Category of Student) and the **Values** column to assign full labels to the numerical values of the grouping variable Category (such as 1 = 'Psychology Student', 2 = 'Engineering Student'). Ensure that the **Decimals** column is set at 0 for each variable to avoid needless clutter in **Data View**.

See Section 2.3

Click the **Data View** tab and enter the data into **Data View** (Figure 1). If values rather than labels appear in the variable Category, enter the **View** menu and click **Value Labels**.

Case	Category	Triangle	Square	Rectangle
1	Psychology Student	2	12	7
2	Psychology Student	8	10	9
3	Psychology Student	4	15	3
4	Psychology Student	6	9	7
5	Psychology Student	9	13	8
6	Psychology Student	7	14	8
7	Engineering Student	13	3	35
8	Engineering Student	21	4	30
9	Engineering Student	26	10	35
10	Engineering Student	22	8	30
11	Engineering Student	20	9	28
12	Engineering Student	19	8	27

Figure 1. The data from Table 1 in **Data View**

10.2.2   Exploring the results: Boxplots

As usual, the first step is to explore the data set. The boxplot was described in Section 4.4.2. Here, however, the **clustered boxplot** (which clusters the levels of the within subjects factor within levels of the between subjects factor) is appropriate.

To obtain a clustered boxplot, proceed as follows:
• Click **Analyze➔Descriptive Statistics➔Explore…** to open the **Explore** dialog box.
• Complete the details as in Section 9.2.2, but with the addition of the variable label Category of Student transferred to the **Factor List** panel.
• Click **OK**.

The edited boxplot is shown in Output 2. Notice the extreme score (case 3) for the number of rectangles identified by a Psychology student and the outlier (case 7) for the number of triangles identified by an Engineering student. In a real research situation, it might have been worth eliminating the two deviant scores and comparing the analyses with and without the outliers, but here we shall work with the entire data set. Extreme scores may simply be clerical errors or the results of misunderstandings; but they might also be authentic scores in the tail of the distribution.

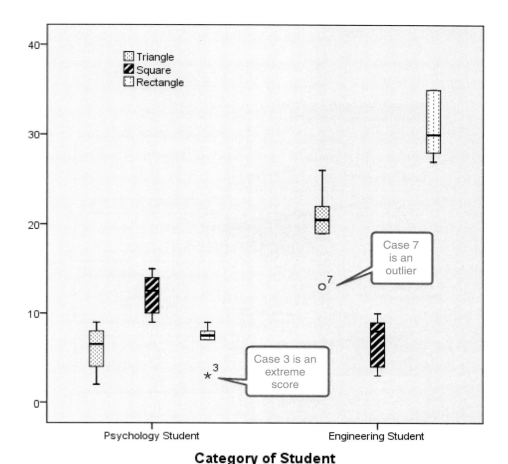

Output 2. Edited boxplots of the three shapes for each student category

10.2.3   Running the ANOVA

As we observed in Chapter 9, the analysis of a within subjects experiment begins with three variables in Data View. There is no mention of the name of any treatment factor. SPSS must be told that there is, in fact, a single dependent variable (the measure), which has been taken at the different levels making up a within subjects treatment factor. In the current example, Data View will contain the name of the between subjects (group) factor; but the within subjects factor (Shape) has yet to be defined.

- Select **Analyze➜General Linear Model➜Repeated Measures...** to open the **Repeated Measures Define Factor(s)** dialog box. (The partially completed dialog is shown in Figure 2.)
- In the **Within-Subject Factor Name** box, delete factor1 and type a generic name (such as *Shape*) for the repeated measures factor. This variable name must not be that of any of the three levels making up the factor. It must also conform to the rules governing the assignment of variable names: e.g. no spaces are allowed. (Spaces can be approximated,

however, by use of the shift and hyphen keys.) In the **Number of Levels** box, type the number of levels (3) making up the repeated measures factor. Click **Add** and, in the middle box in Figure 2, the entry Shape(3) will appear. As the **Measure Name** (the name of the dependent variable in the experiment), enter *Score*. Clicking on the **Add** button will cause the name Score to appear in the bottom panel.

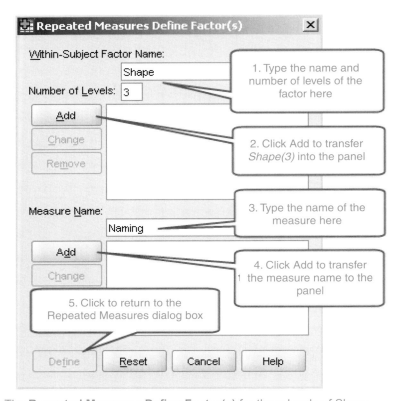

Figure 2. The **Repeated Measures Define Factor(s)** for three levels of Shape

- Click **Define** to open the **Repeated Measures ANOVA** dialog box.
- Transfer the variable names Triangle, Rectangle and Square to the **Within-Subjects Variables** box as shown in Figure 3.
- The new element is the presence of the between subjects factor Category of Student. Transfer this factor name to the **Between-Subjects Factor(s)** box as shown in Figure 3.
- There are some useful additional options. A profile plot of the levels of the within subjects factor Shape for each level of the between subjects variable Category is requested by clicking **Plots...** and following the steps shown in Figure 9 in Chapter 9. Click **Continue** to return to the **Repeated Measures** dialog box.
- A table of **descriptive statistics**, **estimates of effect size** and a table of **Bonferroni adjusted pairwise comparisons** among the levels of the within subjects factor Shape are requested by clicking **Options...** and following the steps shown in Figure 10 in Chapter 9. Click **Continue** to return to the **Repeated Measures** dialog box.

- Had there been more than two levels in the between subjects variable Category, a Tukey post-hoc test could have been requested by clicking **Post Hoc...**, transferring the variable name Category to the **Post Hoc Tests for** box, and clicking the **Tukey** check box. Click **Continue** to return to the original dialog box.
- Click **OK** to run the ANOVA.

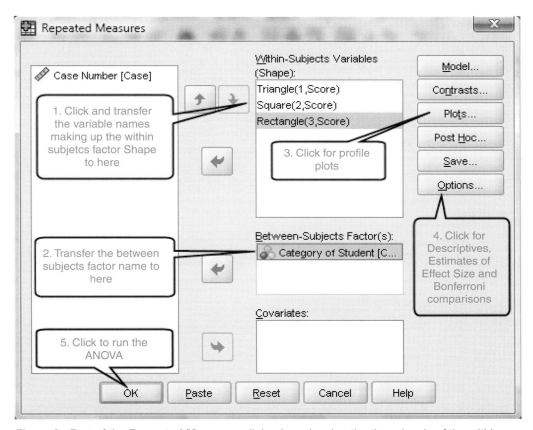

Figure 3. Part of the **Repeated Measures** dialog box showing the three levels of the within subjects factor Shape and the between subjects factor Category

10.2.4 Output for the two-factor mixed ANOVA

The output from a mixed ANOVA is extensive, particularly for more complex experiments with three or more factors. The first step is to do some editing and remove some of the items.

10.2.4.1 The list of output contents

You will find the table of contents in the **SPSS Statistics Viewer** particularly helpful for navigating the extensive output.

Output 3 shows the left-hand pane of the **Viewer**, in which the various items appearing in full in the right-hand pane are listed as labelled icons.

Two items, **Multivariate Tests** and **Tests of Within-Subjects Contrasts**, can be deleted immediately by highlighting each in turn and pressing the **Delete** key on the keyboard. In the **Estimated Marginal Means** section, the **Multivariate Tests** table can also be deleted.

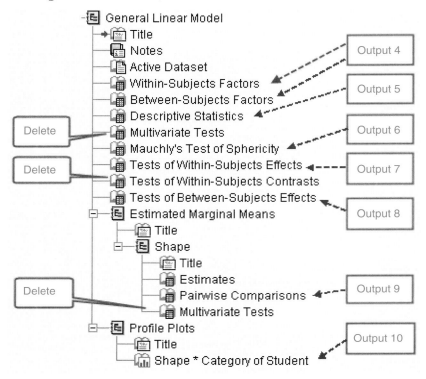

Output 3. The left-hand pane of **Viewer** listing the output items for the mixed ANOVA

10.2.4.2   Design specifications

It is important to check that the nature of the design has been correctly communicated to SPSS. Output 4 shows the two SPSS tables identifying the levels of the **Within-Subjects Factors** and the levels of the **Between-Subjects Factors**.

Within-Subjects Factors

Measure: Score

Shape	Dependent Variable
1	Triangle
2	Square
3	Rectangle

Between-Subjects Factors

		Value Label	N
Category of Student	1	Psychology Student	6
	2	Engineering Student	6

Output 4. The **Within-Subjects Factors** list of levels and the **Between-Subjects Factors** list of levels

Check that the levels of each of the factors have been correctly labelled. Check that the value labels for the between subjects factor have been correctly assigned. Make sure also that the levels of the within subjects factor are listed in the order that they appear from left to right in Data View.

10.2.4.3   The descriptive statistics

Output 5 shows the table of descriptive statistics requested in **Options**. Inspection of the means shows different profiles across the factor Shape for the two student categories, suggesting the presence of an interaction between the two factors.

Descriptive Statistics

	Category of Student	Mean	Std. Deviation	N
Triangle	Psychology Student	6.00	2.61	6
	Engineering Student	20.17	4.26	6
	Total	13.08	8.13	12
Square	Psychology Student	12.17	2.32	6
	Engineering Student	7.00	2.83	6
	Total	9.58	3.65	12
Rectangle	Psychology Student	7.00	2.10	6
	Engineering Student	30.83	3.43	6
	Total	18.92	12.74	12

Output 5. The optional table of **Descriptive Statistics**

10.2.4.4   The Mauchly test

The next table, in Output 6, reports the result of the **Mauchly's Test of Sphericity** for homogeneity of covariance. (Section 9.2.4 describes the correct procedure when the Mauchly statistic is significant.)

See
Section
9.2.4

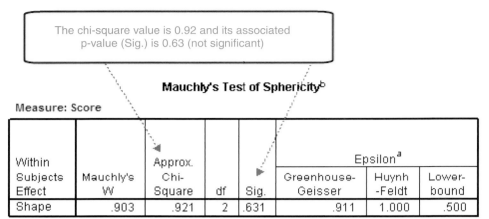

The chi-square value is 0.92 and its associated p-value (Sig.) is 0.63 (not significant)

Mauchly's Test of Sphericity[b]

Measure: Score

Within Subjects Effect	Mauchly's W	Approx. Chi-Square	df	Sig.	Epsilon[a]		
					Greenhouse-Geisser	Huynh-Feldt	Lower-bound
Shape	.903	.921	2	.631	.911	1.000	.500

Tests the null hypothesis that the error covariance matrix of the orthonormalized transformed dependent variables is proportional to an identity matrix.

a. May be used to adjust the degrees of freedom for the averaged tests of significance. Corrected tests are displayed in the Tests of Within-Subjects Effects table.

b.
Design: Intercept+Category
Within Subjects Design: Shape

Output 6. **Mauchly's Test of Sphericity** and values of **Epsilon** for more conservative tests

In the present case, the **Mauchly** statistic has a p-value of 0.63, so there is no evidence of heterogeneity of covariance. The usual (**Sphericity Assumed**) F test can therefore be used. You should therefore simplify the ANOVA table, as in Output 6, by removing the information about the conservative F tests.

10.2.4.5   Tests for within subjects and interaction effects

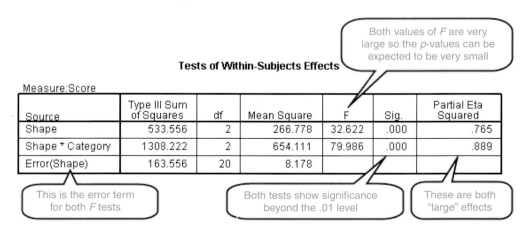

Both values of F are very large so the p-values can be expected to be very small

Tests of Within-Subjects Effects

Measure:Score

Source	Type III Sum of Squares	df	Mean Square	F	Sig.	Partial Eta Squared
Shape	533.556	2	266.778	32.622	.000	.765
Shape * Category	1308.222	2	654.111	79.986	.000	.889
Error(Shape)	163.556	20	8.178			

This is the error term for both F tests

Both tests show significance beyond the .01 level

These are both "large" effects

Output 7. The edited **ANOVA summary table** for the within-subjects factor Shape and its interaction with the between-subjects factor Category

Note that in Output 7, the factor Shape is significant beyond the 1 per cent level: the *p*-value (**Sig.**) .000 is computerese for 'less than .0005'. Write $p < .01$ (or p <.001), not .000. This result would be reported as follows:

> The mean scores for the three shapes differed significantly beyond the .01 level: $F(2, 20) = 32.62$; $p < .01$. Partial eta squared = .765, a 'large' effect.

The Category × Shape interaction is also significant beyond the 1% level: the *p*-value is less than .0005. This result would be reported as follows:

> There was a significant interaction between Category and Shape: $F(2, 20) = 79.99$; $p < .01$. Partial eta squared = .889, a large effect.

10.2.4.6   Test for between subjects effects

Output 8 shows the ANOVA summary table for the between subjects factor Category.

Ignore the terms **Intercept** and **Type III**: these refer to the regression method that was used to perform the analysis. With a *p*-value (**Sig.**) of less than .0005, there is clearly a significant difference in performance between the two groups of students. This result would be reported as follows:

> The mean scores for the categories of student differed significantly at the 1% level: $F(1,10) = 98.95$; $p < .01$. Partial eta squared = .91, a 'large' effect.

The ANOVA strongly confirms the patterns discernible in Table 3: the Shape and Category factors both have significant main effects; and the interaction between the factors is also significant. You will notice, however, that although the value given for *F* is exactly the same as in the one-way ANOVA of the mean scores of the participants over all three shapes, the mean squares for the Category and Error sources have three times the values in the one-way table shown in Output 1. For each of the six means for each group, there were three times that number of raw scores, increasing the multiplier of the sum of the squares of the deviations by a factor of three.

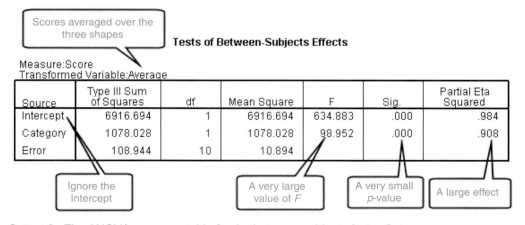

Output 8. The ANOVA summary table for the between-subjects factor Category

Output 9 shows the pairwise comparisons requested in **Options**.

Pairwise Comparisons

Measure: Score

(I) Shape	(J) Shape	Mean Difference (I-J)	Std. Error	Sig.^{a}	95% Confidence Interval for Difference^a Lower Bound	Upper Bound
1	2	3.50*	.97	.015	.71	6.29
	3	-5.83*	1.22	.002	-9.34	-2.32
2	1	-3.50*	.97	.015	-6.29	-.71
	3	-9.33*	1.28	.000	-13.02	-5.65
3	1	5.83*	1.22	.002	2.32	9.34
	2	9.33*	1.28	.000	5.65	13.02

Based on estimated marginal means
  *. The mean difference is significant at the .05 level.
  a. Adjustment for multiple comparisons: Bonferroni.

| Differences significant at .01 level | | Differences significant at .05 level |

Output 9. The **Bonferroni pairwise comparisons** for the factor Shape

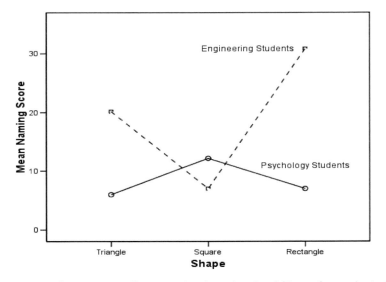

Output 10. The performance profiles over the three levels of Shape for each student category

The requested profile plot is shown (edited) in Output 10. The plot confirms the pattern of the boxplots in Output 2. With squares, the Psychology students improved, while the Engineering students' scores tended to slump in that condition.

10.2.5   Simple effects analysis with syntax

Given that the Group × Shape interaction has proved significant, the researcher might wish to 'unpack' this interaction by making tests for the simple effects of Group at each of the three levels of the Shape factor. The use of the **Syntax Editor** is described in Section 8.5.1.

See
Section
8.5.1

The syntax for testing for simple main effects of a factor in a mixed design at specific levels of a factor of the opposite type (i.e. a between factor at one level of a within factor and vice versa) is tricky, because the /DESIGN subcommand permits the explicit mention of between subjects factors only; while the /WSDESIGN subcommand permits reference to within subjects factors only. In other words, for an experiment of mixed factorial A × (B) design, a phrase such as A WITHIN B(1) will not be permitted in either the /DESIGN or the /WSDESIGN subcommand.

10.2.5.1   Simple main effects of the between subjects factor at specific levels of the within subjects factor

The trick here is that, when (in the two-factor mixed factorial A × (B) experiment) we want to specify the simple main effect of the between subjects factor A at each level of B, we use the keyword MWITHIN to refer to the effects of A. This reference, however, is in the /WSDESIGN subcommand which, hitherto, we have used exclusively for within subjects sources (Figure 4).

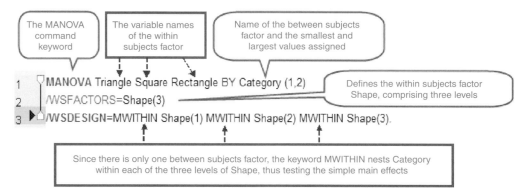

Figure 4. Syntax for simple main effects of the between factor at each level of the within factor

In this particular example, where there is only one between subjects factor, there will be an automatic link between that factor and the MWITHIN statements. In more complex mixed designs, where there are two or more between subjects factors, we shall need to write an additional /DESIGN subcommand to resolve the ambiguity and make the link between the specific between subjects effect that we want to test and the MWITHIN phrase in the /WSDESIGN subcommand.

The results of the tests for simple main effects of the Group factor at the three levels of the Shape factor are shown in Output 11 (edited). The desired simple main effects are labelled as if they were interactions: that is, the keyword BY which, hitherto has always indicated an interaction, appears before MWITHIN. The simple main effect of Group at the first level of Shape is labelled as 'Category BY MWITHIN SHAPE(1); the simple main effect of Group at the second level of Shape is 'Category BY MWITHIN SHAPE(2)'. These are NOT interactions: they are simple effects. The sources labelled 'MWITHIN SHAPE(1)' and 'MWITHIN SHAPE(2)' test the null hypothesis that the average score across the groups is zero within each level of Shape. Unless we are dealing with difference scores, this test is not usually of interest, because the null hypothesis will always be false.

We can see from Output 11 that formal testing has confirmed the existence of simple main effects of Group at all three levels of Shape. Since there were only two groups, we can infer that the difference between the two group means is significant at all three levels of the Shape factor.

```
Tests involving 'MWITHIN SHAPE(1)' Within-Subject Effect.

  Tests of Significance for T1 using UNIQUE sums of squares
  Source of Variation              SS   DF      MS       F  Sig of F

  WITHIN+RESIDUAL        ┌─Ignore─┐  124.83  10    12.48
  MWITHIN SHAPE(1)       └────────┘ 2054.08   1  2054.08  164.55   .000
  Category BY MWITHIN SHAPE(1) 602.08   1   602.08   48.23   .000
                        The simple main effect of Category at the first level of Shape

Tests involving 'MWITHIN SHAPE(2)' Within-Subject Effect.

  Tests of Significance for T2 using UNIQUE sums of squares
  Source of Variation              SS   DF      MS       F  Sig of F

  WITHIN+RESIDUAL        ┌─Ignore─┐   66.83  10     6.68
  MWITHIN SHAPE(2)       └────────┘ 1102.08   1  1102.08  164.90   .000
  Category BY MWITHIN SHAPE(2)  80.08   1    80.08   11.98   .006
                        The simple main effect of Category at the second level of Shape

Tests involving 'MWITHIN SHAPE(3)' Within-Subject Effect.

  Tests of Significance for T3 using UNIQUE sums of squares
  Source of Variation              SS   DF      MS       F  Sig of F

  WITHIN+RESIDUAL        ┌─Ignore─┐   80.83  10     8.08
  MWITHIN SHAPE(3)       └────────┘ 4294.08   1  4294.08  531.23   .000
  Category BY MWITHIN SHAPE(3) 1704.08   1  1704.08  210.81   .000
                        The simple main effect of Category at the third level of Shape
```

Output 11. Results of the tests for simple main effects of Category at each level of Shape

The syntax for testing for simple main effects of Shape at each level of the Group factor is shown in Figure 5.

Note once again that, although we are testing for simple main effects of the within subjects factor, we use the /DESIGN subcommand, not /WSDESIGN. This is because only the /DESIGN subcommand allows you to name a between subjects factor. Since there are only two factors, the link between MWITHIN and the within subjects factor is unambiguous.

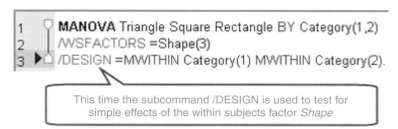

```
1    MANOVA Triangle Square Rectangle BY Category(1,2)
2    /WSFACTORS =Shape(3)
3    /DESIGN =MWITHIN Category(1) MWITHIN Category(2).
```

This time the subcommand /DESIGN is used to test for simple effects of the within subjects factor *Shape*

Figure 5. Syntax for testing for simple main effects of the within subjects factor (Shape) at each level of the between groups factor

The results of the simple effects analysis are shown in Output 12.

Tests of Between-Subjects Effects.

These are not generally of interest. Ignore!

Tests of Significance for T1 using UNIQUE sums of squares

Source of Variation	SS	DF	MS	F	Sig of F
WITHIN+RESIDUAL	108.94	10	10.89		
MWITHIN CATEGORY(1)	1266.72	1	1266.72	116.27	.000
MWITHIN CATEGORY(2)	6728.00	1	6728.00	617.56	.000

Tests involving 'SHAPE' Within-Subject Effect.

Tests for simple main effects of *Shape* at each level of *Group*.

AVERAGED Tests of Significance for MEAS.1 using UNIQUE sums of squares

Source of Variation	SS	DF	MS	F	Sig of F
WITHIN+RESIDUAL	163.56	20	8.18		
MWITHIN CATEGORY(1) BY SHAPE	131.44	2	65.72	8.04	.003
MWITHIN CATEGORY(2) BY SHAPE	1710.33	2	855.17	104.57	.000

Despite the keyword BY, these are simple *main* effects.

Output 12. Tests for simple main effects of the within subjects factor Shape at each level of the between groups factor

The arrangement of this output is somewhat different from the output for the simple main effects of Group at each level of Shape: the output is divided explicitly into between subjects and within subjects effects. The same points about the output, however, apply here too. In the between subjects output, the sources MWITHIN GROUP(1) and MWITHIN GROUP(2) test the hypothesis that, within each group, the mean score averaged across the three shapes is zero. In the context of our example, this hypothesis is a non-starter. The results we are looking for are in the within subjects section. Once again, the labels of the simple effects contain the keyword BY as if they were interactions. Output 12 (edited) shows that there are significant simple main effects of Shape at both levels of Group. Should you wish to make multiple comparisons among the cell means, this might be seen as justification for defining the comparison family in relation to the three means at each level of the Group factor, rather than the six means in the entire experiment.

Figure 6 presents the syntax for testing for simple main effects of either factor in the A × (B) design in more abstract notation, representing the scores obtained under the conditions of the within subjects factor B as B1 and B2. In the current example, B1, B2, B3 and A are Triangle, Square, Rectangle and Student Category, respectively.

10.2.5.3 Including both /DESIGN and /WSDESIGN subcommands in the same MANOVA command

In Figure 6, the /DESIGN and /WSDESIGN subcommands are presented as alternatives, the choice between them depending upon which set of simple main effects are required. Both subcommands, however, can be run on a single MANOVA command. Have a separate subcommand for each set of simple main effects: the two sets of simple effects are alternative partitions of the same interaction and main effect terms in the model.

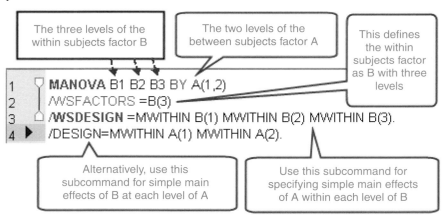

Figure 6. Using the MWITHIN keyword to test for simple main effects in the A × (B) mixed design. (The period at the end of line 3 can be dispensed with, in which case both subcommands will be run.)

10.2.5.4 Including comments with SPSS syntax

As an *aide-memoire*, it can be useful, in syntax files, to include reminders of the purpose of various subcommands and phrases. If added in the proper format, such comments are ignored by the computer and the syntax will run in the usual way. The rules for comments are as follows.

- If a comment requires several lines, write it before or after a command.
- If a comment occurs in the middle of a command, it must not spill over into a second line.
- All comments begin with an asterisk * and end with a period or full stop.
- When a comment occurs before or after a command, the asterisk and full stop, respectively, are all that is necessary.
- A comment in the middle of a line of syntax must begin with the /* and end with a full stop, followed by the two characters */ . (There is no full stop after the solidus /.)
- When a comment comes in the middle of a command, but at the end of a line, the right-hand sequence of characters */ after the period is unnecessary.

The format for comments in various positions is illustrated in Figure 7.

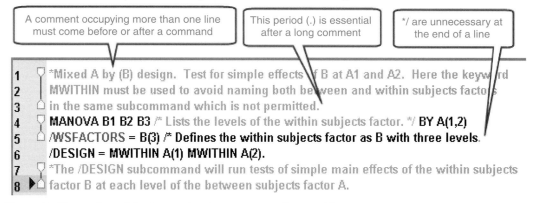

Figure 7. Illustration of the formatting for comments inserted in syntax

10.3   THE THREE-FACTOR MIXED ANOVA

The procedures described in Section 10.2 can readily be extended to the analysis of data from mixed factorial experiments with three treatment factors. To make the correct ANOVA choice, however, the user must be clear about the different possible experimental designs, for each of which there is a particular model and ANOVA procedure.

10.3.1   The two three-factor designs

In Table 4 below are shown the most common mixed ANOVA designs, all of which can be seen as elaborations of between subjects experiments, the simplest of which we shall term the 'Type A' design. In Table 4, the within subject factors are bracketed.

There are two possible three-factor mixed factorial experiments:
1. Two within subjects factors and one between subjects factor: A × (B × C)
2. One within subjects factor and two between subjects factors: A × B × (C).

Table 4. The 'mixed' or 'split-plot' experimental designs, as elaborations of the simple, two-group between subjects experiment (Type A)

(a)	Women	Men	
Type A design	Group 1	Group 2	

(b)	**Gender**	**Task:**	Task 1	Task 2	Task3
Type A × (B)	Women			Group 2	
design	Men			Group 2	

(c)		**Task:**	Task 1		Task 2		Task3	
Type A × (B×C)	**Gender**	**Hand:**	L	R	L	R	L	R
design	Women				Group 1			
	Men				Group 2			

(d)	**Gender**	**Hand**	**Task:**	Task 1	Task 2	Task 3
Type A × B × (C)	F	R			Group 1	
design		L			Group 2	
	M	R			Group 3	
		L			Group 4	

10.3.2 Two within subjects factors

Suppose that to the experiment described in Section 10.2, we were to add an additional within subjects factor, such as Solidity (of the shape), with two levels, Solid or Outline. The participants (either Psychology or Engineering students) now have to try to recognise both Solid and Outline Triangles, Squares, and Rectangles.

10.3.2.1 Entering the data

Since there are six combinations of the Shape and Solidity factors, we shall need to have six variables in **Data View** to contain all the scores. Prepare the named columns systematically in **Variable View** by taking the first level of one factor (say, Shape) and combining it in turn with each of the levels of the second factor (Solidity), and then doing the same with the second and third levels of the first factor. The top part of **Data View** might appear as in Figure 8, which shows the headings of the columns and the data for the first few participants. As we read from left to right across the variable labels for the various combinations of Shape and Solidity, we see that, whereas the second column is still a triangle (we are still at the first level of the Shape factor, i.e., Triangle), the level of the Solidity factor has changed to Outline. In this sense, the levels of the Shape factor can be said to 'change more slowly' than those of the Solidity factor as we scan the variable names from left to right.

TriangleSolid	TriangleOutline	SquareSolid	SquareOutline	RectangleSolid	RectangleOutline
2	12	3	1	4	5
13	22	5	9	6	8
14	20	8	7	5	7
12	1	3	9	6	10

Figure 8. The variable names for a three-factor mixed factorial experiment with two within subjects factors

10.3.2.2 Running the analysis

As usual, we must define our within subjects factors to create a framework into which the variables in Data View can be slotted. If the data are arranged as in Figure 8, the within subjects factors will be defined in the order: Shape (3), Solidity (2). The 'slower' factor in the sense described above is defined first. Once the factors have been defined, a grid will appear, waiting for the appropriate variable names to be inserted in the slots.

When you are working in the **Repeated Measures** dialog box, take care when transferring variable names from the list in the panel on the left to the slots in **Within-Subjects Variables** panel on the right. If, in **Data View**, you have arranged the variables systematically as we have described, you will be able to transfer the variables *en bloc* to the Within-Subjects Variables panel, where each will occupy the correct slot. The numerical contents of the slots in the panel are determined by the order in which the factors were defined and the numbers of levels that were given for each factor. In this case, since the Shape factor (with 3 levels) was defined first, the contents of the brackets should read as follows: (1, 1), (1, 2), (2, 1), (2, 2), (3, 1), (3, 2). Should the order of the variables in the left-hand panel fail to correspond with the numbering in the right-hand panel, something has gone wrong. You may, for instance, have defined the factors in the wrong order. Had you defined the factors in the order Solidity(2), Shape(3), the numbering in the slots would have been wrong for some of the variables: the third slot would still contain the data for the variable SquareSolid, but the programme would treat this variable as the scores for the solid triangle; and the slot that should contain data for the solid triangle would be treated as an outline square.

The upper part of the completed dialog box is shown in Figure 9.

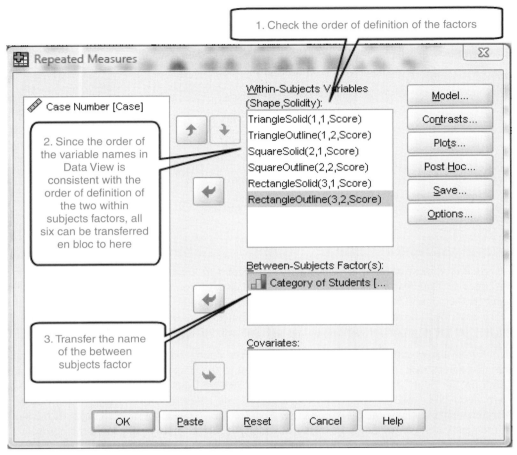

Figure 9. The upper part of the **Repeated Measures** dialog box for a three-factor mixed factorial experiment, with two within subjects factors and one between subjects factor

10.3.2.3   The ANOVA summary tables

The output includes Output 13, which shows the tests for the main effects of the within subjects factors and their various interactions with each other and with the between subjects factor. Output 14 shows the test for the between subjects factor.

Tests of Within-Subjects Effects

Measure:**Score**

Source	Type III Sum of Squares	df	Mean Square	F	Sig.	Partial Eta Squared
Shape	166.17	2	83.08	7.11	.017	.640
Shape * Category	109.06	2	54.53	4.67	.045	.539
Error(Shape)	93.44	8	11.68			
Solidity	25.00	1	25.00	11.25	.028	.738
Solidity * Category	28.44	1	28.44	12.80	.023	.762
Error(Solidity)	8.89	4	2.22			
Shape * Solidity	15.17	2	7.58	2.74	.124	.407
Shape * Solidity * Category	193.39	2	96.69	34.98	.000	.897
Error(Shape*Solidity)	22.11	8	2.76			

Output 13. The edited **Within-Subjects Effects** table showing the **F ratio** and **Partial Eta Squared** for the within subjects factors Shape and Solidity and their various double and triple interactions with each other and with the between subjects factor Category

Tests of Between-Subjects Effects

Measure:Score
Transformed Variable:Average

Source	Type III Sum of Squares	df	Mean Square	F	Sig.	Partial Eta Squared
Category	18.78	1	18.78	.538	.504	.119
Error	139.56	4	34.89			

Output 14. The edited **Between-Subjects Effects** table showing the **F ratio** and **Partial Eta Squared** for the between subjects factor Category

In the ANOVA, having equal sample sizes ensures that the sums of squares for the various effects can vary independently. Nevertheless, a significant higher order effect is often of more interest than a lower order effect and supersedes the former as the focus of attention and further analysis. In Output 13, for example, we see that the Shape × Solidity interaction is not significant. The finding that there is a significant three-way Shape × Solidity × Category interaction, however, shows that a more fine-grained analysis of the two-way interaction within the data from each group of participants is indicated. One obvious possibility is that the Shape × Solidity interaction may occur in one participant category but not in the other; on the other hand, there may be simple interactions in both groups of participants, but the patterns they show may be different.

10.3.2.4   The profile plots

The profile plots of Shape against Solidity for the two student groups are shown in Output 15. Comparison of the profile plots in the two groups strongly suggests heterogeneity of the simple interactions: the Engineers show a striking cross-over pattern; whereas the psychologists' profiles converge. The patterns shown by the two sets of profiles are quite consistent with the finding from the ANOVA that the three-way interaction is significant.

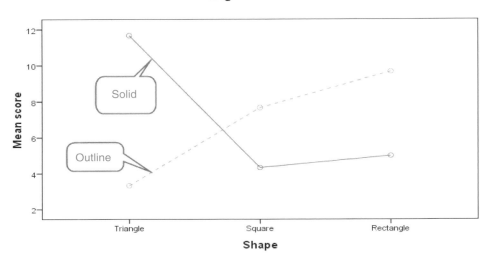

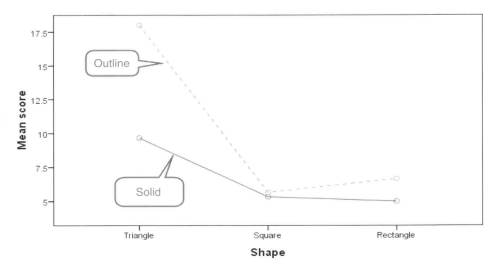

Output 15. Profile plots of Solidity against Shape for the two groups of participants

10.3.3 Using syntax to test for simple effects

Since the three-way interaction has proved to be significant, the researcher might wish to 'unpack' it by making further tests. Should at least one of the simple interactions turn out be significant, one might consider further analysis of simple, simple main effects of Solidity at different levels of the Category factor (i.e. in the psychologists and the engineers considered separately).

As we observed in our discussion of the syntax for simple effects in the two-factor A × (B) mixed factorial experiment, in order to avoid naming both a between subjects factor and a within subjects factor in the same subcommand (whether that is /DESIGN or /WSDESIGN), we shall need to use the keyword MWITHIN. If the experimental design is of the type A × (B × C), for instance, a statement such as B BY C at A(1), for instance, is unacceptable in either subcommand, because it names both within subjects and between subjects factors. Once again, the MWITHIN keyword is included in the subcommand we would normally use for effects of the other type: that is, if we want simple effects of within subjects factors (or their simple interactions), the MWITHIN keyword is included in the /DESIGN command, not the /WSDESIGN subcommand, as might be expected. The same is true of simple effects and (in designs with more than one between subjects factor) interactions among between subjects sources: in such cases, the MWITHIN keyword occurs in the /WSDESIGN, not the /DESIGN, subcommand.

For a mixed factorial design of type A × (B × C), that is, one in which factor A is between subjects and B and C are within subjects as in the current example, the following syntax (Figure 10) will run the full ANOVA:

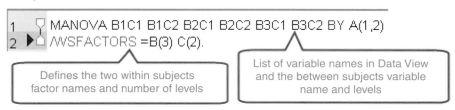

```
1   MANOVA B1C1 B1C2 B2C1 B2C2 B3C1 B3C2 BY A(1,2)
2   /WSFACTORS =B(3) C(2).
```

Defines the two within subjects factor names and number of levels

List of variable names in Data View and the between subjects variable name and levels

Figure 10. Syntax for a mixed factorial design of type A × (B × C)

In terms of the factors and the names of the variables in Data View in our current example, the syntax for the mixed ANOVA will appear as in Figure 11.

```
MANOVA TriangleSolid TriangleOutline SquareSolid SquareOutline
RectangleSolid RectangleOutline BY Category(1,2)
    /WSFACTORS = Shape(3) Solidity(2).
```

Figure 11. Syntax for the current example with Shape and Solidity as within subjects factors and Category as the between subjects factor

We shall be testing the simple interactions between Shape and Solidity at each level of the Category factor. As a check on the output, we shall want to satisfy ourselves that the sum of the sums of squares for the simple interactions is equal to the sum of squares for the three-way interaction plus the sums of squares for the two-way interaction between Shape and Solidity.

We expect this because, in general,

$$\sum_{j} SS_{BC \ at \ A_j} = SS_{BC} + SS_{ABC} \quad \text{- - - (1)}$$

Alternative partitioning of interaction terms

We shall not show the MANOVA output for the full ANOVA again, since the values given are identical with those shown in Outputs 13 and 14. We note from Output 13 that

$$SS_{Shape \times Solidity} + SS_{Shape \times Solidity \times Category} = 15.17 + 193.39 = 208.56$$

We shall make use of this value when we examine the output for the tests for simple interactions.

The syntax for testing for simple interactions between two within subjects factors at specified levels of a between subjects factor is shown in Figure 12.

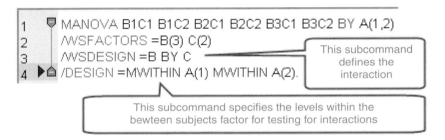

Figure 12. Syntax for testing simple interactions between two within subjects factors

Notice that, since there are three factors in the current experiment, we shall need both /DESIGN and /WSDESIGN subcommands to link the simple interactions to the MWITHIN statements. In terms of the variable names in the current example, the syntax for testing for simple interactions between Shape and Solidity at each level of the Category factor is as shown in Figure 13.

Figure 13. Syntax for testing simple interactions at each level of a between subjects factor

The results of the tests for simple interactions are shown in Output 16, which forms the final part of an extensive list of test results, the rest of which has been omitted. Notice that, once again, the second occurrence of the keyword BY in connexion with the keyword MWITHIN suggests a three-factor interaction; but these are simple two-factor interactions of Shape with Solidity at each level of the Category factor.

When we add together the sums of squares for the sources labelled as MWITHIN CATEGORY(1) BY SHAPE BY SOLIDITY and MWITHIN CATEGORY(2) BY SHAPE BY SOLIDITY, we obtain the value 208.56, which, as we have seen (1), is the sum of the sums of squares for the Shape × Solidity interaction and the Shape × Solidity × Category interaction. This is further confirmation that our interpretation of the output is correct.

```
Tests involving 'SHAPE BY SOLIDITY' Within-Subject Effect.

AVERAGED Tests of Significance for MEAS.1 using UNIQUE sums of squares
Source of Variation            SS       DF       MS         F  Sig of F

WITHIN+RESIDUAL              22.11        8      2.76
MWITHIN CATEGORY(1)         55.11        2     27.56      9.97     .007
BY SHAPE BY SOLIDITY

MWITHIN CATEGORY(2)        153.44        2     76.72     27.76     .000
BY SHAPE BY SOLIDITY
```

Output 16. Tests for simple interactions Shape and Solidity at both levels of the Category factor

Our formal tests have confirmed the existence of simple interactions between Shape and Solidity in both groups of participants. Arguably, therefore, we can proceed to test for simple, simple main effects of solidity in order to cast further light on the profile patterns in Output 15. The syntax for these tests is as shown in Figure 14.

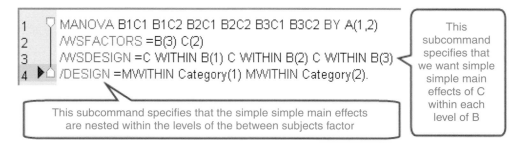

Figure 14. Syntax for simple simple main effects for an A × (B × C) design

In terms of the variable names of the current example, the syntax reads as in Figure 15.

```
1  ▽  MANOVA TriangleSolid TriangleOutline SquareSolid SquareOutline
2  │   RectangleSolid RectangleOutline BY Category(1,2)
3  │   /WSFACTORS = Shape(3) Solidity(2)
4  │   /WSDESIGN = Solidity WITHIN Shape(1) Solidity WITHIN Shape(2) Solidity WITHIN Shape(3)
5  △  /DESIGN =MWITHIN Category(1) MWITHIN Category(2).
```

Figure 15. Syntax for testing simple simple main effects

Since the MWITHIN keywords in the /DESIGN subcommand nest the three simple main effects within each level of the between subjects factor Category, the analysis will run tests of six simple, simple main effects: Solidity at Shape(1), Shape(2) and Shape(3) at Category(1); and Solidity at Shape(1), Shape(2) and Shape(3) at Category(2).

Output 17 shows the results of the six tests for simple simple main effects of Solidity at the six combinations of the Shape and Solidity factors.

	Source of Variation	SS	DF	MS	F	Sig of F
	WITHIN+RESIDUAL	13.67	4	3.42		
C at B(1)A(1)	MWITHIN CATEGORY(1) BY SOLIDITY W SHAPE(1)	104.17	1	104.17	30.49	.005
C at B(1)A(2)	MWITHIN CATEGORY(2) BY SOLIDITY W SHAPE(1)	104.17	1	104.17	30.49	.005
	WITHIN+RESIDUAL	15.67	4	3.92		
C at B(2)A(1)	MWITHIN CATEGORY(1) BY SOLIDITY W SHAPE(2)	.17	1	.17	.04	.847
C at B(2)A(2)	MWITHIN CATEGORY(2) BY SOLIDITY W SHAPE(2)	16.67	1	16.67	4.26	.108
	WITHIN+RESIDUAL	1.67	4	.42		
C at B(3)A(1)	MWITHIN CATEGORY(1) BY SOLIDITY W SHAPE(3)	4.17	1	4.17	10.00	.034
C at B(3)A(2)	MWITHIN CATEGORY(2) BY SOLIDITY W SHAPE(3)	32.67	1	32.67	78.40	.001

Output 17. Tests for simple, simple main effects of Solidity at each of the six combinations of Shape and Category

Since the factor of Solidity has only two levels, a significant simple, simple main effect implies that the difference between the means for the Solid and Outline conditions is also significant. Had we tested for simple, simple main effects of Shape at each of the four combinations of the Solidity and Category factors, further testing of pairwise comparisons would have been required. Once again, the presence of a significant simple, simple main effect might be seen as justification for defining the size of the comparison family on the basis of three means only.

10.3.4   One within subjects factor and two between subjects factors: the A × B × (C) mixed factorial design

Suppose the experiment described in Section 10.3.2 were to have an additional between subjects factor, such as Sex (Male, Female) but just one within subjects factor Shape. Our mixed factorial design is now of type A × B × (C). The participants (Psychology and Engineering Students, Male and Female) are asked to try to recognise targets of three different shapes (Triangles, Squares and Rectangles).

10.3.4.1   Preparing the data set

The data for this final example of a mixed factorial ANOVA are given on our website at www.psypress.com/spss-made-simple.

In **Variable View**, it will now be necessary to add a second grouping variable, Sex. Figure 16 shows the first row of values in Data View. The names of the two grouping variables, Category and Sex, can also be seen.

Case	Category	Sex	Triangle	Square	Rectangle
1	Psychology Student	Male	2	12	7

Figure 16. The variable names for a three-factor mixed factorial experiment with one within subjects and two between subjects factors

10.3.4.2   Running the ANOVA

The completed **Repeated Measures ANOVA** dialog box is shown in Figure 17. Notice that the Between-Subjects Factor(s) box now contains the labels of two grouping variables, Category of Student and Sex.

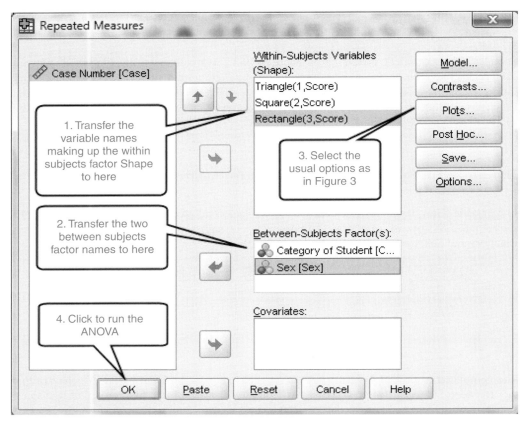

Figure 17. The upper part of the **Repeated Measures** dialog box for a three-factor mixed factorial experiment with one within subjects factor and two between subjects factors

10.3.4.3   The output

The output, as usual, is extensive, so we shall draw your attention to the key tables only. Output 18 shows the tests of the within subjects factor Shape and its various interactions with the two between subjects factors. Output 19 shows the tests of the between subjects factors Category and Sex. The results in Output 18 show that Shape and the interaction between Shape and Category are significant beyond the 1% level; but neither the interaction between Shape and Sex nor the triple interaction is significant. The results in Output 19 show that the factor Category is significant at the 1% level but neither the factor Sex nor the interaction between Sex and Category is significant.

Tests of Within-Subjects Effects

Measure: Score

Source	Type III Sum of Squares	df	Mean Square	F	Sig.	Partial Eta Squared
Shape	519.62	2	259.81	29.39	.000	.786
Shape * Category	1277.74	2	638.87	72.27	.000	.900
Shape * Sex	14.92	2	7.46	.84	.448	.095
Shape * Category * Sex	7.86	2	3.93	.44	.649	.053
Error(Shape)	141.44	16	8.84			

Output 18. The edited **Within-Subjects Effects** table showing the **F ratio** and **Partial Eta Squared** for the within subjects factor Shape and its interactions with the two between subjects factors Category and Sex

Tests of Between-Subjects Effects

Measure: Score
Transformed Variable: Average

Source	Type III Sum of Squares	df	Mean Square	F	Sig.	Partial Eta Squared
Category	1093.34	1	1093.34	107.69	.000	.931
Sex	22.75	1	22.75	2.24	.173	.219
Category * Sex	6.28	1	6.28	.62	.454	.072
Error	81.22	8	10.15			

Output 19. The edited **Between-Subjects Effects** table showing the **F ratio** and **Partial Eta Squared** for the two between subjects factors Category and Sex together with their interaction

10.3.4.4   The profile plot

Output 20 shows that the profiles of the psychologists and engineers show a cross-over pattern, hence the significant interaction between Shape and Category.

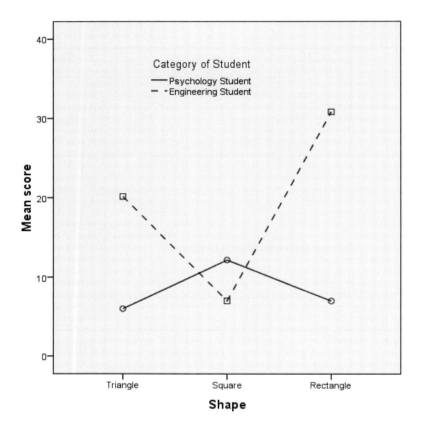

Output 20. The profile plot showing the significant interaction of Shape and Category

10.3.4.5   Testing for simple main effects and interactions

In the event of a significant two-factor interaction, the researcher might well proceed to test for simple main effects. Since the procedure presents no new issues, we shall not describe the syntax for the tests for simple main effects here.

Since, in the current example, the three-factor interaction is statistically insignificant, we would not go on to test for simple interactions. Had the interaction proved to be significant, however, we would certainly have considered testing the simple interactions for significance.

In general notation, the syntax for testing for a simple interaction between factors A and B at each of the three levels of factor C is shown in Figure 18.

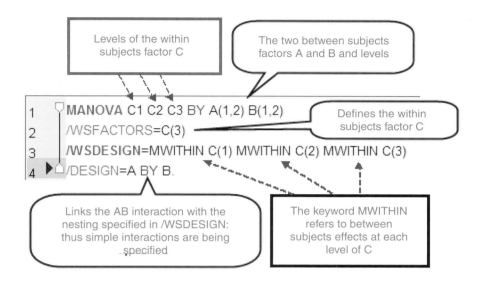

Figure 18. Syntax for testing for a simple AB interaction at each level of the within subjects factor C

The syntax for our current example is shown in Figure 19.

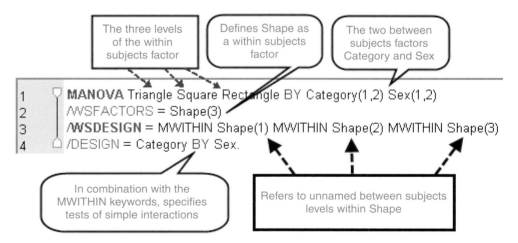

Figure 19. Syntax for testing for a simple Category by Sex interaction at each level of the within subjects factor Shape

Output 21 shows the output for the test for a simple interaction between Category and Sex at one level only of the Shape factor: Triangle.

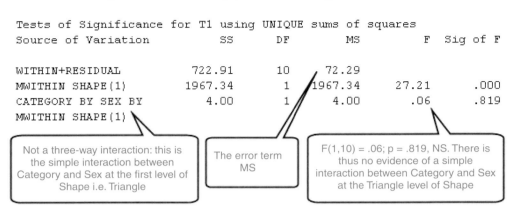

Tests involving 'MWITHIN SHAPE(1)' Within-Subject Effect.

Tests of Significance for T1 using UNIQUE sums of squares
Source of Variation   SS   DF   MS   F   Sig of F

WITHIN+RESIDUAL   722.91   10   72.29
MWITHIN SHAPE(1)   1967.34   1   1967.34   27.21   .000
CATEGORY BY SEX BY   4.00   1   4.00   .06   .819
MWITHIN SHAPE(1)

> Not a three-way interaction: this is the simple interaction between Category and Sex at the first level of Shape i.e. Triangle

> The error term MS

> F(1,10) = .06; p = .819, NS. There is thus no evidence of a simple interaction between Category and Sex at the Triangle level of Shape

Output 21. Some of the output, showing that there is no significant simple interaction between Category and Sex in the data from the Triangles condition

Testing for simple, simple main effects following a significant three-factor interaction

Since, in the current example, there was no three-factor interaction, the question of unpacking the interaction by testing for simple, simple main effects does not arise. Should a test for a simple interaction show significance, you might wish to proceed to make tests of simple, simple main effects. The syntax is shown in Figure 20.

Here, we are asking for tests of simple, simple main effects of factor A at combinations of factors B and C: B(1)C(1), B(2)C(1), B(3)C(1) and so on. In the output (not shown here), these simple, simple main effects will look like interactions, because their labels contain the keyword BY with MWITHIN.

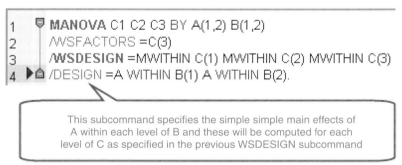

```
1    MANOVA C1 C2 C3 BY A(1,2) B(1,2)
2    /WSFACTORS =C(3)
3    /WSDESIGN =MWITHIN C(1) MWITHIN C(2) MWITHIN C(3)
4    /DESIGN =A WITHIN B(1) A WITHIN B(2).
```

> This subcommand specifies the simple simple main effects of A within each level of B and these will be computed for each level of C as specified in the previous WSDESIGN subcommand

Figure 20. Syntax for testing simple simple main effects in an A × B × (C) design

In the current example, the syntax for testing simple, simple main effects appears as in Figure 21.

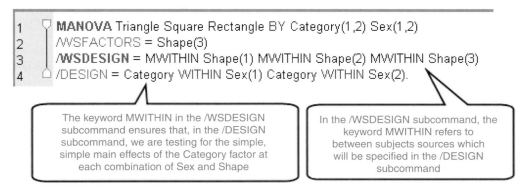

Figure 21. Syntax for testing for simple simple main effects of Category at each combination of Shape and Sex

Notice that, once again, although we can use the keyword MWITHIN in the /WSDESIGN subcommand to refer to between subjects sources, we need an additional /DESIGN subcommand to specify that we want an interaction.

Output 22 shows a fragment of the output: the test for simple simple effects of Category at the combinations of Triangle Shape with Male and Female Participants.

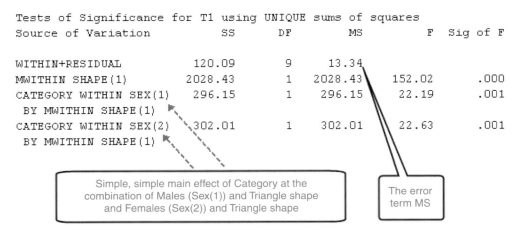

Output 22. Tests for simple simple main effects of Category at the combinations of Triangle Shape with Male and Female participants

Finally, we should perhaps say that the foregoing testing of simple, simple main effects is included for the sake of completeness: although both of the tests for simple, simple main effects reported in Output 22 show significance beyond the .01 level, we should not normally proceed with such further testing were the test for the three-factor interaction to prove insignificant, which is the case in our present example.

10.4   THE MULTIVARIATE ANALYSIS OF VARIANCE (MANOVA)

In the analysis of variance (ANOVA), there is just ONE dependent variable. There may, as we have seen, be several factors (that is, independent variables) and, as a consequence, **Data View** will contain several variables. Such a data set, however, is still regarded as **univariate**, because it contains only one measured variable, namely the DV, that is of central interest and is recorded during the investigation. This is still essentially true if the researcher has further data on the participants in the form of measurements on a **covariate**, that is, a variable which correlates (or covaries) with the DV and may inflate the error term in the F tests. We shall have two measured variables; but interest still focuses on the DV and the purpose of the technique known as **analysis of covariance (ANCOVA)** is to 'purify' the data by removing the effects of the covariate, thereby reducing data 'noise' and enabling the researcher to make more powerful ANOVA F test.

A researcher, however, will often wish to study the effects of experimental or group factors upon *two or more* DVs. For example, in an experiment on the influence of drugs upon skilled performance, the researcher might wish to take measures of speed and errors, as well as the participant's performance score. Such an experiment will result in a **bivariate** or **multivariate** data set, that is, one in which two or more of the variables are measured during the course of the investigation with a view to investigating how they are affected by the factors in the experimental design. Such additional DVs are quite different from covariates, in that, far from being merely potential contributors to data noise, they are of central interest in their own right.

A researcher with a multivariate data set of this kind might consider running a univariate ANOVA on each of the DVs in the study. This, indeed, has been (and still is) a very common approach to the analysis of multivariate data. A major problem, however, is that the DVs are highly likely to be correlated, because the same people are being measured on the different DVs. As a result, the outcomes of the various univariate ANOVAs are not independent. This can have serious consequences for the interpretation of the p-values from the F tests: the type I error rate, for example, may increase to an unacceptably high level.

The **multivariate analysis of variance (MANOVA)** is a set of techniques designed specially for the purpose of analysing simultaneously the results of experiments with several DVs.

10.4.1   What the MANOVA does

The MANOVA is an extension or generalisation of the univariate ANOVA to multivariate data sets. We have seen that the one-way ANOVA tests the null hypothesis that any differences there may be among the group means on a single DV have arisen merely through sampling error. In MANOVA, the object of the exercise is, firstly, to find a linear function of the DVs with respect to which the groups are spread as widely as possible. This linear function of the DVs is known as a **discriminant function**; in fact, the one-way MANOVA was originally termed **discriminant analysis**. The next step is to determine whether differences among the group means with respect to participants' scores on the discriminant function (these means are known as **centroids**) could have arisen merely through sampling error, the null hypothesis being that, in the population, the mean discriminant score or centroid is the same for all groups.

A discriminant function has the following general form.   If we suppose that there are p dependent variables in the experiment, $DV_1, DV_2, ..., DV_p$,   the formula for the discriminant function is

$$D = b_0 + b_1 DV_1 + b_2 DV_2 + ... + b_p DV_p \quad \text{- - - (2)}$$

A discriminant function

Each of the participants in the experiment will receive, in addition to scores on the DVs, an additional score on the discriminant function D.   The values of the constants $b_0, b_1, ... b_p$ are chosen so that the distributions of D among the groups (i.e., the group means or centroids) are spread out across the range of variation of D to the greatest possible extent: that is, the variability of D between groups is maximised.   In this sense, the function D can be said to 'discriminate' among the groups.

If there are more than two groups, more than one discriminant function can be extracted.   If there are k groups, $k - 1$ uncorrelated (or **orthogonal**) discriminant functions can be extracted. During the MANOVA, the extraction of the first discriminant function D_1 is followed by the extraction of the second discriminant function D_2, which is uncorrelated with (or **orthogonal to** D_1).   The process continues until all $k - 1$ discriminant functions have been extracted.   Each participant will now have, in addition to a score on each DV, $k - 1$ extra scores, one on each of the discriminant functions.

We have already said that the one-way MANOVA is identical with the technique known as discriminant analysis (DA). Both the MANOVA and DA, however, are options in SPSS. The choice between them depends upon the research situation. The MANOVA is applicable in experimental (or quasi-experimental research), where the researcher is primarily interested in comparing groups or conditions.   DA, on the other hand, is applicable in correlational research, in which the researcher is more interested in possible associations among a set of measured variables and wants to predict category membership from other measures in the data set. The researcher, for instance, might use a DA to predict patients' diagnostic categories from their scores on a battery of clinical scales.   The use of discriminant functions to categorise people in this way is known as **classification**. The output from SPSS's discriminant analysis procedure (see Chapter 14) reflects the difference in orientation between the MANOVA and DA. Although the DA and MANOVA outputs contain the same core statistics, the DA output also includes additional statistics of particular interest to the researcher who is trying to predict group membership.

While the discriminant functions from the MANOVA could each be analysed with a univariate, one-way ANOVA to compare the group centroids or means, additional techniques are available for measuring the relative contribution of each discriminant function to the between groups variance and of the DVs to the variance accounted for by each discriminant function.

10.4.2   How the MANOVA works

The presence of several DVs makes the mathematics of the MANOVA more complicated than that of the ANOVA. In the one-way ANOVA, the total variability, as measured by the total sum of squares, is partitioned into between groups and within groups components and (after adjustments for their different degrees of freedom), the two variance estimates are compared by means of an F ratio to test the null hypothesis of equality, in the population, of the group means. Each of the two variance estimates has a single (or **point**) value.

Something basically similar happens in the MANOVA as well; but the analogues of point values such as the between and within sums of squares in the univariate ANOVA are rectangular arrays of numbers known as **matrices**. Conceptually, though, the parallels are close.

We have already encountered the **variance-covariance** matrix in Chapter 9, where we discussed the within subjects ANOVA. The values running along the principal diagonal of the variance-covariance matrix (the line of cells running from the top left to the bottom right) are variances and the off-diagonal values are covariances between pairs of the repeated measures. The safe use of the within subjects ANOVA requires that the variance-covariance matrix must have the property of **sphericity**, that is, the values of the covariances must be (within sampling error) uniform. One of the great advantages of the MANOVA over the within subjects ANOVA is that sphericity is not a requirement. This is especially relevant when the MANOVA is used as an alternative to the ANOVA for the analysis of data from within subjects experiments (see below).

10.4.2.1   Variance-covariance matrices in MANOVA

In the MANOVA, the point values embodying the total variability, the between groups variability and the within groups variability that are used in the ANOVA, namely, SS_{total}, $SS_{between}$ and SS_{within}, respectively, are replaced by equivalent values calculated from variance-covariance matrices. In Chapter 9, we saw that the building block from which a covariance is calculated is the **cross-product** $(X - M_X)(Y - M_Y)$. The numerator of the covariance is the sum of cross-products SP, where $SP = \sum (X - M_X)(Y - M_Y)$. If we take deviations of the scores on the DVs from their respective grand means, ignoring the group means, we have a variance-covariance matrix T which is the analogue of the total sum of squares in the ANOVA. If we take the deviations of the group means from the grand means, we have a matrix B corresponding to the between groups sum of squares in ANOVA. If we take the deviations of the scores from their group means, we have a matrix W corresponding to the within groups sum of squares in the ANOVA. Rather than merely measuring variance or variability, however, as in the ANOVA, these matrices also measure covariance, or shared variability.

10.4.2.2   Partition of the total variance-covariance matrix

Matrices, such as T, B and W, that all have r rows and c columns (that is, they have the same **dimensions**), can be added to produce another matrix with r rows and c columns, whose elements are the sums of the corresponding elements in the component matrices. For example,

$$\begin{pmatrix} 2 & 1 & 3 & 1 \\ 5 & 0 & 1 & 2 \end{pmatrix} + \begin{pmatrix} 6 & 0 & 9 & 1 \\ 3 & 3 & 4 & 6 \end{pmatrix} = \begin{pmatrix} 8 & 1 & 12 & 2 \\ 8 & 3 & 5 & 8 \end{pmatrix}$$
$$\begin{array}{ccc} M_1 & M_2 & M_3 = M_1 + M_2 \quad \text{- - - (3)} \\ (2 \times 4) & (2 \times 4) & (2 \times 4) \end{array}$$

Matrix addition

In the MANOVA, the between groups and within groups variance-covariance matrices of cross-products have the same dimensions (same number of rows, same number of columns) and can therefore be added together. It can be shown that when this is done, we have the total variance-covariance matrix. So, in MANOVA, we have a partition of the total variance-covariance matrix into between groups and within groups components thus:

$$T = B + W \quad \text{- - - (4)}$$

Partition of the total variance-covariance

matrix in the MANOVA

10.4.2.3 A multivariate analogue of the variance: the determinant and Wilks' lambda

We have stressed that T, B and W are *matrices*, that is, rectangular arrays of values, not point values. From such a matrix, however, a point analogue of the variance can be calculated, namely, the **determinant** of the variance-covariance matrix. The determinant can be thought of as measuring variance plus covariance. A determinant is denoted by the use of two vertical lines: | |. The determinants of the between groups and within groups matrices are $|B|$ and $|W|$, respectively.

In the one-way ANOVA, the F statistic is used to test the null hypothesis of equality of the group means. In MANOVA, several statistics have been proposed for testing the null hypothesis of equality of the group centroids. These statistics include **Wilks's lambda**, **Pillai's criterion**, **Hotelling's trace** and **Roy's principal root**. Wilks' lambda divides the determinant of the within groups matrix by the sum of the determinants of the within groups and between groups matrices:

$$\Lambda = \frac{|W|}{|W| + |B|} \quad \text{- - - (5)} \quad \textbf{Wilks' lambda}$$

We can think of Wilks' lambda as expressing the error variance as a proportion of the total variance. From Wilks' lambda, an approximate F statistic can be calculated. (An approximate chi-square statistic can also be used.) The degrees of freedom of F are given by complex formulae with which we shall not concern ourselves here (see Tabachnick & Fidell, 2007, p.259). The values of the degrees of freedom are included in the SPSS output.

10.4.2.3 Wilks' lambda and eta squared

Recall that in univariate one-way ANOVA, a measure of effect size is **eta squared (η^2)**, where

$$\eta^2 = \frac{SS_{between}}{SS_{total}} \quad \text{- - - (6)} \quad \textbf{Eta squared}$$

Eta squared is the proportion of the total variability in the scores that is accounted for by variability among the group means.

For simplicity, **Wilks's lambda (Λ)**, can be thought of as the proportion of the total variance that is *within* groups, rather than *between* groups, as in eta squared: in fact, in the context of the one-way ANOVA (where there is just one DV), lambda is simply 1 minus eta squared:

$$\Lambda = 1 - \eta^2 \quad \text{- - -} \quad (7)$$

Wilks' lambda and eta squared in the special case of one DV

This comparison extends to the situation where, rather than one DV, we have a discriminant function of several DVs. The value of Λ, like that of η^2, can range in value from 0 to 1. Since, however, lambda is measuring *within* groups rather than *between* groups variability, a value of Λ close to zero indicates a *large* separation among the means; whereas a value close to unity indicates a *small* separation.

10.4.2.4 How discriminant functions are constructed: eigenvectors and eigenvalues

A **vector** is a row or column of values, as opposed to a **scalar**, which is a single value. In a matrix, any row or column is a vector. From some matrices, it is possible to calculate a special vector known as an **eigenvector**. In the MANOVA, the values in an eigenvector are the coefficients of a discriminant function: there is an eigenvector for each discriminant function extracted by the MANOVA. Associated with each eigenvector and discriminant function is an **eigenvalue (λ)** (or **characteristic root**). The eigenvalue measures the proportion of the variance accounted for by that function. An eigenvalue has a maximum value of 1, which would mean that its discriminant function accounts for 100% of the variance.

Eigenvectors and eigenvalues are ubiquitous in multivariate statistics: 'Most of the multivariate procedures rely on eigenvalues and their corresponding eigenvectors (also called characteristic roots and vectors) in one way or another because they consolidate the variance in a matrix (the *eigenvalue*) while providing the linear combination of variables (the *eigenvector*) to do it' (Tabachnick & Fidell, 2007; p.931).

10.4.2.5 Eigenvalues and Wilks' lambda

We have already looked at Wilks's lambda in the context of the comparison between within groups and between groups variance-covariance matrices. Lambda can also be expressed in terms of eigenvalues:

$$\Lambda = \prod_{i}^{d} \frac{1}{1 + \lambda_i} \quad \text{- - -} \quad (8)$$

Wilks's lambda expressed in terms of eigenvalues

In formula (8), d is the number of discriminant functions extracted by the MANOVA. The symbol $\prod$ (pi) stands for 'product': it is an operator, like Σ, but this time the d terms $1/(1 + \lambda_i)$ are multiplied together, not added. The greater the eigenvalues, the smaller the value of Wilks's lambda, bearing in mind that lambda is the *error* variance-covariance expressed as a proportion: the *smaller* the value of lambda, the *greater* the power of the discriminant function to discriminate among the groups.

The other principal statistics that appear in the SPSS MANOVA output, namely, the **Pillai-Bartlett trace**, **Hotellings T^2 (Hotelling-Lawley trace)** and **Roy's largest root**, are all functions of the eigenvalues λ. The simplest of these measures, Roy's largest root, is simply the largest value of λ. Since the first eigenvector (and discriminant function) to be extracted has the largest eigenvalue, Roy's statistic is the ratio of the between groups to the within groups variance/covariance for the first discriminant function.

10.4.3   Assumptions of the MANOVA

In univariate ANOVA, the data should be normally distributed. In MANOVA, the distributions of the DVs should be **multivariate normal**: if there are k DVs, then for any set of fixed values of $k - 1$ of them, the distribution of the remaining variable is also normal. The assumption of multivariate normality is the counterpart, in multivariate statistics, of the assumption of normality of distribution in the univariate ANOVA.

In the univariate ANOVA, the data should meet the requirement of homogeneity of variance. In MANOVA, the counterpart of this assumption is **homogeneity of variance-covariance matrices**: that is, it is assumed that the variance-covariance matrices in the different groups have all been sampled from the same population and so can be combined to give a pooled estimate of error, just as in the ANOVA, the cell variances are combined in the within groups mean square. The assumption of homogeneity of variance-covariance matrices (which is tested by **Box's test**) is quite a separate property from **sphericity**, that is, the homogeneity of the covariances among the repeated measures in the within subjects ANOVA, which is tested with the Mauchly test: variance-covariance matrices can be homogeneous across groups, but the individual matrices may not have the property of sphericity. The great advantage of MANOVA is that homogeneity of covariance is not a requirement and for this reason, some prefer to use MANOVA for the analysis of data from within subjects experiments.

To some extent, MANOVA is robust to violation of the assumptions of multivariate normality and homogeneity of variance-covariance matrices. As in the case of between subjects ANOVA, when sample sizes are large and equal among groups, all is likely to be well as far as Type I and Type II error rates are concerned. In the ANOVA, the greatest threat to the accuracy of the p-values of the F tests is a combination of unequal sample sizes and heterogeneity of variance. In the MANOVA, the parallel of these contraindications is a combination of unequal sample sizes and disparities among the variance-covariance matrices in different groups: if the larger samples have larger variances and covariances, the p-values are likely to be too large; whereas if the smaller samples have larger variances and covariances, the p-values are likely to be too small (Tabachnick & Fidell, 2007; p252). This consideration has implications for the choice between the various test statistics that are available.

The presence of strong associations among the variables is known as **multicollinearity**. In the extreme case of a perfect correlation between two of the DVs, the variance-covariance matrix is **singular**, that is, the determinant does not exist and the key statistics cannot be calculated. If the data show multicollinearity, one or more of the dependent variables must be removed before the MANOVA can run successfully.

10.4.4   Application of MANOVA to the shape recognition experiment

In Section 10.2, we described the analysis of data from an experiment of design A × (B), specifically, Category × Shape, using the mixed or split-plot ANOVA. This technique is available through the **Repeated Measures** procedure in the GLM menu. Included in the SPSS output is a table of **Multivariate Tests** which we omitted from that section, but which is shown in Output 23 below.

Multivariate Tests[b]

Effect		Value	F	Hypothesis df	Error df	Sig.	Partial Eta Squared
Shape	Pillai's Trace	.841	23.884[a]	2.000	9.000	.000	.841
	Wilks' Lambda	.159	23.884[a]	2.000	9.000	.000	.841
	Hotelling's Trace	5.308	23.884[a]	2.000	9.000	.000	.841
	Roy's Largest Root	5.308	23.884[a]	2.000	9.000	.000	.841
Shape * Category	Pillai's Trace	.941	71.159[a]	2.000	9.000	.000	.941
	Wilks' Lambda	.059	71.159[a]	2.000	9.000	.000	.941
	Hotelling's Trace	15.813	71.159[a]	2.000	9.000	.000	.941
	Roy's Largest Root	15.813	71.159[a]	2.000	9.000	.000	.941

a. Exact statistic

b. Design: Intercept + Category
Within Subjects Design: Shape

Output 23. Table of results of multivariate tests for the data in Table 1

Output 23 shows the output from the MANOVA of the same data. The results of the tests made by the MANOVA are clearly in agreement with those of the ANOVA: there is a significant main effect of the Shape factor and also a significant Shape by Category interaction. (We should note, however, that the ANOVA and the MANOVA don't always produce the same results.) You will notice that the values of partial eta squared for the Shape factor and Shape by Category interaction are somewhat larger than those given for the same sources of variance in the Repeated Measures ANOVA output. The values given in Output 23 are 1 minus the value of Wilks' lambda for each source of variance.

The results of the approximate F test can be reported in the usual way, including information about the degrees of freedom, the p-values and measures of effect size, as when reporting the results of a univariate ANOVA F test.

10.4.4.1   Testing within subjects sources for significance

The MANOVA procedure is obtainable by choosing the **Multivariate** option in the **GLM** menu. If, in the MANOVA dialog box, you were to enter Category of Student as the Fixed Factor and Triangle, Square and Rectangle as the dependent variables and run the MANOVA procedure, you would obtain a test of the Category of Student factor. The procedure would find a discriminant function of Triangle, Square and Rectangle that maximises the separation of the group means or centroids and tests the null hypothesis that, in the population, the two group centroids are equal. The output would also include comparisons of the two groups on each of the three dependent variables considered separately. The output, however, would contain neither a test of the within subjects Shape factor nor of its interaction with the grouping factor Category of Student.

Essentially, the Repeated Measures procedure uses MANOVA to test within subjects sources of variance by creating, from the variables in the data set, certain additional variables and entering those (rather than Triangle, Square and Rectangle) into the MANOVA. The output will then include the desired tests of within subjects sources.

10.4.4.2 How the Repeated Measures procedure uses MANOVA to test within subjects sources

You might wish to choose the Multivariate option and use MANOVA yourself to see how the Repeated Measures procedure makes tests of within subjects factors and their interactions.

In Figure 22, is shown the original data set, including participants' scores under the Triangle, Square and Rectangle conditions, plus two new variables, SquareMinusTriangle and RectangleMinusSquare. These were produced by using the **Compute** command in the **Transform** menu to produce two columns of difference scores: the first was obtained by subtracting each Triangle score from the same participant's Square score; the second was obtained by subtracting the Square score from the corresponding Rectangle score (Figure 23).

	Case	Category	Triangle	Square	Rectangle	SquareMinus Triangle	RectangleMinus Square
1	1	1	2	12	7	10	-5
2	2	1	8	10	9	2	-1
3	3	1	4	15	3	11	-12
4	4	1	6	9	7	3	-2
5	5	1	9	13	8	4	-5
6	6	1	7	14	8	7	-6
7	7	2	13	3	35	-10	32
8	8	2	21	4	30	-17	26
9	9	2	26	10	35	-16	25
10	10	2	22	8	30	-14	22
11	11	2	20	9	28	-11	19
12	12	2	19	8	27	-11	19

Figure 22. **Data View**, showing the addition to the data set of two difference variables

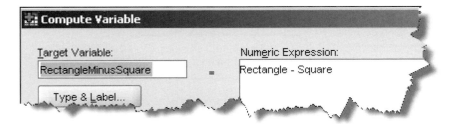

Figure 23. Compute Rectangle – Square with the **Compute Variable** command

Considering first the within subjects factor Shape, the null hypothesis holds that, in the population, the mean scores for the three shapes, Triangle, Square and Rectangle, are equal. If this is true, the values, in the population, of the means of the difference scores SquareMinusTriangle and RectangleMinusSquare are both zero. If the two difference variables are input as DVs into the MANOVA, the procedure will test this hypothesis and we shall have a test for a main effect of Shape.

If, in addition to the two difference variables, we input the grouping variable Category, the MANOVA procedure will compute a discriminant function of the two difference scores, which maximises the difference between the group means or centroids. Think of that discriminant function as a simple contrast between the two difference scores. If there is no interaction present, the value of that contrast will be similar in the two groups and the discriminant function will not be able to discriminate reliably between them. If an interaction is present, the mean values of the function (the centroids) will be further apart and the discriminant function will be able to discriminate reliably between the two groups.

Running the MANOVA

To run the MANOVA
- Select **Analyze→General Linear Model→Multivariate…** to open the **Multivariate** dialog box (Figure 24).
- Transfer the DVs, that is, the two difference variables, to the **Dependent Variables** box.
- Click **Options** and select **Descriptive statistics**, **Estimates of effect size**, and **Homogeneity tests** for checking the assumption of homogeneity of the variance-covariance matrix. Click **Continue** to return to the **MANOVA** dialog box.
- Click **OK** to run the MANOVA.

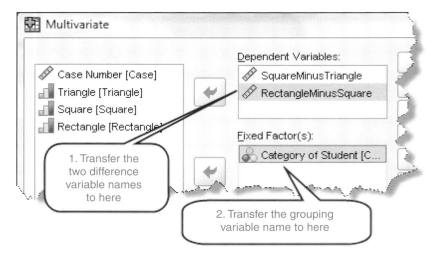

Figure 24. The **Multivariate** dialog box with the two difference scores transferred to the **Dependent Variables** box and the IV to the **Fixed Factor(s)** box

10.4.4.4 The MANOVA output

The results of the MANOVA are summarised in Output 24.

The multivariate equivalent of the main effect of Shape

Multivariate Tests[b]

Effect		Value	F	Hypothesis df	Error df	Sig.
Intercept	Pillai's Trace	.841	23.884[a]	2.000	9.000	.000
	Wilks' Lambda	.159	23.884[a]	2.000	9.000	.000
	Hotelling's Trace	5.308	23.884[a]	2.000	9.000	.000
	Roy's Largest Root	5.308	23.884[a]	2.000	9.000	.000
Category	Pillai's Trace	.941	71.159[a]	2.000	9.000	.000
	Wilks' Lambda	.059	71.159[a]	2.000	9.000	.000
	Hotelling's Trace	15.813	71.159[a]	2.000	9.000	.000
	Roy's Largest Root	15.813	71.159[a]	2.000	9.000	.000

a. Exact statistic

b. Design: Intercept + Category

The multivariate equivalent of the Shape*Category interaction

Output 24. Results of the MANOVA of the difference variables SquareMinusTriangle and RectangleMinusSquare

Although the upper and lower part of the table are labelled 'Intercept' and 'Category', respectively, we have the same results of the tests for a main effect of the Shape factor and the Shape × Category interaction as were presented in Output 17 from the **Repeated Measures** procedure. The use of difference variables rather than raw scores as input for the MANOVA has captured both the main effect of Shape and the Shape × Category interaction. The Repeated Measures procedure creates difference variables in a similar way and inputs them to the MANOVA, but outputs a table in which the name of the within subjects factor and the interaction are correctly labelled.

There are several ways of proceeding when a MANOVA main effect or an interaction is significant, but the details of these lie beyond the scope of this book. SPSS provides a step-by-step tutorial - click the **Help** button in the **MANOVA** dialog box and then click **Show me** at the foot of the resulting text box. Statistical textbooks, such as Tabachnick & Fidell (2007) and Field (2005, 2009), suggest further procedures such as Roy-Bargmann Stepdown Analysis and Discriminant Analysis.

10.5   A FINAL WORD

In this chapter, we have described the analysis of data from experiments of mixed factorial (or split-plot) design, in which some (but not all) factors have repeated measures. Experiments of this type are very widespread in research.

On the positive side, the presence of within subjects factors has both convenience and improved power for the statistical tests. On the negative side, the difficulties with within subjects designs that we discussed in Chapter 9, together with their implications for the determination of power and effect size and their consequences for error rates, all apply to the designs we have described in this chapter. The main problem is that having repeated measures on some factors produces correlated data; and the patterns of those correlations can have consequences for the statistical tests. Should the variance-covariance matrices lack the property of homogeneity of covariance or sphericity, the F tests will produce too many significant results. Conservative tests are available to attempt to control the **Type I error rate**; but there has been considerable debate about how effective they really are.

An alternative approach to the analysis of data from experiments of mixed factorial design is the multivariate analysis of variance (MANOVA). The MANOVA does not assume sphericity; however, the variance-covariance matrices in the various groups should be homogeneous.

We have taken only a very brief look at MANOVA using a simple example. MANOVA designs can have two or more factors and DVs as well as covariates, and can include contrast analyses. To learn more about these techniques, you should consult textbooks such as those already cited before embarking on a MANOVA.

Recommended reading

There are many readable textbooks on ANOVA, which provide extensive coverage of within subjects ANOVA. These include:

Dugard, P., Todman, T., & Staines, H. (2010). *Approaching multivariate analysis: A practical introduction (2nd ed.).* London & New York: Routledge.

Field, A. (2009). *Discovering Statistics Using SPSS (3nd ed.).* London: Sage.

Howell, D. C. (2007). *Statistical methods for psychology (6th ed.).* Belmont, CA: Thomson/Wadsworth.

Keppel, G., & Wickens, T. D. (2004). *Design and analysis: A researcher's handbook (4th ed.).* Upper Saddle River, New Jersey: Pearson Prentice Hall.

There are now several excellent textbooks on multivariate statistics, including MANOVA. These include:

Tabachnick, B. G., & Fidell, L. S. (2007). *Using multivariate statistics (5th ed.).* Boston: Allyn & Bacon (Pearson International Edition).

Exercises

Exercise 15 *Mixed ANOVA: two-factor experiment* and Exercise 16 *Mixed ANOVA: three-factor experiment* are available in www.psypress.com/spss-made-simple and click on Exercises.

CHAPTER 11

Measuring statistical association

11.1   INTRODUCTION

So far, this book has been concerned with comparing the averages of different samples with respect to one variable, measured at the continuous or scale level: for example, on a measure of skilled performance, a drug group might be compared with a placebo group; right-handed people might be compared with left-handed people; the trained might be compared with the untrained; males might be compared with females. In such data sets, there is only one measured variable, the dependent variable: the other variables are grouping variables specifying the conditions under which the participants were tested or the natural groups to which they belonged; or the research might focus upon the performance of the same participants under the different conditions making up a within subjects factor. In this chapter, we move to correlational as opposed to experimental reseach and consider situations in which participants, rather than being assigned to different conditions created by the experimenter, are simply measured on two or more characteristics without any manipulation of conditions by the experimenter. Here interest centres on the question of whether there exists an association between the measured variables and, if so, the strength of the association.

In the early part of the chapter, we shall be concerned with data at the continuous or scale level of measurement only. Later, however, we shall turn to the analysis of nominal and ordinal data.

In the final part of the chapter, we shall be concerned with some issues that arise in correlational research and some of the ways in which they can be resolved.

11.1.1 A correlational study

In Chapter 1, we described a correlational study designed to investigate the extent to which children's Actual violence is related to their level of Exposure to screen violence.

The researcher measures these variables in the expectation that they will show a positive association: there should be a tendency for those with high Exposure also to score highly on Actual violence; those low on Exposure should also be low on Actual violence; and those with average Exposure should fall within the normal range on Actual violence. This strategy will not yield the strong evidence for causation that a true experiment would yield; however, an association would at least be consistent with the researcher's view that exposure to screened violence encourages actual violence in children.

Correlational research like this results in a **bivariate** data set, which can be pictured in a **scatterplot**. The scatterplot of the children's actual violence against their exposure to screen violence is shown in Figure 1. In the scatterplot, each person is represented as a point, the coordinates of which are the person's scores on the Exposure and Actual scales, which are marked out on the horizontal and vertical axes, respectively.

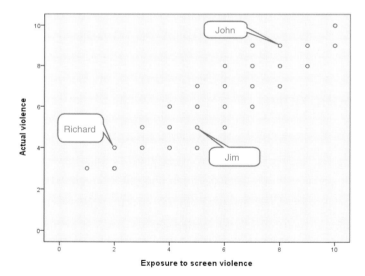

Figure 1. Scatterplot of Actual Violence against Exposure to Screen Violence

It is evident from the scatterplot that there is indeed an association between the variables of Exposure to and Actual violence: John was highest on Exposure and he was also the most violent of the three children identified in the figure; Richard, with least Exposure, was also the least violent; Jim had intermediate scores on both variables. On the other hand, the association is imperfect: four children, including Jim, scored 5 on Exposure; but their Actual violence scores ranged from 4 to 7.

11.1.2 Linear relationships

One variable is said to be a **linear function** of another if the graph of the first upon the second is a straight line. Temperature in degrees Fahrenheit is a linear function of temperature in degrees Celsius, as shown in Figure 2.

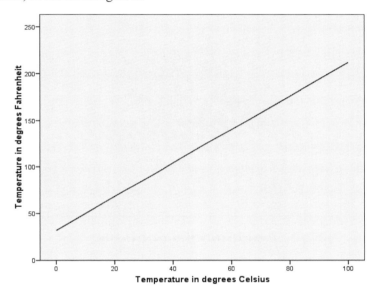

Figure 2. A linear (straight line) relationship

11.1.3 Error in measurement

In many empirical disciplines, including medicine, biology and psychology, measurements have associated with them a considerable random, or **error** component. This means that, even if two variables have a linear relationship, the random error component in the scores ensures that the points in their scatterplot will never lie exactly on a straight line as in Figure 2. Provided, however, that the scatterplot has a roughly elliptical shape as in Figure 1, the relationship between the variables can be assumed to be basically linear.

If the slope of the longer axis (the **major axis**) of the ellipse is positive, the variables are said to be **positively correlated**; if it is negative, they are **negatively correlated**. The thinner the ellipse, the stronger the degree of the linear relationship; the more circular the ellipse, the weaker the relationship.

If two variables are dissociated or independent, their scatterplot will be a circular cloud of points. Suppose two coins are each tossed 100 times and the number of heads recorded for each. The experiment is repeated 1000 times. There are two variables here: Number of Heads on the First coin and Number of Heads on the Second coin. Each repetition of the experiment will produce another pair of scores, one on each variable, so that at the end of the exercise we shall have 1000 pairs of scores. Here, however, the pairing is arbitrary: the outcomes should be independent and we should not expect any association between the two variables. The scatterplot will appear as in Figure 3.

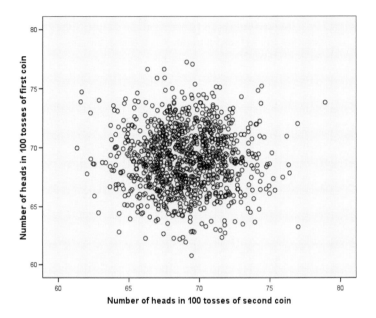

Figure 3. Scatterplot showing dissociation between two variables

11.2 THE PEARSON CORRELATION

The Pearson correlation is a measure of a supposed linear relationship between two variables, both measured at the continuous or scale level. The word 'supposed' is important here. Should the variables be in a nonlinear relationship (i.e., the graph of one against the other is curved in some way), the Pearson correlation can be highly misleading as a measure of strength of association. The true nature of the relationship between two continuous variables will be evident from the appearance of their scatterplot and the plot should always be viewed when that is possible.

11.2.1 Formula for the Pearson correlation

There are several different formulae for the Pearson correlation, one of the most common of which is as follows:

$$r_{XY} = \frac{\sum(X - M_X)(Y - M_Y)}{\sqrt{\sum(X - M_X)^2 \sum(Y - M_Y)^2}} = \frac{SP}{\sqrt{SS_X SS_Y}} \quad \text{- - -} (1)$$

The Pearson correlation

In the SS/SP version of this formula, SS stands for 'Sum of Squares' (i.e. the squared deviations from the mean summed over all the participants in the study) and SP stands for 'Sum of Products' (i.e. the product of the deviations from M_X and M_Y summed over all participants).

11.2.2 The range of values of the Pearson correlation

It can be shown that the value of r can vary only within the range from -1 to $+1$, inclusive.

$$-1 \leq r \leq +1 \quad \text{- - -} \ (2)$$

Range of possible values of r

This property confers upon the Pearson correlation a great advantage over another measure of association known as the **covariance**, which was described in Chapter 9. The covariance has no upper or lower limit; moreover, its value depends upon the scale on which each of the two variables is measured: if a data set comprises the heights and weights of 100 people, measured in feet and stones, respectively, and these measurements are transformed to inches and pounds, the value of the covariance will also change. The value of the correlation coefficient, on the other hand, remains unchanged by any linear transformation of the units of measurement. A correlation between the heights and weights of fifty people measured in centimetres and grams respectively has the same value as the correlation between their heights and weights measured in inches and pounds. The correlation thus has the great advantage of being 'unit-free', and can be used to compare the degrees of association between pairs of variables measured in different units.

The Pearson correlation is actually the covariance between two sets of scores X and Y after they have been transformed to standard (z) scores z_X and z_Y by subtracting their respective means and dividing these deviation scores by their respective standard deviations. The formula for the Pearson correlation may be written as follows:

$$r_{XY} = \frac{\sum z_X z_Y}{n-1} \quad \text{- - -} \ (3)$$

Standard score formula for the Pearson correlation

Comparison for formula (3) with formula (2) in Chapter 9 shows that the Pearson correlation is indeed the covariance between two standardised variables.

11.2.3 The sign of a correlation

The sign of a correlation may reflect the intrinsic natures of the variables being measured: for instance, one would not expect height to correlate negatively with weight. Often, however, the sign of a correlation is merely a matter of definition and scaling and therefore arbitrary. If we label an obsessive-compulsive scale as Decisiveness, the zero point will represent extreme indecisiveness and the highest value extreme decisiveness; but if we label the same scale Indecisiveness, the zero point will represent extreme decisiveness. Since the purpose of a correlation coefficient is primarily to measure the strength of a statistical association, the researcher's attention often focuses upon the *absolute* value of r, that is, its numerical value with the sign ignored. Figure 4 shows two scatterplots: the first is the scatterplot of Actual violence upon Exposure to violence; the second is a scatterplot with the direction of the Exposure scale reversed by multiplying the original Exposure scores by −1. (The reversal would make psychological sense if the variable name Exposure were to be changed to Degree of Censorship.) In either case, the absolute value of the Pearson correlation is .90. A negative correlation of −.90 represents the same (strong) degree of linear association as a positive correlation of +.90.

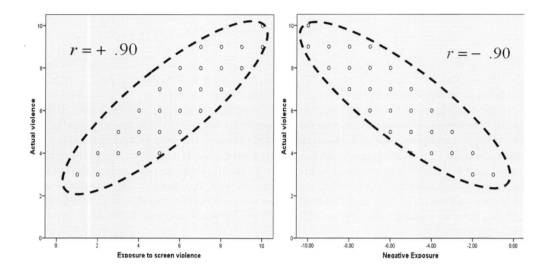

Figure 4. Scatterplots of data sets showing the same degree of association, but with correlations of opposite sign

A perfect linear association, with all the points in the scatterplot lying along the same straight line, would be reflected either in a correlation of +1 or a correlation of −1: either value would represent a perfect linear relationship.

11.2.4 Testing an obtained value of *r* for significance

The test for the significance of a correlation coefficient presupposes that the data have the property of **bivariate normality**, that is, at any particular value of either variable, the other variable has a normal distribution. If that requirement is met, the test of the null hypothesis that, in the bivariate normal population, the correlation is zero is made with the statistic *t*, where

$$t(n-2) = \frac{r\sqrt{(n-2)}}{\sqrt{(1-r^2)}} \quad \text{--- (4)}$$

Testing *r* for significance

In formula (3), *n* is the number of pairs of scores. If the assumption of bivariate normality holds, this test statistic is distributed approximately as *t* on *n* − 2 degrees of freedom.

11.2.5   A word of warning about the correlation coefficient

It is quite possible, from inspection of a scatterplot, to do two useful things:

1. Establish that there is indeed a linear relationship between the variables, in which case the Pearson correlation would be a meaningful statistic to use;
2. Guess fairly accurately what the value of the Pearson correlation would be if it were to be calculated.

In other words, from inspection of the scatterplot alone, one can discern the most important features of the true relationship (if any) between two variables. So if we reason from the scatterplot to the statistics, we shall never go seriously wrong.

The converse, however, is not true: given only the value of a Pearson correlation, one can say nothing whatsoever about the relationship between two variables. Many years ago, in a famous paper, the statistician Anscombe (1973) presented some bivariate data sets which illustrate how misleading the value of the Pearson correlation can be. In one set, for instance, the correlation was high, yet the scatterplot showed no association whatsoever; in another, the correlation was zero, but the scatterplot showed a perfect, but nonlinear, association. The moral of this cautionary tale is clear: when studying the association between two variables, always construct a scatterplot, and interpret (or disregard) the Pearson correlation accordingly.

In the same paper, Anscombe gave us a useful rule for deciding whether there really is a robust linear relationship between two variables: should the shape of the scatterplot be unaltered by the removal of a few observations at random, the plot is an accurate depiction of the true relationship between the variables. In one of the sets Anscombe devised, a substantial correlation is driven by one outlier and disappears when the outlier is removed.

To sum up, the Pearson correlation is a measure of a *supposed* linear relationship between two variables; but the supposition of linearity must always be confirmed by inspection of the scatterplot.

11.2.6   Effect size

Unlike t, F or chi-square, the value of a correlation is, in itself, a measure of 'effect' size, bearing in mind that correlation does not imply causation. However, for the purposes of comparison with other measures of effect size, the **square** of the correlation r^2, which is known as the **coefficient of determination**, is often used instead. The reason for this will be explained more fully in Chapter 12, where we shall see that the square of the Pearson correlation is the proportion of the variance of the scores on the target or criterion variable that is accounted for by regression upon another variable. In the data set depicted in Figure 1, the Pearson correlation between the Actual and Exposure scores is +.89. The value of the coefficient of determination (CD) is therefore $.89^2 = .80$. This means that 80% of the variance of the Actual scores is accounted for by regression upon Exposure.

The coefficient of determination is the proportion of the variance of either variable that is shared with the other variable. This sharing of variance can be depicted by two overlapping circles, where the overlapping area represents the proportion of the variance of either variable that is shared with the other (Figure 5).

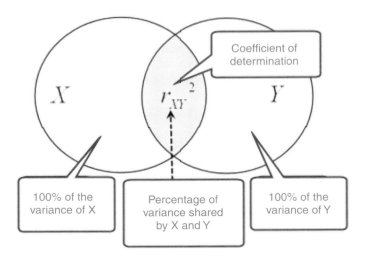

Figure 5. The coefficient of determination as the percentage of the variance of either variable that is shared with the other

In the coefficient of determination (r^2), we have a measure of effect size, which can be interpreted along guidelines suggested by Cohen (1988).   Cohen's guidelines are shown in Table 1.

Table 1. Guidelines (from Cohen, 1988) for classifying association strength, as measured by a correlation coefficient		
Absolute value of r	r squared	Size of effect
$.1 \leq |r| < .30$	$.01 \leq r^2 < .09$	Small
$.30 \leq |r| < .50$	$.09 \leq r^2 < .25$	Medium
$|r| \geq .50$	$r^2 \geq .25$	Large

In words …

A correlation less than .1 is trivial.

If a correlation is between .1 and .3 (ignoring the sign), the association is SMALL. Between 1% and 8% of the variance is shared.

If a correlation is between .3 and .5, the association is MEDIUM. Between 9% and 25% of the variance is shared.

If a correlation is .5 or greater, the association is LARGE. At least 25% of the variance is shared.

11.3   CORRELATION WITH SPSS

Table 2 shows the raw data that were pictured in the scatterplot in Figure 1.

Table 2. The raw data from the violence study						
	Exposure	Violence			Exposure	Violence
1	1	3	15	5	7
2	2	3	16	6	7
3	2	4	17	7	7
4	3	4	18	8	7
5	4	4	19	6	8
6	5	4	20	7	8
7	3	5	21	8	8
8	4	5	22	9	8
9	5	5	23	7	9
10	6	5	24	8	9
11	4	6	25	9	9
12	5	6	26	10	9
13	6	6	27	10	10
14	7	6			

11.3.1 Preparing the SPSS data set

As usual, begin in **Variable View**. Name the variables *Actual* and *Exposure* and assign full variable labels, such as *Actual Violence* and *Exposure to Screen Violence*. Set the **Decimals** specification to zero in order to avoid unnecessary clutter in **Data View**. Switch to **Data View** and enter the data. Save the data set.

11.3.2 Obtaining the scatterplot

The procedure for plotting a scatterplot using **Chart Builder** is described in Section 5.7. Here we want a scatterplot of Actual against Exposure.

The default scatterplot will not show the zero point on the vertical scale. The complete vertical scale can be displayed either by editing the obtained scatterplot or, in the **Chart Builder**, by altering the specifications in the **Element Properties** dialog box. Follow the steps in Figure 6 to plot the scatterplot with the scale starting at zero on the **Y-Axis**.

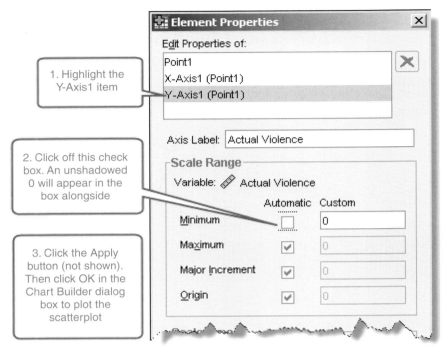

1. Highlight the Y-Axis1 item

2. Click off this check box. An unshadowed 0 will appear in the box alongside

3. Click the Apply button (not shown). Then click OK in the Chart Builder dialog box to plot the scatterplot

Figure 6. Editing the **Element Properties** dialog box to obtain a scatterplot showing the entire Y-Axis scale starting at zero

11.3.3   Obtaining the Pearson correlation

- Choose   **Analyze→Correlate→Bivariate...**   (Figure   7)   to   open   the   **Bivariate Correlations** dialog box (Figure 8).
- Complete the dialog as in Figure 8.

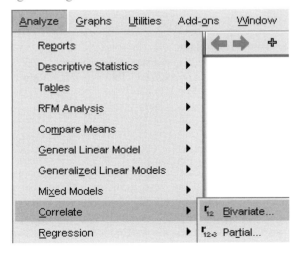

Figure 7. The **Correlate** menu with **Bivariate** highlighted

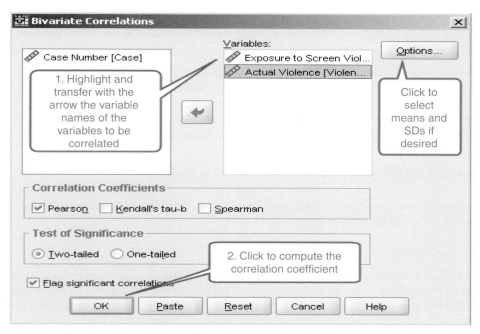

Figure 8. The **Bivariate Correlations** dialog for computing the Pearson correlation coefficient

11.3.4 Output for the Pearson correlation

Output 1 tabulates the Pearson correlation, with its *p*-value. The value for *r* is .892, which is significant beyond the .01 level. This is written as:

$$r(27) = .892; p < .01. \text{ Effect size } r^2 = .80, \text{ a Large effect.}$$

Since 80% of the variance is shared, the association is obviously a strong one.

Correlations

		Exposure to Screen Violence	Actual Violence
Exposure to Screen Violence	Pearson Correlation	1	.892**
	Sig. (2-tailed)		.000
	N	27	27
Actual Violence	Pearson Correlation	.892**	1
	Sig. (2-tailed)	.000	
	N	27	27

**. Correlation is significant at the 0.01 level (2-tailed).

r = 0.892 and is significant at .01 level

There are 27 pairs of values

Since the correlation of Exposure with Actual is the same as the correlation of Actual with Exposure, the second row is a repeat of the first row

Output 1. The Pearson **Correlations** table

Notice that in Output 1, the information we need in the upper right cell of the table (the value of r, the number of pairs of data and the p-value) is duplicated in the lower left cell of the table. This is because the correlation of A with B is the same as the correlation of B with A.

Were we to have more than two variables, the results would have appeared in the form of a square matrix with entries above the principal diagonal (from top left to bottom right) being duplicated in the cells below it. When there are more than two variables, SPSS can be commanded to construct this **correlation matrix (or R-matrix)** simply by entering as many variable names as required into the **Variables** box (Figure 8).

11.4   OTHER MEASURES OF ASSOCIATION

The Pearson correlation is suitable only for data on continuous or scale variables. With ordinal or nominal data, other statistics must be used.

11.4.1   Spearman's rank correlation

The term **ordinal data** includes both ranks and assignments to ordered categories. When the same objects are ranked independently by two judges, the question arises as to the extent to which the two sets of ranks agree. This is a question about the strength of association between two variables which, although quantitative, are measured at the ordinal level. Suppose that the ranks assigned to ten paintings by two judges are as in Table 3.

Table 3. Ranks assigned by two judges to each of ten paintings										
Painting	A	B	C	D	E	F	G	H	I	J
First Judge	1	2	3	4	5	6	7	8	9	10
Second Judge	1	3	2	4	6	5	8	7	10	9

It is obvious that the judges generally agree closely in their rankings: at most, their assignments differ by a single rank. One way of measuring the level of agreement between the two judges is by calculating the Pearson correlation between the two sets of ranks. This correlation is known as the **Spearman rank correlation** (r_S) or as **Spearman's rho** (ρ). Like eta squared, Spearman's rho is a *statistic*, not a parameter, and is thus an exception to the general rule about reserving Greek and Roman letters for parameters and statistics, respectively. While the defining formula for the Spearman rank correlation looks very different from that for the Pearson correlation, the two formulae are actually equivalent, provided that no ties are allowed.

The use of the Spearman rank correlation is not confined to ordinal data. Suppose the scatterplot of the bivariate distribution of two continuous variables shows that they are in a **monotonic** (increasing or decreasing together) but non-linear relationship, rendering the Pearson correlation an unsuitable measure of degree of association. The scores on both variables can be converted to ranks and the Spearman rank correlation calculated instead.

Arguably, in this situation, the value of the rank correlation is a truer reflection of the degree of association between the two variables than is the value of the Pearson correlation.

11.4.2   Kendall's tau statistics

The **Kendall's tau** (τ) statistics offer an alternative to the Spearman rank correlation as measures of agreement between rankings, or assignments to ordered categories. The basic idea is that one set of ranks can be converted into another by a succession of reversals of pairs of ranks in one set: the fewer the reversals needed to achieve the conversion (in relation to the total number of possible reversals), the larger the value of tau. The numerator of Kendall's tau is the difference between the number of pairs of objects whose ranks are concordant (i.e. they go in the same direction) and the number of discordant pairs. If the former predominate, the sign of tau is positive; if the latter predominate, tau is negative.

There are three different versions of Kendall's tau: **tau-a**, **tau-b** and **tau-c**. All three measures have the same numerator, the difference between the numbers of concordant and discordant pairs. In their denominators, however, they differ in the way they handle tied observations.

The denominator of the correlation **tau-a** is simply the total number of pairs. The problem with tau-a is that when there are ties, its range quickly becomes restricted, to the point where it becomes difficult to interpret.

The correlation **tau-b** has terms in the denominator that consider, in either variable, pairs that are tied on one variable but not on the other. (When there are no ties, the values of tau-a and tau-b are identical.)

The correlation **tau-c** was designed for situations where one wishes to measure agreement between assignments to unequal-sized sets of ordered categories. Provided the data meet certain requirements, the appropriate tau correlation can vary throughout the complete range from -1 to $+1$.

Note that the calculation of Kendall's statistics with ordinal data, in the form of assignments of target objects to ordered categories, is best handled by the **Crosstabs** procedure (see next section); indeed, **tau-c** can be obtained only in **Crosstabs**.

11.4.3   Rank correlations with SPSS

In **Variable View**, name two variables, *Judge1* and *Judge2*. Click the **Data View** tab to switch to **Data View** and, from Table 3, enter the ranks assigned by the first judge into the Judge1 column and those assigned by the second judge into the Judge2 column.

- Choose **Analyze➔Correlate➔Bivariate…** to obtain the **Bivariate Correlations** dialog box (the completed version of which is shown in Figure 9). By default, the **Pearson** check box will be marked. Click off the **Pearson** check box and click the **Kendall's tau-b** and the **Spearman** check boxes.
- Transfer the variable names Judge1 and Judge2 to the **Variables:** box.
- Click **OK** to obtain the correlations shown in Output 2.

Table 4. A nominal data set showing observed and expected frequencies			
	A	B	C
O	20	41	29
E	30	30	30

The test is 'approximate' because the true chi-square variable is defined in the context of a normally distributed variable and is therefore continuous. The statistic we are about to describe is only approximately distributed as χ^2. The chi-square statistic is defined as follows:

$$\chi^2 = \sum \frac{(O-E)^2}{E} \quad \text{---} \ (5)$$

Approximate chi-square statistic

(In formula 5, the symbol Σ means 'Sum': the formula instructs us to add the values of $\frac{(O-E)^2}{E}$ for toy A, toy B and toy C together.)

A chi-square distribution has one parameter, the **degrees of freedom (df)**. In the context of nominal data in a one-way classification, the value of the degrees of freedom (df) is one less than the number of categories in the one-way classification. In this example, $df = 3 - 1 = 2$. A chi-square variate has a lower limit of zero, but no upper limit. The distribution is positively skewed, with a long tail to the right. The critical region lies above the 95th percentile of the distribution of chi-square on 2 degrees of freedom, which is 6.0 .

How well does the theoretical **uniform distribution** fit the observed distribution? It is clear from the formula that the greater the differences between the observed and expected frequencies, the greater will be the magnitude of the χ^2 statistic. The value of chi-square is:

$$\chi^2 = \frac{(-10)^2}{30} + \frac{(11)^2}{30} + \frac{(-1)^2}{30} = \frac{222}{30} = 7.4$$

The null hypothesis that the distribution is uniform is rejected: $\chi^2(2) = 7.4$; $p = .03$.

11.5.2 Running a chi-square goodness-of-fit test on SPSS

The results of the three toys experiment can either be entered into the data editor on an individual basis (in which case there would be 90 rows in **Data View**) or as frequencies (in which case there would only be three rows). We shall assume that the researcher has already computed the frequency distribution and that **Data View** appears as in Figure 10.

	Preference	Frequency
1	Toy A	20
2	Toy B	41
3	Toy C	29
4		

Figure 10. Data View showing data in the form of a frequency distribution

If the data are entered in the form of a frequency distribution as in Figure 10, it is essential to make this clear to SPSS by following the **Weight Cases** procedure (in the Data menu). In this case, the values of the variable Preference must be weighted with those in the Frequency variable. The procedure is shown in Figure 11:

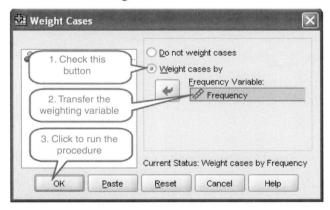

Figure 11.   The **Weight Cases** procedure

The **Chi-square goodness-of-fit test** is run as follows:

- In **Variable View** name the variables *Preference* and *Frequency*. The Preference variable comprises 3 categories. Assign the value 1 for Toy A, 2 for Toy B, and 3 for Toy C. Change **Scale** to **Nominal** for Preference.
- Enter the data in **Data View**.
- Use **Weight Cases…** to weight the values in Frequency as in Figure 11.
- Choose **Analyze➜Nonparametric Tests➜Chi-Square…** to open the **Chi-Square Test** dialog box (Figure 12).
- Follow the steps in Figure 12.
- Click **OK**.

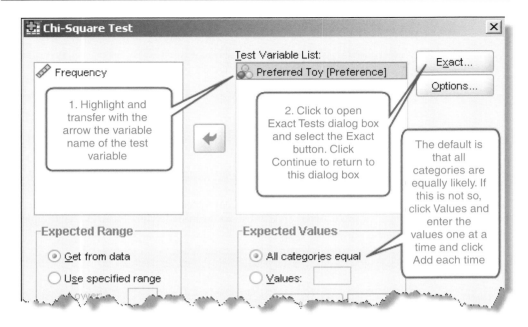

Figure 12. The **Chi-Square Test** dialog box with Preferred Toy transferred to the **Test Variable List** box

The first table (Output 3) in the output shows the observed and expected frequencies.

Preferred Toy

	Observed N	Expected N	Residual
Toy A	20	30.0	-10.0
Toy B	41	30.0	11.0
Toy C	29	30.0	-1.0
Total	90		

Output 3. The observed and expected frequencies

Any transcription errors will immediately be apparent here. Notice that the expected frequencies are 30 for each choice, because if there is no preference, the three choices are equally likely, and we should have approximately equal numbers of children choosing A, B and C.

The next table (Output 4) presents the results of the Chi-square goodness-of-fit test.

Test Statistics

	Preferred Toy
Chi-Square [a]	7.400
df	2
Asymp. Sig.	.025
Exact Sig.	.026
Point Probability	.003

The value of Chi-square

The test shows significance beyond the .05 level

a. 0 cells (.0%) have expected frequencies less than 5. The minimum expected cell frequency is 30.0.

Output 4. The output for the **Chi-square goodness-of-fit test**

Output 3 showed marked discrepancies between the expected and observed frequencies, and it is not surprising that the **Exact Sig.** (i.e. the p-value) given in Output 4 is small (.026). The results of the test might be reported as follows:

> "Inspection of the frequency distribution shows that twice as many children (41) chose Toy B as chose Toy A (20). Approximately the expected number (29) preferred Toy C. A chi-square test of the null hypothesis that the three toys were equally attractive to the children showed significance beyond the .05 level: $\chi^2(2) =$ 7.4; exact $p = .03$ ".

The interpretation of the results of this test requires care. The experimenter may have had theoretical reason to expect that Toy B would be preferred to the other toys. All the chi-square test has shown, however, is that the hypothesis of no preference among the three toys is untenable. We have not demonstrated that any one toy was preferred significantly more (or less) than either of the others. Had the purpose of the investigation been to show that Toy B was preferable to the other two, a better analytic strategy would have been to dichotomise a child's choice as either B or NotB. This can be done by dichotomising the data into B and NotB: 49 for B and 41 for NotB. A binomial test would test the null hypothesis that the number of children choosing B exceeded the expected value. In the **Binomial Test** dialog box, the **Test Proportion** would be set at $1/3 = .33$. The binomial test shows significance beyond the .05 level: $p = .01$. This result does support the scientific hypothesis that Toy B is preferred to either of the other two toys.

11.5.3   Measuring effect size following a chi-square test of goodness-of-fit

As an effect size index for the chi-square goodness-of-fit test, Cohen (1988) has proposed the statistic w. If P_O and P_E are the observed and expected proportions, obtained from the values of O and E by dividing them by the total frequency N, the formula for w is

$$w = \sqrt{\sum \frac{(P_o - P_E)^2}{P_E}} \quad \text{- - - (6)}$$

Cohen's effect size index

The value of w can be calculated very easily from that of chi-square. In our current example, $N = 90$ and $\chi^2 = 7.4$. The value of w, therefore, is:

$$w = \sqrt{\sum \frac{(P_O - P_E)^2}{P_E}} = \sqrt{\frac{\chi^2}{N}} = \sqrt{\frac{7.4}{30}} = .50$$

Cohen suggests the values .1, .3 and .5 as Small, Medium and Large effects respectively. We have interpreted these guidelines in Table 5. Our obtained value .50, therefore, is a Large effect.

Table 5. Guidelines (from Cohen, 1988) for interpreting the effect size index	
Value of *w*	Size of effect
.1 ≤ *w* < .3	Small
.3 ≤ *w* < .5	Medium
w ≥ .5	Large
In words … A value less than .1 is trivial. A value between .1 and .3 is a Small effect. A value between .3 and .5 is a Medium effect. A value of at least .5 is a Large effect.	

To sum up, we have just discussed the use of the approximate **chi-square statistic** χ^2 to test the **goodness-of-fit** of a theoretical distribution of expected frequencies E to the distribution of the observed frequencies O over a set of categories making up a single qualitative variable or attribute.

In the general case, if the attribute has k categories, the value of chi-square for the goodness-of-fit test is given by

$$\chi^2(k-1) = \sum_{\text{all categories}} \frac{(O - E)^2}{E} \quad \text{- - - (7)}$$

Chi-square goodness-of-fit test

11.5.4 Testing for association between two qualitative variables in a contingency table

In Chapter 1, we saw that when people's membership of two sets of mutually exclusive and exhaustive categories is recorded, it is possible to construct a **crosstabulation**, or **contingency table**. In the analysis of nominal data, the crosstabulation is the equivalent of the scatterplot. Like the scatterplot, the contingency table provides an excellent means of inspecting a discrete bivariate distribution in order to ascertain the presence of an association between the variables concerned.

See
Section
1.5.3

A researcher has reason to believe that there should be a higher incidence of a potentially harmful antibody in patients whose tissue is of a certain 'critical' type. In a study of 79 patients, the incidence of the antibody in patients of four different tissue types, including the 'critical' category, are recorded. The results are presented in Table 6.

Table 6. Contingency table with a pattern of observed frequencies suggesting an association between Tissue Type and Presence of an antibody

Tissue type	Presence		Total
	No	Yes	
Critical	6	21	27
A	5	7	12
B	11	7	18
C	14	8	22
Total	36	43	79

11.5.4.1 The chi-square statistic

The pattern of the frequencies appears to confirm the research hypothesis: there is a noticeably higher incidence of the antibody in the Critical group.

The researcher's hypothesis is that there is an association between the variables of Group (the type of tissue) and the Presence (Yes or No) of the antibody. The null hypothesis H_0 is the negation of this: there is no association between the two attributes. While it would appear from Table 6 that the null hypothesis is false, a formal statistical test is required to confirm this.

The null hypothesis that there is no association between the Group and Presence variables can be tested with the **chi-square test for association**. For each cell of the contingency table, the expected frequency E is calculated on the assumption that the attributes of Group and Presence are independent, and the values of E are compared with the corresponding observed frequencies O by means of the statistic χ^2, where

$$\chi^2(3) = \sum_{\text{all cells}} \frac{(O-E)^2}{E} \quad \text{---} \ (8)$$

Chi-square test for association

In general, if variables A and B comprise a and b categories, respectively, the value of the degrees of freedom of this chi-square statistic is given by

$$df = (a-1)(b-1) \quad \text{---} \ (9)$$

General formula for the degrees of freedom

in two-way contingency tables

In the present example, $df = (4 - 1)(2 - 1) = 3$. In a 4×2 table with fixed marginal totals, the assignment of frequencies to only three cells completely determines the values of the frequencies in the remaining five cells.

The expected frequencies are calculated using estimates of probability derived from the marginal totals and the total frequency N in the following way. If R and C are the marginal totals of the row and the column that locate the cell in the contingency table, the expected frequency E_{RC} is given by

$$E_{RC} = \frac{R \times C}{N} \quad \text{---} \ (10) \ \textbf{Expected frequency}$$

For example, for the top left cell in the contingency table, E = (27×36)/79 = 12.30. The expected frequencies (referred to by SPSS as **Expected Counts**) in all eight cells of the table are shown in Output 5.

Tissue Type * Presence Crosstabulation

			Presence		Total
			No	Yes	
Tissue Type	Critical	Count	6	21	27
		Expected Count	12.3	14.7	27.0
	Type C	Count	5	7	12
		Expected Count	5.5	6.5	12.0
	Type B	Count	11	7	18
		Expected Count	8.2	9.8	18.0
	Type A	Count	14	8	22
		Expected Count	10.0	12.0	22.0
Total		Count	36	43	79
		Expected Count	36.0	43.0	79.0

Output 5. The observed and expected frequencies of observations in the cells of the contingency table in Table 6

The value of chi-square is

$$\chi^2 = \sum_{all\ cells} \frac{(O-E)^2}{E} = \frac{(6-12.3)^2}{12.3} + \frac{(21-14.7)^2}{14.7} + ... + \frac{(14-10.0)^2}{10.0} + \frac{(8-12.0)^2}{12.0} = 10.66$$

The p-value of the chi-square value 10.66 on $df = 3$ is $< .05$. The null hypothesis is therefore rejected and we report this result as follows:

$$\chi^2(3) = 10.66;\ p < .05$$

Formula (10) is a straightforward application of the multiplication rule for independent events in elementary probability. Events are independent if the probability of their joint occurrence is the product of their separate probabilities: for example, if a coin is tossed and a die is rolled, the joint probability of a head and a six is $1/2 \times 1/6 = 1/12$. If, in a two-way contingency table, the row and columns represent attributes A and B, respectively, and R and C are the marginal totals of the row and column intersecting in a cell of the table, the probabilities of those particular levels of A and B are R/N and C/N, respectively. According to the null hypothesis, the occurrence of this level of A with that level of B are independent events, so the probability of their joint occurrence $p = (R/N)(C/N)$. We can regard the total frequency N as the number of times an experiment of chance is replicated, so the expected cell frequency E is given by $E = (R/N)(C/N)N = RC/N$.

11.5.4.2 Measuring effect size in contingency tables

The rejection of the null hypothesis establishes the presence of an association between the two attributes. The chi-square statistic itself, however, is not a satisfactory measure of association strength, because its magnitude is affected by the total frequency of observations in the contingency table. From the chi-square statistic itself, however, several statistics designed to measure strength of association have been devised.

An ideal measure of association should mimic the correlation coefficient by having a maximum absolute value of 1 for a perfect association, and a value of 0 for dissociation or independence. The choice of the appropriate statistic depends on whether the contingency table is 2×2 (each variable has two categories) or larger. Some statistics, such as the **phi coefficient**, cannot achieve the full range of variation from 0 to 1 when the number of columns is not equal to the number of rows.

A useful measure of effect size for use with two-way contingency tables is what SPSS calls Cramer's V, the formula for which is as follows:

$$V = \sqrt{\frac{\chi^2}{N(a-1)}} \quad \text{- - - (11) \textbf{Cramer's } V}$$

Formula (11) is applicable to an $a \times b$ contingency table, in which a is no greater than b.

In our current example, $V = .367$.

For the purposes of evaluating Cramer's V, we can transform Cramer's V into the equivalent value of Cohen's index of effect size w by applying the following formula:

$$w = V\sqrt{(a-1)} \quad \text{- - - (12) \textbf{Obtaining Cohen's } w \textbf{ from } V}$$

Applying formula (12) to the current example, we have

$$w = V\sqrt{(a-1)} = .367\sqrt{(2-1)} = .367$$

We can now consult Cohen's table and interpret the effect size (Table 5). The value .367 is of Medium size.

Some measures of association, such as **Goodman & Kruskal's lambda**, measure the proportional reduction in error achieved when membership of a category on one attribute is used to predict category membership on the other.

More information on the various measures of association can be found by clicking the SPSS **Help** box in the **Crosstabs: Statistics** dialog box.

11.5.4.3 Likelihood ratio (or Maximum Likelihood) chi-square

So far, both in testing for goodness-of-fit and association, we have used the traditional **Pearson chi-square** statistic. Both types of tests, however, can also be made with another approximate chi-square statistic known variously as the **likelihood ratio**, **maximum likelihood** or **log-likelihood** chi-square. Like the Pearson chi-square, the likelihood ratio chi-square is distributed approximately as a true chi-square variable on the same number of degrees of freedom; although for small samples, the Pearson chi-square is perhaps the better approximation (Agresti, 1990).

For a test of goodness-of-fit with a single qualitative variable comprising g categories, the formula for the likelihood-ratio chi-square is

$$\chi^2(g-1) = 2 \sum_{\text{all categories}} O \ln\left(\frac{O}{E}\right) \quad \text{---(13)}$$

LR goodness-of-fit chi-square

where the function ln is the natural log (to the base e) of the ratio of the observed to the expected frequency. For a test of association, the formula is

$$\chi^2(r-1)(c-1) = 2 \sum_{\text{all cells}} O \ln\left(\frac{O}{E}\right) \quad \text{---(14)}$$

LR association chi-square

where r and c are the numbers of rows and columns, respectively, in the contingency table. The likelihood ratio chi-square is distributed approximately as chi-square on $(r-1)(c-1)$ degrees of freedom.

For the data in Table 6, the value of the likelihood ratio chi-square is

$$\chi^2(3) = 2 \sum_{\text{all groups}} O\left[\ln\left(\frac{O}{E}\right)\right]$$

$$= 2\left[6 \ln\left(\frac{6}{12.3}\right) + 21 \ln\left(\frac{21}{14.7}\right) + \ldots + 14 \ln\left(\frac{14}{10.0}\right) + 8 \ln\left(\frac{8}{12.0}\right)\right]$$

$$= 11.09$$

which is close to 10.66, the value of the value of the Pearson chi-square.

The likelihood ratio chi-square is ubiquitous in log-linear analysis (Chapter 13) because, unlike the Pearson chi-square, the values of chi-square associated with the various components in a model add up to the total chi-square value: the likelihood chi-square is thus said to have the **additive property**.

11.5.4.4 Two by two contingency tables: the odds and odds ratio

Table 7 is a contingency table in which both attributes (Presence of the antibody and tissue Group) are dichotomous, i.e., they consist of only two categories. (Table 7 was constructed from Table 6 by 'collapsing' across the three non-critical tissue types to produce a single category named 'Other'.)

Table 7. A 2 × 2 contingency table

Tissue type	Presence		Total
	No	Yes	
Critical	6	21	27
Other	30	22	52
Total	36	43	79

The **Odds** is a measure of likelihood which, like probability, arises in the context of an experiment of chance, that is, a procedure with an uncertain outcome, such as tossing a coin or rolling a die. The odds in favour of an outcome is the number of ways in which the outcome could occur divided by the number of ways in which it could fail to occur.

$$Odds = \frac{\left[\begin{array}{c}\text{number of ways in which}\\\text{an outcome can occur}\end{array}\right]}{\left[\begin{array}{c}\text{number of ways in}\\\text{which it can fail to occur}\end{array}\right]} \quad \text{- - - (15) } \textbf{The Odds}$$

When a die is rolled, for example, the odds in favour of a six are 1 to 5 or, to express this as a fraction, 1/5.

We can compare the incidence of an outcome in two groups of participants simply by dividing the odds in favour of the outcome in one category by the odds in favour of the same outcome in the other category, the resulting statistic being known as the **odds ratio (OR)**:

$$OR = \frac{\left[\text{odds in favour in first group}\right]}{\left[\text{odds in favour in second group}\right]} \quad \text{- - - (16) } \textbf{The Odds Ratio}$$

In Table 7, we see that for the Critical category, the value of the odds in favour of the presence of the antibody is $21/6 = 3.5$ and for the category Other, $Odds = 22/30 = .7333$. The odds ratio is calculated simply by dividing the odds for the Critical group by the odds for the Other group: $OR = 3.5/.7333 = 4.77$. The odds ratio tells us that when we move from the category Other to the Critical category, the odds in favour of the occurrence of the antibody increase nearly fivefold.

The odds ratio is useful for exploring any contingency table where at least two of the attributes are dichotomous. We shall make use of this statistic later, when we consider multi-way frequency tables in Chapter 13.

11.5.5   Analysis of contingency tables with SPSS

To illustrate the computerisation of the analysis, we shall return to the contingency table shown in Table 7. We shall enter the data in the form of a frequency distribution, rather than case by case. When the data have already been grouped in this way, the data set for a contingency table must include two grouping variables to identify the various cell counts, one representing the rows (Group), and the other the columns (Presence) of the contingency table in Table 6. In this example, since the data are counts, not individual records of presence or absence, a third variable (Count) is needed for the cell frequencies.

- In **Variable View**, name the variables *Group*, *Presence*, and *Count*.
- In the **Values** column, define the numerical values and their labels for the two grouping variables. For the Group variable, assign the code numbers 1, 2, 3 and 4 to tissue types A, B, C and Critical, respectively. For the Presence variable, assign the numbers 1 and 2 to No and Yes, respectively.
- When you have finished working in Variable View, Click the **Data View** tab to switch to **Data View** and enter the data into the three columns, as shown in Figure 13.

	Group	Presence	Count
1	Type A	No	14
2	Type A	Yes	8
3	Type B	No	11
4	Type B	Yes	7
5	Type C	No	5
6	Type C	Yes	7
7	Critical	No	6
8	Critical	Yes	21

Figure 13. **Data View** showing the two grouping variables and the counts of presence or absence of the antibody

When you have grouped data as in this example, the next step is essential. Since the data in the Count column represent cell frequencies of a variable (not values), SPSS must be informed of this by means of the **Weight Cases** procedure in the **Data** menu. The procedure for weighting cases is illustrated in Figure 14.

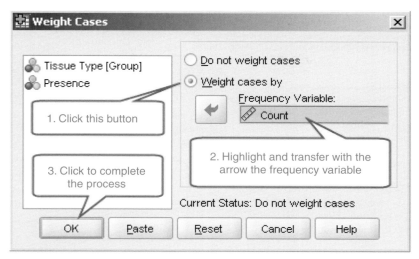

Figure 14. The **Weight Cases** procedure

Had the data been recorded case by case in the data file (i.e. not collated), there would have been no need to use the **Weight Cases** procedure because the **Crosstabs** procedure would have counted up the cases automatically.

- Find the **Crosstabs** procedure in the **Descriptives** submenu as shown in Figure 15.

Figure 15. Finding **Crosstabs** in the **Descriptives** submenu

- To obtain the contingency table and make the chi-square test, proceed as shown in Figure 16.
- Complete the **Statistics...**, **Cells...**, and **Format...** dialog boxes as shown in Figures 17 - 19. The **Format...** dialog controls the order in which rows for the values of the grouping variable appear in the contingency table. The default setting is **Ascending**, meaning that the top row of entries in the table will be the data for the value 1 and the bottom row will be the data for the value 4 (the Critical group). By changing the setting to **Descending**, this order will be reversed: the row with the value 4 (the Critical group) will now appear at the top and the row with the value 1 will appear at the bottom.

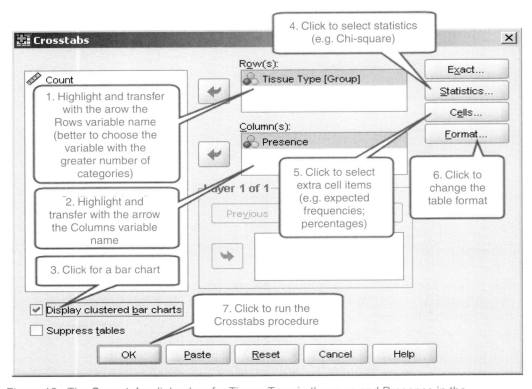

Figure 16. The **Crosstabs** dialog box for Tissue Type in the rows and Presence in the columns

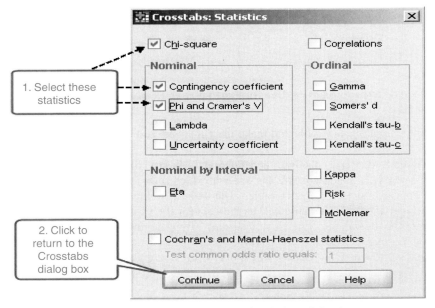

Figure 17. Appropriate choices of statistics in the **Statistics** dialog box

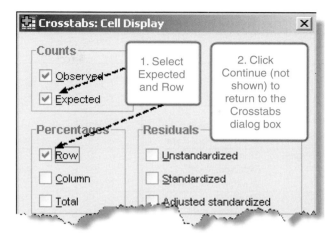

Figure 18. The **Cell Display** dialog box with **Expected** and **Row** ticked

The option of **Expected** cell frequencies in **Counts** enables the user to check that the prescribed minimum requirements for the valid use of chi-square have been fulfilled. Although there has been much debate about these, some leading authorities have proscribed the use of chi-square when:

1. In 2 × 2 tables, any of the expected frequencies is less than 5;
2. In larger tables, any of the expected frequencies is less than 1 or more than 20% are less than 5.

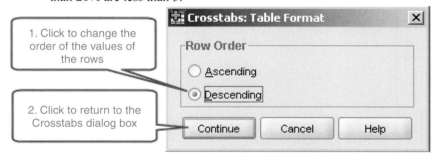

Figure 19. Changing the order of listing the rows with the **Table Format** dialog box

Output 6 shows the contingency table in Output 5, to which have been added the row percentages. In the Critical group, 77.8% of cases had the antibody; whereas the highest percentage in any of the other groups was 58.3%.

Tissue Type * Presence Crosstabulation

			Presence		
			No	Yes	Total
Tissue Type	Critical	Count	6	21	27
		Expected Count	12.3	14.7	27.0
		% within Tissue Type	22.2%	77.8%	100.0%
	Type C	Count	5	7	12
		Expected Count	5.5	6.5	12.0
		% within Tissue Type	41.7%	58.3%	100.0%
	Type B	Count	11	7	18
		Expected Count	8.2	9.8	18.0
		% within Tissue Type	61.1%	38.9%	100.0%
	Type A	Count	14	8	22
		Expected Count	10.0	12.0	22.0
		% within Tissue Type	63.6%	36.4%	100.0%
Total		Count	36	43	79
		Expected Count	36.0	43.0	79.0
		% within Tissue Type	45.6%	54.4%	100.0%

Output 6. The contingency table, to which have been added the row percentages

Output 7 shows the (edited) clustered bar chart, in which the colours in the original chart have been replaced by black and white patterns. The chart provides a striking demonstration of the predominance of the antibody in the Critical tissue group.

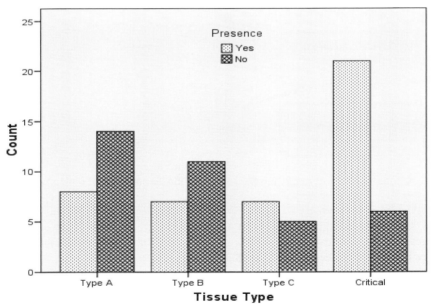

Output 7. Clustered bar chart showing the relatively high incidence of the antibody in the Critical tissue group

Chi-Square Tests

	Value	df	Asymp. Sig. (2-sided)
Pearson Chi-Square	10.655[a]	3	.014
Likelihood Ratio	11.093	3	.011
Linear-by-Linear Association	9.850	1	.002
N of Valid Cases	79		

Chi-square has a p-value .014 (significant at .05 level)

a. 0 cells (.0%) have expected count less than 5. The minimum expected count is 5.47.

As shown in Output 4, none of the expected counts was <5

Output 8. Result of the chi-square test

Output 8 shows the results of the chi-square test. The chi-square value 10.66 is significant beyond the .05 level:

$$\chi^2 (3) = 10.66; \quad p < .05$$

Note the remark under the table in Output 8 about expected cell frequencies, which assures the user that the data are sufficiently plentiful to permit the usual chi-square test.

Output 9 gives the values of the tests of strength of association. In this particular example, where one of the attributes is a dichotomy, the values of phi and Cramer's V are the same. That would not necessarily be so in more complex tables.

Symmetric Measures

		Value	Approx. Sig.
Nominal by Nominal	Phi	.367	.014
	Cramer's V	.367	.014
	Contingency Coefficient	.345	.014
N of Valid Cases		79	

a. Not assuming the null hypothesis.

b. Using the asymptotic standard error assuming the null hypothesis.

Output 9. Statistics measuring the strength of the association between Tissue Type and presence in the antibody

11.5.6   Getting help with the output

Should any item in the SPSS output be unfamiliar, you can find an explanation by double-clicking on the item to highlight it and right-clicking with the mouse (Figure 20).

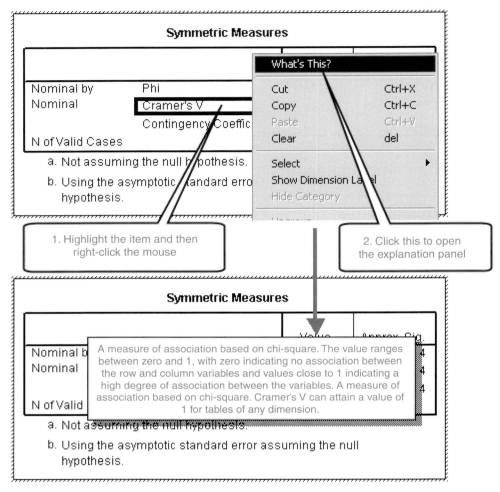

Figure 20. Getting help with unfamiliar terms in the output

11.5.7 Some cautions and caveats

As with any other statistical technique, the making of an approximate chi-square test implies that the requirements of the underlying statistical model have been met.   One requirement is that there must be sufficient data.   The frequencies in the cells of the contingency table must also meet certain requirements.

11.5.7.1 Low expected frequencies

A word of warning about the misuse of chi-square should be given here. In the first place, it is important to bear in mind that the 'chi-square' statistic is only *approximately* distributed as a true chi-square variable. The greater the expected frequencies, the better the approximation, hence the rule about minimum expected frequencies. When the expected frequencies fall below the recommended levels, the approximation can be poor and the *p*-value of the approximate chi-square statistic can be misleading.   SPSS, however, can provide **exact *p*-values**, which should be requested when the data are scarce.

Returning to our current example, suppose that the study had involved only 19 patients. The contingency table (Output 10) shows the same pattern as before: there is a clear predominance of the antibody in the Critical tissue group.

Tissue Type * Presence Crosstabulation

Count

		Presence		Total
		No	Yes	
Tissue Type	Critical	2	7	9
	Type C	1	0	1
	Type B	3	0	3
	Type A	4	2	6
Total		10	9	19

Output 10. A contingency table summarising a small data set

Were you to proceed to use the Pearson chi-square statistic to test the null hypothesis of independence, you would find that the *p*-value of chi-square was greater than .05 and be forced to accept the null hypothesis. With the table displaying the 'asymptotic' *p*-value, however, would come a warning that there are too many cells with low expected frequencies. The correct procedure here is to request an exact test.

When completing the Crosstabs dialog, click the **Exact …** button at the side of the dialog box (see Figure 16), enter the **Exact Tests** dialog box, and activate the **Exact** radio button (Figure 21).

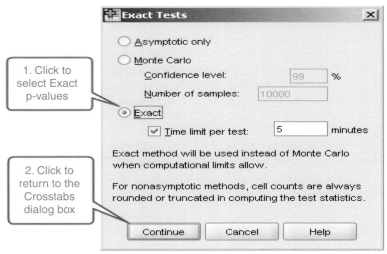

Figure 21. Choosing an exact test

The results of both the approximate (Asymptotic) chi-square test and the exact test are shown in Output 11. The exact tests do not agree with the asymptotic tests: on the exact tests, the result is significant beyond the .05 level. This is the result we should accept. We have evidence for a greater presence of the antibody in the Critical group.

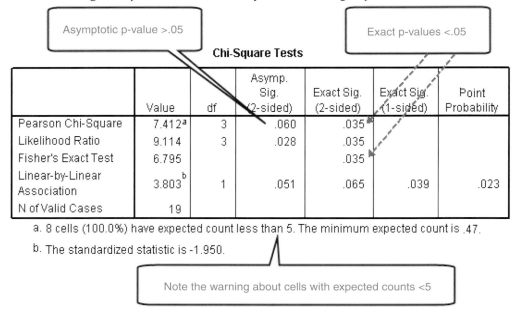

Output 11. Results of the exact tests

11.5.7.2 Non-independent observations: correlated nominal data

The use of the chi-square test requires that each individual studied contributes to the count in only one cell of the contingency table. In other words, the observations must be independent. Suppose that a researcher is interested in the effects of hearing a debate upon people's response to a contentious political issue. One hundred people are asked whether they support the motion before and after hearing the debate. One might be tempted simply to count the proportions of the participants in favour of the motion before and after hearing the debate and proceed with a chi-square test for a possible association between the variables of Stage of Monitoring (Before/After) and Response (Yes/No). To analyse the data in this way, however, would be to violate the requirement that each person must contribute to the tally in only one cell of the two-way frequency table. There would be twice as many responses as there were participants! Since the same people are giving their Yes/No response on different occasions, an experiment of this kind will yield **correlated nominal data**. We shall see that correct approach here is to follow a different data-gathering strategy and make a test of **goodness-of-fit**, rather than a test for association.

The way to proceed is to identify the individuals as they give their responses to the motion before and after hearing the debate. It can then be seen whether a person's views have changed or not. Suppose the participants' responses are as shown in Table 8.

Table 8. Number of people supporting a political motion		
Before	After	Frequency
Yes	Yes	27
	No	13
No	Yes	38
	No	22

The **McNemar test** uses only the data on those participants who *changed* their views. We can see from Table 8 that a total of 51 participants changed their minds after hearing the debate; but while only 13 participants changed their minds against the motion, 38 changed their minds in favour of the motion. If the null hypothesis is true and listening to the debate had no effect, we could expect as many participants to change their responses in the negative direction as in the positive direction. Under the null hypothesis, if a participant's responses can be assumed to be independent of those of the other participants, we have a series of 51 **Bernoulli trials** like tosses of a coin (see Chapter 6). We could test the null hypothesis by running a **binomial test**, setting the expected proportion at .5, as described in Chapter 6. The McNemar test uses an approximate chi-square test of goodness-of-fit to test the same null hypothesis.

To run the McNemar test on SPSS Statistics 18, prepare the data file by defining two nominal variables named *Before* and *After* and a scale variable named *Frequency*. When defining the nominal variables, label the values 1 and 2 as Yes and No, respectively. When the data have been entered, Data View should appear as in Figure 22.

Before	After	Frequency
Yes	Yes	27
Yes	No	13
No	Yes	38
No	No	22

Figure 22. The appearance of Data View before running the McNemar test

At this point, SPSS must be instructed to weight the rows by their frequencies of occurrence. Choose **Data➔Weight Cases…** and, in the **Weight Cases** dialog box, transfer the variable label Frequency into the **Frequency Variable** box.

- To run the **McNemar** test, choose **Analyze➔Nonparametric Tests➔2 Related Samples…** to open the **Two-Related-Samples Tests** dialog box.
- Follow the steps shown in Figure 23.

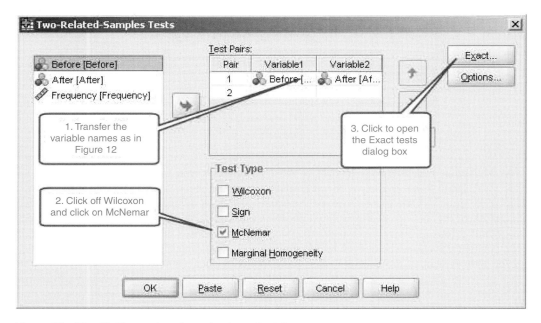

Figure 23. The **McNema**r test for paired nominal data

The results of the test are shown in Output 12. The very low *p*-value of .001 is strong evidence against the null hypothesis. We have evidence that listening to the debate tended to change more people's views in the direction of the motion rather than against it.

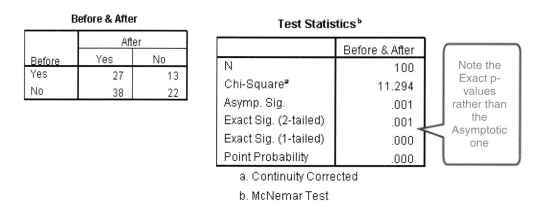

Output 12. The contingency table (left) and the McNemar Test results (right)

Since the McNemar test (or the binomial test) is a test of goodness-of-fit, we can use Cohen's measure *g* (which we described in Chapter 6) as a measure of effect size, where *g* is the difference between P, the proportion of outcomes in the target category and p is the probability of the outcome under the null hypothesis:

$$g = |P - p| \quad \text{- - -} (17)$$

Cohen's Effect size index

In Table 9, we reproduce our interpretation of the guidelines suggested by Cohen (1988).

Table 9. Guidelines (from Cohen, 1988) for interpreting the effect size index g

Value of g	Size of effect
$.05 \le g < .15$	Small
$.15 \le g < .25$	Medium
$g \ge .25$	Large

In words …

A value less than .05 is trivial.
A value between .05 and .15 is a Small effect.
A value between .15 and .25 is a Medium effect.
A value of at least .25 is a Large effect.

Output 12 shows that of the 51 participants who changed their responses, 38 changed in a positive direction, that is, the proportion who changed in a positive direction was $38/51 = .75$. The proportion under the null hypothesis is .5. Substituting in formula (17), we have

$$g = |P - p| = .75 - .5 = .25$$

which, according to Table 9 is a Large effect.

11.5.8   Other problems with traditional chi-square analyses

There are several other potential problems with the making of chi-square tests that the user should be aware of. A lucid account of the rationale and assumptions of the chi-square test is given by Howell (2007) and would be an excellent starting-point for further reading on this topic.

11.6   DO DOCTORS AGREE? COHEN'S KAPPA

Suppose that two psychiatrists assign each of 50 patients to one of a set of five diagnostic categories, A, B, C, D and E. Their assignments are shown in Table 10.

Table 10. Assignments of patients to categories A to E					
Doctor1	Doctor2	Count	Doctor1	Doctor2	Count
A	A	4	C	D	1
A	B	1	C	E	1
A	C	1	D	A	1
A	D	1	D	B	1
A	E	1	D	C	2
B	A	1	D	D	8
B	B	4	D	E	2
B	C	0	E	A	1
B	D	4	E	B	0
B	E	2	E	C	1
C	A	2	E	D	3
C	B	0	E	E	2
C	C	6			

When these assignments are cast into the form of a contingency table, the data appear as in Table 11.

The marked diagonal cells in Table 11 contain the numbers of patients who were assigned to the same diagnostic category by the two doctors. Intuitively, it might seem reasonable to divide the sum of the judgements on the marked diagonal by the total number of judgements and argue that the percentage of agreement is 24/50 = 48%. As with the analysis of any contingency table, however, we must take into consideration the different numbers of patients with different kinds of problem, as indicated by the varying row and column frequencies. Such discrepancies may merely reflect a tendency to make more use of some diagnostic categories than others, rather than truly reliable diagnosis. Accordingly, we need to obtain the **expected frequencies (E)** for the cells along the marked diagonal, given the values of the marginal row and column totals. We obtain the value of E for each cell by multiplying the marginal totals in the row and column and dividing by the total frequency (50). For example, four patients were assigned to diagnostic category B by both doctors. Since the row and column totals for the assignments by the first and second doctor are 6 and 11, respectively, $E = 66/50 = 1.32$.

Table 11. Contingency table showing the diagnoses of 50 patients by two doctors

(The observed frequencies are given in the rows labelled O; the expected frequencies are given in the rows labelled E.)

Second Doctor * First Doctor Crosstabulation

			First Doctor					Total
			A	B	C	D	E	
Second	A	O	4	1	2	1	1	9
Doctor		E	1.4	2.0	1.8	2.5	1.3	9.0
	B	O	1	4	0	1	0	6
		E	1.0	1.3	1.2	1.7	.8	6.0
	C	O	1	0	6	2	1	10
		E	1.6	2.2	2.0	2.8	1.4	10.0
	D	O	1	4	1	8	3	17
		E	2.7	3.7	3.4	4.8	2.4	17.0
	E	O	1	2	1	2	2	8
		E	1.3	1.8	1.6	2.2	1.1	8.0
Total		O	8	11	10	14	7	50
		E	8.0	11.0	10.0	14.0	7.0	50.0

Cohen (1960) suggested the statistic **kappa (κ)** as a measure of agreement between the doctors. Kappa is defined as

$$\kappa = \frac{\sum_{diagonal} O - \sum_{diagonal} E}{N - \sum_{diagonal} E} \quad \text{- - - (18)} \quad \textbf{Kappa coefficient}$$

where O and E are, respectively, the observed and expected frequencies *for the diagonal cells only* in Table 11 and N is the *total* number of patients. (For the *entire* contingency table, the totals for O and E would be equal.) Substituting in the formula, we have

$$\sum_{diagonal} O = 4 + 4 + 6 + 8 + 2 = 24$$

$$\sum_{diagonal} E = 1.44 + 1.32 + 2.00 + 4.76 + 1.12 = 10.64$$

$$\kappa = \frac{24 - 10.64}{50 - 10.64} = 0.34$$

The value .34 is even lower than the 48% agreement we arrived at using the intuitive measure.

Cohen's kappa statistic is available in SPSS.

- In **Variable View**, set up the variables *Doctor1* and *Doctor2* as nominal variables and *Count* as a scale variable. For the nominal variables Doctor1 and Doctor2, assign to the values 1, 2, …, 5 the labels A, B, …,E respectively. Enter all the data for each combination of doctors (Table 10).

- Follow the path **Data➜Weight Cases...** to weight the cases by Count.
- Choose **Analyze➜Descriptive Statistics➜Crosstabs...** to open the **Crosstabs** dialog box.
- Highlight and transfer the grouping variable names to the **Row(s)** and **Column(s)** boxes respectively
- Click the **Statistics...** button and select the **Kappa** check box (see earlier Figure 17). Click **Continue** to return to the **Crosstabs** dialog box and then click **OK**.

The output starts with a **Case Processing Summary** table and then the **Doctor1*Doctor2 Crosstabulation** table. The value of κ is shown in the next table (Output 13).

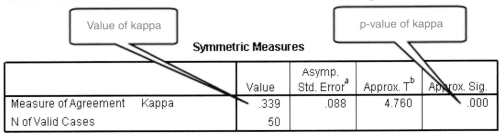

a. Not assuming the null hypothesis.

b. Using the asymptotic standard error assuming the null hypothesis.

Output 13. The kappa statistics

The value of kappa is given as .34, as calculated previously. The output also contains a test of the significance of kappa which is of little importance, because a value such as .34, while significant beyond the .01 level, is much too low for a reliability: a minimum value of .75 would be expected with a reliable diagnostic system.

The result should be reported as follows:

> "Cohen's kappa statistic was used as a measure of diagnostic agreement between the two doctors: κ = .34; p < .01".

11.7   PARTIAL CORRELATION

11.7.1   Correlation does not imply causation

In experimental (as opposed to correlational) research, provided there are adequate controls, the independent variable (IV) can be shown to have a causal effect upon the dependent variable (DV). In correlational research, however, in which variables are measured as they occur in participants, it can be difficult or impossible to demonstrate unequivocally that one variable in any sense 'causes' another. In some situations, in fact, even when two variables are substantially correlated, *neither* variable causes the other: both are at least partly determined by a third variable. In such circumstances, although the correlation between the two variables may be both statistically significant and substantial, it is a 'spurious' correlation, in the sense that it suggests the presence of a direct causal link between the two variables when actually there is none.

Suppose that, as a continuation of the research described at the beginning of this chapter, further data were gathered with fresh participants, not only on Actual violence and Exposure to screened violence, but also their parents' attitudes towards aggression, violence and their preparedness to use violence in certain situations.   Let us call this new variable Parental Aggression.

Once again, as in the earlier study, Actual violence and Exposure to screened violence turned out to be highly positively correlated: $r(27) = .707$; $p < .01$.

The hypothesis that motivated the original study was that Exposure to screened violence increases Actual violence. This hypothesis can be represented diagrammatically as a simple **causal model**:

Model 1

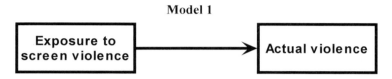

The high correlation between Exposure and Actual obtained in both studies is certainly consistent with this model.   The existence of a positive correlation, however, is equally compatible with the view that the amount of screen violence a child watches is a reflection of his or her own violent tendencies:

Model 2

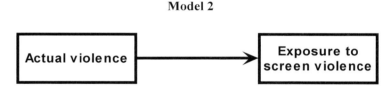

Here then, we have two contradictory models, each able to live quite happily with the high correlations yielded by the two studies.

There is, however, still another possibility.   In the second study, the correlations of the Parental variable with Actual violence and Exposure to violence were even higher than the correlation between Actual and Exposure: the correlation between Parental aggression and Actual violence was .801 and the correlation between Parental aggression and Exposure was .845.   Such a pattern of correlations is consistent with – indeed suggestive of – a third hypothesis, namely, that the Parental variable has a strong causal influence on both Exposure to and Actual violence, as shown in Model 3:

Model 3

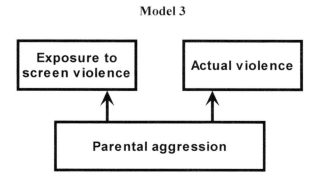

If Model 3 is correct, the high correlation observed between Exposure to and Actual violence in our two studies has been driven entirely by the variable of Parental aggression.

We have not exhausted the possibilities for models of causation here.   The point is that it is often impossible to determine unequivocally which model is the correct interpretation of a correlation coefficient, unless additional, collateral data are available or theoretical considerations compel the acceptance of one particular model and rejection of the others.

Had we no additional evidence beyond a high correlation between Exposure and Actual, we should have to accept that the findings were compatible with any of the three models of causation that we have described, and perhaps with others that we have not described.   The high correlations of both variables with Parental aggression, however, show the original correlation between Exposure and Actual in a different light, as we shall see in the next section.

11.7.2   Meaning of partial correlation

A **partial correlation** is what remains of the correlation between two variables when their correlations with a third variable have been taken into consideration. If r_{AC} and r_{BC} are, respectively, the correlations of variables A and B with a third variable C, the partial correlation between A and B with C 'partialled out' ($r_{AB.C}$) is given by the following formula:

$$r_{AB.C} = \frac{r_{AB} - r_{AC}r_{BC}}{\sqrt{\left(1 - r_{AC}^{\,2}\right)\left(1 - r_{BC}^{\,2}\right)}} \quad \text{- - - (19)} \ \textbf{Partial correlation}$$

If the two variables correlate substantially with the third variable, the partial correlation between them may be much smaller than the original correlation; indeed, an initially high correlation may be reduced to insignificance. In that case, it may be reasonable to interpret the original correlation as having been driven by the third variable, as in the third causal model shown above.

To run a partial correlation within SPSS, proceed as follows:

• Select **Analyze➔Correlate➔Partial…** to enter the **Partial Correlations** dialog box.

• Complete the dialog box as shown in Figure 24.

• By clicking the **Options** button and checking the **Zero-order correlations** box in the **Options** dialog, you can obtain the original Pearson correlation between Exposure and Actual violence for comparison.

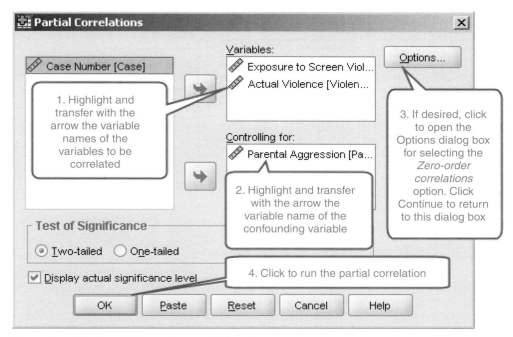

Figure 24. The **Partial Correlations** dialog box

The upper part of the edited output (Output 14) gives the Pearson correlations among the three variables. The lower part of the table gives the partial correlation between Actual Violence and Exposure to Screen Violence, after the potential confounding variable of Parental Aggression has been controlled or **partialled out**. The original value of .707 has been reduced to .095: in other words, little remains of the original correlation when the correlations of Exposure to Screen Violence and Actual Violence with the Parental Aggression variable have been taken into consideration. It would appear that the original correlation was driven largely by Parental Aggression.

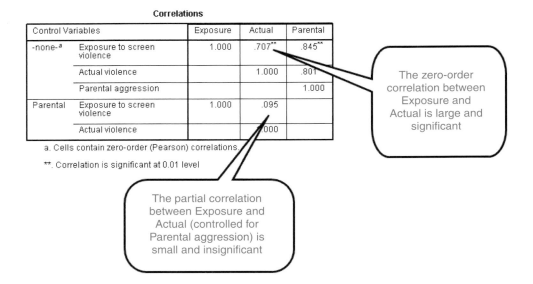

Correlations

Control Variables		Exposure	Actual	Parental
-none-[a]	Exposure to screen violence	1.000	.707**	.845**
	Actual violence		1.000	.801
	Parental aggression			1.000
Parental	Exposure to screen violence	1.000	.095	
	Actual violence		1.000	

a. Cells contain zero-order (Pearson) correlations.

**. Correlation is significant at 0.01 level

The zero-order correlation between Exposure and Actual is large and significant

The partial correlation between Exposure and Actual (controlled for Parental aggression) is small and insignificant

Output 14. Edited table of correlations showing the original (zero-order) correlations and the partial correlation. (The original table also gave the *p*-value of the partial correlation, which appears in the report below.)

Report this result as follows:

> The partial correlation between Actual violence and Exposure with Parental Aggression partialled out is insignificant: $r_{partial}$ (27) = .095; p = .644.

11.8   CORRELATION IN MENTAL TESTING: RELIABILITY

A psychological test must have two attributes:
1. It must be **reliable**;
2. It must be **valid**.

A **reliable** test gives *consistent* results: a person, if tested with the instrument on different occasions by different testers, should score at similar percentile levels.   Implicit in this definition is that scores on the test must have an appropriate distribution, so that the variance reflects natural individual differences in the property concerned. Ceiling and floor effects, whereby everyone either achieves perfection or fails the test completely, vitiate reliability.

A **valid** test is one that measures what it is supposed to measure. The brevity of that definition belies the complexity of the problems involved in the establishment of the validity of a test: in his Dictionary of Psychology, Reber (1985) gives more than twenty definitions of validity. In this section, however, we shall be concerned with reliability only. Reliability is a necessary (but not a sufficient) condition for validity. An unreliable measuring instrument would be like an elastic tape measure or a rubber ruler: even when used to measure a property of the same object, such an instrument would never give the same result twice. In particular, we shall be concerned with how the reliability of a composite test consisting of a set of items increases with the number of items.

There are several approaches to the measurement of reliability, all of which utilise the Pearson correlation. Three of these are:
1. **Test-retest**;
2. **Parallel forms**;
3. **Split-half**.

In the first two methods, each participant is tested twice, either (as in 1) with the same test or (as in 2) with parallel (or equivalent) forms of the same test. A Pearson correlation is then used to measure the association between the participants' scores on the two occasions of testing and thus determine the reliability of the test. It is generally accepted that the reliability of a test should be at least .80 for the test to be useful. In the **split-half** approach to the determination of reliability, the component items are divided into two equal-sized equivalent subgroups, perhaps the odd-numbered and even-numbered items. Each participant receives two subtotal scores: one for the even items, the other for the odd. The split-half reliability is the Pearson correlation between the odd totals and the even totals. In the split-half approach, the participant is tested only once. Split-half reliability can be viewed as a special case of the general problem of establishing the reliability of the total score on any composite test consisting of several items, some of which may themselves be of low reliability.

In psychometric theory, a score X on a test is regarded as the sum of two components:
1. A **true** component t, which is that part of x that truly expresses the property;
2. An **error** component e.

Thus

$$X = t + e \quad \text{- - - (20)} \quad \textbf{Components of a test score}$$

On the basis of some reasonable assumptions, such as the independence of the true and error components, it can be shown that

$$\sigma^2_{\text{total}} = \sigma^2_{\text{true}} + \sigma^2_{\text{error}} \quad \text{- - - (21)}$$

Partition of the total variance of the scores

In words, the total variance of a score is the sum of the variances of the true component and random error, remembering that different participants will be in possession, to varying degrees, of the property we are trying to measure.

The **reliability** $\left(r_{xx} \right)$ of a test is defined as the ratio of the true to the total variance:

$$r_{xx} = \frac{\sigma^2_{\text{true}}}{\sigma^2_{\text{total}}} \quad \text{- - - (22)} \quad \textbf{Reliability as a ratio of variances}$$

The notion of a reliability as a ratio of true to total variance extends to composite scores that are aggregates of scores on individual items. The relability of a measuring instrument can also be conceptualised as the correlation between the scores on a test given to the same individuals on two different occasions.

11.8.1   Reliability and number of items: coefficient alpha

Psychometric theory shows that the reliability of a test increases with the number of items it contains. **Coefficient alpha** $\left(\textbf{Coeff}\,\alpha\right)$, the reliability of a test that is a composite of several items, is defined as follows:

$$\text{Coeff}\,\alpha = \frac{i}{i-1}\left(\frac{\sigma_X^2 - \sum_{\text{items}} \sigma_{\text{item}}^2}{\sigma_X^2}\right) \; \text{---} \; (23) \; \textbf{Coefficient alpha}$$

where i is the number of items in the test and σ_X^2 is the variance of the complete test.

Formula (23) makes explicit the intimate connection between variance and reliability. The relationship between number of items and reliability obtains because the items in a test constitute a sample from a domain of possible items and, other things being equal, the statistics of large samples are less subject to variability than those of small samples.

There are several equivalent versions of the formula for **coefficient alpha**, one of which is the **Spearman-Brown formula**, which expresses the reliability of a test in terms of the mean of the correlations between every possible pair of items:

$$r_{xx} = \frac{iM_r}{1+(i-1)M_r} \; \text{---} \; (24)$$

The Spearman-Brown formula

where i is the number of items in the test and M_r is the mean of the correlations between all pairs of items. It is clear from (24) that even if the average inter-item correlation is low, the total score on a test with many items can achieve a very high level of reliability.

Suppose that a test contains four items, all of which are intended to measure the same property. Table 12 shows the scores of six people on the test. (These data have been borrowed from Winer, 1962, p127.)

Table 12. The scores of six participants on a four-item test				
Participant	Item 1	Item 2	Item 3	Item 4	Sum
1	2	4	3	3	12
2	5	7	5	6	23
3	1	3	1	2	7
4	7	9	9	8	33
5	2	4	6	1	13
6	6	8	8	4	26

From the **Spearman-Brown** formula, we can expect the reliability of the sum of the four test items to be greater than that of any of the individual items.   Table 13 shows the intercorrelations among the four items. The mean inter-item correlation is +.84.

Table 13. Intercorrelations among the four items in the test

Inter-Item Correlation Matrix

	Item 1	Item 2	Item 3	Item 4
Item 1	1.000	1.000	.865	.865
Item 2	1.000	1.000	.865	.865
Item 3	.865	.865	1.000	.586
Item 4	.865	.865	.586	1.000

Applying the Spearman-Brown formula, we find that the estimate of the reliability for the aggregate test score is

$$r_{xx} = \frac{iM_r}{1+(i-1)M_r} = \frac{4(0.84)}{1+3(0.84)} = .95$$

There were only four items in this test; but the reliability of a test with many items can be expected to be very high indeed – even if the mean inter-item correlation is much lower than it is in this example.

11.8.2 Measuring agreement among judges: the intraclass correlation

So far, we have been considering the question of the consistency of a test when used repeatedly to test the same individuals. A related problem is the measurement of the level of agreement among *different* measuring instruments when used on the same set of objects or people. A particular instance is the measurement of the extent to which judges agree when, for example, rating the performance of musicians or skaters on a 10-point scale. Table 14 shows the marks assigned by four judges to six performers.

Table 14. Marks assigned by four judges to six performers

Performer	Judge1	Judge2	Judge3	Judge4	MeanRating
1	2	4	3	3	3.00
2	5	7	5	6	5.75
3	1	3	1	2	1.75
4	7	9	9	8	8.25
5	2	4	6	1	3.25
6	6	8	8	4	6.50

The four marks given to each performer can be regarded as belonging to a category or **class**: they all refer to the same person and should tend to be more similar to one another than they are to the marks assigned to the other performers. The total variance of the ratings σ^2_{total} is made up of two components:

1. The variance of the true extent to which people possess the property, which we shall term σ^2_{people} ;

2. The error variance $\sigma^2_{within\ people}$, which depends partly upon differences among the judges. The larger the first component of the total variance in relation to the second, the closer the agreement among the judges.

In summary, we can break down the total variance of the ratings as follows:

$$\sigma^2_{total} = \sigma^2_{between\ people} + \sigma^2_{within\ people} \quad - - - (25)$$

Partition of the total sum of squares

Conceptually, the **intraclass correlation (*ICC*)** is defined as follows:

$$ICC = \frac{\sigma^2_{between\ people}}{\sigma^2_{between\ people} + \sigma^2_{within\ people}} \quad - - - (26)$$

Intraclass correlation

Comparison of (26) with (22) shows that the *ICC* is actually the ratio of the variance of the hypothetical true scores to the total variance and is therefore a reliability. This is why (26) is termed a 'correlation'. In fact, measuring agreement among the judges and assessing the reliability of an aggregate score are actually one and the same problem. In our second example, the judges are the equivalent of separate test items measuring one and the same property in the person being tested. The *ICC* is, at the same time, both a measure of agreement among judges and a measure of the reliability of their average ratings of the performers. In fact, the *ICC* is yet another form of coefficient alpha.

11.8.3   Reliability analysis with SPSS

We shall illustrate SPSS's computation of reliability using the scores of six people on four items (Table 12).

- Select **Analyze➔Scale➔Reliability Analysis...** (Figure 25) to open the **Reliability Analysis** dialog box (Figure 26).
- Complete the **Reliability Analysis** dialog boxes as shown in Figures 26 and 27.

In choosing the default **Two-Way Mixed** model from the **Statistics** menu, we have assumed that the four judges are the only ones of interest (a fixed effects source), whereas the performers are a random sample from a large pool of potential performers (a random effects source).

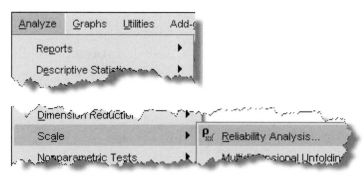

Figure 25. The menu for **Reliability Analysis**

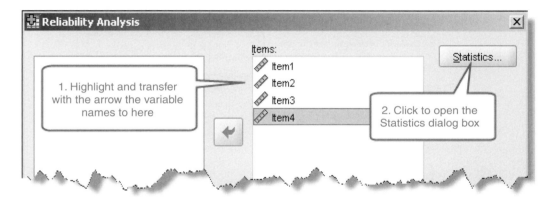

Figure 26. The completed **Reliability Analysis** dialog box

It can be seen in Output 15 that both **Cronbach's Alpha** and the **Intraclass Correlation Coefficient** (*ICC*) for **Average Measures** have the value .95, as calculated previously from the Spearman-Brown formula. As we should expect, the value of *ICC* for individual items (.825) is lower than it is for the whole test (.950).

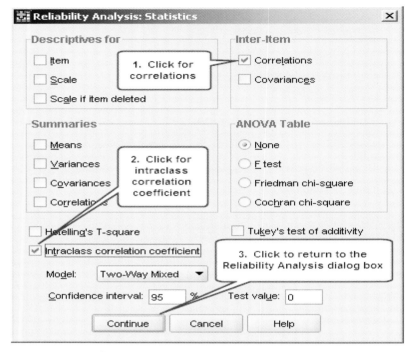

Figure 27. The completed **Statistics** dialog box for **Reliability Analysis**

The value of Alpha

Reliability Statistics

Cronbach's Alpha	Cronbach's Alpha Based on Standardized Items	N of Items
.950	.955	4

Intraclass Correlation Coefficient

	Intraclass Correlation[a]	F Test with True Value 0			
		Value	df1	df2	Sig
Single Measures	.825[b]	19.865	5.0	15	.000
Average Measures	.950[c]	19.865	5.0	15	.000

Two-way mixed effects model where people effects are random and measures effects are fixed.

a. Type C intraclass correlation coefficients using a consistency definition-the between-measure variance is excluded from the denominator variance.

b. The estimator is the same, whether the interaction effect is present or not.

c. This estimate is computed assuming the interaction effect is absent, because it is not estimable otherwise.

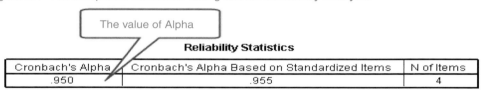

The value of *ICC* and its significance (p <.01)

Output 15. The values of Alpha and ICC and its significance for the aggregate and single items

11.9   A FINAL WORD

In this chapter, we switched out attention from statistics that were designed to compare means (or other averages such as the median) to those designed to measure association. In particular, we discussed two of the most used (and misused) of all statistics, namely, the Pearson correlation and the chi-square statistic. A correlation should never be taken at its face value without first examining the scatterplot; and the user of the approximate chi-square test for association should make sure that the contingency table conforms to the requirements of minimum expected frequencies and independence of responses.

Recommended reading

Howell (2007) has excellent chapters on correlation (Chapter 9) and on the analysis of contingency tables (Chapter 6).

Howell, D. C. (2007). *Statistical methods for psychology (6th ed.).* Belmont, CA: Thomson/Wadsworth.

Exercises

Exercise 17 *The Pearson correlation*, Exercise 18 *Other measures of association* and Exercise 19 *The analysis of nominal data* are available in www.psypress.com/spss-made-simple . Click on Exercises.

Regression

12.1   INTRODUCTION

The associative coin has two sides. On the one hand, a single number, a correlation coefficient, can be calculated which expresses the *strength* of the association between two variables. On the other, however, there is a set of techniques, known as **regression**, which utilise the presence of an association between two variables to predict the values of one variable (the **dependent**, **target** or **criterion** variable) from those of another (the **independent variable**, or **regressor**). In **simple** regression, there is just one IV or regressor; in **complex** regression there are two or more IVs. It is with this predictive aspect of association that the present chapter is concerned.

Prediction of an individual's score on one variable from the same person's scores on other variables has obvious practical value. Another, equally important aspect of regression, however, is the determination of the extent to which the variance of the dependent variable can be accounted for or explained by the variance of one or more independent variables.

12.1.1   Simple, two-variable regression

Returning to the study of the association between Actual violence and Exposure to screened violence (Chapter 11), our starting point in this chapter is the same elliptical scatterplot that served as our point of departure in the earlier chapter. The cautions and caveats about the use and abuse of the Pearson correlation all apply, with equal force, to regression as well. In particular, the scatterplot must either be elliptical in shape, indicating a basically linear relationship between the DV and the IV, or circular, indicating that they are independent.

Figure 1 shows the **regression line** drawn through the points in the scatterplot. The equation of this line is

$$Y' = 2.09 + .74X$$

where Y' is the point on the line above X. (It is important to distinguish carefully between the observed value Y and Y', which is the corresponding point on the line for the same value of X.)

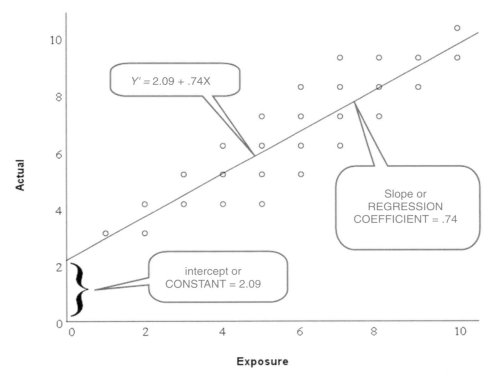

Figure 1. The regression line of Actual violence upon Exposure to screen violence

The general form of this **linear regression equation** is

$$Y' = b_0 + b_1 X \quad \text{- - -} \quad (1)$$

The linear regression line

where b_0 is the **intercept** of the line and b_1 is its **slope**. The intercept is the distance from the origin to the point at which the line cuts the y-axis. At this point, $X = 0$: that is, $Y' = b_0$ (equation 1). In SPSS output, the intercept b_0 is referred as the **constant**.

The slope of the regression line b_1 is known as the **regression coefficient**. The regression coefficient measures the estimated average change in the dependent variable Y that results from increasing the value of X, the regressor or IV, by one unit. In our example, $b_1 = .74$, so an increase of one unit in Exposure results in an estimated average increase of .74 units in the Actual violence score.

Suppose that we had no access to the regression statistics at all and were to be told only that the mean score on Actual violence is 6.37 and that John has an Exposure score of 8. Without further information, our best guess of John's Actual score would be the mean Actual score M_Y, that is, 6.37. We should be obliged to make this guess whatever the value of John's Exposure score. We could do much better, of course, if we knew the equation of the regression line and were to take as our guess of John's Actual score the point on the line above $X = 8$. From (1), we see that John's predicted Actual score (the point on the regression line above Exposure = 8) is

$$Y' = 2.091 + .7359 \times 8 = 8.0$$

This estimate is much closer to John's real score Y on Actual violence, which was 9 (Figure 2).

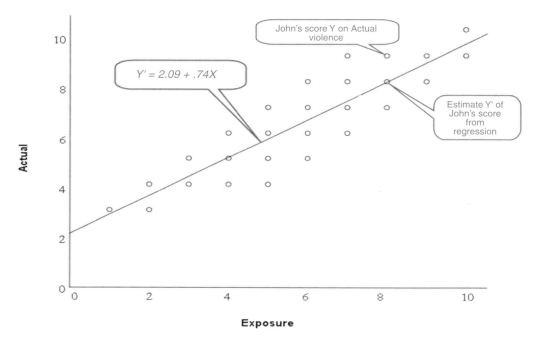

Figure 2. Estimating John's score using the regression line

12.1.2 Residuals

Although we can predict the participant's real score on Actual violence more accurately when we use the regression line, we shall still make errors. The error or **residual** (e) is the participant's real score on Actual violence minus the prediction from regression:

$$e = Y - Y' \; \text{-- -} \; (2) \; \textbf{The residual score}$$

In John's case, since $Y = 9$ and $Y' = 8$, $e = 9 - 8 = 1$. John's residual score is shown in Figure 3.

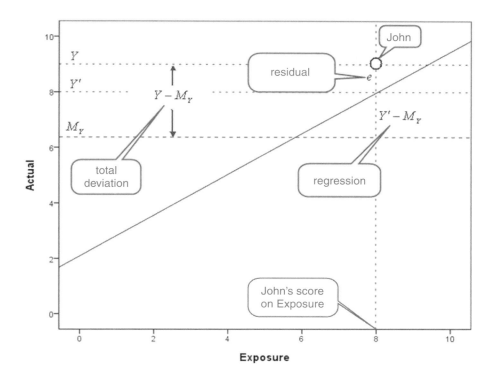

Figure 3. John's residual score

In regression, the study of the residuals is of great importance, because they form the basis for measures of the accuracy of the estimates and of the extent to which the regression model gives a good account of the data in question. (See Tabachnick & Fidell, 2007 for advice on **regression diagnostics**, which are based largely upon residuals and their transformations.)

The building-block from which the variance of the DV is calculated is the deviation score $(Y - M_Y)$: $SS_Y = \Sigma (Y - M_Y)^2$. It is clear from Figure 3 that this deviation is the sum of two components: (1) the residual $e = (Y - Y')$; (2) the regression component $(Y' - M_Y)$. For a given value of X, the closer the line is to the point (X,Y), the smaller will be the residual and the greater will be the regression component $(Y' - M_Y)$. The sums of squares of the total, regression and residual deviations are SS_Y, $SS_{regression}$ and $SS_{residual}$, respectively.

12.1.3   The least squares criterion for 'the best-fitting line'

The regression line shown in Figure 1 is the line that 'fits' the data best according to what is known as the **least squares criterion**, whereby the values of b_0 and b_1 must be such that the sum of squares of the residuals $\Sigma e^2 = SS_{residual}$ is a minimum. There is a unique mathematical solution to this problem. The values of b_0 and b_1 that meet the criterion are given by the following formulae:

$$b_1 = \frac{SP}{SS_X}$$

--- (3) **Slope and intercept of the regression line**

$$b_0 = M_Y - b_1 M_X$$

where *SS* and *SP* are, respectively, the sum of squares and cross-products, as in the formula for the Pearson correlation (Chapter 11):

$$SS_X = \Sigma(X - M_X)^2 \qquad SP = \Sigma(X - M_X)(Y - M_Y)$$

The technique we have been describing is known as **ordinary least squares (OLS)** regression. There are other kinds of regression (such as logistic regression) that do not work in this way. It is not our intention here to present a comprehensive account of regression, simple or complex. There are, however, certain features that are common to all types of regression and therefore particularly deserving of attention.

12.1.4   Regression and correlation

In view of the foregoing considerations, especially the similarity of the formulae involved, one might expect the regression and correlation formulae to be intimately related. In fact, they are. The regression coefficient b_1 is directly proportional to the correlation coefficient r_{XY} thus:

$$b_1 = r_{XY} \frac{s_Y}{s_X} \quad \text{--- (4)}$$

**Relation between the regression coefficient
and the Pearson correlation**

It is clear from formula (4) that the regression and correlation coefficients must always have the same sign. In Figure 4, are shown scatterplots showing positive and negative associations. Notice that the regression and correlation coefficients have the same sign in each plot.

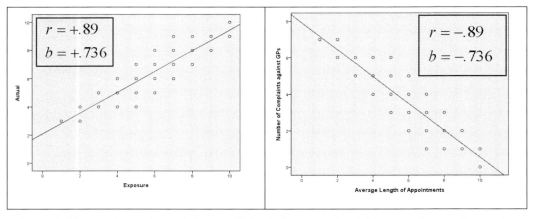

Figure 4. Regression and correlation coefficients for pairs of variables showing positive and negative association

Figure 5 shows the scatterplot of two uncorrelated variables, namely, two random samples of 10,000 values from a normal population with a mean of 100 and a standard deviation of 25. As expected, the scatterplot is circular, which is characteristic of dissociated variables. Notice that, in this case, the regression line is horizontal: its slope is zero, as indicated by the value of the regression coefficient.

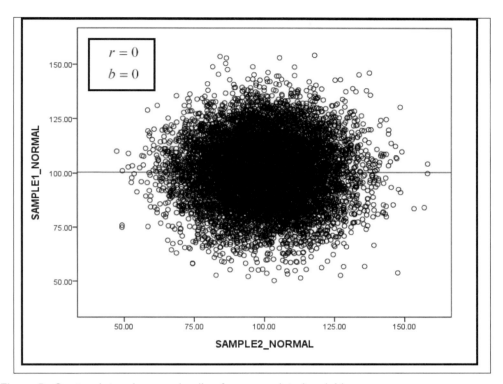

Figure 5. Scatterplot and regression line for uncorrelated variables

12.1.5   The coefficient of determination revisited

In Chapter 11, it was observed that the **coefficient of determination (*CD*)** can be represented diagrammatically as the proportion of overlap between two circles, the total area of each circle representing 100% of the variance of one of the variables (Figure 6). In this section, we shall review the coefficient of determination in terms of regression rather than correlation.

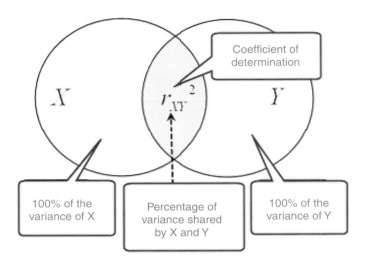

Figure 6. Diagrammatic representation of the coefficient of determination (CD)

12.1.5.1 Partition of the sum of squares of the DV in regression

In Chapter 7, we saw that, although a variance estimate is made by dividing a sum of squares by its degrees of freedom, we can, for the purposes of comparison within the same data set, regard the sums of squares of the treatment and error terms in the ANOVA as measures of spread or dispersion in their own right.

We have already seen (Figure 3) that the total deviation score on variable Y can be partitioned according to equation (5).

$$Y - M_Y \quad = \quad \left(Y' - M_Y\right) \quad + \quad \left(Y - Y'\right)$$

$$\begin{bmatrix} \text{total} \\ \text{deviation} \end{bmatrix} \quad \begin{bmatrix} \text{regression} \\ \text{component} \end{bmatrix} \quad \begin{bmatrix} \text{residual} \\ \text{component } (e) \end{bmatrix} \text{--- (5)}$$

Breakdown of the total deviation score on Y

It can be shown that if the squares of these deviation scores are summed over all the participants in the study, the sum of squares for the dependent variable Y can be broken down into regression and residual components according to the following equation:

$$SS_Y = SS_{\text{regression}} + SS_{\text{residual}} \quad \text{--- (6)}$$

**Partition of the sum of squares of the DV
in simple regression**

In words, equation (6) states that the total spread of scores on the dependent variable is the sum of an error or residual component and a regression component.

The breakdown in equation (6) is strongly reminiscent of the partition of the total sum of squares in the ANOVA. As in that equation, the cross-product terms disappear, basically because deviations about the mean sum to zero.

12.1.5.2 Degrees of freedom of the regression sums of squares

The degrees of freedom of SS_Y can be partitioned in a manner similar to the sum of squares:

$$df_Y = df_{regression} + df_{residual}$$
$$(n-1) \qquad\qquad 1 \qquad\qquad (n-2) \quad \text{--- (7)}$$

Partition of the degrees of freedom of the DV

If we assume that there are n (X,Y) pairs in the data set, the degrees of freedom of SS_Y is $(n-1)$, because the specification of $(n-1)$ deviations from M_Y fixes the remaining deviation. The element of the residual degrees of freedom is $Y - Y' = Y - M_Y - b_1(X - M_X)$, from which it is clear that TWO parameters have been estimated: M_Y and b_1. As a result, another degree of freedom is lost and so the residual sum of squares has $(n-2)$ degrees of freedom. This leaves only one degree of freedom for the regression sum of squares.

The degrees of freedom of the residual or error sum of squares is important in formal statistical tests of the estimates of the regression parameters.

12.1.5.3 The coefficient of determination again

It is clear from equation (6) that if the points in the scatterplot all lie along a straight line, the residual sum of squares would be zero and the regression sum of squares would be equal to SS_Y. If, on the other hand, the scatterplot shows dissociation, then the regression sum of squares would be zero and SS_Y would consist entirely of error variance. The coefficient of determination (CD) expresses the regression sum of squares as a proportion of SS_Y and can be shown to be given by the square of the Pearson correlation:

$$CD = r^2 = \frac{SS_{regression}}{SS_Y} \quad \text{--- (8)}$$

The coefficient of determination

The Pearson correlation between the Actual and Exposure scores is .89. The value of the coefficient of determination is therefore $.89^2 = .80$. This means that 80% of the variance of Actual scores is accounted for by regression of Actual violence upon Exposure to violent programmes.

In the coefficient of determination, we have a useful measure of effect size applicable to regression. In Table 1, we reproduce part of a table from Chapter 11, which offers a rough guide to the classification of effect size in regression.

Table 1. Guidelines (from Cohen, 1988) for classifying association strength, as measured by a correlation coefficient and the coefficient of determination

Absolute value of r	r squared	Size of effect
$.1 \leq \lvert r \rvert < .30$	$.01 \leq r^2 < .09$	Small
$.30 \leq \lvert r \rvert < .50$	$.09 \leq r^2 < .25$	Medium
$\lvert r \rvert \geq .50$	$r^2 \geq .25$	Large

12.1.6   Shrinkage with resampling

So far, all the statistics we have described refer to a single sample of scores. The purpose of the regression exercise, however, is ultimately to generalise beyond our data to the bivariate population or joint distribution of Actual violence and Exposure, which can be visualised as a scatterplot with an infinite number of points.   The statistics of our sample, including the coefficient of determination, will tend to overstate the predictive power of regression in the population, with the consequence that predictive power will be lost if the regression equation we have just arrived at is re-applied to a fresh data set. This loss in predictive power with re-sampling is known as **shrinkage**. The *CD*, as calculated from a set of data, is positively biased as an estimate of the corresponding parameter (population value).   In practice, where we are attempting to generalise beyond our own data to the population, we need to use the degrees of freedom of the relevant statistics to adjust the value of r^2 downwards to remove its positive bias.   This is the reason for the 'adjustment' referred to in the SPSS output for various regression-related routines; in fact, **adjusted R^2** is referred to by some authors as '**shrunken R^2**'.

12.1.7   Beta-weights

The **beta weight** β_1 is the slope of the regression line when the DV and IV have both been transformed to the standardised variables z_Y and z_X , respectively, where

$$z_Y = \frac{Y - M_Y}{s_Y} \text{ and } z_X = \frac{X - M_X}{s_X} \text{ --- (9)}$$

Standardised variables

It follows immediately from (3) that since the mean and standard deviation of a set of standardised scores are 0 and 1, respectively, the intercept in the regression equation of z_Y upon z_X is zero and the regression equation of z_Y upon z_X is

$$z'_Y = \beta_1 z_x \text{ --- (10)}$$

Standardised form of the simple regression equation

where z'_Y , a point on the regression line, is the estimate of the observed standard score z_Y for a particular value of z_X.

The slope β_1 of the standardised form of the regression equation is the average change in the DV Y, measured in standard deviation units, produced by an increase of one standard deviation in the IV or regressor X. The beta-weight therefore has the advantage of providing a unit-free measure of the slope of the regression line.

We have seen that the slope of the regression line is directly proportional to the Pearson correlation, the constant being the ratio of the standard deviations of Y and X. Since the standard deviations of z_Y and z_X are both unity, the slope of the standardised regression line is simply the Pearson correlation r and we can write:

$$z'_Y = \beta_1 z_X = r z_X \; \text{- - -} \; (11)$$

Identity of beta with r in
the standardised simple regression equation

12.1.8   Effects of linear transformations on the correlation and regression coefficients

It would be most unsatisfactory if, having calculated the correlation between the heights and weights of a hundred people, measured in inches and pounds, respectively, we were to find that the correlation changed when the measurements were converted to centimetres and kilograms! It would not, of course: a *linear* transformation of either X or Y leaves the *absolute* value of the correlation unaltered; if the slope of the transformation is negative, however, the sign of the correlation changes. For example, if the correlation between X and Y is $+ .6$, the correlation between X and $100Y$ is still $+ .6$; but the correlation between X and $- 100Y$ is $- .6$.

12.1.9   Significance testing in simple regression

In Chapter 11, we saw that, provided the data have a bivariate normal distribution, the null hypothesis of independence (which states that in the population, the correlation is zero) can be tested with the statistic t on $(n - 2)$ degrees of freedom, where

$$t = \frac{r\sqrt{(n-2)}}{\sqrt{(1-r^2)}} \; \text{- - -} \; (12)$$

***t* test for the significance of a correlation**

We have seen that the Pearson correlation r is closely related to the regression coefficient b_1, so that the value of one fully determines that of the other:

$$r = b_1\left(\frac{s_Y}{s_X}\right)$$

A test of the significance of the sample correlation r, therefore, is also a test of the significance of the regression coefficient b_1. The testing of a regression coefficient for significance can be approached in two equivalent ways:

1.   Make a point estimate of the population value and divide that by an estimate of the standard error of the regression coefficient to produce a t statistic.

2. Use the ANOVA to test the coefficient of determination for significance. In simple regression (one IV), $F = t^2$.

In the t test approach, the test statistic t, on $(n-2)$ degrees of freedom, is

$$t = \frac{b_1}{s_{b_1}} \quad \text{---} \ (13)$$

t test for the significance of the regression coefficient

where the standard error estimate in the denominator is given by

$$s_{b_1} = \sqrt{\frac{SS_{\text{residual}} / (n-2)}{SS_X}} \quad \text{---} \ (14)$$

Standard error of the regression coefficient

In the ANOVA approach, the test statistic is

$$F\left(1, df_{\text{residual}}\right) = \frac{MS_{\text{regression}}}{MS_{\text{residual}}} = \frac{SS_{\text{regression}} / 1}{SS_{\text{residual}} / (n-2)} = \frac{SS_{\text{regression}} (n-2)}{SS_{\text{residual}}} \quad \text{---} \ (15)$$

F test for the significance of the regression coefficient

remembering that the residual sum of squares has $(n-2)$ degrees of freedom (Section 12.1.5.2).

Since $SS_{\text{regression}} = r^2 SS_Y$ and $SS_{\text{residual}} = \left(1 - r^2\right) SS_Y$, we see that

$$F\left(1, df_{\text{residual}}\right) = \frac{r^2 SS_Y (n-2)}{\left(1 - r^2\right) SS_Y} = \frac{r^2 (n-2)}{\left(1 - r^2\right)} \quad \text{---} \ (16)$$

The F statistic as a function of the correlation

Notice that (16) is t^2 (compare formula 12). In words, the value of t fully determines that of F, and vice versa, because $F = t^2$. The two tests are exact equivalents.

12.2   SIMPLE REGRESSION WITH SPSS

As always, we recommend that you should get to know your data before making any formal statistical tests. In regression, as well as correlation, the graphical approach is the best way of doing this. In this example, we shall want to see the scatterplot and regression line first.

12.2.1   Drawing scatterplots with regression lines

Our starting point is the scatterplot of Actual violence upon Exposure (Figure 1). To add a regression line to this scatterplot, double-click on the plot to enter the **Chart Editor**, then click on the icon marked by the white cursor in Figure 7 labelled **Add Fit Line at Total**.

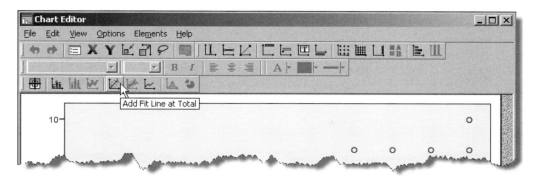

Figure 7. Choosing **Fit Line at Total** to draw the regression line

Clicking on **Fit Line at Total** will access the **Properties** dialog box, in which the **Linear** radio button is checked as the default setting. Close the **Properties** dialog box to see the regression line (Output 1).

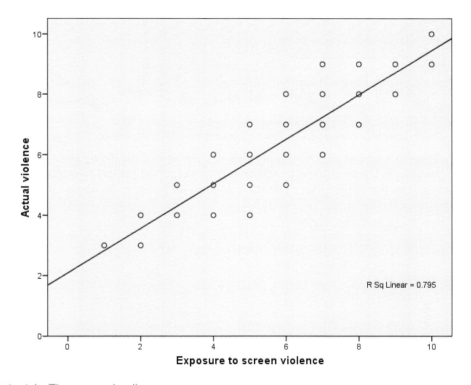

Output 1. The regression line

In Output 1, the vertical axis has been displaced slightly to the left, with the result that the intercept appears to be nearer the origin that the correct value of 2.09 (the intercept or regression constant). To rectify this, enter the **Chart Editor** again and click the icon labelled **Add a reference line to the X axis** (Output 2).

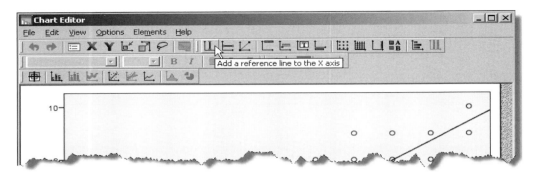

Output 2. Adding a vertical reference line to the X axis

Clicking this icon will access the **Properties** dialog box (Figure 8).

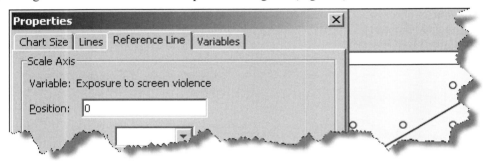

Figure 8. The **Properties** dialog box for drawing a vertical reference line on the X axis

Set the **Position** to zero and click the **Apply** button at the foot of the dialog box. The graph will now appear as in Output 3. The regression line intercepts the vertical reference line 2.09 units above zero on the vertical axis. The value 2.09, as we know, is the correct value of the intercept.

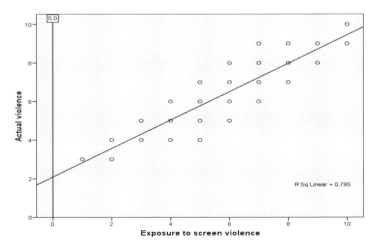

Output 3. Scatterplot with regression line and vertical reference line above the zero point on the X axis

12.2.2   A problem in simple regression

In some North American universities, there is concern with the efficacy of the methods used to select students for entry. How closely are scores on the entrance tests and final exam results associated? If there is an association, how accurately can we predict university performance from students' marks on the entrance tests?

Given that we have each student's final exam mark and entrance test mark, a Pearson correlation can be used to measure the degree of statistical association between these two variables. Simple regression can be used to predict final exam performance from marks on the entrance test.

12.2.3   Procedure for simple regression

In Table 2, the score Fin is a student's mark in the Final University Exam, and Ent is the same student's mark in the Entrance Exam. The full data set is available at www.psypress.com/spss-made-simple, so only the first 2 cases are shown in Table 2.

Table 2. Table of the Final University Exam (Fin) and the Entrance Exam (Ent) scores

Case	Fin	Ent	Case	Fin	Ent	Case	Fin	Ent	Case	Fin	Ent
1	38	44	10	81	53	19	105	43	28	142	56
2	49	40	11	86	47	20	106	55	29	145	60
3	6		12	91		21	107	48		50	

The table contains the marks of 34 students: Student 1 (whose data are in the first row of the first two columns from the left) got 44 in the Entrance Exam and 38 in the Final University Exam. Student 34, on the other hand, (whose data are shown in the seventh row of the last two columns on the right), got 49 in the Entrance Exam and 195 in the Final University Exam.

12.2.3.1   Preparing the SPSS data set

Using the techniques described in Chapter 2, Section 2.3, enter **Variable View** and name the variables *Case*, *FinalExam* and *EntranceExam*. In the **Label** column, add more informative variable labels such as *Case Number*, *Final University Exam* and *Entrance Exam*. In **Data View**, enter the data in the pre-labelled columns.

> See
> Section
> 2.3

12.2.3.2   Exploring the data

Normally the user would explore the data to check for incorrect entries and examine the scatterplot to detect any outliers. Here, in the interests of brevity, we shall proceed directly with the regression analysis and rely upon the regression procedure itself to find any problem cases.

12.2.3.3   Running simple regression

- Choose **Analyze➔Regression** (see Figure 9) and click **Linear...** to open the **Linear Regression** dialog box (the completed dialog is shown in Figure 10).
- Transfer the variable names as shown in Figure 10, taking care to select the appropriate variable names for the dependent variable (target) and the independent variable (regressor).

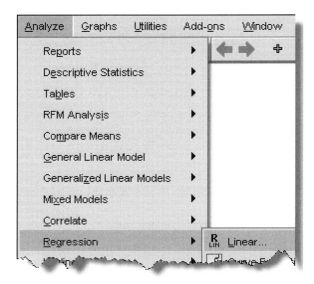

Figure 9. Finding the **Linear Regression** procedure

- Request additional descriptive statistics and a residuals analysis by clicking the **Statistics...** button to open the **Linear Regression: Statistics** dialog box (Figure 11) and activating the **Descriptives** checkbox. Analysis of the residuals gives a measure of how good the prediction is and whether there are any cases that are so discrepant as to be considered outliers and perhaps dropped from the analysis. Click the **Casewise diagnostics** checkbox to include a listing of any exceptionally large residuals in the output. Click **Continue** to return to the **Linear Regression** dialog box.
- Since systematic associations between the predicted values and the residuals can indicate violations of the assumption of linearity, we also recommend that a plot of the standardised residuals (*ZRESID) against the standardised predicted values (*ZPRED) should be requested. Click **Plots...** to open the **Linear Regression: Plots** dialog box (Figure 12) and transfer *ZRESID to the **Y:** box and *ZPRED to the **X:** box. Click **Continue** to return to the **Linear Regression** dialog box.
- Back in the **Linear Regression** dialog box, predicted values and residuals can be saved to **Data View** by clicking the **Save...** button. Click **OK** to run the regression.

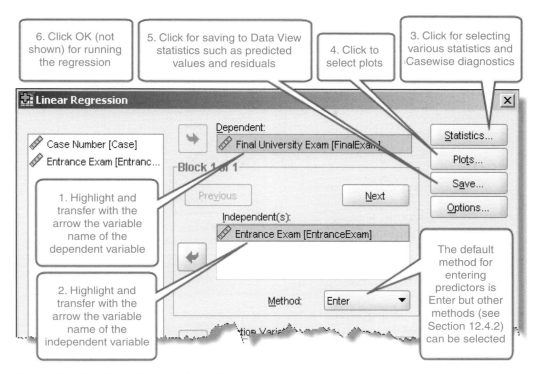

Figure 10. The **Linear Regression** dialog box

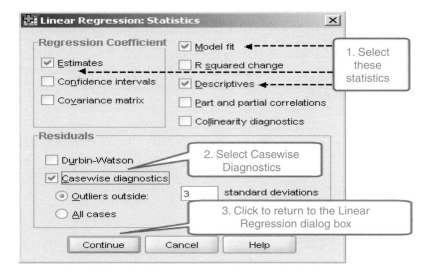

Figure 11. The **Statistics** dialog box with extra options **Descriptives** and **Casewise diagnostics** selected

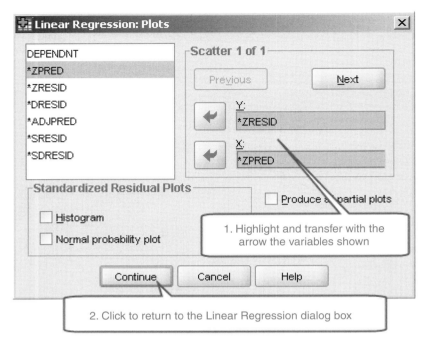

Figure 12. The **Plots** dialog box with *ZRESID (standardised residuals) and *ZPRED (standardised predicted scores) selected for the axes of the plot

12.2.4   Output for simple regression

The various tables and charts in the output are listed as icons in the left-hand pane of **SPSS Statistics Viewer**, as shown in Output 4. After the requested descriptive statistics and correlations (plus several other tables), the first table to scrutinise is **Casewise Diagnostics**. The information it contains may indicate that the regression analysis should be terminated and re-run after outliers have been removed from the data set. The table can be selected directly by moving the cursor to **Casewise Diagnostics** in the left-hand pane and clicking the left-hand mouse button.

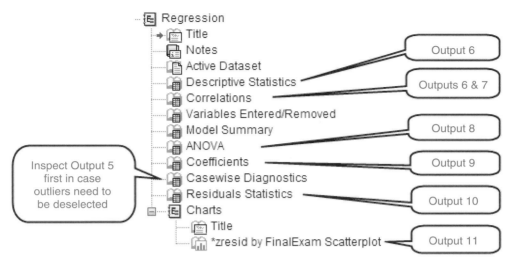

Output 4. The left-hand pane of the Output Viewer listing the tables and charts in the right-hand pane

12.2.4.1   Indication of residual outliers

The table of cases (**Casewise Diagnostics**) in Output 5 shows only one outlier with an absolute standardised residual greater than 3. This is Case 34, with a score of 195 for Final University Exam. From past experience, this is a suspiciously high mark and is almost certainly a typo; moreover, the candidate concerned managed a mark of only 49 in the entrance exam, which did not show great promise. The next section describes how to eliminate this outlier and re-run the regression analysis.

Casewise Diagnostics [a]

Case Number	Std. Residual	Final University Exam	Predicted Value	Residual
34	3.12	195	110.95	84.05

a. Dependent Variable: Final University Exam

Output 5. A list of cases with residuals greater than ± 3 standard deviations

12.2.4.2   Elimination of outliers

A more robust regression analysis can be obtained by eliminating suspicious outliers. Use the **Select Cases** procedure described in Section 3.3.1.

See Section 3.3.1

- Choose **Data➔Select Cases…** to open the **Select Cases** dialog box.
- Click the **If condition is satisfied** radio button and define the condition as *Case ~=34* (the symbol ~= means 'not equal to').
- Click **Continue** and then **OK** to deselect this case.

If there are several suspicious outliers (arising from the same systematic typographical error, perhaps), it might be simpler to deselect them all by using a cut-off value for one of the variables (e.g. defining the condition with an inequality operator, as in the specification: *FinalExam* > 190). Sometimes, in order to see what value to use in the inequality, it is convenient to arrange scores in order of value by entering the **Data** menu and choosing **Sort Cases…** .

When the regression analysis is re-run after deleting the original output, there will be no table of **Casewise Diagnostics**, since no cases will now have outlying residuals. We can therefore begin with the various tables and plots in the output. In Output 6, are the tables of descriptive statistics and the correlation coefficient for the 33 cases remaining in the data set.

Descriptive Statistics

	Mean	Std. Deviation	N
Final University Exam	102.82	32.633	33
Entrance Exam	47.27	7.539	33

Correlations

		Final University Exam	Entrance Exam
Pearson Correlation	Final University Exam	1.00	.73
	Entrance Exam	.73	1.00
Sig. (1-tailed)	Final University Exam	.	.00
	Entrance Exam	.00	.
N	Final University Exam	33	33
	Entrance Exam	33	33

Output 6. The **Descriptive Statistics** and **Correlations** tables for the data set without the outlier

Output 7 gives the value of **Multiple R**, where **R** is the **multiple correlation coefficient**. We shall explain the meaning of **R** fully when we discuss multiple regression; here we shall simply note that, in this example, R is equal to the Pearson correlation between scores on the two examinations.

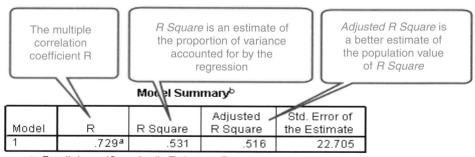

The multiple correlation coefficient R

R Square is an estimate of the proportion of variance accounted for by the regression

Adjusted R Square is a better estimate of the population value of R Square

Model Summary^b

Model	R	R Square	Adjusted R Square	Std. Error of the Estimate
1	.729ᵃ	.531	.516	22.705

a. Predictors: (Constant), Entrance Exam

b. Dependent Variable: Final University Exam

Output 7. The values of the multiple correlation coefficient *R* and other statistics

In general, when, as in the present example, there is only one regressor, **R** is the *absolute value* of the Pearson correlation between the DV or criterion and the IV or regressor. Had the correlation between the two exams been negative, the value of R would still have been .729 .

The other statistics listed in Output 7 are the coefficient of determination **R Square** (a positively biased estimate of the proportion of the variance of the dependent variable accounted for by regression), **Adjusted R Square** (which corrects this bias and therefore has a lower value than the coefficient of determination), and the **Standard Error of the Estimate** (the standard deviation of the residuals). The **effect size**, as estimated by **adjusted R^2** is .516 (52%). This, following Cohen's classification, is a 'large' effect.

Output 8 shows the regression ANOVA, which tests for a linear relationship between the variables. The **F** statistic is the ratio of the mean square for regression to the residual mean square. In this example, the value of **F** in the ANOVA Table is significant beyond the .01 level. *It should be noted, however, that only an examination of the scatterplot can confirm that the relationship between two variables is genuinely linear.*

The value of *F* and its associated p-value (significant at the .01 level)

ANOVA^b

Model		Sum of Squares	df	Mean Square	F	Sig.
1	Regression	18096.33	1	18096.3	35.10	.000^a
	Residual	15980.58	31	515.50		
	Total	34076.91	32			

a. Predictors: (Constant), Entrance Exam

b. Dependent Variable: Final University Exam

Output 8. The **ANOVA** for the regression

Output 9 presents the kernel of the regression analysis, the regression equation. The values of the **regression coefficient** and **constant** are given in column **B** of the table. Two further features of Output 9 are worthy of note. In the column headed 'Standardized Coefficients', there is no entry in the row labelled 'Constant'. This is because, as we have seen, the intercept of the regression equation disappears when the scores are standardised. In the same column, the regression coefficient is given as .73, which is the value of the Pearson correlation r because, as we have seen, when the variables are standardised, the slope of the regression line is the Pearson correlation.

Coefficients^a

Model		Unstandardized Coefficients		Standardized Coefficients	t	Sig.
		B	Std. Error	Beta		
1	(Constant)	-46.30	25.48		-1.82	.079
	Entrance Exam	3.15	.53	.73	5.92	.000

a. Dependent Variable: Final University Exam

The regression equation includes this constant and coefficient	*Beta* is the regression coefficient when all the variables are expressed in standardised form	This tests the null hypothesis that there is no linear relationship between the variables (i.e. H_0 states that the regression coefficient is 0)

Output 9. The regression equation and associated statistics

From the values for the intercept and slope given in Output 9, the regression equation is

$$(\text{Final University Exam})' = -46.30 + 3.15 \times (\text{Entrance Exam})$$

where (Final University Exam)$'$ is the predicted value of the actual Final University Exam mark. Thus a person scoring 60 in the Entrance Exam would have a predicted Final mark of

$$-46.30 + 3.15 \times 60 = 142.7 \quad (\text{i.e. } 143).$$

Notice that in Table 2, the person who scored 60 on the Entrance Exam actually scored 145 on the Final University Exam. So $Y' = 143$ and $Y = 145$. The residual $e = (Y - Y')$ is

$$145 - 143 = +2.$$

Other statistics are also listed in Output 9. The **Std. Error** is the standard error of the regression coefficient, B. **Beta** is the beta coefficient, which is the estimated average change in the dependent variable (expressed in standard deviation units) that would be produced by a positive increment of one standard deviation in the independent variable. The t statistic tests the regression coefficient for significance, and **Sig.** is the p-value of t. (Here .00 means $< .01$, i.e. t is significant beyond the .01 level for the variable Entrance Exam. Write this p-value as '$<.01$', not as '.00'.)

Output 10 is a table of the statistics of the residuals. The row labelled **Predicted Value** summarises the unstandardised predicted values. The row labelled **Residual** summarises the unstandardised residuals. The row labelled **Std. Predicted Value** (identified as *ZPRED in the **Plots** dialog box in Figure 12) summarises the standardised predicted values (i.e. Predicted Value transformed to a scale with mean 0 and SD 1). You can see that the calculated value for the SD (.98) is approximately 1. The row labelled **Std. Residual** (identified as *ZRESID in the **Plots** dialog box in Figure 12) summarises the standardised residuals (with mean = 0 and SD = 1).

Residuals Statistics [a]

	Minimum	Maximum	Mean	Std. Deviation	N
Predicted Value	60.95	152.43	102.82	23.780	33
Residual	-54.49	30.97	.00	22.35	33
Std. Predicted Value	-1.76	2.09	.00	1.00	33
Std. Residual	-2.40	1.36	.00	.98	33

a. Dependent Variable: Final University Exam

Output 10. Table of statistics relating to the residuals

Output 11 is the scatterplot of the standardised residuals (*ZRESID) against the standardised predicted values (*ZPRED). The plot shows an essentially shapeless pattern, thereby confirming that the assumptions of linearity and homogeneity of variance are tenable. A crescent-shape or a 'funnel' would have indicated that a linear regression model was not a convincing interpretation of the data.

Other diagnostic plots could have been selected from within the **Standardized Residual Plots** box in Figure 12: for example, we could obtained a histogram of the standardised residuals (see Output 11) and a cumulative normal probability plot (in which, ideally, the points should lie along or adjacent to the diagonal).

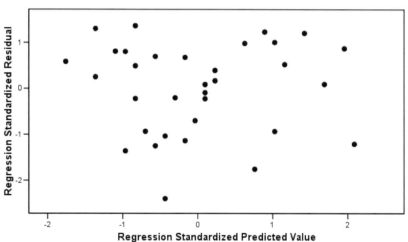

Output 11. Scatterplot of standardised residuals against standardised predicted scores

12.3 MULTIPLE REGRESSION

In **multiple regression**, the values of one variable (the dependent variable, target or criterion, Y) are estimated from those of two or more (in the general case, p) independent variables or regressors $(X_1, X_2, ..., X_p)$. This is achieved by the construction of a **multiple linear regression equation** of the general form:

$$Y' = b_0 + b_1 X_1 + b_2 X_2 + \ldots + b_p X_p \quad \text{- - -} \quad (17)$$

Multiple linear regression equation

where the parameters b_1, b_2, ..., b_p are the **partial regression coefficients** and the intercept b_0 is the **regression constant**. This equation is known as the **multiple linear regression equation of Y upon X_1, X_2, ... X_p.**

In simple regression, where there is only one IV or regressor, the graph of the regression equation is a straight line. In multiple regression, where there are two or more IVs, the graph is a plane or an abstract generalisation of a plane known in mathematics as a **hyperplane**.

Associated with each IV or regressor is a **partial regression coefficient**, which is the average change in the criterion variable that would be produced by a positive increase of one unit in the IV, with all the other IVs being held constant. Consider the partial regression coefficient b_1. Suppose we were to fix the values of all variables except regressor X_1, regress the criterion Y upon X_1 and calculate the regression coefficient. If we were to do this for every possible combination of fixed values for the other regressors and average the regression coefficients, we should have the partial regression coefficient b_1.

12.3.1   The multiple correlation coefficient R

One simple measure of the efficacy of regression for the prediction of Y is the Pearson correlation between the true values of the target variable Y and the estimates Y' obtained from the multiple regression equation. The correlation between Y and Y' is known as the **multiple correlation coefficient R**. Notice that the upper case is used for the multiple correlation coefficient, to distinguish it from the correlation between the DV and any one IV considered separately.

12.3.1.1   Range of the multiple correlation coefficient

Returning for a moment to simple regression, where there is only one IV, recall that, while a linear transformation of one of the variables in a correlation leaves the absolute value of the correlation unaltered, a negative slope changes the sign of the correlation. Even in simple regression, the multiple correlation coefficient is defined, because R is simply the correlation between the predictions from regression, Y', that is, a linear function of the IV (X), and Y, the true values of the scores on the DV. The linear function Y', as we have seen, must always have the same sign as the correlation. The value of R can never be negative, because if the Pearson correlation is negative, the negative sign of the regression coefficient ensures that the correlation between Y and Y' is positive in that case also. This is true however many IVs there may be in the regression equation. The multiple correlation R, therefore, unlike the Pearson correlation, can only take values in the range from 0 to +1, inclusive. (In practice, with measured variables, neither of these theoretical limits is ever achieved.)

As in simple regression, a measure of **effect size** in multiple regression is provided by the **coefficient of determination R^2** which, by analogy with bivariate regression, is the proportion of variance in the dependent variable that can be accounted for by regression upon the independent variables or regressors. The positive bias in R^2 is reduced in the statistic known as **adjusted R^2**.

12.3.2   Significance testing in multiple regression

Statistical testing is more complex in multiple regression than it is in simple regression. As in simple regression, an overall F test can be made of the null hypothesis of complete independence. In multiple correlation, however, the significance of F does not imply that any one of the partial regression coefficients is significant. Another problem is that when there are two or more correlated IVs, it is impossible to attribute variance in the DV unequivocally to any particular IV, without additional collateral evidence or a well-conceived and empirically supported causal model.

If we assume that there are p independent variables, the (very unlikely) null hypothesis that all the regression coefficients are zero is, by analogy with (16), tested with the statistic

$$F\left(p, df_{\text{residual}}\right) = \frac{MS_{\text{regression}}}{MS_{\text{residual}}} = \frac{SS_{\text{regression}} / p}{SS_{\text{residual}} / (n-1-p)} = \frac{R^2(n-1-p)}{(1-R^2)p} \quad \text{--- (18)}$$

**F ratio for testing the null hypothesis
that all regression coefficients are zero**

By way of explanation of the rightmost term in (18), recall that in simple regression, the regression sum of squares has one degree of freedom, so that the residual sum of squares has ($n - 1 - 1$) = ($n - 2$) degrees of freedom. When there are p independent variables or regressors in the regression equation, the degrees of freedom are ($n - 1 - $p).

Associated with the independent variable X_k is the regression coefficient b_k. The null hypothesis that, in the population, this regression coefficient is zero is tested with the statistic

$$t_k = \frac{b_k}{s_{b_k}} \quad \text{where } s_{b_k} = \sqrt{\frac{SS_{\text{residual}} / (n-1-p)}{SS_{X_k}(1-R^2)}} \quad \text{--- (19)}$$

t test for significance of a partial regression coefficient

where the s_{b_k} is the estimated standard error of the partial regression coefficient b_k. Here, R is the multiple correlation coefficient between the DV and the estimates from regression Y' when all p IVs or regressors are in the regression equation.

Provided various assumptions are met, this statistic is distributed as t on ($n - 1 - p$) degrees of freedom. Formula (19) is an obvious generalisation from the case of one IV (formula 13) to the case of p IVs.

12.3.3   Partial and semipartial correlation

12.3.3.1   Partial correlation

We made the acquaintance of partial correlation in Chapter 11. The **partial correlation** between two variables is what remains of the association between them when their associations with a third variable have been taken into account. Consider the multiple regression of Y (the DV) upon X_1 and X_2 (the IVs). Let e_Y and e_1 be the residuals of Y and X_1 when both variables are regressed upon the other independent variable X_2. The correlation between the residuals e_Y

and e_1 is the partial correlation between Y and X_1. In Chapter 11, we saw that this correlation is readily obtained from the values of the correlations among the three variables.

In this chapter, we shall denote the partial correlation between Y and X_1 by using subscript notation thus $r_{Y1.2}$. In the subscript, the IV or regressor on the right of the point has been removed or 'partialled out' of the variables on the left of the point: i.e., X_2 has been removed from both Y and X_1.

We gave a formula for the partial correlation in Chapter 11. Amending the notation to apply to the present (regression) situation, the partial correlation $r_{Y1.2}$ is given by

$$r_{Y1.2} = \frac{r_{Y1} - r_{Y2}.r_{12}}{\sqrt{(1 - r_{Y2}^2)(1 - r_{12}^2)}} \quad \text{--- (20) } \textbf{Partial correlation}$$

The partial correlation is tested for significance with

$$t = \frac{r\sqrt{(n-3)}}{\sqrt{(1 - r^2)}} \quad \text{--- (21) } t \textbf{ test for significance of partial correlation}$$

on $(n - 3)$ degrees of freedom. A degree of freedom has been lost from the residual variance because an additional regression coefficient has been estimated.

12.3.3.2   Semipartial (or part) correlation

Since in multiple regression we are trying to account for the variance of the DV in terms of regression upon two or more IVs, interest centres upon the proportion of the *total* variance of the DV that is accounted for, rather than the residual variance when the effects of other variables have been removed. To determine this proportion, we need to know the correlation between Y and the residual variance of X_1 after the influence of X_2 has been removed from X_1 only. The **semipartial** (or **part**) **correlation** between Y and the residuals of X_1 after the influence of X_2 has been removed is written as $r_{Y(1.2)}$. In the subscript of r, $Y(1.2)$, the dot between the numbers 1 and 2 inside the brackets indicates that X_2 has been partialled out of X_1, but not of Y.

The semipartial correlation $r_{Y(1.2)}$ is given by

$$r_{Y(1.2)} = \frac{r_{Y1} - r_{Y2}.r_{12}}{\sqrt{(1 - r_{12}^2)}} \quad \text{--- (22) } \textbf{Semipartial correlation}$$

The formulae for the partial and semipartial correlations are very similar. The only difference is the additional factor in the denominator of the partial correlation, which ensures that its value is always at least as great as that of the semipartial correlation. Generally, the value of the partial correlation will be greater: it is highly unlikely that either Y or X_1 will show a correlation of exactly zero with X_2, in which case the partial and semipartial correlations would have the same value. The semipartial correlation can be tested for significance in the same way as the partial correlation. If, however, the partial correlation is significant, so also must be the semipartial correlation and vice versa.

Figure 13 depicts the relationships among the three variables when Y is regressed upon two independent variables X_1 and X_2.

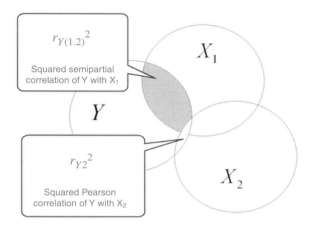

Figure 13. Variance interpretation of the semipartial correlation

Figure 13 shows that the square of the *semipartial* correlation $r^2_{Y(1.2)}$ (the grey area) is the additional proportion of the *total* variance of Y that is accounted for when the independent variable X_1 is added to the regression equation of Y upon X_2. The square of the *partial* correlation $r^2_{Y1.2}$, on the other hand, is the proportion of the *unexplained* variance of Y (the residuals when Y is regressed upon X_2) that is accounted for when X_1 is added to the regression equation. In the figure, the partial correlation is the grey area divided, not by 100% (the area of the whole circle), but by the area of the circle from which the white area of overlap has been subtracted. (The denominator of the partial correlation is thus smaller, making its value greater than that of the semipartial correlation.)

The foregoing notation for the semipartial correlation generalises to any number of independent variables. Suppose there are, not two but four independent variables X_1, X_2, X_3, X_4 and that we regress X_1 upon the other independent variables X_2, X_3, X_4. The semipartial correlation of Y with X_1 is the correlation between Y and the residuals of X_1 when X_2, X_3 and X_4 have been removed by multiple regression. This semipartial correlation is written as $r_{Y(1.234)}$, the subscripts 234 to the right of the point and the brackets signifying that the effects of X_2, X_3, X_4 have been removed from X_1 but not from Y.

If we regress Y upon two independent variables X_1 and X_2, the Pearson correlation between Y and the estimates from regression Y' is the multiple correlation coefficient, which we shall write as $R_{Y.12}$. In this expression, the subscript '$Y.12$' indicates that Y is being correlated with a function of X_1, X_2 (the linear regression function). As we have seen, the square of the multiple correlation $R^2_{Y.12}$ is the proportion of the total variance of the dependent variable Y that is accounted for by regression upon the independent variables X_1 and X_2 and is known as the **coefficient of determination**.

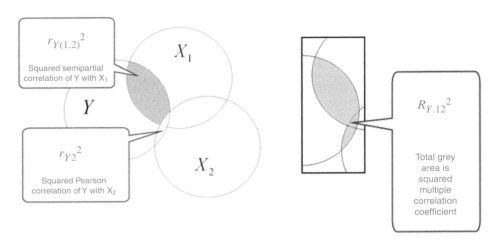

Figure 14. Relation between total proportion of variance accounted for by regression (R^2) and the squared semipartial correlation

In Figure 14, the total grey area in the right part of the figure is the coefficient of determination, that is, the total proportion of the variance of Y that is accounted for by multiple regression upon the two independent variables. The left-hand part of Figure 14 shows that the coefficient of determination can be partitioned into two components:

1.   The square of the Pearson correlation between Y and X_2;
2.   The squared semipartial correlation between Y and the residuals of X_1 after regression of X_1 upon X_2. We can therefore write

$$R^2_{Y.12} = r_{Y2}^2 + r_{Y(1.2)}^2 \; \text{--- (23) \textbf{Partition of } } R^2_{Y.12}$$

We can also partition the coefficient of determination $R^2_{Y.12}$ as if the initial regression had been Y upon X_1 as follows:

$$R^2_{Y.12} = r_{Y1}^2 + r_{Y(2.1)}^2 \; \text{--- (24) \textbf{Alternative partition of } } R^2_{Y.12}$$

where $r^2_{2.1}$ is the squared semipartial correlation between Y and the residuals of X_2 after regression upon X_1.

12.3.3.5   Obtaining semipartial correlations from multiple correlations: ΔR^2

We now consider a more complex example, in which there are four independent variables X_1, X_2, X_3, X_4. In this case, the multiple correlation coefficient is $R_{Y.1234}$, the subscripts indicating that the dependent variable Y is being correlated with a linear function of X_1, X_2, X_3, X_4.

We can partition the squared multiple correlation $R^2_{Y.1234}$ as follows:

$$R^2_{Y.1234} = r_{Y4}^2 + r_{Y(3.4)}^2 + r_{Y(2.34)}^2 + r_{Y(1.234)}^2 \; \text{--- (25) \textbf{Partition of } } R^2_{Y.1234}$$

The first three terms on the right of equation (25), however, are a partition of the squared multiple correlation when Y is regressed upon the three independent variables X_2, X_3, X_4:

$$r_{Y4}^2 + r_{Y(3.4)}^2 + r_{Y(2.34)}^2 = R_{Y.234}^2 \quad \text{- - -} (26) \; \textbf{Partition of } \boldsymbol{R_{Y.234}^2}$$

We may therefore express the squared semipartial correlation of Y with X_1 as the difference between the two squared multiple correlation coefficients thus

$$r_{Y(1.234)}^2 = R_{Y.1234}^2 - R_{Y.234}^2 \quad \text{- - -} (27) \; \textbf{Delta } \boldsymbol{R^2}$$

From (27), we see that the squared semipartial correlation is the increase in R^2 that results from adding that particular independent variable to the regression equation. For this reason, the squared semipartial correlation is referred to by some authors as ΔR^2 (**delta R^2**). This expression also appears in the output of several statistical computing packages. (SPSS Statistics, however, uses the term **R squared change** instead of **delta R^2**.)

12.3.3.6 Uncorrelated independent variables

If, in the example of four independent variables, those variables were to be uncorrelated, we could represent the situation as in Figure 15. In Figure 15, none of the independent variables overlaps with any of the others, reflecting the total lack of correlation among them. In this case, the coefficient of determination (the total proportion of the variance of the dependent variable that is accounted for by regression) is given by

$$R_{Y.1234}^2 = r_{Y1}{}^2 + r_{Y2}{}^2 + r_{Y3}{}^2 + r_{Y4}{}^2 \quad \text{- - -} (28)$$

Partition of $R_{Y.1234}^2$ when the IVs are uncorrelated

The partition in (28) permits an unequivocal attribution of a portion of the variance of Y accounted for by regression to a particular independent variable. Unfortunately, however, the situation in which all the IVs are totally independent never arises in practice, with the result that it is impossible to attribute variance of the DV unequivocally to any one IV.

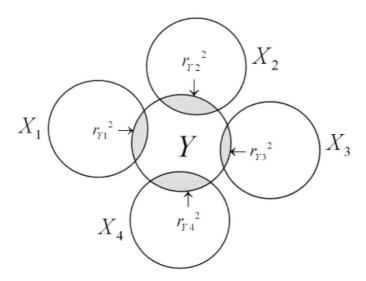

Figure 15. Regression with uncorrelated independent variables – a situation which never occurs in practice

The situation depicted in Figure 15 is, in practice, never encountered when the independent variables X are measured in the units of study, because such measurements are always subject to error.   More typically, the IVs are correlated, as in Figure 14.   There, the squared semipartial correlation between Y and either dependent variable is less than the square of the simple Pearson correlation between Y and that independent variable alone.   The squared semipartial correlation effectively places an independent variable 'at the end of the queue', as far as the attribution of variance in Y to each IV is concerned.

It can be shown that the test for the significance of a regression coefficient b_k, that is,

$$t_k = \frac{b_k}{s_{b_k}}$$

is equivalent to the test of the significance of the squared semipartial correlation, or ΔR_k^2 :

$$F\left(1, n-1-p\right) = \frac{\Delta R_k^2}{SS_{\text{residual}} / \left(n-1-p\right)} = \frac{R_{Y.\text{all}}^2 - R_{Y.\text{all except } X_k}^2}{\left(1 - R_{Y.12...k}^2\right) / \left(n-1-p\right)} \quad \text{- - -} \quad (29)$$

F ratio for significance of squared semipartial correlation

where ΔR_k^2 is the squared semipartial correlation between Y and X_k when all the other $p - 1$ independent variables or regressors have been entered into the regression equation first.

The sharing of variance among the independent variables in multiple regression makes it impossible to assign variance in Y unequivocally to any one independent variable.   There is, therefore, a large literature on the question of which of the variables in a multiple regression is the 'most important' in explaining the variance of the dependent variable.   The paper and textbook by Darlington (1968, 1990) provide a lucid discussion of the problems with the various measures of 'importance' that have been proposed.

We have already seen that the unstandardised regression coefficient is unsuitable as a measure of 'importance'.   It might be thought that the simple Pearson correlation between an independent variable and the criterion would be an appropriate measure; but there are situations in which the largest squared semipartial correlation ΔR^2 is not obtained with the variable showing the highest Pearson correlation with the criterion.

Some independent variables in a regression analysis are 'important', not in the sense that they predict the dependent variable, but because when their effects are removed from other independent variables (with which they correlate substantially), those other variables predict the criterion with greater accuracy.   Such variables are known as **suppressors**. It should be noted that a suppressor variable may itself show a negligible correlation with the criterion.

12.4 MULTIPLE REGRESSION WITH SPSS

One potential problem with multiple regression is that if we have measured several variables, some of which are highly correlated, the multiple regression package the researcher is using may not work at all. This is known as the problem of **multicollinearity**. A key measure here is the **tolerance** of a regressor, that is, one minus the square of the multiple correlation between the regressor and estimates of its values from its regression upon all the other regressors. If the tolerance is too low, the multiple regression will fail to run.

After the data have been thoroughly explored, it is often a good idea to **centre** the variables by converting each to a set of deviation scores by subtracting its mean value from the raw values. As we have seen, such a transformation of the variables leaves the correlations among them unaltered; but the computing algorithm is often happier with deviation scores than with the raw data.

Even if multiple regression is feasible, there remains the problem of ascertaining which of the many variables in a study are crucial. In a situation where everything correlates with everything else, it is impossible to attribute variance in the dependent variable unequivocally to any one independent variable. Should the researcher be armed with a well-developed causal model, this can drive both the selection of appropriate IVs and establish their relative importance. Often, however, especially in the early stages of research in an area, the researcher has no such model; indeed, the motivation for the research may be little more than the suspicion that certain variables might be important.

In Table 3, three extra variables, the subject's Age, the score obtained on a relevant academic Project, and IQ have been added to the original variables in Table 2. The outlier that was detected in the preliminary regression analysis, however, has been removed. Only a few cases are shown in Table 3. The full data set is available at www.psypress.com/spss-made-simple.

Table 3. An extension of Table 2, with data on three additional independent variables

Case	Fin	Ent	Age	Pro	IQ	Case	Fin	Ent	Age	Pro	IQ
1	38	44	21.9	50	110	18	103	48	22.3	53	134
2	49	40	22.6	75	120	19	105	43	21.8	72	140
3	61	43	21.8	54	119	20	106	55	21.4	69	127

In the following discussion, we shall be concerned with two main questions:
1. Does the addition of more independent variables improve the accuracy of predictions of the value of Final University Exam?
2. Of these new variables, are some more useful than others for prediction of the dependent variable?

We shall see that the answer to the first question is 'Yes, up to a point'. It can be shown, in fact, that (providing the tolerance is sufficient) adding more regressors will result in a value for R which is at least as high as the previous value, provided that multicollinearity is not an issue. On the other hand, this does not mean that more IVs should necessarily be added as a matter of course because, in some circumstances, that can result in highly unstable estimates. More is not necessarily better.

The second question, concerning the relative importance of the various regressors, is particularly problematic, and none of the available approaches to it is entirely satisfactory (see, for example, the references to Darlington's work above and Howell, 2007, for a review).

In this section, we shall consider two general approaches to multiple regression. In **simultaneous** multiple regression, all the relevant regressors are entered in the equation directly, so that the tests for each regression coefficient effectively put it 'at the end of the queue' and test ΔR^2 in the presence of all the other variables. In **stepwise** multiple regression, the more controversial of the two techniques, the independent variables are added to (or taken away from) the equation one at a time, the order of entry (or removal) being determined by preset statistical criteria. Many would say, however, that no statistical model alone can justify such 'queue-jumping': a substantive causal model is also essential.

In this section, we shall begin with an example of the use of simultaneous regression. After that, for the sake of completeness (and with considerable reservations), we shall turn to stepwise regression. In fact, despite the theoretical problems with stepwise regression, we have found that the method often yields sensible results that are very similar to those from a simultaneous regression on the same data.

To construct the SPSS data file, restore the original data set (minus the outlier) to **Data View**. In **Variable View**, name the three new variables (e.g. *Age*, *Project* and *IQ*). Use the **Label** column to assign a variable label such as *Project Mark*. Now enter the scores in **Data View**. The first three cases are shown in Figure 16.

Case	FinalExam	EntranceExam	Age	Project	IQ
1	38	44	21.9	50	110
2	49	40	22.6	75	120
3	61	43	21.8	54	119

Figure 16. The first three cases in **Data View**

12.4.1   Simultaneous multiple regression

- In the **Linear Regression** dialog box, transfer the variable name Final University Exam into the **Dependent Variable:** and Entrance Exam, Age, Project Mark and IQ into the **Independent Variables:** box.
- Select the other optional items as in Section 12.2.3, then click **OK**.

12.4.1.1   Output for simultaneous multiple regression

The first table in the output is a table of the requested descriptive statistics for each variable (Output 12).

Descriptive Statistics

	Mean	Std. Deviation	N
University Exam	102.82	32.63	33
Entrance Exam	47.27	7.54	33
Age	22.518	3.046	33
Project Mark	67.94	9.14	33
IQ	129.03	9.66	33

Output 12. The Descriptive Statistics table

The next item is an edited table of correlations (Output 13) showing that the target variable Final University Exam correlates significantly with three of the regresssors but not with the fourth (Age).

Correlations

		University Exam
Pearson Correlation	University Exam	1.00
	Entrance Exam	.73
	Age	-.03
	Project Mark	.40
	IQ	.65
Sig. (1-tailed)	University Exam	.
	Entrance Exam	.00
	Age	.43
	Project Mark	.01
	IQ	.00

Output 13. Edited table of correlations

Output 14 lists the variables entered in the model.

Variables Entered/Removed [b]

Model	Variables Entered	Variables Removed	Method
1	IQ, Age, Project Mark, Entrance Exam [a]	.	Enter

a. All requested variables entered.

b. Dependent Variable: Final University Exam

Output 14. List of variables entered, the dependent variable and the method of analysis

Output 15 shows that the multiple correlation coefficient R is .87 and the **Adjusted R Square** is .73. The effect size represented by adjusted R^2 is 73% i.e. a **large** effect.

Model Summary [b]

Model	R	R Square	Adjusted R Square	Std. Error of the Estimate
1	.87[a]	.76	.73	16.92

a. Predictors: (Constant), IQ, Age, Project Mark, Entrance Exam

b. Dependent Variable: Final University Exam

Output 15. Value of *R* and other statistics

Recall that when one regressor (Entrance Exam) was used to predict Final University Exam, the value of R was .73 and **Adjusted R Square** (the estimate of the proportion of variance accounted for by regression) was .52 (52%). With R now at .87 and **Adjusted R Square** up from 52% to 73%, we see that the answer to the question of whether adding more independent variables improves the predictive power of the regression equation is definitely 'Yes'. There remains, however, the question of which of the new variables is responsible for the improvement.

Not surprisingly, the ANOVA (Output 16) shows that the regression is significant beyond the .01 level.

ANOVA[b]

Model		Sum of Squares	df	Mean Square	F	Sig.
1	Regression	26059.63	4	6514.91	22.75	.000[a]
	Residual	8017.28	28	286.33		
	Total	34076.91	32			

a. Predictors: (Constant), IQ, Age, Project Mark, Entrance Exam

b. Dependent Variable: Final University Exam

Output 16. The **ANOVA** for regression

Output 17 tables the values of the regression coefficients. From column **B**, we see that the multiple regression equation of Final University Exam upon Entrance Exam, Age, Project Mark and IQ is:

$$\text{Final}' = -272.13 + 2.49 \times \text{Entrance} + 1.24 \times \text{Age} + 0.50 \times \text{Project} + 1.51 \times \text{IQ}$$

where Final' is the predicted Final University Exam mark.

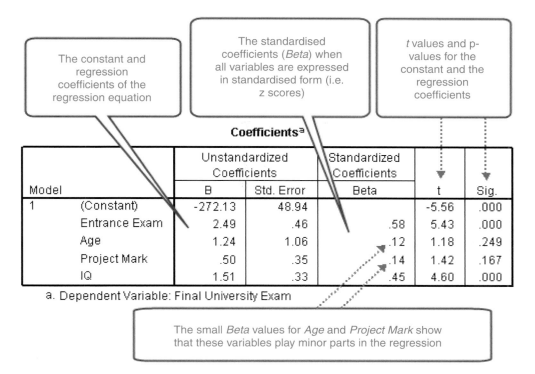

The constant and regression coefficients of the regression equation

The standardised coefficients (*Beta*) when all variables are expressed in standardised form (i.e. *z* scores)

t values and p-values for the constant and the regression coefficients

Coefficients[a]

Model		Unstandardized Coefficients		Standardized Coefficients		
		B	Std. Error	Beta	t	Sig.
1	(Constant)	-272.13	48.94		-5.56	.000
	Entrance Exam	2.49	.46	.58	5.43	.000
	Age	1.24	1.06	.12	1.18	.249
	Project Mark	.50	.35	.14	1.42	.167
	IQ	1.51	.33	.45	4.60	.000

a. Dependent Variable: Final University Exam

The small *Beta* values for *Age* and *Project Mark* show that these variables play minor parts in the regression

Output 17. The regression equation and associated statistics

A person with Age 21.6 and scoring 60 on the Entrance Exam, 84 on the Project and having an IQ of 132 would have an estimated score of

$$-272.13 + 2.49\times(60) + 1.24\times(21.6) + .50\times(84) + 1.51\times(132) = 145.37$$

Notice that case 29, who meets these specifications, actually scored 145 in the Final University Exam. However, not all cases have estimates so close to the actual values: for case 6, the estimate is 113.34, but the actual value is 73.

But what about the second question? Do all the new variables contribute substantially to the predictive power of the regression equation, or are some IVs merely 'passengers' in the equation? We can learn little about the relative importance of the variables from the sizes of their regression coefficients *B*, because the values of the partial regression coefficients reflect the original units in which the variables were measured. For this reason, although the coefficient for Age is larger than that for Project, we cannot thereby conclude that Age is the more important predictor.

The **beta coefficients** (in the column headed **Beta**) tell us rather more, because each gives the estimate of the average number of standard deviations change in the criterion that will be produced by a change of one standard deviation in the regressor concerned. On this count, Entrance Exam still makes by far the greatest contribution, because a change of one standard deviation on that variable produces a change of .58 standard deviations on Final University Exam. Next is IQ with a change of .45, but Project Mark produces a change in Final University Exam of only .14 standard deviations and Age a change of .12 SDs. This ordering of the standardised beta coefficients is supported by consideration of the correlations between the criterion and each of the three regressors (Output 13). If **R square change** (ΔR^2) had been selected in Figure 11, the output would have shown that the regressor with the largest beta coefficient also has the largest value of R square change.

The remaining items of output (the table of **Residual Statistics** and the scatterplot of standardised predicted values against standardised residuals) are not shown here. There were no residual outliers. Residuals are the basis of **regression diagnostics**, that is, set of procedures for identifying rogue scores that can distort the values of multiple regression statistics. The raw residuals e are themselves valuable measures of **distance**. But distances exert more **leverage** on the regression statistics if they are far from the mean of the IV concerned than if they are near. Leverage is captured by the statistic known as h_i, where h stands for 'hat'. To have influence, however, a score must have both distance and leverage. The statistic known as **Cook's D** is a respected measure of influence, which is sensitive to both distance and leverage. (See Howell, 2007, pages 515-520, for a helpful introduction to regression diagnostics.)

12.4.2   Stepwise multiple regression

If, in the **Linear Regression** dialog box, the choice of **Method** is changed to **Stepwise**, rather than **Enter**, a stepwise regression will be run, whereby predictors are added to (or subtracted from) the equation one at a time. In **Forward selection**, predictors are added one a time, provided they meet an entry criterion: we could decide, for example, that a variable makes a robust contribution if the increase in the variance it explains is significant beyond the .05 level. In **Backward deletion**, the predictors are all present initially and are removed one at a time if they do not meet a retention criterion: we could decide, for example, that a variable will be removed if the resulting reduction in the value of R^2 has an associated p-value of greater than .10. The SPSS **Stepwise regression** routine is a combination of these two processes: a variable, having been added at an early stage, may subsequently be removed. Selected portions of the results of a **Stepwise regression** analysis are shown in Outputs 18-22.

Variables Entered/Removed[a]

Model	Variables Entered	Variables Removed	Method
1	Entrance Exam	.	Stepwise (Criteria: Probability-of-F-to-enter <= .050, Probability-of-F-to-remove >= .100).
2	IQ	.	Stepwise (Criteria: Probability-of-F-to-enter <= .050, Probability-of-F-to-remove >= .100).

a. Dependent Variable: Final University Exam

First variable entered in Model 1	No variables were removed	Second variable added to the first in Model 2. No other variables were entered so there are no more Models

Output 18. List of variables entered (only two achieved entry in the stepwise regression)

Output 18 contains information about the variables entered in and removed from the model. In this example, no variables were removed.

Output 19 shows that the value of R for Model 2 is smaller than the value (.87) given for simultaneous regression of Final University Exam upon Entrance Exam, Project Mark, Age and IQ but only slightly so. This shows the lack of predictive value of the two excluded variables (Age and Project Mark). The values of adjusted R^2 for Model 1 and Model 2 are large (52% & 71%, respectively) so the **effect sizes** are large.

Model Summary^c

Note the increase in the value of R (and R^2) after the addition of a second variable

Model	R	R Square	Adjusted R Square	Std. Error of the Estimate
1	.73^a	.53	.52	22.70
2	.85^b	.73	.71	17.62

a. Predictors: (Constant), Entrance Exam
b. Predictors: (Constant), Entrance Exam, IQ
c. Dependent Variable: Final University Exam

Output 19. Value of **R** and associated statistics for each Model

The ANOVA (Output 20) for each regression Model is significant.

ANOVA^c

Model		Sum of Squares	df	Mean Square	F	Sig.
1	Regression	18096.33	1	18096.33	35.10	.000^a
	Residual	15980.58	31	515.50		
	Total	34076.91	32			
2	Regression	24757.87	2	12378.93	39.85	.000^b
	Residual	9319.04	30	310.63		
	Total	34076.91	32			

a. Predictors: (Constant), Entrance Exam
b. Predictors: (Constant), Entrance Exam, IQ
c. Dependent Variable: Final University Exam

Output 20. The **ANOVA** for each regression Model

The decision of the SPSS stepwise procedure is that, since the increment in R with the inclusion of either of the remaining variables (Project Mark and Age) does not reach the necessary statistical criterion, these variables are excluded from the final equation (Output 21).

From column **B** in Output 21, we see that the multiple regression equation of Final University Exam upon Entrance Exam and IQ is

$$(\text{Final University Exam})' = -219.07 + 2.51 \times (\text{Entrance Exam}) + 1.58 \times \text{IQ}$$

where (Final University Exam)$'$ is the predicted value of the Final University Exam mark.

Thus the estimated score of a person with Age 21.6 scoring 60 on the Entrance Exam and having an IQ of 132 is

$$-219.07 + 2.51 \times (60) + 1.58 \times (132) = 140.09$$

Notice that case 29, who meets these specifications, scored 145 in the Final University Exam. In this case the 'simultaneous' regression equation provides a better estimate than the stepwise regression equation; but there are other cases in which the opposite is true.

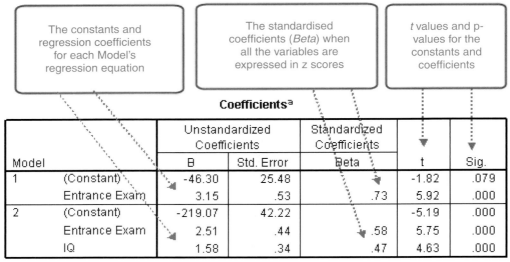

The constants and regression coefficients for each Model's regression equation	The standardised coefficients (*Beta*) when all the variables are expressed in z scores	t values and p-values for the constants and coefficients

Coefficients[a]

Model		Unstandardized Coefficients		Standardized Coefficients		
		B	Std. Error	Beta	t	Sig.
1	(Constant)	-46.30	25.48		-1.82	.079
	Entrance Exam	3.15	.53	.73	5.92	.000
2	(Constant)	-219.07	42.22		-5.19	.000
	Entrance Exam	2.51	.44	.58	5.75	.000
	IQ	1.58	.34	.47	4.63	.000

a. Dependent Variable: Final University Exam

Output 21. The regression coefficients tables for the single variable (Model 1) and the two variables (Model 2) remaining in the stepwise regression analysis

Output 22 lists the statistics for the excluded variables. Note the low values of t and their correspondingly high (i.e. $> .05$) p-values.

Excluded Variables [c]

Model		Beta In	t	Sig.	Partial Correlation	Collinearity Statistics Tolerance
1	Age	.18[a]	1.42	.167	.25	.93
	Project Mark	.21[a]	1.69	.102	.29	.92
	IQ	.47[a]	4.63	.000	.65	.90
2	Age	.15[b]	1.56	.129	.28	.92
	Project Mark	.17[b]	1.77	.088	.31	.91

a. Predictors in the Model: (Constant), Entrance Exam

b. Predictors in the Model: (Constant), Entrance Exam, IQ

c. Dependent Variable: Final University Exam

Output 22. The variables excluded from the stepwise regression analysis

In the table in Output 22, **Beta In** is the standardised regression coefficient that would result if the variable were entered into the equation at the next step. The t test is the usual test of significance of the regression coefficient.

To sum up, the **stepwise regression** confirms the conclusion from the beta coefficients in the simultaneous regression that only the variables Entrance Exam and IQ are useful for predicting Final University Exam marks. The other two variables are superfluous and can be dropped from the analysis.

12.5 MULTILEVEL REGRESSION MODELS

Underlying all the methods described so far in this chapter has been a very important assumption, namely, that the observations are independent. Suppose, however, that we are interested in the factors that lead to school success and that we have data on the exam results of a large number of children, together with their scores on a reading test, as well as information about their school's gender admission policy and other variables.

If we are interested in the effect of the children's reading levels on their exam success at school, it might seem natural to regress their school exam scores on their reading scores in the manner described earlier in this chapter. We could easily enter the data into SPSS and apply the methods of least squares regression to estimate the regression coefficient and test it for significance. The difficulty with this approach is that the assumption of independence of observations is manifestly false: it is well known that schools vary considerably in the stringency of their selection processes, their policy with regard to the issue of segregation of boys and girls and so on. For a variety of reasons, therefore, observations from one school will tend to be more similar to one another than they are to observations from another school.

Data of this kind are not a simple random sample from a pool of possible observations, as required by ordinary least squares regression models: on the contrary, they are clustered in a hierarchical fashion: students are nested within schools; schools are nested within districts and so on. Just as the data of children within a particular school will be more similar than the data of children from different schools, there may be characteristics of a district that tend to make data from that district more similar than data from another district. Research in many areas of study (e.g. education and health psychology) typically yield data that are hierarchically clustered in this way.

If the hierarchical dependencies in such a data set are ignored, the consequences can be serious. Ordinary least squares (OLS) regression will produce underestimates of the standard errors of the test statistics and the researcher may be led to conclude that there is strong evidence for non-existent effects. Rasbash *et al.* (2004) provide some striking examples of the consequences of inappropriate use of OLS regression with clustered data and the different conclusions the researcher would come to using multilevel modelling.

There is now available some excellent software for multilevel or hierarchical modelling, including the SPSS MIXED procedure. Jon Rasbash and his associates (Rasbash *et al.*, 2004) have developed MLwiN, a dedicated package which provides excellent graphical feedback and an interactive learning environment for the user, backed up by an excellent manual and other documentation.

12.6   PATH ANALYSIS

When two variables are highly correlated, as were children's Exposure to screened violence and their Actual violence in the data we analysed in Chapter 11, it may be tempting to conclude that there is a direct causal link between them.   As we have seen, however, correlation does not imply causation. The correlation between Exposure to and Actual violence may be driven by their joint causation by a third variable.   In Section 11.7, we examined the correlations among three variables, Actual violence, Exposure to violence and Parental aggression, and concluded that the high correlation between Exposure to and Actual violence arises because Parental aggression determines both the aggression levels of their children and the amount of screened violence that their children watch.   We obtained evidence for this conclusion by calculating the **partial correlation** between Exposure to and Actual violence after the associations between those variables and Parental aggression had been removed.   The correlation between Exposure and Actual was much reduced by the removal, or **partialling out**, of Parental aggression.   In discussing this partial correlation, we considered three different **causal models** of the associations among the three variables, all three of which were consistent with a high correlation between Actual violence and Exposure; the almost negligible partial correlation, however, gave credence to the model of common causation, rather than to either of the other models.

In this chapter, we introduced the technique known as **multiple regression**, the purpose of which is to ascertain the extent to which a dependent variable (DV) can be accounted for (or predicted) by two or more independent variables (IVs) and, if so, the relative importance of the IVs in accounting for the variance of the DV.   **Path analysis**, which we shall consider in this section, is a development of multiple regression, the purpose of which is to utilise the associations among a set of variables to help to determine, with the assistance of a special graphical representation known as a **path diagram**, the most convincing causal model for the data.   Since correlation does not imply causation, however, any interpretation of a path analysis must be tentative.

12.6.1   A path diagram

A **path diagram** is a formalised diagram of a causal model, conforming to a set of established conventions.   In a multiple regression equation, the DV is the subject of the equation and, as such, appears on the left; the IVs appear to the right of the equals sign.   In contrast, in a path diagram (Figure 17), the DV or DVs appear on the extreme right of the diagram, with the causal variables to the left.   The supposed causal sequence is read from left to right across the diagram.   Thus in Figure 17, a Parental predisposition to violence determines both the manner in which they Control their children's behaviour and the children's Exposure to screen violence.   Both Control and Exposure directly affect the child's Actual violence.   We should also note that in a path diagram, the distinction between independent and dependent variables tends to break down and instead, a distinction is made between **exogenous** variables, the causation of which is not depicted, and **endogenous** variables, to which causal pathways lead. In a path diagram, exogenous variables have arrows leaving them but none entering them; whereas endogenous variables always have at least two arrows entering them: a causal path arrow from one or more input variables and an additional arrow representing an error term of some kind.   In Figure 17, there is one exogenous variable, Parental, and three endogenous variables: Actual violence, Control and Exposure.   Notice that, in this causal model, the

Parental variable has no *direct* effect upon Actual violence: the effects of the Parental variable are mediated by the Control and Exposure variables.

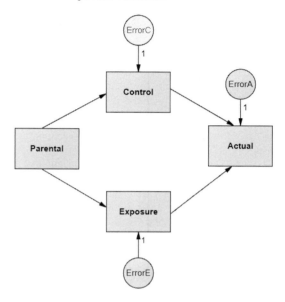

Figure 17. An input path diagram of the causation of Actual violence in children by a Parental predisposition to violence through the mediating variables of method of Control and Exposure to screen violence

The path diagram shown in Figure 17 is an **input path diagram**, that is, a diagram showing only the causal pathways among the three variables: no estimates of any parameters are given. The input path diagram is the researcher's causal model, which is to be put to the test against the data in comparison with other possible causal models. The outcome of a path analysis is an **output path diagram**, which comprises the input path diagram plus various statistics, most notably **path coefficients**. Path coefficients are regression coefficients. As with multiple regression, the user has the option of calculating **unstandardised coefficients**, which are based upon the raw data, or **standardised coefficients**, which are based upon data that have been transformed to standard (z) scores. In some ways, standardised coefficients are more informative, because they express the effects of variables measured originally in different units as the number of standard deviations of change resulting from a unit change in the causal variable.

As an example of a path analysis, we shall return to the situation in which we have measurements on only three variables, Parental, Exposure and Actual, and are attempting to interpret a high positive correlation between Exposure and Actual in terms of the most convincing model of causality.

Figure 18 depicts the input path diagram of the common causality model of the situation, in which a high correlation between Actual violence and Exposure to violence is interpreted in terms of direct common causation of both variables by the Parental variable.

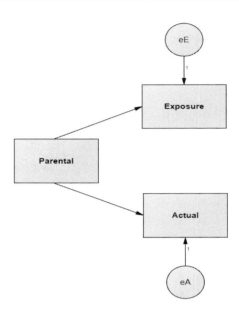

Figure 18. An input path diagram of direct common causation of Actual violence and Exposure to screen violence by a Parental variable

Figure 19 shows the **output path diagram** for the same model. The path coefficients are **standardised path coefficients**.   The values beside the boxes are squared multiple correlations. Some other conventions for path diagrams should be noted. Observed variables, such as Screen Violence and Actual Violence, are represented by rectangles. The circles labelled eE and eA (errorExposure and errorActual) represent the error components of the two DVs. In path analysis, these error components are treated as additional independent variables, hence the arrows from the circles to the corresponding rectangles. These error components, however, are **latent variables**, because they are inferred from the data and are not part of the original data set. By convention, latent variables are represented as circles in path diagrams. Error variables are not the only kind of latent variables to appear in path diagrams. In Chapter 15, we shall encounter **factors**, which are hypothetical dimensions underlying the correlations among a set of observed variables.

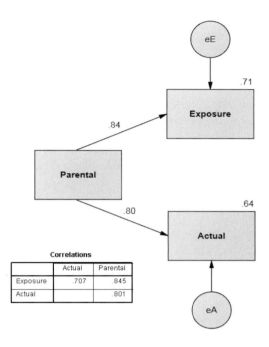

Correlations

	Actual	Parental
Exposure	.707	.845
Actual		.801

Figure 19. Output path diagram of the model of common causation

The output path diagram in Figure 19 summarises two simple regressions: Exposure on Parental and Actual on Parental. Since the statistics on the output path diagram in Figure 19 are standardised estimates, their values are the correlations and squared multiple correlations between the Parental variable and the Exposure and Actual variables, as can be seen from the correlations in the SPSS output superimposed upon the figure. Since these are simple regressions, the squared multiple correlations are the squares of the Pearson correlations.

12.6.2   Path analysis with AMOS

AMOS is an acronym for Analysis Of Moment Structures. In statistics, a **moment** is the long run average or **expectation** of a power of a random variable. For example, the expectation of the mean is the **first moment** of the mean, the expectation of the square of the mean is the **second moment** of the mean, and so on. The expectation of the deviation from the mean (the first moment of the deviation) is zero. The expectation of the square of the deviation (the second moment) is the **variance**. With two random variables, X and Y, the **product-moment** is the expectation of the product of the deviations of X and Y from their respective means. In samples, the product-moment is estimated by the cross-product of deviations in the numerator of statistics such as the Pearson correlation and the regression coefficient. The product-moment, then, appears in measures of *association*. The AMOS package utilises the associations among variables to run path analysis and certain other techniques, such as **factor analysis**, which we shall consider in Chapter 15.

In order to access AMOS, you must have a data set in the **Data Editor**, preferably the set that you want to analyse. The AMOS 18 command appears at the bottom of the **Analyze** menu. If the Data Editor contains no data and you click on the AMOS 18 command, you will receive an error message prompting you to enter some data.

We suggest that, while you are still in SPSS, you enter as variable labels either the variable names or very short labels (for example, you might abbreviate the label 'Exposure to Screen Violence' to 'Exposure'). This will make life easier for you when working in AMOS, because in some dialogs, you will be required to enter both variable names and variable labels when labelling the rectangles or circles representing the variables.

The AMOS window appears as in Figure 20.

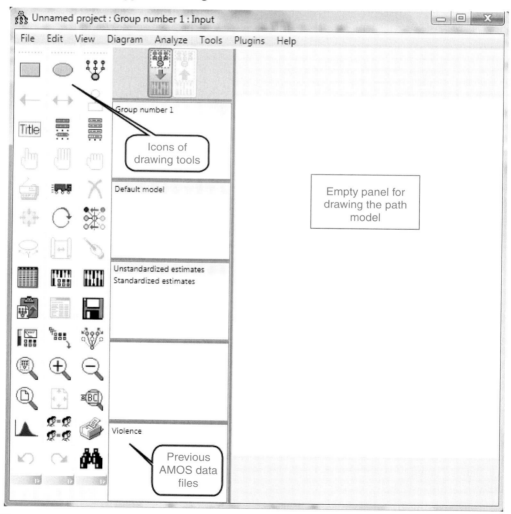

Figure 20. The AMOS window

Across the top of the AMOS window is a row of drop-down menus, including **File** and **Edit**. On the left underneath, is an extensive palette of drawing tools. Clicking on the top left rectangle, for example, will enable you to draw a rectangle in the drawing space on the right of the window. In the central grey pillar are icons requesting a display of the input or output path diagrams, a drop-down menu specifying standardized or unstandardized estimates and a list of practice files already in AMOS.

Once in AMOS, you must make a file active. Choose **File➔Data Files** to access the **Data Files** dialog box (Figure 21). To make the data in the SPSS Data Editor active in AMOS also, click the button labelled **Working File** and then **OK**. When this has been done, the file name will be replaced by the indicator **<working>**.

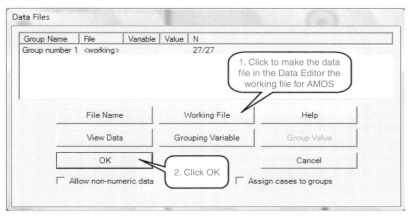

Figure 21. The **Data Files** dialog box

If you are ever in doubt about which SPSS data set is active in AMOS, or you want to remind yourself of the variable names and variable labels when completing dialogs, you have only to choose **View➔Variables in Dataset** in order to see a list of both the names and the labels of the variables in the current AMOS dataset (Figure 22). This facility is very useful when you are labelling figures in drawings, because the display of variable names and labels remains on screen while you are completing the **Object Properties** dialog.

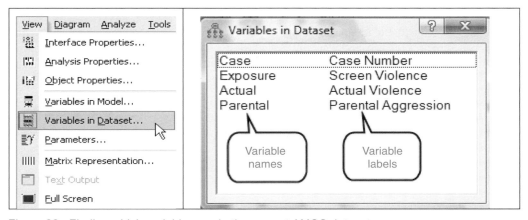

Figure 22. Finding which variables are in the current AMOS dataset

12.6.2.2 Stages in a path analysis in AMOS

A path analysis in AMOS takes place in six stages:
1. An input path diagram is drawn.
2. A choice is made between unstandardized and standardized estimates.
3. The analysis properties (items in the output) are specified.
4. The estimates are calculated.
5. The output path diagram is displayed.
6. The text output is accessed and examined.

12.6.2.3 Constructing the input path diagram

Click the cursor on the top left rectangle in the toolbar. This will enable you to draw a rectangle (by left-clicking and dragging) in the drawing area on the right (Figure 23). Initially, the rectangle will be red; but its colour will change to black when the cursor is removed.

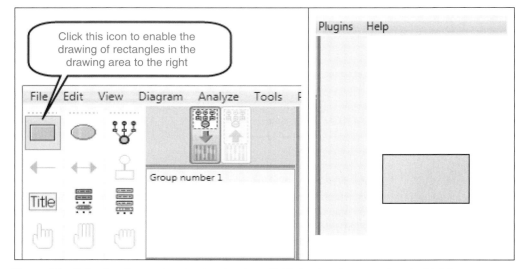

Figure 23. Selecting the rectangle drawing icon (left) for drawing a rectangle (right)

We want to draw three identical rectangles, one for each of the three variables Actual Violence, Screen Violence and Parental Aggression. To do this, click on the copier icon (Figure 24) and (starting with the cursor inside the rectangle we want to copy) click-and-drag two identical copies of the original rectangle to the appropriate places in the drawing area as shown in Figures 25 and 26.

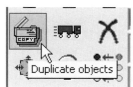

Figure 24. The copier icon

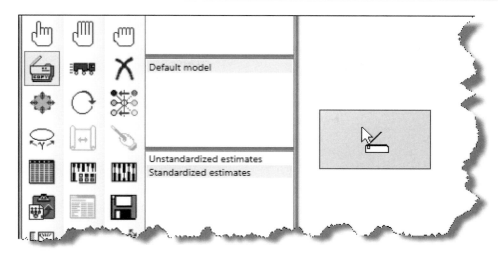

Figure 25. An image of the copier appears in the rectangle when that object is clicked

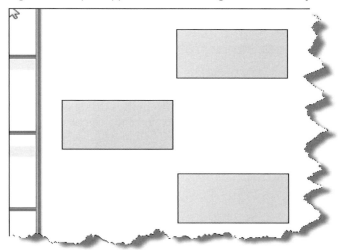

Figure 26. Produce two replicas of the original rectangle by dragging to their desired positions

Once the duplicates of the original rectangle have been drawn, the three rectangles can be named according to the variables they represent. In AMOS, a part of a diagram (a rectangle, an arrow, a circle) is known as an **object**. Objects can be individually selected and edited. Right-click on the leftmost rectangle, which is going to represent the (exogenous) Parental variable, choose **Object Properties➔Text** (See Figure 27) and enter the variable name and label in the appropriate slots in the dialog box. At this point, it is very useful to see the variable names and labels on screen, which is achieved by choosing **View➔Variables in the Dataset**. Note that you must enter both the variable name and the variable label; otherwise you will receive an error message to the effect that the figure has not been labelled. You can experiment with different font sizes and bold font to try to achieve the clearest possible diagram.

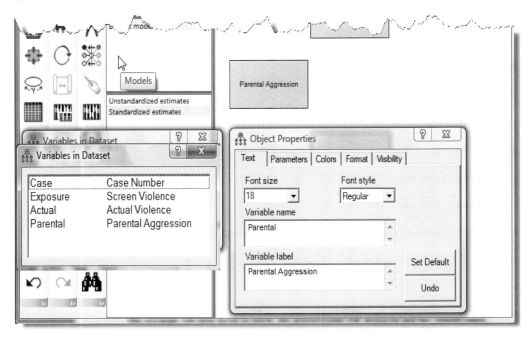

Figure 27. Naming an object. It is convenient to have both the names and the labels of the
variables simultaneously displayed, as shown

Note that there is no **OK** button in the **Object Properties** dialog box. To complete the entry
of the variable name and label, click on the cross in the top right corner of the dialog window.
The rectangle will then revert to black, the dotted border will disappear and the variable name
will now appear in the figure. Follow the same procedure to label the other two rectangles.

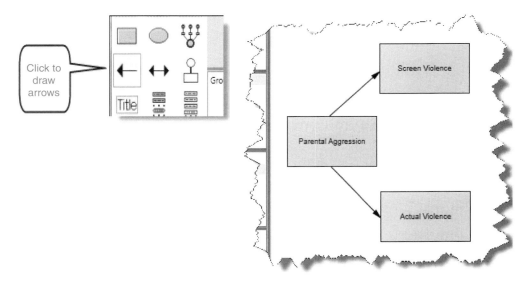

Figure 28. Click the arrow icon (left) and then move the cursor to the drawing panel and drag
the cursor between the appropriate points on the rectangles (right)

Draw the paths from the Parental Aggression to the Screen Violence and to the Actual Violence rectangles by using the one-headed arrow as shown in Figure 28. Simply click on the arrow icon, move the cursor to the leftmost rectangle in the drawing area and drag the arrow to the Screen Violence rectangle. Follow the same procedure to draw the path from the Parental Aggression rectangle to the Actual Violence rectangle.

Each endogenous variable must have a residual or error component. Click on the **Add a unique variable** icon (Figure 29) and left-click the upper of the two rectangles on the right (Screen Violence).

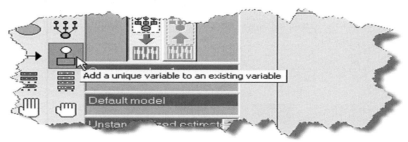

Figure 29. The **Add a unique variable** icon

A circle with an arrow pointing to the Screen Violence rectangle will now appear as shown in Figure 30. Note that the orientation of the circle is exactly as we wanted it. When we follow the same procedure to attach a unique variable circle and arrow to the Actual rectangle, however, we find that the circle appears above the rectangle and threatens to clutter up the path diagram. On clicking the rectangle, however, you will see the circle and arrow rotate clockwise through 45%. Click three more times to position the circle and arrow below the rectangle as desired.

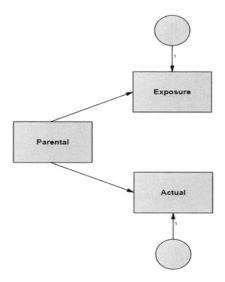

Figure 30. Unique variable objects (circles) have now been added to the Screen Violence and Actual Violence rectangles

The residual circles can be named by right-clicking, selecting **Object Properties** and completing the dialogs in the usual way. We can label the residual variables *e*E and *e*A (for errorExposure and errorActual, respectively). We have now completed the input path diagram.

Drawing path diagrams in AMOS requires some practice. For example, the rectangles representing the observed variables must be positioned in the drawing area to leave sufficient room for the error variables. Should you find that there is insufficient room, click the **Select all objects** icon (Figure 31a) and click on any of the rectangles to effect the selection. Now click on the **Move** icon (Figure 31b) and click-and-drag the complete figure to the desired position on the drawing board. Deselect objects by clicking on the fist icon beside the open hand.

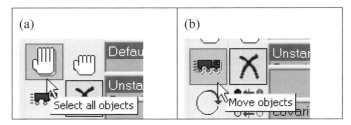

Figure 31. The **Select all objects** and **Move objects** icons

12.6.2.4   Choosing standardized estimates

In the central grey pillar, you will see a drop-down menu with **Unstandardized estimates** as the default selection (Figure 32). Click on the downward-pointing arrow on the right and choose **Standardized estimates**.

Figure 32. Choosing standardized estimates

12.6.2.5   Specifying the Analysis Properties

Analysis Properties can be found in the **View** menu (Figure 33). Click on that option to open the **Analysis Properties** dialog box (Figure 34).

Select the **Output** tab and tick the boxes as shown. Click on **Standardized estimates** and **Squared multiple correlations**.

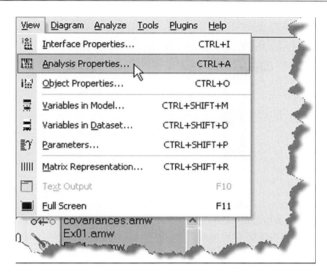

Figure 33. Accessing the **Analysis Properties** dialog box

When you first click on Analysis Properties, you will access the Estimation tab and will see that the radio button is set at Maximum Likelihood. That's as it should be, so click on the Output tab and activate the buttons shown in Figure 34.

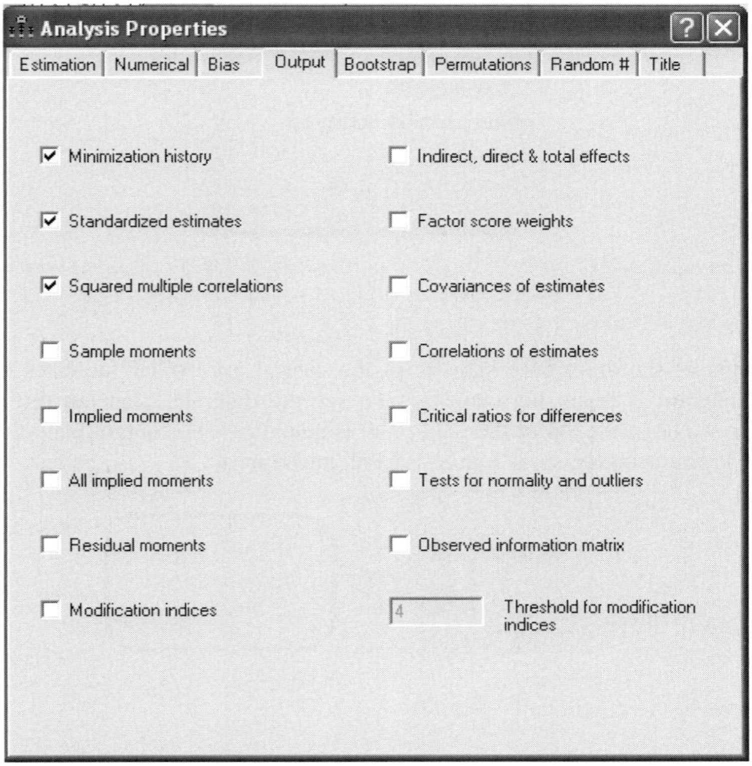

Figure 34. The **Analysis Properties** dialog box

12.6.2.6   Running the analysis

To run the analysis, click on the **Calculate estimates** icon (Figure 35).

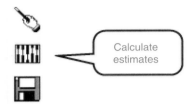

Figure 35. The **Calculate estimates** icon

An immediate consequence of clicking the Calculate estimates icon is the appearance, in the grey central pillar of the value of a chi-square statistic with its degrees of freedom (Output 23). We shall discuss the meaning of this statistic more fully when we come to consider the written output of the analysis. For the moment, we note that the value of chi-square on one degree of freedom is 0.2, which falls well short of significance: the *p*-value is .627. The result of the chi-square test indicates that the model we have been testing is a very good fit for the data. The value of chi-square reflects the degree to which the model *fails* to account for the data, so the smaller the value of chi-square, the better the fit.

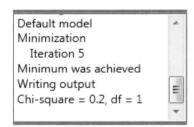

Output 23. The value and number of degrees of freedom of the chi-square statistic

12.6.2.7   Viewing the output path diagram

The appearance of the chi-square statistic in the central grey pillar indicates that the final output path diagram is ready for viewing. To see the diagram, click on the **output path diagram** viewer icon at the top of the grey pillar (Figure 36). The output path diagram shown in Output 24 (reproduced earlier as Figure 19) will now appear.

Figure 36. Viewing the output path diagram

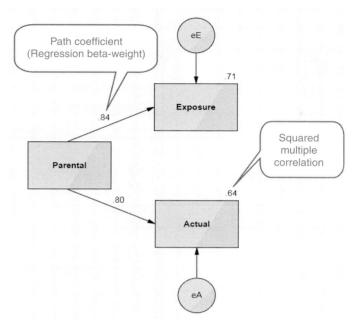

Output 24. Output path diagram

The values of the path coefficients and R^2 can be confirmed by returning to SPSS and regressing Screen Violence and Parental Aggression and Actual Violence and Parental Aggression. The outputs (edited) are shown in Output 25.

It is clear from Outputs 24 and 25 that Parental Aggression has a slightly greater effect on exposure to Screen Violence than on Actual Violence.

Model Summary		
Model	R	R Square
1	.845[a]	.713

a. Predictors: (Constant), Parental Aggression

Coefficients[a]

Model		Unstandardized Coefficients	Standardized Coefficients
		B	Beta
1	(Constant)	-.614	
	Parental Aggression	1.004	.845

a. Dependent Variable: Screen Violence

Model Summary		
Model	R	R Square
1	.801[a]	.642

a. Predictors: (Constant), Parental Aggression

Coefficients[a]

Model		Unstandardized Coefficients	Standardized Coefficients
		B	Beta
1	(Constant)	2.064	
	Parental Aggression	.735	.801

a. Dependent Variable: Actual Violence

Output 25. The values of R^2 and Beta weights from the regression of Screen Violence and Parental Aggression (upper row) and of Actual Violence and Parental Aggression (lower row) as shown in Figure 19 and Output 24

12.6.2.8   The text output of the analysis

The details of the statistical tests can be viewed by clicking on the **View Text** icon (Figure 37). When this is done, a **navigation tree** will appear, as shown in Output 26. The output is quite extensive and we shall not consider all of it in detail here. Some items, however, are worthy of note at this stage (see next Section).

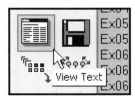

Figure 37. Viewing the text output

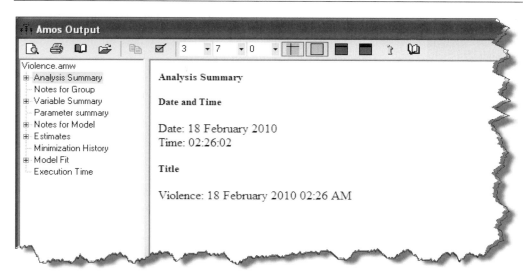

Output 26. The output navigator (the list of contents in the left-hand panel)

12.6.2.9 The purpose of the chi-square test: level of identification of path models

We have seen that the chi-square statistic measures the extent to which a model *fails* to account for the data. In this subsection, we shall consider the circumstances in which chi-square is defined and a test of the applicabilty of the model can be made.

The degrees of freedom of *any* statistic are given by the following formula:

$$df = \begin{bmatrix} \text{Number of} \\ \text{independent} \\ \text{observations} \end{bmatrix} - \begin{bmatrix} \text{Number of} \\ \text{parameters} \\ \text{estimated} \end{bmatrix} \quad \text{- - - (30)}$$

General formula for the degrees of freedom

In the context of the testing of path models, formula (30) is to be interpreted as follows:

$$df = \begin{bmatrix} \text{Number of} \\ \text{variances and} \\ \text{covariances} \end{bmatrix} - \begin{bmatrix} \text{Number of} \\ \text{parameters} \\ \text{in the model} \end{bmatrix} \quad \text{- - - (31)}$$

Degrees of freedom of chi-square in path analysis

If the number of parameters in the model exceeds the number of variances and covariances (which, in this context, is to be viewed as the number of data points), the model is said to be **underidentified**, meaning that no unique solution to the problem of estimating the parameters can be found.

If the number of data points (i.e. the number of variances and covariances) is equal to the number of parameters, formula (31) indicates that the chi-square statistic has no degrees of freedom. In this situation, the model is said to be **just-identified** or **saturated**, and is a perfect fit to the data, whatever the values of the data points. The value of chi-square, therefore, must be zero and the fitting of the model to the data is a trivial exercise. The production of a saturated model, however, is not without its value, because estimates of its constituent parameters (such as path coefficients) can be tested for significance.

The testing of a model for goodness-of-fit is meaningful only when the number of data points exceeds the number of parameters in the model, in which case the model is said to be **overidentified**. Only if the situation permits the calculation of a value of chi-square on at least one degree of freedom, can the question of the adequacy of the model arise and a formal test of goodness-of-fit be made.

If, in the output navigator, we click on **Notes for Model**, we shall obtain the information shown in Outputs 26 and 27. We learn that the number of distinct sample moments (i.e. the number of data points) is 6 and the number of parameters in the model is 5. The degrees of freedom of chi-square is therefore 1. Note, however, that the chi-square referred to here is the *log likelihood* chi-square; whereas the chi-square shown in the central pillar is the Pearson chi-square. The two statistics have slightly different values.

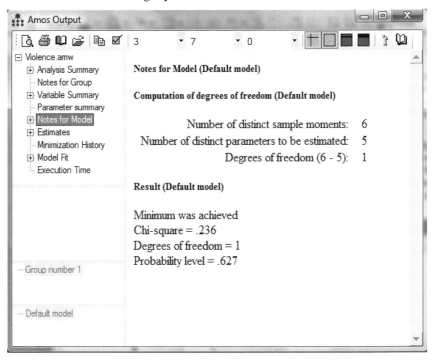

Output 27. Notes on the model

12.6.2.10 The model fit summary

Clicking the **Model Fit** option in the output navigator will produce a display of the goodness-of-fit statistics, only part of which is shown in Output 28. The **CMIN** statistic is the log likelihood chi-square, which we already known from the notes on the model to have the value .236.

The problem with both the Pearson and log likelihood chi-square statistics is that their values are affected by the size of the sample. There are other measures, such as the **normed fit index (NFI)** and the **comparative fit index (CFI)**, which are less sensitive to sample size.

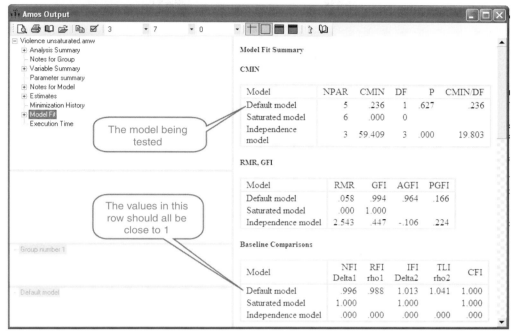

Output 28. Some goodness-of-fit statistics

Note that in the table of **CMIN** statistics, the **default model** is the one we are testing. The independence model assumes, almost certainly wrongly, that there are no associations whatsoever among the variables in the data set. The chi-square statistic for that model (59.409), however, serves as a measure of the total variance remaining to be explained by a model positing associations among the variables. Compared with this value, the value of CMIN for the default model (.236) is tiny, indicating that the model we are testing accounts for most of the variance unaccounted for by the total independence model.

Several other measures in the output, such as the **normed fit index (NFI)** and the **comparative fit index (CFI)**, compare the goodness-of-fit of the model being tested with that of the complete independence model. Their values should be close to 1, because the model being tested should account for most of the residual 'variance'. Inspection of the table headed **Baseline Comparisons** shows that the comparative statistics for the 'default model' do indeed have values close to 1.

The import of the goodness-of-fit statistics that we have reviewed is that dropping a parameter from the saturated model makes very little difference to the accuracy with which the model predicts the values of the 'data points' (i.e, the variances and covariances in the variance-covariance matrix, not the scores that individuals received on the three variables).

12.6.3   A brief look at a saturated model

The model we have tested holds that the correlation between the variables of Exposure to and Actual violence is actually driven by their common causation by the Parental variable. The possibility remains that, although the Parental variable plays the most important role in driving the correlation between Exposure and Actual, Exposure in its own right may still exert some causal influence upon Actual violence. Output 29 shows the input path diagram of this model. We shall see that this model, in which there are as many parameters as there are data points, is a **saturated model**.

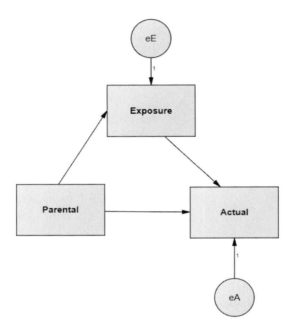

Output 29. The input path diagram of a saturated model

The exercise of fitting a saturated model to the data is trivial, because the model will predict the data points (variances and covariances) exactly and the chi-square statistic, with no degrees of freedom, will be zero. It can be seen from Output 30 that, since the number of data points (6) is equal to the number of parameters to be estimated (6), the chi-square statistic has no degrees of freedom. It is, however, instructive to examine the saturated model, because it clarifies some aspects of path analysis.

Notes for Model (Default model)

Computation of degrees of freedom (Default model)

$$\begin{aligned} \text{Number of distinct sample moments:} &\quad 6 \\ \text{Number of distinct parameters to be estimated:} &\quad 6 \\ \text{Degrees of freedom (6 - 6):} &\quad 0 \end{aligned}$$

Result (Default model)

Minimum was achieved
Chi-square = .000
Degrees of freedom = 0
Probability level cannot be computed

Output 30. Notes for the saturated model

It is instructive, before running the path analysis for the saturated model to choose **View➔Analysis Properties** and, in the Output tab of the **Analysis Properties** dialog, check the boxes labelled Implied moments, All implied moments and Residual moments (Figure 38).

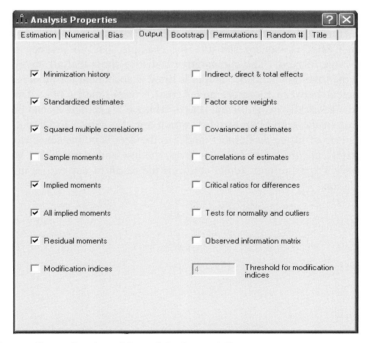

Figure 38. Requesting estimates of the original correlations

Output 31 shows the output path diagram for the saturated model. The standardised path coefficient between Exposure to and Actual violence is only .11, a value which the Text Output shows is too small to be robust.

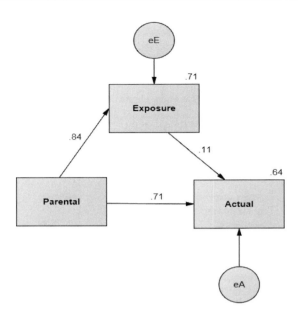

Output 31. The output path diagram of the saturated model

Output 32 shows the Model Fit Summary from the AMOS output. Notice that the model is a perfect fit: the CMIN chi-square statistic, for example, has no degrees of freedom and therefore has a value of zero. The comparative statistics show that all the residual variance remaining when the total independence model is fitted is accounted for by the saturated model. The path coefficient between Exposure and Actual is very small (.11). This value is both substantially and statistically insignificant: the *p*-value (.627) is high, as can be seen from the results of the tests of the regression weights, which are also shown in Output 32. Note that, although the exercise of fitting a saturated model to the data is in one sense trivial, tests of the parameter estimates can still be made. Moreover, the low and insignificant value of the path coefficient between Exposure and Actual confirms the result of our earlier investigation with the partial correlation.

Regression Weights: (Group number 1 - Default model)

			Estimate	S.E.	C.R.	P	Label
Exposure	<---	Parental	1.004	.125	8.044	***	
Actual	<---	Exposure	.082	.168	.486	.627	
Actual	<---	Parental	.652	.200	3.259	.001	

Model Fit Summary

CMIN

Model	NPAR	CMIN	DF	P	CMIN/DF
Default model	6	.000	0		
Saturated model	6	.000	0		
Independence model	3	59.409	3	.000	19.803

RMR, GFI

Model	RMR	GFI	AGFI	PGFI
Default model	.000	1.000		
Saturated model	.000	1.000		
Independence model	2.543	.447	-.106	.224

Baseline Comparisons

Model	NFI Delta1	RFI rho1	IFI Delta2	TLI rho2	CFI
Default model	1.000		1.000		1.000
Saturated model	1.000		1.000		1.000
Independence model	.000	.000	.000	.000	.000

Output 32. Tests of the regression weights and the Model Fit Summary for a saturated model

Output 33 shows some more of the Estimates from the AMOS output.

Implied Correlations (Group number 1 - Default model)

	Parental	Exposure	Actual
Parental	1.000		
Exposure	.845	1.000	
Actual	.801	.707	1.000

Residual Covariances (Group number 1 - Default model)

	Parental	Exposure	Actual
Parental	.000		
Exposure	.000	.000	
Actual	.000	.000	.000

Output 33. The estimates of correlations and residual covariances from the saturated model

Notice that the estimated correlations are exactly those in the SPSS output shown in Figure 19. The saturated model, being a perfect fit, reproduces the data points exactly. Notice, too, that the residuals, that is, the discrepancies between the covariances estimated from the model and the actual values of the covariances, are all zero.

In this section, we have only touched on path analysis. Further consideration of this important topic is beyond the scope of this book. As your next port of call, we suggest you might try the second edition of Dugard, Todman & Staines (2010), which has a very readable chapter on path analysis, which includes more complex (and therefore more realistic) examples than the very simple ones we have used here.

12.7   A FINAL WORD

Multiple regression is a highly complex topic and a full treatment is beyond the scope of this book. The following is a small selection from the wide choice of excellent books available.

Recommended reading

Ordinary least squares regression

Many years ago Jacob Cohen co-authored a book on multiple regression which, perhaps more than any other, has made this difficult topic accessible to those other than professional statisticians. The book has continued to be updated and the latest edition has kept fully abreast with recent developments. It is strongly recommended to anyone wishing to make progress in multiple regression.

Cohen, J., Cohen, P., West, S. G., & Aiken, L. S. (2003). *Applied multiple regression/correlation analysis for the behavioral sciences (3rd ed.)*. Mahwah, NJ: Lawrence Erlbaum Associates.

Dugard, Todman and Staines have written a readable practical guide to multivariate analysis, including multiple regression:

Dugard, P., Todman, J., & Staines, H. (2010). *Approaching multivariate analysis: a practical introduction (2nd ed.)*. London & New York: Routledge.

A more comprehensive, in-depth treatment of multiple regression will be found in

Tabachnick, B. G., & Fidell, L. S. (2007). *Using multivariate statistics (5th ed.)* Boston: Allyn & Bacon (Pearson International Edition).

The article and book by Darlington are still well worth reading:

Darlington, R. B. (1968). Multiple regression in psychological research and practice. *Psychological Bulletin*, 69, 161 – 182.

Darlington, R. B. (1990). *Regression and linear models*. New York: McGraw-Hill.

Multilevel modelling

The topic of multilevel modelling is introduced in Tabachnick & Fidell (2007), Chapter 15. The manual by Jon Rasbash and his associates would be an excellent follow-up:

Rasbash, J., Steele, F., Browne, W., & Prosser, B. (2004). *A User's Guide to MLwiN Version 2.0.* London: Centre for Multilevel Modelling, University of London.

Exercises

Exercise 20 *Simple, two-variable regression* and Exercise 21 *Multiple regression* are available in www.psypress.com/spss-made-simple and click on Exercises.

CHAPTER 13

Analyses of multiway frequency tables

13.1   INTRODUCTION

A contingency table is a crosstabulation showing the frequencies of observations in different combinations of the categories making up qualitative or categorical variables. The construction of a contingency table is the first step in the investigation of a possible association between categorical variables in a set of nominal data. The two-way contingency table is the equivalent, for nominal data, of the scatterplot used to investigate associations in continuous bivariate (or multivariate) data sets. In Chapter 11, we described the use of approximate chi-square tests to test for the presence of an association between two categorical variables: 1. Tissue Type; 2. Presence of an Antibody.

In this chapter, we shall consider the investigation of associations among the variables in multivariate nominal data sets with three or more attributes. The traditional Pearson chi-square test was designed for use with two-way frequency tables. The situation often arises, however, in which the researcher has nominal data on three or more attributes and wants to test for associations among the attributes. For many years, the standard approach to this problem was to combine or 'collapse' the frequencies across the categories of some of the variables, thus creating a two-way table, upon which the usual chi-square test could then be made. This is a dangerous practice. Todman & Dugard (2007), for example, show how an apparent association between sex and mathematical ability (seemingly revealed by collapsing across a third variable and testing in the usual way) actually arises from the association of both gender and mathematical aptitude with a third variable, namely, the relative lengths of the index and third fingers. (Later in this chapter, we shall see that there are circumstances in which multiway frequency tables can safely be collapsed across the categories of some variables, but this move must be justified by preliminary analysis.) It is also possible to generalise the traditional chi-square test to multi-way tables without collapsing across any of the attributes. Such an approach, however, as we shall see, rarely answers the researcher's specific questions.

Recent years have seen great advances in the analysis of multi-way contingency tables, and these new methods, collectively known as **loglinear analysis**, are now available in computing packages such as SPSS. Loglinear analysis allows the user to do much more than merely reject the hypothesis of independence of all the variables in the classification, which (when there are three or more attributes) is very unlikely to be true anyway. The great advantage of loglinear analysis is that it makes possible the formulation of a model of the data that shows the unique contribution of each attribute and of its interactions with the other attributes.

13.2   SOME BASICS OF LOGLINEAR MODELLING

There is general agreement that there is little or no advantage in using loglinear analysis to analyse a two-way contingency table: the Pearson and likelihood ratio chi-square tests which we described in Chapter 11 (together with follow-up measures of strength of association) are sufficient for this purpose. In the simple context of the two-way table, however, the essential features of loglinear modelling emerge very clearly; moreover, the comparison with the traditional chi-square analysis of the same data is also instructive. In this section, therefore, we shall apply loglinear analysis to the same data that we analysed in Chapter 11, namely, the incidence of an antibody in four different tissue groups. The data are reproduced in Table 1 below.

Table 1. Contingency table with a pattern of observed frequencies suggesting an association between Tissue Type and Presence of an antibody

Tissue type	Presence		Total
	Yes	No	
A	8	14	22
B	7	11	18
C	7	5	12
Critical	21	6	27
Total	43	36	79

13.2.1   Loglinear models and ANOVA models

The full loglinear model of a two-way contingency table is very similar in appearance to the fixed-effects model for the two-factor, between subjects ANOVA. In this subsection, we shall review the ANOVA model before discussing the loglinear model.

In the ANOVA model, each score X is expressed as the sum of several components:
1.   The **grand mean** μ;
2.   A **main effect** of factor A which, in the population, is the deviation of a marginal group mean on the A classification from the grand mean;
3.   A **main effect** of factor B, which is the deviation of a marginal mean on the B classification from the grand mean;
4.   The **interaction** AB, which is what remains of the deviation of a cell mean from the grand mean when the two main effects have been subtracted;
5.   A random **error** component.

The **two-way ANOVA model** states that:

$$X = \begin{bmatrix} \text{grand} \\ \text{mean} \end{bmatrix} + \begin{bmatrix} \text{main effect} \\ \text{of factor A} \end{bmatrix} + \begin{bmatrix} \text{main effect} \\ \text{of factor B} \end{bmatrix} + \begin{bmatrix} \text{AB} \\ \text{interaction} \end{bmatrix} + \begin{bmatrix} \text{random} \\ \text{error} \end{bmatrix} \text{- - - (1)}$$

The two-way ANOVA model

A main effect of factor A is estimated with $M_j - M$, the deviation of the mean on the A classification from the grand mean. A main effect of factor B is estimated with $M_k - M$, the deviation of the mean on the B classification from the grand mean. The interaction component AB is what is left of the deviation of the cell mean from the grand mean when the main effects have been removed: $M_{jk} - M_j - M_k + M$.

With the exception of the grand mean, the components of the fixed effects ANOVA model are deviation scores, which have the property that they sum to zero at any level of either factor.

The full loglinear model for the cell frequencies in a two-way contingency table is similar in form to the ANOVA model:

$$\ln E = \text{constant} + \begin{bmatrix} \text{main effect} \\ \text{of A} \end{bmatrix} + \begin{bmatrix} \text{main effect} \\ \text{of B} \end{bmatrix} + \begin{bmatrix} \text{interaction} \\ \text{AB} \end{bmatrix} \text{- - - (2)}$$

A Loglinear model

In equation 2, $\ln E$ is the natural logarithm of the cell frequency.

Notice that, rather than modelling the individual score X as in the two-way ANOVA, we are modelling the cell frequency in the contingency table. There is no separate random error term in the loglinear model. Moreover, rather than modelling the cell frequency itself, we are modelling the natural logarithm of the cell frequency. The reason for this is basically that, as we said in Chapter 11, values of the expected frequencies are derived from *products* of the marginal frequencies in the contingency table. Equation 2 is linear in form because the log of a product is the *sum* of the logs of the factors involved. In fact, there is a multiplicative equivalent of the model in equation 2, in which the expected frequencies themselves (rather than their logs) are modelled as a *product* of main effect and interaction terms. This multiplicative model can be obtained from (2) by taking antilogs of both sides of the equation.

These differences aside, there are important similarities between the ANOVA and loglinear models. The 'constant' in the loglinear model is the equivalent of the grand mean in the ANOVA model: it is the mean of the logs of the cell frequencies. The main effects are the deviations of the logs of the marginal frequencies from the grand mean of the logs. The interaction effect (there is one for each cell in the table) is what remains of the deviation of the log of the cell mean from the grand mean when the main effects have been removed. Once again, the main effects sum to zero over all the levels of either factor; and the interaction effects sum to zero at any level of either factor.

Although the ANOVA is predicated upon a score model, the ANOVA is not an exercise in modelling as such: the various components of the model (main effects and interactions) are tested for significance and the results are interpreted accordingly. Throughout the testing process, however, the same model remains intact with all its original components, regardless of the outcomes of the tests.

In contrast, loglinear analysis is a process of **model-building**, the aim of the exercise being to find the model which, while having as few components as possible, accounts for the cell frequencies adequately. In the tissue type example, for instance, the hypothesis that the two attributes are independent implies that the cell frequencies can be modelled adequately by omitting the interaction term and retaining only the main effect components of the model.

13.2.2   Model-building and the hierarchical principle

Having identified important similarities with the ANOVA model, we must now draw your attention to a very important difference. In the ANOVA, we are dealing with the means of samples of scores. The values of means are independent of the numbers of observations from which they are calculated. In ANOVA, therefore, the values of the various effects are unaffected by the sizes of the samples. In loglinear analysis, however, we are modelling cell frequencies as a function of other frequencies. As a consequence, the values of the marginal frequencies do affect estimates of the main effects and the interaction.

In loglinear analysis, therefore, model-building should generally follow what is known as the **hierarchical principle**: that is, if an interaction term is included in the model, the main effects of all the factors involved in the interaction must also be included; and if the interaction involves three or more factors, the model must include all the lower-order interactions involving those factors. For example, if the model includes the three-way interaction term ABC, it must also include the main effects A, B and C, plus the two-way interactions AB, AC and BC. In most (though not all) SPSS loglinear procedures, only the interaction term of highest order need be specified: the procedure will automatically **generate** the lower-order effects. Hence a model which includes the effects A, B, C, D, BC, BD, CD and BCD is said to be of **generating class** A, BCD: the term BCD implies the presence in the model of the main effects B, C and D, and also of the two-way interactions BC, BD and CD.

13.2.2.1   Saturated models

A loglinear model that contains all the possible effect terms is known as a **saturated model**. A saturated model will always predict the observed cell frequencies exactly. In our current example, since the interaction has been defined as the residual difference between the (logs of the) cell frequencies and the grand mean when the main effects have been removed, the sum of the main effects plus the interaction is the (log of the) cell frequency.

Each effect term in a loglinear model has an associated number of degrees of freedom and parameters that must be estimated. In our 4×2 contingency table, the Group variable has $(4 - 1) = 3$ degrees of freedom, the Presence variable has $(2 - 1) = 1$ degree of freedom and the Group $\times$ Presence interaction has $(4 - 1)(2 - 1) = 3$ degrees of freedom. That makes 7 degrees of freedom in total, making 7 parameters that would be estimated with the saturated model. If we add the grand mean, we have as many parameters as there are cells in the contingency table, leaving no room for any deviation from the observed cell frequencies.

13.2.2.2　Unsaturated models

The purpose of a loglinear analysis is often to see whether the cell frequencies can be adequately approximated by a model that contains *fewer* than the full set of possible treatment effects, subject to the hierarchical constraint. A model that contains fewer than the total number of possible terms is known as an **unsaturated model**.

When there is no association between two variables, the expected frequencies can be accounted for adequately in terms of the marginal frequencies in the table and the model will contain no interaction terms. This model is known as the **total independence** or **main-effects-only** model:

$$\ln E = \text{constant} + \begin{bmatrix} \text{main effect} \\ \text{of A} \end{bmatrix} + \begin{bmatrix} \text{main effect} \\ \text{of B} \end{bmatrix} \text{ - - - (3)}$$

Loglinear main-effects model

Note the absence of the interaction term from this unsaturated model.

13.2.2.3　The role of the chi-square test in loglinear model-building

When we make a traditional chi-square test for an association in a contingency table, the null hypothesis states that the attributes are independent. On that assumption, expected frequencies are calculated from the marginal frequencies in the table and the chi-square test statistic expresses the extent to which the observed cell frequencies O deviate from the corresponding expected frequencies E. The greater the values $(O - E)$ tend to be, the greater the value of chi-square and the stronger the evidence against the null hypothesis of independence. In Chapter 11, we described two versions of the chi-square statistic: the Pearson version and the likelihood ratio version. It is the likelihood ratio chi-square that receives the greater emphasis in loglinear analysis.

In Chapter 11, we observed that the traditional chi-square test is used for two purposes. When we have data on a single variable, we can use the chi-square statistic to measure the extent to which our data are approximated by a theoretical distribution and test the null hypothesis that the data have been sampled from this theoretical population. This is a **goodness-of-fit** test. Where we have data on two attributes in the form of a contingency table, we can use chi-square to test for an **association** between the two attributes. In a test of goodness-of-fit, a *small* value of chi-square indicates a *good* fit. In a test for association, a *large* value of chi-square indicates the presence of an association.

In loglinear modelling, the (likelihood ratio) chi-square statistic is used as a measure of goodness-of-fit of the model to the data. A small value for chi-square indicates a good fit; a large value indicates a poor fit. There are several approaches to loglinear modelling. In the **backward hierarchical** approach, we begin with the saturated model, which we know in advance will predict the cell frequencies perfectly. Next, we remove the most complex interaction term from the model. The expected frequencies and LR chi-square are now recalculated on the basis of the simpler model. The effect of this simplification of the model will be to increase the value of chi-square from zero, because there are now fewer parameters in the model than there are cells in the table and the degrees of freedom of the chi-square statistic will increase from zero to the degrees of freedom of the effect that has been removed. This increment in chi-square can be tested to see whether the removal of the interaction significantly worsens the goodness-of-fit of the model to the data. If the goodness-of-fit is not significantly worse, that is, the value of chi-square has not been significantly increased, we remove the term from the model. We continue the process of removing terms, recalculating the expected frequencies and re-testing with chi-square. The process ends when the removal of a term from the model results in a significant increase in chi-square, indicating that the term should be retained in the model. (If the term is an interaction, we must also, in accordance with the hierarchical principle, retain any lower order interactions and the main effects of all the factors involved.)

In the context of loglinear modelling, the likehihood ratio chi-square measure of goodness-of-fit is often known as G^2 (or as the **Goodman statistic**, in honour of Goodman's pioneering work in this area). A great advantage of the Goodman statistic over the traditional Pearson chi-square is that it has the **additive property**: that is, its total value can be apportioned among the different terms being tested, enabling us to see whether the removal of any term from the model makes a significant difference to the model's goodness-of-fit. By 'total value' here, we mean the value of chi-square that we should obtain if we tried to fit the data with a model containing only a constant and no effect terms at all.

The significance of any particular interaction effect is tested with G^2_{effect} , where

$$G^2_{\text{effect}} = G^2_{\text{effect present}} - G^2_{\text{effect absent}} \text{ - - - (4)}$$

Partition of the LR chi-square (using the Goodman statistic)

which is distributed approximately on chi-square with degrees of freedom equal to that of the effect itself.

13.2.3 The main-effects-only loglinear model and the traditional chi-square test for association

The **main-effects-only** model is the equivalent, in loglinear analysis, of the null hypothesis of no association between two variables that is tested by the traditional chi-square test. In the loglinear analysis of a two-way contingency table, the value of the Goodman statistic will be exactly that of the likelihood ratio chi-square, obtained from the formula:

$$\chi^2 (r-1)(c-1) = 2 \sum_{\text{all cells}} O \ln\left(\frac{O}{E}\right) \text{ - - - (5) } \textbf{Likelihood ratio chi-square}$$

where r and c are the numbers of rows and columns, respectively. The likelihood ratio chi-square is distributed approximately as chi-square on $(r-1)(c-1)$ degrees of freedom. For the data in Table 1, the value of the likelihood ratio chi-square is

$$\chi^2(3) = 2 \sum_{\text{all cells}} O\left[\ln\left(\frac{O}{E}\right)\right]$$

$$= 2\left[6 \ln\left(\frac{6}{12.3}\right) + 21 \ln\left(\frac{21}{14.7}\right) + \ldots + 14 \ln\left(\frac{14}{10.0}\right) + 8 \ln\left(\frac{8}{12.0}\right)\right]$$

$$= 11.09$$

We shall see that this is exactly the value of G^2 when the interaction term has been removed from the loglinear model and the main effects model is tested for goodness-of-fit.

Note carefully that when we apply the main-effects-only model to the data and run a test of significance, we are not testing the *main effects* for significance: we are testing the increase in the value of chi-square resulting from the *removal* of the interaction term from the model. We are, in fact, testing the *interaction term* for significance.

13.2.4   Analysis of the residuals

As in regression analysis, it is good practice to assess the goodness-of-fit of a loglinear model by examining the distribution of the **residuals** (the differences between the observed and expected frequencies). There are different kinds of residuals, designed for different purposes. The **raw** residuals are obtained by subtracting the expected frequencies generated by the model from the observed frequencies. Other residuals have been rescaled, so that they have a mean of zero and a standard deviation of 1. Examples are **Adjusted residuals** and **deviance residuals**, which are more useful than raw residuals for identifying outliers and cells where the estimates of the expected frequencies are particularly poor.

13.2.4.1   Quantile-quantile Q-Q plots

A special kind of graph, which will be included in the SPSS output if requested, displays the distribution of the residuals. A **quantile-quantile Q-Q plot** is a plot of the quantiles of the standardised scores of the obtained distribution against the values of the standard normal distribution that have the same quantile values. (Quantiles are points taken at regular intervals from the cumulative distribution function of a random variable – the **100-quantiles** are called **percentiles**.) The same range of values of the standard normal variable Z is stepped out on both axes. If the points tend to lie (approximately) along the straight line running diagonally from bottom left to top right, the obtained distribution is normal; non-normal distributions have points that deviate systematically from the line in an obviously non-linear fashion.

13.2.4.2   Detrended Q-Q plots

In a **detrended Q-Q plot**, the deviations of the scores from the line in the Q-Q plot (i.e. their deviations from expectation) are plotted against their standard scores. If the distribution is normal, all values will lie reasonably close to the horizontal baseline through zero on the vertical axis. The points in the detrended plot should show no obvious pattern: should, for instance, those points on the left tend to lie above the horizontal baseline and those to the right below (or vice versa), non-normality of distribution is indicated.

13.3   MODELLING A TWO-WAY CONTINGENCY TABLE

We shall now run a loglinear analysis of the Tissue Type × Presence contingency table in Table 1. Since we have already explored this table thoroughly in Chapter 11, we can dispense with the preliminaries here and proceed with the loglinear analysis proper.

Follow the usual procedure to enter the data into the **Data Editor**, which will appear as in Figure 1.

	Group	Presence	Count
1	Type A	No	14
2	Type A	Yes	8
3	Type B	No	11
4	Type B	Yes	7
5	Type C	No	5
6	Type C	Yes	7
7	Critical	No	6
8	Critical	Yes	21

Figure 1. **Data View** showing the two grouping variables and the counts of presence or absence of the antibody

(To view the value labels rather than the numerical values themselves, check **Value Labels** in the **View** menu or click the label icon at the tops of either of the **Data Editor** windows.)

13.3.1   SPSS procedures for loglinear analysis

Figure 2 shows the menu for loglinear analysis.

Any of the three choices on the **Loglinear** menu will fit a loglinear model to the data. **Model Selection**, however, accesses the HILOGLINEAR program; whereas the **General** and **Logit** choices access the GENLOG program. Here we shall concentrate on the **Model Selection** choice.

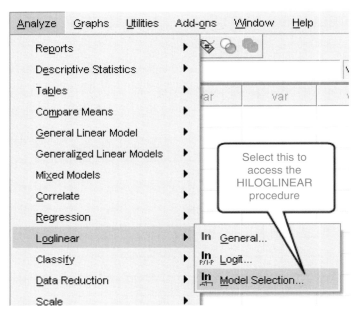

Figure 2. The **Loglinear** menu

13.3.1.1 Procedure

There are important differences between the HILOGLINEAR and GENLOG programs. All three choices from the **Loglinear** menu will produce parameter estimates and tests of significance of these estimates. **Model Selection**, however, will run a backward elimination analysis and report direct tests of significance of the various components of the model. In our view, this is the easiest way of testing the components of the loglinear model. Tests of the significance of model components can also be made in GENLOG; but in order to make such tests, the user must take extra steps. We shall therefore take the **Model Selection** approach first.

Select **Data➜Weight Cases…** to open the **Weight Cases** dialog box and transfer the variable Count to the **Frequency Variable** box. Click **OK**.   (This move is not necessary for a loglinear analysis; however, loglinear analysis should be run in conjunction with the Crosstabs procedure, which does require that the cases be weighted according to frequency.)

Select Analyze➜Loglinear➜Model Selection… to enter the Model Selection Loglinear Analysis dialog box (Figure 3).

Transfer the variable names Group and Presence to the **Factor(s)** panel on the right. Each factor name in the **Factor(s)** box will be followed by the expression (? ?), which is a request for the minimum and maximum values of the code numbers that have been selected for the categories.

Follow the steps described in Figure 3 to specify the minimum and maximum values of each factor.

Click **OK** to run the procedure.

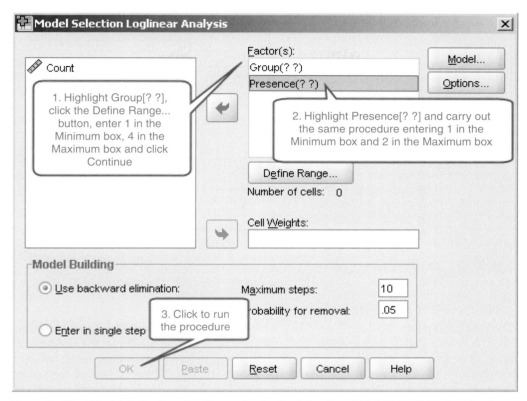

Figure 3. The **Model Selection Loglinear Analysis** dialog box (HILOGLINEAR) showing how to define the range of the factor values

13.3.1.2   Table of contents of the Output window

The output of many SPSS procedures is extensive. SPSS has therefore provided a useful navigational aid. In the SPSS Output window, there is a vertical grey pillar, to the left of which is a table of contents of the output, each item appearing as a labelled icon. Clicking on any item in the table will bring it into view in the pane on the right of the pillar (Figure 4).

13.3.1.3   The output

An early item in the output (not shown here) is a table headed **Convergence Information**. In this table, check that the generating class is given as Group*Presence, which means that SPSS has applied a saturated model to the data.

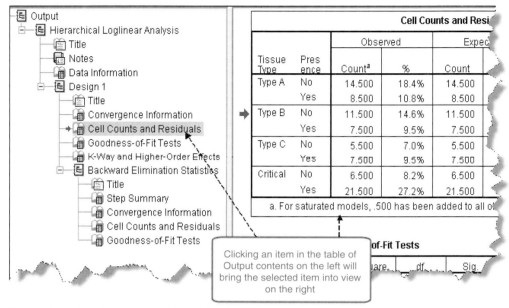

Figure 4. Table of contents of the Output window

The next item (partly shown in Figure 4) is a table of **Cell Counts and Residuals**. From this table, it is immediately apparent that the saturated model is a perfect fit: all the residuals are zero.   For technical reasons, however, the frequency in every cell in the table has been incremented by .5.   Later in the **Backward Elimination Statistics** section of the output, however, another table, also with the caption **Cell Counts and Residuals**, appears with the observed frequencies as they were in the original data set. This table is shown in Output 1.

Cell Counts and Residuals							
Tissue Type	Presence	Observed		Expected		Residuals	Std. Residuals
		Count	%	Count	%		
Type A	No	14.000	17.7%	14.000	17.7%	.000	.000
	Yes	8.000	10.1%	8.000	10.1%	.000	.000
Type B	No	11.000			13.9%	.000	.000
	Yes	7.000			8.9%		
Type C	No	5.000			6.3%		
	Yes	7.000			8.9%		
Critical	No	6.000	7.6%	6.000	7.6%	.000	.000
	Yes	21.000	26.6%	21.000	26.6%	.000	.000

In every cell, the expected frequency predicted from the saturated model is equal to the observed frequency.

Since the saturated model predicts the frequencies exactly, the residuals are all zero.

Output 1. Table of **Cell Counts and Residuals**, showing that the saturated model predicts the cell frequencies perfectly

The table headed **Goodness-of-fit Tests** (Output 2) shows that the chi-square statistic has no degrees of freedom and hence a value of zero: this is entirely consistent with information in the table of cell counts and residuals.

Goodness-of-Fit Tests

	Chi-Square	df	Sig.
Likelihood Ratio	.000	0	.
Pearson	.000	0	.

Output 2. The **Goodness-of-Fit Tests**. The saturated model leaves chi-square with no degrees of freedom

Note carefully that the test reported in Output 2 is not a test of the significance of any of the components of the model: the chi-square statistic measures any residual difference that might remain (in this case there is none) between the predictions of the model and the actual cell frequencies.

The tests of significance for individual components of the model are reported in the table of **Backward Elimination Statistics**, which is shown in Output 3. In this table, it can be seen that when the interaction term is removed from the model, the value of the **LR chi-square** (i.e. G^2) increases from zero to 11.093 on 3 degrees of freedom. Since this value is significant beyond the .05 level, the interaction term must be retained in the model. Note that the value 11.093 is *exactly the value we obtained when we applied the likelihood ratio chi-square formula to the same contingency table.*

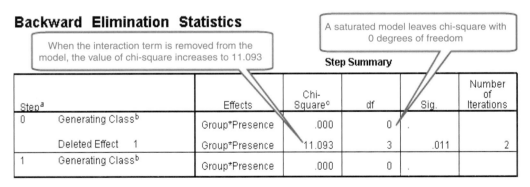

Backward Elimination Statistics

When the interaction term is removed from the model, the value of chi-square increases to 11.093

A saturated model leaves chi-square with 0 degrees of freedom

Step Summary

Step[a]		Effects	Chi-Square[c]	df	Sig.	Number of Iterations
0	Generating Class[b]	Group*Presence	.000	0	.	
	Deleted Effect 1	Group*Presence	11.093	3	.011	2
1	Generating Class[b]	Group*Presence	.000	0	.	

a. At each step, the effect with the largest significance level for the Likelihood Ratio Change is deleted, provided the significance level is larger than .050

b. Statistics are displayed for the best model at each step after step 0

c. For 'Deleted Effect', this is the change in the Chi-Square after the effect is deleted from the model

Output 3. Table of backward elimination statistics

The process of backward elimination ceases after the first step because, by the hierarchical principle, the retention of an interaction necessitates also the retention of its component factors.

Output 4 is part of a table with the caption **K-Way and Higher Order Effects**. (In the original table, the Pearson chi-square values were also given. They present a very similar picture to the LR chi-square statistics.) Here the term **Order** refers to the number of factors involved in the effects concerned: a first-order effect (K=1) is a main effect; a second-order effect (K = 2) is a two-way interaction, and so on.

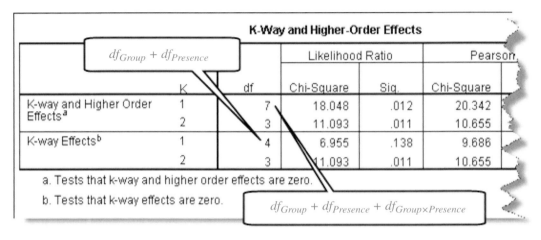

	K	df	Likelihood Ratio Chi-Square	Sig.	Pearson Chi-Square
K-way and Higher Order Effects[a]	1	7	18.048	.012	20.342
	2	3	11.093	.011	10.655
K-way Effects[b]	1	4	6.955	.138	9.686
	2	3	11.093	.011	10.655

a. Tests that k-way and higher order effects are zero.

b. Tests that k-way effects are zero.

Output 4. Table showing the chi-square values associated with the effects at different levels. The upper part of the table gives the chi-square value associated with effects at a level as high as or higher than a specified level; the lower part gives the total chi-square associated with the effects at each level alone

In the upper part of Output 4, the chi-square value opposite each level of effect is the chi-square attributable to all effects at that level, *plus* those associated with any (and every) higher-order effect. The chi-square value for K = 1 (18.048) is the total chi-square value of the two main effects, plus the chi-square value for the two-way interaction. Since there are no effects of order higher than K = 2, the chi-square for K = 2 is, in this example, the chi-square associated with the interaction alone, namely, 11.093.

The meaning of the terms in Output 4 may be clearer upon consideration of the values in the degrees of freedom column. In the upper part of the table, the entries are the total degrees of freedom of all effects at each level, *plus* the degrees of freedom of the effects at all higher levels. Thus at level K = 1, we have the main effect of Group (df = 3), plus the main effect of Presence (df = 1), *plus* the degrees of freedom of the interaction (3), making seven degrees of freedom in all. At level K = 2, there is only one effect, namely, the interaction ($df = 3$).

In the lower half of the table, the *df* value for K = 1 is now 4 (not 7), because here we are being given the total degrees of freedom of the effects at one level only. The total degrees of freedom for the two main effects is 4 (1 for Presence plus 3 for Group), which is the value opposite K = 1.

The topmost entry for the LR chi-square (or G^2) is 18.048. This is the total value of chi-square: it is the increment in G^2 that would result from applying a model that contained no effects at all, that is, one containing the constant only. You will see that when we add the two values in the lower part of the table (those associated with the main effects and the interaction), we obtain 18.048, which is exactly the value of the total G^2 in the upper part of the table. (This is also approximately true of the corresponding Pearson chi-square values.)

Notice also that the value of G^2 given for the interaction alone (11.093) is what remains of the total G^2 when the portion attributable to the main effects only (6.955) has been subtracted.

Finally, we note from the entry for K = 1 in the lower part of Output 4 that the tests for main effects do not show significance. The only significant component in the model, therefore, is the interaction.

13.3.2   Fitting an unsaturated model

A saturated model, which contains all possible effect terms, must (as explained earlier) always predict the cell frequencies exactly, as in the present example.

We have also seen, however, that in order to account adequately for the pattern of frequencies in Table 1, we must include the interaction term in the model; otherwise, the value of chi-square increases significantly. We know, therefore, that an unsaturated model containing only main effect terms will fit the data poorly. It is, however, instructive to apply an (albeit ill-fitting) main-effects-only model to the data of our current example, so that we can obtain some of the graphs from SPSS's regression diagnostics. The goodness-of-fit of a model is readily apparent from the appearance of such diagnostic graphs. We shall begin at the point where we have completed the dialog shown in Figure 3. In that exercise, we were then able to proceed with the backward elimination simply by clicking **OK**.

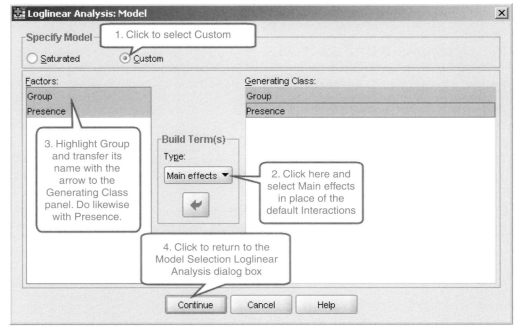

Figure 5. The completed **Loglinear Analysis: Model** dialog, showing that a main-effects-only model has been specified

- This time, click the **Model** button in the top right-hand corner of the dialog box, to obtain the **Loglinear Analysis: Model** dialog box (Figure 5). Follow the steps shown in Figure 5 to specify a main-effects-only model. In the central pillar in the dialog box is the **Build Term(s)** caption, with the **Type** button underneath. The default setting is **Interactions**. Change this setting to **Main effects** and return to **Model Selection Loglinear Analysis**.
- In the **Model Selection Loglinear Analysis** dialog box, click the **Options** button to open the **Loglinear Analysis: Options** dialog box (Figure 6). Select a **Residuals** plot and click **Continue** to return to **Model Selection Loglinear Analysis**.
- Finally click **OK** to run the procedure.

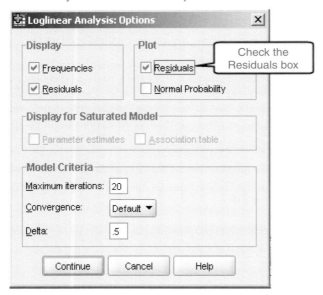

Figure 6. The completed **Loglinear Analysis: Options** dialog

13.3.2.1   Output for an unsaturated model

The first table in the output (not shown here) is **Convergence Information**. Check that the generating class is given as Group, Presence, not Group*Presence, as when we were fitting a saturated model.

Output 5 shows the plots of observed counts and residuals for our current data set. The fit is now clearly far from perfect: the expected and observed frequencies no longer match and there are non-zero entries in the **Residuals** and **Standardised Residuals** columns.

Cell Counts and Residuals							
Tissue Type	Presence	Observed		Expected		Residuals	Std. Residuals
		Count	%	Count	%		
Type A	No	14.000	17.7%	10.025	12.7%	3.975	1.255
	Yes	8.000	10.1%	11.975	15.2%	-3.975	-1.149
Type B	No	11.000	13.9%	8.203	10.4%	2.797	.977
	Yes	7.000	8.9%	9.797	12.4%	-2.797	-.894
Type C	No	5.000	6.3%	5.468	6.9%	-.468	-.200
	Yes	7.000	8.9%	6.532	8.3%	.468	.183
Critical	No	6.000	7.6%	12.304	15.6%	-6.304	-1.797
	Yes	21.000	26.6%	14.696	18.6%	6.304	1.644

Output 5. **Cell Counts and Residuals** table when the main-effects-only model is applied

Output 6 summarises the **Goodness-of-fit Tests**. The significant increase in G^2 shows that the main-effects-only (independence) model is not a good fit for these data.

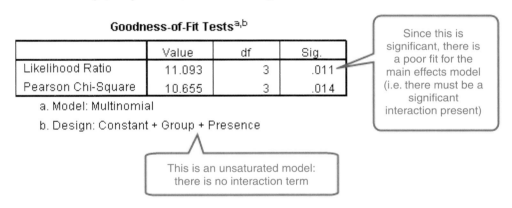

Goodness-of-Fit Tests[a,b]

	Value	df	Sig.
Likelihood Ratio	11.093	3	.011
Pearson Chi-Square	10.655	3	.014

a. Model: Multinomial

b. Design: Constant + Group + Presence

Since this is significant, there is a poor fit for the main effects model (i.e. there must be a significant interaction present)

This is an unsaturated model: there is no interaction term

Output 6. Summary of the **Goodness-of-Fit Tests**

The values of the **Likelihood Ratio** and **Pearson Chi-Square** are exactly the same as those we obtained by the backward elimination analysis in the previous section. They are also the values we obtain when we make the traditional chi-square test of association between Presence and Group. The significance test for the goodness-of-fit of a main-effects-only loglinear model is the exact equivalent of the traditional likelihood-ratio chi-square test for association, in which the null hypothesis is that the two variables are independent.

It may be worth repeating our earlier point that the test reported in Output 6 is a test of the component *omitted* from the model, not of those remaining in the model. The test of G^2 when the main-effects-only model is applied is a test of the *interaction* component of the full model.

13.3.2.2 The residual plots

If a loglinear model is a good fit and the observed cell counts are plotted against the expected counts from the loglinear model, the points on the graph should lie close to a straight line. Another characteristic of a good fit is that both the adjusted and deviance residuals should have approximately normal distributions. Thirdly, a plot of either kind of residual against the expected values should result in an amorphous cloud of points, and there should be no outstandingly large values.

Output 7 shows what the residual plots would look like if the main-effects-only model were a good fit for the data, as it would be with a data set showing no association between Group and Presence. Only the cells either above or below the diagonal of blank cells are relevant: the other three cells simply reproduce the same plots with the axes reversed.

Hiloglinear Model

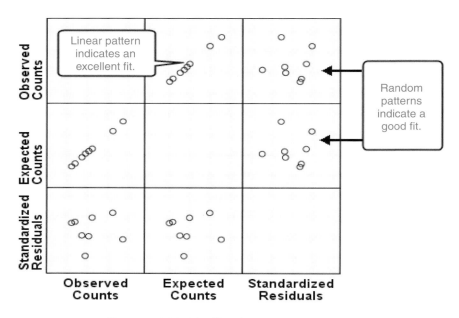

Cases weighted by Count

Output 7. Plots of **Observed Counts, Expected Counts** and **Standardized Residuals** when a model fits the data well

The strongly linear pattern in the plot of observed counts against expected counts indicates an excellent fit, as do the shapeless plots of observed counts against standardised residuals.

Output 8 shows the plots of counts and residuals for the data in our current example (the data in Table 1). The plots clearly do not meet the criteria for a good fit: the plot of observed counts against expected counts is far from linear; and the plots of the observed and expected counts against the standardised residuals show patterns that are far from random.

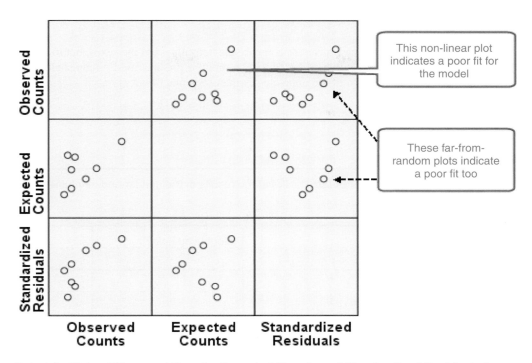

Output 8. Plots of **Observed Counts**, **Expected Counts** and **Standardized Residuals** for the data in Table 1 showing that the main-effects model fits the data poorly

13.3.3   Summary

The purpose of the foregoing sections has been to introduce the fundamentals of loglinear modelling in the simplest possible context and to familiarise the reader with the general procedure and the main features of the output. As we said in Section 13.1, if you actually have a two-way contingency table you want to analyse, you should use one of the chi-square tests described in Chapter 11: there would be no advantage in running a loglinear analysis (although that would produce the same result). In the next section, however, the essential features we have discussed in this section will be put to good use in the analysis of a three-way frequency table, where the loglinear analysis has great advantages over the traditional chi-square approach. Faced with a more complex table, loglinear modelling can not only confirm the existence of associations among the data, but also pinpoint the precise nature of those associations.

13.4   MODELLING A THREE-WAY FREQUENCY TABLE

We shall illustrate the application of loglinear modelling of a three-way frequency table with some data from an imaginary experiment on gender and helpfulness. Suppose that male and female interviewers asked 50 male and 50 female participants whether, in a hypothetical situation, they would offer to help someone in difficulties. The factors of sex of interviewer and sex of participant were varied orthogonally, so that each of 50 male and 50 female interviewers interviewed 25 male and 25 female participants.

The purpose of the investigation was not to compare the helpfulness of the sexes, but to test the opposite-sex dyadic hypothesis, which holds that, in certain pre-specified circumstances, we are more likely to help someone of the opposite sex than someone of our own.

13.4.1   Exploring the data

The data are shown in Table 2.

Table 2. Three-way contingency table showing the results of the gender and helpfulness experiment

		Would you help?		
Sex of Interviewer	Sex of Participant	Yes	No	Total
Male	Male	4	21	25
	Female	16	9	25
Female	Male	11	14	25
	Female	11	14	25
	Total	42	58	100

The measures known as the **odds** and the **odds ratio (*OR*)** were introduced in Chapter 11. There, we used them to explore the pattern of the frequencies in a two-way contingency table. These measures can also be used to explore more complex frequency tables, provided at least two of the factors are dichotomies.

What is the effect of the sex of the interviewer on whether male participants will help or not? When the interviewer is male (first data row in the table), the odds in favour of males helping are $4/21 = .190$.   When the interviewer is female (third data row in the table), the odds in favour of males helping are $11/14 = .786$.   Male participants, then, are more likely to help when the interviewer is female.   The *OR* is $.786/.190 = 4.13$: that is, male participants are four times as likely to help when the interviewer is a female.

When we turn to the female participants, we find that, when we compare their helpfulness with male and female interviewers, the odds ratio is 2.26.   Again, the participants are more likely to help someone of the opposite sex than one of their own.   A superficial exploration of the data, therefore, seems to confirm the opposite-sex dyadic hypothesis.

Suppose for a moment that instead of recording whether someone was prepared to help or not, we had taken some continuous measure of helpfulness on an independent scale with units.   We should then have had an experiment of between subjects, two-factor design and could consider running an ANOVA on the data.   The opposite-sex dyadic hypothesis implies what, in the context of ANOVA, would be a two-way interaction between Sex of Participant and Sex of Interviewer.   In the present context of loglinear modelling, however, the same hypothesis implies a *three-way* interaction between the factors of Sex of Participant, Sex of Interviewer and whether Help was given. Here, the Help × Sex of Participant interaction has replaced the continuous measure of helpfulness. In Chapter 9, we saw that a three-way interaction is said to occur when the interaction between two of the variables is not homogeneous across the levels of the third factor. In the present example, the opposite-sex dyadic hypothesis implies that the interaction between Gender and Help will be different with male and female interviewers: with male interviewers, females will be more helpful than they would be with female interviewers; with female interviewers, the reverse pattern should be obtained.

We have used the odds ratio to explore the three-way frequency table. The clustered bar charts offered as options in SPSS's crosstabulation procedure can also be illuminating.

Output 9 shows rather different patterns for the Male and Female interviewers. A pattern consistent with the opposite-sex dyadic hypothesis is clearly evident when the interviewer is male. With a female interviewer, however, the incidence of help is rather less than 50% in both male and female participants; nevertheless, comparisons between the heights of the bars in the graphs on the right and on the left show that once again, the males were more helpful when the interviewer was female, and vice versa for the females, again a pattern consistent with the hypothesis.

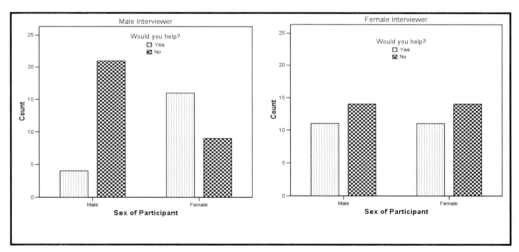

Output 9. Bar charts of the helpfulness of male and female participants with male and female interviewers showing an interaction pattern

13.4.2 Loglinear analysis of the data on gender and helpfulness

An important consideration before embarking upon a loglinear analysis of a multiway frequency table is whether the data are sufficiently numerous to meet the requirements of loglinear modelling. According to Tabachnick and Fidell (2007; p862), there should be at least five times as many cases as there are cells in the multi-way table. Those authors also recommend that, in every possible two-way contingency table, all expected frequencies must be greater than 1 and no more than 20% should be less than 5. Since, in our data set, there are 100 cases and 8 cells in the multiway table, the first criterion is satisfied. We can test the data on the second criterion by using **Crosstabs** to create three two-way tables (Interviewer × Help,

Participant × Help and Participant × Interviewer) and calculate the expected frequencies for each table.

Proceed as follows:

*   In **Variable View**, create three grouping variables: *Participant (Sex of Participant), Interviewer (Sex of Interviewer), Help (Would you help?)* and a fourth variable, *Count*, for the frequencies. Use the **Values** column to assign values to the code numbers, such as, for the *Help* variable, 1 = Yes, 2 = No. The complete SPSS data set is shown in Figure 7.

	Interviewer	Participant	Help	Count
1	Male	Male	Yes	4
2	Male	Male	No	21
3	Female	Male	Yes	11
4	Female	Male	No	14
5	Male	Female	Yes	16
6	Male	Female	No	9
7	Female	Female	Yes	11
8	Female	Female	No	14

Figure 7. **Data View** showing the Gender and Helping data set

*   We now need to weight the cases with the frequencies in Count. (This step would not be required if the data consisted of records of individual cases.) Choose **Data→Weight Cases...** to open the **Weight Cases** dialog box and transfer the variable Count to the **Frequency Variable** box. Click **OK**.
*   The next stage is to confirm, with **Crosstabs**, that the expected frequencies are sufficiently large. (The procedure is described in Section 11.5.5.) The output tables (which we have omitted) show that no cell has an expected frequency of less than 1 and over 80% of cells have expected frequencies of 5 or more. We have, therefore, sufficient data for a loglinear analysis. See Section 11.5.5
*   Select **Analyze→Loglinear→Model Selection...** to open the **Model Selection Loglinear Analysis** dialog box (the completed version is shown in Figure 8).
*   Follow the steps in Figure 8. You will notice that, since each variable contains two categories, to which we have consistently assigned the values 1 and 2, we need only complete the **Define Range** dialog once; had the variables had different numbers of categories or different values been used from variable to variable, it would have been necessary to enter the ranges separately for each grouping variable.
*   The default model is **backward elimination**. Makes sure its radio button is on.
*   Click **OK**.

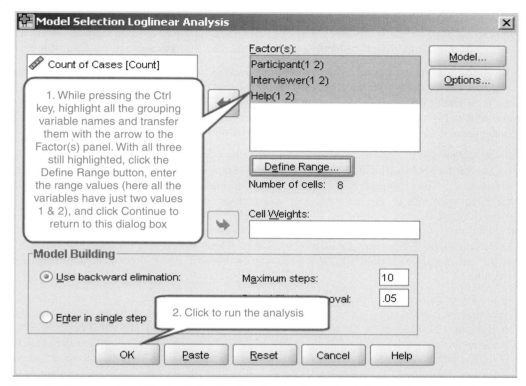

Figure 8. The completed **Model Selection Loglinear Analysis** dialog box for three factors

13.4.2.2 The output for the loglinear analysis

The first table in the output (Output 10) lists the number of cases and the names of the variables (factors) in the analysis. Check that the information is consistent with the design of the experiment as we have described it: in this example, there should be three factors, each having two levels. In Output 10, the factors, Help, Interviewer and Participant, are listed under the heading 'Categories'.

Data Information

		N
Cases	Valid	8
	Out of Range ᵃ	0
	Missing	0
	Weighted Valid	100
Categories	Help	2
	Interviewer	2
	Participant	2

a. Cases rejected because of out of range factor values.

Output 10. Information about the number of cases and the category names (factors)

The next item (not shown here) is a table listing the observed and expected counts for the combinations of the three factors. At this stage, SPSS is fitting a **saturated model**, with generating class Sex of Interviewer × Sex of Participant × Help to the cell frequencies. In this section of the output, therefore the observed and expected frequencies have the same values.

The third item in the output, with the caption **K-Way and Higher-Order Effects** (Output 11), lists the results of the statistical tests for the various effects. As explained in Section 13.3, the term **Order** denotes the number of factors involved in the effect concerned: a first-order effect (K=1) is a main effect; a second-order effect (K = 2) is a two-way interaction, and so on. In the present example, there is one three-way interaction (K = 3).

In the upper part of Output 11, the chi-square value opposite each level of effect is the chi-square attributable to all effects at that level, *plus* that associated with any (and every) higher-order effect. The chi-square value for K = 1 (15.382) is the *total* of the chi-squared values for the three main effects, the three two-way interactions and the three-way interaction. This is clear from the degrees of freedom: 3 (main effects) + 3 (two-way interactions) + 1 (three-way interaction) = 7, the value given in the degrees of freedom column opposite K = 1 in the upper half of the table. Since there are no effects of order higher than K = 3, the chi-square for K = 3 is the chi-square associated with the three-way interaction alone (6.659), on one degree of freedom.

In the lower half of the table, the value of the degrees of freedom for K = 1 is now 3 (not 7), because now we are being given the degrees of freedom associated with *one* level only. The total degrees of freedom for the three main effects alone is 3, which is the value opposite K = 1 in the lower part of the table. The chi-square value (and degrees of freedom) are the same for K = 3 in both the upper and the lower parts of the table, because in either case, there is just one three-way interaction. From the entries for K = 3 in either half of the table, we see that, as we should expect from the hypothesis, there is indeed a significant three-way interaction (Sex of Interviewer × Sex of Participant × Help) : Chi-Square = 6.659 on one degree of freedom; $p = .01$.

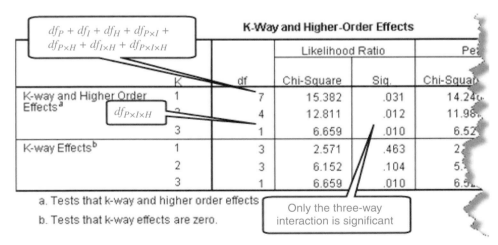

Output 11. Part of the **Tests of Effects** table. The subscripts P, I and H represent Participant, Interviewer and Help respectively

From the lower part of Output 11, which gives the results of tests of the individual components of the model, we also learn that no other effect makes a significant contribution to the total chi-square value, as can be seen from the *p*-values in the rows for K = 1 and K = 2. Loglinear analysis, therefore, has given us something that the traditional chi-square test cannot offer: a direct test for a three-way interaction.

The fourth part of the SPSS output, the **Backward Elimination Statistics** (Output 12) shows that the saturated model containing the three-way interaction is the best one for the data, because removal of the interaction term would result in a significant increase in Chi-square. At Step 1, the saturated model is therefore adopted as the final model.

Backward Elimination Statistics

Since deletion of the three-way interaction term results in a significant increase in chi-square, this term must be retained in the final model

Step Summary

Step[a]	Effects		Chi-Square[c]	df	Sig.	Number of Iterations
0	Generating Class[b]	Participant*Interviewer*Help	.000	0	.	
	Deleted Effect 1	Participant*Interviewer*Help	6.659	1	.010	2
1	Generating Class[b]	Participant*Interviewer*Help	.000	0	.	

a. At each step, the effect with the largest significance level for the Likelihood Ratio Change is deleted, provided the significance level is larger than .050
b. Statistics are displayed for the best model at each step after step 0
c. For 'Deleted Effect', this is the change in the Chi-Square after the effect is deleted from the model

Output 12. The final model for the gender and professed helpfulness data

The loglinear analysis has confirmed the opposite-sex dyadic hypothesis, which implies that the best-fitting loglinear model contains the three-way interaction term.

13.4.3   The main-effects-only model and the traditional chi-square test

The formula for the likelihood ratio chi-square statistic (and indeed the Pearson formula also) can readily be adapted for use with multiway contingency tables. We can represent a three-way frequency table as a set of two-way tables, one at each level of the third attribute, where *r* and *c* are the number of rows and columns in each table and each table is said to be at a different **layer** of the third attribute, which has *l* layers. Let *R*, *C* and *L* be the marginal totals associated with a particular combination of the categories of the three attributes. By extension of the reasoning for the two-way contingency table, the expected cell frequency *E* under the null hypothesis of total independence among the three attributes is given by

$$E = \frac{R}{N} \times \frac{C}{N} \times \frac{L}{N} \times N = \frac{RCL}{N^2} \quad \text{- - - (6)}$$

Expected cell frequency for total independence model

For the three-way frequency table, the likelihood ratio chi-square statistic is

$$\chi^2(r-1)(c-1)(l-1) = 2 \sum_{\text{all cells}} O \ln\left(\frac{O}{E}\right) \text{ - - - (7) } \textbf{The LR Chi-square}$$

which is distributed approximately as chi square on $(r-1)(c-1)(l-1)$ degrees of freedom.

Table 3 shows the observed frequencies O, together with the expected frequencies E for each of the eight cells in the frequency table of the results of the helping experiment. Also given are the marginal total frequencies for the three variables: Sex of Participant; Sex of Interviewer; Help.

Table 3. Observed and expected frequencies for the data in Table 2. (In (a), the expected frequencies are shown in brackets.)

(a) Table of observed and expected frequencies

		Would you help?	
Sex of Interviewer	Sex of Participant	Yes	No
Male	Male	4 (10.5)	21 (14.5)
	Female	16 (10.5)	9 (14.5)
Female	Male	11 (10.5)	14 (14.5)
	Female	11 (10.5)	14 (14.5)

(b) Marginal row frequencies

Sex of Interviewer		Sex of Participant		Was Help Given?	
Male	Female	Male	Female	Yes	No
50	50	50	50	42	58

For example, we can use (6) to calculate the expected frequency of the first cell in Table 3(a) (Male Interviewer, Male Participant, Help Given) using the values of the marginal totals in Table 3(b) i.e. $(50 \times 50 \times 42)/100^2 = 10.5$. The expected frequencies for the other cells are found in a similar way. Applying the likelihood ratio chi-square formula, we have

$$\chi^2(1) = 2 \sum_{\text{all cells}} O \ln\left(\frac{O}{E}\right)$$

$$= 2\left[4 \times \ln\left(\frac{4}{10.5}\right) + 21 \times \ln\left(\frac{21}{14.5}\right) + \dots + 14 \times \ln\left(\frac{14}{14.5}\right)\right]$$

$$= 12.81$$

This value is significant beyond the .05 level: $\chi^2(1) = 12.81$; $p = .016$. If you follow the procedure described in Section 13.3.2 and apply a main-effects-only model to the three-way frequency table, you will find that the value for chi-square given in the output is exactly the value that we have just obtained by applying the likelihood-ratio formula. Output 13 shows the result of the goodness-of-fit test of the main-effects-only model. The value of chi-square is exactly the same as the one we have just calculated from the extension of the usual likelihood ratio formula.

Goodness-of-Fit Tests

	Chi-Square	df	Sig.
Likelihood Ratio	12.811	4	.012
Pearson	11.987	4	.017

Output 13. The result of the goodness-of-fit test of the main-effects-only model

The main-effects-only model is the exact equivalent, in loglinear analysis, of the traditional chi-square test for an association. The problem with the traditional chi-square test is that it can merely reject the total independence (main-effects-only) model. This is fine if there are only two attributes: since in that situation only one association is possible, the interpretation of a significant result is unequivocal. With multi-way frequency tables, however, a significant result tells us only that there are at least some dependencies among the variables: it cannot tell us which of several possible effects is responsible for the pattern of frequencies in the frequency table. Could these cell frequencies have arisen from one or more of the possible two-way interactions? Does the three-way interaction account for a significant portion of the chi-square value? Only modern methods such as loglinear analysis can provide the answers to such questions.

13.4.4 Collapsing a multi-way table: the requirement of conditional independence

We might reasonably ask another question of our data: are female participants more inclined to help than male participants? The traditional approach to this question was to create a two-way table by 'collapsing' across the levels of the Interviewer variable. By adding the data for the male interviewers to that of the female interviewers, we can produce a two-way table in which only the variables of Sex of Participant and Help remain. We have already said, however, that there are dangers in 'collapsing' a table in this way. In Output 14, the variable Sex of Interviewer has disappeared and, in both the table and the clustered bar chart, we see a pattern of cell frequencies suggesting that there may be a tendency for female participants to be more helpful. Moreover, this impression is seemingly confirmed by formal statistical testing: **Fisher's Exact** two-tailed probability = .03. On the other hand, we have previously seen that the loglinear analysis does not confirm *any* of the two-way interactions: the only statistically robust effect to emerge from the loglinear analysis is a three-way interaction.

Our variables are Help, Participant and Interviewer. In collapsing the three-way table across the Interviewer variable to obtain a two-way Help × Participant table, we have ignored the fact (confirmed by the three-way interaction that emerged from the loglinear analysis) that the Interviewer variable is correlated with the interaction between the other two variables and therefore confounds the simple comparison of males and females on helpfulness.

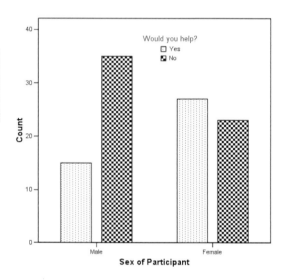

Helpfulness in male and female participants: p = .025

Count

Sex of Participant		Would you help?		
		Yes	No	Total
Sex of Participant	Male	15	35	50
	Female	27	23	50
Total		42	58	100

Output 14. Collapsed table, showing levels of helpfulness in male and female participants

An important concept in loglinear modelling is that of **conditional independence**. Two variables A and B are said to be conditionally independent at one level of a third variable C if, at that level of C, they show no association. Only if A & B are conditionally independent at *every* level of C, is it permissible to collapse the frequency table across C to investigate the association between A and B with a traditional chi-square test. In our example, A, B and C are Help, Participant and Interviewer, respectively. If we follow the Select Cases procedure and test for an association between Help and Participant in the male inverviewers, we find a striking tendency for the females to be more helpful: $\chi^2(1) = 12.647$; $p < .01$. (If, however, we make a similar test with the female interviewers, we find no such tendency: $\chi^2(1) = 0$; $p = 1$.) Clearly the requirement of conditional independence of A and B (Help and Participant) at all levels of C (male and female interviewers) has not been met and it is unsafe to collapse the three-way table by combining the data for the male and female interviewers.

A better case can be made for collapsing the data across the Participant variable and studying the association between Interviewer and Help. It will be found that if tests for association between Interviewer and Help are made on the data from the male and female participants separately, the chi-square test fails to show significance in either case. When the three-way table is collapsed across Participants (i.e. the data for male and female participants are combined so that we have a two-way Interviewer × Help table), the chi-square test fails to provide evidence for an association. This result is consistent with that of the loglinear analysis.

13.4.5 An alternative data set for the gender and helpfulness experiment

The presence of a three-way interaction, together with the absence of any other significant effects, made the interpretation of the output of the gender and helping experiment very simple. Often, however, several steps will be needed to locate the significant effects. Let us suppose that the data from the gender and helping experiment had been as in Table 4.

<table>
<tr><td colspan="5">Table 4. Three-way contingency table showing a more complex outcome of the gender and helping experiment.</td></tr>
<tr><td></td><td></td><td colspan="2">Would you help?</td><td></td></tr>
<tr><td>Sex of Interviewer</td><td>Sex of Participant</td><td>Yes</td><td>No</td><td>Total</td></tr>
<tr><td>Male</td><td>Male</td><td>4</td><td>10</td><td>14</td></tr>
<tr><td></td><td>Female</td><td>10</td><td>20</td><td>30</td></tr>
<tr><td>Female</td><td>Male</td><td>47</td><td>10</td><td>57</td></tr>
<tr><td></td><td>Female</td><td>58</td><td>17</td><td>75</td></tr>
<tr><td></td><td>Total</td><td>119</td><td>57</td><td>176</td></tr>
</table>

Notice that in Table 4, the row marginal totals show some variation: there were differences both in the numbers of male and female interviewers and in the numbers of male and female participants.

In the table of **Convergence Information** (Output 15), we learn that the generating class is Interviewer*Help, Participant. Remembering the hierarchical principle by which the retention of an interaction term in the model requires the retention of all lower order effect involving the factors in the interaction, we write the final model as follows:

$$\ln(E) = \text{constant} + \begin{bmatrix} \text{main effect} \\ \text{of} \\ \text{Interviewer} \end{bmatrix} + \begin{bmatrix} \text{main effect} \\ \text{of} \\ \text{Help} \end{bmatrix} + \begin{bmatrix} \text{Interviewer} \times \text{Help} \\ \text{interaction} \end{bmatrix} + \begin{bmatrix} \text{main effect} \\ \text{of} \\ \text{Participant} \end{bmatrix} \text{ - - (8)}$$

Final loglinear model

This unsaturated model fits the data quite well: the table of **Cell Counts and Residuals** (not shown) shows no residual value larger than .713. The **Goodness-of-Fit Tests** (Output 16) show that G^2 is small and insignificant, confirming the appearance of the table of observed and expected frequencies.

Convergence Information[a]

Generating Class	Interviewer*Help, Participant	
Number of Iterations		.000
Max. Difference between Observed and Fitted Marginals		.000
Convergence Criterion		.250

a. Statistics for the final model after Backward Elimination.

Output 15. The Convergence Information table in the Backward Elimination Statistics section of the output

Goodness-of-Fit Tests

	Chi-Square	df	Sig.
Likelihood Ratio	2.435	3	.487
Pearson	2.393	3	.495

Output 16. **Goodness-of-Fit Tests** for the unsaturated model

Output 17 shows the table of **K-Way and Higher-Order Effects**. The total **Likelihood Ratio Chi-Square** (G^2) is 110.282; but, unlike the equivalent table from the analysis of the previous data set, most of this value is accounted for by main effects and two-way interactions. There is no evidence for a three-way interaction in these data. There is, therefore, here no evidence to support the opposite-sex dyadic hypothesis.

K-Way and Higher-Order Effects

	K	df	Likelihood Ratio		Pearson		Number of Iterations
			Chi-Square	Sig.	Chi-Square	Sig.	
K-way and Higher Order Effects[a]	1	7	110.282	.000	123.000	.000	0
	2	4	35.310	.000	37.077	.000	2
	3	1	.431	.512	.425	.514	4
K-way Effects[b]	1	3	74.972	.000	85.923	.000	0
	2	3	34.879	.000	36.651	.000	0
	3	1	.431	.512	.425	.514	0

a. Tests that k-way and higher order effects are zero.

b. Tests that k-way effects are zero.

Output 17. The K-Way and Higher-Order Effects table

Output 18 shows the **Backward Elimination Statistics**. At Step 0, a saturated model is applied first, after which the three-way interaction is tested by fitting a model with the three-way component absent. Since there is no significant increase in G^2 , the three-way interaction term is dropped from the model.

At Step 1, each of the three two-way interactions is tested by removing it from the model. Only for the Interviewer $\times$ Help interaction is the increase in G^2 significant. At Step 2, therefore, the other two two-way interactions are removed from the model. At Step 3, it is found that if either Interviewer × Help or Participant is removed from the model, G^2 is significantly increased. At Step 4, therefore, both terms are retained and the final model is of generating class Interviewer × Help, Participant.

Backward Elimination Statistics

Step[a]	Generating Class[b] / Deleted Effect		Abbreviations for Participant, Interviewer and Help, respectively — Effects	Step Summary Chi-Square[c]	df	Sig.	Number of Iterations
0	Generating Class[b]		P*I*H	.000	0	.	
	Deleted Effect	1	P*I*H	.431	1	.512	4
1	Generating Class[b]		P*I, P*H, I*H	.431	1	.512	
	Deleted Effect	1	P*I	1.029	1	.310	2
		2	P*H	.198	1	.656	2
		3	I*H	32.098	1	.000	2
2	Generating Class[b]		P*I, I*H	.629	2	.730	
	Deleted Effect	1	P*I	1.806	1	.179	2
		2	I*H	32.875	1	.000	2
3	Generating Class[b]		I*H, P	2.435	3	.487	
	Deleted Effect	1	I*H	32.875	1	.000	2
		2	P	6.610	1	.010	2
4	Generating Class[b]		I*H, P	2.435	3	.487	

a. At each step, the effect with the largest significance level for the Likelihood Ratio Change is deleted, provided the Significance level is larger than .050.

b. Statistics are displayed for the best model at each step after Step 0.

c. For 'Deleted Effect', this is the change in the Chi-square after the effect is deleted from the model.

Output 18. The Backward Elimination Statistics table

While the loglinear analysis of this second data set does not confirm the opposite-sex dyadic hypothesis, it should serve as an illustration of how this technique can pinpoint the key associations among the variables in a multi-way frequency table.

From inspection alone, it is much more difficult to discern any clear-cut pattern in the data of Table 4 than it is in Table 3. The import of the loglinear analysis is that the only robust effects are an Interviewer × Help interaction and a main effect of Sex of Participant. Since the interaction has received confirmation from the loglinear analysis, there is justification for creating a two-way table by collapsing across the factor of Sex of Participant.

The significant main effect of the Participant factor arises simply because there were more male participants in the study. While that fact is of no scientific interest, the Participant factor must be retained in the model to achieve an adequate goodness-of-fit to the cell frequencies.

The cross-tabulation of the Interviewer × Help interaction is shown in Output 19. There is an obvious tendency for the participants to be helpful when the interviewer is female:

$$\mathrm{LR}\,\chi^2\,(1) = 32.875;\ p < .01.\ \ OR = 8.33.$$

This odds ratio $(105/27)/(14/30)$ is very large indeed.

Sex of Interviewer * Was help given? Crosstabulation				
Count				
		Was help given?		
		Yes	No	Total
Sex of Interviewer	Female	105	27	132
	Male	14	30	44
	Total	119	57	176

Output 19. Crosstabulation showing that participants were more likely to help a female interviewer

13.4.6   Reporting the results of a loglinear analysis

Reports of loglinear analyses in the literature have yet to follow a standard format. For example, once a model has been fitted, it would be possible to write out the equation of the loglinear model and report the estimates of each of the terms in the equation. Many journal editors, however, would take the view that such a mathematical presentation is unnecessary and would serve only to obscure the findings of the research.

One of the many excellent features of the book by Tabachnick & Fidell (2007) is their inclusion of sample write-ups of the results of the multivariate procedures they describe, including a report of a loglinear analysis on pages 906-908. In their report they (quite rightly, in our view) do not include any formal equations. They do, however, include the following:

1. Details of the data that were used in the analysis, including information about the incidence of cells with low expected frequencies and the presence of outliers. It is essential to establish that there are no contraindications against the use of loglinear analysis. Make sure that you have sufficient data.
2. The maximum likelihood chi square and p-value for the final model.
3. A table showing the results of the significance tests of the various effects on an individual basis. The entries in the table are chi-square tests of partial association, each on one degree of freedom.
4. A larger table showing the parameter estimates and the ratios of the estimates to their standard errors. This table, however, is very extensive, so the researcher submitting an article might omit it from the first draft (or include it as an appendix): the table can always be included in the body of the text in a revision of the article should the editor require this.

13.5   A FINAL WORD

In this chapter, we have described how loglinear analysis can be used to analyse data in the form of multiway contingency tables. This powerful technique makes it possible to tease out and confirm associations among the attributes in a multivariate nominal data set much more effectively and safely than if the researcher were to adapt the traditional Pearsonian analysis and collapse the multiway table across factors in the classification.

Recommended reading

Howell (2007) has a lucid introductory chapter on the theory of loglinear analysis. Tabachnick & Fidell (2007) have an extensive chapter on loglinear analysis with various computing packages, including SPSS. Todman and Dugard (2007) and Dugard, Todman & Staines (2010) take a more informal, hands-on approach.

Dugard, P., Todman, J., & Staines, H. (2010). *Approaching multivariate analysis: A practical introduction (2nd ed.).* London & New York: Routledge.

Howell, D. C. (2007). *Statistical methods for psychology (6th ed.).* Belmont, CA: Thomson/Wadsworth.

Tabachnick, B. G., & Fidell, L. S. (2007). *Using multivariate statistics (5th ed.).* Boston: Allyn & Bacon (Pearson International Edition).

Todman, J., & Dugard, P. (2007). *Approaching multivariate analysis: An introduction for psychology.* Hove: Psychology Press.

Exercise

Exercise 22 *Loglinear analysis* is available in www.psypress.com/spss-made-simple and click on Exercises.

CHAPTER 14

Discriminant analysis and logistic regression

14.1   INTRODUCTION

In Chapter 12, it was shown how the methods of regression could be used to predict scores on one dependent or **criterion** variable from knowledge of scores on one or more independent variables or **regressors**. In the situations we discussed, both the dependent variable and the independent variables were always scale or continuous data. There are circumstances, however, in which one might wish to predict, not scores on a quantitative dependent variable, but category membership: that is, the DV is qualitative, rather than quantitative.

Suppose that a premorbid blood condition (indicated by the presence of a protein) has been discovered, which is suspected to arise in middle age partly because of smoking and drinking. A hundred people are tested for the presence of the condition and a record made of their smoking and alcohol consumption. Can people's levels of smoking and drinking be used to predict whether they have the blood condition?

Here, although the independent variables (smoking and alcohol consumption) are continuous variables, the dependent variable is qualitative, consisting merely of the categories Yes (condition present) and No (condition absent). Could we assign arbitrary code numbers to the categories (dummy coding: $0 = $ No; $1 = $ Yes) and carry out an OLS (Ordinary Least Squares) regression in the usual way? Well, yes, we could; but there are many problems with that approach, and it is not recommended.

In this Chapter, we shall discuss two regression techniques that have been specially designed to predict category membership:
1.   **Discriminant analysis**.
2.   **Logistic regression**.

14.1.1 Discriminant analysis

The topic of discriminant analysis (DA) was alluded to in Chapter 10, in the context of multivariate analysis of variance (MANOVA). Mathematically, the one-way MANOVA and discriminant analysis are equivalent and the outputs from the two techniques contain a common core of key statistics. The difference is one of perspective: in the MANOVA, the focus is on the making of comparisons; whereas in DA, the researcher is more interested in the prediction of category membership than in the comparison of levels of performance among different groups. At the same time, however, it must be said that, although discriminant analysis is more at home in the context of correlational, rather than experimental, research, the technique can also be used as an effective follow-up to the MANOVA.

14.1.1.1 Discriminant functions

In discriminant analysis, the IVs are combined into a new variable known as a **discriminant function D** which, like the estimate of the DV in multiple regression, is a linear function of the IVs.

Let Y be the dependent variable which, we shall assume, consists of two number-coded categories: 1 = Condition Present; 0 = Condition Absent. Let $X_1, X_2, ..., X_p$ be p independent variables from which we hope to predict category membership. The purpose of discriminant analysis is to find a linear function D of the independent variables, that is, a function of the form

$$D = b_0 + b_1 X_1 + b_2 X_2 + ... + b_p X_p \; \text{--- (1)} \; \textbf{Discriminant function}$$

where the values of the coefficients and intercept of the discriminant function are chosen so that to the greatest possible extent, the group means on D (which are known as the **group centroids**) are separated as widely in their values as possible. If the discriminant function D separates the two group means/centroids, we can imagine two overlapping, bell-shaped distributions (normality is an assumption in discriminant analysis) centred on the values of the group centroids.

In discriminant analysis, the value of the discriminant function D is used to classify the individuals in the study by assigning them to the Condition Present group ($Y = 1$) if their score on D exceeds a criterion cut-off value and to the Condition Absent group ($Y = 0$) if their score fails to reach the cut-off. If the group centroids (means on D) are different, the number of correct assignments will exceed chance. In this situation, errors of assignment are inevitable. Since the distributions overlap, some participants will be wrongly assigned to the Condition Present group when actually they do not have the condition; whereas others, who have the condition may, because their score on D falls short of the cut-off point, will be wrongly assigned to the Condition Absent category. The more widely separated the distributions of D in the two groups, however, the less will be the overlap and the more successful the procedure will be in predicting group membership from a particular value of D.

Returning briefly to the MANOVA, in which discriminant functions also play a central role, the formula for a discriminant function was there expressed in terms of *dependent*, rather than *independent* variables. Exactly the same function is determined in either case: the difference is one of supposed direction of causation. In the present context, the variables X are termed IVs because they are viewed as *independent variables* or regressors from which category membership is to be predicted. In the experimental context, it is assumed that group membership (the treatment factor) causes or influences the continuous variables, which in MANOVA are thus seen as DVs, not IVs.

As with multiple regression, given that a discriminant function can be constructed which reliably separates the group centroids, tests are available to ascertain which of its component independent variables contribute reliably to the separation of the group centroids and hence to accuracy of classification. There are many other parallels between multiple regression and discriminant analysis; indeed, with discriminant analysis, we find all the ambiguities and other difficulties that one finds with multiple regression.

14.1.1.2   Measuring the predictive power of discriminant functions

Two statistics serve as measures of the power of discriminant functions to discriminate among the groups. The **canonical correlation** is the correlation between scores on a discriminant function and scores on the coding variables defining group membership. The **eigenvalue** is another measure of the separation achieved by a discriminant function, which can readily be converted to the percentage of the between groups variance that is accounted for by a discriminant function.

14.1.2   Types of discriminant analysis

There are three types of discriminant analysis (DA): **direct**, **hierarchical**, and **stepwise**, where these terms have exactly the same meaning as they do in multiple regression. **Direct DA** is the equivalent of simultaneous multiple regression: *all* the variables are entered into the regression equation at once. In **hierarchical DA**, they are entered according to a schedule set by the researcher on the basis of theory or collateral evidence. In **stepwise DA**, statistical criteria alone determine the order of entry.

Since in most analyses, the researcher has no sound theoretical rationale for giving some predictors higher priority than others, the third (**stepwise**) method is the most frequently used. On the other hand, the same uncertainties arise with stepwise discriminant analysis as with the use of stepwise methods in multiple regression. A *statistical* model alone cannot resolve theoretical issues: a substantive, *causal* model is also required. On those grounds, it might be argued that the direct approach, in which all the independent variables are entered simultaneously, is the safest one to adopt. The direct approach is also the one consistent with the MANOVA, in which the DVs (here they are the IVs) are entered simultaneously. Here, nevertheless, we shall opt for the stepwise approach, in order to illustrate some of the criteria for inclusion and exclusion of variables. Were we to use discriminant analysis as a follow-up to a MANOVA, we should take the direct approach.

14.1.3   Stepwise discriminant analysis

The statistical procedure for stepwise discriminant analysis is similar to stepwise multiple regression, in that the effect of the addition or removal of an IV is monitored by a statistical test and the result is used as a basis for the inclusion of that IV in the final analysis. When there are only two groups, there is just one discriminant function. With more than two groups, however, there can be several functions (one fewer than the number of groups), although it is unusual for more than the first two or three discriminant functions to be statistically robust.

Variables are added or removed from the analysis according to changes in the value of **Wilks' Lambda (Λ)**, a statistic which was described in Chapter 10. When a new variable is added, the value of Wilks' lambda will *decrease*: that is, the discriminant function will be *more* effective in separating the groups. (Recall from the discussion in Section 10.4.2.3 that lambda measures *error* variance and covariance, not variance accounted for.) At the same time, when any variable is removed, lambda will generally increase; though sometimes this increase will be minimal, in which case the variable is a candidate for removal from the discriminant function. The significance of the change in Λ when a variable is entered or removed is obtained from an approximate F test. A criterion is set for values of F deemed to be sufficiently large to justify adding a variable to the function: this criterion is known as **F to Enter**. Similarly, a small value of F is set, below which a variable will be removed. At each step of adding a variable to the analysis, the variable with the largest F that exceeds **F to Enter** is included. This process is repeated until there are no further variables with an F value greater than **F to Enter**. Sometimes a variable, having been included at one point, is removed later when its F value falls below **F to Remove**. (This can happen with the stepwise multiple regression procedure as well – see Section 12.4.2.)

Eventually, the process of adding and subtracting variables is completed, and a summary table is shown indicating which variables were added or subtracted at each step. The variables remaining in the analysis are those used in the discriminant function(s). The next table shows which functions are statistically reliable. The first function provides the best means of predicting group membership. Later functions may or may not contribute reliably to the prediction process. Additional tables displaying the functions and their success rates for correct prediction can (and should) be requested. Plots can also be specified.

14.1.4 Assumptions of discriminant analysis

As with the MANOVA, the safe use of discriminant analysis requires that the data meet certain criteria. The distribution of the data should be **multivariate normal**: for any fixed set of values for $p - 1$ variables, the remaining variable is normally distributed. The discriminant analysis tests are sufficiently robust to cope with some skewness, provided the samples are not too small. The problem of outliers, however, is potentially more serious. It is best to remove extreme values, if that can be justified. As in the MANOVA (to which DA is mathematically equivalent), there is also the assumption of **homogeneity of variance-covariance matrices**. Heterogeneity of variance-covariance matrices is most serious when the sample sizes are unequal. It is also important to avoid **multicollinearity** (high correlations among the independent variables). In particular, no variable must be an exact linear function of any of the others, a condition known as **singularity**.

While it is assumed that the independent variables will usually be quantitative, it is also possible to include the occasional qualitative independent variable (e.g. sex, marital status), just as it is in multiple regression. In general, however, discriminant analysis does not 'like' categorical IVs, the presence of which can inflate the error rates.

14.2 DISCRIMINANT ANALYSIS WITH SPSS

A school's vocational guidance officer would like to be able to help senior pupils to choose which subjects to study at university. Fortunately, some data are available from a project on the background interests and school-leaving examination results of architectural, engineering and psychology students. The students also filled in a questionnaire about their extra-curricular interests, including outdoor pursuits, drawing, painting, computing, and kit construction. Our research question is this: can knowledge of the pupils' scores on these nine variables be used to predict their subject category at university? In this study, subject category at university (psychologists, architects or engineers) is the dependent variable, and all the others are independent variables. Since the dependent variable is not continuous but a set of categories and the independent variables are continuous, discriminant analysis is an obvious approach to the analysis.

14.2.1   Accessing the data set

Since the data for this example are the scores of 118 participants on ten variables (the nine IVs plus Study Subject), it would be extremely tedious for readers to type the data into **Data View**. The data are available at: www.psypress.com/spss-made-simple. Select *Ch14 Vocational guidance data* and save it to the hard disk (or your stick) for easier access.

A section of the data set in **Data View** is shown in Figure 1.

Case	StudySubject	Sex	ConKit	ModelKit	Drawing	Painting	Outdoor	Computing	VisModel	Quals
32	Architect	Male	4	2	7	4	2	2	4	9
33	Architect	Female	4	10	7	3	5	1	6	7
34	Psychologist	Male	2	2	0	0	1	1	2	9
35	Psychologist	Female	2	4	3	1	1	1	6	9

Figure 1. Some cases in the Vocational Guidance data set

14.2.2   Exploring the data

Before embarking on the discriminant analysis, the user should probe the data for possible violations of the underlying assumptions. A full treatment of this topic is beyond the scope of this book, but the interested reader should consult a statistical text such as Tabachnick & Fidell (2007) for more details.

Here we suggest you check for extreme scores and outliers by using the **Explore** command (see Chapter 4, Section 4.4.3) to examine the distributions of the variables within the different categories of the grouping factor (Study Subject).

> See Section 4.4.3

- In the **Explore** dialog box, click the **Plots** radio button in the **Display** options, and transfer the variable names of all the predictors except Sex into the **Dependent List** box. Transfer the variable name Study Subject into the **Factor List** box, and the variable name Case Number into the **Label Cases by** box.
- Click **OK** to plot all the boxplots and stem-and-leaf displays.

Most of the boxplots are satisfactory except for Interest in Painting (see Output 1). Here one box is much longer than the others; moreover, in the Engineers' box, the median line is positioned close to the lower side of the box, rather than centrally. There are also two outliers. (See Table 2 in Section 4.4.2 for a reminder of the layout of a boxplot.) The corresponding **stem-and-leaf**

> See Section 4.4.2

displays also show discrepancies among the distributions and marked skewness of the distribution in the engineers. Should the first run of the discriminant procedure indicate that there are problems with the data, it might be advisable to omit the independent variable Interest in Painting.

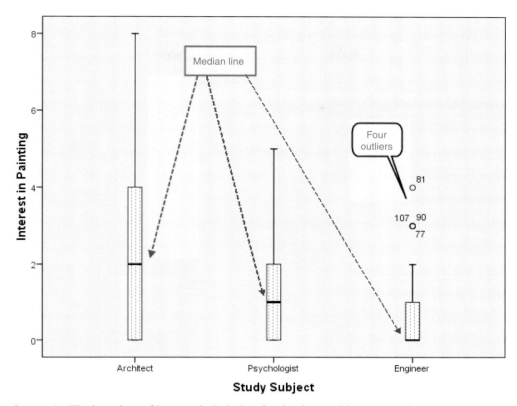

Output 1. The boxplots of Interest in Painting for the three subject categories

Running discriminant analysis

- Choose **Analyze→Classify→Discriminant...** to access the **Discriminant Analysis** procedure. (Figure 2 shows part of the Analyze menu.)

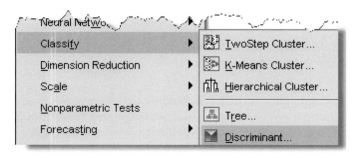

Figure 2. Finding the **Discriminant** procedure in the **Analyze** menu

- Complete the **Discriminant Analysis** dialog as shown in Figure 3.

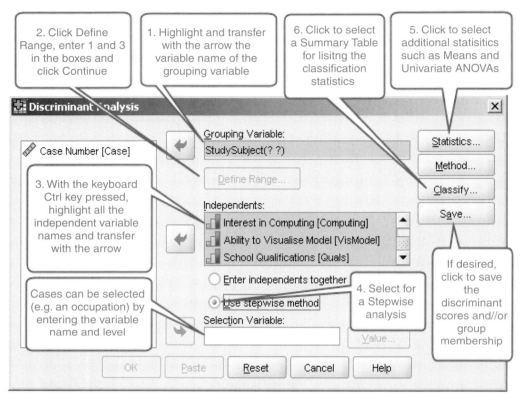

Figure 3. The **Discriminant Analysis** dialog box for the grouping (with three levels) and several independent variables, using the **stepwise method**

- Transfer StudySubject (the categorical DV) to the **Grouping Variable** slot.
- Click the **Define Range** button, enter 1 and 2 in the boxes and click **Continue**.
- Holding down the **Control** key, drag the cursor down the names of the nine independent variables to highlight them and transfer them all to the **Independents** box by clicking the central arrow.
- Activate the radio button marked **Use stepwise method**.

On the upper right of the **Discriminant Analysis** dialog box are buttons labelled **Statistics...** and **Classify...**. Clicking them will open further dialogs offering a variety of useful extra items for the output.

We shall certainly want descriptive statistics. Should we find, for instance, that the means on a variable are very similar across the three groups, this would indicate that the groups are not well differentiated by that variable. We can expect our best discriminating variables to show differences between the groups. For exploratory purposes, it will also be useful to have the univariate ANOVAs for the variables considered separately. Since the IVs are likely to be correlated, we can take the p-values of the ANOVAs with a pinch of salt: this is essentially the same problem that we discussed in Chapter 10, in the context of experiments with more than one DV. Nevertheless, the statistics of the univariate tests will highlight those variables that are playing the most important roles.

The **Discriminant Analysis: Statistics** dialog box (not shown) offers means, univariate ANOVAs and **Box's M**. (Box's test is for homogeneity of the variance-covariance matrices across groups – see Chapter 10.) These should all be selected, together with the unstandardised function coefficients. We shall also want the total covariance matrix, which will give us the variances and covariances of the independent variables in the data as a whole, ignoring the grouping factor. The separate-groups covariance will be useful as well.

Clicking the **Classify...** button will open the **Discriminant Analysis: Classification** dialog box (not shown). The most important item here is the summary table, which shows how successfully the discriminant functions assigned the participants to the categories of the dependent variable.

If you click the **Method** button, you will obtain the **Discriminant Analysis: Stepwise** dialog box (not shown). You will see that Wilks' lambda has been selected by default as the statistic that will be used for the addition and subtraction of variables to and from the discriminant functions. You will also see that the criteria for entry and removal have been set at 3.84 and 2.71, respectively. Here, you have the option of checking the lower radio button labelled Use probability of *F*, which will set the *p*-values for entry and removal at .05 and .01, respectively. Since we have plenty of data, we shall stay with the default criteria.

If you click the **Save...** button, you will open the **Discriminant Analysis: Save** dialog box, which offers discriminant scores and predicted group membership. It will be useful to have these values in **Data View** for further consideration and experiment.

- To obtain the means and one-way ANOVAs for each of the variables across the three levels of the independent variable, click **Statistics...** and select **Means** and **Univariate ANOVAs**. Click **Continue** to return to the original dialog box.
- To obtain a final summary table showing the success or failure of the discriminant functions to assign participants to their subject categories, click **Classify...** and select **Summary table**. Click **Continue** to return to the original dialog box.
- In some analyses there may be a grouping variable of which just one level is of interest. For example, we could have excluded Sex from the list of **Independents** and then carried out the analysis on males only by entering the variable name Sex in the **Selection Variable** box and then 1 for males in the **Value** box which would have appeared as soon as Sex was entered.
- Click **OK** to run the **Discriminant Analysis**.

Output for discriminant analysis

The output, as listed in the left-hand pane of the **SPSS Statistics Viewer** (Output 2), is rather daunting. Fortunately, as with the regression output, not all of it is required.

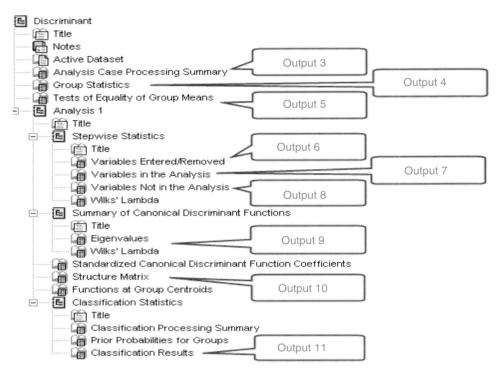

Output 2.　The left-hand pane of the **SPSS Statistics Viewer**

14.2.4.1　Information about the data and the number of cases in each category of the grouping variable

Output 3 shows how many valid cases were used in the analysis. Ten cases, which were missing a score on one or more of the independent variables, have been excluded.

Analysis Case Processing Summary

Unweighted Cases		N	Percent
Valid		108	91.5
Excluded	Missing or out-of-range group codes	0	.0
	At least one missing discriminating variable	10	8.5
	Both missing or out-of-range group codes and at least one missing discriminating variable	0	.0
	Total	10	8.5
Total		118	100.0

Output 3.　Information about the number of valid cases

The next table (Output 4) is part of the **Group Statistics** table, which shows the optional statistics and the number of cases for each independent variable at each level of the grouping variable and all of them together (here only those for the Architect category are shown).

Group Statistics

Study Subject		Mean	Std. Deviation	Valid N (listwise) Unweighted
Architect	Sex of Student	1.27	.45	30
	Interest in Construction Kits	3.33	1.58	30
	Interest in Modelling Kits	3.97	2.68	30
	Interest in Drawing	5.10	2.29	30
	Interest in Painting	2.50	2.18	30
	Interest in Outdoor Pursuits	2.30	2.07	30
	Interest in Computing	1.77	1.45	30
	Ability to Visualise Model	5.53	1.25	30
	School Qualifications	6.63	2.86	30

Output 4. An edited table showing part of the optional statistics and the number of cases for each independent variable at each level of the grouping variable Study Subject

The **Univariate ANOVAs** (Output 5) show whether there is a statistically significant difference among the mean scores of the three study groups on each independent variable. (Since Sex of Student is a nominal variable with arbitrary values 1 = Male and 2 = Female, the first row of statistics in the table can be ignored.) Most of the remaining differences are significant (as shown in the column **Sig.**), except for the variables Interest in Computing and Interest in Modelling Kits. We can therefore expect that neither of those two variables will play an important role in the discriminant functions.

Tests of Equality of Group Means

	Wilks' Lambda	F	df1	df2	Sig.
Sex of Student	.77	15.99	2	105	.00
Interest in Construction Kits	.84	9.71	2	105	.00
Interest in Modelling Kits	.96	2.11	2	105	.13
Interest in Drawing	.90	6.09	2	105	.00
Interest in Painting	.83	10.41	2	105	.00
Interest in Outdoor Pursuits	.94	3.24	2	105	.04
Interest in Computing	1.00	.00	2	105	1.00
Ability to Visualise Model	.84	9.74	2	105	.00
School Qualifications	.88	7.38	2	105	.00

All ANOVAs are significant except those with p-value >0.05

Output 5. Univariate **ANOVAs**

Returning to the point we made at the end of Chapter 10, when we were discussing the MANOVA, the *p*-values of F tests on each of a set of correlated DVs must be viewed with scepticism. This is also true of the tests reported in Output 5; although in the present context, the DVs have become IVs. The very small *p*-values of some of the tests, however, indicate that at least some of the differences are robust.

14.2.4.3 The summary table

The **Stepwise Statistics** section begins with a summary table (Output 6) showing which variables were entered and removed (though in this analysis none, having at first been included was then subsequently removed), along with values of **Wilks' Lambda** and the associated probability levels. Notice the values of **F to Enter** and **F to Remove** in footnotes b and c. These are the default criteria, which can be changed in the **Stepwise Method** dialog box. As a result of this process, only seven of the original nine IVs survived to appear in Output 6. The casualties were Interest in Modelling kits and Interest in Drawing.

Variables Entered/Removed [a,b,c,d]

		Wilks' Lambda				Exact F			
Step	Entered	Stat-istic	df1	df2	df3	Stat-istic	df1	df2	Sig.
1	Sex of Student	.77	1	2	105	16.0	2	105	.00
2	Interest in Painting	.64	2	2	105	16.0	4	208	.00
3	School Qualifications	.54	3	2	105	12.4	6	206	.00
4	Ability to Visualise Model	.48	4	2	105	11.3	8	204	.00
5	Interest in Outdoor Pursuits	.44	5	2	105	10.3	10	202	.00
6	Interest in Construction Kits	.40	6	2	105	9.59	12	200	.00
7	Interest in Computing	.37	7	2	105	8.99	14	198	.00

At each step, the variable that minimizes the overall Wilks' Lambda is entered.

a. Maximum number of steps is 18.

b. Minimum partial F to enter is 3.84.

c. Maximum partial F to remove is 2.71.

d. F level, tolerance, or VIN insufficient for further computation.

Output 6. Summary table of variables entered and removed

Note the increments in Wilks' lambda are tested using *three* parameters: *df1*, *df2* and *df3*. The value of *df1* is the number of predictors that have so far been added to the function, including the potential predictor. You can see that, as we move down through steps 1 to 7, the value of *df1* increases in value from 1 to 7. The value of *df2* is (number of groups $-$ 1) = 2. The parameter *df3* is the degrees of freedom of the within groups mean square. Had the groups been of equal size, the value of *df3* would have been $3(n-1)$, where *n* was the number in each group. In this case, however, the groups are not of equal size, so the value of *df3* is

$$\left(n_1 - 1\right) + \left(n_2 - 1\right) + \left(n_3 - 1\right) = 29 + 36 + 40 = 105$$

which is the value given in Output 6. The value of the approximate F statistic is calculated from those of *df1*, *df2* and *df3* by using the formula shown in Tabachnick & Fidell (2007; p. 385).

14.2.4.4   Entering and removing variables step by step

The next table, **Variables in the Analysis**, lists the variables in the analysis at each step. Output 7 shows only Steps 1-3 and the final stage, Step 7.

Variables in the Analysis

Step		Toler-ance	F to Remove	Wilks' Lambda
1	Sex of Student	1.00	15.99	
2	Sex of Student	.88	15.71	.83
	Interest in Painting	.88	10.19	.77
3	Sex of Student	.88	15.26	.70
	Interest in Painting	.85	12.34	.67
	School Qualifications	.95	9.78	.64
7	Sex of Student	.59	7.47	.43
	Interest in Painting	.73	10.92	.46
	School Qualifications	.91	10.83	.46
	Ability to Visualise Model	.90	7.96	.43
	Interest in Outdoor Pursuits	.84	3.96	.40
	Interest in Construction Kits	.80	4.33	.41
	Interest in Computing	.70	3.85	.40

Output 7. **Variables in the Analysis** at Steps 1 to 3, and finally at Step 7

In Output 7, the column labelled **Tolerance** is one minus the square of the multiple correlation coefficient between the variable being considered for entry and all the other variables already entered. (Its value is 1 for Sex, because no other variable has yet been entered.) Very small values of the Tolerance suggest that a variable can contribute little to the analysis. The column **F to Remove** tests the significance of the decrease in discrimination should that variable be removed. Since, however, no F-ratio is less than the criterion value of 2.71 (the default criterion), all the variables have been retained.

The table **Variables not in the Analysis** (Output 8) shows the variables not in the analysis at the start and at each step thereafter until the final step (Output 8 shows only Steps 0 & 1, then Step 7). It can be seen that Sex of Student had the highest **F to Enter** value initially (and the lowest **Wilks' Lambda**) and is, therefore, selected as the first variable to enter at Step 1 (Output 7).

At Step 1, the variable with the next highest **F to Enter** value is Interest in Painting, which is then entered at Step 2 as shown in Output 7. Finally at Step 7, the variables Interest in Modelling Kits and Interest in Drawing are never entered because their **F to Enter** values are smaller than the default criterion of 3.84.

Variables Not in the Analysis

Step		Toler-ance	Min. Toler-ance	F to Enter	Wilks' Lambda
0	Sex of Student	1.00	1.00	15.99	0.77
	Interest in Construction Kits	1.00	1.00	9.71	0.84
	Interest in Modelling Kits	1.00	1.00	2.11	0.96
	Interest in Drawing	1.00	1.00	6.09	0.90
	Interest in Painting	1.00	1.00	10.41	0.83
	Interest in Outdoor Pursuits	1.00	1.00	3.24	0.94
	Interest in Computing	1.00	1.00	0.00	1.00
	Ability to Visualise Model	1.00	1.00	9.74	0.84
	School Qualifications	1.00	1.00	7.38	0.88
1	Interest in Construction Kits	0.93	0.93	3.43	0.72
	Interest in Modelling Kits	0.94	0.94	2.20	0.74
	Interest in Drawing	1.00	1.00	6.04	0.69
	Interest in Painting	0.88	0.88	10.19	0.64
	Interest in Outdoor Pursuits	0.98	0.98	1.49	0.75
	Interest in Computing	0.75	0.75	4.20	0.71
	Ability to Visualise Model	1.00	1.00	8.83	0.66
	School Qualifications	0.98	0.98	7.69	0.67
7	Interest in Modelling Kits	0.72	0.57	0.36	0.37
	Interest in Drawing	0.63	0.52	0.91	0.37

> This variable is entered at Step 1 (Output 7) with the largest *F* to Enter value

> This variable is entered at Step 2 (Output 7) with the largest *F* to Enter value

> These variables at Step 7 are excluded because their *F* to Enter values are <3.84

Output 8. Part of the table of **Variables Not in the Analysis** at Steps 0, 1 and 7

The next table in the output, **Wilks' Lambda**, is a repeat of the table given in Output 5 and is not reproduced.

14.2.4.5   Statistics of the discriminant functions

Output 9 shows the percentage (**% of Variance**) of the between groups variance accounted for by each discriminant function and how many of them (if any) are significant (see the **Sig.** column in the **Wilks' Lambda** table). Here we see that both functions are highly significant. The **Canonical Correlation** for a discriminant function is the square root of the ratio of the between-groups sum of squares to the total sum of squares. The square of the canonical correlation is the proportion of the total variability explained by differences between groups. The canonical correlation is essentially **eta** (see Chapter 7), as applied to the one-way ANOVA of participants' scores on the discriminant function.

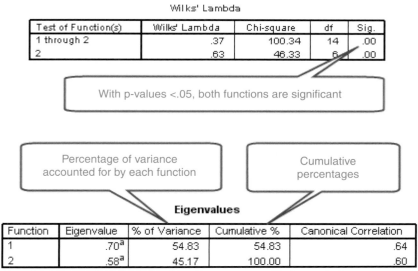

Wilks' Lambda

Test of Function(s)	Wilks' Lambda	Chi-square	df	Sig.
1 through 2	.37	100.34	14	.00
2	.63	46.33	6	.00

With p-values <.05, both functions are significant

Percentage of variance accounted for by each function

Cumulative percentages

Eigenvalues

Function	Eigenvalue	% of Variance	Cumulative %	Canonical Correlation
1	.70[a]	54.83	54.83	.64
2	.58[a]	45.17	100.00	.60

a. First 2 canonical discriminant functions were used in the analysis.

Output 9. Statistics of the discriminant functions

In Output 9, note also that the eigenvalues (and hence the values of the percentage of between groups variance accounted for by each discriminant function) are smaller in the second function to be extracted. The canonical correlation (i.e. eta) is also smaller in the second function. The value of Wilks' lambda is higher for the second function, again reflecting that this function accounts for less of the variance: the Wilks' statistic is the error variance expressed as a proportion of the total, so the smaller its value, the greater the proportion of between groups variance accounted for.

14.2.4.6   Standardised coefficients and within groups correlations with discriminants

Two tables follow in the listing, the first (not reproduced here) being the **Standardized Canonical Discriminant Function Coefficients**, and the second (Output 10) the **Structure Matrix**, which is a table of pooled within groups correlations between the independent variables and the discriminant functions.

Structure Matrix

	Function	
	1	2
Ability to Visualise Model	-.51*	-.10
School Qualifications	.43*	-.16
Interest in Painting	-.42*	.36
Interest in Drawing a	-.22*	.12
Interest in Modelling Kits a	-.12*	.07
Interest in Computing	.01*	.00
Sex of Student	.19	.70*
Interest in Construction Kits	-.15	-.54*
Interest in Outdoor Pursuits	.19	.25*

Pooled within-groups correlations between discriminating
variables and standardized canonical discriminant functions
Variables ordered by absolute size of correlation within function.

*. Largest absolute correlation between each variable and
any discriminant function

a. This variable not used in the analysis.

Output 10. The **Structure Matrix**

It is clear from the information in Output 10 that the first function is contributed to positively by School Qualifications and their interest in painting, and negatively by their ability to visualise models. The second function is contributed to positively by Sex and negatively by Interest in Modelling Kits and Interest in Outdoor Pursuits. The asterisks mark the correlations with the higher value for each variable (row).

The next table in the output (not reproduced), **Functions at Group Centroids**, lists the group means (for Architect, Psychologist, Engineer) for each discriminant function.

14.2.4.7   Success of predictions of group membership

The optional selection of **Summary table** from the **Classify** options in the **Discriminant Analysis** dialog box provides an indication of the success rate for predictions of group membership using the discriminant functions developed in the analysis (see Output 11). The footnote to the table indicates that the overall success rate is 72.2%.

Classification Results[a]

	Study Subject	Predicted Group Membership			Total
		Architect	Psychologist	Engineer	
Count	Architect	22	2	6	30
	Psychologist	4	25	8	37
	Engineer	5	5	31	41
%	Architect	73.3	6.7	20.0	100.0
	Psychologist	10.8	67.6	21.6	100.0
	Engineer	12.2	12.2	75.6	100.0

a. 72.2% of original grouped cases correctly classified.

Output 11. **Classification Results** table showing the predicted group membership

Output 11 also shows that the Engineers were the most accurately classified, with 75.6% of the cases correct. The Architects were next with 73.3%. The Psychologists were the least accurately classed, with a success rate of 67.6%. Notice also that incorrectly classified Architects were more likely to be classified as Engineers than as Psychologists, and that incorrectly classified Psychologists are more likely to be classified as Engineers than as Architects!

14.2.5 Predicting group membership

Section 14.2 posed the question of whether knowledge of pupils' scores on a number of variables could be used to predict their subjects of study at university. The analysis has demonstrated that two discriminant functions can be generated using all the variables except Interest in Modelling Kits and Interest in Drawing, and that these functions can predict 72.2% of the cases correctly, with some variation in levels across subjects. So far, however, we have not seen what the predicted subject of study was for any particular individual. The vocational guidance officer in our example wants to make predictions of the subjects that future students will eventually take on an individual basis, given knowledge of their scores on the same independent variables. It is easy to do either or both of these things with the **Discriminant** procedure.

To compare the actual subject of study with the predicted subject of study, proceed as follows:
- Complete the **Discriminant Analysis** dialog box as before but, in addition, click **Save…** and then click the radio button for **Predicted group membership**. Click **Continue** and **OK**.
- The predicted group membership will appear in a new column labelled **Dis_1** in **Data View**, along with the predictions for all the other cases.
- We suggest that you actually try this and, once **Dis_1** appears in **Data View**, switch to **Variable View** and rename the variable *PredictDiscrim*. Figure 4 is a section from **Data View** showing some of the predictions of choice of subject from the discriminant analysis.

To predict the subject of study for a future student, proceed as follows:
- Enter the data for the potential students at the end of the data in **Data View**. Leave the grouping variable (StudySubject) blank or enter an out-of-range number so that the analysis does not include these cases when it is computing the discriminant functions.
- Then after completing the steps described above, the predicted group membership will appear in a new column labelled PredictDiscrim in **Data View**, along with the predictions for all the other cases.

Case	StudySubject	Sex	ConKit	ModelKit	Drawing	Painting	Outdoor	Computing	VisModel	Quals	PredictDiscrim
96	Engineer	Male	4	2	4	0	2	1	4	7	Engineer
97	Engineer	Male	3	2	2	0	0	2	4	0	Architect
98	Engineer	Male	4	1	5	1	0	2	7	7	Architect
99	Engineer	Female	1	0	0	0	6	0	2	6	Psychologist
100	Engineer	Male	6	2	2	0	4	2	4	7	Engineer
101	Engineer	Female	4	2	5	1	4	1	4	9	Psychologist

Figure 4. Section of **Data View** showing the predictions from discriminant analysis of choice of main university subject

Before leaving the topic of discriminant analysis, some further consideration of the consequences of violation of the assumptions is in order. The procedure is vulnerable to the presence of extreme scores and outliers. In our preliminary exploratory analysis of the data, we found that the distribution of the scores on Interest in Painting was markedly skewed, with several outliers. It would be a worthwhile exercise to repeat the analysis with the outliers removed, and perhaps even with this variable omitted altogether.

With samples this size, departures from multivariate normality are unlikely to have serious consequences for the **Type I error rate**. Discriminant analysis, however, also requires that the variance-covariance matrices should be homogeneous across groups. If **Box's Test** is requested (as it should be), the result will be as shown in Output 12.

Box's Test of Equality of Covariance Matrices

Log Determinants

Study Subject	Rank	Log Determinant
Architect	7	4.518
Psychologist	7	3.419
Engineer	7	2.768
Pooled within-groups	7	4.432

The ranks and natural logarithms of determinants printed are those of the group covariance matrices.

Test Results

Box's M		100.520
F	Approx.	1.620
	df1	56.000
	df2	27655.091
	Sig.	.002

Tests null hypothesis of equal population covariance matrices.

Output 12. Result of **Box's Test** for homogeneity of variance-covariance matrices

We can see from Output 12 that the Box test has indicated that the variance-covariance matrices are not homogeneous across the groups. The Box test, however, is notoriously sensitive and, provided the researcher has large samples of equal size, a significant result can be ignored with impunity (Tabachnick & Fidell, 2007; p. 252). This robustness, however, does not necessarily extend to situations in which, although some of the samples are large, there is much variation in size. If the smaller samples have larger variances and covariances, there will be too many significant results; if, on the other hand, the larger samples have larger variances and covariances, the tests are conservative (Tabachnick & Fidell, op. cit.). In the present data set, we can see from Output 12 that the variance-covariance matrix for the data from the Engineers has the largest determinant. Since this is also the largest sample ($n = 41$), we can be more confident that the p-values of the test statistics do not overstate the case against the null hypothesis.

In the next section, we shall consider an alternative approach to regression with a categorical DV. The methods we shall describe carry fewer assumptions than does discriminant analysis: they do not require multivariate normality; nor need there be homogeneity of the variance-covariance matrices.

14.3   BINARY LOGISTIC REGRESSION

The method we shall describe in this section is applicable to situations in which the dependent variable consists of two categories only. It is not, therefore, applicable to the data set we have just analysed with discriminant analysis, in which the dependent variable consisted of three categories. Those data on subject choices at university, however, can be analysed by a more general method of logistic regression known as **multinomial logistic regression**, which we shall touch upon in the final section of this chapter.

14.3.1   Logistic regression

Logistic regression is another approach to category prediction. This method carries fewer assumptions than does discriminant analysis: neither multivariate normality nor homogeneity of variance-covariance matrices is required. Discriminant analysis, moreoever, is also sensitive to the inclusion of qualitative IVs such as sex, blood group or nationality; logistic regression, on the other hand, can cope with any number of qualitative regressors: in fact, *all* the predictors can be categorical.   For these reasons, logistic regression is fast overtaking discriminant analysis as the preferred technique for prediction of dichotomous category membership.

Returning to the example of the premorbid blood condition mentioned at the start of this Chapter, suppose that of the hundred people studied, forty-four people have the condition and fifty-six do not. We shall assign code numbers to the two categories: to those who have the condition, we assign 1; and to those who do not, we assign 0. In this section, we shall outline the use of logistic regression to predict category membership.

On the basis of the foregoing information about the patients, a prediction of category membership can be made without running any regression at all. Since the probability that a person selected at random will have the condition is $44/100 = .44$ (44%) and the probability that they will not have the condition is $56/100 = .56$ (56%), our best a priori prediction of category membership for any particular person selected at random is to assign them to the 'condition absent' category. If we do that, we shall be right in 100% of the cases in which the condition was absent, but wrong in the 44% of cases in which the condition was present, giving us a net success rate of 56% over the hundred assignments. This prediction, which does not require any regression model, is the equivalent, in logistic regression, of 'intercept-only' prediction in multiple regression, in which we assign the mean value of the criterion variable, irrespective of the values of the regressors. The purpose of logistic regression is to improve upon this baseline success rate by exploiting any association between the dependent and independent variables to predict category membership (the dependent variable) with the greatest possible accuracy.

In what follows, it is assumed that, although the condition can only be present or absent, variables such as number of cigarettes smoked and amount of alcohol consumed actually increase the probability of developing the condition **continuously** throughout the range of consumption. This probability, however, cannot be expected to be a linear function of the independent variables: it is likely to rise with increasing rapidity as scores on the independent variable increase from zero and decelerate at a later stage, so that the probability graph would be rather like a flattened S (see Figure 5).

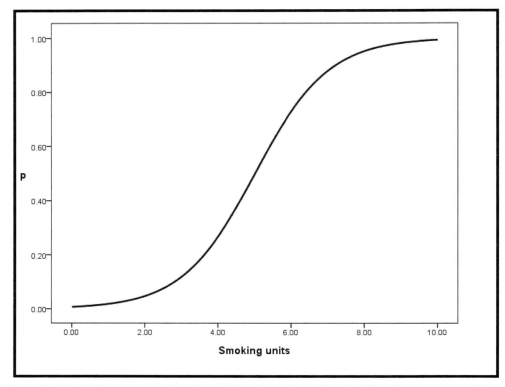

Figure 5. A logistic regression function, giving the estimated probability of a person smoking a certain number of cigarettes having the premorbid blood condition

This theoretical curve expressing the probability of the blood condition as a function of the number of cigarettes smoked is known as the **logistic regression function**. The purpose of logistic regression is to estimate this curve from the data. On the basis of the number of cigarettes that a person smokes, the estimate of the logistic regression function assigns a probability of belonging to the condition-present category. As in multiple regression with a continuous DV, further IVs, such as alcohol intake, can be added to improve predictive accuracy.

Probability estimates from the logistic regression function can be used to assign individuals to either of the two categories of the dependent variable. This is achieved by fixing a criterion probability (most commonly .5) and, should the probability estimate for a participant exceed the criterion, that person is assigned to the 'condition present' category. A value less than .05 will result in assignment to the 'condition absent' category (see Figure 6).

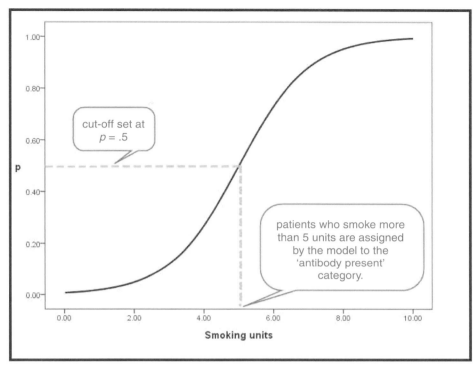

Figure 6. Decision rule for assigning a participant to a category using the logistic regression function

14.3.2 How logistic regression works

We have seen that in the context of an experiment of chance, such as tossing a coin, or rolling a die, the **odds** in favour of an event is the number of ways in which the event could occur divided by the number of ways in which it could fail to occur. If a die is rolled, the odds in favour of a six are 1/5 and the odds in favour of an even number are 3/3 = 1. If we know that among 100 patients, 44 have the blood condition and a patient is selected at random, the odds in favour of the patient selected having the antibody are 44/56 = 11/14.

Another measure of likelihood applicable in the same situation is the **probability**. The probability of an event is the number of ways in which the event could occur divided by the total number of possible outcomes. If a die is rolled, the probability of a six is 1/6 and the probability of an even number is 3/6 = ½ . The two measures of likelihood, the odds and the probability, are closely related:

$$p = \frac{odds}{1+ odds} \quad \text{- - - (2)}$$

Relation between probability and the odds

If we substitute the odds in favour of a six (1/5) into (2), we have p = (1/5)/(6/5) = 1/6. If we substitute the odds in favour of the blood condition (11/14) into (2), we have p = (11/14)/(25/14) = 11/25 = .44.

14.3.2.1   The logit

As a measure of likelihood, the odds has the disadvantage of asymmetry of range. If we start at fifty-fifty (i.e. odds = 1) and regard events with odds greater than 1 as 'likely' and those with odds less than 1 as 'unlikely', there is, in principle, no limit to how great the odds in favour of a 'likely' event could be; whereas those of an 'unlikely' event – however unlikely that event might be short of being an impossibility – can only have a small fractional value.

The **logit** is the natural logarithm (log to the base e) of the odds:

$$log\,it = \ln\left(odds\right) = \log_e\left(odds\right) \quad \text{- - - (3)}$$

The logit or log odds

When the logit of an event is zero, the odds themselves are 50/50, because the log of 1 is 0. We have seen that the odds in favour of the blood condition are 11/14. The logit, therefore, is $\ln(11/14) = -.24$. Had the number of patients with the antibody been 56 instead of 44, the odds would have been 14/11, and the logit would have been $\ln(14/11) = +.24$, which is the same distance from zero, but in the opposite direction. In contrast with the odds, the logit has symmetry of range.

The log of a number is the power to which the base must be raised to equal the number itself. So the base raised to the power of the log of a number (i.e. the **antilogarithm** of the logarithm) is the number itself. From the definition of a logarithm, therefore, we can express the odds as an antilogarithm, that is, as the base e raised to the power of the log of the odds (i.e. to the power of the logit). So if x and y are odds, they can be expressed as $x = e^{\ln(x)} = e^{\text{logit}(x)}$ and $y = e^{\ln(y)} = e^{\text{logit}(y)}$, respectively.

14.3.2.2   The logistic regression function

Recall that in **multiple regression**, the dependent variable Y is predicted from p independent variables $X_1, X_2, ..., X_p$ by means of the regression equation

$$Y' = b_0 + b_1 X_1 + b_2 X_2 + ... + b_p X_p \quad \text{- - - (4)}$$

Multiple regression equation

where b_0 is the regression constant and $b_1, b_2, ...,b_p$ are the regression coefficients.

The logistic regression function is, as we have seen, nonlinear. Expressing the probability in terms of the odds as in (2) and expressing the adds as an antilog, we have:

$$p = \frac{odds}{1+odds} = \frac{e^{log\,it}}{1+e^{log\,it}} \quad \text{- - - (5)}$$

Probability as a function of the logit

In the present context, p is the probability of a patient having the blood condition and the logit is the natural log of the odds in favour of having the condition.

In logistic regression, it is assumed that the logit is a linear function of the independent variables thus:

$$logit = b_0 + b_1 X_1 + b_2 X_2 + ... + b_p X_p \quad \text{- - - (6)}$$

The logit equation

If so, we can estimate the probability p of the antibody with $\hat{p}$, where

$$\hat{p} = \frac{e^{logit}}{1 + e^{logit}} = \frac{e^{b_0 + b_1 X_1 + b_2 X_2 + ... + b_p X_p}}{1 + e^{b_0 + b_1 X_1 + b_2 X_2 + ... + b_p X_p}} \quad \text{- - - (7)}$$

The logistic regression equation

14.3.2.3   Estimating the regression parameters

In logistic regression, as in ordinary multiple regression, the values of the parameters b_0, b_1, ..., b_p in the logit equation (6) are chosen so that the logistic regression equation predicts the independent variable (in this case category membership) as accurately as possible.

We should note that, in contradistinction to ordinary least squares (OLS) regression, there is no mathematical solution to the problem of determining the values of the parameter estimates in the logit equation. Instead, a highly computing-intensive algorithm is used to arrive at the estimates by a series of repetitions or **iterations**. If all goes well, the estimates of the parameters from successive iterations approximate ever more closely to, or **converge** upon, stable values for the parameter estimates. It is essential, however, when running logistic regression, that the user checks the iteration history to make sure that convergence really has been achieved; otherwise the output may contain bizarre and self-contradictory information!

14.3.2.4   Centring the independent variables

As with OLS regression, it is often a good idea to **centre** continuous IVs by subtracting the mean from each score. While this transformation does not affect the correlations among the variables, it can sometimes enable the logistic regression algorithm to converge upon stable estimates that it could not produce from the raw data. Centring the variables is particularly important if the researcher is testing a model containing interaction terms.

14.3.2.5   The meaning of a logistic regression coefficient

A logistic regression coefficient b is the increase in the logit produced by an increase of one unit in the independent variable. The logit, however, is the log of the odds, so if the logit increases by b units, the raw odds are *multiplied* by the antilog of b, that is by e^b. Suppose, for instance, that we were to find that for the IV Smoking, $b = 1.1$. This means that if the amount of smoking were to increase by one unit, the odds in favour of having the antibody would increase by a factor of $e^b = e^{1.1} = 3.0$. In other words, an increase of one unit in Smoking multiplies the odds in favour of having the antibody by three.

14.3.3   An example of a binary logistic regression with quantitative independent variables

For our first example, we return to the data set on the premorbid blood condition, smoking and drinking. Table 1 shows the data on the first eight cases only - the complete data set is available at www.psypress.com/spss-made-simple. We shall assume that at the point when the data were being transcribed, convenient units for smoking and alcohol were decided upon: one smoking unit might have been ten cigarettes; one drinking unit might have been the equivalent of a large glass of wine or a half-pint of beer.

Table 1. The first eight cases in a hypothetical set of data showing the presence or absence of a blood condition, together with levels of smoking and alcohol consumption							
Case	Blood	Smoke	Alcohol	Case	Blood	Smoke	Alcohol
1	Yes	7	18	5	Yes	5	11
2	Yes	6	15	6	Yes	2	18
3	Yes	1	10	7	Yes	0	0
4	Yes	7	16	8	No	6	12

14.3.3.1   Exploring the data

As usual, we recommend that you explore the data first before embarking upon any formal analysis. For example, an examination of the correlations among the three variables (see Output 13) shows that Presence of the antibody correlates substantially with the Smoking variable ($r = +.586$). and with Alcohol intake ($r = +.267$). The independent variables of Alcohol intake and Smoking level are also correlated ($r = +.443$).

See Section 11.2

Correlations

		Blood Condition	Number Smoked	Alcohol consumption
Blood Condition	Pearson Correlation	1.000	.586[**]	.267[**]
	Sig. (2-tailed)		.000	.007
	N	100.000	100	100
Number Smoked	Pearson Correlation	.586[**]	1.000	.443[**]
	Sig. (2-tailed)	.000		.000
	N	100	100.000	100
Alcohol consumption	Pearson Correlation	.267[**]	.443[**]	1.000
	Sig. (2-tailed)	.007	.000	
	N	100	100	100.000

[**]. Correlation is significant at the 0.01 level (2-tailed).

Output 13. **Correlations** among category membership (presence or absence of the premorbid blood condition), amount of smoking and level of alcohol consumption

14.3.3.2 Centring the independent variables

You will find from running **Descriptives** that the means for the smoking and alcohol variables are 1.38 and 3.87, respectively, with standard deviations 2.461 and 4.907. To centre the smoking and alcohol scores, use **Compute** to subtract their means from the raw values of their respective variables. The new smoking and alcohol means will now be zero. You may wish to confirm that the standard deviations are still 2.461 and 4.907, respectively, and that the correlations among the three variables are still exactly as they are in Output 13.

14.3.3.3 Running binary logistic regression

In its logistic regression dialog box, SPSS uses the term **covariate** to denote continuous independent variables. In this example, both IVs are continuous, so they are both covariates.

- Choose **Analyze➔Regression➔Binary Logistic ...** to open the **Logistic Regression** dialog box (Figure 7).
- Follow the steps in Figure 7.
- Click **Options...** to obtain the **Options** dialog box (Figure 8). Select **Hosmer-Lemeshow goodness-of-fit** and **Iteration history**. (The iteration history is essential.) Click **Continue** to return to the **Logistic Regression** dialog box.
- Click **OK** to run the logistic regression.

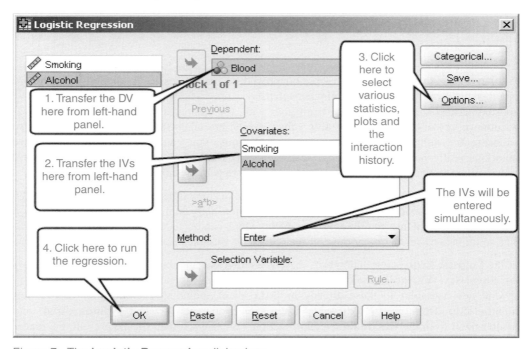

Figure 7. The **Logistic Regression** dialog box

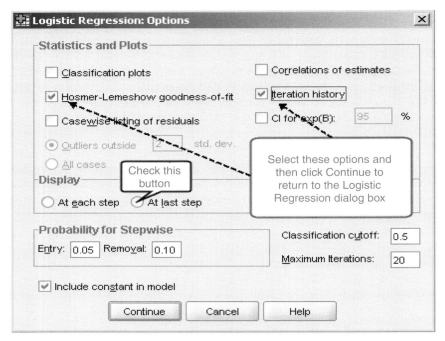

Figure 8. The **Options** dialog box with Hosmer-Lemeshow goodness-of-fit and Iteration history selected

We have seen that the logistic regression procedure maximises its predictions of category membership by a highly computer-intensive process which generates successive approximations called **iterations**. If all goes well, the estimates should converge upon (i.e. become progressively closer to) stable values, which are taken to be the best estimates. By choosing the item **Iteration history** in the **Options**, you can check that the successive iterations really have converged. (It may sometimes be necessary to increase the number specified in the Maximum Iterations slot to, say, 100 to achieve convergence.)

The analysis of a data set with many variables may take some time to complete. If some of the IVs are highly inter-correlated, the logistic regression algorithm may fail to converge upon stable estimates (the **multicollinearity** problem, which can occur with any regression method). The solution is to delete one or more of the redundant variables from the analysis.

In the **Logistic Regression** dialog box, there is another button labelled **Save...** which accesses the **Save New Variables** dialog box (not shown). Selecting items from this box will add several new variables to those already in **Data View**, including **Probabilities** and **Group membership** from the **Predicted Values** selection section, and **Standardized** and **Studentized** from the **Residuals** selection section. We suggest that, for the present, the reader might focus on the basic regression only and experiment with the **Save...** button options later.

The output for logistic regression is extensive (see Output 14), even if no options are selected. Notice that the output, after the preliminaries, essentially consists of two Blocks. The first, **Block 0: Beginning Block**, gives the statistics of the baseline, intercept-only or guessing approach to prediction of category membership. The second, **Block 1: Method = Enter**, gives the statistics of prediction from the regression model with both IVs present in the regression equation.

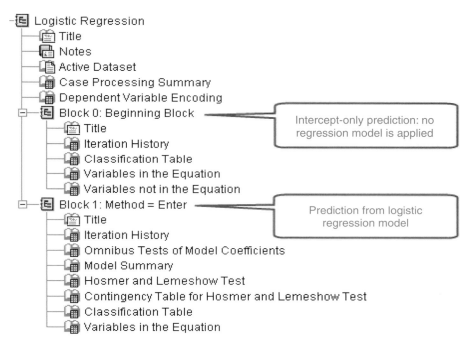

Output 14. The left-hand pane of **SPSS Statistics Viewer** showing the details of the output

In logistic regression, pivotal use is made of a statistic termed the **likelihood ratio**, which, in the output for logistic regression, is written as **– 2 Log likelihood**. This statistic behaves as chi-square: it has a large value when a model fits poorly, and a small value when the model fits well. The log likelihood statistic is analogous to the residual sum of squares in multiple regression: the larger its value, the more the variance that remains to be accounted for. A small, statistically insignificant value indicates that the regression model fits the data well.

The first two tables in the output (not shown here) are a **Case Processing Summary** table specifying how many cases were selected and a **Dependent Variable Encoding** table tabulating the numerical values and value labels of the dependent variable. Examine both tables to make sure that the logistic regression procedure has processed all the data and that the value labels have been correctly assigned to the numerical values of the categorical dependent variable.

Next there is a block of tables under the heading **Block 0: Beginning Block** in which the logistic regression procedure applies a model containing neither of the independent variables (i.e. the 'intercept only' model). Block 0 begins with the **Iteration History** (Output 15).

Iteration History[a,b,c]

Iteration		-2 Log likelihood	Coefficients Constant
Step 0	1	137.186	-.240
	2	137.186	-.241
	3	137.186	-.241

a. Constant is included in the model.

b. Initial -2 Log Likelihood: 137.186

c. Estimation terminated at iteration number 3 because parameter estimates changed by less than .001.

Output 15. **Iteration History** for Step 0 (the intercept-only model)

Notice that the convergence to stable values for the likelihood ratio and the estimate of the regression constant was almost instantaneous: the values in the second and third rows agree to three places of decimals.

In the introduction, we saw that, in the absence of any information about regression, the best bet of a person's category membership is the more frequently occurring category (i.e. condition absent). This 'guessing stage' is called **Step 0** by SPSS. Included in this block is the Step 0 **Classification Table** (see Output 16). There are no surprises here: we have already seen that the success rate without any regression is 56%.

Classification Table[a,b]

			Predicted		
			Blood Condition		
Observed			No	Yes	Percentage Correct
Step 0	Blood Condition	No	56	0	100.0
		Yes	44	0	.0
		Overall Percentage			56.0

a. Constant is included in the model.

b. The cut value is .500

Correct! If we always predict absence, we shall be correct for those without the condition

Wrong! These people actually have the condition

Our net success rate

Output 16. The 'no regression' or 'intercept only' **Classification Table**

Two other tables in Block 0 (not shown here) are **Variables in the Equation** and the **Variables not in the equation**. The first table gives the statistics of the intercept, which are not generally of interest. The second table tells us that neither of the independent variables is in the regression equation.

The next block of tables of output is headed **Block 1: Method = Enter**. The first item in the block is the **Iteration History** (Output 17).

Iteration History[a,b,c,d]

		-2 Log likelihood	Coefficients		
Iteration			Constant	Smoking	Alcohol
Step 1	1	98.522	-.906	.472	.004
	2	88.269	-1.030	.875	-.029
	3	80.474	-1.202	1.530	-.061
	4	78.107	-1.355	2.108	-.078
	5	77.999	-1.392	2.256	-.079
	6	77.999	-1.394	2.264	-.078
	7	77.999	-1.394	2.264	-.078

a. Method: Enter

b. Constant is included in the model.

c. Initial -2 Log Likelihood: 137.186

d. Estimation terminated at iteration number 7 because parameter estimates changed by less than .001.

Output 17. The **Iteration History** for Step 1, the simultaneous regression of presence of the antibody upon smoking and alcohol intake

In the last three rows of entries in the iteration history table, the entries agree to three places of decimals, indicating that convergence to stable estimates has been achieved.

The next three items, **Omnibus Tests of Model Coefficients**, **Model Summary** and **Hosmer-Lemeshow test**, are shown in Output 18. The first table shows that the regression model improves significantly upon chance in predicting category membership: all the p-values are very small. In the **Model Summary** table, the **Nagelkerke R Square** statistic imitates the coefficient of determination R^2 in multiple regression: it can be interpreted as the proportion of variance of the dependent variable that is accounted for by the regression model. The other statistic in the table, **Cox & Snell R Square**, compares the log likelihood for the model with the log likelihood for the baseline, intercept-only model. The Nagelkerke R Square, unlike the Cox & Snell R^2, can take values over the full range from 0 to 1. The size of R^2 (60% after Step 2) indicates that the model contributes powerfully to the prediction of the presence or absence of the blood condition.

In the Hosmer-Lemeshow table, the p-value is high, which indicates that all the systematic variance has been accounted for by the model: the rest is error.

Omnibus Tests of Model Coefficients

		Chi-square	df	Sig.
Step 1	Step	59.187	2	.000
	Block	59.187	2	.000
	Model	59.187	2	.000

Model Summary

Step	-2 Log likelihood	Cox & Snell R Square	Nagelkerke R Square
1	77.999ᵃ	.447	.599

a. Estimation terminated at iteration number 7 because parameter estimates changed by less than .001.

Hosmer and Lemeshow Test

Step	Chi-square	df	Sig.
1	6.155	7	.522

Output 18. Some output statistics indicating that regression accounts significantly for presence of the antibody

Output 19 shows the **Contingency Table for the Hosmer and Lemeshow Test**. The first column categorises, in order of increasing magnitude, the probabilities assigned by the regression model into divisions known as **deciles** (deciles divide the distribution into ten parts): the lowest probabilities are in deciles 1 and 2; the highest are in deciles 8 and 9. The table shows the association between assigned probability and presence or absence of the blood condition. Notice that, in general, there is close agreement between the **Expected** frequencies (the assignments by the regression model and category assignment on the basis of the cut-off point of .05 for probability) and the **Observed** or actual frequencies of patients in those categories. In particular, notice that in deciles 1 and 2 (the first two rows of entries), both Observed and Expected frequencies are very low; whereas in deciles 8 and 9 (the last two rows of entries), both the Observed and Expected frequencies are considerably higher – and in complete agreement.

Contingency Table for Hosmer and Lemeshow Test

		Blood Condition = No		Blood Condition = Yes		
		Observed	Expected	Observed	Expected	Total
Step 1	1	13	11.254	0	1.746	13
	2	12	11.004	1	1.996	13
	3	4	3.311	0	.689	4
	4	17	19.523	7	4.477	24
	5	5	6.087	3	1.913	8
	6	4	4.134	10	9.866	14
	7	1	.687	9	9.313	10
	8	0	.000	9	9.000	9
	9	0	.000	5	5.000	5

Output 19. Contingency table showing the association between the size of the probability assigned by the regression model and presence or absence of the antibody

Output 20 is the Classification Table showing the proportion of correct assignments when the regression model has been applied to the data. The new success rate of 85% is a spectacular improvement upon the baseline, intercept-only rate of 56%.

Classification Table^a

			Predicted		
			Blood Condition		
	Observed		No	Yes	Percentage Correct
Step 1	Blood Condition	No	51	5	91.1
		Yes	10	34	77.3
		Overall Percentage			85.0

a. The cut value is .500

Output 20. The **Classification Table** with the regression model applied

Output 21 tabulates the variables that are included in the regression equation. Since we chose the **Enter** method, both DVs will be entered in the equation, even if one does not make a significant contribution when added to the other. It can be seen from the p-values that Alcohol, although correlating substantially with the incidence of the antibody, does not make a significant contribution when the Smoking variable is also present in the equation.

Variables in the Equation

		B	S.E.	Wald	df	Sig.	Exp(B)
Step 1	Smoking	2.264	.513	19.490	1	.000	9.623
	Alcohol	-.078	.085	.846	1	.358	.925
	Constant	-1.394	.373	13.979	1	.000	.248

Output 21. The table of **Variables in the Equation**

The **Wald statistic** tests a regression coefficient (or the constant) for significance. As with OLS regression, the null hypothesis is that, in the population, the value of the parameter is zero. The Wald statistic is defined as follows:

$$Wald = \frac{b^2}{s_b^2} \quad \text{--- (8)}$$

The Wald statistic

and is distributed approximately as chi-square on one degree of freedom.

The first column of entries in Output 21 contains the estimates of the regression parameters: the constant and the two regression coefficients. We see that $b_0 = -1.394$, $b_{Smoking} = 2.264$ and $b_{Alcohol} = -0.078$. Substituting these values in (7), the logistic regression equation is

$$\hat{p} = \frac{e^{\log it}}{1 + e^{\log it}} = \frac{e^{-1.394 + 2.264\,Smoking - 0.078\,Alcohol}}{1 + e^{-1.394 + 2.264\,Smoking - 0.078\,Alcohol}}$$

In Output 21, the entries in the rightmost column, under Exp(B), are the factors by which the raw odds in favour of the occurrence of the blood condition are *multiplied* by increasing the independent variable by one unit. The term Exp(B) is e^B , the **exponential function** of B. It is the antilog of the regression coefficient. For example, in the first row of entries in Output 21, the value of B for Smoking is given as 2.264. This means that an increase in smoking level of one unit produces, on average, an increase of 2.264 units in the logit (i.e. the natural log of the odds) in favour of having the blood condition. But an increase of 2.264 units in the logarithm corresponds to *multiplication* of the raw odds by $Exp(2.264) = e^{2.264} = 9.623$. In words, an increase of one unit in Smoking, multiplies the likelihood of having the blood condition by ten.

It is clear from Output 21 that Smoking makes both a significant and a substantial contribution to the regression: p < .01; Exp(B) = 9.623. Alcohol, on the other hand, makes neither a significant ($p = .358$) nor a substantial [Exp(B) = .925] contribution. That suggests that, in our regression exercise, we might dispense with the services of the Alcohol variable altogether.

We have been describing the output resulting from **simultaneous** regression, that is, regression with both the IVs entered into the regression equation in a single step. Returning to the **Logistic Regression** dialog box, the drop-down menu for **Method** gives us several other possible approaches. If we select, say, **Backward LR** (i.e. Backward Likelihood Ratio), we shall find that the regression will eliminate the Alcohol variable from the regression and still achieve a hit rate of 85% of accurate classifications. (As a matter of fact, you will obtain the same result if you select any of the other methods.) We suggest that, as an analytic strategy, it is often helpful to begin with simultaneous regression, the output of which is easier to understand, and then proceed to the sequential methods in order to clarify the results of the simultaneous regression.

14.3.4   Binary logistic regression with categorical independent variables

Neither binary nor multinomial regression has any problems with the inclusion of categorical independent variables: in fact, all the independent variables can be qualitative, as the following example will illustrate.

In Chapter 13, we described an experiment on gender and professed helpfulness, in which participants were asked by a male or female interviewer whether they would be prepared to help in a certain situation. The research hypothesis was the opposite-sex dyadic hypothesis, which holds that one is more inclined to help someone of the opposite sex than someone of one's own sex. The results are reproduced in Table 2.

Table 2. Three-way contingency table showing the results of the Gender and professed helpfulness experiment

Incidence of helping by male and female participants with male and female interviewers

Count

Sex of Interviewer			Would you help?		Total
			Yes	No	
Male	Sex of Participant	Male	4	21	25
		Female	16	9	25
	Total		20	30	50
Female	Sex of Participant	Male	11	14	25
		Female	11	14	25
	Total		22	28	50

Here the implicit dependent variable was Help, a categorical, dichotomous variable with two values: 1 = Yes; 2 = No. The independent variables were Sex of Interviewer and Sex of Participant. As we saw in Chapter 13, however, the loglinear analysis does not frame the problem in regression terms. Instead, the analysis models the expected cell frequencies in the multiway contingency table. Confirmation of the opposite-sex dyadic hypothesis would take the form of a three-way interaction among the factors: in participants of either sex, there would be a higher helping rate when the interviewer was of opposite sex to that of the participant.

We have here a data set that also meets all the requirements for logistic regression: there is a categorical dependent variable Help; and there are two categorical IVs, Sex of Participant and Sex of Interviewer. In the present regression context, however, confirmation of the opposite-sex dyadic hypothesis would take the form of a two-way interaction between Sex of Participant and Sex of Interviewer.

The running of logistic regression with these data involves two new moves: 1. an interaction term must be included in the model; 2. SPSS must be informed that the IVs are categorical, not continuous.

The data are available at www.psypress.com/spss-made-simple. The file is *Ch13 Helping(3WayInteractionOnly).sav*. With this file in the **Data Editor**, proceed as follows:
- Choose **Analyze➔Regression➔Binary Logistic …** to open the **Logistic Regression** dialog box (Figure 9).

- Transfer the name of the DV to the **Dependent** slot and the names of the two IVs to the **Covariates** panel.
- Add the interaction term by selecting both IVs. The button marked >**a*b**> will become active. Click to transfer the interaction term Interviewer*Participant to the Covariates panel.

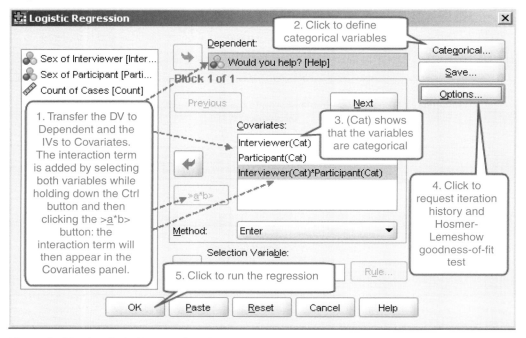

Figure 9. The **Logistic Regression** dialog box. The IVs (covariates) are registered as categorical by clicking the **Categorical** button and completing the **Define Categorical Variables** dialog box (see Figure 10)

- Click the **Categorical…** button to obtain the **Define Categorical Variables** dialog box (see Figure 10). Transfer the names Participant and Interviewer to the **Categorical Covariates:** box. The default type of **Contrast** is **Indicator**, which registers the presence or absence of the target category. Click **Continue** to return to the **Logistic Regression** dialog box, where you will now see the variable names marked with **(Cat).**
- Click the **Options** button and select **Iteration history** and the **Hosmer-Lemeshow goodness-of-fit test** from the **Options** dialog box. Click **Continue** to return to the **Logistic Regression** dialog box.
- Click **OK** to run the regression.

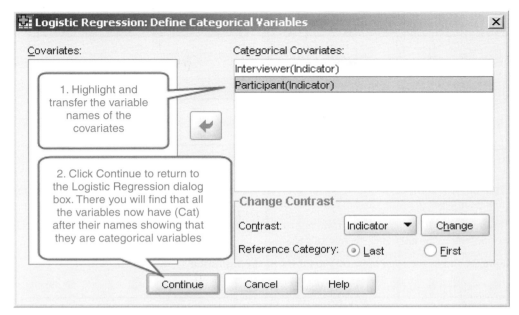

Figure 10. The completed dialog box for **Define Categorical Variables**

14.3.4.1 Output of binary logistic regression with categorical independent variables

As usual, following the preliminaries, the output is presented under the headings Step 0 (intercept-only prediction) and Step 1 (prediction from the regression model).

Output 22 shows the classification table at Step 0. The baseline success rate is 58%.

Classification Table[a,b]

			Predicted		
			Would you help?		
Observed			Yes	No	Percentage Correct
Step 0	Would you help?	Yes	0	42	.0
		No	0	58	100.0
		Overall Percentage			58.0

a. Constant is included in the model.

b. The cut value is .500

Baseline, 'intercept-only' success rate

Output 22. The baseline classification success rate with 'intercept-only' prediction

Output 23 shows the classification success rate when the regression model is applied.

Classification Table[a]

			Predicted		
			Would you help?		
Observed			Yes	No	Percentage Correct
Step 1	Would you help?	Yes	16	26	38.1
		No	9	49	84.5
		Overall Percentage			65.0

a. The cut value is .500

Success rate when regression model is applied

Output 23. **Classification Table** showing an increase in the success rate when the regression model is applied

The classification success rate from regression is 65%, which is an improvement upon the baseline, intercept-only success rate of 58%.

Output 24 shows the final table of **Variables in the Equation**.

Variables in the Equation

		B	S.E.	Wald	df	Sig.	Exp(B)
Step 1	Interviewer(1)	-.817	.580	1.985	1	.159	.442
	Participant(1)	.000	.570	.000	1	1.000	1.000
	Interviewer(1) by Participant(1)	2.234	.892	6.268	1	.012	9.333
	Constant	.241	.403	.358	1	.549	1.273

Output 24. Final table of **Variables in the Equation**

It can be seen from Output 24 that the only significant term in the regression is the **Interviewer × Participant** interaction. Notice that the value of Exp(B), the multiplier of the raw odds, is much greater than it is for the other terms in the regression equation. This result is the equivalent, in logistic regression, of the significant three-way interaction that we obtained when we used loglinear analysis to model the cell frequencies of the same contingency table. The outcome of the logistic regression is in complete agreement with that of the loglinear analysis of the same data.

14.4 MULTINOMIAL LOGISTIC REGRESSION

In Section 14.2, **discriminant analysis** was used to predict the university subject chosen by students on the basis of several independent variables. In Section 14.3, we introduced **logistic regression**, which carries fewer assumptions than does **discriminant analysis**. SPSS's **binary logistic regression** can only be used for predicting a dichotomous (two-category) dependent variable. If there are more than two categories, we must use **multinomial logistic regression**. The purpose of the following exercise is to see whether **multinomial logistic regression** can predict choice of Subject at University with the same level of accuracy as can **discriminant analysis**. In multinomial logistic regression, the independent variables can be either **factors** or **covariates**. Factors are categorical variables (e.g. Sex of Student) and covariates are continuous variables (as are all the remaining variables in our example).

14.4.1   Running multinomial logistic regression

To run the multinomial logistic regression procedure with the choice of subject data:

- Choose **Analyze➔Regression➔Multinomial Logistic...** to open the **Multinomial Logistic Regression** dialog box (Figure 11).
- Transfer StudySubject to the **Dependent** box, Sex of Student to the **Factor(s)** box and the remaining quantitative independent variables into the **Covariate(s)** box.
- Click **Model...** at the side of the **Multinomial Logistic Regression** dialog box to open the **Model** dialog box (Figure 12). Follow the steps shown in Figure 12. Click **Continue** to return to the main dialog box.

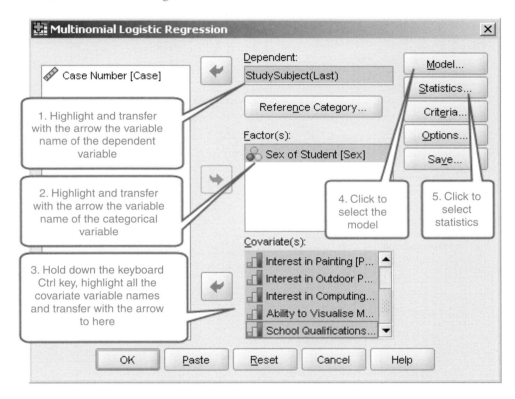

Figure 11. The **Multinomial Logistic Regression** dialog box

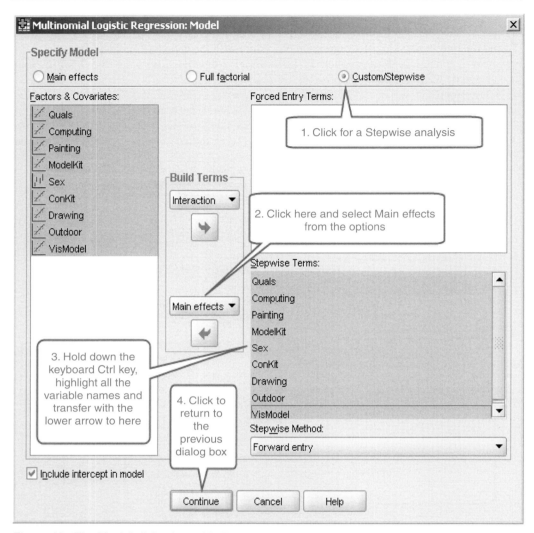

Figure 12. The **Model** dialog box with **Forward entry** selected

- Click **Statistics** to see a dialog box labelled **Multinomial Logistic Regression: Statistics** (Figure 13). Check the boxes as shown in the figure.
- Click **Continue** to return to the **Multinomial Logistic Regression** dialog box.
- Click **OK** to run the multinomial logistic regression.

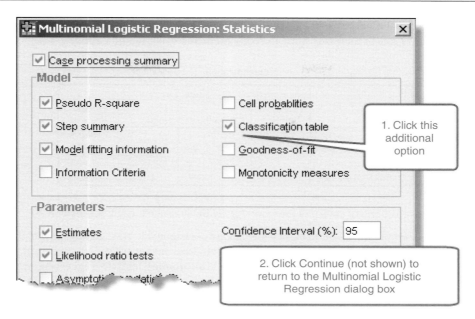

Figure 13. The upper part of the **Statistics** dialog box with **Classification table** selected in addition to those already highlighted when the dialog box is opened

14.4.1.1 Output of multinomial logistic regression

The output consists of several tables. First there is a **Case Summary Table** (not shown here) listing the levels of the dependent variable (Study Subject) and the numbers of each, and also the levels of the factor Sex and the numbers of males and females.

Next there is a **Step Summary** table (Output 25) showing which covariates were entered and in which order. Note that the variables Drawing and Model Kit were never entered, the same two that were omitted from the **discriminant analysis** model.

Step Summary

Model	Action	Effect(s)	-2 Log Likelihood	Chi-Square	df	Sig.
0	Entered	Intercept	235.548			
1	Entered	Sex	208.820	26.727	2	.000
2	Entered	Painting	191.144	17.677	2	.000
3	Entered	Quals	171.760	19.384	2	.000
4	Entered	VisModel	159.182	12.578	2	.002
5	Entered	Computing	146.761	12.422	2	.002
6	Entered	Outdoor	140.055	6.705	2	.035
7	Entered	ConKit	133.221	6.834	2	.033

Stepwise Method: Forward Entry

Output 25. The **Step Summary** table showing which IVs were entered in the model

Finally after several other tables not shown here, there is the **Classification** table (Output 26) showing that 72.2% of the cases were correctly predicted using the final model.

Classification

Observed	Predicted			
	Architect	Psychologist	Engineer	Percent Correct
Architect	20	2	8	66.7%
Psychologist	2	28	7	75.7%
Engineer	5	6	30	73.2%
Overall Percentage	25.0%	33.3%	41.7%	72.2%

Output 26. Predictions of category membership by multinomial logistic regression

Recall that a level of 72.2% accuracy of category assignment was also achieved by using **discriminant analysis**. For the three Study Subjects, however, the numbers of correct predictions differ slightly in the two outputs. **Multinomial logistic regression** was more successful at predicting Psychologists and slightly less successful at predicting Architects. Engineers differ by just one case.

Although the general level of accuracy of assignment is the same with the two procedures, you will find that, if you use the **Save** button to obtain the assignments by both techniques in **Data View**, there is some disagreement between the category assignments by the two procedures in individual cases. We should bear in mind that this data set failed to meet one of the criteria for discriminant analysis, namely, homogeneity of the variance-covariance matrices. Since that property is not a requirement for multinomial logistic regression, perhaps we should place more reliance upon the multinomial logistic regression.

14.5   A FINAL WORD

In this chapter, we have described some regression methods that have been specially designed for data sets in which the DV is a set of categories, rather than a continuous variable. We began with discriminant analysis, which assumes multivariate normality and homogeneity of variance-covariance matrices across the categories of the DV. We then described binary logistic regression, which assumes neither multivariate normality nor homogeneity of variance-covariance matrices. Finally, we touched upon multinomial logistic regression which is applicable when the DV consists of more than two categories. We found that, with the same data set on choices of subjects at university, discriminant analysis and multinomial logistic regression gave very similar results.

The use of logistic regression encounters many of the problems of interpretation that arise with multiple regression. In particular, when independent variables are correlated, there is always doubt about which IV makes the greatest contribution to the variance of the dependent variable. The design of any multiple regression project and the interpretation of the output require the guidance of a *causal* model: a *statistical* model is insufficient.

Recommended reading

Howell (2007), Todman & Dugard (2007) and Dugard, Todman & Staines (2010) have lively and helpful chapters on logistic regression. Tabachnick & Fidell (2007) go into the technicalities in most detail. We suggest you might begin with David Howell's chapter, which sets the scene very nicely.

Dugard, P., Todman, T., & Staines, H. (2010). *Approaching multivariate analysis: A practical introduction (2nd ed.).* London & New York: Routledge.

Howell, D. (2007). *Statistical methods for psychology (6th ed.).* Belmont, CA: Thomson/Wadsworth.

Tabachnick, B. G., & Fidell, L. S. (2007). *Using multivariate statistics (5th ed.)* Boston: Allyn & Bacon (Pearson International Edition).

Todman, J., & Dugard, P. (2007). *Approaching multivariate analysis: An introduction for psychology.* Hove: Psychology Press.

Exercise

Exercise 23 *Predicting category membership: Discriminant analysis and binary logistic regression* is available in www.psypress.com/spss-made-simple and click on Exercises.

CHAPTER 15

The search for latent variables: factor analysis

15.1   INTRODUCTION

Suppose that some schoolchildren are tested on several variables, perhaps an assortment of school subjects such as foreign languages, music, mathematics and related activities such as mapwork. The correlations of performance on each test with every other test in the battery can be arranged in a rectangular array known as a **correlation matrix**, or **R-matrix** (Table 1).

Table 1. A correlation matrix (as output by SPSS) showing, in the off-diagonal elements of each row or column, the correlations of one test with each of the other tests. In each cell along the principal diagonal from top left to bottom right is the correlation of a test with itself.

Correlation Matrix

		French	German	Latin	Music	Maths	Mapwork
Correlation	French	1.000	.836	.742	.032	.083	.312
	German	.836	1.000	.715	-.081	.008	.118
	Latin	.742	.715	1.000	.022	.222	.131
	Music	.032	-.081	.022	1.000	.713	.783
	Maths	.083	.008	.222	.713	1.000	.735
	Mapwork	.312	.118	.131	.783	.735	1.000

In its basic form, a correlation matrix is **square**, that is, there are as many rows as there are columns. The diagonal of cells running from top left to bottom right is known as the **principal**

diagonal of the matrix. The values in the off-diagonal cells are the same above and below the principal diagonal: e.g., the correlation of French with German is the same as that of German with French. Each row (or column) of the R-matrix contains all the correlations involving one particular test in the battery. Since the variables are labelled in the same order in the rows and columns of the R-matrix, each of the cells along the principal diagonal contains the correlation of one of the variables with itself (i.e. 1). The R-matrix is the starting point for a variety of multivariate statistical procedures, but in this chapter we shall consider just one technique: **factor analysis.**

Factor analysis is a set of techniques designed to enable the researcher to classify data on several variables with reference to a smaller number of supposed underlying dimensions or **factors**. Is it possible, for example, to account for the patterns shown by the correlations in Table 1 in terms of fewer factors than there were tests in the battery?

Since the entries below the principal diagonal of the R-matrix in Table 1 are identical with those above it, we shall concentrate on the upper half of the table only. In Figure 1, we see that there are two groups of subjects showing high correlations with one another: 1. German, French and Latin; 2. Music, Maths and Mapwork.

Correlation Matrix

		French	German	Latin	Music	Maths	Mapwork
Correlation	French	1.000	.836	.742	.032	.083	.312
	German	.836	1.000	.715	-.081	.008	.118
	Latin	.742	.715	1.000	.022	.222	.131
	Music	.032	-.081	.022	1.000	.713	.783
	Maths	.083	.008	.222	.713	1.000	.735
	Mapwork	.312	.118	.131	.783	.735	1.000

Group 1: French, German and Latin show high intercorrelations, but each shows low correlations with the subjects in Group 2

Group 2: Maths, Mapwork and Music show high intercorrelations, but each shows low correlations with the subjects in Group 1

Figure 1. Exploring the R-matrix

While the members of each group correlate strongly with the other group members, they show much lower correlations with the members of the other group. For example, German (Group 1) correlates .008 with Maths and .118 with Mapwork. And Maths (Group 2) correlates .083 with French and .222 with Latin.

It is tempting to surmise that the clustering among the tests in the R-matrix arises because, although the tests in each group are measuring the same underlying ability (or very similar abilities), the two groups are tapping different abilities. The tests in Group 1 might be tapping general linguistic ability; whereas those in Group 2 might be tapping nonverbal, visuo-spatial ability.

It would appear, therefore, that the 15 correlations among the six tests in the R-matrix can be accounted for in terms of just two underlying, independent dimensions. The purpose of factor analysis is to quantify these dimensions.

The **factors** produced by factor analysis are mathematical entities, which can be thought of as classificatory axes for plotting the tests as points on a graph. The greater the value of a test's co-ordinate, or **loading**, on a factor/axis, the more important that factor is in accounting for the variance of scores on that test. Theoretically, a loading can vary throughout the range from -1 to $+1$, inclusive. In practice, however, errors in measurement restrict this theoretical range considerably.

The term **factor** has also an equivalent algebraic interpretation as a linear function of the observed scores that people achieve on the tests in a battery. If a battery contains six tests (as in the present example), and each person tested were also to be assigned a seventh score consisting of the sum of the six test scores, that seventh (summative) score would be a **factor score**, and it would make sense to speak of correlations between the factor scores and the real test scores. Factor scores, in fact, can be used as representative variables for input into subsequent analyses.

We have seen that the loading of a test on a factor is, geometrically speaking, the co-ordinate of the test point on the factor axis. But that axis also represents a 'factor' in the second, algebraic sense, and the loading is the correlation between the original test scores and those on the factor. Ultimately, however, a factor (a mathematical entity) is assumed to represent an underlying or latent variable, in terms of which the correlations in the R-matix can be accounted for or explained and the tests in the battery can be classified.

In **exploratory factor analysis**, the aim is to determine the number and nature of the factors necessary to account adequately for the correlations in the R-matrix. The researcher will hope that the correlations among the observed variables can be accounted for in terms of comparatively few factors. In **confirmatory factor analysis**, on the other hand, the researcher hypothesises that there should be a predetermined number of factors, on which the tests in the battery should show specified patterns of loadings. Such a model can then be put to the test by gathering data and testing the favoured model against other models of the same data, positing different number of factors and other specifications. Recent years have seen dramatic developments in what is known as **structural equation modelling (SEM)**, of which confirmatory factor analysis is one aspect. (See, for example, Tabachnick & Fidell, 2007, Chapter 14.)

At present, SPSS itself offers exploratory factor analysis only. Under the aegis of SPSS, however, there is also AMOS, a structural equation modelling (SEM) package, which can be accessed through the **Analyze** menu. A detailed treatment of SEM is beyond the scope of this book. Later in this chapter, however, we shall take a brief look at how AMOS can be used to run a confirmatory factor analysis.

15.1.1 Stages in an exploratory factor analysis

An exploratory factor analysis usually takes place in three stages:
1. A **matrix of correlation coefficients** is generated for all possible pairings of the variables (i.e. the tests).
2. From the correlation matrix, **factors** are **extracted.** The most common method of extraction is called **principal factors** or **principal components**. (Technically, there is a difference between factors and components, but this need not concern us at the moment.)
3. The factors (axes) are **rotated** to facilitate the interpretation of the results of the factor analysis.

15.1.2   The extraction of factors

The factors (or axes) in a factor analysis are **extracted** one at a time, leaving after each extraction a residual data set of scores that do not correlate with the extracted factor. The process is repeated with the residual data set until it is possible, from the loadings of the tests on the factors so far extracted, to generate good approximations to the correlations in the original R-matrix. One of the main purposes of exploratory factor analysis is to ascertain the number of factors necessary to achieve an adequate reconstruction of the R-matrix.

15.1.3   The rationale of rotation

We can think of the tests in the battery and the origin of the classificatory axes or factors as stationary points and rotate the axes around the origin of this graph to produce a new pattern of loadings known as a **rotated factor matrix**. We can do this because, although rotation will cause the values of all the loadings to change, the new set of loadings on the axes, *whatever the new position of the axes*, can still be used to produce exactly the same estimates of the correlations in the R-matrix. In this sense, the position of the axes is arbitrary: the factor matrix (or **F-matrix**) only tells us *how many* axes are necessary to classify the data adequately: it does not thereby establish that the initial position of the axes is the best position. There is, in fact, no unique position for the axes that is 'best' in every possible respect.

The factors or axes are rotated in order to make the results of the factor analysis easier to interpret. In general, it is easier to endow mathematical factors with substantive meaning if the tests in the R-matrix are loaded substantially on comparatively few factors, as opposed to having small loadings on many factors. The position of the axes (or rotated factor matrix) that best achieves this economy is said to have the property of **simple structure**. That term, however, coined many years ago by Thurstone, is open to different interpretations and there exists no method of achieving, in a single rotation, all the properties that Thurstone described. Modern computing packages such as SPSS offer a selection of rotation methods, each based upon a different (but reasonable) interpretation of simple structure.

15.1.4   Some issues in factor analysis

As we have described it so far, the outcome of a factor analysis will have seemed entirely objective and automatic. While the researcher will almost certainly have expectations about how many factors are likely to emerge, the process of factor extraction proceeds automatically until a criterion for termination is reached. The results of a factor analysis, however, are notoriously dependent upon the manner in which the participants and the test materials have been sampled by the researcher and the type of factor analysis the researcher is using.

When children are selected from the full range of ability, the pattern of correlations shown in Figure 1 is extremely unlikely. Years of research with normal primary school children have shown the predominance of a factor on which *every* test has substantial loadings. This is known as the **general factor (g)**. Study after study has confirmed the pattern known as the **positive manifold**, that is, substantial correlations among all the tests in the battery. Figure 1 shows an unusual predominance of **group factors**, that is, factors on which only *some* of the tests in the battery have substantial loadings. Such a **group factor profile** is characteristic of of children selected for their high academic ability.

Even when the same battery of tests has been used in different projects, the precise number of factors extracted and the nature of the hypothetical dimensions they represent have been found to vary from study to study. The goal of **factor invariance** has, in detail, proved to be somewhat elusive.

The pattern shown by the loadings in the final rotated factor matrix depends upon the method of rotation used. The most commonly used method of rotation is **varimax**, which maintains independence among the mathematical factors. Geometrically, this means that during rotation, the axes remain **orthogonal** (i.e. they are kept at right angles). Orthogonal axes represent uncorrelated factors. There are other methods of rotation, however, which allow the axes to be non-orthogonal or **oblique**, so that they represent correlated factors. There has been much argument about which method of rotation is best, and the preferred method tends to reflect the theoretical views of the user. In view of the multiplicity of considerations that can influence the outcome of a factor analysis, it has often been argued that traditional factor analytic methods are ill-suited to the testing of specific hypotheses and are appropriate only in the early, exploratory stages of research. Confirmatory factor analysis, however, in contrast with exploratory factor analysis, allows the formulation of hypotheses that are sufficiently specific to be put to the empirical test.

15.1.5   Some key technical terms

An understanding of the SPSS output requires at least an intuitive grasp of the meaning of several technical terms.
- Provided the factors remain uncorrelated or orthogonal during rotation, the **loading** of a test on a factor, as we have seen, is the correlation between the test and the factor.
- The **communality** of a test is the total proportion of its variance that is accounted for by the extracted factors. The communality is the **squared multiple correlation R^2** between the test and the factors emerging from the factor analysis. If the factors are orthogonal or independent (as they will be in the example we shall consider), the communality is given by the sum of the squares of the loadings of the test on the extracted factors. The communality of a test is a measure of its reliability.
- The **eigenvalue** (or **latent root**) of a factor is a measure of the total variance (taken across all the tests) accounted for by the factor. If the total variance of each test is unity, the eigenvalue of the first factor extracted has a theoretical maximum equal to the number of tests in the battery. (In practice, of course, this cannot be achieved with variables having an element of measurement error.) The eigenvalue can be converted to a measure of the proportion of the total variance by dividing by the total number of tests in the battery. Before the rotation phase, the first factor extracted always has the largest eigenvalue, the second the next largest, and so on. The process of extraction continues until the factors extracted account for negligible proportions of the total variance.
- If the eigenvalues of successive factors are plotted against the ordinal numbers of the factors, the curve eventually flattens out and its appearance thereafter has been likened to the rubble or scree on a mountainside. The eigenvalue plot is therefore known as a **scree plot** (see Output 6). There is general agreement that the factorial litter begins when the eigenvalues fall below one.
- The process of **rotation** changes the eigenvalues of the factors that have been extracted, so that the common factor variance accounted for by the extraction is more evenly distributed among the rotated factors. The communalities, on the other hand, are unchanged by rotation, because their values depend only upon the number of factors and the correlations among the tests.

15.1.6 Preliminaries

Before you proceed with a factor analysis, it is advisable to inspect the R-matrix first. Since the purpose of factor analysis is to account for associations among the tests, the exercise is pointless if no substantial associations exist. By convention, all variables should show at least one correlation of the order of .3 before it is worth proceeding with a full factor analysis. Should any variables show no substantial correlation with any of the others, they should be removed from the R-matrix. It is also advisable to check that the correlation matrix does not possess the highly undesirable property of **multicollinearity**, that is, the presence of very high correlations arising from the inclusion of very similar tests in the battery. Should the R-matrix show multicollinearity, some of the variables must be omitted from the analysis; otherwise the factor analysis will not run.

The process of preparing the data for a factor analysis includes checking them for transcription errors, the presence of extreme scores and outliers and missing values. Some writers insist that at least 300 cases are required for a factor analysis; others, however, accept fewer cases. Should the data be less plentiful than one would wish, however, extreme scores and outliers can distort the correlations in the R-matrix.

Missing data present problems for any kind of analysis. One approach is to exclude cases from the analysis; another is to substitute the mean score for the variable concerned. **Listwise** exclusion removes from the analysis any case that does not have values on all the variables in the set. This is a strict criterion: should even a single score be missing, all the data from the case concerned are excluded. **Pairwise** exclusion removes only those cases that do not have both scores for any one pair of variables, so that data from a case may be included in the calculation of some correlations, but not for others. This is clearly a less stringent criterion than listwise exclusion.

A potential problem with pairwise exclusion is that the correlations in the R-matrix may be based upon data from different samples of participants. The result may be what is known as an **ill-conditioned** matrix, that is, one that does not yield stable solutions to mathematical operations essential to factor analysis and other multivariate methods.

The **Kaiser-Meyer-Olkin (KMO)** statistic tests for **sampling adequacy**, that is, absence of multicollinearity among the variables. It is generally recommended that its value should be at least 0.6 .

A preliminary inspection of the R-matrix in order to check for the presence of correlations among the variables must be supported by some statistical analysis. **Bartlett's test** of sphericity, which is included in the SPSS output, is rather too sensitive to be very useful and typically shows significance with large data sets. SPSS ouput, however, also includes tests for the significance of the correlations in the R-matrix, which is more helpful.

The claim that a subset of the tests in a battery really do measure a particular underlying factor must be supported by additional statistics, such as **Cronbach's alpha**, which are obtained from a separate reliability analysis.

15.2 AN EXPLORATORY FACTOR ANALYSIS

Table 2 contains the raw data from which the correlations in Table 1 were calculated.

Table 2. Marks of 10 children in six examinations					
Case	French	German	Latin	Music	Maths	Mapwork
1	56	66	53	47	50	48
2	46	48	43	53	69	55
3	56	51	43	40	49	45
4	29	42	39	53	56	48
5	71	67	84	66	67	60
6	56	47	58	59	67	74
7	62	69	48	59	58	66
8	46	42	38	46	38	42
9	66	73	85	34	49	42
10	36	42	48	53	59	48

From these raw data, we can run a factor analysis by choosing from menus and completing dialogs. Were we, however, to start from a correlation matrix such as that shown in Table 1, rather than the raw data, we should have to use SPSS syntax. We shall describe how that is done in a later section.

15.2.1 Entering the data for a factor analysis

Enter the data using the procedures described in Section 2.3. In **Variable View**, name the six variables for the factor analysis. It's good practice to include an extra variable for the case number. Ensure that there are no decimals by changing the value in the **Decimals** column to 0. Click the **Data View** tab at the foot of **Variable View** and enter the data in **Data View**.

15.2.2 Running a factor analysis on SPSS

To run the factor analysis, proceed as follows:
- Choose **Analyze➜Dimension Reduction➜Factor...** (Figure 2) to open the **Factor Analysis** dialog box (Figure 3).
- Transfer all the variable names except Case Number to the **Variables** box.

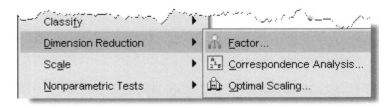

Figure 2. Finding the **Factor Analysis** dialog box in the **Analyze** menu

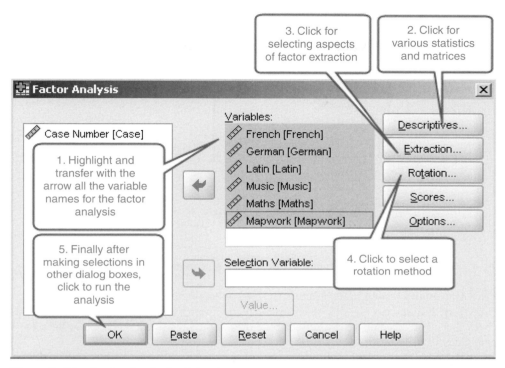

Figure 3. The **Factor Analysis** dialog box

Before running the analysis, you should select some options to control the analysis and add some useful extra items to the output.

- Click **Descriptives...** to open the **Descriptives** dialog box (Figure 4). Click the following check boxes: **Univariate descriptives**, to tabulate descriptive statistics; **Initial solution**, to display the original communalities, eigenvalues and the percentage of variance explained; **Coefficients**, to tabulate the R-matrix; **Reproduced**, to obtain an approximation of the R-matrix from the loadings of the factors extracted by the analysis; **Significance levels**, to identify the significant correlations in the R-matrix; **KMO and Bartlett's test of sphericity** for tests of sampling adequacy and complete independence. The **Reproduced** option will also obtain communalities and the residual differences between the observed and reproduced correlations.

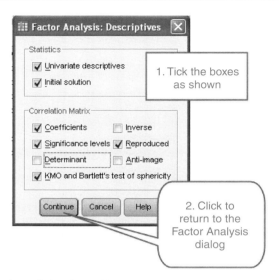

Figure 4. The Descriptives dialog box with appropriate selections

- Click **Continue** to return to the **Factor Analysis** dialog box.
- Click **Extraction…** to open the **Extraction** dialog box (Figure 5). Click the **Scree plot** check box. The scree plot is a useful display showing the relative importance of the factors extracted.

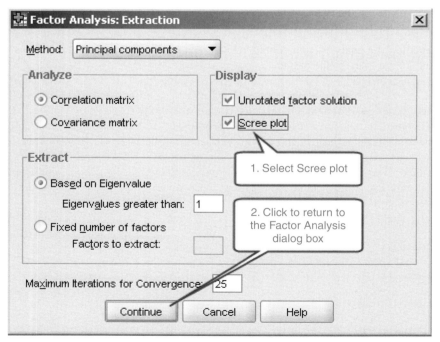

Figure 5. The **Extraction** dialog box with **Scree plot** selected

- Click **Continue** to return to the **Factor Analysis** dialog box.
- To obtain the rotated F-matrix, click **Rotation…** to obtain the **Rotation** dialog box (Figure 6). In the **Method** box, click the **Varimax** radio button. In the Display panel, check the boxes labelled **Rotated solution** and **Loading plots**.
- Click **Continue** and then **OK** to run the factor analysis procedure.

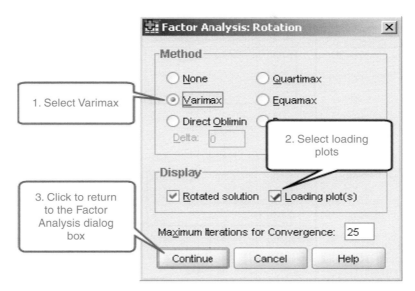

Figure 6. The **Rotation** dialog box with **Varimax** selected

15.2.3   Output for factor analysis

The output of the factor analysis is extensive, as shown by the length of the list of items in the **SPSS Statistics Viewer**. Any desired item can be viewed immediately, however, by clicking on its name in the list.

15.2.3.1   Descriptive statistics

Output 1 shows the specially requested descriptive statistics for the variables.

Descriptive Statistics

	Mean	Std. Deviation	Analysis N
French	52.00	13.167	10
German	55.00	12.561	10
Latin	54.00	17.233	10
Music	51.04	9.524	10
Maths	56.18	9.854	10
Mapwork	52.74	10.854	10

Output 1. Descriptive statistics for the variables

The correlation matrix (edited by adding additional shading) is shown in the upper part of Output 2. This is exactly the same R-matrix that we discussed in Section 15.1. (The shaded groups in Output 2 look larger than the ringed groups in Figure 1; but note the duplication of correlations with the inclusion of elements on both sides of the principal diagonal.)

Correlation Matrix

		French	German	Latin	Music	Maths	Mapwork
Correlation	French	1.000	.836	.742	.032	.083	.312
	German	.836	1.000	.715	-.081	.008	.118
	Latin	.742	.715	1.000	.022	.222	.131
	Music	.032	-.081	.022	1.000	.713	.783
	Maths	.083	.008	.222	.713	1.000	.735
	Mapwork	.312	.118	.131	.783	.735	1.000
Sig. (1-tailed)	French		.001	.007	.465	.410	.190
	German	.001		.010	.411	.491	.373
	Latin	.007	.010		.476	.269	.359
	Music	.465	.411	.476		.010	.004
	Maths	.410	.491	.269	.010		.008
	Mapwork	.190	.373	.359	.004	.008	

Output 2. The correlation matrix (**R-matrix**) with additional shading (see text) and the *p*-values of the correlations

In the lower part of Output 2 are the *p*-values of the correlations in the upper part. The *p*-values corresponding to the correlations in the shaded areas in the upper table, which are shown in similarly shaded and correspondingly placed rectangles in the lower table, are all very small, indicating that the correlations are both substantial and statistically robust.

We saw in Section 15.1 that we should be able to account for the pattern of correlations in terms of two independent dimensions of ability. The important question now is whether this view is confirmed by the results of the formal factor analysis. Are two factors sufficient to account for the correlations among the tests? Are the results of the factor analysis consistent with the simple interpretation we have arrived at through inspection of the R-matrix?

It can be seen from Output 3 that the value of the KMO statistic is .606, which is within the acceptable range. There is unlikely to be a problem with multicollinearity. In view of the large (and statistically significant) correlations in the R matrix, it would be very surprising if Bartlett's test were not significant, even with such a small data set as the present one.

KMO and Bartlett's Test

Kaiser-Meyer-Olkin Measure of Sampling Adequacy.		.606
Bartlett's Test of Sphericity	Approx. Chi-Square	28.455
	df	15
	Sig.	.019

Output 3. A measure of sampling adequacy and Bartlett's test

15.2.3.4 Communalities

Output 4 is a table of communalities assigned to the variables by the factor analysis. The communality of a test is, as we have seen, the proportion of the variance of the test that has been accounted for by the factors extracted. For example, we see that 89% of the variance of the scores on French is accounted for by the factoring.

Communalities

	Initial	Extraction
French	1.000	.888
German	1.000	.870
Latin	1.000	.783
Music	1.000	.852
Maths	1.000	.801
Mapwork	1.000	.862

Extraction Method: Principal Component Analysis.

Output 4. Table of the communalities of the six variables

The next table (Output 5) displays information about the factors (SPSS calls them 'components') that have been extracted. Technically, a 'component' is not identical with a 'factor'. In principal components analysis (as opposed to factor analysis), the analysis produces as many components as there are tests in the battery. You can see that this is so in Output 5, where 6 components are listed. A principal components analysis accounts for *all* the variance of the test scores, including error. In contradistinction, a factor analysis accounts only for that portion of the variance that is common factor variance, that is, variance that is shared among the tests in the battery. The common factor variance is the *reliable* part of the total variance.

A principal components analysis begins with the R-matrix and proceeds until the entries in R can be produced exactly. This includes all the values in R, including the unit entries along the principal diagonal, each of which represents 100% of the variance of the test in the row or column of R. Exact reproduction of the unit entries will require as many components as there are tests. In a true factor analysis, an initial estimate of the communality of each test is made and that value is substituted for the initial unit value in the cell of the principal diagonal. The amended R-matrix (known as the **reduced R-matrix**) is sometimes denoted by R*. A factor analysis attempts to reproduce this reduced R-matrix, rather than the original R-matrix, which has ones along the principal diagonal. We can see the results of a true factor analysis in the last six columns on the right of Output 5, each of which contains only two entries.

Earlier, we saw that the **eigenvalue** of a factor is a measure of the total test variance that is accounted for by that factor alone. The eigenvalue is an aggregate of the proportions of the variances of the individual tests that are accounted for by the factor and is the sum of the squares of the loadings of the tests on the factor. Since each loading is the correlation between a test and the factor, the square of the loading gives the proportion of test variance that is accounted for by regression of the test scores upon the factor scores. The squared loading is the **coefficient of determination**. Since the maximum value of each component of the eigenvalue is 1, the theoretical total value of an eigenvalue is the number of tests in the battery. If, therefore, we divide the eigenvalue by the number of tests and multiply by 100, we shall have the percentage of the total test variance that is accounted for by each factor.

In Output 5, the first block of three columns, labelled **Initial Eigenvalues**, contains the eigenvalues and the contributions they make to the total variance. The eigenvalues determine which factors (components) remain in the analysis: following Kaiser's criterion, factors with an eigenvalue of less than 1 (i.e. factors 3-6) are excluded. From the eigenvalues, the proportions of the total test variance accounted for by the factors are readily obtained. For example, the eigenvalue of the first factor is 2.81. Since the total test variance that could possibly be accounted for by a factor is 6 (the total number of tests), the proportion of the total test variance accounted for by the first factor is 2.81 ÷ 6 = 46.82%, the figure given in the **% of Variance** column. In this analysis, the two factors that meet the Kaiser criterion account for over 84% of the variance (see the column labelled **Cumulative %**).

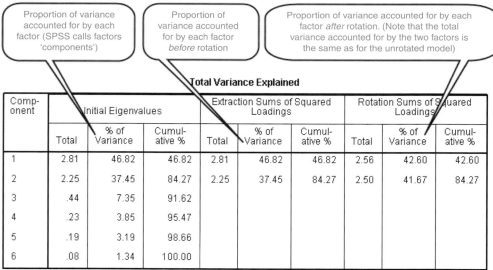

Comp-onent	Initial Eigenvalues			Extraction Sums of Squared Loadings			Rotation Sums of Squared Loadings		
	Total	% of Variance	Cumul-ative %	Total	% of Variance	Cumul-ative %	Total	% of Variance	Cumul-ative %
1	2.81	46.82	46.82	2.81	46.82	46.82	2.56	42.60	42.60
2	2.25	37.45	84.27	2.25	37.45	84.27	2.50	41.67	84.27
3	.44	7.35	91.62						
4	.23	3.85	95.47						
5	.19	3.19	98.66						
6	.08	1.34	100.00						

Extraction Method: Principal Component Analysis.

Output 5. Edited table of statistics relating to the two components extracted

The second block of three columns (**Extraction Sums of Squared Loadings**) repeats the output of the first block, but only for the two factors that have met Kaiser's criterion.

The third block (**Rotation Sums of Squared Loadings**) tabulates the output for the rotated factor solution. Notice that the proportions of variance explained by the two factors are more similar in the rotated solution than they are in the unrotated solution, in which the first factor accounts for a much greater percentage of the variance. Notice also that the accumulated proportion of variance from the two components/factors is the same for the unrotated and rotated solutions.

15.2.3.5 Scree plot

Output 6 (edited) shows the **scree plot**, which was specially requested in the **Factor Analysis: Extraction** dialog box. The eigenvalues are plotted against the ordinal numbers of the factors extracted. The amount of variance accounted for (the eigenvalue) by successive components initially plunges sharply as successive factors (components) are extracted.

The point of interest is where the curve begins to flatten out. It can be seen that the 'scree' begins to appear between the second and third factors. Notice also that Component 3 has an eigenvalue of less than 1, so only the first two components have been retained.

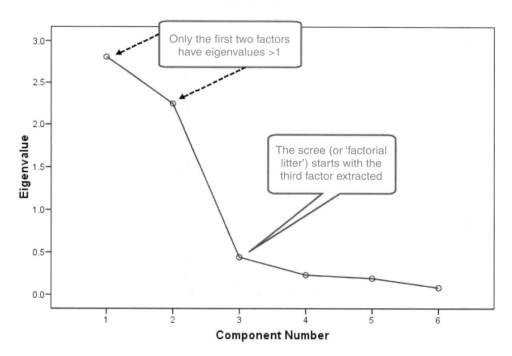

Scree Plot

Output 6 (annotated). The scree plot

15.2.3.6 The component matrix (unrotated factor matrix)

Output 7 shows the component (factor) matrix containing the loadings of the six tests on the two factors extracted.

Component Matrix[a]

	Component	
	1	2
French	.764	-.551
German	.661	-.659
Latin	.714	-.523
Music	.566	.729
Maths	.647	.618
Mapwork	.735	.568

Extraction Method: Principal Component Analysis.

a. 2 components extracted.

Output 7. The component matrix (correlations between the variables and the unrotated components)

Since the components or factors can be thought of as graphical axes, each test can be plotted as a point on the graph with its loadings on the factors as coordinates. When this is done, the graph appears as in Output 8.

Component Plot

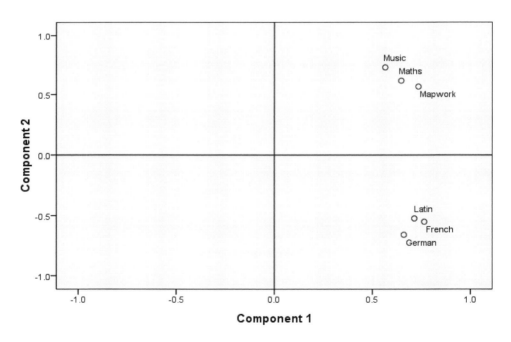

Output 8. Plot of the unrotated factor matrix, in which each of the six tests in the battery appears as a point in space with its loadings on the axes (factors) as coordinates

(The plot of the unrotated factor matrix shown in Output 8 will not appear in the output if a rotation has been requested. This graph can be obtained in a second run of the factor analysis procedure by clicking the **Rotation** button in the **Factor Analysis** dialog box and, in the **Factor Analysis: Rotation** dialog box, changing the choice of rotation from **Varimax** to **None** and checking the square labelled **Loading plots**.)

It can be seen that, in agreement with the impression given by the correlation matrix, the factor analysis has extracted two factors. On the other hand, it is not easy to interpret the unrotated factor matrix; nor does the graph in Output 8 really help. Both groups of tests show substantial loadings on both factors, which is not in accord with the obvious psychological interpretation of the pattern of correlations in the original R-matrix, which seemed to arise from two independent abilities, each required for one of the two clusters of tests with high correlations.

Another awkward feature of the unrotated factor matrix is that, whereas the mathematical group of tests loads positively on both factors, the verbal group is negatively loaded on the second factor. In other words, the higher one's score on the language subjects, the lower one's score on the first factor/component, whatever that factor may be. A factor such as factor 1, upon which one group of tests loads negatively and the other loads positively, is known as a **bipolar factor**. Bipolar factors are very difficult to interpret without collateral evidence or a sound theoretical rationale.

15.2.3.7 Reproduced correlation matrix and residuals

Reproduced Correlations

		French	German	Latin	Music	Maths	Mapwork
Reproduced Correlation	French	.888[a]	.868	.834	.031	.154	.249
	German	.868	.870[a]	.816	-.107	.020	.111
	Latin	.834	.816	.783[a]	.022	.139	.228
	Music	.031	-.107	.022	.852[a]	.817	.830
	Maths	.154	.020	.139	.817	.801[a]	.826
	Mapwork	.249	.111	.228	.83?	.826	.862[a]
Residual[b]	French		-.032	-.092	.00?	-.071	.063
	German	-.032		-.101			.007
	Latin	-.092	-.101				-.096
	Music	.002	.025	-.001			-.046
	Maths	-.071	-.012	.083			-.091
	Mapwork	.063	.007	-.096			

The diagonal entries are the communalities

The residual correlations are small

The reproduced correlations are close to the values in the R-matrix

Extraction Method: Principal Component Analysis.

a. Reproduced communalities

b. Residuals are computed between observed and reproduced correlations. There are 8 (53.0%) nonredundant residuals with absolute values greater than 0.05.

Output 9 The reproduced correlation matrix and residuals

Output 9 shows the **reproduced correlation matrix** of coefficients, computed from the extracted factors (components), together with the **residuals**, which are the differences between the values in the R-matrix and the corresponding values in the reproduced matrix. The residuals are small, indicating that the two factors extracted give a good account of the correlations in the R-matrix.

Each reproduced correlation between two tests is the sum of the products of their loadings on the factors emerging from the analysis. For example, the sum of the products of the loadings of French and German on the two factors extracted is, from the loadings in the unrotated F-matrix in Output 7, $[(.764 \times .661) + (-.551 \times - .659)] = .868$, which is the value given for the reproduced correlation between French and German in Output 9. The diagonal values labelled **a** are the communalities listed in Output 4. Each communality is the sum of the squares of the loadings of a test on the two factors extracted: so the sum of the squares of the entries in the first row of Output 7 is .888, the value given as the communality for French in Output 9. Notice that all the communalities are very large – at least 78%.

The **residuals** are the differences between the actual and reproduced correlations. For example, the actual correlation between French and German is .836 (Output 2) and the reproduced correlation is .868, so the difference is –.032, which is the residual shown in the lower half of Output 9. Footnote *b* gives the number and proportion of residuals (i.e. the differences) that are greater than .05. There are eight such residuals (53%); but none is greater than .10.

15.2.3.8   The rotated factor (component) matrix

Output 10 shows the rotated factor (component) matrix, which should be compared with the unrotated matrix in Output 7.

Rotated Component Matrix [a]

	Component	
	1	2
French	.936	.105
German	.932	-.045
Latin	.880	.092
Music	-.070	.920
Maths	.065	.892
Mapwork	.163	.914

Extraction Method: Principal Component Analysis.
Rotation Method: Varimax with Kaiser Normalization.
   [a.] Rotation converged in 3 iterations.

Output 10. The rotated component matrix

Output 11 is a graph of the rotated F-matrix, in which each of the six tests is plotted as a point in space with its new loadings on the rotated axes as coordinates.

Component Plot in Rotated Space

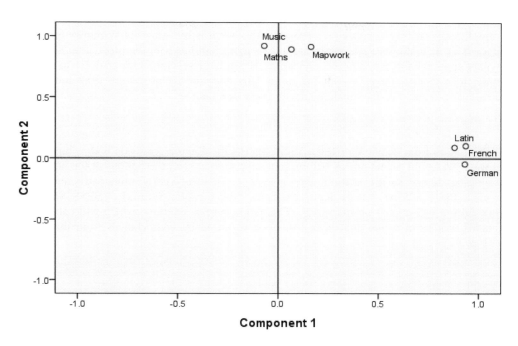

Output 11. Graph of the rotated R-matrix

The purpose of rotation is not to change the number of components extracted, but to try to arrive at a new position for the axes (components) that is easier to interpret in substantive terms. In the previous Section, we showed that the sum of the products of the loadings of any two tests on the factors extracted gives the 'reproduced' value of the correlation between the two tests in R. You will find that you will arrive at exactly the same value for the reproduced correlation if you take the sum of the products of the loadings of the tests on the rotated factors given in Output 10. This will be so whatever the position of the axes.

It can be seen from the graph in Output 11 that the rotated component/factor matrix is much easier to interpret than the unrotated matrix in Output 7. The three language tests now have high loadings on one factor only (Component 1); whereas Mapwork, Mathematics and Music have high loadings on the other factor only (Component 2). Since the rotation was orthogonal, that is, the axes were kept at right angles, the two factors are uncorrelated. This is quite consistent with what we concluded from our inspection of the original R-matrix, namely, that the correlations among the six tests in our battery could be accounted for in terms of two independent psychological dimensions of ability and that each group of tests measured a separate dimension of ability.

Tests with high loadings on one factor only are said to be **indicators** of the factor concerned. Clearly, Output 11 shows that Music, Maths and Mapwork are indicators of Factor 1; whereas Latin, French and German are indicators of Factor 2.

15.3   USING SPSS SYNTAX TO RUN AN EXPLORATORY FACTOR ANALYSIS

Initially, the easiest way to run a factor analysis on SPSS is by using the Windows graphical interface with its dialog boxes. When the user is more familiar with the procedure, however, the syntax approach has much to recommend it. If you have several factor analyses to run, for example, it is much quicker to edit the syntax file and run the procedure from the syntax window, rather than complete the dialogs with every new data set.

15.3.1 Running a factor analysis with syntax

With the scores from Table 1 in **Data View**, access the **Factor Analysis** dialog box in the usual way. Make the selections as before, remembering to select the buttons at the bottom of the dialog box to specify the rotation, order a scree test, request a correlation matrix and so on. Now click **Paste**. When this is done, a window with the title **Syntax1 – SPSS Statistics Syntax Editor** will appear on the screen. This is the **syntax window**, which will contain the commands written in syntax that have just been specified by your choices from the dialog boxes (see Figure 7).

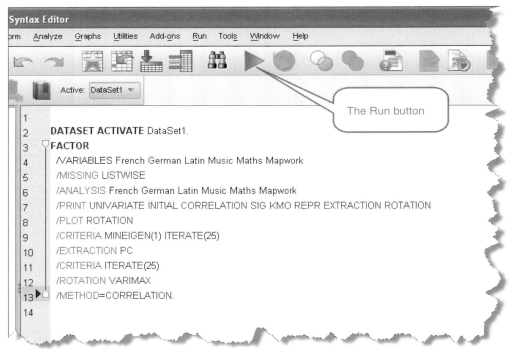

Figure 7. The syntax window after clicking **Paste** in the completed **Factor** dialog box

To run the factor analyis, you can select the entire command (by left-clicking and dragging the cursor from its initial position at the beginning of the top line) and clicking the run button in the toolbar above the window (see Figure 8).

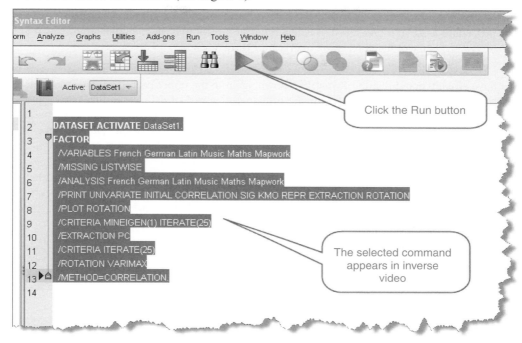

Figure 8. One way of running the factor analysis from the Syntax Editor

You can also run the procedure by choosing **Run➜All** from the drop-down menu at the top of the syntax window.

It is easy to see that with another data set, consisting of scores on a different battery of tests, it would be easy to edit the **FACTOR** command by changing the variable names and other specifications to match the active data set in **Data View**. Inevitably, the experienced user of syntax will have built up a library of written commands, because it is quicker to carry out the analysis by editing the display in the **SPSS Statistics Syntax Editor** than to complete all the dialog and subdialog boxes again.

15.3.2 Using a correlation matrix as input for factor analysis

The Windows graphical interface with its dialog boxes is a comparatively recent development. SPSS (like several other major statistical packages) was originally designed to be run with syntax exclusively. The translation of all the SPSS procedures to dialog boxes is as yet incomplete: there are some procedures that cannot yet be accessed through the graphical interface. We have seen, for example, that in order to test for simple effects following the ANOVA, the user must run a syntax command: simple effects are not an option in the dialogs.

So far, we have concentrated on running the factor analysis procedure from the raw data, that is, participants' scores on the various tests. There are occasions when we might wish to run a factor analysis with the R-matrix, not the raw data, as our starting-point. It is not possible to do this using the SPSS graphical interface, but it can easily be done using syntax.

15.3.2.1 Running a factor analysis from a correlation matrix

The procedure has two stages, each of which requires a separate syntax command:
1. the entry of the correlation matrix into **Data View**;
2. the running of the factor analysis.

We have already noted that the R-matrix (shown again in the upper part of Figure 9) is square and symmetric: the correlations below the principal diagonal of cells extending from top left to bottom right are duplicates of the values above the principal diagonal. In such cases, a lower triangular matrix (Figure 9, lower part), which contains only the values along the principal diagonal and below, contains all the correlations in the full square matrix.

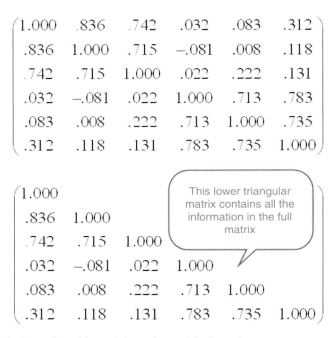

Figure 9. R-matrix (upper) and lower triangular matrix (lower)

When we come to enter the correlations in the R-matrix into the SPSS syntax editor, we shall enter the matrix in lower diagonal form. There are other modes of entry, but they require more complicated syntax.

15.3.2.2 Preparation of the correlation matrix

- Choose **File→New→Syntax** to open the **SPSS Statistics Syntax Editor** window.
- Type in the words MATRIX DATA, as shown in Figure 10.
- On the same row, type VARIABLES=ROWTYPE_ exactly as we have it here. (The lower case can be used.) There must be no spaces at all between the two words, only the hyphen. Create the final underline by pressing and holding down the shift key and pressing the hyphen key.

- Click on the **Variables** icon and paste the names of the six tests into the row, finishing with a full stop.

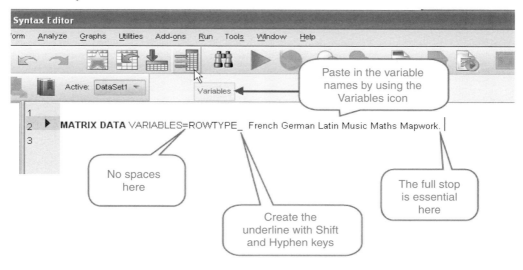

Figure 10. The MATRIX DATA command

This first command, MATRIX DATA, prepares SPSS to receive a matrix with dimensions equal to the number of variables in the list. As with all commands, there is a full stop at the end.

In the expression VARIABLES=ROWTYPE_ , ROWTYPE_ is a special string variable which prepares the syntax editor for rows of data, each row beginning with another keyword indicating the type of data in that row. If the first word is CORR, the row contains correlations; if the first word is N, the data in the row will be the sample sizes of each of the variables listed in the MATRIX DATA command. Had means and standard deviations been available (which we shall suppose is not the case in this example), they could be given in rows beginning with MEAN and STDEV, respectively.

The next step is to write the BEGIN DATA command and enter the correlation matrix in lower triangular form, beginning each line of values with the keyword CORR. The lower triangular form of the R-matrix is not obligatory; but other forms, such as the upper triangular, would require a special format command. Note that BEGIN DATA is a command in itself and ends with a full stop.

The complete syntax for entering the R-matrix into the SPSS Data Editor is shown in Figure 11. We have entered the sample sizes underneath the correlations; but they could also have been entered above the correlations, just underneath the BEGIN DATA command. We should note that the information about samples sizes is not required for the basic factor analysis; however, it is needed for some of the additional statistics.

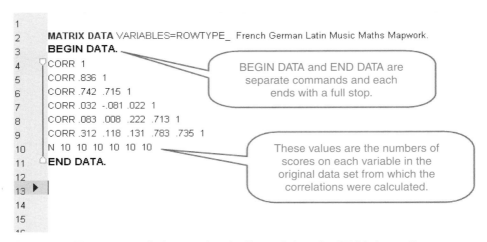

Figure 11. The commands for entering the R-matrix into the SPSS data editor

To execute the MATRIX DATA command, proceed as follows:

- Click **Run** in the toolbar above the syntax window and select **All**.
- The matrix will appear in **Data View** (Figure 12), not in the **SPSS Statistics Viewer**.
- If there are any errors in the syntax, they will be flagged in the SPSS Statistics Viewer.

ROWTYPE_	VARNAME_	French	German	Latin	Music	Maths	Mapwork
N		10.000	10.000	10.000	10.000	10.000	10.000
CORR	French	1.000	.836	.742	.032	.083	.312
CORR	German	.836	1.000	.715	-.081	.008	.118
CORR	Latin	.742	.715	1.000	.022	.222	.131
CORR	Music	.032	-.081	.022	1.000	.713	.783
CORR	Maths	.083	.008	.222	.713	1.000	.735
CORR	Mapwork	.312	.118	.131	.783	.735	1.000

Figure 12. The data set that appears in Data View after the **MATRIX DATA** command has been run

15.3.2.3   Syntax of the FACTOR command

Return to the syntax window and type the **FACTOR** command below the previous syntax, as shown in Figure 13.

- Notice that the identification of the matrix in the /**MATRIX =IN** subcommand is given as (**CORR=***). This informs SPSS that the input will be a correlation matrix (and not, say, a factor matrix), and that it is in the current data file (represented by *), which can be seen in the **Data View** window. The /**PRINT** options are those selected in the **Descriptives** dialog box and the /**PLOT** option is that selected in the **Extraction** dialog box. It is not necessary to enter /**ROTATION VARIMAX**, because that is the default rotation method. *Again note the full stop at the end of the command: it is absolutely essential.*

```
1  ▽ FACTOR
2    /MATRIX =IN (CORR=*)
3    /PRINT INITIAL EXTRACTION ROTATION CORRELATION REPR
4    /PLOT EIGEN
5  ▶◻ /ROTATION VARIMAX.
```

Figure 13. The **FACTOR** command for running a factor analysis from a correlation matrix in **Data View** with various options as chosen in Section 15.2.2

* Run the **FACTOR** command by clicking **Run** in the toolbar at the top of the syntax window and selecting **All**. The output for the factor analysis will be more or less identical with that previously described in Section 15.2.3, depending upon which statistics were specified in the /PRINT subcommand.

15.3.3   Progressing with SPSS syntax

As we said earlier, we believe that the best way of learning SPSS syntax is by pasting the minimal basic commands into the **syntax window** from the appropriate dialog boxes in the usual way, and observing how the syntax becomes more elaborate when extra options are chosen from the subdialog boxes.

You can obtain more information about a command by selecting it and clicking on the Syntax Help icon at the top of the syntax window (Figure 14).

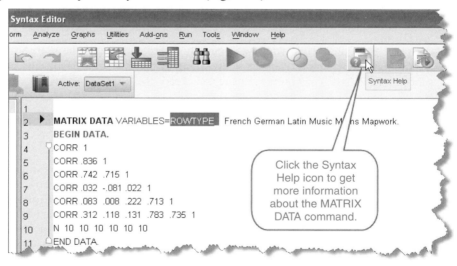

Figure 14. Getting help with syntax

Figure 15 shows **the Online Help** window.

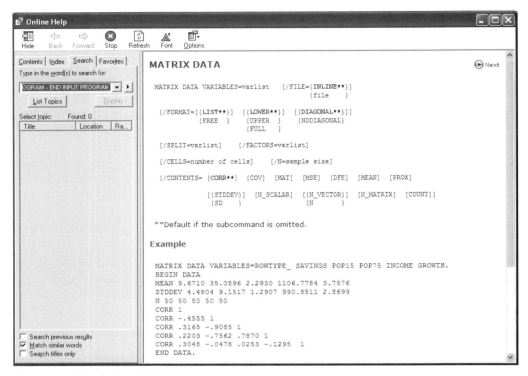

Figure 15. The **Online Help** window

The appearance of the Online Help window is initially rather daunting. The user, however, will find the examples very helpful. In the **syntax map** at the top, square brackets indicate optional subcommands and (within the square brackets) the curly brackets {} indicate alternatives.

15.4   CONFIRMATORY FACTOR ANALYSIS WITH AMOS

So far, we have concentrated on the use of factor analysis to determine the number of common factors that contribute substantially to the correlations in an R-matrix. Often, however, the researcher will have a strong theoretical or empirical basis for expecting that a particular factor structure will emerge from the analysis and will wish to test a specific factor analytic model against competing alternatives. The building and testing of different factor analytic models is known as **confirmatory factor analysis**. In this section, we shall briefly describe the use of the AMOS package to run a confirmatory factor analysis. The manner in which AMOS is accessed and the use of the palette of drawing tools to produce an input path diagram have already been described in detail in Section 12.6, so we can dispense with some of the details here.

Suppose that the researcher who produced the data we have been analysing has a sound theoretical and empirical basis for expecting that the R-matrix can best be explained in terms of a model with two independent or orthogonal factors, Verbal and Spatial, and that French, German and Latin are indicators of the Verbal factor and Music, Maths and Mapwork are indicators of the Spatial factor. Although the researcher is well aware of the preponderance of the general factor in most analyses of such data, the fact that all the children in the study belonged to a group with high academic ability points to a solution in terms of group factors rather than a general factor. The researcher is anxious to show that the two-factor model fits the data better than the competing one-factor model.

A confirmatory factor analysis takes place in stages similar to those in a path analysis:

- The **input path diagram** is constructed.
- A choice between **unstandardised or standardised estimates** is made.
- The **Analysis Properties**, that is, the items in the output, are specified.
- The **estimates are calculated**.
- The **output path diagram** is displayed.
- The **Text Output** is displayed.

15.4.1   Input path diagram for a confirmatory factor analysis

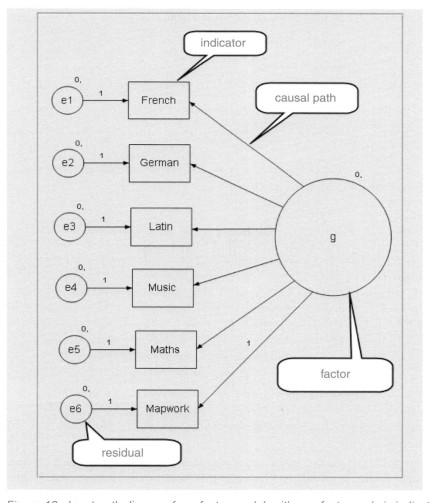

Figure 16. Input path diagram for a factor model with one factor and six indicators

In a path diagram of a factor analysis (such as Figure 16), factors, which are latent variables and, as such, not part of the data set, are represented as circles. The factors, since they supposedly underlie test performance, are represented as 'causing' some or all of the observed variables in the data set, the latter being **indicators** of the factors. The causal path from factor to indicator is represented by a unidirectional arrow in the input path diagram. Figure 16 shows the input path diagram for a factor model positing that a single general factor accounts adequately for the associations among all the tests in the battery.

You will notice that, in Figure 16, some of the pathways have been marked with a 1. We shall explain this when we come to consider the identification of factor analytic models. (We have already touched on the topic of model identification in Chapter 12 in the context of path analysis.)

Figure 17 shows the input path diagram for a two-factor model. While this is superficially similar to our researcher's two-factor model, there is an important difference: the two factors are allowed to correlate, rather being independent or orthogonal. Correlation between factors is indicated by a curved double-headed arrow, as shown in Figure 17.

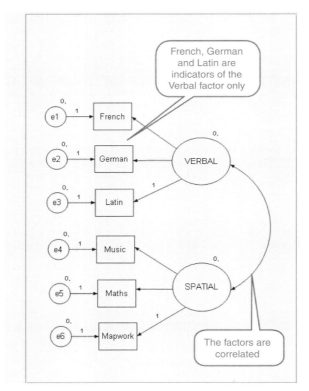

Figure 17. Input path diagram for a two-factor model with correlated factors and three indicators of each factor

Since our researcher holds that the two factors are independent or orthogonal, the path diagram for that model would be similar to Figure 17, except that there would be no curved double-headed arrow.

15.4.2 Drawing the input path diagram for the researcher's two-factor model

- Open SPSS and place the data on the children's school marks in the **Data Editor**. Access AMOS by choosing **Analyze➔AMOS**.
- Choose **File➔Data Files** and, in the **Data Files** dialog, click on the **Working File** button. This move will make the children's marks file active within AMOS.
- Use the **Draw observed variables** (the rectangle) and **Duplicate objects** (the copier) icons (Figure 18) to create a column of six identical smallish rectangles to represent the six observed variables in the data set. Make sure you leave sufficient room on the left of the rectangles for the residual variables and plenty of space on the right for the paths and the two factors. Since the factors are orthogonal, we shall not need additional space for a curved arrow at the extreme right of the diagram, as in Figure 17. Should you run out of space in the drawing area, you can always reposition objects by selecting them and repositioning them with the mover icon as described in Section 12.6.2.3 (Figure 31).

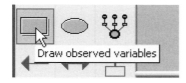 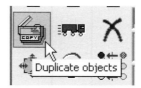

Figure 18. The **Draw observed variables** (rectangle) and **Duplicate objects** (copier) icons

Use the **Add a unique variable** icon (Figure 19) to add a residual variable to the rectangle representing each of the six observed variables. Recall from Section 12.6.2.3 that, from an initial orientation at twelve o'clock, each left mouse click rotates the arrow pointing from the residual circle clockwise through 45%. Click seven times to position the residual circle to the left of the rectangle representing the observed variable.

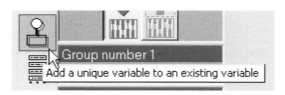

Figure 19. The **Add a unique variable to an existing variable** icon

When, having clicked the **Add a unique variable** icon and placed the cursor on a rectangle in the drawing space, a circle representing the error or residual variance will appear above the rectangle, as shown in Figure 20 (left side). We shall want the residual on the left of the rectangle. Clicking on the object again, however, will rotate the position of the error circle 45 degrees in a clockwise direction. The seventh click will place the residual circle to the left of the rectangle as required, as shown in Figure 20 (right side).

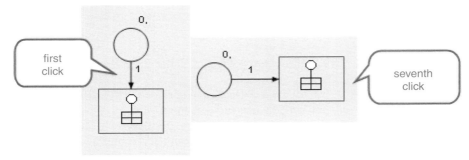

Figure 20. Repositioning the representation of the residual variable

Use the **Draw unobserved variables** (oval) (Figure 21) and **Duplicate objects** (copier) icons to draw, one above the other, two circles (one for each factor) to the right of the rectangles. The circles will represent the factors in the model.

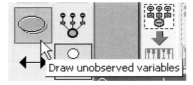

Figure 21. The **Draw unobserved variables** (oval) icon

Use the **Draw paths (single-headed arrow) key** (Figure 22) to draw six paths: three from each factor to its three indicator variables.

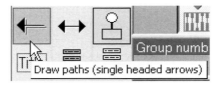

Figure 22. The **Draw paths** (single-headed arrow) icon

Right-click on each of the fourteen shapes and Choose **Object Properties** to assign labels to the variables, as shown in Figure 23. In the **Object Properties** dialog, you must assign both a variable name and a variable label thus:

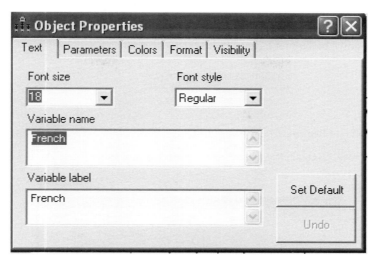

Figure 23. Naming the variables with the **Object Properties** dialog box

When completing the **Object Properties** dialog, it is helpful to choose **View➔Variables in dataset** to open the **Variables in Dataset** window, which will display both the variable names and the variable labels. (You will probably need to click-and-drag the right border of the window to view the complete variable labels.) The program will not run until both the variable name and the variable label have been entered into the appropriate slots of the **Object Properties** dialog.

Complete the path diagram by choosing **Object Properties➔Parameters** (Figure 24) and then touching each of the paths in turn from the rectangles to the circles on the right (the arrow will turn red when it has been properly selected) and assigning a regression weight of 1 in the Object Properties dialog box. Each arrow should then have a little 1 above it. This operation is known as **constraining parameters** and is essential for the factor analysis to run.

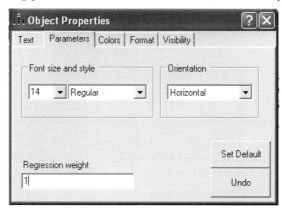

Figure 24. Constraining the regression weight with the **Object Properties** dialog

15.4.3   Running the analysis

From the drop-down menu in the central pillar, choose standardized estimates (Figure 25).

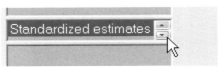

Figure 25. Choosing **Standardized Estimates**

- Choose **View→Analysis Properties→Output** and tick some (or all) of the boxes (Figure 26).

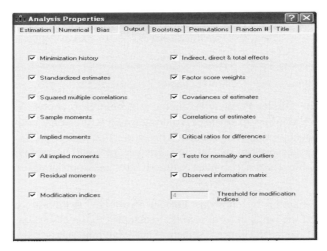

Figure 26. Completing the **Analysis Properties** dialog

- Click the **Calculate estimates** icon (Figure 27).

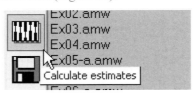

Figure 27. Calculating the estimates by clicking the **Calculate estimates** button

In our researcher's model, the factors are uncorrelated. If the factors are not joined by a double-headed curved arrow in the input path diagram, you will receive a prompt warning that, in the analysis, the factors will be uncorrelated or orthogonal (Figure 28). Click the **Proceed with the analysis** button.

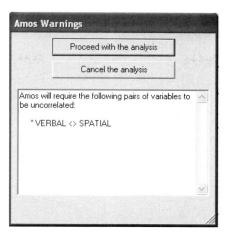

Figure 28. Warning that the factors will be independent or orthogonal

15.4.5   Result of the chi-square goodness-of-fit test and the output path diagram

On the grey central pillar, the results of the chi-square goodness-of-fit test for the two-factor model will appear (Figure 29):

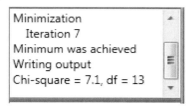

Figure 29. Results of the chi-square goodness-of-fit test of the two-factor model

Note that, in Figure 29, the degrees of freedom of the chi-squared estimate is given as 13. The chi-square value of 7.1 on 13 degrees of freedom has a p-value of .897 (i.e. not significant), which indicates that the model is a very good fit for the data.

To view the output path diagram, click the **Output Path** viewer icon at the top of the central pillar (Figure 30).

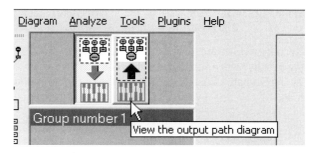

Figure 30. The output path viewer

The output path diagram now appears, as shown in Figure 31.

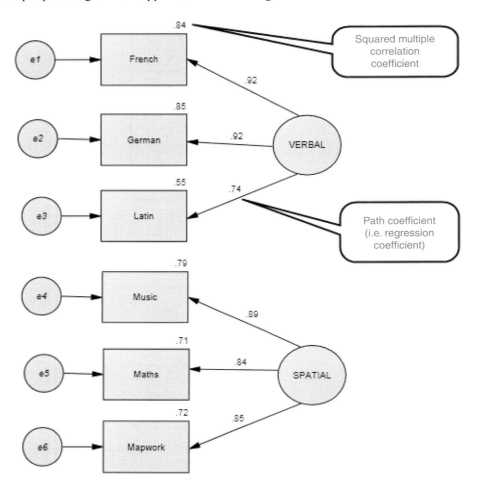

Figure 31. Output path diagram for a two-factor model with orthogonal factors and three indicators of each factor.

Notice that in Figure 31, there is no double-headed, curved arrow linking the two factors, as in Figure 17. In the model we have been testing, the factors have been made orthogonal or uncorrelated.

We shall consider the output in more detail in the next section. First, however, we shall compare the foregoing results with output path diagram and the value of chi-square for the one-factor model. The output path diagram for the one-factor model is shown in Figure 32.

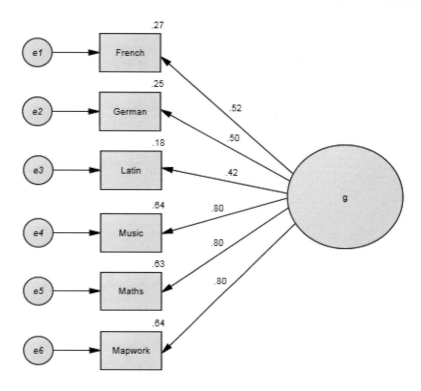

Figure 32. Output path diagram for a one-factor model

It can be seen from Figure 32 that, while the squared multiple correlations are high for Music, Maths and Mapwork, they are low for French, German and Latin. The one-factor model would appear to be a bad fit for those tests. This impression of poorness-of-fit is confirmed by the value of chi-square: 29.0 (on 14 degrees of freedom), which is much larger than the value of chi-square for the two-factor model: 7.1. The larger the value of chi-square, the poorer the fit of the model to the data.

15.4.5 Text output from a confirmatory factor analysis

We can obtain a detailed output by clicking on the **View Text** icon (Figure 33).

Figure 33. The **View Text** icon

The output is extensive and we shall not consider it in detail here. (For a fuller treatment, see the Recommended reading section at the end of the chapter.) The **navigation tree** is shown in Figure 34.

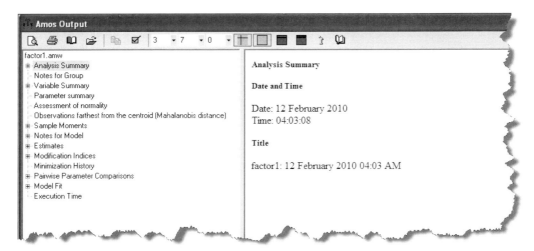

Figure 34. The navigation tree for the output of a factor analysis

The item **Notes for Model** (Figure 35) contains information about the number of data points and the degrees of freedom of the path model. It also gives the value (and the p-value) of the chi-square statistic. As in Chapter 12, we note that the value for chi-square given in the Notes is the value of the log-likelihood chi-square, not the Pearson chi-square, the value of which appears in the grey central pillar once the analysis has been run.

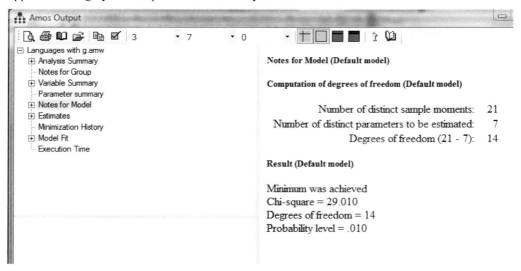

Figure 35. Notes on the statistics of the two-factor model, including the degrees of freedom of the chi-square statistic

We can compare models for goodness-of-fit by examining the statistics of their residuals, bearing in mind that different models may involve the estimation of different numbers of parameters, making the values of chi-square impossible to compare directly. (In such cases, we should need to compare the p-values and the values of other goodness-of-fit statistics.) We want to compare our researcher's two-factor model with a one-factor model of the same data.

As it happens, with these two path models, the degrees of freedom of the residual chi-square statistic are the same, so a comparison of the values of chi-square is meaningful.

Recall that the general formula for the degrees of freedom of any statistic is given by:

$$df = \begin{bmatrix} \text{Number of} \\ \text{independent} \\ \text{observations} \end{bmatrix} - \begin{bmatrix} \text{Number of} \\ \text{parameters} \\ \text{in the model} \end{bmatrix} \quad \text{---} \ (1)$$

General formula for the degrees of freedom

From the model notes in Figure 35, we see that with this data set, there are 21 distinct sample moments, that is, the number of independent observations is 21. Since the number of parameters in the model is 12, the degrees of freedom of the residual chi-square measure of goodness-of-fit is 9. In the classification of model identification (see Section 12.6.2.9), this model is **over-identified** and the statistics of goodness-of-fit make sense. By similar reasoning, we find that the degrees of freedom of the chi-square statistic for goodness-of-fit for the one-factor model is also 9, so the two chi-square values are directly comparable.

The values of the **CMIN** statistic (the log likelihood chi-square) are shown in Figure 36. The independence model is most unlikely to be adequate for any real set of data; however, it serves as a useful comparison for the value of CMIN for the model being tested (the Default model), which is relatively small.

Model	NPAR	CMIN	DF	P	CMIN/DF
Default model	7	29.010	14	.010	2.072
Saturated model	21	.000	0		
Independence model	6	41.529	15	.000	2.769

Figure 36. Statistics based on the log-likelihood chi-square

Figure 37 shows the values of the comparative statistics of goodness-of-fit, which are displayed in the table headed **Baseline Comparisons**. As we said in Chapter 12, the statistics in this table were designed to be (in comparison with both the Pearson and log-likelihood chi-square statistics) relatively independent of sample size. The values of these statistics should be fairly close to 1, indicating that most of the residual variance (that is, the residual variance left by the total independence model) has been accounted for by the model being tested.

Model	NFI Delta1	RFI rho1	IFI Delta2	TLI rho2	CFI
Default model	.301	.252	.455	.394	.434
Saturated model	1.000		1.000		1.000
Independence model	.000	.000	.000	.000	.000

Figure 37. The comparative statistics of goodness-of-fit

The **Text** output contains many other items of interest, including a table of reproduced correlations which, since this model is a very good fit, are close in value to those in the original R-matrix. For a full discussion of the output, however, we must refer you to a more advanced book, such as Dugard, Todman & Staines (2010), who have a very readable chapter on factor analysis.

15.4.6   Structural equation modelling

A **structural equation model (SEM)** is a statistical model of the causal relationships among a set of variables which culminates, on the other hand, in a path diagram, which depicts the direction of causality and a parallel, equivalent set of regression equations with associated statistics. In this book, we have briefly described two applications of SEM, namely, path analysis and factor analysis.

Neither path analysis nor factor analysis, each a useful research tool in its own right, qualifies as a full SEM. A full SEM contains both observed and latent variables (i.e., factors) and has two aspects:
1.   a **measurement model**, which depicts the relationships between the factors and their indicators;
2.   a **latent variable model**, which depicts the causal relationships among the factors.

A confirmatory factor analysis culminates in a measurement model. Its purpose is to account for the correlations among a set of observed variables as efficiently as possible. A latent variable model specifies the regression structure of the latent variables in the full SEM model. We have not considered any latent variable models in this book. Model-building of any kind, however, including the development of a full SEM, is an essentially *comparative* exercise, in which the contending models are compared for goodness-of-fit to the observed data.

15.5   A FINAL WORD

In this chapter, we have described techniques designed to classify variables with reference to relatively few reference variables or factors, which are taken to represent underlying substantive (medical, social or psychological) characteristics. In exploratory factor analysis, the aim is to ascertain the minimum number of factors needed to generate reasonably close approximations to the correlations in the original R-matrix. Another important aspect of exploratory analysis is rotation, whereby the factors, viewed as mathematical axes with respect to which each variable can be plotted as a point in space, are rotated in order to achieve the 'simple structure' needed to interpret the factors.

In confirmatory factor analysis, the researcher tests the applicability of different factor models to the same set of data, with a view to confirming that one of the possible models gives the best account of the data, in the sense that its estimates fit the observed data better than do those of any of its rivals. We described the use of the AMOS package to run a confirmatory factor analysis and show that a two-factor model gives a better account of the data than does a one-factor model.

Confirmatory factor analysis is only one aspect of structural equation modelling (SEM), which also includes latent variable modelling, that is, a regression or path structuring of latent variables bringing out their causal relationships. Latent variable models are distinct from measurement models, which link factors to their indicators. The testing of a complete structural equation model, with both measurement and latent structure aspects, is beyond the scope of this book.

Recommended reading

If you are unfamiliar with factor analysis, we suggest you read the lucid texts by Kim and Mueller (1978a, 1978b), before proceeding to more difficult books, such as Tabachnick and Fidell (2007). (Tabachnick and Fidell also have a chapter on structural equation modelling.)

A strong feature of the books by Kim and Mueller is that they present factor analysis as an aspect of the analysis of covariance structures, which makes these texts an admirable preparation for books such as *Structural Equation Modeling with AMOS* (Byrne, 2001), which lucidly describes confirmatory factor analysis.

Dugard, Todman & Staines (2010) take a practical approach to SEM and factor analysis and have some interesting examples.

Byrne, B. M. (2001). *Structural equation modeling with AMOS: basic concepts, applications and programming.* Mahwah, NJ: Lawrence Erlbaum Associates.

Dugard, P., Todman, J., & Staines, H. (2010). *Approaching multivariate analysis: a practical introduction (2nd ed.)* London & New York: Routledge.

Kim, J., & Mueller, C. W. (1978a). *Factor analysis: statistical methods and practical issues.* Newbury Park, CA: Sage.

Kim, J., & Mueller, C. W. (1978b). *Introduction to factor analysis: what it is and how to do it.* Newbury Park, CA: Sage.

Tabachnick, B. G., & Fidell, L. S. (2007). *Using multivariate statistics (5th ed.).* Boston: Allyn & Bacon (Pearson International Edition).

Exercise

Exercise 24 *Factor analysis* is available in www.psypress.com/spss-made-simple and click on Exercises.

Glossary

Adjusted R squared   A measure of effect size in Regression and Analysis of Variance (ANOVA). The adjustment corrects for positive bias.

Alternative hypothesis (H_1)   In hypothesis-testing, the proposition that the null hypothesis is false.

Analysis of covariance (ANCOVA)   In the context of analysis of variance (ANOVA), an ancillary technique which corrects for the association between the dependent variable and one or more additional variables known as covariates.   A covariate is a potential nuisance variable, which may inflate the error term of the F-ratio and result in an incorrect decision about the null hypothesis.

Analysis of variance (ANOVA)   A set of univariate statistical techniques for comparing means from experiments with three or more treatment conditions or groups.   In the one-way ANOVA, the total variance is divided into treatment and error components, which are compared by means of an F ratio.

Behrens-Fisher problem   A problem with making an independent samples t test when the population variances are heterogeneous. Underlying the t test for independent samples is the assumption of homogeneity of variance.   If that assumption is true, the t statistic is distributed as t on $n_1 + n_2 - 2$ degrees of freedom.   With heterogeneity of variance, particularly when the sample sizes are unequal, the ordinary t statistic, in which there is a pooled estimate of the supposedly constant population variance, does not have this distribution.   In such cases, the sample variances are no longer pooled for the calculation of the test statistic.   The Behrens-Fisher T statistic is used instead and the df are adjusted downwards by means of the Welch-Satterthwaite formula or an equivalent.

Between groups   See Between subjects designs.

Between subjects designs   Comparative experimental designs yielding independent samples of data, in which each participant is tested under only one condition and there is no basis for pairing the scores from one group with those in another.   The term between groups is also used to describe this kind of design.   (cf. Repeated measures and Within subjects.)

Bivariate normality   Two variables are said to have a bivariate normal distribution if, given a value of one variable, the distribution of the other variable at that value is normal.   More technically, the conditional distributions must be normal.   The correct application of the Pearson correlation assumes bivariate normality, which is indicated by an elliptical (or, where there is dissociation or independence, circular) scatterplot.   (cf. Multivariate Normality.)

Bonferroni correction   A procedure, based on the Bonferroni inequality in probability theory, for controlling the familywise (or experimentwise) Type I error rate.   A more stringent criterion for significance can be set by dividing the ordinary (per comparison) significance level by the number of planned comparisons or (with unplanned or post hoc comparisons) by the number of pairwise comparisons possible from an array of means of specified size.   An equivalent procedure is to multiply the p-value by the same factor.

Canonical Correlation In discriminant analysis, the correlation between a discriminant function and the categorical dependent variable.

Centring In multiple regression, the computing algorithm may not produce a solution when the correlations among the independent variables or regressors are high. (The extreme case is multicollinearity.) The risk of failure is greater if interaction terms or powers are included in the regression model. The program is more likely to run if the raw scores on a variable are first transformed into deviations by subtracting the mean, an operation known as centring.

Chi-square distribution The sum of the squares of n independent squared standard normal variables has a chi-square distribution on n degrees of freedom. A chi-square variable has a continuous distribution. The familiar chi-square statistic used in the analysis of nominal data is only an approximation to a true chi-square variable, and the approximation becomes poor when expected cell frequencies are low. The (controversial) correction for continuity (Yates' correction) is an attempt to improve the approximation.

Coefficient alpha (Cronbach's alpha) A measure of the reliability of a psychological test, which is applicable to tests consisting of several items and yielding a final score which is an aggregate of scores on the component items. (See Spearman-Brown formula.)

Coefficient of determination (CD) In simple regression, the proportion of the variance of the target, criterion or dependent variable that is accounted for by regression upon another variable (the regressor or independent variable). Its value is given by the square of the Pearson correlation. In multiple regression, the coefficient of determination is the square of the multiple correlation coefficient.

Cohen's d A measure of effect size, defined as the difference between the two treatment means divided by the standard deviation.

Cohen's kappa A measure of agreement between raters who are assigning cases to the same set of mutually exclusive categories, as when following a diagnostic system.

Communality In factor analysis, the total proportion of the variance of scores on a variable that is accounted for by the common factors extracted in the analysis.

Comparison See Contrast.

Confidence interval An interval constructed around the value of a statistic such as the mean which would 'cover' or include the population value in a specified proportion of samples.

Confirmatory factor analysis A set of techniques designed to account for an R-matrix in terms of a model in which the number of factors and other aspects of the model are pre-specified. Confirmatory factor analysis is an aspect of structural equation modelling.

Contingency table A table classifying individuals with respect to two or more sets of categories (see Qualitative variables). The entries in the cells of a contingency table are the frequencies of individuals with various combinations of attributes. For example, if patients are classified with respect to tissue type and presence or absence of an antibody, the contingency table would show the numbers of patients with and without the antibody in each tissue category. A contingency table is the starting point for various statistical analyses. For example, with a two-way contingency table, an approximate chi-square test can be used to test for an association between the two attributes. Complex multi-attribute contingency tables can be analysed with loglinear analysis.

Continuous variable   A quantitative variable that can have an infinite number of values within a specified interval. Height and weight are examples. SPSS uses the term scale to denote variables at the continuous level of measurement.

Contrast   The comparison between two of an array of k treatment means (or combinations of means) can be written as a linear contrast, which is a weighted sum of the treatment means, such that the coefficients (weights) add up to zero. (See Orthogonal contrasts.)

Correction for continuity   When a discrete variable is used as an approximation to a continuous one or vice versa (as when using the normal distribution as an approximation to a binomial distribution or an approximate chi-square statistic with frequency data), the value 0.5 is first subtracted from the difference between the observed and expected values before the test statistic is calculated.

Correlation A measure of a supposed linear relationship between two continuous variables X and Y, the value of which can vary only within the range from -1 to $+1$, inclusive.

Correlation ratio See eta.

Correlational research A research strategy whereby variables are measured as they occur in the individuals studied. Correlational research contrasts with experimental research, in which the supposedly causal variable is manipulated by the experimenter, independently of the characteristics of the participants.

Covariance   A measure of a supposed linear association between two variables.   The covariance is the sum of the cross-products of the deviations of pairs of scores on the two variables from their respective means divided by the number of pairs of scores minus one. If the scores on both variables are standardised, the covariance is identical with the Pearson correlation.

Covariate[1]   In the context of the analysis of variance (ANOVA), a variable that may be correlated with the measure or dependent variable and therefore must be taken into consideration in the analysis.

Covariate[2] In some SPSS procedures, such as logistic regression and canonical correlation, a covariate is a continuous independent variable.

Cross-validation A procedure for attempting to generalise the results of a multiple regression. One approach is to divide the original data set into two sub-samples, fit a regression model to the first sub-sample and then assess the predictive value of the model when applied to the second sub-sample. Applying a regression model to a fresh sample will show a weakening of predictive power known as shrinkage. Shrinkage will be minimal with very large samples: Howell (2007, p506) reviews various recommendations, including the stipulation that in multiple regression we should have at least 40 or 50 more participants than there are predictors in the regression equation. The guiding principle is that, with multiple regression (as with many other techniques), the more data one has, the better.

Cumulative probability The probability of a value of a random variable or variate less than or equal to a specified value. Cumulative probabilities are given by distribution functions.

Degrees of freedom A term borrowed from physical science, in which the degrees of freedom of a system is the number of constraints needed to determine its state completely at any point. In statistics, the degrees of freedom *df* are given by the number of independent observations minus the number of parameters estimated.

Deleted residual In regression diagnostics, it is often important to determine the influence of one particular case upon the regression statistics. Two regressions are run: the first with the entire data set; the second with the case omitted. The difference in magnitude between the raw residual (with all the data present) and the deleted residual (with the case removed) is a measure of the influence of the target case upon the regression statistics.

Dependent (or outcome) variable In the context of a true experiment, the variable (such as performance) that is measured during the course of the investigation, as opposed to the variable that is manipulated by the experimenter (the independent variable or IV). The purpose of an experiment is to determine whether the IV has a causal effect upon the DV.

Discriminant analysis (DA) A multivariate statistical technique which is mathematically equivalent to the one-way multivariate analysis of variance (MANOVA). In DA, the objective is to predict group membership from two or more measured variables, which are therefore regarded as independent (rather than dependent variables, as in the MANOVA). Linear discriminant functions of the independent variables, which are constructed so that they maximise inter-group differences, are used to predict group membership.

Discriminant function See Discriminant analysis.

Distribution Any table, display or formula that pairs each of the values of a variable with a frequency or a probability. With continuous variables, the distribution function gives the cumulative probability of specific values; the density function gives the probability density of a particular value, that is, the derivative of the distribution function at that point. (Note that with a continuous variable, the probability of any particular value is zero.)

Distribution function See Distribution.

Dummy variables Variables consisting of the values 0 and 1. In several contexts, dummy variables are used to code group membership.

Eigenvalue or latent root In factor analysis, a measure of the variance accounted for by a factor extracted by the analysis. If the eigenvalue is divided by the total number of variables or tests in the R-matrix, the measure becomes the proportion of the total variance that is accounted for by the treatment factor.

Eta The correlation ratio, a measure of effect size in the analysis of variance (ANOVA). In the one-way ANOVA, eta is the correlation between the scores and their group means. Eta squared or R^2 is a measure of the proportion of the total variance that is accounted for by differences among the treatment means. In the one-way ANOVA, eta squared is the ratio of the between groups sum of squares to the total sum of squares. As an estimator, eta squared is positively biased. Statistics such as adjusted R squared and omega squared correct the bias.

Event An outcome of an experiment of chance.

Event space In an experiment of chance, the subset of the sample space containing those elementary outcomes that qualify as instances of a defined event.

Experiment   A research technique in which the independent variable (IV) is manipulated to ascertain its effects upon the dependent variable (DV). Such direct manipulation is the hallmark of a true comparative experiment, as opposed to a correlational study or a quasi-experiment.

Experimentwise Type I error rate   See Familywise Type I error rate.

Experiment of chance   In probability theory, a procedure with an uncertain outcome, such as tossing a coin or rolling a die. The entire set of possible elementary outcomes (an elementary outcome is one of the simplest possible ways in which the experiment can turn out) is termed the sample space. An event space is a subset of the sample space.

Exploratory factor analysis   A set of techniques designed to account for an R-matrix in terms of the minimum number of classificatory axes or dimensions, the latter being known as factors. (See Confirmatory factor analysis.)

F distribution   The distribution of the ratio of two chi-square variables, each of which has been divided by its degrees of freedom. An F distribution has two parameters, namely, df_1 and df_2, the degrees of freedom of the chi-square variables. The mean of the distribution is $df_1/(df_2 - 2)$, provided that $df_2 > 2$. It can be shown that the ratio of two independent estimates of the variance of a normal population is distributed as $F(df_1, df_2)$. The F test in analysis of variance (ANOVA) is an application of this result.

F ratio   See F distribution.

Factor[1]   In Analysis of Variance (ANOVA), a set of related categories, treatments or conditions. A factor is thus a qualitative or categorical independent variable.

Factor[2]   See Factor analysis.

Factor analysis (FA)   A set of techniques enabling the researcher to account for the correlations among a battery of tests in terms of a relatively small number of classificatory axes or factors, which are assumed to represent theoretical dimensions, latent variables or hypothetical constructs. Since a factor is also a function of the observed variables, individuals receive, in addition to scores on the tests in the battery, a factor score locating them on the dimension concerned. (See R-matrix.)

Factor score   An individual's aggregate score on a combination of the scores on the tests in a battery.

Factorial experiments   Experiments in which there are two or more independent variables or factors. If each level of one factor is found in combination with every level of another factor, the two factors are said to cross and the factors are independent or orthogonal. In nested or hierarchical factorial designs, on the other hand, the levels of some factors are distributed among the levels of other factors, so that not every combination of conditions can be found in the experimental design.

Familywise Type I error rate   This term, which we owe to Tukey, has largely replaced the older term experimentwise. Following the analysis of variance of data from an experiment with three or more conditions, the researcher will often wish to make planned or unplanned comparisons among the means for specified groups or conditions. If the null hypothesis is true, the probability of at least one comparison showing significance is known as the familywise Type I error rate. The familywise Type I error rate may be considerably higher than the significance level set for any one comparison (the Type I error rate per comparison) and increases with the size of the array of treatment means. With large sets of comparisons, the familywise error rate greatly exceeds the per comparison significance level, which is usually set at .05: for example, if we have a set of 5 treatment means and make all 10 possible pairwise comparisons, the probability that at least one comparison will show significance (the familywise error rate) is approximately $1 - .95^{10} = .40$. (This is an approximation, because the comparisons are not independent.) Conservative tests such as the Bonferroni and Tukey methods are designed to control the experimentwise Type I error rate.

The problem with basing the familywise Type I error rate on the entire experiment is that the criteria for the significance of comparisons can become extremely stringent. There may be grounds for defining the reference set of means as those making up only part of the experiment and thus working with a smaller 'family' of comparison. Such a redefinition of the comparison 'family' must first be justified by, for example, demonstrating the presence of simple effects.

Greenhouse-Geisser correction In within subjects or repeated measures experiments, the data may not have the property of sphericity, or homogeneity of covariance. If so, the ordinary F test may be positively biased, that is, it may give too many significant results when the null hypothesis is true. The correction adjusts the numerator and denominator degrees of freedom of the F ratio downwards by multiplying them by a constant (epsilon), which takes its maximum value of 1 when there is homogeneity of covariance. Another corrective procedure is the Huynh-Feldt method, which is less conservative than the Greenhouse-Geisser correction. SPSS offers a choice of several different corrections.

Grouping variable In SPSS, a qualitative variable consisting of a set of arbitrary code numbers indicating group membership. In Variable View, the numbers, or values, should always be assigned meaningful value labels.

Homogeneity of covariance (sphericity) A property of the variance-covariance matrix, which is calculated from the data obtained from an experiment with a repeated measures factor.

Hypothesis A supposition about the state of nature. In statistics, a hypothesis is a statement about a population, such as the value of a parameter or the nature of the distribution. (See Null hypothesis; Alternative hypothesis; Hypothesis testing.)

Hypothesis testing A statistical procedure for testing the null hypothesis (H_0) against the alternative hypothesis (H_1). On the basis of the null hypothesis, the range of possible values of the test statistic (e.g., t, F, χ^2) is divided into an acceptance region and a critical region. The critical region contains values of the test statistic that are unlikely under H_0: that is, under H_0, there is a low probability α that the value of the test statistic will fall within the critical region. The value of α is known as the significance level and is conventionally set at .05, .01 (or sometimes .001), depending on the research area. Should the value of the test statistic fall within the critical region, the statistic is said to be significant beyond the pre-specified alpha-level. Such a significant result is regarded as evidence against the null hypothesis and therefore, by implication, as evidence for the alternative hypothesis. The location of the critical region depends upon the alternative hypothesis. In a t test, for example, if H_1 is the two-sided assertion that the population mean is not that specified by H_0 (i.e. μ_0), the critical region is located symmetrically in both tails of the distribution, that is, above the $(1 - \alpha/2)^{th}$ percentile and below the $\alpha/2^{th}$ percentile. If, on the other hand, H_1 states that the mean is greater than μ_0, that is, H_1 is a one-sided alternative, the critical region is located entirely in the upper tail of the t distribution, above the $(1 - \alpha)^{th}$ percentile. This is known as a one-tailed test.

Independent samples   Two samples are said to be independent if the values in each have been drawn at random from their respective populations and there is no basis for pairing the data they contain.

Independent variable   In a true experiment, a variable manipulated by the experimenter, to determine whether it has a causal effect upon the dependent variable. In correlational research, the term is used to denote a predictor variable or regressor, a variable that is being investigated as possibly having a causal effect upon a target, criterion or independent variable. In that context, the 'independent variable' is not manipulated by an experimenter, but is measured as a characteristic of the participant during the course of the investigation.   The investigator attempts to neutralise the influence of possible confounds by statistical, rather than experimental means.   Where natural groups are being compared, the researcher attempts to balance potential confounding variables across groups by following an appropriate sampling strategy.

Interaction   In analysis of variance (ANOVA), two factors are said to interact when the effects of one factor are not the same at all levels of the other. In other words, the simple main effects of one factor are not homogeneous across all levels of the other factor.

Interval data   Data yielded by the measurement on a scale whose units are equally spaced on the property concerned.   There has been much debate about whether data in the form of ratings (and other psychological measures) have the interval property.   Those who argue that ratings do not have the interval property tend to eschew the use of parametric tests and favour nonparametric or distribution-free tests.   Others, however, take the view that this issue is irrelevant to the choice of a statistical test.

Latent variable   A variable supposedly underlying associations among the variables in a multivariate data set.   In several multivariate methods, such as factor analysis and structural equation modelling (of which confirmatory factor analysis is an application), linear functions are constructed which serve as reference variables or axes with reference to which the observed variables can be classified. Such linear functions are taken to represent latent variables.

Level   In Analysis of Variance, one of the conditions or categories that make up an qualitative independent variable or factor[1].   Since, in the general case, a factor is a set of qualitatively different categories rather than a continuous independent variable, the term 'level' does not, in this special context, carry its usual comparative meaning.

Levene's test   Tests for homogeneity of variance, a requirement for the independent samples t test.   A significant result on Levene's test indicates that the homogeneity assumption is untenable, a contraindication against the use of the traditional t test, which uses a pooled estimate of the supposedly uniform population variance.

Leverage   The values of some statistics can be unduly influenced by atypical cases or outliers. In regression, for example, measures are available for measuring the influence or leverage that outliers exert upon the regression model yielded by the analysis. The further from the mean an outlier is, the greater the leverage it can exert.

Linear Of the nature of a straight line. The straight line function is the simplest in the family of linear equations. The analogues of the straight line when there are two or more IVs are, respectively, the plane (two IVs) and the hyperplane (three or more IVs). (See Regression.)

Loading In factor analysis, the loading of a test on a factor is the correlation between scores on the test and the scores of the participants on that particular factor (i.e., their factor scores). The loading is thus a measure of the extent to which performance on the test can be accounted for in terms of the factor concerned. The square of the loading is the proportion of the common factor variance of the test that is accounted for by that particular factor.

Logistic regression A method of regression applicable when the dependent variable is a set of categories. The independent variables may be either continuous or categorical.

Loglinear analysis A set of techniques for modelling the expected frequencies of observations in the cells of a multi-way contingency table. The expected raw cell frequencies can be estimated by multiplicative functions of the relevant marginal frequencies, in which the factors are estimates of main effects and interactions. Since, however, the logarithm of a product is the sum of the logarithms of its factors, the logarithm of the expected cell frequency can be modelled by a linear function of the various effect terms, which are estimated from the logarithms of the marginal frequencies.

Main effect In factorial analysis of variance (ANOVA), a factor is said to have a main effect if, in the population, the means on the dependent variable do not have the same value at all levels of the factor (ignoring the other factors in the design).

Mann-Whitney test The nonparametric equivalent of an independent samples t test. In the Mann-Whitney test, the null hypothesis is that the two populations have identical distributions. Wilcoxon's rank-sum test, another nonparametric test, is the exact equivalent of the Mann-Whitney test.

MANOVA See Multivariate analysis of variance.

Model An interpretation of data, usually in the form of an equation or a path diagram, in which an observed score is presented as the sum of systematic and error components. The use of any formal statistical test requires that the assumptions of a specific model are applicable to the data.

Multiple correlation coefficient R In regression, the Pearson correlation between the target or criterion variable and the estimates of its values from the regression equation. The value of R, however, unlike the Pearson correlation, cannot be negative, because the slope of the regression line, plane or hyperplane is always consistent with the orientation of the cloud of points in the scatterplot.

Multiple responses The compiler of a questionnaire may be interested in the mode of transport used by the respondents to get to their work. A single question in the form of a checklist inviting respondents to tick those modes of transport they use is likely to receive two, three or more responses, which would create problems for entry of the data into SPSS. Another approach, however, is to have a Yes/No question for each item in the list and record the response to each question as a separate dummy variable. SPSS has a Multiple Response procedure which computes and displays the frequencies with which different modes of transport are used by the respondents.

Multivariate analysis of variance (MANOVA) A generalisation of the analysis of variance (ANOVA) from the univariate to the multivariate situation, where there are two or more dependent variables.

Multivariate data A data set containing observations on three or more variables.

Multivariate normality A set of k variables is said to have a multivariate normal distribution if, given any set of values of $k - 1$ of them, the remaining variable is normally distributed. More technically, not only is the distribution of each variable considered separately (its marginal distribution) normal, but also the conditional distributions are normal. Techniques such as Multivariate analysis of variance (MANOVA) and Discriminant Analysis (DA) assume multivariate normality.

Multivariate statistics Statistical techniques for analysing data sets with two or more dependent variables. Examples are Multivariate analysis of variance (MANOVA), Factor analysis (FA) and Principal components analysis (PCA). (See Univariate statistics.)

Nagelkerke's R^2 In logistic regression, a statistic which mimics the coefficient of determination (R^2) in ordinary least squares (OLS) regression. Nagelkerke's statistic was designed to overcome the inability of another measure, Cox and Snell's R^2, to achieve its maximum value.

Nominal data Numerical data consisting of records of category membership. Nominal data result from observations of qualitative variables.

Non-parametric or distribution-free test A test, such as the Mann-Whitney test or the Friedman test, which does not make specific assumptions about the population distribution such as normality or homogeneity of variance. Such tests, however, do carry the assumption that the distributions are identical in all conditions or groups.

Normal (or Gaussian) distribution The famous 'bell curve', upon which much of classical statistical theory is based. A normal distribution has two parameters, the mean and the variance. Some naturally occurring variables, such as height and weight, have an approximately normal distribution. Since a linear function of two normal variables has itself a normal distribution, the mean of a sample of fixed size n drawn from a normal distribution is itself normally distributed, even if $n = 2$. Moreover, according to the Central Limit Theorem, the mean of a large sample of fixed size n from a non-normal distribution, provided n is sufficiently large, has an approximately normal distribution.

Null hypothesis In statistical hypothesis-testing, the null hypothesis (H_0) is the supposition of 'no effect': there is *no* difference between the means; there is *no* association between two variables; the sample we have selected has *not* been drawn from a population with a mean different from that of the standardisation sample, and so on. The null hypothesis, therefore, is usually the negation of the scientific hypothesis. The null hypothesis cannot be proved. This truth reflects the logical asymmetry of truth and falsification. In classical, Fisherian hypothesis-testing, should a statistical test fail to show significance, the null hypothesis is not regarded as 'proved', but is 'retained' or 'accepted'. In Neyman-Pearson hypothesis testing on the other hand, the emphasis shifts to the alternative hypothesis (H_1), the supposition that the null hypothesis is false. In that system, the null hypothesis can be confirmed.

Odds In an experiment of chance, the number of ways in which an event can occur, divided by the number or ways in which it can fail to occur. (cf. Probability)

Omega squared   A measure of effect size in analysis of variance (ANOVA) which corrects for the positive bias of eta squared.

One-tailed versus two-tailed tests   In hypothesis testing, a critical region of values for the test statistic is set up such that, under the null hypothesis, the probability of a value in the region is equal to a small value known as the significance level (usually .05). In a two-tailed test, the critical region is distributed equally between the tails of the sampling distribution of the test statistic. Some argue, however, that the location of the critical region should depend upon the scientific or alternative hypothesis. There are situations in which it makes sense to look for a difference in one direction only: e.g. since brain injury is unlikely to improve test performance, the critical region for a suspiciously low performance on a diagnostic test should, arguably, be located entirely in the lower tail of the t-distribution. Since the null and alternative hypotheses are complementary (i.e. they exhaust the possibilities), the null hypothesis is the asymmetrical proposition that the population mean is 'equal to or greater than', rather than 'equal to' a specified value. An unexpected result in the 'wrong' direction, therefore, cannot be declared to be significant.

Ordinal data   Data containing only information about order or sequencing. Examples of ordinal data are sets of ranks and lengths of sequences of dichotomous outcomes over a set of trials.

Ordinary least squares (OLS) regression   A set of techniques designed to predict value of a continuous target, criterion or dependent variable from values of one, two or more continuous predictors, regressors or independent variables. The regression line, plane or hyperplane is positioned (by assigning values to its parameters) so as to minimise the sum of the squares of the residuals $Y - Y'$, where Y and Y' are the target variable and the estimate from the regression equation, respectively. This is known as the least-squares criterion.

Orthogonal contrasts   Two contrasts are said to be orthogonal (independent) if the products of their corresponding coefficients sum to zero. In the one-way ANOVA of data from an experiment with k treatment groups, a set of $k - 1$ orthogonal contrasts can be constructed, each member of which accounts for a portion of the between groups sum of squares, so that the total of the sums of squares of the contrasts is the between groups sum of squares itself.

Orthogonal polynomial coefficients   A matrix of orthogonal contrast coefficients, each row of which contains different values of a polynomial of the same order, the order increasing with the 2nd and subsequent rows. Where the levels of a treatment factor vary along a quantitative dimension, the sum of squares of each polynomial contrast captures a particular component of trend (linear, quadratic, cubic) in the data.

Orthogonal rotation   In factor analysis, the classificatory axes (factors) can be rotated around the origin in relation to the test points in order to produce a pattern of loadings that is easier to interpret than the original pattern. If the axes are kept at right angles during rotation, the process is known as orthogonal rotation. Axes at right angles represent uncorrelated factors. In oblique rotation, however, the axes are not maintained at right angles: that is, the axes represent correlated factors.

Outcome variable   See Dependent variable.

p-value   In statistical testing, the probability, under the null hypothesis, of obtaining a value of the test statistic at least as unlikely as the value that has been calculated from the data. If the p-value is smaller than 0.05 or 0.01, the test has shown significance beyond the 0.05 or the 0.01

level, respectively. If the alternative hypothesis is one-sided, the p-value must refer to values of the test statistic in one tail only of the distribution: extreme values in the opposite direction must result in acceptance of H_0.

Part correlation   See Semipartial correlation.

Partial correlation   What remains of the correlation between two variables when their relationships with a third variable have been neutralised or 'partialled out'.   A partial correlation is a correlation between the residuals of two variables that have been regressed upon a third variable.

Path analysis   A development of multiple regression, the purpose of which is to utilise the associations among a set of variables to help to determine, with the assistance of a special graphical representation known as a path diagram, the most convincing causal model for the data.   In path analysis, regression coefficients are termed path coefficients.

Path coefficient See Path analysis.

Path diagram   A graphical representation of a causal model, which makes explicit the supposed causal relationships among variables.   An input path diagram depicts only the supposed causal pathways among the variables; whereas an output path diagram shows the path coefficients also.

Pearson correlation A measure of the strength of a supposed linear (straight line) association between two quantitative variables, each measured on a continuous scale with units, which is so constructed that it can take values only within the range from –1 to +1, inclusive.   (See Coefficient of determination.)   The supposition of linearity must always be checked by examining the scatterplot.

Percentile A score or value below which a specified proportion of the distribution lies: the 95th percentile is the score below which 95% of the distribution lies; the 5th percentile is the value below which 5% of the distribution lies.   The median (or middle score) is the 50th percentile.

Point-biserial correlation $r_{pt\text{-}bis}$ The Pearson correlation between a dichotomous qualitative variable (such as gender) and a continuous or scale variable.   The sign of the point-biserial correlation is of no importance, because it reflects only the ordinal relation between the arbitrary code numbers used to denote the two categories.   If the t test between the group means on the scale variable is significant, then so will be the point-biserial correlation, because the two statistics are related according to:

$$r_{pt-bis}^2 = \frac{t^2}{t^2 + df}$$

where $df = n_1 + n_2 - 2$.

Polynomial A sum of terms, each of which is a product of a constant and a power of the same variable thus

$$y = a_0 + a_1 x + a_2 x^2 + \ldots + a_n x^n$$

The highest power n is the degree or order of the polynomial.

Post hoc comparisons Unplanned comparisons of the sort one inevitably makes at the data-snooping stage of a statistical analysis, after the data have been gathered. Planned or *a priori* comparisons are decided upon before the data are gathered. Since the family of possible post hoc comparisons is usually considerably larger than a set of planned comparisons, the familywise error rate associated with post hoc comparisons may also be much higher than the nominal per comparison error rate. In either case, the per family error rate can be controlled by the Bonferroni correction, whereby the *p*-value for each comparison is multiplied by the number of comparisons in the family.

Power The probability, assuming that the null hypothesis is false, that when a statistical test is made, the null hypothesis will be rejected. The power P of a statistical test is related to the Type II error rate (β) according to the equation: $P = 1 - \beta$. Power is affected by several factors, including the significance or alpha-level, the minimum effect size that the researcher considers worth reporting, the number of participants in the experiment, the design of the experiment (especially whether it is between subjects or within subjects) and the reliability of measurement.

Principal components (PC) A set of techniques enabling the researcher to account for the correlations among a battery of tests in terms of classificatory dimensions or components. In contrast with factor analysis (FA), principal components is designed to account for 100% of the variance of each of the tests in the battery, rather than the variance it shares with the other tests.

Probability A measure of likelihood so constructed that it can have values only within the range from 0 (for an impossible event) to 1 (a certainty). Probabilities arise in the context of experiments of chance, in which an event is viewed as a subset of the entire set of possible elementary outcomes. The results of an experiment can be viewed as an experiment of chance: the researcher's observations are a sample from a reference set or population of possible observations. On that basis, we can assign probabilities to ranges of values within which the sample mean (or other statistic) might fall, assuming that the null hypothesis (or some other statistical hypothesis) is true.

Probability density function (frequency function) A continuous random variable X assigns an infinite number of possible values within any specified interval in its range. The probability of any particular value of X, therefore, is zero. A probability density function, however, assigns a probability density to values of X. A probability density can be regarded informally as the probability of a value in the neighbourhood of a specified value. More technically, a probability density is the rate of change (i.e., the derivative) of the cumulative probability at that point.

Qualitative variables Characteristics or properties, such as nationality, gender and blood group, which can be possessed only in kind (not in degree) and comprise sets of categories, rather than numerical values.

Quantitative variables Characteristics or properties, such as height, weight or intelligence, that are possessed in degree, so that one individual can have more or less of the property than another. A quantitative variable consists of a set of values. The term continuous variable is often used for variables of this kind.

Quasi-experiment A hybrid of a true comparative experiment and correlational research, in which sampling strategy is used in the attempt to create control groups for the purposes of comparison. In studies of the effects of smoking upon health and longevity, for example, sampling strategies are used in the attempt to equalise possible confounding variables such as education level and lifestyle. The quasi-experiment, however, has the same fundamental weakness as correlational research, namely, that the supposedly causal variable (e.g. smoking) is observed in the participants studied, rather than being manipulated by an experimenter, with the result that other characteristics of the participants are varying at the same time. As a consequence, however much the researcher attempts to make the samples comparable, it can never be claimed that all possible confounds have been controlled.

Random variable (or variate) In probability theory, a rule for assigning a numerical value to outcomes in the sample space: 'Let X be the number of spots on the upper face when a die is rolled'; 'When a coin is tossed, Let Y be 1 for a head and 0 for a tail'.

Regression The prediction of a dependent, target or criterion or variable from other variables known as independent variables or regressors. The prediction is made by constructing a regression equation, the subject of which is the estimate of the dependent variable from the independent variables.

Reliability The extent to which a measuring instrument produces consistent results, in the sense that participants achieve scores at similar percentile levels with different testers or from occasion to occasion of testing. The various approaches to the determination of reliability include test-retest, parallel (or equivalent) forms and split-half. (See Validity.)

Repeated measures (or within subjects) design Experimental designs in which observations are made on the same participants on two or more occasions. The repeated measures design is a special case of the randomised blocks design, a block being a set of observations that are linked in some way, as when fertilizer is applied to plants in the same flowerbed. Such experiments yield sets of observations that can be paired or matched across samples: these four observations are John's scores; those four are Mary's. Repeated measures designs yield correlated data, as do experiments with different groups of participants who are matched in some way. (Compare Between subjects design.)

R-matrix A square array, or matrix, displaying the correlations of each of the tests in a battery with every other test. An R-matrix can be the starting point for factor analysis, which is a set of techniques for accounting for the correlations among the tests in terms of relatively few underlying variables or factors.

Rotation In factor analysis, the factors can be regarded as classificatory axes with respect to which the tests in the battery can be plotted as points. When the axes are orthogonal (at right angles to one another), the co-ordinates of each test point are the correlations between the test and the factors emerging from the analysis. Such a correlation is known as the loading of a test on the factor concerned. Should the axes be rotated around the origin in relation to the test points, all the loadings will change. The sum of the products of the loadings of any two tests on all the axes, however, will remain constant and affords the same estimate of the observed correlation between the two tests. Rotation makes it easier to interpret the results of a factor analysis because, in relation to the original pattern of loadings, each test tends after rotation to have higher loadings on fewer factors. (See Orthogonal rotation.)

Sample space In an experiment of chance, the set of all elementary outcomes, each of which is assumed to be equally likely (thus introducing the element of circularity into the classical definition of probability).

Scale data A term in SPSS denoting data in the form of independent measurements on a scale with units. Examples are heights, weights, IQs, scores on questionnaires and ratings. Equivalent terms are continuous data and interval data.

Scatterplot A graphical display depicting a bivariate distribution, in which the axes represent the scales on the two variables and the individuals are represented as points with co-ordinates equal to their scores on the variables. An elliptical cloud of points indicates a linear association between the two variables: the narrower the ellipse, the stronger the association. A circular cloud of points indicates independence or dissociation. The Pearson correlation is a measure of a supposedly linear association between two variables and, wherever possible, the supposition of linearity should be checked by inspecting the scatterplot.

Semipartial correlation In multiple regression, what remains of the correlation between a dependent variable (DV) and one of a set of independent variables (IVs) when the variance shared by the IV with the other IVs has been partialled out of the predictor (but not the DV) by regression.

Shrinkage The tendency for the predictive power of a regression model to weaken with resampling.

Simple effects In factorial analysis of variance, the effect of one factor at one particular level of another. Simple effects analysis provides a way of analysing significant interactions. A two-way interaction can be explored by testing the simple main effects of one factor at different levels of the other. Heterogeneity of simple effects, as when they act in opposite directions, helps to explain a significant interaction. A significant three-way interaction can be further explored by testing the simple two-way interactions between two of the factors at specific levels of the third. In unplanned (post hoc) multiple pairwise comparisons, a significant simple effect is sometimes used as a justification for defining a smaller comparison family, rather than one based upon all the cell means involved in the interaction.

Simple main effect See Simple Effects.

Spearman-Brown formula A formula, equivalent to coefficient alpha, which expresses the reliability of a test in terms of mean of the correlations between every possible pair of items thus:

$$reliability = \frac{iM_r}{1+(i-1)M_r}$$

where i is the number of items in the test and M_r is the mean of the correlations between pairs of items. It is clear from the formula that even if the average inter-item correlation is low, the total score on a test with many items can achieve a very high level of reliability.

Standard deviation The positive square root of the variance, often written as s, where

$$s = +\sqrt{\frac{\sum (X-M)^2}{n-1}}$$

Unlike the variance, the standard deviation measures spread or dispersion in the original units of measurement. The square root operation, however, does not negate the distorting effects of extreme scores or outliers on the value of the standard deviation. Adding a constant k to each score leaves the standard deviation unaltered. If each score is multiplied by a constant k, the standard deviation is multiplied by k. (Compare Variance.)

Standard normal variable See z.

Structural equation modelling A structural equation model (SEM) is a statistical model of causal relationships among the variables in a set of multivariate data. Such a model takes the dual form of a set of regression equations and a pictorial representation showing the causal relationships among the variables. SEM can be used for confirmatory factor analysis (CFA), the culmination of which is a measurement model. A latent variable (LV) model specifies the regression structure among latent variables. A complete or full structural equation model comprises both a measurement model (CFA) and a latent variable model.

Sum of squares (SS) The sum of the squares of the deviations of scores X from their mean M. The sum of squares is the numerator of the variance estimate s^2.

t distribution In the one-sample case, the distribution of the statistic t, where

$$t = \frac{M - \mu}{s/\sqrt{n}}$$

and M is the mean of a sample of size n drawn from a normal population. The distribution of t has one parameter, the degrees of freedom df, the value of which is given by $df = n - 1$. A t distribution resembles the standard normal distribution in being bell-shaped and symmetrical, and in having a mean of zero. The t distribution, however, has thicker tails and its variance is $df/(df - 2)$. As n increases, the t distribution approximates the standard normal distribution ever more closely.

Test statistic In hypothesis testing, a statistic, such as t, F or chi-square, with a known sampling distribution, which can be used to test the null hypothesis. If the value of the test statistic is sufficiently improbable under the null hypothesis, the result is said to be statistically significant and the null hypothesis is rejected.

Trend analysis In analysis of variance (ANOVA), the independent variable, rather than merely being a set of related treatments, groups or experimental conditions, may be quantitative and continuous, as when different groups of patients ingest different measured quantities of a drug. If so, the question arises as to the nature of the functional relationship between the dependent variable and the independent variable. In trend analysis, the treatment sum of squares is divided into orthogonal (independent) components accounted for by linear, quadratic and more complex polynomial functions. Each component of trend can be tested for significance. (See Orthogonal polynomial coefficients.)

Type I error The rejection of the null hypothesis when it is actually true. The probability of a Type I error is the significance level α and is also known as the alpha-level, or the alpha-rate.

Type II error The acceptance of the null hypothesis when it is actually false. Its probability β is known as the beta-level or beta-rate. The beta-level is determined by several factors, including the sample size and the significance level. (See Power.)

Univariate statistics Analyses in which there is only one dependent variable. Examples are the t tests and analysis of variance (ANOVA). (Compare Multivariate statistics.)

Unrelated samples See Independent Samples.

Validity[1] In psychological testing (psychometrics), a test is said to be valid if it measures what it is supposed to measure. This beguilingly simple definition is open to many interpretations, which is why, in Reber's Dictionary of Psychology (1985), there are more than 25 definitions of validity. In personnel selection, the predictive or criterion validity is the Pearson correlation between scores on a psychological test and a target or criterion variable (job efficiency, academic grade). In order to be valid in this sense, a psychological test must also be reliable. Reliability, however, does not ensure validity. A vocabulary test may be highly reliable; but it may have low validity as a predictor of success on an IT course.

Validity[2] An experiment is said to have ecological validity when the dependent variable is a characteristic actually seen in everyday life. Is the result of a scenario study of bystander intervention generalisable to a real situation in which the protagonist is asked for (or should offer) help? This is a question of ecological validity.

Validity[3] An experiment is said to be internally valid if the independent variable has been shown unequivocally to have had a causal effect upon the dependent variable. The internal validity of an experiment is threatened by such influences as placebo effects, extraneous variables, demand characteristics and experimenter effects.

Validity[4] In psychometrics, a test is said to be have high internal validity if its component items correlate with the aggregate total score on the test.

Variable A property or characteristic consisting of a set of values or categories. (See Qualitative variables, Quantitative variables.)

Variance A measure of the extent to which scores are spread (or dispersed) around their mean. The variance estimate s^2 of a set of n scores is the sum of the squares of their deviations from the mean, divided by $n - 1$: that is, $s^2 = SS/(n - 1)$. The denominator of the variance estimate is also known as the degrees of freedom df, and the variance estimate can be expressed as SS/df. The variance is of great theoretical importance but, as a descriptive measure, its value is limited by the fact that it expresses the spread of a set of scores in squares of the original units of measurement. The positive square root of the variance estimate is known as the standard deviation s, which expresses spread in the original units of measurement. In the population, the variance is the mean squared deviation of scores from the population mean and the standard deviation is the root mean square. The df appears in the denominator of the sample variance to remove negative bias: that is, the expected value of the sample mean squared deviation is less than the value of the population variance. Adding a constant k to each score leaves the variance unaltered. Multiplying by k multiplies the variance by k^2.

Wald-Wolfowitz runs test There are situations, as when a participant makes a series of choices over a series of trials, in which the investigator is concerned with whether sequences of the same choice indicate a lack of randomness in the participant's strategy. The Wald-Wolfowitz tests for non-randomness.

Welch's F test A variation of the F test which is applicable when the assumption of homogeneity of variance has been violated.

Welch-Satterthwaite formula A formula used to adjust the degrees of freedom for a variant of the t statistic in which separate variance estimates are retained. See Behrens-Fisher problem.

Wilks' Lambda (Λ) In the univariate one-way ANOVA, variance estimates or mean squares (MS) are made by dividing the sums of squares SS by their degrees of freedom and using the F statistic to compare the between groups and within groups estimates $MS_{between}$ and MS_{within}. In multivariate analysis of variance (MANOVA), where there are several DVs, the analogue of the variance estimate is the determinant of a matrix of cross-products of deviations. There is a between groups cross-product matrix $S_{between}$ and a within groups matrix S_{within}, which are analogous to the between groups and within groups sums of squares in the one-way ANOVA. There is also a total cross-product matrix S_{total} which, in a manner similar to the univariate ANOVA total sum of squares, can be partitioned by expressing it as the sum of the between groups and within groups matrices:

$$S_{total} = S_{between} + S_{within}$$

Wilks' lambda Λ is defined as a ratio of determinants:

$$\Lambda = \frac{|S_{error}|}{|S_{between} + S_{error}|}$$

In the univariate one-way ANOVA, where there is only one DV, the formula for Λ simplifies to:

$$\Lambda = \frac{SS_{within}}{SS_{within} + SS_{between}} = \frac{SS_{within}}{SS_{total}} = 1 - \eta^2$$

where η is the correlation ratio. It is therefore clear that while Λ, like η^2, can take values in the range from 0 to 1, inclusive, small values of Λ indicate *large* differences among the group means, while large values of Λ indicate small differences. An approximate F statistic can be used to test a value of Λ for significance.

Within subjects designs See **Repeated measures**.

Yates' correction A modification of the approximate chi-square formula. See **Correction for continuity**.

z The standard normal variable, with a mean of zero and a standard deviation of 1. Any normally distributed variable X can be transformed to z by subtracting the mean and dividing by the standard deviation. A z-score expresses a value in units of standard deviation, not the original units. A positive sign for z indicates that the value is so-many standard deviations above the mean; a negative sign indicates that the value is so-many standard deviations below the mean. Standardising a variable does NOT normalise its distribution: if the raw scores have a skewed distribution, so will the standardised scores.

References

Agresti, A. (1990). *Categorical data analysis*. New York: Wiley.

American Psychological Association. (2001). *Publication manual of the American Psychological Association (5th ed.)*. Washington, D. C.: American Psychological Association.

Anscombe, F. J. (1973). Graphs in statistical analysis. *American Statistician, 27*, 17 - 21.

Brown, M.B., & Forsythe, A.B. (1974). The ANOVA and multiple comparisons for data with heterogeneous variances. *Biometrics, 30*, 719-724.

Byrne, B. M. (2001). *Structural equation modeling with AMOS: Basic concepts, applications and programming*. Mahwah, N. J.: Lawrence Erlbaum Associates.

Cohen, J. (1960). A coefficient of agreement for nominal scales. *Educational and Psychological Measurement, 10*, 37-46.

Cohen, J. (1962). The statistical power of abnormal-social psychological research: A review. *Journal of Abnormal and Social Psychology, 65,* 145 - 153.

Cohen, J. (1988). *Statistical power analysis for the behavioral sciences (2nd ed.)*. Hillsdale, N.J.: Lawrence Erlbaum Associates.

Cohen, J., Cohen, P., West, S. G., & Aiken, L. S. (2003). *Applied multiple regression/correlation analysis for the behavioral sciences (3rd ed.).* Mahwah, NJ: Lawrence Erlbaum Associates.

Darlington, R. B. (1968). Multiple regression in psychological research and practice. *Psychological Bulletin, 69*, 161 – 182.

Darlington, R. B. (1990). *Regression and linear models*. New York: McGraw-Hill.

Dodd, D. H., & Schultz, R. F. (1973). Computational procedures for estimating magnitude of effect for some analysis of variance designs. *Psychological Bulletin, 79*, 391-395.

Dugard, P., Todman, J., & Staines, H. (2010). *Approaching multivariate analysis: A practical introduction (2nd ed.)*. London & New York: Routledge.

Erdfelder, E., Faul, F., & Buchner, A. (1996). GPOWER: A general power analysis program. *Behavior Research Methods, Instruments, and Computers, 28,* 1 - 11.

Faul, F., Erdfelder, E., Lang, A-G., and Buchner, A. (2007). G*Power 3: A flexible statistical power analysis program for the social, behavioral and biomedical sciences. *Behavior Research Methods, 39*, 175 – 191.

Field, A. (2005). *Discovering Statistics Using SPSS: and sex and drugs and rock 'n' roll (2nd ed.)*. London: Sage.

Field, A. (2009). *Discovering statistics using SPSS: and sex and drugs and rock 'n' roll (3rd ed.)*. London: Sage.

Field, A., & Hole, G. (2003). *How to design and report experiments*. London: Sage.

Howell, D. C. (2007). *Statistical methods for psychology (6th ed.)*. Belmont, CA: Thomson/Wadsworth.

Keppel, G., & Wickens, T. D. (2004). *Design and analysis: A researcher's handbook (4th ed.)*. Upper Saddle River, NJ: Pearson Prentice Hall.

Kim, J., & Mueller, C. W. (1978a). *Factor analysis: Statistical methods and practical issues.* Newbury Park, CA: Sage.

Kim, J., & Mueller, C. W. (1978b). *Introduction to factor analysis: What it is and how to do it.* Newbury Park, CA: Sage.

King, B. M., & Minium, E. M. (2003). *Statistical reasoning in psychology and education (4th ed.)* New Jersey: John Wiley & Sons, Inc.

Neave, H. R., & Worthington, P. L. (1988). *Distribution-free tests.* London: Unwin Hyman.

Nelson, D. (2004). *The Penguin dictionary of statistics.* London: Penguin Books.

Rasbash, J., Steele, F., Browne, W., & Prosser, B. (2004). *A user's guide to MLwiN (Version 2.0)*. London: Centre for Multivel Modelling, Institute of Education, University of London.

Reber, A. S. (1985). *The Penguin dictionary of psychology.* Harmondsworth, Middlesex, England: Penguin Books.

Sani, F., & Todman, J. (2006). *Experimental design and statistics for psychology: A first course.* Oxford: Blackwell.

Tabachnick, B. G., & Fidell, L. S. (2007). *Using multivariate statistics (5th ed.).* Boston: Allyn & Bacon (Pearson International Edition).

Todman, J., & Dugard, P. (2007). *Approaching multivariate analysis: An introduction for psychology.* London: Psychology Press.

Tukey, J. W. (1977). *Exploratory data analysis.* Reading, Mass. : Addison-Wesley series in behavioral science.

Welch, B.L. (1951). On the comparison of several mean values: An alternative approach. *Biometrika, 38*, 330-336.

Winer, B. J. (1962). *Statistical principles in experimental design.* New York: McGraw-Hill.

Winer, B. J., Brown, D. R., & Michels, K. M. (1991). *Statistical principles in experimental design (3rd ed.).* New York: McGraw-Hill.

Index